All-Terrain Vehicle 1988-1992

MAINTENANCE MANUAL ■ VOLUME 2 ■ 1ST EDITION

PRIMEDIA Business Directories & Books
P.O. Box 12901 ■ Overland Park, KS 66282-2901
Phone: 800-262-1954 Fax: 800-633-6219
www.primediabooks.com

June, 2002
June, 2003

This book can be recycled. Please remove cover.

Cover photo courtesy of:
Mark Clifford
Los Angeles, California

All-Terrain Vehicle *1988-1992*

MAINTENANCE MANUAL ■ VOLUME 2 ■ 1ST EDITION

All-Terrain Vehicle Manufacturers:

■ Honda
TRX125, TRX200, TRX200SX, TRX250R (1986-1989), TRX250X, TRX300, TRX300FW, TRX350 (1986-1987),TRX350D (1987-1989)

■ Kawasaki
KLF110, KLF185, KLF220, KSF250, KXF250, KLF300, KLF300 4 x 4

■ Polaris
Big Boss, Trail Blazer, Trail Boss, Trail Boss 350L

■ Suzuki
LT80, LT160E, LT230E, LT230S, LT250S, LT250R, LT300E, LT-F300, LT500R, LT-4WD, LT-F4WD, LT-F4WDX, LT-F250

■ Yamaha
YFM80, YFM100, YFA1, YFM200DX, YFM225, YFM250, YFU1, YFU1T, YFS200, YFB250, YFM350ER, YFM350FW, YFM350X, YFZ350

PRIMEDIA Business Magazines & Media

President & Chief Executive Officer Charles McCurdy
Senior Vice President, Sales Operation John French
Vice President, PRIMEDIA Business Directories & Books Bob Moraczewski

EDITORIAL

Editor
Mike Hall

Technical Writers
Ben Evridge
Rodney J. Rom

Editorial Production Manager
Dylan Goodwin

Senior Production Editors
Greg Araujo
Shirley Renicker

Production Editors
Holly Messinger
Shara Pierceall
Darin Watson

Associate Production Editor
Susan Hartington

Technical Illustrators
Matt Hall
Bob Meyer
Mike Rose

MARKETING/SALES AND ADMINISTRATION

Publisher
Shawn Etheridge

Marketing Manager
Elda Starke

Advertising & Promotions Coordinators
Melissa Abbott
Wendy Stringfellow

Art Directors
Tony Barmann
Chris Paxton

Sales Managers
Ted Metzger, Manuals
Dutch Sadler, Marine
Matt Tusken, Motorcycles

Sales Coordinator
Marcia Jungles

Operations Manager
Patricia Kowalczewski

Customer Service Manager
Terri Cannon

Customer Service Supervisor
Ed McCarty

Customer Service Representatives
Shawna Davis
Courtney Hollars
Susan Kohlmeyer
Jennifer Lassiter
April LeBlond
Ernesto Suarez

Warehouse & Inventory Manager
Leah Hicks

The following product lines are published by PRIMEDIA Business Directories & Books.

More information available at *primediabooks.com*

CONTENTS

FUNDAMENTALS SECTION

Engine Fundamentals
Operating Principles. 7
Carburetion. 9
Ignition System. 13

Service Fundamentals
Troubleshooting 19
Maintenance:
    Spark Plug. 21

Service Fundamentals (Cont.)
Maintenance: (Cont.)
    Carburetor 23
    Ignition 23
    4-Stroke Valve System 29
    Lubrication 29
    Clutch Control 29

METRIC CONVERSION CHARTS 423

MAINTENANCE SECTION

(Note: Basic model designations are listed below; refer to section for listing of specific model numbers.)

HONDA
    TRX125 30
    TRX200, TRX200SX 44
    TRX250R(1986-1989) 62
    TRX250X 77
    TRX300,
        TRX300FW. 92
    TRX350 (1986-1987),
        TRX350D (1987-1989) 112

KAWASAKI
    KLF110. 128
    KLF185, KLF220 139
    KSF250 150
    KXF250 162
    KLF300. 174
    KLF300 4 × 4 186

POLARIS
    Big Boss, Trail Blazer, Trail Boss,
        Trail Boss 350L 198

SUZUKI
    LT80 218
    LT160E. 230
    LT230E, LT230S, LT250S 244
    LT250R. 262
    LT300E, LT-F300 275
    LT500R. 291
    LT-4WD, LT-F4WD, LT-F4WDX, LT-F250 304

YAMAHA
    YFM80, YFM100 321
    YFA1 332
    YFM200DX, YFM225, YFM250, YFU1, YFU1T 342
    YFS200 359
    YFB250 370
    YFM350ER, YFM350FW. 382
    YFM350X 397
    YFZ350 411

INTRODUCTION

This All-Terrain Vehicle (ATV) Maintenance Manual contains the specifications and procedures necessary for someone with average mechanical ability to properly maintain an ATV covered herein.

In addition to maintenance specifications, extensive service specifications such as clearances and tolerances are also listed in the CONDENSED SERVICE DATA sections. The service specifications are provided for the mechanic experienced with ATVs or related equipment. When in doubt, service work should be performed by a qualified mechanic.

Also included in this ATV Maintenance Manual are fundamentals sections which include information concerning engine design and general service information. These sections provide general information which may increase the reader's maintenance capability by explaining how components operate and discussing general maintenance procedures.

DUAL DIMENSIONS

This service manual provides specifications in both the Metric (SI) and U.S. Customary systems of measurement. The first specification is given in the measuring system used during manufacture, while the second specification (given in parenthesis) is the converted measurement. For instance, a specification of "0.28 mm (0.011 inch)" would indicate that the equipment was manufactured using the metric system of measurement and the U.S. equivalent of 0.28 mm is 0.011 inch.

Intertec Publishing thanks the following firms for their cooperation and technical assistance:

Browning Yamaha & Honda, Paola, Kansas
Freedom Honda Kawasaki, Grandview, Missouri
Northland Kawasaki, Gladstone, Missouri
Honda Yamaha North, North Kansas City, Missouri
Polaris Ind., Inc., Roseau, Minnesota
Shawnee Cycle Plaza, Shawnee, Kansas
Shrout Yamaha, Blue Springs, Missouri
U.S. Suzuki Motor Corporation, Brea, California
Yamaha Suzuki South, Belton, Missouri

ENGINE DESIGN FUNDAMENTALS
OPERATING PRINCIPLES

ENGINE TYPES

The engines used to power all-terrain vehicles and many other items of power equipment in use today are basically similar. All are technically known as "Internal Combustion Reciprocating Engines."

The source of power is heat formed by the burning of a combustible mixture, usually petroleum products and air. In a reciprocating engine, this burning takes place in a closed cylinder containing a piston. Expansion resulting from the heat of combustion applies pressure on the piston to turn a shaft by means of a crank and connecting rod.

The fuel-air mixture may be ignited by means of an electric spark (Otto Cycle Engine) or by heat formed from compression of air in the engine cylinder (Diesel Cycle Engine). The complete series of events that must take place in order for the engine to run may occur in one revolution of the crankshaft (two strokes of the piston in cylinder), which is referred to as a "Two-Stroke Cycle Engine," or in two revolutions of the crankshaft (four strokes of the piston in cylinder), which is referred to as a "Four-Stroke Cycle Engine."

OTTO CYCLE. In a spark ignited engine, a series of five events is required in order for the engine to provide power. This series of events is called the "Cycle" (or "Work Cycle") and is repeated in each cylinder of the engine as long as work is being done. This series of events that comprise the "Cycle" is as follows:

1. The mixture of fuel and air is pushed into the cylinder by atmospheric pressure when the pressure within the engine cylinder is reduced by the piston moving downward in the cylinder (or by applying pressure to the fuel-air mixture as by crankcase compression in the crankcase of a "Two-Stroke Cycle Engine," which is described in a later paragraph).

2. The mixture of fuel and air is compressed by the piston moving upward in the cylinder.

3. The compressed fuel-air mixture is ignited by a timed electric spark.

4. The burning fuel-air mixture expands forcing the piston downward in the cylinder, thus converting the chemical energy generated by combustion into mechanical power.

5. The gaseous products formed by the burned fuel-air mixture are exhausted from the cylinder so that a new "Cycle" can begin.

The above described five events that comprise the work cycle of an engine are commonly referred to as (1) INTAKE; (2) COMPRESSION; (3) IGNITION; (4) EXPANSION (POWER); and (5) EXHAUST.

TWO-STROKE CYCLE. Two-stroke cycle engines may be of the Otto Cycle (spark ignition) or Diesel Cycle (compression ignition) type. However, because the two-stroke cycle engines listed in the repair section of this manual are all of the Otto Cycle type, operation of two-stroke Diesel Cycle engines will not be discussed in this section.

In two-stroke cycle engines, the piston is used as a sliding valve for the cylinder intake and exhaust ports. The intake and exhaust ports are both open when the piston is at the bottom of its downward stroke (bottom dead center or BDC). The exhaust port is open to atmospheric pressure; therefore, the fuel-air mixture must be elevated to a higher than atmospheric pressure in order for the mixture to enter the cylinder. As the crankshaft is turned from BDC and the piston starts on its upward stroke, the intake and exhaust ports are closed and the fuel-air mixture in the cylinder is compressed. When the piston is at or near the top of its upward stroke (top dead center or TDC), an electric spark across the electrode gap of the spark plug ignites the fuel air mixture. As the crankshaft turns past TDC and the piston starts on its downward stroke, the rapidly burning fuel-air mixture expands and forces the piston downward. As the piston nears the bottom of its downward stroke, the cylinder exhaust port is opened and the burned gaseous products from combustion of the fuel-air mixture flows out the open port. Slightly further downward travel of the piston opens the cylinder intake port and a fresh charge of fuel-air mixture is forced into the cylinder. Because the exhaust port remains open, the incoming flow of fuel-air mixture helps clean (scavenge) any remaining burned gaseous products from the cylinder. As the crankshaft turns past BDC and the piston starts on its upward stroke, the cylinder intake and exhaust ports are closed and a new cycle begins.

Because the fuel-air mixture must be elevated to a higher-than-atmospheric pressure to enter the cylinder of a two-stroke cycle engine, a compressor pump must be used. Coincidentally, downward movement of the

Engine Design Fundamentals

piston decreases the volume of the engine crankcase. Thus, a compressor pump is made available by sealing the engine crankcase and connecting the carburetor to a port in the crankcase. When the piston moves upward, volume of the crankcase is increased, which lowers pressure within the crankcase to below atmospheric. Air then will be forced through the carburetor, where fuel is mixed with the air, and on into the engine crankcase. In order for downward movement of the piston to compress the fuel-air mixture in the crankcase, a valve must be provided to close the carburetor-to-crankcase port. Three types of valves are used: In Fig. 1-1, a reed-type

inlet valve is shown in the schematic diagram of the two-stroke cycle engine. Reeds (R) are forced open by atmospheric pressure as shown in view "B" when the piston is on its upward stroke and pressure in the crankcase is below atmospheric. When the piston reaches TDC, the reeds close, as shown in view "A," and fuel-air mixture is trapped in the crankcase to be compressed by downward movement of the piston. In Fig. 1-2, a schematic diagram of a two-stroke cycle engine is shown in which the piston is used as a sliding carburetor—crankcase port (third port) valve. In Fig. 1-3, a schematic diagram of a two-stroke cycle engine is shown in which a slotted disc (rotary valve) attached to the engine crankshaft opens the carburetor-crankcase port when the piston is on its upward stroke. In each of the three basic designs shown, a transfer port (TP—Fig. 1-2) connects the crankcase compression chamber to the cylinder; the transfer port is the cylinder intake port through which the compressed fuel-air mixture in the crankcase is transferred to the cylinder when the piston is at bottom of stroke as shown in view "A."

Due to rapid movement of the fuel-air mixture through the crankcase, the crankcase cannot be used as a lubricating oil sump because the oil would be carried into the cylinder. Lubrication is accomplished by mixing a small amount of oil with the fuel or by a separate oil metering system. In either case, the engine lubricating oil is carried through the crankcase and eventually is forced into the combustion chamber where it is burned. Where an oil metering system is used, ratio of oil to fuel by volume is varied by throttle opening and engine speed. When oil is premixed with the fuel, manufacturer's recommended fuel-oil ratio should be strictly observed.

FOUR-STROKE CYCLE. In a four-stroke cycle engine operating on the Otto Cycle (spark ignition), the five events of the cycle take place in four strokes of the piston, or in two revolutions of the engine crankshaft.

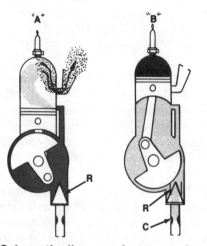

Fig. 1-1—Schematic diagram of a two-stroke cycle engine operating on the Otto Cycle (spark ignition). View "B" shows piston near top of upward stroke and atmospheric pressure is forcing air through carburetor (C), where fuel is mixed with the air, and the fuel-air mixture enters crankcase through open reed valve (R). In view "A," piston is near bottom of downward stroke and has opened the cylinder exhaust and intake ports; fuel-air mixture in crankcase has been compressed by downward stroke of piston and flows into cylinder through open port. Incoming mixture helps clean burned exhaust gases from cylinder.

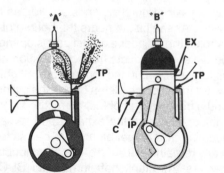

Fig. 1-2—Schematic diagram of two-stroke cycle engine operating on Otto Cycle. Engine differs from that shown in Fig. 1-1 in that piston is used as a sliding valve to open and close intake (carburetor-to-crankcase) port (IP) instead of using reed valve (R—Fig. 1-1).

C. Carburetor	IP. Intake port (carburetor-to-crankcase)
EX. Exhaust port	TP. Transfer port (crankcase-to-cylinder)

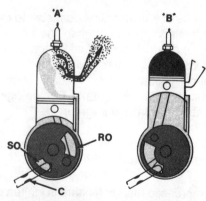

Fig. 1-3—Schematic diagram of two-stroke cycle engine similar to those shown in Figs. 1-1 and 1-2 except that a rotary carburetor-to-crankcase port valve is used. Disc driven by crankshaft has rotating opening (RO) that uncovers stationary opening (SO) in crankcase when piston is on upward stroke. Carburetor is (C).

Thus, a power stroke occurs only on alternate downward strokes of the piston.

In view "A" of Fig. 1-4, the piston is on the first downward stroke of the cycle. The mechanically operated intake valve has opened the intake port and, as the downward movement of the piston has reduced the air pressure in the cylinder to below atmospheric pressure, air is forced through the carburetor (where fuel is mixed with the air) and into the cylinder through the open intake port. The intake valve remains open and fuel-air mixture continues to flow into the cylinder until the piston reaches the bottom of its downward stroke. As the piston starts on its first upward stroke, the mechanically operated intake valve closes and, because the exhaust valve is closed, the fuel-air mixture is compressed as in view "B."

Just before the piston reaches the top of its first upward stroke, a spark at the spark plug electrode ignites the compressed fuel-air mixture. As the engine crankshaft turns past top center, the burning fuel-air mixture expands rapidly and forces the piston downward on its power stroke as shown in view "C." As the piston reaches the bottom of the power stroke, the mechanically operated exhaust valve starts to open and, as the pressure of the burned fuel-air mixture is higher than atmospheric pressure, it starts to flow out the open exhaust port. As the engine crankshaft turns past bottom center, the exhaust valve is almost completely open and remains open during the upward stroke of the piston as shown in view "D." Upward movement of the piston pushes the remaining burned fuel-air mixture out of the exhaust port. Just before the piston reaches the top of its second upward or exhaust stroke, the intake valve opens and the exhaust valve closes. The cycle is completed as the crankshaft turns past top center and a new cycle begins as the piston starts downward as shown in view "A."

In a four-stroke cycle engine operating on the Diesel Cycle, the sequence of events of the cycle is similar to that described for operation on the Otto Cycle, but with the following exceptions: On the intake stroke, air only is taken into the cylinder. On the compression stroke, the air is highly compressed, which raises the temperature of the air. Just before the piston reaches top dead center, fuel is injected into the cylinder and is ignited by the heated, compressed air. The remainder of the cycle is similar to that of the Otto Cycle.

CARBURETORS

Function of the carburetor on a spark-ignition engine is to atomize the fuel and mix the atomized fuel in proper proportions with air flowing to the engine intake port or intake manifold. Carburetors used on engines that are to be operated at constant speeds and under even loads are of simple design because they only have to mix fuel and air in a relatively constant ratio. On engines operating at varying speeds and loads, the carburetors must

be more complex because different fuel-air mixtures are required to meet the varying demands of the engine.

Requirements

To meet the demands of an engine being operated at varying speeds and loads, the carburetor must mix fuel and air at different mixture ratios. Gasoline-air mixture

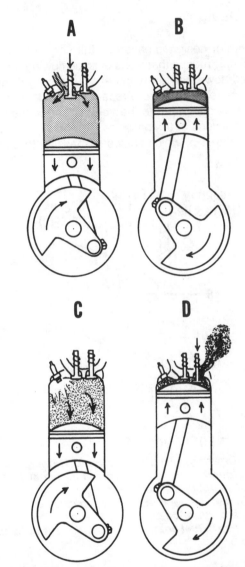

Fig. 1-4—Schematic diagram of four-stroke cycle engine operating on the Otto (spark ignition) cycle. In view "A," piston is on first downward (intake) stroke and atmospheric pressure is forcing fuel-air mixture from carburetor into cylinder through the open intake valve. In view "B," both valves are closed and piston is on its first upward stroke, compressing the fuel-air mixture in cylinder. In view "C," spark across electrodes of spark plug has ignited fuel-air mixture and heat of combustion rapidly expands the burning gaseous mixture, forcing the piston on its second downward (expansion or power) stroke. In view "D," exhaust valve is open and piston is on its second upward (exhaust) stroke, forcing the burned mixture from cylinder. A new cycle then starts as in view "A."

Engine Design Fundamentals

ratios required for different operating conditions are approximately as follows:

	Fuel	Air
Starting, cold weather	1 lb.	7 lbs.
Accelerating	1 lb.	9 lbs.
Idling (no-load)	1 lb.	11 lbs.
Part open throttle	1 lb.	15 lbs.
Full load, open throttle	1 lb.	13 lbs.

Basic Design

Carburetor design is based on the venturi principle, which simply means that a gas or liquid flowing through a necked-down section (venturi) in a passage undergoes an increase in velocity (speed) and a decrease in pressure as compared to the velocity and pressure in full-size sections of the passage. The principle is illustrated in Fig. 1-5, which shows air passing through a

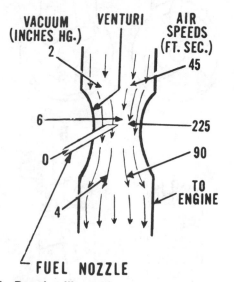

Fig. 1-5—Drawing illustrating the venturi principle upon which carburetor design is based. Figures at left are inches of mercury vacuum and those at right are air speeds in feet per second that are typical of conditions found in a carburetor operating at wide-open throttle. Zero vacuum in fuel nozzle corresponds to atmospheric pressure.

carburetor venturi. The figures given for air speeds and vacuum are approximate for a typical wide-open throttle operating condition. Due to low pressure (high vacuum) in the venturi, fuel is forced out through the fuel nozzle by the atmospheric pressure (0 vacuum) on the fuel; as fuel is emitted from the nozzle, it is atomized by the high velocity air flow and mixes with the air.

Although some carburetors may be very basic, the varying requirements of ATV engines make it necessary to incorporate features to provide variable fuel-air ratios for different operating conditions. These design features will be described in the following paragraphs outlining the different carburetor types.

Carburetor Types

Carburetors used on ATV engines are usually classified by type of throttle valve, venturi and starting (enriching) method used. The following paragraphs describe different operating principles. Various combinations of the following features are used in each ATV carburetor.

THROTTLE VALVES. In order to vary the speed, a valve is installed between the fuel nozzle and engine that limits the volume of combustible mixture available to the combustion chamber. When less mixture is available to the combustion area, there will be less expansion resulting in less rpm and less power. The two types of throttle valves commonly used are the disc (butterfly) valve (Fig. 1-6) and the variable venturi (slide) valve (Fig. 1-9).

If, after the engine has been started, the throttle valve is in the wide-open position, the engine can obtain enough fuel and air to run at dangerously high speeds so the throttle valve must be partly closed. At no load, the engine requires very little air and fuel to run at its rated speed and the throttle must be moved nearer the closed position. As more load is placed on the engine, more fuel and air mixture is required for the engine to operate at its rated speed. When the engine is required to develop maximum power or speed, the throttle must be in the wide-open position.

DISC (BUTTERFLY) VALVE. A typical disc-type throttle valve is shown in Figs. 1-6, 1-7 and 1-8. As the throttle disc is turned toward the closed position, the opening of

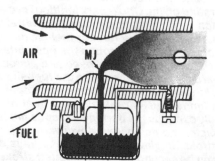

Fig. 1-6—View of carburetor showing disc-type throttle valve completely open for high-speed operation.

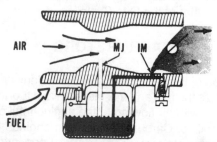

Fig. 1-7—As disc-type throttle valve is moved toward the closed position, vacuum at the main jet (MJ) may not be enough to draw fuel into the passing air and an intermediate jet (IM) is provided.

the throttle bore is decreased. When disc is in position shown in Fig. 1-8, the throttle opening is nearly closed. Idle speed adjustment is accomplished by stopping rotation of the valve before throttle bore is completely closed. When throttle is nearly closed, vacuum at the venturi is insufficient to provide correct fuel-air ratio by using only one fuel nozzle. Usually an additional idle jet (Fig. 1-8) and intermediate jet (Fig. 1-7) are incorporated.

VARIABLE VENTURI (SLIDE) VALVE. A typical slide-type carburetor is shown in Fig. 1-9. When the slide is completely open, the small step in the throttle bore serves as a large diameter venturi for high speed. As the slide is lowered, the venturi size is decreased as shown in Fig. 1-10. Decreasing the venturi size slows the speed by decreasing the amount of fuel and air mixture that can be drawn into the engine and also increases the vacuum at the venturi fuel nozzle. A valve needle attached to the throttle slide is incorporated to lower the amount of fuel drawn in by the high vacuum created by the small venturi. An idle jet is sometimes installed, as shown in Fig. 1-10, to provide an additional mixture adjustment for low-speed settings. Idle speed is controlled by stopping the throttle slide before it completely closes the throttle bore. If the valve needle is raised in the throttle slide, it will increase the fuel flow from the main nozzle at intermediate throttle settings.

VENTURI. As previously explained, a gas or liquid flowing through a necked-down section (venturi) in a passage increases in velocity (speed) and decreases in pressure as shown in Fig. 1-5. When movement of the piston draws air through the carburetor, this change of pressure is what causes the fuel to be drawn into the air as it passes the fuel nozzle. The venturi must be matched to the engine to provide the right amount of pressure drop at the venturi for correct fuel-air mixture. Some adjustment can be accomplished by making the fuel flow less (or more) restricted by changing the jet sizes; however, manufacturer's recommendation of carburetor and jet sizes should be closely followed.

VARIABLE VENTURI (SLIDE) VALVE. The sliding variable venturi that is commonly used as a throttle is explained in a previous paragraph. If a larger carburetor of this same type is installed, it is possible that low-speed (part throttle) operation will function normally, but

at full-open throttle, the venturi will be too large to provide the correct fuel-air mixture.

VACUUM-CONTROLLED VENTURI. Some models use a vacuum-controlled, variable venturi as shown in Fig. 1-11. These models use a disc-type throttle plate that controls the amount of fuel-air mixture available to the engine. When the engine is running at slow speed (throttle nearly closed), the venturi piston is lowered as shown in Fig. 1-11. As the throttle disc is opened (Figs. 1-12 and 1-13), the vacuum at the venturi is transferred into chamber (V) via port (P) and atmospheric pressure is admitted under venturi piston via port (A). The high pressure below the venturi and low pressure above causes the piston to raise as shown in Figs. 1-12 and 1-13. As with the slide-type variable venturi, a valve needle is attached to the venturi to limit the amount of fuel drawn from the main nozzle at low speed. An idle mixture jet (IJ—Fig. 1-11) and intermediate jet (IM—Fig.

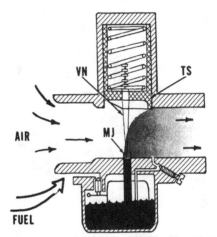

Fig. 1-9—View of variable venturi, slide-type throttle valve. Throttle slide (TS) is in the fully raised high-speed position. Valve needle (VN) is raised allowing main jet (MJ) to be completely open.

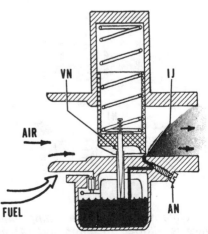

Fig. 1-10—With throttle slide lowered to idle speed position, only a small amount of air is allowed to pass. The valve needle (VN) is lowered, closing the main jet and fuel is drawn from the idle jet (IJ). Idle mixture adjustment needle (AN) controls fuel-air ratio.

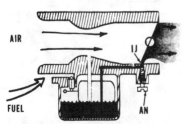

Fig. 1-8—With throttle disc nearly closed, the idle jet (IJ) is used. Usually, an adjustment needle (AN) is provided to adjust the idle mixture fuel-air ratio.

Engine Design Fundamentals

1-12) are provided to correct the fuel to air ratio throughout the entire speed range. It is extremely important that the venturi piston is free to move easily in its bore and that it fits tightly enough to seal the different pressures. Idle speed is controlled by stopping the throttle disc before it closes the throttle bore.

STARTING ENRICHMENT. The ratio of fuel to air must be much richer when starting in cold weather than when running at full open throttle. Two methods of obtaining a rich starting mixture are commonly used.

1. CHOKE PLATE: Fig. 1-14 shows a typical choke plate installation in relation to the carburetor venturi.

At cranking speeds, air flows through the carburetor venturi at a slow speed; thus, the pressure in the venturi does not usually decrease to the extent that atmospheric pressure on the fuel will force enough fuel from the nozzle. If the choke plate is closed, as shown by the broken line in Fig. 1-14, air cannot enter into the carbu-

retor and pressure in the carburetor decreases greatly as the engine is turned at cranking speed. Fuel is then forced from the fuel nozzle. In manufacturing the carburetor choke plate or disc, a small hole or notch is cut in the plate so that some air can flow through the plate when it is in closed position to provide air for the starting fuel-air mixture. In some instances after starting a cold engine, it is advantageous to leave the choke plate in a partly closed position as the restriction of air flow will decrease the air pressure in the carburetor venturi, thus, causing more fuel to flow from the nozzle resulting in a richer fuel-air mixture. The choke plate or disc should be in fully open position for normal engine operation.

2. STARTING VALVE: Fig. 1-15 shows a simplified starting system typical of the type found in many carbu-

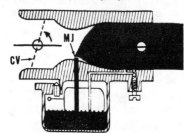

Fig. 1-13—As engine speed and throttle opening are increased, vacuum at venturi port (P) and above venturi piston (V) increases until venturi is completely open. Needle jet (NJ) is completely open.

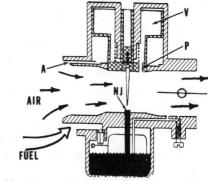

Fig. 1-14—As choke valve (CV) is closed (shown by the broken lines), vacuum is increased at main jet (MJ).

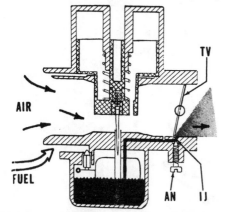

Fig. 1-11—View of vacuum-controlled, variable venturi-type carburetor with throttle valve (TV) nearly closed. Idle mixture adjustment needle (AN) is shown. Fuel is discharged from idle jet (IJ).

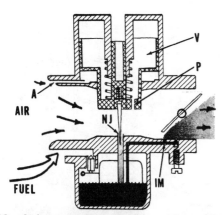

Fig. 1-12—At intermediate throttle setting, atmospheric air pressure is allowed to enter port (A) under the venturi piston and venturi vacuum is transferred to top of piston (V) via port (P). The vacuum above the piston and atmospheric pressure below causes the venturi piston to raise. Fuel is discharged at partially open needle jet (NJ) and intermediate jet (IM).

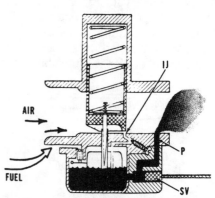

Fig. 1-15—View of simplified starting valve enrichment method. With starting valve (SV) open, the normal idle mixture supplied by idle jet (IJ) is further enriched by starting port (P).

retors. A combination of two principles is used to enrich the fuel-air mixture. First, the passage is normally less restricted (larger) than the normal idle passage and, second, the starting port is located between the throttle slide and engine. With the starting port (P) located as shown in Fig. 1-15, closing the throttle slide increases the vacuum at the starting port in much the same way as the choke plate previously described. It is obvious that this rich mixture normally should not be used, so a shut-off valve is incorporated in the system. The starter jet shut-off valve (SV—Fig. 1-15) is sometimes actuated by a control on the carburetor; however, it is often remotely controlled by a handlebar-mounted lever via a control cable.

IGNITION SYSTEM

The timed spark that ignites the fuel charge in the cylinder may be supplied by either a magneto or battery ignition system. To better understand the operation of the components and the differences and similarities of the two systems, this section will combine the various units, and explain and compare their functions.

Theory

In the modern ignition system, a relatively weak electric current of 6 to 12 volts and 2 to 5 amperes is transformed into a momentary charge of minute amperage and extremely high (10,000-25,000) voltage capable of jumping the spark plug gap in the cylinder and igniting the fuel charge.

To understand the ignition system theory, electricity can be thought of as a stream of electrons flowing through a conductor. The force of the stream can be increased by restricting volume, or the volume increased by reducing the resistance to movement, but the total amount of power cannot be increased except by employing additional outside force. The current has an inertia of motion and resists being stopped once it has started flowing. If the circuit is broken suddenly, the force will tend to pile up temporarily, attempting to convert the speed of flow into energy.

Here is a short list of useful electrical terms and a brief explanation of their meanings:

AMPERE—A unit of measurement used to designate the amount or quantity of flow of an electrical current.

OHM—The unit of measurement used to designate the resistance of a conductor to the flow of current.

VOLT—The unit of measurement used to designate the force or pressure of an electrical current.

WATT—The unit of measurement that designates the ability of an electrical current to perform work or to measure the amount of work performed.

The four terms are directly interrelated: one ampere equaling the flow of current produced by one volt against a resistance of one ohm. One watt designates the work potential of one ampere at one volt in one second.

Ignition Coil

When an electrical current is flowing through a conductor, a magnetic field exists at right angles to the current flow. As long as the conductor is relatively straight, nothing much happens, but if the conductor is coiled around a soft iron core, then the length of the iron core is at approximately right angles to the wire. A path is provided for the magnetic field and the iron core becomes a magnet as long as the current flows.

A second phenomenon of electrical action happens when a magnetic field is interrupted—a pulsation of electrical energy is formed at right angles to the lines of magnetic flow.

In a battery ignition system, these two peculiarities are combined to form an ignition coil as shown in Fig. 1-16. The inner and outer laminations are composed of soft iron and form a continuous path for a magnetic field. Around the inner laminations, but insulated from it, are many coils of fine copper wire. Around this coil of fine wire, but insulated from it and the iron core, are several windings of heavier copper wire. These windings are encased in the outer laminations, then in a protective case.

The outer winding of heavier wire is connected to the two screw terminals on the coil case and form the primary circuit of the coil. The inner winding of fine wire is grounded at one end and the other end is connected to the insulated, high-tension terminal and forms the secondary circuit.

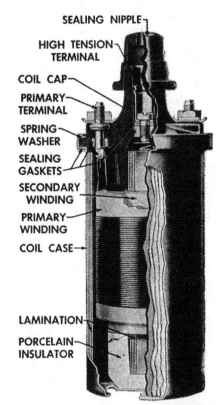

SEALING NIPPLE

HIGH TENSION TERMINAL

COIL CAP

PRIMARY TERMINAL

SPRING WASHER

SEALING GASKETS

SECONDARY WINDING

PRIMARY WINDING

COIL CASE

LAMINATION

PORCELAIN INSULATOR

Fig. 1-16—Sectional view of a typical ignition coil.

Engine Design Fundamentals

Primary Circuit

The primary circuit is attached to the power source in both the battery and magneto electrical systems.

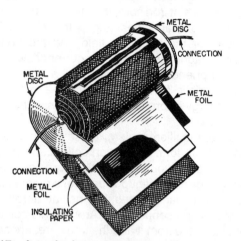

Fig. 1-17—*A typical condenser consists of two metal conductors separated by layers of insulating paper and rolled into a tight cylinder.*

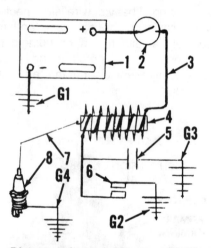

Fig. 1-18—*Diagram of a typical battery ignition system. Refer to text for principles of operation.*

1. Battery
2. Ignition switch
3. Primary circuit
4. Ignition coil
5. Condenser
6. Contact points
7. Secondary circuit
8. Spark plug
G1-G4. Ground connections

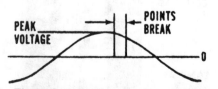

Fig. 1-19—*The primary current of a magneto ignition system is an alternating current. Thus, voltage varies from zero to a predetermined peak during each positive and negative cycle. To produce an adequate spark to ignite the fuel charge, the contact points must break at or near the voltage peak as shown.*

In the battery system, the primary circuit consists of the battery, ignition switch, primary windings, contact points, condenser and the necessary connecting wiring as shown at (3—Fig. 1-18). When the ignition switch (2) and contact points (6) are closed, the primary circuit (3), primary windings of coil (4) and the closed contact points (6), the ground connections (G1 at battery and G2 at points) plus the engine casting or frame complete the circuit. As the current flows, a magnetic field is built up in the soft iron laminations of coil (4), which is surrounded by the primary and secondary windings. When contact points (6) open to break the circuit, the current tries to flow through the path of least resistance, which is the condenser (5) until condenser capacity is reached. Then, the primary current ceases to flow and the magnetic field starts to collapse. This collapse is hastened by the condenser, which tries to discharge its stored energy backward through the primary circuit. When the magnetic field collapses, extremely high voltage is induced in the coil secondary windings. The high voltage flows through the secondary circuit (7) to spark plug (8) where it jumps the plug gap and is dissipated in the engine frame through ground (G4).

In a magneto ignition system, the same principles are involved but the method of application is somewhat different. Instead of stored chemical energy of a battery that produces a constant direct current, the source of energy is a pulsating alternating current induced in the magneto primary windings and derived from permanent magnets. Because of variation in voltage and direction of current flow (see Fig. 1-19), the ignition points must not only be correctly timed with relation to the piston, but also to break at or near peak voltage. The proper position with relation to the position of the permanent magnet is decided by laboratory tests and sometimes becomes a part of the service specifications. This position is referred to as "edge gap."

Secondary Circuit

The secondary circuit carries the high-voltage current from the coil to the spark plug or plugs. The secondary circuit ground at the spark plug should be of negative polarity. On systems with a separate high-tension coil, the secondary current polarity can be reversed by changing the primary circuit leads at the coil or by reversing the connections. The potential voltage available in the secondary circuit, when the system is in good condition, may be 18,000 to 25,000 volts. The actual voltage depends on the resistance of the secondary circuit, and the type and condition of the spark plug plays an important part in establishing the operating resistance. When the secondary current is induced in the coil, current strength continues to build up until a spark is formed across the plug gap, then the energy will be dissipated and voltage will not rise higher.

SOLID-STATE IGNITION SYSTEM

BREAKERLESS MAGNETO SYSTEM. The solid-state (breakerless) magneto ignition system operates somewhat on the same basic principles as the conventional-type flywheel magneto previously described. The main difference is: The breaker contact points are replaced by a solid-state electronic Gate Controlled Switch (GCS) that has no moving parts. In a conventional system, breaker points are closed over a longer period of crankshaft rotation than in the "GCS," so a diode has been added to the circuit to provide the same characteristics as closed breaker points.

BREAKERLESS MAGNETO OPERATING PRINCIPLES. The same basic principles for electromagnetic induction of electricity and formation of magnetic fields by electrical current, as outlined for the conventional flywheel-type magneto, also apply to the solid-state magneto. Therefore, the principles of the different components (diode and GCS) will complete the operating principles of the solid-state magneto.

The diode is represented in wiring diagrams by the symbol in Fig. 1-20. The diode is an electronic device that permits passage of electrical current in one direction only. In electrical schematic diagrams, current flow is opposite direction the arrow part of symbol is pointing.

The symbol in Fig. 1-21 represents the gate controlled switch (GCS) in wiring diagrams. The GCS acts as a switch permitting current passage from cathode (C) terminal to anode (A) terminal when in "ON" state and will not permit electric current to flow when in "OFF" state. The GCS can be turned "ON" by a positive surge of electricity at the gate (G) terminal and will remain "ON"

as long as current remains positive at the gate terminal or as long as current is flowing through the GCS from cathode (C) terminal to anode (A) terminal.

Basic components and wiring diagram for the solid-state breakerless magneto are shown schematically in Fig. 1-22. In Fig. 1-23, the magneto rotor (flywheel) is

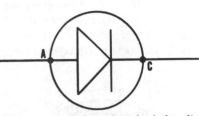

Fig. 1-20—In a diagram of an electrical circuit, the diode is represented by this symbol. The diode will allow current to flow in one direction only, from cathode (C) to anode (A).

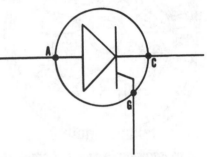

Fig. 1-21—This is the symbol used for a Gate Controlled Switch (GCS) in an electrical diagram. The GCS will permit current to flow from cathode (C) to anode (A) when "turned on" by a positive electrical charge at gate (G) terminal.

Fig. 1-22—Schematic diagram of typical breakerless magneto ignition system. Refer to Figs. 1-23, 1-24 and 1-25 for schematic views of operating cycle.

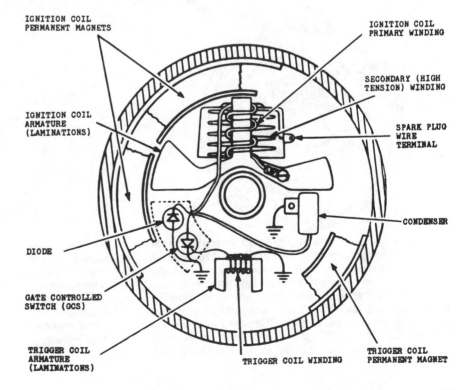

IGNITION COIL PERMANENT MAGNETS

IGNITION COIL PRIMARY WINDING

SECONDARY (HIGH TENSION) WINDING

IGNITION COIL ARMATURE (LAMINATIONS)

SPARK PLUG WIRE TERMINAL

DIODE

CONDENSER

GATE CONTROLLED SWITCH (GCS)

TRIGGER COIL ARMATURE (LAMINATIONS)

TRIGGER COIL WINDING

TRIGGER COIL PERMANENT MAGNET

turning and the ignition coil magnets have just moved into position so that their lines of force are cutting the ignition coil windings and producing a negative surge of current in the primary windings. The diode allows current to flow opposite to the direction of diode symbol arrow and action is same as conventional magneto with breaker points closed. As rotor (flywheel) continues to turn, as shown in Fig. 1-24, direction of magnetic flux lines will reverse in the armature center leg. Direction of current will change in the primary coil circuit and the previously conducting diode will be shut off. At this point, neither diode is conducting. As voltage begins to build

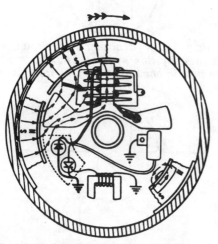

Fig. 1-23—View showing flywheel of breakerless magneto system at instant of rotation where lines of force of ignition coil magnets are being drawn into left and center legs of magneto armature. The diode (see Fig. 1-20) acts as a closed set of breaker points in completing the primary ignition circuit at this time.

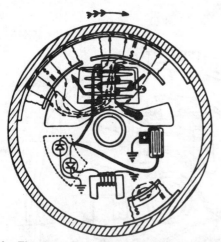

Fig. 1-24—Flywheel is turning to point where magnetic flux lines through armature center leg will reverse direction and current through primary coil circuit will reverse. As current reverses, diode that was previously conducting will shut off and there will be no current. When magnetic flux lines have reversed in armature center leg, voltage potential will again build up, but because GCS is in "OFF" state, no current will flow. To prevent excessive voltage buildup, the condenser acts as a buffer.

up as rotor continues to turn, the condenser acts as a buffer to prevent excessive voltage build up at the GCS before it is triggered.

When the rotor reaches the approximate position shown in Fig. 1-25, maximum flux density has been achieved in the center leg of the armature. At this time, the GCS is triggered. Triggering is accomplished by the triggering coil armature moving into the field of a permanent magnet, which induces a positive voltage on the gate of the GCS. Primary coil current flow results in the formation of an electromagnetic field around primary coil that inducts a voltage of sufficient potential in the secondary coil windings to "fire" the spark plug.

When the rotor (flywheel) has moved the magnets past the armature, the GCS will cease to conduct and revert to the "OFF" state until it is triggered. The condenser will discharge during the time that the GCS was conducting.

CAPACITOR DISCHARGE SYSTEM. The capacitor discharge (CD) ignition system uses a permanent magnet rotor (flywheel) to induce a current in a coil, but unlike the conventional flywheel magneto and solid-state breakerless magneto described previously, the current is stored in a capacitor (condenser). Then the stored current is discharged through a transformer coil to create the ignition spark. Refer to Fig. 1-26 for a schematic of a typical capacitor discharge ignition system.

CAPACITOR DISCHARGE OPERATING PRINCIPLES. As the permanent flywheel magnets pass by the input generating coil (1—Fig. 1-26), the current produced charges the capacitor (6). Only half the generated current passes through diode (3) to charge the capaci-

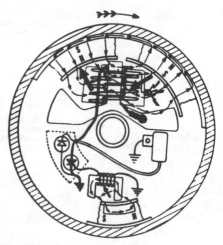

Fig. 1-25—With flywheel in the approximate position shown, maximum voltage potential is present in windings of primary coil. At this time, the triggering coil armature has moved into the field of a permanent magnet and a positive voltage is induced on the gate of the GCS. The GCS is triggered and primary coil current flows resulting in the formation of an electromagnetic field around the primary coil that inducts a voltage of sufficient potential in the secondary windings to "fire" the spark plug.

tor. Reverse current is blocked by diode (3) but passes through zener diode (2) to complete the reverse circuit. Zener diode (2) also limits maximum voltage of the forward current. As the flywheel continues to turn and magnets pass the trigger coil (4), a small amount of electrical current is generated. This current opens the gate controlled switch (5) allowing the capacitor to discharge through the pulse transformer (7). The rapid voltage rise in the transformer primary coil induces a high voltage secondary current that forms the ignition spark when it jumps the spark plug gap.

Spark Plug

In any spark ignition engine, the spark plug provides the means for igniting the compressed fuel-air mixture in the cylinder. Before an electric charge can move across an air gap, the intervening air must be charged with electricity, or ionized. The spark plug gap becomes more easily ionized if the spark plug ground (G4—Fig.

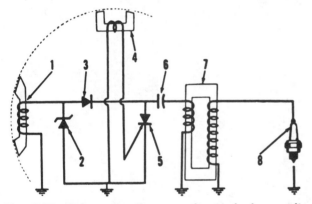

Fig. 1-26—Schematic diagram of a typical capacitor discharge ignition system.

1. Generating coil
2. Zener diode
3. Diode
4. Trigger coil
5. Gate controlled switch
6. Capacitor
7. Pulse transformer (coil)
8. Spark plug

1-18) is of negative polarity. If the spark plug is properly gapped and the system is not shorted, not more than 7,000 volts may be required to initiate a spark. Higher voltage is required as the spark plug warms up, or if compression pressures or the distance of the air gap is increased. Compression pressures are highest at full throttle and relatively slow engine speeds. Therefore, high voltage requirements, or a lack of available secondary voltage, most often shows up as a miss during maximum acceleration from a slow engine speed. There are many different types and sizes of spark plugs that are designed for a number of specific requirements.

THREAD SIZE. The threaded shell portion of the spark plug and the attaching holes in the cylinder are manufactured to meet certain industry-established standards. The diameter is referred to as "thread size." Those commonly used are: 10 mm, 14 mm, 18 mm, 7/8- and 1/2-in. pipe.

REACH. The length of thread and the thread depth in cylinder head or wall are also standardized throughout the industry. This dimension is measured from gasket seat of plug to cylinder end of thread (Fig. 1-27).

HEAT RANGE. During engine operation, part of the heat generated during combustion is transferred to the spark plug and from the plug to the cooling medium through the shell threads and gasket. The operating temperature of the spark plug plays an important part in engine operation. If too much heat is retained by the plug, the fuel-air mixture may be ignited by contact with the heated surface before the ignition spark occurs. If not enough heat is retained, partially burned combustion products (soot, carbon and oil) may build up on the plug tip resulting in "fouling" or shorting out of the plug. If this happens, the secondary current is dissipated uselessly as it is generated instead of bridging the plug gap as a useful spark and the engine will misfire.

Fig. 1-27—Views of spark plugs of various "reaches." A 3/8-inch reach spark plug measures 3/8 inch from firing end of shell to gasket surface of shell. The two plugs at left illustrate the difference in plugs normally used in two-stroke cycle and four-stroke cycle engines; refer to the circled electrodes. Spark plug at left has a shortened ground electrode. The short ground electrode will operate cooler then a longer ground electrode.

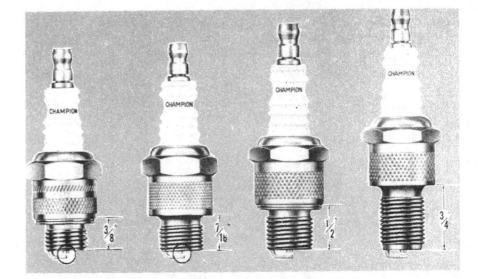

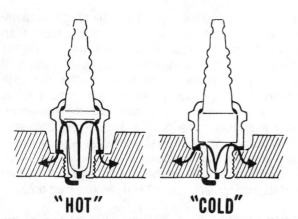

"HOT"　　　"COLD"

Fig. 1-28—Spark plug tip temperature is controlled by the length of the path heat must travel to reach cooling surface of the engine cylinder head.

The operating temperature of the plug tip can be controlled, within limits, by altering the length of the path the heat must follow to reach the threads and gasket of the plug (Fig. 1-28). Thus, a plug with a short, stubby insulator around the center electrode will run cooler than one with a long slim insulator. Most plugs in the more popular sizes are available in a number of heat ranges that are interchangeable within the group. The proper heat range is determined by engine design and type of service. Like most other elements of design, the plug type installed as original equipment is usually a compromise and is either the most suitable plug for average conditions or the best plug to meet the two extremes of service expected. No one spark plug, however, can be ideally suited for long periods of slow-speed operation and still be the best type for high-speed operation.

SERVICE FUNDAMENTALS

TROUBLESHOOTING

Most performance problems, such as failure to start, failure to run properly or missing out, are caused by malfunction of the ignition system or fuel system. The experienced serviceman generally develops and follows a logical sequence in troubleshooting that will most likely lead him quickly to the source of trouble. One such sequence might be as follows:

FAILS TO START

1. Remove and examine spark plugs. If fuel is reaching the cylinder in proper amount, there should be an odor of gasoline on the plugs if they are cold. Too much fuel can foul the plugs causing engine not to start. Fouled plugs are wet in appearance and easily detected. The presence of fouled plugs is not a sure indication that the trouble has been located, however. The engine might have started before fouling occurred if ignition system had been in good shape.

2. With spark plug removed, hold wire 1/8 to 1/4 inch from an unpainted part of the cylinder head or cylinder and crank engine sharply. The resulting spark may not be visible in bright daylight, but a distinct snap should be heard as the spark jumps the gap.

If carburetor and ignition were both apparently in good condition when tested in (1) and (2) above, check other elements of the engine such as crossed spark plug wires, improper timing, etc. A systematic search will usually pinpoint the cause of trouble with minimum delay or confusion.

DIAGNOSIS. If the presence of fuel was not apparent when checked as in (1) above and the spark seemed satisfactory when checked as in (2), systematically check the fuel system for the cause of trouble. The following are some of the probable causes:
- No fuel in tank
- Fuel shut-off valve closed
- Fuel tank vent closed or plugged
- Carburetor not primed
- Choke or starting valve incorrectly used or malfunctioning
- Water or dirt in the fuel
- Fuel line pinched or kinked
- Clogged fuel shut off, fuel line or filter
- Carburetor dirty or incorrectly adjusted
- Inlet or exhaust valve stuck open

If ignition trouble was indicated when checked as outlined in (2) above, check the electrical system for causes of trouble. Some probable causes are as follows:
- Battery voltage low (battery ignition models)
- Ignition breaker points improperly adjusted
- Shorted wire or stop switch
- Open (broken) wire
- Loose or corroded connections
- Condenser shorted
- Incorrect gap between primary coil and flywheel magnets (magneto and energy transfer ignition)
- Flywheel loose
- Faulty coil
- Ignition breaker points stuck open
- High-tension coil not properly grounded (energy transfer ignition)
- Ignition breaker point contacts pitted, burned or dirty (new ignition points are sometimes coated with protective oil)

FAULTY RUNNING ENGINE

The diagnosis of trouble in a running engine depends on experience, knowledge and acute observation. A continuous miss on one cylinder of a two-cylinder engine usually can be isolated by observing the items listed in the previous paragraphs under FAILS TO START.

Faults, such as not enough power or speed, usually can be traced to improper tuning. Make sure that air filter is clean and in good condition, and the exhaust pipe and muffler are open (not clogged). Ignition timing and carburetor(s) must be correctly adjusted. The carburetor jet sizes, clip position in valve needle and idle mixture needle settings listed in the individual service sections in this manual are "normal" settings. Altitude above sea level, rider's weight, driving habits, etc., may require different sizes and settings than those listed. On engines with two carburetors, make certain the throttles are synchronized to open exactly the same amount. Ignition timing on two-cylinder engines must be the same for each cylinder. In addition to normal engine tuning procedures, check the following: sprocket sizes incorrect; drive chain too tight or too loose; tire pressure too low; brakes dragging; clutch slipping; damaged pistons, rings and/or cylinders; loose cylinder head nuts; leaking head gasket; leaking crankcase seals.

SPECIAL NOTES ON TROUBLESHOOTING

ENGINE OVERHEATS. Probable causes of engine overheating include:

1. Dirt or debris accumulation on or between cooling fins on cylinder and head.

Fig. 2-1—Normal plug appearance. Insulator is light tan to gray in color and electrodes are not burned. Renew plug at regular intervals as manufacturer recommends.

Fig. 2-2—Appearance of spark plug indicating cold fouling, which may be caused by use of a too-cold plug, excessive idling or light loads, carburetor choke (or starting valve) out of adjustment, carburetor adjusted too "rich" or air filter dirty or wet.

Fig. 2-3—Appearance of spark plug indicating wet fouling: a wet, black oil film over entire firing end of plug. Cause may be incorrect fuel-oil ratio, incorrectly adjusted oil pump or leakage of transmission oil into crankcase (through crankshaft seals).

2. Too lean fuel-air adjustment of carburetor.

3. Improper ignition timing. Check breaker-point gap and ignition timing.

4. Two-stroke engines, operating with an improper fuel-lubricating oil mixture, may overheat due to lack of lubrication. Refer to appropriate engine service section in this manual for recommended lubrication requirements.

5. Missing or bent shields or blower housing. (On models with cooling blower, never attempt to operate without all shields and blower housing in place.)

6. Engines operating under loads in excess of rated engine horsepower, or at extremely high ambient (surrounding) air temperatures, may overheat.

TWO-STROKE CYCLE ENGINE EXHAUST PORTS. Two-stroke engines, especially those operating on an overly rich fuel-air mixture, or with too much lubricating oil mixed with the fuel, will tend to build up carbon in the cylinder exhaust ports. It is recommended that the muffler be removed periodically and the carbon removed from the exhaust ports, exhaust pipe and muffler.

On two-stroke engines that are hard to start, or where complaint is loss of power, it is wise to remove the exhaust pipe and inspect the exhaust ports for carbon buildup.

TWO-STROKE CYCLE ENGINES WITH REED VALVE. On two-stroke cycle engines, the incoming fuel-air mixture must be compressed in engine crankcase in order for the mixture to properly reach the engine cylinder. On engines using reed-type carburetor-to-crankcase intake valve, a bent or broken reed will not allow compression buildup in the crankcase. Thus, if such an engine seems to be all right otherwise, remove and inspect the reed valve unit. Refer to an appropriate engine repair manual for information on individual two-stroke cycle engine models.

SPARK PLUG. The appearance of the spark plug will be altered by use, but careful examination of the plug tip can contribute useful information. It must be remembered that contributing factors differ in two-stroke cycle and four-stroke cycle engine operation and, although the appearance of two spark plugs may be similar, the corrective measures may depend on whether the engine is of two-stroke or four-stroke design. The accompanying pictures (Figs. 2-1 through 2-8) are provided by Champion Spark Plug Company to illustrate typical conditions. Listed also are the probable causes and suggested corrective measures.

MAINTENANCE

SPARK PLUG

The recommended type of spark plug, heat range and electrode gap is listed in the appropriate MAINTENANCE section for each vehicle.

The spark plug electrode gap should be adjusted on most plugs by bending the ground electrode. Refer to Fig. 2-9. The ground electrode for some extremely cold (racing) plugs is constructed as shown by "COLD PLUG" in Fig. 2-10 and electrode gap is preset or adjusted with a special tool.

Spark plugs are usually cleaned by abrasive action commonly referred to as "sand blasting." Actually, ordinary sand is not used. Rather, a special abrasive is used that is a nonconductor of electricity even when melted, thus the abrasive cannot short out the plug current. Extreme care should be used in cleaning the plugs after

sand blasting; any abrasive particles left on the plug may cause damage to piston rings, piston or cylinder walls.

After plug is cleaned by abrasive, and before gap is set, the electrode surfaces between the grounded and insulated electrodes should be cleaned and returned as nearly as possible to original shape by filing with a point file. Failure to properly dress the electrodes can result in high secondary voltage requirements and plug misfire.

Fig. 2-6—Gap bridging usually results from excessive carbon deposits from prolonged usage, improper oil or incorrect oil-to-fuel ratio, or high-speed operation immediately upon starting.

Fig. 2-4—Appearance of spark plug indicating splash fouling. Carbon deposits, accumulated over a long period, may be loosened suddenly when new spark plugs are installed. When the engine is placed under load, excess carbon deposits shed off the piston and are thrown against the hot insulator surface. These deposits can foul the plug, but can be removed from the plug by cleaning.

Fig. 2-7—If plug has been in use for some time, electrodes may be badly eroded. Could be caused by lean carburetor mixture, fast timing, overloading, improper cooling or spark plug heat range too hot.

Fig. 2-5—Appearance of spark plug indicating core bridging. This condition is similar to, and caused by, the same combustion chamber deposits that cause splash fouling (Fig. 2-4). When the deposits become lodged between the insulator and the spark plug shell, an electrical bridge is formed, resulting in plug misfire.

Fig. 2-8—Gray, metallic aluminum deposits on plug. This condition is caused by internal engine damage. Engine should be overhauled and cause of damage corrected.

Service Fundamentals

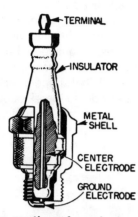

Fig. 2-9—*Cross-section of spark plug showing typical construction and nomenclature. Recommended gap between center electrode and ground electrode is listed in appropriate section for each vehicle.*

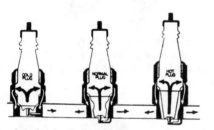

Fig. 2-10—*A principal characteristic of a "COLD" plug is that it has a shorter path for heat to travel from the insulator tip to the metal shell than the "HOT" plug shown at right.*

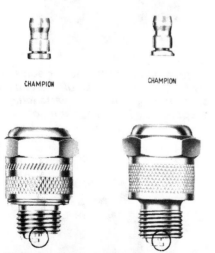

Fig. 2-11—*View of a Champion J-8J spark plug (left) and a similar J-8 plug on right. The J suffix indicates that ground electrode is slightly shorter as shown. Plugs with short ground electrodes usually require less ignition voltage than standard type and lessen the chance of bridging between electrodes. The short ground electrode operates cooler than standard length even though plugs are considered in same heat range.*

CAUTION: Use special caution when filing the electrodes of spark plugs using precious-metal electrodes. Fig. 2-12 shows the center electrode of a Champion "Gold Palladium" spark plug that has been bent by filing. Precious-metal electrodes are usually softer than normal plugs and can be easily damaged by filing. Electrode gap for plugs with precious-metal electrodes usually can be set for less gap than other spark plugs.

It is usually necessary to clean or renew spark plugs shortly after overhauling the engine. The oil used to coat engine parts during assembly may foul the plugs quickly. During the break-in period, a higher (hotter) heat range plug may be used to reduce fouling.

The following may be used to compare standard types to "Gold Palladium" spark plugs:

14 mm	⅜ in. Reach		14 mm	.472 in. Reach
....	....	HOT	....	....
J-8J	....	↑	L-86	....
....	UJ-11G	│	....	....
J-7J	....	│	....	....
....	UJ-7G	│	L-81	L-6G
J-6J	....	│	....	....
J-4J	....	↓	L-78	L-3G
J-57R	....	COLD	L-77J	L-2G

14 mm	¾ in. Reach		18 mm	.445 in. Reach
....	....	HOT	K-13	....
....	....	↑	....	K-12G
N-5	....	│	K-9	....
....	....	│	....	K-8G
N-4	N-4G	│	K-8	....
....	....	│	....	K-5G
N-3	N-3G	│	K-7	....
N-2	N-2G	↓	K-60R*	K-3G
....	....	COLD	K-57R*	K-2G

* .500 in. Reach

Fig. 2-12—*Use care to prevent damage to the electrodes, especially those made of precious metals. The center electrode shown here has been roughened, shortened and bent by filing. The plug shown is a Champion "Gold Palladium" type.*

CARBURETOR

The bulk of carburetor service consists of cleaning, inspection and adjustment. After considerable service, it may become necessary to overhaul the carburetor and renew worn parts to restore original operating efficiency. Although carburetor condition affects engine operating economy and power, ignition and engine compression also must be considered to determine and correct causes.

Before dismantling carburetor for cleaning and inspection, clean all external surfaces and remove accumulated dirt and grease. If fuel starvation is suspected, all filters in carburetor, shut-off valve and tank should be inspected. Because of inadequate fuel handling methods, rust and other foreign matter may sometimes block, or partially block, these filters. Under no circumstances should these filters be removed from the fuel system. If filters are removed, the blockage will most likely occur within the carburetor, and cleaning will be frequent and more difficult.

Refer to appropriate maintenance section for exploded or cross-sectional views of carburetors. Disassemble the carburetor and note any discrepancies that may cause a malfunction. Thoroughly clean and inspect each part. Wash jets and passages and blow clear with clean, dry, compressed air.

NOTE: Do not use a drill or wire to clean jets because the possible enlargement of holes will affect calibration.

Measurement of jets to determine extent of wear is difficult and installation of new parts usually ensures satisfaction. Sizes are usually stamped on each jet.

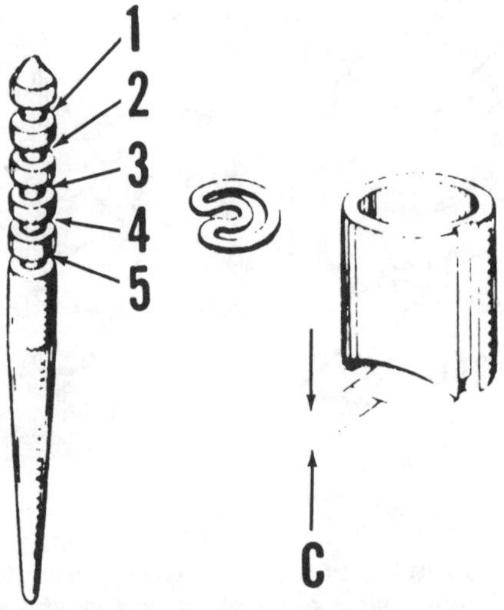

Inspect float pin and needle valve for wear and renew if necessary. Check metal floats for leaks and dual-type floats for alignment of float sections.

NOTE: Do not attempt to resolder leaky floats.

Check fit of all moving parts. Binding or excessive clearance of all parts should be corrected. Mixture adjustment needles must not be worn or grooved.

When reassembling, be sure float level (or fuel level) is properly adjusted as listed in the CARBURETOR paragraph of the appropriate maintenance section.

Normal adjustment will be limited to replacement of recommended standard-size jets and turning idle mixture needle (screw). However, the following procedure may be useful for carburetors that are particularly hard to adjust. Refer to the appropriate CARBURETOR paragraph within the specific maintenance section for further explanation and views of carburetors.

Idle mixture adjustment needle controls mixture from idle to approximately $1/8$ throttle opening. Throttle slide cut away (Fig. 2-13) on variable venturi carburetors controls mixture from $1/8$ to $1/4$ throttle opening. A larger cut away leans the mixture in this range. The valve needle located in sliding venturi controls mixture from $1/4$ to $3/4$ throttle opening. Lowering the needle in the slide leans mixture. The size of the main jet controls mixture from $3/4$ to full-open throttle.

IGNITION AND ELECTRICAL

The fundamentals of ignition and electrical system service are outlined in the following paragraphs. Refer to the appropriate heading for type of system being inspected or overhauled. A simple, easily constructed test lamp is shown in Fig. 2-14. A similar test lamp or ohmmeter can be used to facilitate repair.

Fig. 2-13—View of slide-type throttle valve. A large cut-away (C) leans the mixture in the 1/8-1/4 throttle opening range. Installation of clip in a groove nearer the top (such as No. 1) of valve needle, leans the mixture in the 1/4-3/4 throttle opening range.

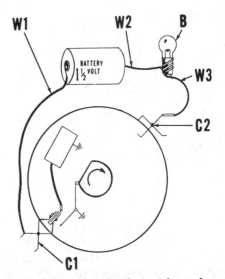

Fig. 2-14—Drawing of a simple test lamp for checking ignition timing and various other complete circuits.

Service Fundamentals

BATTERY IGNITION. Repair is usually limited to renewal of breaker points and/or condenser and adjustment of ignition timing. Refer to the appropriate MAINTENANCE section for recommended breaker-point gap and ignition timing for each model.

BREAKER POINTS. Using a small screwdriver, separate and inspect condition of contacts. If burned or deeply pitted, points should be renewed. If contacts are clean to grayish in color, disconnect condenser and coil lead wires from breaker-point terminal. Connect one

lead (C1—Fig. 2-14) to the insulated breaker-point terminal and the other (C2) to engine (ground). Light should burn with points closed and go out with points open. If light does not burn, little or no contact is indicated and points should be cleaned or renewed, and contact maximum gap should be reset.

NOTE: In some cases, new breaker-point contact surfaces may be coated with oil or wax.

If light does not go out when points are opened, breaker arm insulation is defective and points should be renewed.

Adjust breaker-point gap as follows unless manufacturer specifies adjusting breaker-point gap to obtain correct ignition timing. First, turn engine so points are closed to be sure the contact surfaces are in alignment and seat squarely. Then, turn engine so breaker-point opening is maximum and adjust breaker gap to manufacturer's specification. Be sure to recheck gap after tightening breaker-point base retaining screws.

CONDENSER. To check condition of the condenser without special test equipment, proceed as follows: The condenser case and wire should be visually checked for any obvious damage. Connect one end of the test lamp (C1—Fig. 2-14) to terminal at end of condenser wire and other end to condenser case. If light goes on, condenser is shorted and should be renewed. It is usually a good practice to renew condenser when breaker points are renewed.

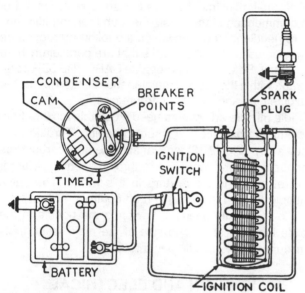

Fig. 2-15—Drawing of a typical battery ignition system for single-cylinder engine. Ignition switch closes to complete the circuit.

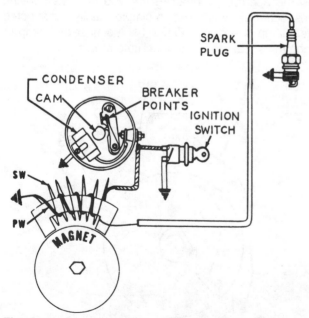

Fig. 2-16—Drawing of a typical magneto ignition system. Coil primary winding is shown at (PW) and secondary winding at (SW). Ignition switch grounds the primary circuit to stop engine.

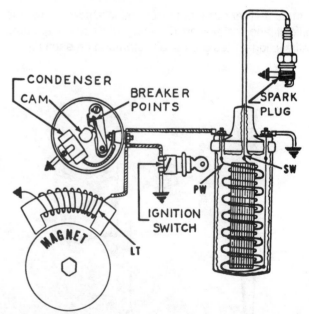

Fig. 2-17—Drawing of a typical energy transfer ignition system. Low-tension generating coil is shown at (LT). When breaker points are closed, current completes circuit through the points. When breaker points open, current rushes into the high-tension coil primary winding (PW) and induces voltage in the secondary (SW). Ignition switch grounds low-tension circuit to stop engine.

IGNITION COIL. If a coil tester is available, condition of coil can be checked. However, if tester is not available, a reasonably satisfactory performance test can be made as follows:

Disconnect high-tension wire from spark plug. Turn engine so cam has allowed breaker points to close. With ignition switch on, open and close points with small screwdriver while holding high-tension lead about ⅛ to ¼ inch from engine ground. A bright blue spark should snap across the gap between spark plug wire and ground each time the points are opened. If no spark occurs, or spark is weak and yellow-orange, renewal of the ignition coil is indicated.

Sometimes an ignition coil may perform satisfactorily when cold, but fail after engine has run for some time and coil is hot. Check coil when hot if this condition is indicated.

IGNITION TIMING. On some engines, ignition timing is non-adjustable and a certain breaker-point gap is specified. On other engines, timing is adjustable by changing the position of the stator plate with a specified breaker-point gap or by simply varying the breaker-point gap to obtain correct timing. Ignition timing is usually specified either in degrees or engine (crankshaft) rotation or in piston travel before the piston reaches top dead center position.

Some engines may have timing marks or locating pin to locate the crankshaft at proper position for the ignition spark to occur (breaker points begin to open). If not, it will be necessary to measure piston travel or install a degree wheel on engine crankshaft. Refer to Figs. 2-18 and 2-19.

A timing light as shown in Fig. 2-14 is a valuable aid in checking or adjusting engine timing. After disconnecting the ignition coil lead from the breaker-point terminal, connect the leads of the timing light as shown. If timing is adjustable by moving the stator plate, be sure the breaker-point gap is adjusted as specified. Then, to check timing, slowly turn engine in normal direction of rotation past the point where ignition spark should occur. The timing light should be on, then go out (breaker points open) just as the correct timing location is passed. If not, turn engine to proper timing location and adjust timing by relocating the breaker-point base plate or varying the breaker contact gap as specified by appropriate section for each model. Recheck timing to be sure adjustment is correct.

If ignition is equipped with advancing mechanism (manual control or automatic, centrifugal advance), make sure timing is checked when fully advanced. On some models, timing can be checked using an automotive power timing light when engine is running.

Flywheel Magneto

Repair is usually limited to renewal of breaker points and/or condenser and adjustment of ignition timing. Refer to appropriate MAINTENANCE section for recommended breaker-point gap and ignition timing for each model.

BREAKER POINTS. The same general service procedure is used as in the preceding paragraph for BATTERY IGNITION. Holes are usually provided in the flywheel for adjustment; however, flywheel usually must be removed for renewal of ignition points.

CONDENSER. The same general procedure is used to check condenser as outlined in previous BATTERY IGNITION system. Condenser is usually located under the flywheel.

ARMATURE AIR GAP. To fully concentrate the magnetic field of the flywheel, magnets pass as closely to the armature core as possible without danger of metal-to-metal contact. The clearance between the flywheel magnets and the legs of the armature core is called the armature air gap.

Fig. 2-18—On some engines, it will be necessary to measure piston travel with rule, dial indicator or special timing gauge when adjusting or checking ignition timing. Arrows show direction to move chain to position piston Before Top Dead Center after TDC has been located.

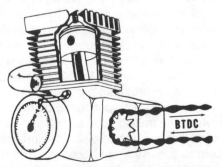

Fig. 2-19—View of typical degree wheel installation to check ignition timing. Degree wheel also can be used to check rotary valve timing and piston port opening.

Service Fundamentals

On magnetos where the armature and high-tension coil are located outside the flywheel rim, adjustment of the armature air gap is made as follows: Turn the engine so the flywheel magnets are located directly under the legs of the armature core and check the clearance between the armature core and flywheel magnets. If the measured clearance is not within manufacturer's specifications, loosen the armature mounting screws and place shims of thickness equal to minimum air gap specifications between the magnets and armature core. The magnets will pull the armature core against the shim stock. Tighten the armature core mounting screws, remove the shim stock and turn the engine through several revolutions to be sure the flywheel does not contact the armature core.

Where the armature core is located under or behind the flywheel, the following methods may be used to check and adjust armature air gap: On some engines, slots or openings are provided in the flywheel through which the armature air gap can be checked. Some engine manufacturers provide a cut-away flywheel that can be installed temporarily for checking the armature air gap.

Another method of checking the armature air gap is to remove the flywheel and place a layer of plastic tape equal to the minimum specified air gap over the legs of the armature core. Reinstall flywheel and turn engine through several revolutions and remove flywheel. No evidence of contact between the flywheel magnets and plastic tape should be noticed. Then, cover the legs of the armature core with a layer of tape equal to the maximum specified air gap. Reinstall flywheel and turn engine through several revolutions. Indication of the flywheel magnets contacting the plastic tape should be noticed after the flywheel is again removed. If the magnets contact the first thin layer of tape applied to the armature core legs, or if they do not contact the second thicker layer of tape, armature air gap is not within specifications and should be adjusted.

NOTE: Before loosening armature core mounting screws, scribe a mark on mounting plate against edge of armature core so air gap adjustment can be gauged.

MAGNETO EDGE GAP. The point of maximum acceleration of the movement of the flywheel magnetic field through the high-tension coil (and, therefore, the point of maximum current induced in the primary coil windings) occurs when the trailing edge of the flywheel magnet is slightly past the last leg of the armature core. The exact point of maximum primary current is determined by using electrical measuring devices, the distance between the trailing edge of the flywheel magnet and the leg of the armature core at this point is measured and becomes a service specification. This distance, which is stated either in thousandths of an inch or in degrees of flywheel rotation, is called the Edge Gap or "E" Gap.

For maximum strength of the ignition spark, the breaker points should just start to open when the flywheel magnets are at the specified edge gap position. Usually, edge gap is nonadjustable and will be maintained at the proper dimension if the contact breaker points are adjusted to the recommended gap and the correct breaker cam is installed. However, magneto edge gap can change and, thereby, reduce spark intensity due to the following:

a. Flywheel drive key sheared
b. Flywheel drive key worn (loose)
c. Keyway in flywheel or crankshaft worn (oversized)
d. Loose flywheel retaining nut, which also can cause any above listed difficulty
e. Excessive wear on breaker cam
f. Breaker cam loose on crankshaft
g. Excessive wear on breaker point rubbing block so that points cannot be properly adjusted.

Unit-Type Magneto

Improper functioning of the carburetor, spark plug or other components often causes difficulties that are thought to be an improperly functioning magneto. Because a brief inspection will often locate other causes for engine malfunction, it is recommended that one be certain the magneto is at fault before opening the magneto housing.

BREAKER POINTS AND CONDENSER. The same general procedure is used to service and check as outlined in previous paragraphs for BATTERY IGNITION system. Usually, complete magneto housing is rotated when adjusting ignition timing.

COIL. The ignition coil can be tested without removing the coil from the housing. The instruction provided with coil tester should have coil test specifications listed.

ROTOR. Usually, service on the magneto rotor is limited to renewal of bushings or bearings if damaged. Check to be sure rotor turns freely and does not drag or have excessive end play.

MAGNETO INSTALLATION. When installing a unit-type magneto on an engine, refer to IGNITION paragraph in appropriate engine repair section for magneto-to-engine timing information.

Energy Transfer System

The energy transfer ignition system operates very much as the previously described flywheel magneto system except the components are not in one area of the engine. Refer to Fig. 2-17. The rotor (rotating magnet) is attached to the crankshaft with the low-tension coil around it. As the magnet revolves, current generated in the low-tension coil (LT) is grounded by the closed ignition breaker points. When the current generated in the low-tension coil reaches its maximum voltage, the ignition points open causing a rapid buildup of primary current in the high-tension ignition coil. The rapid buildup of current in the high-tension coil primary windings (PW) induces a high-tension current in the secondary windings (SW) in much the same way as the rapid collapse in a battery ignition system. A special high-tension coil is used and cannot be interchanged with a battery ignition coil.

If the ignition timing cam and rotating magnet (rotor) are separately mounted, each must be individually timed with crankshaft to obtain correct magneto edge gap. Refer to preceding paragraph in FLYWHEEL MAGNETO section for explanation of EDGE GAP. On models where rotor is keyed to the crankshaft, advancing time of ignition breaker point opening causes a low voltage in the primary winding resulting in insufficient secondary voltage. If the rotor is movable on the crankshaft, it is important that the rotor position and ignition breaker-point opening not be changed from the recommended settings listed in the repair section of this manual.

Make certain the high-tension coil is securely attached. On many models, the attaching screws provide the ground for the high-tension coil. If not mounted correctly, ignition will be affected.

Capacitor Discharge System

This system differs radically from conventional units in that a relatively high-voltage current is fed into a capacitor that discharges through a pulse transformer (ignition coil) to generate the ignition spark. The secondary current is induced by the rapid buildup rather than by collapse of the primary current. The result is a high-energy ignition spark ideally suited to high-speed, two-stroke engine operation.

One development that made the new system possible was the introduction of semiconductors suitable for ignition system control. Although solid-state technology and the capacitor discharge system are not interdependent, they are uniquely compatible; each has desirable reliability and performance features.

A flywheel magneto is generally used as the primary current source in engines of the size and type found on motorcycles because of the relatively high voltage obtainable and compact, light-weight parts available. If battery current is used as the power source, it must be amplified or converted to obtain necessary voltage.

Introduction of the new ignition system is bringing unfamiliar words into use, which are defined in the following nontechnical terms:

CAPACITOR—Storage capacitor or condenser.
DIODE—A device that allows electrical current to flow in one direction, but blocks a reverse flow.
GATE-CONTROLLED SWITCH—Semiconductor that passes electrical current flow in one direction only

when a second, small "TRIGGER CURRENT" opens the "GATE." Current will not flow in the reverse direction at any time. Properly called "GATE-CONTROLLED SILICON RECTIFIER," it is sometimes called "SCR."
PULSE TRANSFORMER—Similar in purpose and sometimes in appearance to the ignition coil of a conventional ignition system. Contains the primary and secondary ignition coils and converts the primary pulse current into the secondary ignition current that fires the plug. Cannot be interchanged with regular ignition coil.
RECTIFIER—Any device that allows current flow in one direction only, or converts alternating current to direct current. Diodes are sometimes used in combination to form a BRIDGE RECTIFIER.
SCR—See GATE-CONTROLLED SWITCH.
SEMICONDUCTOR—Any of several materials that permit partial or controlled electrical current flow. Used in manufacturing diodes, rectifiers, SCRs, thermistors, thyristors, etc.
SILICON SWITCH—See GATE-CONTROLLED SILICON SWITCH.
SOLID-STATE—That branch of electronic technology that deals with the use of semiconductors as control devices. See SEMICONDUCTOR.
THERMISTOR—A solid-state regulating device that decreases in resistance as its temperature rises. Used for "temperature compensating" a control circuit.
THYRISTOR—A "safety valve" placed in the circuit that will not pass current in either direction, but is used to provide surge protection for other elements.
TRIGGER—The timed, small current that controls or opens the "GATE," thus initiating the spark.
ZENER DIODE—A diode that permits free current flow in one direction, but permits current flow in opposite direction when voltage reaches a predetermined level.

Fig. 2-20 shows a circuit diagram of a typical single-cylinder, capacitor discharge, breakerless ignition sys-

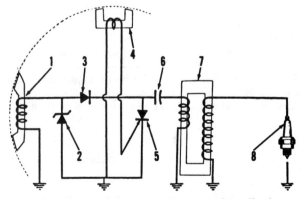

Fig. 2-20—Schematic of a typical capacitor discharge, solid-state ignition system.

1. Generating coil
2. Zener diode
3. Diode
4. Trigger coil
5. Gate-controlled switch (SCR)
6. Capacitor
7. Pulse transformer (coil)
8. Spark plug

Service Fundamentals

tem using permanent flywheel magnets as the energy source. The magnets pass by input generating coil (1) to charge capacitor (6), then by trigger coil (4) to open gate and permit discharge pulse to enter pulse transformer (7) and generate the spark that fires the plug (8). Only half the generated current passes through diode (3) to charge capacitor. Reverse current is blocked by diode (3), but passes through diode (2) to complete the reverse circuit. Diode (2) may be a zener diode to limit maximum voltage of forward current. When the flywheel magnet passes by trigger coil (4), a small electrical current is generated that opens the gate of SCR (5) allowing capacitor to discharge through pulse transformer (7). The rapid voltage rise in transformer primary coil induces a high-voltage secondary current that forms the ignition spark when it jumps the spark plug gap.

Generating System

FLYWHEEL ALTERNATORS. Alternating current is readily available on engines using a flywheel magneto

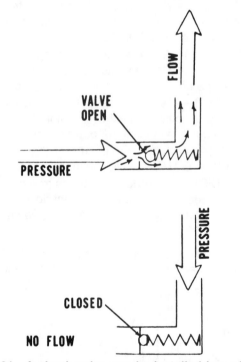

Fig. 2-21—A check valve can be installed in a pipe to allow a liquid to flow in only one direction. A rectifier serves a similar function in an electrical system.

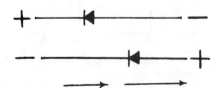

Fig. 2-22—A rectifier serves a similar function to the check valve in Fig. 2-21, allowing current to pass in only one direction.

or energy transfer ignition system by installing an additional armature core (lighting coil) in a position similar to the ignition coil. The principle of this type of system is similar to the flywheel magneto; however, only one winding is necessary. The voltage and amperage can be limited by the resistance (length, diameter, etc.) of the wire used in the lighting coil windings and the alternating current (AC) generated is satisfactory for lighting requirements. However, if a battery is used, the generated alternating current must be changed to direct current (DC), usually via a rectifier.

RECTIFIER. Repair of rectifier is limited to renewal of the unit; however, certain precautions and inspections may be more easily accomplished after a brief description of its operation.

Direct current (DC), like the type available from a battery, has an established negative terminal and a positive terminal. Alternating current, such as generated by a magneto or alternator, changes polarity as the magnetic field of force is broken by the armature core (lighting coil). This simply means that one end of the coil wire is first negative, then, as the flywheel (magnets) move on, the current reverses direction and the same end becomes positive. If the AC current was connected to a battery (DC), the current would first flow into the battery, then, as the AC changed polarity (direction), it would withdraw the same amount.

Electricity in a wire is like liquid in a pipe. In a pipe, a check valve can be installed to allow liquid to flow in only one direction, as shown in Fig. 2-21. A rectifier is a similar valve for an electrical system (see Fig. 2-22). The simplicity of modern rectifier construction is shown in Fig. 2-23. The changing of AC polarity can be shown on elaborate testing equipment like the drawing in Fig. 2-24. Where the curved line crosses the center line, the current reverses polarity. Installation of a rectifier stops current flow in one direction so current flow can be pictured as shown by the solid line in Fig. 2-25. Half the

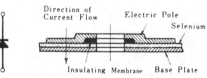

Fig. 2-23—Drawing showing the simplicity of typical modern rectifier construction. Type shown is selenium.

Fig. 2-24—Elaborate testing equipment shows alternating current as a wave. The curved "S" line between the dots is called a cycle.

Fig. 2-25—Alternating current shown by dotted lines is unused when using only one rectifier.

current generated (shown by the broken lines) is lost. A typical, simple, complete system is shown in Fig. 2-26.

In order to use the current that is normally lost in the previously described simple system, a combination of rectifiers can be used. Normally, they are constructed as one rectifying unit. Fig. 2-27 shows a typical complete system.

Rectifiers must be installed to allow current flow from the alternator into the battery. If the rectifier terminals are reversed, current from the battery will be fed into the lighting coil and coil and/or rectifier will be damaged by the resulting short circuit. The rectifier may be damaged if the system is operated without the battery connected or if battery terminals are reversed. Direction of current flow through the rectifier can be easily checked with a battery, light and wire (or ohmmeter) as shown in Fig. 2-28.

If the rectifier will not pass current in either direction using the simple test shown in Fig. 2-28, or if light continues to burn with connections reversed, rectifier may be considered faulty. Paint should not be scraped from rectifier plates and plates should not be discolored (from heat) or bent. The center bolt torque is preset and should NOT be disturbed.

FOUR-STROKE VALVE SYSTEM

Specific settings and procedures for adjusting valve clearances are listed in the appropriate individual sec-

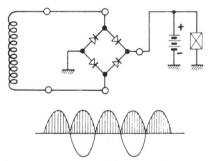

Fig. 2-26—A complete, simple electrical system, using only one rectifier, is basically as shown.

Fig. 2-27—Schematic of a full-wave rectifier system. The four diodes shown are usually constructed as one unit.

tions. Valve clearance should not be changed from the clearances listed. When the valves are closed, heat is transferred from the valve to the cylinder head and valves may burn if set too tight. If the valve clearance is too loose, the engine will have decreased power. The "rattle" usually accompanying too much valve clearance is caused by metal parts of the valve system hitting. Although the noise is sometimes not objectionable, the constant pounding will result in increased wear and/or damage.

Lubrication

Refer to the appropriate MAINTENANCE section for each model for recommended type and quantity of lubrication oils used in engine and gear box.

OIL PUMP ADJUSTMENT. Some models are equipped with a separate oil tank and pump for lubricating the engine. It is important that the oil pump is properly adjusted to provide the correct amount of oil. If the pump does not deliver the correct amount of oil, the engine may be damaged. Refer to the appropriate engine section for adjustment procedure. It is recommended that adjustment be checked periodically to make sure oil delivery is correct. Wear and/or control cable stretch will decrease the amount of oil delivered.

CLUTCH CONTROL

Clutch cable and/or control linkage is usually provided with adjustments to compensate for some stretch in cable and small amount of clutch plate wear. Clutch linkage should not prevent clutch from completely engaging and when the control is actuated, clutch should not drag. Refer to appropriate section for adjustment procedure and requirements of each model.

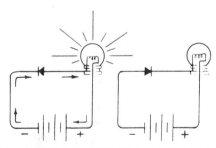

Fig. 2-28—A simple test can be made as shown on a rectifier to show which direction current can flow. Wires should be connected to rectifier so the current is allowed to pass as shown by arrows in schematics.

HONDA

AMERICAN HONDA MOTOR CO., INC.
1919 Torrance Blvd.
Torrance, CA 90501

TRX125

NOTE: Metric fasteners are used throughout vehicle.

CONDENSED SERVICE DATA

MODEL	TRX125
General	
Engine Make	Honda
Engine Type	Four-Stroke; Air-Cooled
Number of Cylinders	1
Bore	54.0 mm (2.12 in.)
Stroke	54.5 mm (2.14 in.)
Displacement	124 cc (7.6 cu. in.)
Compression Ratio	9.0:1
Engine Lubrication	Wet Sump/Oil Pump
Transmission Lubrication	Common With Engine
Engine/Transmission Oil	SAE 10W-40
Forward Speeds	5
Reverse Speeds	1
Tire Size:	
Front	20x7-8
Rear	22x10-8
Tire Pressure:	
Front	17.5 kPa (2.5 psi)
Rear	15 kPa (2.2 psi)
Battery	12V-8AH
Dry Weight (Approx.)	136 kg (300 lbs.)
Tune-Up	
Engine Idle Speed	1400-1600 rpm
Compression Pressure	1230-1430 kPa (178-207 psi)
Spark Plug:	
NGK	DR8ES-L
Nippon Denso	X24ESR-U
Electrode Gap	0.6-0.7 mm (0.024-0.028 in.)
Ignition:	
Type	Breakerless
Timing	8°-12° BTDC

Tune-Up (Cont.)

Carburetor:

Make	Keihin
Model	PB85B
Float Height	10.7 mm
	(0.42 in.)
Main Jet	#92
Idle Jet	#35
Clip Position	2nd Groove
	From Top
Idle Mixture Setting	1⅜ Turns
Throttle Lever Free Play	3-8 mm
	(⅛-5⁄16 in.)

Sizes-Clearances

Valve Clearance (cold):

Intake & Exhaust	0.08 mm
	(0.003 in.)

Valve Face & Seat Angle:

Intake & Exhaust	45°

Valve Seat Width:

Intake	1.2 mm
	(0.05 in.)
Wear Limit	1.5 mm
	(0.06 in.)
Exhaust	1.5 mm
	(0.06 in.)
Wear Limit	1.8 mm
	(0.07 in.)

Valve Stem Diameter:

Intake	5.450-5.465 mm
	(0.2146-0.2152 in.)
Wear Limit	5.42 mm
	(0.213 in.)
Exhaust	5.430-5.445 mm
	(0.2138-0.2144 in.)
Wear Limit	5.40 mm
	(0.213 in.)

Valve Guide Bore Diameter:

Intake & Exhaust	5.475-5.485 mm
	(0.2157-0.2161 in.)
Wear Limit	5.50 mm
	(0.2165 in.)

Valve Stem-to-Guide Clearance:

Intake	0.010-0.035 mm
	(0.0004-0.0014 in.)
Wear Limit	0.08 mm
	(0.003 in.)
Exhaust	0.030-0.055 mm
	(0.0012-0.0022 in.)
Wear Limit	0.10 mm
	(0.004 in.)

Valve Spring Free Length:

Inner	39.4 mm
	(1.55 in.)
Minimum Length	35.5 mm
	(1.40 in.)

Sizes-Clearances (Cont.)

Valve Spring Free Length: (Cont.)

Outer	45.5 mm (1.79 in.)
Minimum Length	41.0 mm (1.61 in.)

Rocker Arm Bore Diameter:

Intake & Exhaust	12.000-12.027 mm (0.4724-0.4735 in.)
Wear Limit	12.05 mm (0.474 in.)

Rocker Shaft Diameter:

Intake & Exhaust	11.977-11.995 mm (0.4715-0.4722 in.)
Wear Limit	11.93 mm (0.470 in.)

Camshaft Lobe Height:

Intake	31.083-31.243 mm (1.2237-1.2300 in.)
Wear Limit	30.98 mm (1.220 in.)
Exhaust	30.681-30.841 mm (1.2079-1.2142 in.)
Wear Limit	30.58 mm (1.204 in.)

Cam Journal Clearance:

Right Journal	0.025-0.059 mm (0.0009-0.0023 in.)
Wear Limit	0.15 mm (0.006 in.)
Left Journal	0.025-0.064 mm (0.0009-0.0025 in.)
Wear Limit	0.15 mm (0.006 in.)

Cylinder Head Distortion (Max.).	0.10 mm (0.004 in.)
Cylinder Bore Diameter	54.00-54.01 mm (2.125-2.126 in.)
Wear Limit	54.10 mm (2.129 in.)
Piston-to-Cylinder Clearance.	0.015-0.055 mm (0.0006-0.0021 in.)
Wear Limit	0.10 mm (0.004 in.)

Piston Diameter—
Measured 10 mm (0.4 in.) From

Skirt Bottom & 90° to Pin Bore	54.955-54.985 mm (2.1242-2.1254 in.)
Wear Limit	53.90 mm (2.555 in.)
Piston Pin Bore	15.002-15.008 mm (0.5906-0.5909 in.)
Wear Limit	15.02 mm (0.591 in.)
Piston Pin Diameter.	14.994-15.000 mm (0.5903-0.5906 in.)
Wear Limit	14.98 mm (0.589 in.)

Sizes-Clearances (Cont.)

Piston-to-Pin Clearance	0.002-0.014 mm (0.0001-0.0006 in.)
Wear Limit	0.02 mm (0.001 in.)
Piston Ring End Gap:	
Top & Second Rings	0.10-0.30 mm (0.004-0.012 in.)
Wear Limit	0.50 mm (0.020 in.)
Oil Ring	0.20-0.80 mm (0.008-0.031 in.)
Piston Ring Side Clearance:	
Top Ring	0.010-0.045 mm (0.0004-0.0018 in.)
Wear Limit	0.12 mm (0.005 in.)
Second Ring	0.015-0.050 mm (0.0006-0.0020 in.)
Wear Limit	0.12 mm (0.005 in.)
Oil Ring	....
Connecting Rod Small End Bore Diameter	15.016-15.034 mm (0.5912-0.5919 in.)
Wear Limit	15.06 mm (0.593 in.)
Connecting Rod Big End Side Clearance (Max.)	0.80 mm (0.031 in.)
Connecting Rod Big End Radial Clearance (Max.)	0.05 mm (0.002 in.)
Crankshaft Runout (Max.):	
Flywheel End	0.08 mm (0.003 in.)
Clutch End	0.10 mm (0.004 in.)

Capacities

Fuel Tank	7.5 L (2.0 gal.)
Engine/Transmission Sump	See Text

Tightening Torques

Axle Nut:	
Front	70-90 N•m (51-65 ft.-lbs.)
Rear	110-150 N•m (80-108 ft.-lbs.)
Cam Chain Tensioner	10-14 N•m (89-124 in.-lbs.)
Camshaft Sprocket	18-20 N•m (13-15 ft.-lbs.)
Clutch Nut	50-60 N•m (36-43 ft.-lbs.)
Cylinder Head Nut	28-30 N•m (20-22 ft.-lbs.)

Tightening Torques (Cont.)

Rewind Starter Cup Cap Screw.........	40-50 N·m (29-36 ft.-lbs.)
Spark Plug.....................	17 N·m (150 in.-lbs.)
Wheel Retaining Nut	50-60 N·m (36-43 ft.-lbs.)
Standard Screws:	
5 mm.........................	3.5-5.0 N·m (31-44 in.-lbs.)
6 mm.........................	7-11 N·m (62-97 in.-lbs.)
Standard Bolts & Nuts:	
5 mm.........................	4.5-6.0 N·m (40-53 in.-lbs.)
6 mm.........................	8-12 N·m (71-106 in.-lbs.)
8 mm.........................	18-25 N·m (13-18 ft.-lbs.)
10 mm........................	30-40 N·m (22-29 ft.-lbs.)
12 mm........................	50-60 N·m (36-43 ft.-lbs.)
Flanged Bolts & Nuts:	
6 mm.........................	10-14 N·m (89-124 in.-lbs.)
8 mm.........................	24-30 N·m (17-22 ft.-lbs.)
10 mm........................	35-45 N·m (25-32 ft.-lbs.)

LUBRICATION

ENGINE AND TRANSMISSION. The engine and transmission are lubricated by a trochoid-type pump located on the right side of the crankcase and driven by a gear on the right end of the crankshaft. The engine and transmission share a common sump. Recommended oil is SAE 10W-40 motor oil with an API classification of SE or SF.

The sump is filled through filler plug (F—Fig. H1-1) opening. Oil level should be maintained at upper mark on filler plug dipstick. Do not screw filler plug in when checking oil level. Oil is drained by removing plug in underside of crankcase. Crankcase capacity after changing oil is 1.3 L (1.4 qt.). Crankcase dry capacity is 1.5 L (1.6 qt.).

Manufacturer recommends changing oil and oil filter after the first week of operation, and then after every 30 days of operation. A sump filter screen located in a compartment in right crankcase half should be removed periodically and cleaned.

The old filter can be renewed after removing filter cover (C). The new filter is inserted with rubber seal side facing toward filter cover (C). Be sure filter spring is correctly positioned between filter and crankcase cover. Renew filter cover "O" ring, if required, and install cover. Sump filter screen is accessible after removing right crankcase cover. With oil drained from crankcase, remove brake pedal and bracket assembly. Remove the reverse cable and shift arm assembly. Remove cap screws securing right crankcase cover and carefully remove cover. Withdraw sump screen from compartment at base of crankcase. Clean screen with a suitable nonflammable solvent and inspect for damage. Renew screen if damaged.

Reinstall by reversing removal procedure. Adjust reverse cable as outlined in REVERSE CABLE ADJUSTMENT section. Fill engine/transmission sump with the appropriate amount of oil and check for leaks.

DRIVE CHAIN. The final drive chain should be lubricated with SAE 80-90 gear oil after the first week of operation and then after every 30 days of operation. An

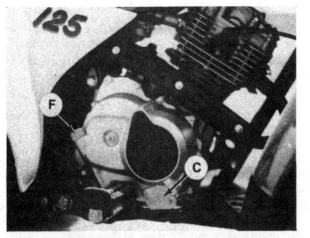

Fig. H1-1—Remove oil fill plug (F) to add oil to engine/transmission sump. Remove cover (C) for access to oil filter element.

"O" ring-sealed drive chain is used. Incorrect chain lubricating oil can cause damage to "O" ring seals.

The drive chain should be removed and cleaned when excessive dirt is evident. Remove chain as outlined in FINAL DRIVE CHAIN AND SPROCKETS section. The chain should be thoroughly washed in kerosene and wiped dry. The use of any cleaning solution other than kerosene can result in drive chain "O" ring seal damage. Lubricate chain with SAE 80-90 gear oil. Reinstall and adjust as described in FINAL DRIVE CHAIN AND SPROCKETS section.

CABLES AND LEVERS. All cables and levers should be inspected and lubricated after the first week of operation and every 30 days of operation thereafter.

AIR CLEANER ELEMENT

The air cleaner element should be removed and cleaned after every 30 days of operation. To remove air cleaner element, first remove seat. Release clips securing element cover and remove cover. Loosen band screw at front of element and withdraw element assembly. Separate foam element from frame.

Thoroughly clean the foam element in a nonflammable solvent. Compress element between hands to remove solvent. Saturate element in clean SAE 80-90 gear oil. Compress element to remove excess oil. Reinstall air cleaner element assembly by reversing removal procedure.

FUEL SYSTEM

CARBURETOR. Refer to Fig. H1-3 for a view of a partially disassembled carburetor similar to type used. The fuel control valve is attached to base of fuel tank. Refer to CONDENSED SERVICE DATA for carburetor specifications.

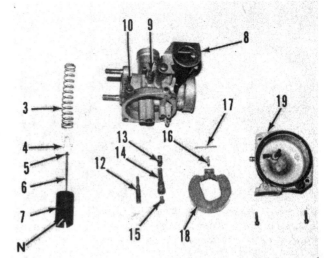

Fig. H1-3—Exploded view of a partially disassembled carburetor similar to type used on TRX125.

3. Spring	12. Idle jet
4. Retainer	13. Needle jet
5. Clip	14. Needle jet holder
6. Jet needle	15. Main jet
7. Throttle slide	16. Fuel inlet valve
8. Body	17. Float pin
9. Idle speed screw	18. Float
10. Idle mixture screw	19. Float bowl

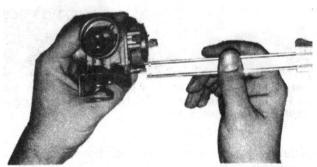

Fig. H1-4—Float height should be 10.7 mm (0.42 in.). Hold carburetor so float is vertical and resting lightly against fuel inlet valve.

Initial setting of idle mixture screw (10—Fig. H1-3) is 1⅜ turns out from a lightly seated position. Rotating idle mixture screw clockwise will lean idle mixture.

Final carburetor adjustment is performed with engine at normal operating temperature. Adjust idle speed screw (9) so engine idles at 1400-1600 rpm. Slowly rotate idle mixture screw (10) clockwise, leaning idle mixture, until engine stalls. Note screw position. Rotate idle mixture screw counterclockwise, richening idle mixture, 1½ turns. Adjust idle speed to 1400-1600 rpm.

When servicing carburetor, note the following: Jet needle clip (5) should be installed in second groove from top of jet needle. Float height should be 10.7 mm (0.42 in.) between bottom of float and carburetor body. Hold carburetor so float is vertical and resting lightly against fuel inlet valve as shown in Fig. H1-4. Float height is not adjustable. Renew float and/or fuel inlet valve if float height is incorrect. Make sure groove in side of throttle

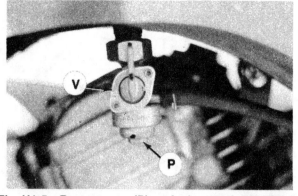

Fig. H1-5—Remove cap (P) on fuel control valve (V) for access to fuel screen. Unscrew valve nut to remove fuel control valve for access to fuel strainer.

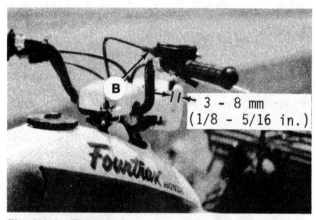

Fig. H1-6—Throttle lever free play should be 3-8 mm (1/8-5/16 in.). Slide dust boot (B) down cable to expose cable adjuster and locknut.

slide is aligned with pin in carburetor body when inserting slide in carburetor.

Suggested main jet size for altitudes above 3300 feet is #88.

FUEL FILTER SCREEN AND STRAINER. A fuel filter screen is located in the fuel control valve and a strainer that extends into the fuel tank is attached to the inlet of the fuel control valve. The filter screen should be cleaned after every 30 days of operation. Periodic cleaning of the fuel strainer should not be required.

To remove the filter screen, be sure fuel control valve is in "OFF" position and unscrew cup (P—Fig. H1-5) on bottom of valve. Remove and clean screen. Reassemble while making sure "O" ring is properly positioned. Tighten cup (do not overtighten), turn valve lever to "ON" and check for leaks.

To remove fuel strainer, disconnect fuel line and drain fuel from fuel tank. Unscrew fuel control valve (V) from fuel tank. Inspect and clean strainer attached to control valve. Reinstall components. Turn control valve lever to "ON" and check for leaks.

THROTTLE LEVER FREE PLAY. Free play at the end of the throttle lever should be 3-8 mm ($\frac{1}{8}$-$\frac{5}{16}$ in.) as shown in Fig. H1-6. To adjust free play, slide back rubber boot (B), loosen knurled nut and rotate cable adjuster. Retighten knurled nut.

IGNITION AND ELECTRICAL

SPARK PLUG. The recommended spark plug for normal operating conditions is a NGK DR8ES-L or Nippon Denso X24ESR-U. Spark plug electrode gap should be 0.6-0.7 mm (0.024-0.028 in.). The spark plug should be removed, inspected, cleaned or renewed, and regapped after every 30 days of operation.

IGNITION. The engine is equipped with a breakerless, capacitor discharge ignition system. The electronic ignition circuit consists of the flywheel, exciter coil, CDI module, pulse generator, ignition coil, spark plug, ignition switch, reverse switch and engine stop switch. To check ignition timing, remove timing plug (T—Fig. H1-8) and connect a power timing light to engine. Ignition timing (8-12° BTDC) at idle speed should occur when "F" mark on flywheel is aligned with stationary mark (M) on case. Advanced ignition timing is 26-30° BTDC at 4000 rpm. Advanced ignition should occur when "=" mark on flywheel is aligned with mark (M) on case. Ignition timing is not adjustable. If ignition timing is not as specified, check condition of ignition components as described in the following test procedures and renew faulty or questionable components.

If ignition malfunction occurs, check condition of spark plug, all wires and connections before troubleshooting the ignition circuit. Using Honda Digital Multi-Tester KS-AHM-32-003 or a suitable ohmmeter, refer to the following test procedures and specifications to aid troubleshooting.

To check condition of exciter coil, separate black/red wire from exciter coil to CDI module at connector. Using

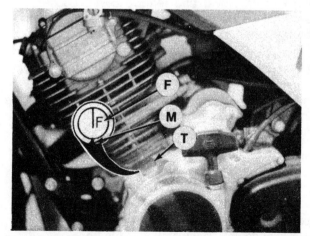

Fig. H1-8—Remove timing plug (T) to view flywheel and timing marks. Ignition at idle speed should occur when "F" mark on flywheel aligns with stationary mark (M).

an ohmmeter, measure resistance between coil end of black/red wire and vehicle ground. Exciter coil is considered satisfactory if resistance is 100-300 ohms.

To check condition of pulse generator, separate wire connector from pulse generator to CDI module. Connect an ohmmeter lead to blue/yellow wire going to engine and remaining ohmmeter lead to vehicle ground. Pulse generator is satisfactory if ohmmeter reading is 290-360 ohms. If reading is incorrect, remove left crankcase cover and repeat test at terminal of pulse generator.

To check condition of ignition coil, detach black/yellow wire and green wire from ignition coil. Disconnect high-tension lead from spark plug. To check primary winding resistance, attach one ohmmeter lead to black/yellow wire terminal on ignition coil and remaining ohmmeter lead to green wire terminal. Ohmmeter should read 0.1-0.3 ohms. Perform two secondary winding tests, one with the spark plug cap attached to coil wire and one without spark plug cap attached. Attach one ohmmeter lead to spark plug cap and remaining ohmmeter lead to coil ground (green wire terminal). Secondary winding resistance through spark plug cap should be 7.4k-11.0k ohms. Remove spark plug cap from high-tension wire. Attach an ohmmeter lead to high-tension wire and remaining ohmmeter lead to coil ground. Secondary winding resistance reading, with spark plug cap removed, should be 3.7k-4.5k ohms. If secondary winding resistance is not within specification, renew spark plug cap.

A neutral/reverse switch is located in the left crankcase cover. The switch turns on the appropriate indicator light when the transmission is in neutral or reverse. When the transmission is in reverse during starting, the ignition is grounded. When the transmission is in neutral during starting, the starter relay circuit can be energized. To check neutral/reverse switch, disconnect the three-wire connector (light green/red wire and two gray wires) in junction box under right rear fender. With transmission in neutral, connect an ohmmeter lead to the light

green/red wire terminal and connect the remaining ohmmeter lead to vehicle ground. The ohmmeter should show continuity. When transmission is in gear, the ohmmeter should read infinity. With transmission in reverse, connect one ohmmeter lead to vehicle ground, then connect remaining ohmmeter lead to one gray wire terminal. Repeat test at other gray wire terminal. The ohmmeter should show continuity. When transmission is in neutral or forward gears, ohmmeter should show infinity.

CHARGING CIRCUIT. The charging circuit consists of the alternator, voltage regulator and maintenance-free battery. Specified battery is rated 12 VDC with 8 amp-hour capacity. Under load, the alternator should produce 14-15 volts and 130 watts at 5000 rpm.

The battery should be charged if the vehicle is stored for an extended period. The battery should be removed during charging. If the battery is charged while in the vehicle, disconnect the battery cables to prevent damage to charging circuit components. The battery should be charged at a minimum rate of 0.9 amperes for five hours or at a maximum rate of 4 amperes for one hour.

The alternator charge coil can be statically tested using a suitable ohmmeter. Separate connector leading to regulator from alternator with two yellow wires. Connect ohmmeter leads to terminals of connector leading to alternator. Resistance reading should be 0.1-1.0 ohm. Connect one tester lead to vehicle ground. Alternately connect remaining tester lead to connector terminals. Ohmmeter should read infinity.

The regulator is mounted on the battery case. To check condition of regulator, disconnect regulator from charging circuit at connector block. Use an ohmmeter in conjunction with chart in Fig. H1-10. Renew regulator if it fails to meet test specifications.

An operational check of the complete charging circuit can be performed with a suitable voltmeter. Attach voltmeter directly to battery terminal. Start and run engine until it is at normal operating temperature. Turn lights on and gradually increase engine speed while reading voltmeter. Regulated voltage should be 14-15 volts.

ELECTRIC STARTER. The engine is equipped with the electric starter shown in Fig. H1-11. Before disassembling starter motor, note alignment marks, or make alignment marks, on center housing and end caps so they can be reinstalled in original positions. When disassembling motor, note location of all shims and washers. Minimum brush length is 5.5 mm (0.22 in.). Note pin on brush holder plate that must align with notch in frame during assembly. Install rear cap so slot engages pin on brush holder plate. Be sure "O" rings are correctly positioned during assembly.

WIRING. If wiring requires repair, always install wire that is the same gauge as original wire. Wires should be routed away from areas of extreme heat or sharp edges.

		+ Tester lead			
		YELLOW	YELLOW	GREEN	RED	BLACK
− Tester lead	YELLOW		A	A	B	A
	YELLOW	A		A	B	A
	GREEN	B	B		C	D
	RED	A	A	A		
	BLACK	E	E	F	G	

Fig. H1-10—Use chart shown above and values listed below to test voltage regulator.

A. Infinite resistance
B. 1k-20k ohms
C. 3k-100k ohms
D. 0.2k-20k ohms
E. 1k-50k ohms
F. 0.2k-10k ohms
G. 3k-10k ohms

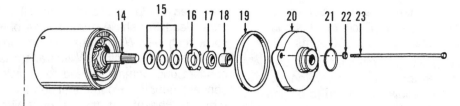

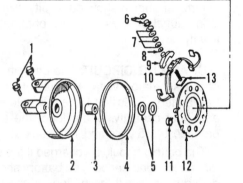

Fig. H1-11—Exploded view of electric starter motor.

1. Screws
2. Rear cap
3. Bushing
4. "O" ring
5. Washers
6. Nut
7. Washers
8. "O" ring
9. Insulator
10. Brush set
11. Spring
12. Brush holder
13. Screw
14. Armature
15. Shims
16. Special washer
17. Oil seal
18. Bushing
19. "O" ring
20. Front cap
21. "O" ring
22. Washer
23. Screw

Attach or hold wires in their original position using plastic tie straps to prevent short circuits.

FASTENERS

After the first week of operation and after every 30 days of operation thereafter, the vehicle should receive an overall inspection. All screws, nuts and other fasteners should be checked and tightened to proper torque specification shown in CONDENSED SERVICE DATA section or in the appropriate maintenance section.

VALVE SYSTEM

The valves are actuated via rocker arms by a single overhead camshaft. The camshaft is driven by a roller chain attached to the left end of the crankshaft. Valve clearance should be adjusted after the first week of operation and then after 30 days of operation. Valve clearance should be adjusted with engine cold.

To adjust valve clearance, remove timing plug (T—Fig. H1-8) and valve adjustment caps (C—Fig. H1-12). Rotate crankshaft until "T" mark (Top Dead Center) on flywheel aligns with stationary mark (M—Fig. H1-8) and piston is on compression stroke. To ensure piston is on compression stroke, rotate crankshaft approximately ¼ turn past TDC while observing intake valve. If valve movement is indicated, rotate crankshaft one complete revolution and align "T" mark with stationary mark again.

Clearance between rocker arm adjusting screw (A—Fig. H1-13) and valve stem should be 0.08 mm (0.003 in.) for both the intake and exhaust valves. Measure clearance with a suitable feeler gauge (G). Adjust clearance by loosening locknut (L) and turning adjusting screw (A). Be sure to recheck clearance after locknuts are tightened.

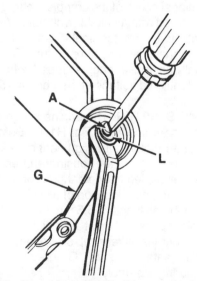

Fig. H1-12—Remove valve adjustment caps (C) to expose rocker arm adjusting screws (A—Fig. H1-13).

Fig. H1-13—Loosen locknut (L) and turn adjusting screw (A) to adjust clearance between valve stem and adjusting screw. Clearance should be 0.08 mm (0.003 in.) for both valves. Measure clearance using feeler gauge (G).

Fig. H1-15—Rear brake lever (B) should have 2-4 mm (6/64-5/32 in.) free travel when reverse button (R) is engaged.

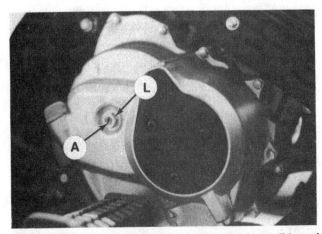

Fig. H1-16—To adjust rear brake lever free travel when reverse button is engaged, loosen nut (N) and adjust cable position in bracket until specified free play is obtained.

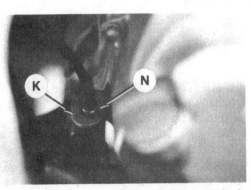

Fig. H1-18—To adjust clutch, loosen locknut (L) and turn adjusting screw (A) counterclockwise until internal resistance is felt, then turn screw 1/4 turn clockwise. Secure adjusting screw with locknut (L).

REVERSE CABLE ADJUSTMENT

The vehicle is equipped with a reverse lock mechanism designed to prevent accidental engagement of reverse gear. The rear brake lever (B—Fig. H1-15) should have 2-4 mm ($^5/_{64}$-$^5/_{32}$ in.) free travel when reverse button (R) is engaged. To adjust free travel, loosen nut (N—Fig. H1-16) and adjust cable position in bracket until specified free play is obtained.

CLUTCH

The engine is equipped with two automatically actuated clutches. A three-shoe centrifugal clutch is mounted on the right end of the crankshaft. The centrifugal clutch is disengaged at idle speed and engages when crankshaft speed increases. A multiple-disc clutch is attached to the transmission mainshaft and is actuated by the gear shift mechanism. When the gear shift lever is operated, the multiple-disc clutch is disengaged to allow smooth transmission gear movement.

The clutch should be adjusted after the first week of operation, and after every 30 days of operation. To adjust clutch, loosen locknut (L—Fig. H1-18). Turn adjusting screw (A) counterclockwise until internal resistance is felt, then turn screw $^1/_4$ turn clockwise. Secure adjusting screw with locknut (L).

The clutch should automatically disengage at engine idle speed. When selecting gears, clutch should engage and disengage freely without excess slippage. Difficult shifting, clutch grabbing or clutch slipping may indicate overhaul is necessary.

MANUAL STARTER

R&R AND OVERHAUL. Refer to Fig. H1-20 for a view of a partially disassembled manual starter. Starter can

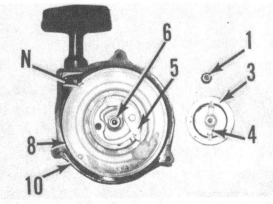

Fig. H1-20—View of partially disassembled manual starter similar to type used on TRX125.

N. Notch	5. Starter pawl
1. Cap screw	6. Friction spring
3. Friction plate	8. Rope pulley
4. Pawl guide	10. Starter housing

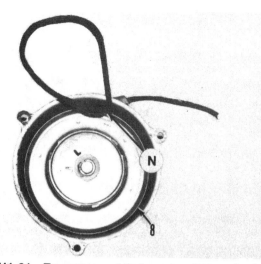

Fig. H1-21—To remove or place tension on rewind spring, pull a loop of rope back through rope outlet so rope engages notch (N) in rope pulley (8). Refer to text.

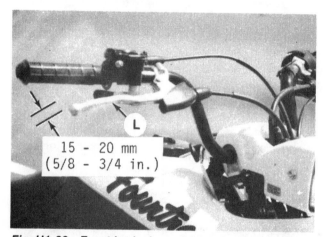

Fig. H1-22—Front brake lever (L) free play measured at end of lever should be 15-20 mm (5/8-3/4 in.). Refer to text for adjustment procedure.

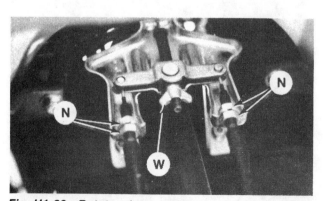

Fig. H1-23—Rotate wing nut (W) to adjust front brake lever free travel. Rotate nuts (N) as outlined in text to equalize front brake action.

be removed from engine as a complete unit after removing the gear shift lever and the four starter retaining cap screws. If starter rope remains under tension, pull starter rope and hold rope pulley with notch (N) adjacent to rope outlet. Pull a loop of rope back through outlet so rope engages notch in pulley and allow pulley to slowly unwind. Remove cap screw (1) and disassemble unit. Be careful when removing rewind spring; a rapidly uncoiling starter spring can cause serious injury.

Rewind spring is wound into starter housing in a clockwise direction. Rope is wound on rope pulley in a clockwise direction as viewed with pulley in housing. Reassemble starter by reversing disassembly procedure. During reassembly, lightly grease pulley shaft and starter pawl.

To place tension on rewind spring after starter assembly, pass rope through rope outlet in housing and install rope handle. Pull a loop of rope back through starter housing outlet and notch (N—Fig. H1-21) in pulley. Turn pulley clockwise two or three complete revolutions to place tension on spring. Do not place more tension on rewind spring than is necessary to draw rope handle up against housing.

FRONT BRAKE SYSTEM

BRAKE LEVER FREE PLAY. Recommended brake lever free travel is 15-20 mm (5/8-3/4 in.) measured at outer end of brake lever (L—Fig. H1-22). Adjust lever free play by rotating brake cable wing nut (W—Fig. H1-23) at equalizer bracket. If uneven brake action is evident at wheels, loosen locknuts (N) on each brake cable and adjust cable position in bracket to equalize brake action. Tighten locknuts (N), then rotate wing nut (W) to adjust brake lever free travel.

OVERHAUL. Brake lining thickness is indicated by position of pointer attached to brake actuating lever when brakes are applied. There is sufficient brake lining remaining if pointer (P—Fig. H1-24) does not align with or pass mark (M) on steering knuckle.

WARNING: Inhaling asbestos brake dust is injurious to human health. Approved OSHA respiration equipment must be worn when working on or around brake components. DO NOT use compressed air to clean brake drums, shoes or nearby components because brake dust will be blown into air. Only vacuum equipment designed to pick up brake dust should be used.

Each front brake assembly is accessible after removing the brake drum. Renew the brake shoes if damaged or if lining is worn to less than 2.0 mm (0.08 in.). Renew the brake drum assembly if inside diameter exceeds 111.0 mm (4.4 in.).

FRONT AXLE

Each front knuckle assembly pivots on the end of the front axle. Front axle tube is bolted to vehicle's frame.

Remove front wheel to service the knuckle assembly. If excessive play between king pin and bushings is noted, then components should be renewed. Renew upper and lower dust seals when renewing king pin and bushings. Grease king pin prior to installation. Tighten king pin bolt to 50-70 N•m (36-51 ft.-lbs.).

STEERING

All Models

TOE-IN SETTING. Place the handlebar in a straight ahead position. Use a suitable measuring tool and measure distance (D—Fig. H1-25), at spindle height, between the center of the tires on the front and rear sides. The measured distance (D) on the front side should be 10 mm (³⁄₈ in.) less or 10 mm (³⁄₈ in.) more than the measured distance on rear side. If not, loosen inside and outside locknuts on the left and right tie rods and rotate tie rod shaft (S) on each side equally until measured distance is within recommended range.

After obtaining the correct setting, securely tighten the locknuts to retain tie rod settings.

INSPECTION. Rotate the steering handlebar through full range of movement and note any binding or roughness. Periodically inspect the steering components for looseness or any other damage. Renew any damaged components. Clean and grease components if binding or excessive effort is noted.

OVERHAUL. To withdraw the steering shaft, remove the handlebar assembly, headlight/choke knob bracket, front fender, front brake equalizer, tie rod ends from steering shaft, upper bushing holder bolts and nuts, then withdraw steering shaft assembly. Unstake and remove the lower nut to withdraw the lower bearing holder. Renew bearing in holder if binding, roughness or other damage is noted.

Tighten nut retaining lower bearing holder to 35-43 N•m (25-31 ft.-lbs.) and stake nut. Upper steering shaft bushing should be a minimum of 2.85 mm (0.112 in.) thick. Renew bushing if excessive wear or other damage is noted. Grease bushing prior to installing steering shaft. Tighten upper bushing holder bolts and lower bearing holder bolts to 24-30 N•m (17-22 ft.-lbs.). Tighten tie rod end nuts to 35-43 N•m (25-31 ft.-lbs.) and install new cotter pins. Complete reassembly in reverse order of disassembly.

REAR BRAKE ASSEMBLY

The rear brake consists of a two-shoe, internally expanding, drum brake mounted on the right end of the rear axle and actuated by either the left handlebar lever or right brake pedal. Information on the front brake is outlined in FRONT BRAKE ASSEMBLY section.

INSPECTION AND ADJUSTMENT. The brake system should be inspected and adjusted after the first week of operation and every 30 days of operation thereafter. The brake drum and shoes should be inspected and renewed annually, if required, as outlined in R&R AND OVERHAUL paragraphs.

To adjust brake pedal free travel, actuate brake pedal and measure free travel at end of pedal. Free travel should be 15-20 mm (⁵⁄₈-³⁄₄ in.) and is adjusted by rotating adjuster (A—Fig. H1-26) at rear brake.

Fig. H1-24—Front brake lining has reached minimum allowable thickness if pointer (P) aligns with or passes mark (M) when brake is applied.

Fig. H1-25—Refer to text for procedure to check toe-in setting. Distance (D) is measured between centerline of wheel at axle height. Tie rod shafts (S) are rotated to adjust toe-in setting after loosening inside and outside tie rod end locknuts.

The rear brake lever should have 15-20 mm (⅝-¾ in.) of free travel measured at end of lever. Rotate lever adjuster (R) at rear brake to adjust lever free travel.

A rear brake lining wear indicator is fitted to the rear brake shoe cam so brake lining wear can be checked externally. To check brake lining wear externally, apply rear brake and note position of pointer (I) at end of indicator in relation to stationary mark on backing plate. Brake shoes should be renewed as outlined in R&R AND OVERHAUL paragraphs if indicator aligns or rotates beyond stationary mark.

Fig. H1-26—Adjust drive chain tension by loosening four axle housing cap screws (C) and rotating tension adjuster nut (T). Brake pedal free travel is adjusted at pedal adjuster (A) and brake lever free travel is adjusted at lever adjuster (R). Rear brake lining has reached minimum allowable thickness if indicator (I) aligns with or passes stationary mark on backing plate when brake is applied.

Fig. H1-27—View showing location of outer brake drum retaining nuts (N) and brake drum cover (3).

R&R AND OVERHAUL. To remove rear brake shoes and drum, first suitably support rear of vehicle and remove right rear axle nut. Pull tire, wheel, hub assembly and hub washer from axle. Loosen brake pedal adjuster (A—Fig. H1-26) and brake lever adjuster (R). Remove two nuts (N—Fig. H1-27) and tapered washer and flat washer located behind nuts (N).

WARNING: Inhaling asbestos brake dust is injurious to human health. Approved OSHA respiration equipment must be worn when working on or around brake components. DO NOT use compressed air to clean brake drum, shoes or nearby components because brake dust will be blown into the air. Only vacuum equipment designed to pick up brake dust should be used.

Remove brake drum cover (3). Remove "O" ring on axle shaft and slide brake drum off axle. Carefully remove brake shoes and springs from backing plate.

Brake shoes should be renewed if linings are worn to 2 mm (0.08 in.) or less. Brake drum should be renewed if inside diameter exceeds 141 mm (5.55 in.).

Reassemble components by reversing disassembly procedures while noting the following: Lightly coat brake shoe cam and anchor pin with grease making sure grease does not contact brake shoe linings. Install tapered washer with cupped side facing toward flat washer. Tighten inner locknut (N) to 40-50 N·m (29-36 ft.-lbs.). Apply Loctite or equivalent to threads of outer locknut (N), install and tighten locknut to 140-150 N·m (101-108 ft.-lbs.) while holding inner nut to prevent rotation. Install wheel hub and tighten axle nut to 110-150 N·m (80-108 ft.-lbs.), then install a new cotter pin. Tighten wheel retaining nuts to 50-60 N·m (36-43 ft.-lbs.).

DRIVE CHAIN AND SPROCKETS

INSPECTION AND ADJUSTMENT. The final drive chain should be inspected and adjusted after the first week of operation and every 30 days thereafter. Improper maintenance and neglect can cause early failure of both drive chain and sprockets. Drive chain free play should be 10-20 mm (⅜-¾ in.) measured midway between sprockets. Drive chain condition and free play can be checked through inspection hole in chain cover.

To adjust chain tension, loosen rear axle housing retaining cap screws (C—Fig. H1-26) and rotate tension adjusting nuts (T). Tighten axle housing cap screws to 50-70 N·m (36-51 ft.-lbs.) and recheck drive chain tension. Renew drive chain if recommended tension adjustment cannot be obtained. Refer to LUBRICATION for drive chain lubrication requirements.

R&R AND OVERHAUL. The drive chain is sealed by "O" rings and fitted with a master link. To remove the

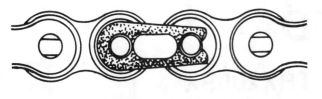

← CHAIN TRAVEL

Fig. H1-28—The drive chain master link retaining clip should always be installed with closed end toward normal direction of chain travel.

drive chain and both sprockets, support rear of vehicle and remove left axle nut. Pull tire, wheel, hub assembly and hub washer from axle. Remove skid plate and chain guard. Loosen rear axle housing cap screws (C—Fig. H1-26) and back off chain tension adjuster nut (T) to slacken chain. Remove drive chain master link while taking care not to damage or lose "O" rings. Remove drive chain. To remove rear sprocket, unscrew sprocket retaining nuts and remove sprocket. To remove engine sprocket, unscrew retaining screw and remove sprocket.

Carefully examine sprockets for excessive wear. Worn sprockets will usually have a hooked-tooth profile. A good test is to place a new chain on a used sprocket and check the fit. If sprockets require renewal due to wear, always renew drive chain. Sprockets should be renewed as a set. Renew drive chain if distance between 40 link pins exceeds 510.5 mm (20.1 in.) with chain straight and all slack removed.

Reassemble by reversing disassembly procedure. Tighten engine sprocket retaining screw to 24-30 N·m (17-22 ft.-lbs.). Tighten rear sprocket retaining nuts to 70-80 N·m (51-58 ft.-lbs.). When assembling chain, be sure "O" rings are properly installed on master link. Install master link clip as shown in Fig. H1-28. Tighten axle nut to 110-150 N·m (80-108 ft.-lbs.), then install a new cotter pin. Tighten wheel retaining nuts to 50-60 N·m (36-43 ft.-lbs.). Refer to previous INSPECTION AND ADJUSTMENT paragraphs for recommended drive chain adjustment procedures.

HONDA

TRX200 AND TRX200SX

NOTE: Metric fasteners are used throughout vehicle.

CONDENSED SERVICE DATA

MODELS General	TRX200, TRX200SX
Engine Make	Honda
Engine Type.	Four-Stroke; Air-Cooled
Number of Cylinders	1
Bore.	65.0 mm (2.56 in.)
Stroke.	60.0 mm (2.36 in.)
Displacement	199.0 cc (12.14 cu. in.)
Compression Ratio:	
TRX200	8.4:1
TRX200SX.	9.0:1
Engine Lubrication	Wet Sump/Oil Pump
Transmission Lubrication	Common With Engine
Engine/Transmission Oil	SAE 10W-40
Forward Speeds.	5
Reverse Speeds	1
Tire Size:	
TRX200:	
Front	21x7-10
Rear.	22x9-8
TRX200SX:	
Front	20x7-8
Rear.	22x11-8
Tire Pressure:	
TRX200:	
Front	21 kPa (2.9 psi)
Rear.	17 kPa (2.5 psi)
TRX200SX:	
Front & Rear	20 kPa (2.9 psi)
Battery	12V-10AH
Dry Weight:	
TRX200	186 kg (409 lbs.)
TRX200SX.	160 kg (352 lbs.)

Tune-Up

Engine Idle Speed	1300-1500 rpm
Compression Pressure:	
TRX200	883-1079 kPa (128-156 psi)
TRX200SX	1200-1400 kPa (174-203 psi)
Spark Plug:	
NGK	DR8ES-L
Nippon Denso	X24ESR-U
Electrode Gap	0.6-0.7 mm (0.024-0.028 in.)
Ignition:	
Type	Breakerless
Timing	10° BTDC
Carburetor:	
Make	Keihin
Model:	
TRX200	PD63B
TRX200SX	PD63A
Float Height	14.0 mm (0.55 in.)
Main Jet:	
TRX200	#95
TRX200SX	#98
Idle Jet	#35
Clip Position	See Text
Idle Mixture Setting	1½ Turns
Throttle Lever Free Play	See Text

Sizes-Clearances

Valve Clearance (cold):	
Intake & Exhaust	See Text
Valve Face & Seat Angle:	
Intake & Exhaust	45°
Valve Seat Width:	
Intake & Exhaust	1.2 mm (0.05 in.)
Wear Limit	1.5 mm (0.06 in.)
Valve Stem Diameter:	
Intake	5.475-5.490 mm (0.2156-0.2161 in.)
Wear Limit	5.45 mm (0.215 in.)
Exhaust	5.455-5.470 mm (0.2148-0.2154 in.)
Wear Limit	5.43 mm (0.214 in.)
Valve Guide Bore Diameter:	
Intake & Exhaust	5.500-5.512 mm (0.2165-0.2170 in.)
Wear Limit	5.52 mm (0.217 in.)

Sizes-Clearances (Cont.)

Valve Stem to Guide Clearance:

Intake . . . . 0.010-0.037 mm (0.0004-0.0015 in.)

    Wear Limit . . . . 0.12 mm (0.005 in.)

Exhaust . . . . 0.030-0.057 mm (0.0012-0.0022 in.)

    Wear Limit . . . . 0.14 mm (0.006 in.)

Valve Spring Free Length (Minimum)
TRX200:

Inner Spring—In. & Ex. . . . . 33.6 mm (1.322 in.)

Outer Spring—In. & Ex.. . . . . 37.6 mm (1.480 in.)

TRX200SX:
Inner Spring—

    Yellow . . . . 29.5 mm (1.16 in.)

    White . . . . 30.5 mm (1.20 in.)

Outer Spring—

    Yellow . . . . 36.5 mm (1.44 in.)

    White . . . . 35.0 mm (1.38 in.)

Rocker Arm Bore Diameter:
Intake & Exhaust . . . . 12.000-12.018 mm (0.4724-0.4731 in.)

    Wear Limit . . . . 12.05 mm (0.474 in.)

Rocker Shaft Diameter:
Intake & Exhaust . . . . 11.966-11.984 mm (0.4711-0.4718 in.)

    Wear Limit . . . . 11.92 mm (0.469 in.)

Camshaft Lobe Height:

Intake. . . . . 34.371 mm (1.3532 in.)

    Wear Limit . . . . 34.191 mm (1.3461 in.)

Exhaust . . . . 34.242 mm (1.3481 in.)

    Wear Limit . . . . 34.062 mm (1.3410 in.)

Cylinder Head Distortion (Max.). . . . . 0.10 mm (0.004 in.)

Cylinder Bore Diameter . . . . 65.000-65.010 mm (2.5590-2.5594 in.)

    Wear Limit . . . . 65.10 mm (2.563 in.)

Piston-to-Cylinder Clearance. . . . . 0.018-0.048 mm (0.0007-0.0019 in.)

    Wear Limit . . . . 0.10 mm (0.004 in.)

Sizes-Clearances (Cont.)

Piston Diameter—
Measured 10 mm (0.4 in.) From
Skirt Bottom & 90° to Pin Bore . . . .
64.962-64.982 mm
(2.5576-2.5583 in.)

    Wear Limit . . . .
64.90 mm
(2.555 in.)

Piston Pin Bore . . . .
15.002-15.008 mm
(0.5906-0.5909 in.)

    Wear Limit . . . .
15.04 mm
(0.592 in.)

Piston Pin Diameter . . . .
14.994-15.000 mm
(0.5903-0.5906 in.)

    Wear Limit . . . .
14.96 mm
(0.589 in.)

Piston-to-Pin Clearance . . . .
0.002-0.014 mm
(0.0001-0.0006 in.)

    Wear Limit . . . .
0.02 mm
(0.001 in.)

Piston Ring End Gap:
Top & Second Rings:
    TRX200 . . . .
0.20-0.60 mm
(0.008-0.024 in.)

        Wear Limit . . . .
0.70 mm
(0.028 in.)

    TRX200SX . . . .
0.20-0.40 mm
(0.008-0.016 in.)

        Wear Limit . . . .
0.50 mm
(0.020 in.)

Oil Ring:
    TRX200 . . . .
0.70-1.0 mm
(0.028-0.039 in.)

    TRX200SX . . . .
0.20-0.80 mm
(0.008-0.031 in.)

Piston Ring Side Clearance:
Top Ring . . . .
0.005-0.045 mm
(0.0002-0.0018 in.)

    Wear Limit . . . .
0.09 mm
(0.004 in.)

Second Ring . . . .
0.015-0.045 mm
(0.0006-0.0018 in.)

    Wear Limit . . . .
0.09 mm
(0.004 in.)

Oil Ring . . . .
....
Connecting Rod Small
End Bore Diameter . . . .
15.010-15.028 mm
(0.5909-0.5917 in.)

    Wear Limit . . . .
15.06 mm
(0.593 in.)

Connecting Rod Big End
Side Clearance (Max.) . . . .
0.80 mm
(0.031 in.)

Connecting Rod Big End
Radial Clearance (Max.) . . . .
0.05 mm
(0.002 in.)

Crankshaft Runout (Max.):
Flywheel End . . . .
0.03 mm
(0.0012 in.)

Sizes-Clearances (Cont.)

Crankshaft Runout (Max.): (Cont.)

Clutch End . . . . 0.06 mm
(0.0024 in.)

Capacities

Fuel Tank:

TRX200 . . . . 8.1 L
(2.1 gal.)

TRX200SX . . . . 8.5 L
(2.2 gal.)

Engine/Transmission Sump . . . . See Text

Tightening Torques

Axle Nut—

Front:

TRX200 . . . . 100 N·m
(74 ft.-lbs.)

TRX200SX . . . . 60-80 N·m
(44-59 ft.-lbs.)

Rear:

TRX200 . . . . 100 N·m
(74 ft.-lbs.)

TRX200SX . . . . 80-140 N·m
(59-103 ft.-lbs.)

Camshaft Bearing Holder . . . . 12 N·m
(106 in.-lbs.)

Clutch Nut . . . . 76-84 N·m
(55-61 ft.-lbs.)

Crankcase . . . . 12 N·m
(106 in.-lbs.)

Crankcase Cover . . . . 10 N·m
(88 in.-lbs.)

Cylinder Head:

Nut . . . . 28-30 N·m
(20-22 ft.-lbs.)

Cap Nut . . . . 10-14 N·m
(88-124 in.-lbs.)

Flywheel Cap Screw . . . . 30-34 N·m
(22-25 ft.-lbs.)

Spark Plug . . . . 17 N·m
(150 in.-lbs.)

Wheel Retaining Nut . . . . 65 N·m
(48 ft.-lbs.)

Standard Screws:

5 mm . . . . 3.5-5.0 N·m
(31-44 in.-lbs.)

6 mm . . . . 7-11 N·m
(62-97 in.-lbs.)

Standard Bolts & Nuts:

5 mm . . . . 4.5-6.0 N·m
(40-53 in.-lbs.)

6 mm . . . . 8-12 N·m
(71-106 in.-lbs.)

8 mm . . . . 18-25 N·m
(13-18 ft.-lbs.)

10 mm . . . . 30-40 N·m
(22-29 ft.-lbs.)

12 mm . . . . 50-60 N·m
(36-43 ft.-lbs.)

Tightening Torques (Cont.)
Flanged Bolts & Nuts:

6 mm	10-14 N·m
	(89-124 in.-lbs.)
8 mm	24-30 N·m
	(17-22 ft.-lbs.)
10 mm	35-45 N·m
	(25-32 ft.-lbs.)

LUBRICATION

All Models

ENGINE AND TRANSMISSION. The engine and transmission are lubricated by a trochoid-type pump located on the right side of the crankcase and driven by a chain via a sprocket on the right end of the crankshaft.

Fig. H3-1—Remove filler plug (F) to check crankcase oil level. Sump screen and centrifugal oil filter are accessible after removing right crankcase cover as outlined in text.

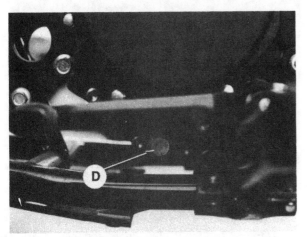

Fig. H3-2—Remove drain plug (D) to drain crankcase oil.

The engine and transmission share a common sump. Recommended oil is SAE 10W-40 with an API classification of SF or SG.

Oil level should be maintained at upper mark on dipstick attached to fill plug (F—Fig. H3-1). Do not screw plug in when checking oil level. Fill sump through opening for fill plug (F). Drain oil by removing drain plug (D—Fig. H3-2) on underside of crankcase. If only oil is changed, fill crankcase with 1.4 L (1.5 qt.) of oil on Model TRX200 or 1.6 L (1.7 qt.) on Model TRX200SX. Crankcase capacity after disassembly is 1.9 L (2.0 qt.).

The manufacturer recommends changing the oil and oil filter after the first week of operation and then after every 30 days of operation. The centrifugal oil filter and sump screen should be cleaned after every 30 days of operation or every three months to coincide with oil change intervals. With oil drained from crankcase, remove reverse cable from bracket and reverse actuator arm, then remove right crankcase cover retaining screws and carefully withdraw cover. The sump filter screen is located in a compartment in the right crankcase half (see Fig. H3-3). Extract, clean and install filter screen (thick side should be out). The centrifugal oil filter is located on the end of the crankshaft. Remove the three oil filter outer cover retaining screws and withdraw cover (see Fig. H3-4). Using a clean lint-free cloth, wipe clean the cover and inside of the centrifugal oil filter

Fig. H3-3—The oil sump screen is located in a cavity in the bottom of the crankcase.

Fig. H3-4—Remove screws for access to centrifugal oil filter.

Fig. H3-5—Periodically inject grease into steering knuckle through grease fitting (F).

housing. Install a new gasket on centrifugal oil filter cover and securely tighten cover screws.

Make sure alignment dowels and gasket are fitted to crankcase and install crankcase cover. Fill engine/transmission sump with appropriate amount of oil and check for leaks. Install reverse actuator arm and cable and adjust as outlined in REVERSE LOCK section.

STEERING KNUCKLE. A grease fitting (F—Fig. H3-5) is located in each steering knuckle to allow lubrication of the king pin and bushings. Periodically inject a good quality multipurpose grease into grease fitting.

SWING ARM. A grease fitting is located on the swing arm to allow lubrication of the swing arm pivot bushings. Periodically inject a good quality multipurpose grease into grease fitting.

DRIVE CHAIN. The drive chain should be lubricated with SAE 80-90 gear oil after the first week of operation and after every 30 days of operation thereafter. The chain uses "O" rings to seal the chain rollers and pins. Incorrect lubrication may damage the "O" rings resulting in premature chain failure.

Remove and clean the drive chain when excessive dirt is evident. Remove chain as outlined in DRIVE CHAIN AND SPROCKETS section. The chain should be thoroughly washed in kerosene and wiped dry. Using any cleaning solution other than kerosene may damage "O" rings. Lubricate chain with SAE 80-90 gear oil, then install and adjust chain as outlined in DRIVE CHAIN AND SPROCKETS section.

CABLES AND LEVERS. All cables and levers should be inspected and lubricated after the first week of operation and after every 30 days of operation thereafter.

AIR CLEANER ELEMENT

All Models

The air cleaner element should be removed and cleaned after every 30 days of operation. To remove the air cleaner element, remove the seat, release four cover clips (S—Fig. H3-7) and remove cover. Loosen air cleaner frame to inlet tube clamp, then withdraw element and frame from case. Remove rear frame bracket, then carefully separate foam element from frame.

Thoroughly clean the foam element in a nonflammable solvent. Compress element between hands to remove solvent. Saturate element in clean SAE 10W-40 engine oil. Compress element to remove excess oil. Install element and reassemble air cleaner components.

Fig. H3-7—Air cleaner element is accessible after removing seat, releasing spring clips (S) and withdrawing cover (C).

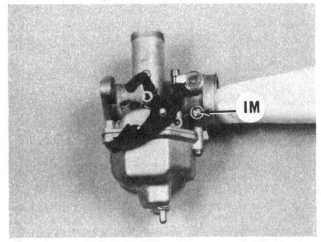

Fig. H3-8—Refer to text for adjustment of idle mixture screw (IM).

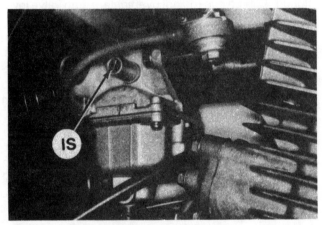

Fig. H3-9—Adjust idle speed screw (IS) so engine idle speed is 1300-1500 rpm.

FUEL SYSTEM

All Models

CARBURETOR. Model TRX200 is equipped with a Keihin PD63B and Model TRX200SX is equipped with a Keihin PD63A carburetor. Initial setting of idle mixture screw (IM—Fig. H3-8) is 1½ turns out. Rotating idle mixture screw clockwise will richen idle mixture. Final adjustment must be performed with engine at normal operating temperature. Adjust idle speed screw (IS—Fig. H3-9) so engine idles at 1300-1500 rpm. Slowly rotate idle mixture screw clockwise until engine stalls and note screw position. While counting turns, rotate idle mixture screw counterclockwise until engine again stalls and note screw position. Set idle mixture screw at midpoint position between two previously noted positions that caused engine stalling. Readjust idle speed.

When servicing carburetor, refer to Fig. H3-10 for an exploded view of carburetor and to carburetor specifications in CONDENSED SERVICE DATA section while

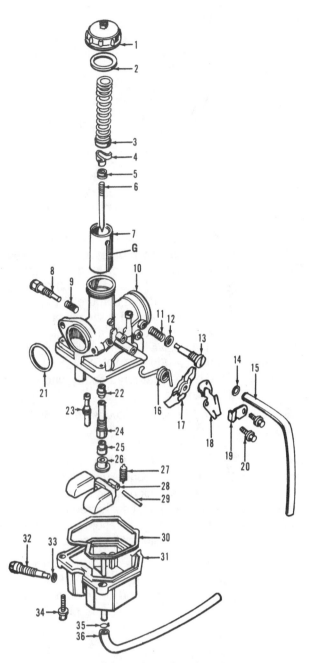

Fig. H3-10—Exploded view of carburetor.

1. Cap	19. Clip
2. Gasket	20. Screw
3. Spring	21. "O" ring
4. Retainer	22. Needle jet
5. Clip	23. Slow jet
6. Jet needle	24. Nozzle
7. Throttle slide	25. Main jet
8. Idle speed screw	26. Baffle
9. Spring	27. Fuel inlet valve
10. Body	28. Float
11. Spring	29. Pin
12. "O" ring	30. Gasket
13. Idle mixture screw	31. Fuel bowl
14. Hose clamp	32. Drain screw
15. Vent hose	33. "O" ring
16. Return spring	34. Screw
17. Choke lever	35. Hose clamp
18. Choke cable clamp	36. Drain hose

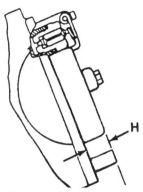

Fig. H3-11—Position carburetor so float rests lightly against fuel inlet valve and measure float height (H).

Fig. H3-13—Slide dust boot (B) down throttle cable, then loosen knurled locknut (L) and rotate cable adjuster (A) until recommended throttle lever free play (F) of 3-8 mm (0.12-0.31 in.) is obtained. Tighten locknut (L) to retain adjustment.

noting the following: Jet needle clip (5) should be installed in third groove from top of jet needle on Model TRX200 or fourth groove from top on Model TRX200SX. Float height (H—Fig. H3-11) should be 14.0 mm (0.55 in.) between bottom of float and carburetor body. Hold carburetor so float is vertical and resting lightly against fuel inlet valve. Float height is not adjustable. Renew float and/or fuel inlet valve if float height is incorrect. Make sure groove (G—Fig. H3-10) in side of throttle slide is aligned with pin in carburetor body when inserting slide in carburetor.

Suggested main jet size for altitudes above 5000 feet is #92 for both models.

FUEL FILTER SCREEN AND STRAINER. A fuel filter screen is located in the fuel control valve and a strainer that extends into the fuel tank is attached to the inlet of the fuel control valve. The filter screen should be cleaned after every 30 days of operation. Periodic cleaning of the fuel strainer should not be required.

To remove the filter screen, be sure fuel control valve is in "OFF" position and unscrew cup (C—Fig. H3-12) on bottom of valve. Remove and clean screen. Reassemble while making sure "O" ring is properly posi-

tioned. Tighten cup (do not overtighten), turn valve lever to "ON" and check for leaks.

To remove fuel strainer, disconnect fuel line and drain fuel from fuel tank. Unscrew fuel control valve (V—Fig. H3-12) from fuel tank. Inspect and clean strainer attached to control valve. Reinstall components and tighten control valve nut to 23 N·m (17 ft.-lbs.). Turn control valve lever to "ON" and check for leaks.

THROTTLE LEVER FREE PLAY. Free play (F—Fig. H3-13) at the end of the throttle lever should be 3-8 mm (1/8-5/16 in.). To adjust free play, slide back rubber boot (B), loosen knurled nut (L) and rotate cable adjuster (A). Retighten knurled nut.

IGNITION AND ELECTRICAL

All Models

SPARK PLUG. The recommended spark plug for normal operating conditions is a NGK DR8ES-L or Nippon Denso X24ESR-U. Spark plug electrode gap should be 0.6-0.7 mm (0.024-0.028 in.). The spark plug should be removed, inspected, cleaned or renewed, and regapped after every 30 days of operation.

IGNITION. The engine is equipped with a breakerless, capacitor discharge ignition system. The electronic ignition circuit consists of the flywheel, exciter coil, CDI module, pulse generator, ignition coil, spark plug, ignition switch, reverse switch and engine stop switch. To check ignition timing, remove timing plug (P—Fig. H3-14) and connect a power timing light to engine. Ignition timing (10° BTDC) at idle speed should occur when "F" mark on flywheel is aligned with stationary mark (M) on case. Advanced ignition timing is 29° BTDC at 4250 rpm on TRX200 models, or 28° BTDC at 3700 rpm on TRX200SX models. Advanced ignition should occur when "=" mark on flywheel is aligned with mark (M) on

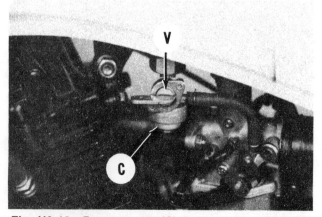

Fig. H3-12—Remove cap (C) for access to fuel filter screen. Detach fuel hose (arrow) and unscrew valve (V) for access to fuel strainer on valve.

Fig. H3-14—Remove timing plug (P) in flywheel cover to view timing marks. "F" mark on flywheel should align with stationary mark (M) for correct idle speed timing.

case. Ignition timing is not adjustable. If ignition timing is not as specified, check condition of ignition components as described in the following test procedures and renew faulty or questionable components.

If ignition malfunction occurs, check condition of spark plug, all wires and connections before troubleshooting the ignition circuit. Using Honda Digital Multi-Tester KS-AHM-32-003 or a suitable ohmmeter, refer to the following test procedures and specifications to aid troubleshooting.

To check condition of exciter coil, disconnect the three-wire connector leading to alternator on connector panel attached to right, rear portion of vehicle frame on Model TRX200, or remove junction box cover on left rear side of Model TRX200SX frame and disconnect black/red wire and green/white wire leading to alternator. Using an ohmmeter, measure resistance between black/red wire and green/white wire. Exciter coil is considered satisfactory if resistance is 100-300 ohms.

To check condition of pulse generator, disconnect the three-wire connector leading to alternator on connector panel attached to right, rear portion of vehicle frame on Model TRX200, or remove junction box cover on left rear side of Model TRX200SX frame and disconnect blue/yellow wire leading to pulse generator. Connect an ohmmeter lead to blue/yellow wire going to engine and remaining ohmmeter lead to vehicle ground. Pulse generator is satisfactory if ohmmeter reading is 290-360 ohms. If reading is incorrect, remove left crankcase cover and repeat test at terminal of pulse generator.

To check condition of ignition coil, detach black/yellow wire and green wire from ignition coil. Disconnect high-tension lead from spark plug. To check primary winding resistance, attach one ohmmeter lead to black/yellow wire terminal on ignition coil and remaining ohmmeter lead to green wire terminal. Ohmmeter should read 0.1-0.3 ohms. Perform two secondary winding tests, one with the spark plug cap attached to coil wire and one without spark plug cap attached. Attach one ohm-

meter lead to spark plug cap and remaining ohmmeter lead to coil ground (green wire terminal). Secondary winding resistance through spark plug cap should be 7.4k-11.0k ohms. Remove spark plug cap from high-tension wire. Attach an ohmmeter lead to high-tension wire and remaining ohmmeter lead to coil ground. Secondary winding resistance reading with spark plug cap removed should be 3.0k-5.0k ohms. If secondary winding resistance is now within specification, renew spark plug cap.

A neutral/reverse switch is located in the left crankcase cover. The switch turns on the appropriate indicator light when the transmission is in neutral or reverse. When the transmission is in reverse during starting, the ignition is grounded. When the transmission is in neutral during starting, the starter relay circuit can be energized. To check neutral/reverse switch on Model TRX200, disconnect the three-wire connector (light green/red, gray and white wires) on connector panel under right rear fender. With transmission in neutral, connect an ohmmeter lead to the light green/red wire terminal and connect the remaining ohmmeter lead to vehicle ground. The ohmmeter should show continuity. When transmission is in gear, the ohmmeter should read infinity. With transmission in reverse, connect one ohmmeter lead to vehicle ground then connect remaining ohmmeter lead to white wire terminal. Repeat test at gray wire terminal. The ohmmeter should show continuity. When transmission is in neutral or forward gears, ohmmeter should show infinity. To check neutral/reverse switch on Model TRX200SX, disconnect light green/red and gray wire connectors in junction box under right rear fender. Follow preceding test procedure for Model TRX200, except no white wire is used on TRX200SX.

CHARGING CIRCUIT. The charging circuit consists of the alternator, voltage regulator, and a maintenance-free battery. Specified battery is rated 12 VDC with 10 amp-hour capacity. Under load, the alternator should produce 13-15 volts and 130 watts at 5000 rpm.

The battery should be charged if the vehicle is stored for an extended period. The battery should be removed during charging. If the battery is charged while in the vehicle, disconnect the battery cables to prevent damage to charging circuit components. The battery should be charged at a minimum rate of 1.2 amperes for five hours or at a maximum rate of 5 amperes for one hour.

The alternator charge coil can be statically tested using a suitable ohmmeter. Separate connector leading to regulator from alternator with two yellow wires. Connect ohmmeter leads to terminals of connector leading to alternator. Resistance reading should be 0.1-1.0 ohm. Connect one tester lead to vehicle ground. Alternately connect remaining tester lead to connector terminals. Ohmmeter should read infinity.

The regulator is mounted on the right rear portion of the vehicle frame on Model TRX200 or on the battery case on Model TRX200SX. To check condition of regulator, disconnect regulator from charging circuit at con-

	+ Tester lead				
– Tester lead	YELLOW	YELLOW	GREEN	RED	BLACK
YELLOW		A	A	B	A
YELLOW	A		A	B	A
GREEN	B	B		C	D
RED	A	A	A		
BLACK	E	E	F	G	

Fig. H3-15—Use chart shown above and values listed below to test voltage regulator.

A. Infinite resistance
B. 1k-20k ohms
C. 3k-100k ohms
D. 0.2k-20k ohms
E. 1k-50k ohms
F. 0.2k-10k ohms
G. 3k-10k ohms

nector block. Use an ohmmeter in conjunction with chart in Fig. H3-15. Renew regulator if it fails to meet test specifications.

An operational check of the complete charging circuit can be performed with a suitable voltmeter. Attach voltmeter directly to battery terminal. Start and run engine until it is at normal operating temperature. Turn lights on and gradually increase engine speed while reading voltmeter. Regulated voltage should be 13-15 volts.

ELECTRIC STARTER. The starting circuit consists of the starter, starter relay, starter switch, diode (not used on Model TRX200), neutral light, neutral/reverse switch and ignition switch. A fuse protects the circuit.

The starter relay is located near the battery on Model TRX200 and inside the junction box on Model TRX200SX. To check relay, disconnect relay pigtail lead and wires from terminals on relay. Connect ohmmeter leads to terminals on top of relay. Ohmmeter should read infinity. Connect a 12-volt battery to terminals of pigtail lead with positive battery lead connected to yellow/red wire terminal and negative battery lead connected to light green/red wire terminal. Ohmmeter should show continuity, if not, renew relay.

To check the neutral/reverse switch, refer to procedure in IGNITION section.

The neutral light must be on for the starter to operate. If the neutral light does not come on when the transmission is in neutral, renew neutral light. On Model TRX200SX, a diode is molded into the neutral light wire near neutral light. If new neutral light does not come on, disconnect wire for light at both ends. Check for continuity between the wire ends using an ohmmeter. After connecting the ohmmeter leads to the wire ends, observe ohmmeter reading, then reverse ohmmeter leads and observe the second reading. There should be continuity during one test and no continuity (infinity) during the other test. If not, renew neutral light wire.

To remove starter motor, remove fuel tank and disconnect battery negative lead. On Model TRX200SX, remove left crankcase cover. On Model TRX200, remove cam tensioner and carburetor. Unscrew two screws securing starter motor and remove motor. Disconnect starter motor cable. Refer to Fig. H3-16 for an exploded view of starter motor. Before disassembling motor, note alignment marks, or make alignment marks, on center housing and end caps so they can be reassembled in original positions. When disassembling motor, note location of all shims and washers. Minimum brush length is 8.5 mm (0.33 in.) on Model TRX200 and 6.5 mm (0.26 in.) on Model TRX200SX. Note pin on brush holder plate that must align with notch in frame during assembly.

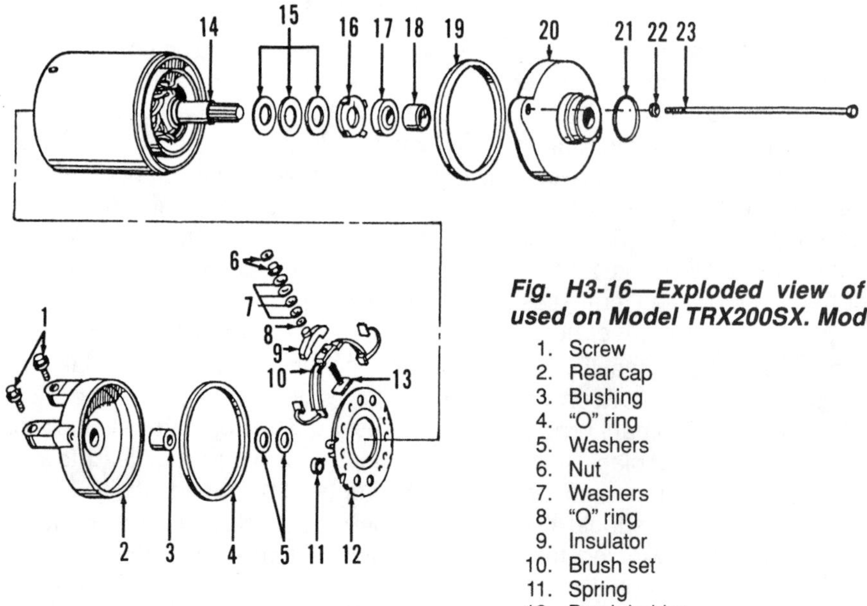

Fig. H3-16—Exploded view of electric starter motor used on Model TRX200SX. Model TRX200 is similar.

1. Screw
2. Rear cap
3. Bushing
4. "O" ring
5. Washers
6. Nut
7. Washers
8. "O" ring
9. Insulator
10. Brush set
11. Spring
12. Brush holder
13. Screw
14. Armature
15. Shims
16. Special washer
17. Oil seal
18. Bushing
19. "O" ring
20. Front cap
21. "O" ring
22. Washer
23. Screw

Install rear cap so slot engages pin on brush holder plate. Be sure "O" rings are correctly positioned during assembly.

WIRING. If wiring requires repair, always install wire that is the same gauge as original wire. Wires should be routed away from areas of extreme heat or sharp edges. Attach or hold wires in their original position using plastic tie straps to prevent short circuits.

FASTENERS

All Models

After the first week of operation and after every 30 days of operation thereafter, the vehicle should receive an overall inspection. All screws, nuts and other fasteners should be checked and tightened to proper torque specification shown in CONDENSED SERVICE DATA section or in the appropriate maintenance section.

VALVE SYSTEM

All Models

The valves are actuated via rocker arms by a single overhead camshaft. Camshaft is timed and driven by a roller drive chain from left end of crankshaft. Valve clearance on all models should be adjusted after the first week of operation then after every 30 days of operation. Valve clearance should be adjusted with engine cold.

To adjust valve clearance, remove valve adjustment cover (V—Fig. H3-17) on left side of cylinder head and timing plug (P—Fig. H3-14). With piston on compression stroke, rotate crankshaft until "T" mark (top dead center) on flywheel aligns with stationary mark (M). Crankshaft can be rotated using the manual starter on Model TRX200SX or by removing left side cover on Model TRX200 and turning flywheel screw. To ensure piston is on compression stroke, remove plug from

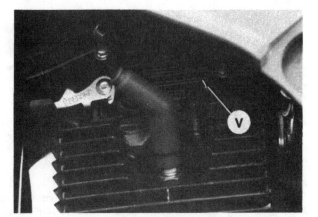

Fig. H3-17—Remove valve adjustment plate (V) on left side of cylinder head to view valve adjustment plates.

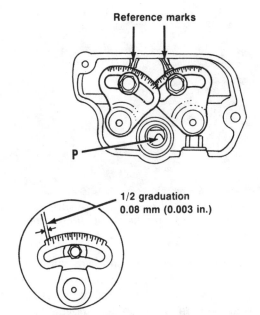

Fig. H3-18—Pointer (P) on end of camshaft must be visible before performing valve adjustment. See text.

inspection hole located between the two valve adjustment plates and note position of pointer (P—Fig. H3-18) on end of camshaft. If pointer is facing upward, then piston is on compression stroke. If pointer is not visible, rotate crankshaft one complete revolution and again align "T" mark on flywheel with stationary mark.

Clearance between rocker arm and valve stem for both intake and exhaust valves should be 0.08 mm (0.003 in.). To adjust, loosen cap screws securing intake and exhaust adjustment plates. Rotate each plate counterclockwise until resistance is felt. Note reference mark (see Fig. H3-18) in relation to marks on adjustment plate. Rotate each plate clockwise one-half graduation and secure adjustment with cap screw. Each one-half graduation on adjustment plate reference scale equals 0.08 mm (0.003 in.), the recommended valve clearance.

CAM CHAIN

All Models

Cam chain tension does not require adjustment. The chain tensioner automatically adjusts cam chain tension as needed.

CLUTCH

All Models

The engine is equipped with two automatically actuated clutches. A three-shoe centrifugal clutch is mounted on the right end of the crankshaft. The centrifugal clutch is disengaged at idle speed and engages when crankshaft speed increases. A multiple-disc clutch

Fig. H3-19—Following procedure outlined in text, loosen locknut (L) and turn adjusting screw (A) to adjust clutch.

is attached to the transmission mainshaft and is actuated by the gear shift mechanism. When the gear shift lever is operated, the multiple-disc clutch is disengaged to allow smooth transmission gear movement.

The clutch should be adjusted after the first week of operation and after every 30 days of operation. To adjust clutch, remove cover on right side of crankcase. Loosen locknut (L—Fig. H3-19). Turn adjusting screw (A) counterclockwise until internal resistance is felt, then turn screw 1/4 turn clockwise. Secure adjusting screw with locknut (L) and install cover.

The clutch should automatically disengage at engine idle speed. When selecting gears, clutch should engage and disengage freely without excess slippage. Difficult shifting, clutch grabbing or clutch slipping may indicate overhaul is necessary.

MANUAL STARTER

Model TRX200SX

R&R AND OVERHAUL. Refer to Fig. H3-20 for an exploded view of manual starter used on Model TRX200SX. Starter can be removed from engine as a complete unit after removing the gear shift lever and the four starter retaining cap screws. If starter rope remains under tension, pull starter rope and hold rope pulley with notch (N) adjacent to rope outlet. Pull a loop of rope back through outlet so rope engages notch in pulley and allow pulley to slowly unwind. Remove nut (9) and disassemble unit. Be careful when removing rewind spring (2); a rapidly uncoiling starter spring can cause serious injury.

Rewind spring is wound into starter housing in a clockwise direction. Rope is wound on rope pulley in a clockwise direction as viewed with pulley in housing. Reassemble starter by reversing disassembly procedure. During reassembly, lightly grease pulley shaft and starter pawl.

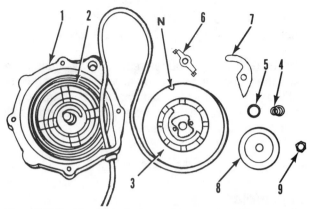

Fig. H3-20—Exploded view of manual starter used on TRX200SX.

N. Notch
1. Starter housing
2. Rewind spring
3. Rope pulley
4. Friction spring
5. Spring guide
6. Pawl guide
7. Starter pawl
8. Friction plate
9. Nut

To place tension on rewind spring after starter assembly, pass rope through rope outlet in housing and install rope handle. Pull a loop of rope back through starter housing outlet and into pulley notch (N). Turn pulley clockwise two or three complete revolutions to place tension on spring. Release rope from notch and allow rope to wind onto pulley. Do not place more tension on rewind spring than is necessary to draw rope handle up against housing.

REVERSE LOCK

All Models

A reverse lock mechanism prevents accidental engagement of reverse gear. There should be 2-4 mm (5/64-5/32 in.) free play at gap (B—Fig. H3-21). Adjust free

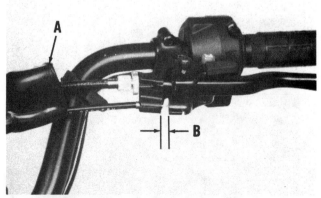

Fig. H3-21—Pull back boot (A) to measure reverse lock lever free play. There should be 2-4 mm (5/64-5/32 in.) free play at gap (B). Adjust free play by loosening locknut (N—Fig. H3-22) and turning adjusting nut (A).

Fig. H3-22—Loosen locknut (N) and rotate adjuster nut (A) to adjust reverse lock lever free travel.

Fig. H3-23—Brake lever free play (F) should be 25-30 mm (1 to 1-1/8 in.) measured at outer end of brake lever (L).

Fig. H3-24—Brake bleed valve (B) is located on back side of wheel cylinder.

play by loosening locknut (N—Fig. H3-22) and turning adjusting nut (A). Retighten locknut.

FRONT BRAKE ASSEMBLY

All Models

A two-shoe hydraulically actuated brake assembly is mounted on each front spindle. A master cylinder and reservoir assembly are mounted on right side of handlebar assembly and actuated by a hand lever.

BRAKE LEVER FREE PLAY. Recommended brake lever free play (F—Fig. H3-23) measured at outer end of brake lever (L) should be 25-30 mm (1-1$\frac{1}{8}$ in.). Brake lever free play is adjusted by removing "ADJUST" plug on outside of brake drum and rotating brake drum so hole is aligned with star wheel on brake shoe adjuster. Use a suitable tool and rotate star wheel until brake shoe locks against drum, then rotate star wheel in opposite direction three adjustment teeth. Repeat adjustment on remaining brake shoe, then adjust both brake shoes on opposite wheel. Make sure no brake drag is noted after adjustment. If brake lever free play is still excessive, then bleed hydraulic system as outlined in BLEEDING section.

BLEEDING. Make sure reservoir (R—Fig. H3-23) is full. Connect a bleed hose to bleed valve (B—Fig. H3-24) on back side of wheel cylinder. Route the bleed hose into a suitable container. Operate brake lever (L—Fig. H3-23) until resistance is felt, then open bleed valve (rotate counterclockwise). Close bleed valve prior to releasing brake lever. Continue bleeding procedure until no air bubbles are noted in fluid discharged from bleed valve.

NOTE: Make sure reservoir (R) remains full during bleeding procedure.

When bleeding procedure is completed, add brake fluid to reservoir until fluid level is at upper level line in reservoir. Make sure fluid level is kept above lower level line adjacent to reservoir sight glass.

R&R AND OVERHAUL. Determining brake shoe thickness is possible by removing "CHECK" plug on outside of brake drum. Brake shoes should be renewed if lining thickness is 2 mm (0.08 in.) or less.

WARNING: Inhalation of asbestos brake dust is injurious to human health. Approved OSHA respiration equipment must be worn when working on or around brake drum and shoes. DO NOT use compressed air to clean brake drum, shoes or nearby components as brake dust will be blown into air.

HONDA TRX200 AND TRX200SX

Only vacuum equipment designed to pick up brake dust should be used.

Support front of vehicle so wheel is off ground and remove wheel. Unscrew axle nut and remove brake drum/hub. While noting location of components, disassemble brake assembly. Detach brake line from wheel cylinder and plug line to reduce fluid loss.

Disassemble and inspect wheel cylinder. Renew complete wheel cylinder if bore is scored, pitted or excessively worn. Minimum allowable bore diameter is 15.923 mm (0.6269 in.) on Model TRX200 and 14.343 mm (0.5647 in.) on Model TRX200SX. Minimum allowable piston diameter is 15.817 mm (0.6227 in.) on Model TRX200 and 14.237 mm (0.5605 in.) on Model TRX200SX. Superficial damage in wheel cylinder bore may be removed using a suitable cylinder hone. After honing, rinse bore with clean brake fluid. Shake out

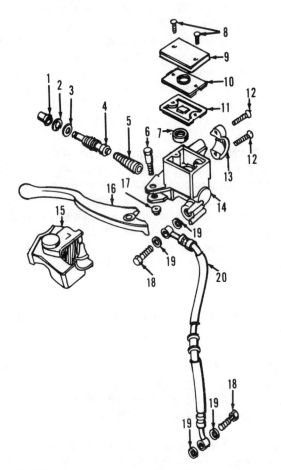

Fig. H3-25—Exploded view of front brake master cylinder.

1.	Boot	11.	Diaphragm
2.	Snap ring	12.	Bolt
3.	Washer	13.	Clamp
4.	Piston & cup	14.	Body
5.	Spring	15.	Rubber boot
6.	Bolt	16.	Brake lever
7.	Seal	17.	Nut
8.	Screw	18.	Union bolt
9.	Cover	19.	Seal washer
10.	Diaphragm plate	20.	Brake hose

excess fluid but do not wipe dry. Using a shop towel or rag to dry cylinder will leave lint particles in bore. Renew boots and piston cups. During reassembly, lubricate components with clean brake fluid.

Apply a suitable sealer to wheel cylinder contact area on backing plate and install wheel cylinder. Attach brake line. Clean brake adjuster and lubricate with silicon grease before installing in housing. Screw adjusters completely in to allow installation of new brake shoes. Apply a light coat of silicone grease to three points on backing plate that will contact edge of brake shoe. Install brake shoes and springs and secure brake shoes with pins and clips. Tighten axle nut to 100 N·m (74 ft.-lbs.) on Model TRX200 or to 60-80 N·m (44-59 ft.-lbs.) on Model TRX200SX. Tighten wheel nuts to 65 N·m (48 ft.-lbs.).

Adjust and bleed brakes as previously outlined.

MASTER CYLINDER. To remove front brake master cylinder (Fig. H3-25), detach brake line from master cylinder. Brake fluid will remove paint; be careful when removing master cylinder. Unscrew two retaining screws and remove master cylinder. Remove brake lever, reservoir cover (9) and diaphragm (11). Remove dust boot (1) and snap ring (2). Disassemble piston assembly while noting location and direction of components. Renew complete master cylinder if bore is scored, pitted or excessively worn. Minimum allowable bore diameter is 12.755 mm (0.5022 in.). Minimum allowable piston diameter is 12.645 mm (0.4978 in.). Superficial damage in master cylinder bore may be removed using a suitable cylinder hone. After honing, rinse bore with clean brake fluid. Shake out excess fluid but do not wipe dry. Using a shop towel or rag to dry cylinder will leave lint particles in bore. Renew boots and piston cups. During reassembly, lubricate components with clean brake fluid. Reassembly is reverse of disassembly. Install spring (5) so small end contacts piston (4). Bleed brakes as previously outlined.

FRONT AXLE

All Models

Each front knuckle assembly (K—Fig. H3-26) pivots within a knuckle holder (H) mounted on the end of a control arm. The upper and lower control arms pivot vertically and are attached to the vehicle frame by bolts. A shock absorber with a coil spring is attached to the vehicle frame and upper end of the steering knuckle. Each steering knuckle is equipped with a grease fitting to allow lubrication of wear surfaces. See LUBRICATION section.

Remove the front wheel to service the knuckle assembly. If excessive play between king pin and bushings is noted, then components should be renewed. Renew upper and lower dust seals when renewing king pin and bushings. Grease king pin prior to installation. Tighten castle nut (C) securing king pin bolt to 60 N·m (44 ft.-lbs.) and install a new cotter pin. If king pin holder and upper and lower control arms were removed, then tighten control arm to frame mounting cap screws to 45 N·m (33 ft.-lbs.) on Model TRX200 and 30-36 N·m (22-26 ft.-lbs.) on Model TRX200SX. Tighten control arm to knuckle holder bolts (B) to 45 N·m (33 ft.-lbs.). Tighten shock absorber upper and lower mounting bolts (T) to 40 N·m (29 ft.-lbs.).

Fig. H3-26—View of front knuckle assembly.

B. Knuckle holder bolts
C. Castle nut
F. Grease fitting
H. Knuckle holder

K. Knuckle
T. Shock absorber
   lower mounting bolt

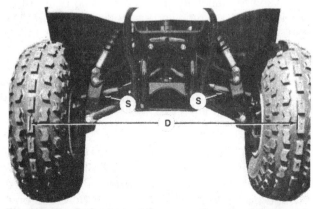

Fig. H3-27—Refer to text for procedure to check toe-in setting. Distance (D) is measured between centerline of wheel at axle height. Tie rod shafts (S) are rotated to adjust toe-in setting after loosening inside and outside tie rod end locknuts.

STEERING

All Models

TOE-IN SETTING. Place the handlebar in a straight-ahead position. Use a suitable measuring tool and measure distance (D—Fig. H3-27), at spindle height, between the center of the tires on the front and rear sides. The measured distance (D) on the front side should be 7 mm (0.28 in.) less than the measured distance on rear side on Model TRX200, or 0-20 mm (0-0.79 in.) less than the measured distance on rear side on Model TRX200SX. If not, loosen inside and outside locknuts on the left and right tie rods and rotate tie rod shaft (S) on each side equally until measured distance is within recommended range.

After obtaining the correct setting, securely tighten the locknuts to retain tie rod settings.

INSPECTION. Rotate the steering handlebar through full range of movement and note any binding or roughness. Periodically inspect the steering components for looseness or any other damage. Renew any damaged components. Clean and grease components if binding or excessive effort is noted.

OVERHAUL. To expose the steering shaft, remove the front fender assembly. Remove screws securing the upper steering shaft clamp and remove clamp. Remove steering shaft bushing and clean old grease from steering shaft. Inspect clamp halves, steering shaft and bushing for damage and excessive wear. Renew components if required. Grease inside of steering shaft bushing and install bushing and clamp. Tighten clamp screws, then rotate shaft and check for binding.

The tie rods are equipped with a ball joint at each end. Tie rod assemblies may be used on either side. Renew tie rod end if ball joint is excessively worn. Tie rod ends are unmarked or marked with an "L" on the hex end as shown in Fig. H3-28. The unmarked tie rod end must be installed on tie rod shaft end that has flats machined along the shaft. The tie rod must be installed so the ball

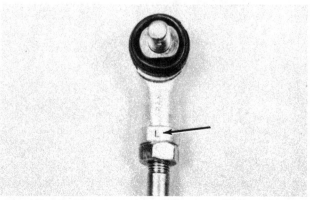

Fig. H3-28—The tie rod must be installed so the ball joint marked "L" is attached to the steering shaft arm.

joint marked "L" is attached to the steering shaft arm and the unmarked ball joint is attached to the steering knuckle. Tighten jam nuts on shaft to 55 N·m (40 ft.-lbs.) on Model TRX200 or to 35-43 N·m (26-32 ft.-lbs.) on Model TRX200SX. Tighten tie rod end retaining nuts to 55 N·m (40 ft.-lbs.) on Model TRX200 or to 35-43 N·m (26-32 ft.-lbs.) on Model TRX200SX. Check toe-in setting as previously outlined.

To remove steering shaft on Model TRX200, detach tie rods and remove front fender assembly and handlebar assembly. To remove steering shaft on Model TRX200SX, detach tie rods and remove front fender assembly, handlebar assembly, headlight and bracket, and air intake assembly. Unscrew upper shaft clamp. On Model TRX200SX, remove lower bearing cover. Detach cotter pin and unscrew lower steering shaft nut. Remove steering shaft. Inspect lower bearing assembly and dust seal and renew if required. The lower bearing is retained by a snap ring on Model TRX200 and by a staked locknut on Model TRX200SX. When installing bearing on Model TRX200SX, tighten locknut to 40-60 N·m (29-43 ft.-lbs.) and stake bearing. Tighten the lower steering shaft nut to 70 N·m (51 ft.-lbs.) and install a new cotter pin. Tighten tie rod end retaining nuts to 55 N·m (40 ft.-lbs.) on Model TRX200 or to 35-43 N·m (26-32 ft.-lbs.) on Model TRX200SX. Tighten handlebar clamp to steering shaft bracket nuts to 40 N·m (29 ft.-lbs.).

REAR BRAKE ASSEMBLY

All Models

The rear brake consists of a two-shoe, internally expanding, drum brake mounted on the right end of the rear axle and actuated by either the left handlebar lever or right brake pedal. Information on the front brake is outlined in FRONT BRAKE ASSEMBLY section.

Fig. H3-29—View of rear axle assembly.

Fig. H3-30—Rear brake lever (R) free travel should be 15-20 mm (5/8-3/4 in.) measured at end of lever. Minor brake lever adjustment can be done by loosening knurled locknut (N) and turning cable adjuster (A).

INSPECTION AND ADJUSTMENT. The brake system should be inspected and adjusted after the first week of operation and every 30 days of operation thereafter. The brake drum and shoes should be inspected and renewed annually, if required, as outlined in R&R AND OVERHAUL paragraphs.

To adjust brake pedal free travel, actuate brake pedal and measure free travel at end of pedal. Free travel should be 15-20 mm (5/8-3/4 in.) and is adjusted by rotating adjuster (P—Fig. H3-29) at rear brake.

The rear brake lever should have 15-20 mm (5/8-3/4 in.) of free travel measured at end of lever (R—Fig. H3-30). Rotate lever adjuster (L—Fig. H3-29) at rear brake to adjust lever free travel. Minor brake lever adjustment can be accomplished by loosening knurled locknut (N—Fig. H3-30) and turning cable adjuster (A) at lever assembly.

A rear brake lining wear indicator is fitted to the rear brake shoe cam so brake lining wear can be checked externally. To check brake lining wear externally, apply rear brake and note position of pointer at end of indicator in relation to stationary mark on backing plate. Brake shoes should be renewed as outlined in R&R AND OVERHAUL paragraphs if indicator aligns or rotates beyond stationary mark.

R&R AND OVERHAUL. To remove rear brake shoes and drum, first suitably support rear of vehicle and remove right rear tire and wheel.

WARNING: Inhaling asbestos brake dust is injurious to human health. Approved OSHA respiration equipment must be worn when working on or around brake drum and shoes. DO NOT use compressed air to clean brake drum, shoes or nearby components as brake dust will be blown into air. Only vacuum equipment designed to pick up brake dust should be used.

Fig. H3-31—Inner (I) and outer (O) locknuts must be unscrewed before removing the brake drum. Loosen cap screws (C) and rotate nuts (N) to adjust drive chain tension.

Remove cotter pin and nut securing wheel hub, then withdraw wheel hub. Remove inner (I—Fig. H3-31) and outer (O) locknuts, lockwasher, drum cover plate and "O" ring. Remove brake drum cover, then withdraw brake drum.

Brake shoes should be renewed if linings are worn to 2 mm (0.08 in.) or less. Brake drum should be renewed if inside diameter exceeds 141 mm (5.55 in.).

Reassemble components by reversing disassembly procedures while noting the following: Lightly coat brake shoe cam and anchor pin with grease making sure grease does not contact brake shoe linings. Install a new gasket on brake drum cover. Lockwasher on outside of drum cover plate must be installed with cupped side facing toward brake drum and side marked "OUTSIDE" toward axle end. Tighten inner locknut (I) to 40 N•m (29 ft.-lbs.). Apply Loctite or equivalent to threads of outer locknut (O), install and tighten locknut to 130 N•m (96 ft.-lbs.). Install wheel hub and tighten axle nut to 100 N•m (74 ft.-lbs.), then install a new cotter pin. Tighten wheel retaining nuts to 65 N•m (48 ft.-lbs.).

DRIVE CHAIN AND SPROCKETS

All Models

INSPECTION AND ADJUSTMENT. The final drive chain should be inspected and adjusted after the first week of operation and every 30 days thereafter. Im-proper maintenance and neglect can cause early failure of both drive chain and sprockets. Drive chain free play is measured midway between sprockets and should be 15-25 mm ($9/16$-1 in.) on Model TRX200 or 30-35 mm ($1^3/16$-$1^3/8$ in.) on Model TRX200SX.

Inspect chain roller and pad near front end of swing arm. Remove ridges worn into roller or pad. Renew roller or pad if groove depth is more than 6 mm ($1/4$ in.) below surface.

To adjust chain tension, loosen rear axle housing retaining cap screws (C—Fig. H3-31) and rotate tension adjusting nuts (N). Tighten axle housing cap screws to 90 N•m (66 ft.-lbs.) and recheck drive chain tension. Renew drive chain if recommended tension adjustment cannot be obtained. Refer to LUBRICATION for drive chain lubrication requirements.

R&R AND OVERHAUL. Remove rear skid plate. Loosen four cap screws (C—Fig. H3-31) and tension adjusting nuts (N) and push axle housing toward front of vehicle to increase drive chain slack. Lift chain off rear sprocket toward left rear wheel. Suitably support rear of vehicle and remove left wheel and hub assembly. De-tach lower end of shock absorber from mount. Remove nut securing swing arm pivot shaft. Support swing arm assembly and withdraw swing arm pivot shaft. Withdraw swing arm assembly far enough to provide clearance for drive chain removal. Remove front (engine) sprocket guard and withdraw drive chain. Remove front sprocket if needed. The rear sprocket on Model TRX200 may be removed by unscrewing retaining nuts. To remove rear sprocket and damper on Model TRX200SX, detach snap ring (R—Fig. H3-29) and remove washer (W) and felt washer, then unscrew sprocket retaining nuts (N) and remove sprocket and damper.

Carefully examine sprockets for excessive wear. Worn sprockets will usually have a hooked-tooth profile. A good test is to place a new chain on a used sprocket and check the fit. If sprockets require renewal due to wear, always renew drive chain. Sprockets should be renewed as a set.

Reassembly is reverse of disassembly. Tighten rear sprocket retaining nuts to 40 N•m (29 ft.-lbs.) on Model TRX200 or to 30-36 N•m (22-26 ft.-lbs.) on Model TRX200SX. Tighten lower shock absorber nut to 45 N•m (33 ft.-lbs.), swing arm pivot shaft nut to 90 N•m (66 ft.-lbs.), axle nut to 100 N•m (74 ft.-lbs.) and wheel retaining nuts to 65 N•m (48 ft.-lbs.). Adjust drive chain slack as outlined in preceding section.

HONDA
TRX250R

NOTE: Metric fasteners are used throughout vehicle.

CONDENSED SERVICE DATA

MODEL	TRX250R
General	
Engine Make	Honda
Engine Type.	Two-Stroke; Liquid-Cooled
Number of Cylinders	1
Bore	66.0 mm (2.60 in.)
Stroke.	72.0 mm (2.83 in.)
Displacement.	246.3 cc (15.03 cu. in.)
Compression Ratio	7.5-7.7:1
Fuel Recommendation:	
Prior to 1989	Leaded
After 1988	Unleaded
Pump Octane Rating	92-100 RON
Engine Lubrication.	Fuel:Oil Premix
Transmission Lubrication.	Oil Sump
Forward Speeds.	6
Reverse Speeds	N/A
Tire Size:	
Front:	
Prior to 1988	21 × 7-10
After 1987	AT22 × 7-10
Rear:	
Prior to 1988	20 × 10-9
After 1987	AT20 × 10-9
Tire Pressure:	
Front	27.5 kPa (4.0 psi)
Rear:	
Prior to 1988	20 kPa (2.9 psi)
After 1987	22.5 kPa (3.3 psi)
Dry Weight (Approx.)	148 kg (326 lbs.)
Tune-Up	
Engine Idle Speed	1350-1650 rpm
Compression Pressure	1079-1275 kPa (110-130 psi)
Spark Plug	
1986 & 1989:	
Champion	RN3C
NGK.	BR8ES

Tune-Up (Cont.)

Spark Plug (Cont.)
1987 & 1988:

Champion	RN2C
NGK	BR9ES
Electrode Gap	0.7-0.8 mm
	(0.028-0.031 in.)

Ignition:

Type	Breakerless
Timing:	
Prior to 1988	19° BTDC
After 1987	21° BTDC

Carburetor:

Make	Keihin
Model	See Text
Float Height	16 mm
	(0.63 in.)
Main Jet	See Text
Idle Jet	See Text
Clip Position	See Text
Idle Mixture Setting	See Text
Throttle Lever Free Play	3-8 mm
	(0.12-0.31 in.)

Sizes-Clearances

Cylinder Head Distortion (Max.)	0.05 mm
	(0.002 in.)
Cylinder Bore Diameter:	
"A" Cylinder	66.030-66.040 mm
	(2.5996-2.6000 in.)
Wear Limit	66.07 mm
	(2.601 in.)
"B" Cylinder	66.020-66.029 mm
	(2.5992-2.5996 in.)
Wear Limit	66.06 mm
	(2.600 in.)
Cylinder Bore Taper (Max.)	0.03 mm
	(0.001 in.)
Cylinder Bore Out-of-Round (Max.)	0.03 mm
	(0.001 in.)
Piston-to-Cylinder Wall Clearance	0.060-0.080 mm
	(0.0023-0.0031 in.)
Wear Limit	0.14 mm
	(0.0055 in.)
Piston Diameter*	
"A" Piston	65.960-65.970 mm
	(2.5968-2.5972 in.)
Wear Limit	65.90 mm
	(2.594 in.)
"B" Piston	65.950-65.959 mm
	(2.5964-2.5968 in.)
Wear Limit	65.89 mm
	(2.594 in.)
Piston Pin Bore	18.007-18.013 mm
	(0.7089-0.7091 in.)
Wear Limit	18.03 mm
	(0.710 in.)

Sizes-Clearances (Cont.)

Piston Pin Diameter	17.994-18.000 mm (0.7084-0.7087 in.)
Wear Limit	17.98 mm (0.708 in.)
Piston-to-Pin Clearance	0.007-0.019 mm (0.0003-0.0007 in.)
Wear Limit	0.03 mm (0.001 in.)
Piston Ring End Gap	0.2-0.4 mm (0.008-0.016 in.)
Wear Limit	0.50 mm (0.020 in.)
Connecting Rod Small End Bore Diameter	21.997-22.009 mm (0.8660-0.8665 in.)
Wear Limit	22.022 mm (0.8670 in.)
Connecting Rod Big End Side Clearance (Max.)	1.0 mm (0.039 in.)
Connecting Rod Big End Radial Clearance (Max.)	0.04 mm (0.002 in.)
Crankshaft Runout (Max.)	0.05 mm (0.002 in.)

*Piston diameter should be measured 25 mm (1 in.) from bottom of skirt on 1986 models or 8 mm (0.3 in.) from bottom of skirt on all other models.

Capacities

Cooling System:	
Drained	1.38 L (1.46 qt.)
Dry	1.52 L (1.6 qt.)
Fuel Tank	10.0 L (2.64 gal.)
Transmission Sump:	
Drained	0.6 L (0.63 qt.)
Dry	0.7 L (0.74 qt.)

Tightening Torques

Axle Nut	
Front:	
Prior to 1988	80-120 N•m (59-88 ft.-lbs.)
After 1987	60-80 N•m (44-59 ft.-lbs.)
Rear	120-170 N•m (88-125 ft.-lbs.)
Clutch Nut	55-65 N•m (40-48 ft.-lbs.)
Cylinder Head	24-29 N•m (18-21 ft.-lbs.)
Drive Sprocket	30-34 N•m (22-25 ft.-lbs.)

Tightening Torques (Cont.)

Flywheel............................	65-75 N.m (48-55 ft.-lbs.)
Primary Drive Gear	40-50 N.m (29-36 ft.-lbs.)
Spark Plug........................	15-20 N.m (132-177 in.-lbs.)
Water Pump Impeller	10-12 N.m (89-106 in.-lbs.)
Wheel Retaining Nut	65 N.m (48 ft.-lbs.)
Standard Screws:	
5 mm	3.5-5.0 N.m (31-44 in.-lbs.)
6 mm	7-11 N.m (62-97 in.-lbs.)
Standard Bolts & Nuts:	
5 mm	4.5-6.0 N.m (40-53 in.-lbs.)
6 mm	8-12 N.m (71-106 in.-lbs.)
8 mm	18-25 N.m (13-18 ft.-lbs.)
10 mm	30-40 N.m (22-29 ft.-lbs.)
12 mm	50-60 N.m (36-43 ft.-lbs.)
Flanged Bolts & Nuts:	
6 mm	10-14 N.m (89-124 in.-lbs.)
8 mm	24-30 N.m (17-22 ft.-lbs.)
10 mm	35-45 N.m (25-32 ft.-lbs.)

LUBRICATION

ENGINE. The engine is lubricated by oil mixed with the fuel. Recommended oil is Honda 2-Stroke oil or a good quality two-stroke oil designed for use in motorcycles. Specified fuel:oil ratio is 20:1.

TRANSMISSION. Recommended transmission oil is SAE 10W-40 oil with API classification SE or SF. The manufacturer recommends changing the transmission oil every two years.

Transmission oil level is checked by removing plug (P—Fig. H7-1). Oil should run from plug hole when plug is removed. Oil can be poured into transmission through opening for fill plug (F). Oil can be drained by unscrewing drain plug on underside of engine. Dry capacity of transmission sump is 0.7 L (0.74 qt.). Refilling transmis-

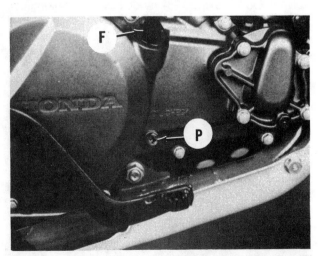

Fig. H7-1—Oil should flow from hole for check plug (P) when plug is unscrewed. Fill transmission sump through hole for fill plug (F).

sion will only require 0.6 L (0.63 qt.) of oil because some oil will be trapped inside case. After refilling transmission, check oil level at check plug (P).

DRIVE CHAIN. The drive chain should be lubricated with SAE 80-90 gear oil after the first week of operation and after every 30 days of operation thereafter. The chain uses "O" rings to seal the chain rollers and pins. Incorrect lubrication may damage the "O" rings resulting in premature chain failure.

Remove and clean the drive chain when excessive dirt is evident. Remove chain as outlined in DRIVE CHAIN AND SPROCKETS section. The chain should be thoroughly washed in kerosene and wiped dry. Using any cleaning solution other than kerosene may damage "O" rings. Lubricate chain with SAE 80-90 gear oil, then install and adjust chain as outlined in DRIVE CHAIN AND SPROCKETS section.

SUSPENSION. After every 30 days of operation the grease fittings on suspension components should be injected with molybdenum disulfide grease. Grease fittings are located at rear shock absorber links and pivots.

CABLES AND LEVERS. All cables and levers should be inspected and lubricated after the first week of operation and after every 30 days of operation thereafter.

AIR CLEANER ELEMENT

The air cleaner element should be removed and cleaned after every 30 days of operation. To remove the air cleaner element, remove the seat/fender, release four cover clips and remove cover (C—Fig. H7-2). Loosen air cleaner frame to inlet tube clamp, then withdraw element and frame from case. Carefully separate foam element from frame.

Thoroughly clean foam element in a nonflammable solvent. Compress element between hands to remove solvent. On 1986 and 1987 models, saturate element in clean SAE 10W-40 engine oil, then compress element

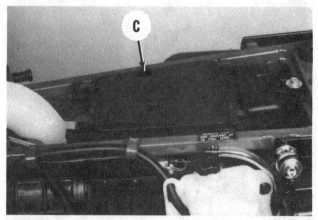

Fig. H7-2—Remove cover (C) for access to air filter element.

Fig. H7-3—Adjust idle speed screw (A) and idle mixture screw (B) as outlined in text.

to remove excess oil. On 1988 and 1989 models, invert air cleaner and fill small compartment with SAE 10W-40 motor oil. Pour oil into filter element, then rub element so oil is distributed throughout. Install element with tab up and reassemble air cleaner components.

FUEL SYSTEM

CARBURETOR. The engine is equipped with a Keihin slide-valve-type carburetor. Keihin carburetor model number applicable to each vehicle model year is as follows: 1986—Model PJ05A; 1987—Model PJ07A; 1988—Model PJ07B; 1989—Model PJ07C. Initial setting of idle mixture screw (B—Fig. H7-3) is $1\frac{7}{8}$ turns out on 1986 and 1987 models, $1\frac{3}{4}$ turns out on 1988 models, and $1\frac{1}{2}$ turns out on 1989 models. Rotating idle mixture screw clockwise will richen idle mixture. Final adjustment must be performed with engine at normal operating temperature. Adjust idle speed screw (A) so engine idles at 1350-1650 rpm. Slowly rotate idle mixture screw clockwise until engine stalls and note screw position. While counting turns, rotate idle mixture screw counterclockwise until engine again stalls and note screw position. Set idle mixture screw at midpoint position between the two previously noted positions that caused engine stalling. Readjust idle speed.

When servicing carburetor, refer to Fig. H7-4 for an exploded view of carburetor while noting the following: Suggested jet sizes are listed below (note that main jet sizes listed apply for average conditions and may not provide optimum performance):

Jet Sizes

	1986	1987	1988	1989
Main Jet:				
Below 5000 ft.	#150	#152	#158	#155
3300-6600 ft.	#148	#150	#155	#152
Above 5000 ft.	#145	#148	#152	#150
Slow Jet	#48	#48	#45	#42

Fig. H7-5—Carburetor float height (C) should be 16.0 mm (0.63 in).

Jet needle clip (7) should be installed in fourth groove from top of jet needle on 1986 and 1989 models or third groove from top on 1987 and 1988 models. Float height (Fig. H7-5) should be 16.0 mm (0.63 in.) between bottom of float and carburetor body. Hold carburetor so float is vertical and resting lightly against fuel inlet valve. Gently bend float arm to adjust float height. When inserting slide (9—Fig. H7-4) in carburetor, insert slide so cutaway is toward air cleaner end of carburetor.

When installing carburetor, note that lug on carburetor must fit into groove of intake rubber tube.

FUEL STRAINER. A fuel strainer attached to the fuel outlet fitting extends into the fuel tank. If fuel flow is reduced or stopped, remove fitting and inspect strainer. To remove fuel strainer, drain fuel from fuel tank. Remove front fender and seat/fender assemblies. Detach fuel lines from fuel control valve, then unscrew and remove fuel tank. Unscrew fuel outlet fitting from fuel tank. Inspect and clean strainer attached to fuel fitting. Reinstall components and check for leaks.

THROTTLE LEVER FREE PLAY. Free play (F—Fig. H7-6) at the end of the throttle lever should be 3-8 mm ($1/8$-$5/16$ in.). To adjust free play, slide back rubber boot (B), loosen knurled nut (L) and rotate cable adjuster (A). Retighten knurled nut.

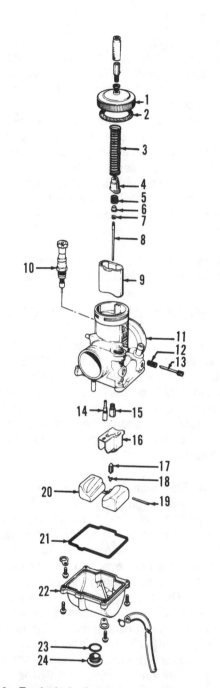

Fig. H7-4—Exploded view of carburetor used on all models. Idle/choke assembly (10) controls idle speed and starter jet. When knob is up (choke on), fuel flows through starter jet circuit. Turning knob when knob is down (choke off) adjusts idle speed.

1.	Cap	13.	Idle mixture screw
2.	Gasket	14.	Slow jet
3.	Spring	15.	Main jet
4.	Cable Holder	16.	Baffle
5.	Spring	17.	Fuel inlet valve
6.	Collar	18.	Clip
7.	Clip	19.	Float pin
8.	Jet needle	20.	Float
9.	Throttle slide	21.	Gasket
10.	Idle/choke assy.	22.	Fuel bowl
11.	Body	23.	Gasket
12.	Spring	24.	Drain screw

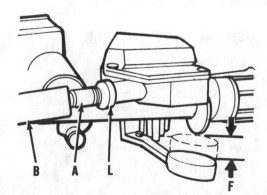

Fig. H7-6—Throttle lever free play (F) should be 3-8 mm (1/8-5/16 in.). To adjust free play, slide back rubber boot (B), loosen knurled nut (L) and rotate cable adjuster (A).

COOLING SYSTEM

INSPECTION. The engine is liquid-cooled by a pressurized cooling system that consists of a radiator, water pump and hoses. System components should be inspected periodically. Replace hoses if cracked, split or otherwise damaged. Inspect radiator for signs of leakage and remove any obstructions. The radiator should be renewed or rebuilt if damage results in a loss of 20 percent or more of the cooling surface area.

CHANGING COOLANT. The manufacturer recommends a mixture of 50 percent distilled water and 50 percent antifreeze.

NOTE: Distilled water must be used to prevent corrosion and clogging in the radiator. Only antifreeze designed for aluminum engines and radiators may be used. A mixture of antifreeze and distilled water must be present at all times. Use of only distilled water will cause corrosion and subsequent damage.

Cooling system capacity is 1.38 L (1.46 qt.) when system is drained or 1.52 L (1.6 qt.) if system is dry.

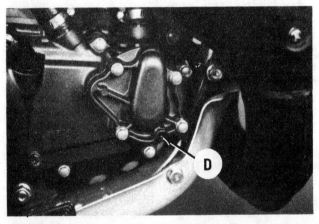

Fig. H7-7—Unscrew drain plug (D) in water pump cover to drain coolant. See also Fig. H7-8.

Fig. H7-8—Unscrew drain plug (P) in cylinder to drain coolant.

To drain coolant, remove radiator cap and unscrew drain plug (D—Fig. H7-7) on water pump and drain plug (P—Fig. H7-8) on cylinder. Catch coolant in a suitable container and dispose of according to prevailing ordinances. Disconnect lower hose from reserve tank then drain and collect coolant. Tip vehicle side-to-side to drain trapped coolant. Reconnect hose to reserve tank and reinstall drain plug.

To refill cooling system, pour coolant into radiator until full. Tip vehicle side-to-side to release trapped air bubbles. Refill radiator. Start and run engine at fast idle, then stop engine. Refill radiator, if necessary, and fill reserve tank to "F" mark. Install radiator cap and run engine until warm, then stop engine, check for leaks and allow engine to cool. Refill radiator, if necessary, and fill reserve tank to "F" mark.

RADIATOR CAP. The radiator cap should have a relief opening pressure of 108-137 kPa (16-20 psi).

IGNITION AND ELECTRICAL

SPARK PLUG. The recommended spark plug for normal operating conditions is a NGK BR8ES or Champion RN3C for 1986 and 1989 models, or a NGK BR9ES or Champion RN2C for 1987 and 1988 models. Spark plug electrode gap should be 0.7-0.8 mm (0.028-0.031 in.). The spark plug should be removed, inspected, cleaned or renewed, and regapped after every 30 days of operation.

IGNITION. The engine is equipped with a breakerless, capacitor discharge ignition system. The electronic ignition circuit consists of the flywheel, exciter coil, CDI module, pulse generator, ignition coil, spark plug, ignition switch and engine stop switch. To check ignition timing, remove gear shift lever and left crankcase cover. Connect a power timing light to engine. Initial ignition timing is 19° BTDC for models prior to 1988 or 21° BTDC for models after 1987. Ignition timing at an idle speed of 1350-1650 rpm should occur when "F" mark (see Fig. H7-10) on flywheel is aligned with index mark on case. When engine speed is increased ignition should occur between "F" mark and "T" mark on flywheel. Ignition timing is not adjustable. If ignition timing is not as specified, check condition of ignition components as described in the following test procedures and renew faulty or questionable components.

If ignition malfunction occurs, check condition of spark plug, all wires and connections before troubleshooting the ignition circuit. Using Honda Digital Multi-Tester KS-AHM-32-003 or a suitable ohmmeter, refer to the following test procedures and specifications to aid troubleshooting.

To check condition of exciter coil, disconnect the black/red wire connector leading to alternator on left frame rail near the fuel tank. Using an ohmmeter, measure resistance between black/red wire and vehicle

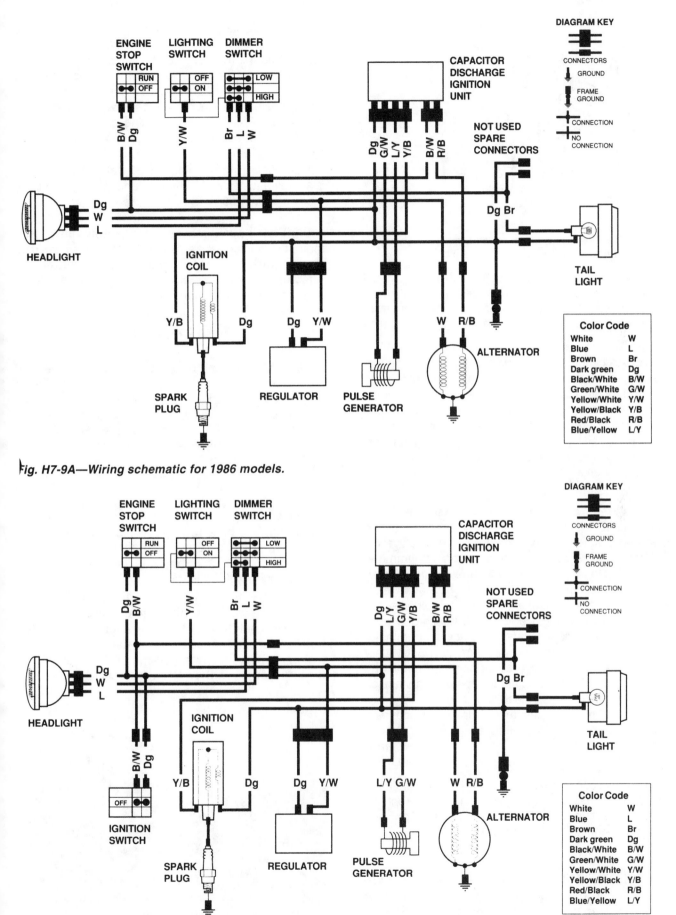

Fig. H7-9A—Wiring schematic for 1986 models.

Fig. H7-9B—Wiring schematic for 1987-1989 models.

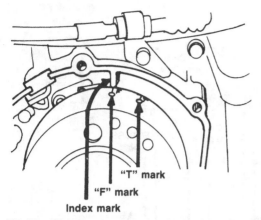

"T" mark
"F" mark
Index mark

Fig. H7-10—The flywheel is marked with "F" and "T" marks to check ignition timing. See text.

ground. Exciter coil is considered satisfactory if resistance is 50-250 ohms. If reading is incorrect, remove left crankcase cover and repeat test at terminal of pulse generator.

To check condition of the pulse generator, disconnect the blue/yellow and green/white wire connector leading to alternator on left frame rail near the fuel tank. Connect ohmmeter leads to blue/yellow wire and green/white wire going to engine. Pulse generator is satisfactory if ohmmeter reading is 50-200 ohms. If reading is incorrect, remove left crankcase cover and repeat test at terminal of pulse generator.

To check condition of ignition coil, detach black/yellow wire and green wire from ignition coil. Disconnect high tension lead from spark plug. To check primary winding resistance, attach one ohmmeter lead to black/yellow wire terminal on ignition coil and remaining ohmmeter lead to green wire terminal. Ohmmeter should read 0.1-0.3 ohms. Perform two secondary winding tests, one with the spark plug cap attached to coil wire and one without spark plug cap attached. Attach one ohmmeter lead to spark plug cap and remaining ohmmeter lead to coil ground (green wire terminal). Secondary winding resistance through spark plug cap should be 7k-11k ohms. Remove spark plug cap from high tension wire. Attach an ohmmeter lead to high tension wire and remaining ohmmeter lead to coil ground. Secondary winding resistance reading with spark plug cap removed should be 3k-5k ohms. If secondary winding resistance is now within specification, renew spark plug cap.

If no faulty component is found and ignition malfunction is still present, renew CDI module and recheck ignition operation. The CDI module is mounted on vehicle frame beneath the front fender assembly.

NOTE: The lighting coil and exciter coil are contained within the magneto stator. If one coil tests defective, then the complete magneto stator assembly must be renewed.

LIGHTING CIRCUIT. The lighting coil is a part of the magneto stator, which is attached on the left crankcase half behind the flywheel. To check condition of lighting coil, disconnect the white/yellow wire connector leading to alternator on left frame rail near the fuel tank. Using an ohmmeter measure resistance between white/yellow wire and vehicle ground. Lighting coil is considered satisfactory if resistance is 0.1-1.0 ohms. See previous NOTE.

Headlight rating is 12 volts-55/60 watts. Taillight rating is 12 volt-8 watt for 1986 models and 12 volt-5 watts for models after 1986.

WIRING. If wiring requires repair, always install wire that is the same gauge as original wire. Wires should be routed away from areas of extreme heat or sharp edges. Attach or hold wires in their original position using plastic tie straps to prevent short circuits.

FASTENERS

After the first week of operation and after every 30 days of operation thereafter, the vehicle should receive an overall inspection. All screws, nuts and other fasteners should be checked and tightened to proper torque specification shown in CONDENSED SERVICE DATA section or in the appropriate maintenance section.

CLUTCH

The engine is equipped with a multiple-disc-type clutch that is actuated by the left handlebar lever. The clutch lever should be adjusted after the first week of operation and then after every 30 days of operation, or more frequently if required.

Clutch lever free play should be 10-20 mm (3/8-3/4 in.) at end of clutch lever. Adjust free play by loosening knurled locknut (A—Fig. H7-11) and rotate adjuster (B). If adjustment cannot be achieved using handlebar adjuster, loosen locknuts (C—Fig. H7-12) at engine bracket shown in Fig. H7-12 and reposition clutch cable.

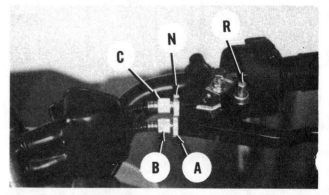

Fig. H7-11—Adjust clutch lever free play by loosening knurled locknut (A) and rotate adjuster (B).

Fig. H7-12—If adjustment limit is reached at clutch lever adjuster, loosen locknuts (C) at engine bracket and reposition clutch cable. Retighten locknuts. If necessary, repeat adjustment procedure at handlebar lever.

Fig. H7-14—Attach bleeder hose to bleed valve (V) on front brake caliper.

Retighten locknuts. If necessary, repeat adjustment procedure at handlebar lever.

Properly operated, the clutch should disengage and engage freely. Difficult shifting, clutch grabbing or clutch slipping may indicate overhaul is necessary.

FRONT BRAKE ASSEMBLY

A disc brake assembly is used on both front wheels. Front brake adjustment for disc pad wear is not required due to the compensating action of the piston in the caliper.

Brake fluid must be rated DOT 4. Maintain brake fluid level between marks on inner side of brake fluid reservoir. To avert spillage, be sure reservoir is horizontal before removing cover.

BLEEDING. Make sure reservoir (R—Fig. H7-13) is full. Connect a bleed hose to bleed valve (Fig. H7-14) on both front brake caliper assemblies. Route the bleed hoses into suitable containers. Operate the brake lever until hard resistance is felt, then open one bleed valve. Close bleed valve prior to releasing brake lever. Con-

tinue bleeding procedure on both wheels until no air bubbles are noted in discharged fluid from bleed valve.

NOTE: Make sure reservoir remains full during bleeding procedure.

When bleeding procedure is completed, add brake fluid to reservoir until fluid level is at upper level line in reservoir.

OVERHAUL. Brake pad thickness can be checked externally by viewing wear indicator arm (A—Fig. H7-15). If pointer (P) on wear indicator arm (A) aligns with or goes beyond raised casting (C) on caliper housing, then brake pads have reached wear limit and must be renewed.

WARNING: Inhaling asbestos brake dust is injurious to human health. Approved OSHA respiration equipment must be worn when working on or around brake calipers and pads. DO NOT use compressed air to clean brake calipers, pads or nearby components as brake dust will be blown into air.

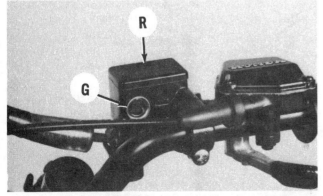

Fig. H7-13—Brake fluid for front brakes is contained in reservoir (R) on handlebar. Fluid level is visible through sight glass (G).

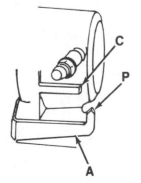

Fig. H7-15—Brake pads must be renewed if pointer (P) on wear indicator arm (A) of front brake caliper is aligned with or below raised casting (C) on caliper.

Only vacuum equipment designed to pick up brake dust should be used.

Brake components are accessible after removing wheel, caliper mounting screws and withdrawing caliper. Refer to Fig. H7-16 for an exploded view of caliper. Brake disc should be renewed if thickness is less than 3 mm (0.118 in.) or runout exceeds 0.3 mm (0.012 in.). Maximum allowable caliper bore diameter is 25.46 mm (1.002 in.). Minimum allowable piston diameter is 25.29 mm (0.996 in.). Tighten brake pad pins to 15-20 N·m (132-176 in.-lbs.). Push piston by hand back into caliper to allow clearance for new brake pads. Tighten brake caliper mounting screws to 24-30 N·m (18-22 ft.-lbs.). After reassembly, operate brake lever until brake lever will not pump up after continuous operation. Do not operate vehicle until brakes are tested and functioning properly.

MASTER CYLINDER. To remove front brake master cylinder (18—Fig. H7-16), detach brake line from master cylinder. Brake fluid will remove paint; be careful when removing master cylinder. Unscrew two retaining screws and remove master cylinder. Remove brake lever, reservoir cover (13) and diaphragm (15). Remove dust boot (1) and snap ring (2). Disassemble piston assembly while noting location and direction of components. Renew complete master cylinder if bore is scored, pitted or excessively worn. Maximum allowable bore diameter is 12.755 mm (0.5022 in.). Minimum allowable piston diameter is 12.645 mm (0.4978 in.). Superficial damage in master cylinder bore may be removed using a suitable cylinder hone. After honing, rinse bore with clean brake fluid. Shake out excess fluid but do not wipe dry. Using a shop towel or rag to dry cylinder will leave lint particles in bore. Renew boots and piston cups. During reassembly, lubricate components with clean brake fluid. Reassembly is reverse of disassembly. Install spring (5) so small end contacts piston (4). Bleed brakes as previously outlined. Do not operate vehicle until brakes are tested and functioning properly.

FRONT AXLE

Both front steering knuckle assemblies pivot on ball joint assemblies at the end of each upper and lower

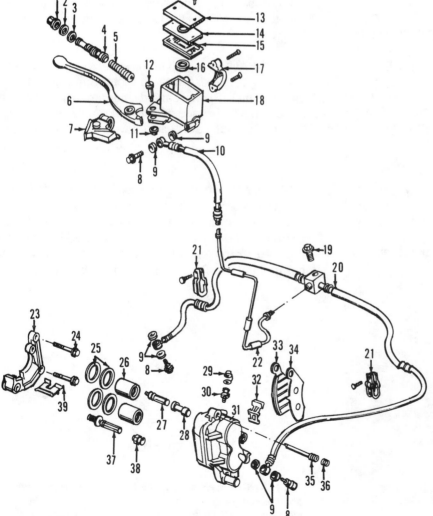

Fig. H7-16—Exploded view of front brake system.

1. Dust boot
2. Snap ring
3. "O" ring
4. Piston
5. Spring
6. Hand lever
7. Boot
8. Union bolt
9. Sealing washer
10. Upper flexible brake hose
11. Nut
12. Bolt
13. Cover
14. Diaphragm plate
15. Diaphragm
16. Separator
17. Clamp
18. Master cylinder body
19. Screw
20. Lower flexible hose
21. Brake hose clamp
22. Metal brake line
23. Caliper bracket
24. Screw
25. Dust and piston seals
26. Piston
27. Caliper pin
28. Boot
29. Bleed valve cap
30. Bleed valve
31. Caliper body
32. Antirattle spring
33. Inboard brake pad
34. Outboard brake pad
35. Pad pin bolt
36. Pad pin bolt cap
37. Caliper pin
38. Boot
39. Clip

control arm. The control arms are bolted at the ends to the vehicle frame and a shock absorber is used to limit and cushion the up and down movement of the control arms. The shock absorbers are adjustable to alter absorber spring setting for different terrain and load conditions.

Remove the front wheel to service the ball joint assemblies. Note that removing the brake components will allow greater access to ball joint assemblies. If any ball joint or control arm is excessively worn or any other damage is noted, then ball joint or control arm must be renewed. Lower ball joint and control arm are a unit assembly on all models. Upper ball joint may be removed from upper control arm on 1986 and 1987 models; ball joint and control arm are a unit assembly on 1988 and 1989 models. Lower control arm and upper control arm retaining nuts should be tightened to 50-60 N·m (36-43 ft.-lbs.) on 1987 models, or to 35-45 N·m (25-33 ft.-lbs.) on 1986, 1988 and 1989 models. Shock absorber retaining nuts should be tightened to 40-50 N·m (29-36 ft.-lbs). Upper ball joint to control arm retain-

ing nut on 1986 and 1987 models should be tightened to 60-80 N·m (43-58 ft.-lbs.). Tighten ball joint to steering knuckle retaining nuts to 50-60 N·m (36-43 ft.-lbs.).

STEERING

TOE-IN SETTING. Place the steering handlebar in a straight ahead position. Use a suitable measuring tool and measure distance (A & B—Fig. H7-17), at spindle height, between the center of the tires on the front and rear sides. The measured distance (A) on the front side should be 0-20 mm (0.0-0.8 in.) shorter than the measured distance on the rear side (B). If not, loosen inside and outside locknuts on the left and right tie rod assemblies and rotate tie rod shaft (S) on each side equally until measured distance is within recommended range.

After obtaining the correct setting, securely tighten the locknuts to retain tie rod settings.

INSPECTION. Rotate the steering handlebar from one extreme to the other and note if any binding or roughness is felt. Periodically inspect the steering components for looseness or any other damage. Renew any damaged component. Clean and grease components if binding or excessive effort is noted.

OVERHAUL. Tie rod assemblies may be interchanged from side to side. Note that gold-colored tie rod end (8—Fig. H7-18) is outer tie rod end and has left-hand threads, as does the adjoining locknut (6). Tighten tie rod mounting nuts to 40-50 N·m (29-36 ft.-lbs.).

On 1986 and 1987 models, steering arm (9) is detachable from steering knuckle. Steering arms are marked "L" or "R" to indicate which steering knuckle they match. Install steering arm with letter side up. Tighten the steering arm retaining nuts to 60-70 N·m (43-51 ft.-lbs.).

To expose the steering shaft, the front fender assembly must be removed. On 1986 and 1987 models, detach the headlight guard. Unscrew the four cap screws securing the upper clamp and remove the clamp

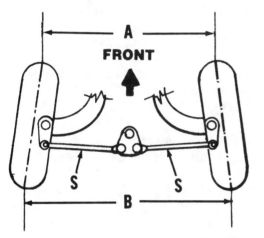

Fig. H7-17—Distance (A) on the front side of tires must be 0-20 mm (0.0-0.8 in.) shorter than the distance on the rear side (B) for desired toe-in. Adjust toe-in by changing length of tie rods (S).

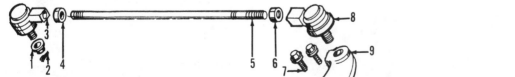

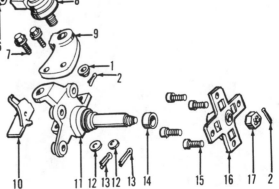

Fig. H7-18—Exploded view of tie rod and knuckle assemblies. Steering arm is integral with knuckle on 1988 and 1989 models. Outer tie rod end (8) and locknut (6) have left-hand threads.

1. Nut
2. Cotter pin
3. Inner tie rod end
4. Locknut
5. Tie rod
6. Locknut (L.H.)
7. Screw
8. Outer tie rod end (gold)
9. Steering arm
10. Brake hose guide plate
11. Steering knuckle
12. Nut
13. Cotter pin
14. Spacer
15. Screw
16. Wheel hub
17. Nut

halves. Extract the steering shaft bushing and clean the old grease from the steering shaft. Inspect the clamp halves, steering shaft and bushing for damage. Renew components if needed. Grease inside of steering shaft bushing and install bushing and clamp halves. Make sure clamp half marked "IN" and half marked "OUT" are properly positioned. Markings are stamped on outside of clamp halves. Tighten the retaining clamp cap screws to 25-30 N•m (18-22 ft.-lbs.).

The tie rod assemblies, handlebar assembly and front skid plate must be removed to withdraw the steering shaft from the vehicle. Remove the lower bearing housing retaining cotter pin and nut to withdraw the steering shaft. Inspect the lower bearing assembly and seals and renew if needed. Bearing retaining snap ring must be removed prior to driving bearing out of housing. Tighten the lower bearing assembly retaining nut to 60-80 N•m (43-58 ft.-lbs.). Tighten tie rod mounting nuts to 40-50 N•m (29-36 ft.-lbs.). Tighten handlebar clamp to steering shaft bracket nuts to 40-50 N•m (29-36 ft.-lbs.).

REAR BRAKE ASSEMBLY

A single disc brake assembly is used for both rear wheels. The running brake is operated hydraulically by a foot pedal on the lower right side. The parking brake is mechanically operated by a cable and handlebar components in conjunction with the clutch lever.

BRAKE PEDAL HEIGHT ADJUSTMENT. Brake pedal height on Model TRX250R is not adjustable.

PARKING BRAKE ADJUSTMENT. Make sure parking brake/clutch lever is in the released position. Loosen locknut (A—Fig. H7-19) and rotate adjuster screw (B) clockwise until resistance is felt, then rotate counterclockwise ⅛ turn and tighten locknut (A). Make sure screw (B) is not overtightened causing rear brake application. To adjust parking brake/clutch lever, apply button (R—Fig. H7-20) and actuate lever. Lever travel should

Fig. H7-19—Attach bleeder hose to bleed valve (V) on rear brake caliper. See text for adjustment of parking brake.

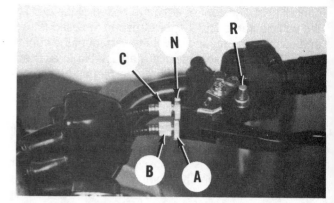

Fig. H7-20—To adjust parking brake/clutch lever travel, loosen locknut (N) and rotate cable adjuster (C).

be 31-39 mm (1¼-1½ in.) on 1986 models or 25-30 mm (1-1⅛ in.) on models after 1986. Slide dust boot down cables, then loosen knurled locknut (N) on upper cable and rotate cable adjuster (C) to adjust travel distance.

BLEEDING. Make sure rear brake master cylinder reservoir is full. Connect a bleed hose to bleed valve (V—Fig. H7-19) on brake caliper assembly. Route the bleed hose into a suitable container. Operate foot pedal until firm resistance is felt, then open bleed valve (V). Close bleed valve prior to releasing foot pedal. Continue bleeding procedure until no air bubbles are noted in discharged fluid from bleed valve.

NOTE: Make sure rear brake master cylinder remains full during bleeding procedure.

When bleeding procedure is completed, add brake fluid to rear brake master cylinder reservoir until fluid level is at "UPPER" level line on reservoir.

OVERHAUL. External determination of brake pad thickness is possible by viewing the brake pads. If brake pads are not worn down to service grooves, then brake pads do not require replacement because of excessive wear. If brake pad wear is down to service grooves or within service grooves, then both brake pads must be renewed.

WARNING: Inhaling asbestos brake dust is injurious to human health. Approved OSHA respiration equipment must be worn when working on or around brake calipers and pads. DO NOT use compressed air to clean brake calipers, pads or nearby components as brake dust will be blown into air. Only vacuum equipment designed to pick up brake dust should be used.

Brake components are accessible after removing caliper mounting screws and withdrawing caliper. Refer to Fig. H7-21 for an exploded view of brake caliper. Brake

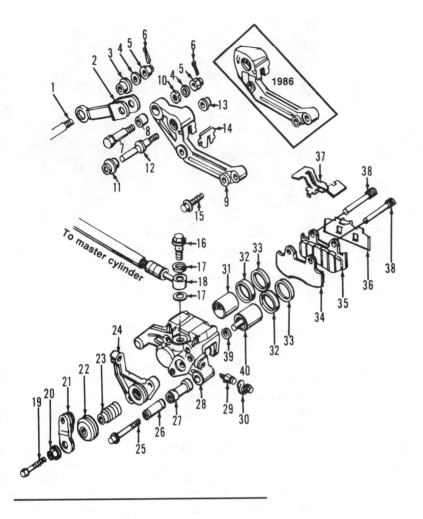

Fig. H7-21—Exploded view of rear brake caliper.

1. Torque link
2. Torque link arm
3. Collar
4. Washer
5. Nut
6. Cotter pin
7. Bolt
8. Collar
9. Caliper mounting bracket
10. Washer
11. Boot
12. Caliper pin
13. Nut
14. Retainer clip
15. Bolt
16. Union bolt
17. Sealing washer
18. Flexible brake hose
19. Parking brake adjust screw
20. Locknut
21. Parking brake arm
22. Boot
23. Parking brake shaft
24. Parking brake base
25. Caliper mounting bolt
26. Caliper pivot collar
27. Collar
28. Caliper
29. Bleed valve
30. Bleed valve cap
31. Piston
32. Piston seal
33. Dust seal
34. Inboard brake pad
35. Outboard brake pad
36. Shim
37. Antirattle spring
38. Pad pin bolts
39. "O" ring
40. Piston

Fig. H7-22—Exploded view of rear brake master cylinder.

1. Screw
2. Screw
3. Fitting
4. "O" ring
5. Master cylinder body
6. Spring
7. Primary cup
8. Piston
9. Push rod
10. Snap ring
11. Nut
12. Boot
13. Pin
14. Joint
15. Nut
16. Washer
17. Cotter pin
18. Hose clamp
19. Reservoir hose
20. Screw
21. Top cover
22. Diaphragm plate
23. Diaphragm
24. Reservoir
25. Collar
26. Rubber grommet
27. Collar
28. Bolt
29. Sealing washer
30. Flexible brake hose
31. Union bolt

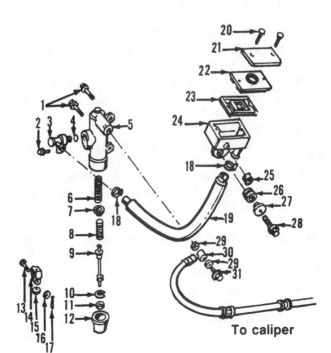

To caliper

disc should be renewed if thickness is 3.0 mm (0.118 in.) or less or disc runout is 0.3 mm (0.012 in.) or more. Maximum allowable caliper bore diameter is 25.46 mm (1.002 in.). Minimum allowable piston diameter is 25.29 mm (0.996 in.). Push piston by hand back into caliper to allow clearance for new brake pads. Tighten brake pad pins to 15-20 N·m (132-176 in.-lbs.). Tighten brake caliper mounting screws to 20-25 N·m (15-18 ft.-lbs.). After reassembly, operate brake pedal until pedal will not pump up after continuous operation. Do not operate vehicle until brakes are tested and functioning properly.

MASTER CYLINDER. To remove rear brake master cylinder (5—Fig. H7-22), disconnect brake plunger from pedal. Detach brake lines from master cylinder and plug line to reservoir. Brake fluid will remove paint; be careful when removing master cylinder. Unscrew retaining screws and remove master cylinder. Remove dust boot (12) and snap ring (10). Disassemble piston assembly while noting location and direction of components. Renew complete master cylinder if bore is scored, pitted or excessively worn. Maximum allowable bore diameter is 14.055 mm (0.5533 in.). Minimum allowable piston diameter is 13.945 mm (0.5490 in.). Superficial damage in master cylinder bore may be removed using a suitable cylinder hone. After honing, rinse bore with clean brake fluid. Shake out excess fluid but do not wipe dry. Using a shop towel or rag to dry cylinder will leave lint particles in bore. Renew boots and piston cups. During reassembly, lubricate components with clean brake fluid. Reassembly is reverse of disassembly. Install spring (6) so small end contacts piston (8). Bleed brakes as previously outlined. Do not operate vehicle until brakes are tested and functioning properly.

DRIVE CHAIN AND SPROCKETS

INSPECTION AND ADJUSTMENT. The drive chain should be inspected and adjusted after the first week of operation and every 30 days of operation thereafter. Improper maintenance and neglect can cause early failure of both drive chain and sprockets. Drive chain free play should be 30-40 mm (1⅛-1½ in.) measured midway between sprockets.

To adjust chain tension, loosen screws (S—Fig. H7-23). Insert a suitable tool into slot (T) and rotate axle housing. Rotate housing toward front of vehicle to increase chain slack or toward rear of vehicle to decrease chain slack. Tighten screws (S) to 19-23 N·m (14-17 ft.-lbs.) to secure chain tension adjustment.

Inspect chain roller and pad near front end of swing arm. Remove ridges worn into roller or pad. Renew roller or pad if groove depth is more than 6 mm (¼ in.) below surface.

R&R AND OVERHAUL. Loosen screws (S—Fig. H7-23) and insert a suitable tool into slot (T). Rotate axle

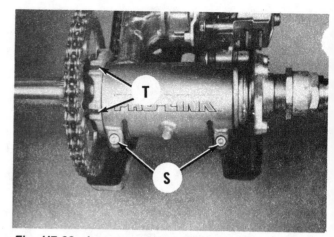

Fig. H7-23—Loosen screws (S) and insert a suitable tool into slot (T) to adjust drive chain tension. Later models are equipped with two screws (S) on each side of axle housing.

housing toward front of vehicle to increase drive chain slack. Detach the master link clip and remove the master link. Do not lose the "O" rings on the master link. Remove the drive chain. Remove front (engine) sprocket guard and remove front sprocket if needed. Remove left rear wheel if rear chain sprocket must be removed.

Carefully examine sprockets for excessive wear. Worn sprockets will usually have a hooked tooth profile. A good test is to place a new chain on a used sprocket and check the fit. If sprockets require renewal due to wear, always renew drive chain. Sprockets should be renewed as a set. Measure length of drive chain between 95 link pins on 1986 and 1987 models, or between 91 link pins on 1988 and 1989 models. Chain must be straight and all slack removed. Renew chain if distance exceeds 1515 mm (59.6 in.) on 1986 and 1987 models, or 1436 mm (56.5 in.) on 1988 and 1989 models.

Tighten rear sprocket nuts to 35-40 N·m (26-29 ft.-lbs.). When assembling chain, be sure "O" rings are properly installed on master link. Install master link clip as shown in Fig. H7-24. Tighten wheel retaining nuts to 65 N·m (48 ft.-lbs.). Refer to previous INSPECTION AND ADJUSTMENT paragraphs for recommended drive chain adjustment procedures.

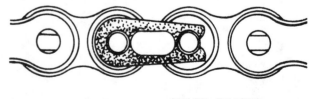

← CHAIN TRAVEL

Fig. H7-24—Drive chain master link clip should always be installed with closed end toward normal direction of chain travel.

HONDA

TRX250X

NOTE: Metric fasteners are used throughout vehicle.

CONDENSED SERVICE DATA

MODEL	TRX250X
General	
Engine Make	Honda
Engine Type	Four-Stroke/Air-Cooled
Number of Cylinders	1
Bore	74.0 mm
	(2.91 in.)
Stroke	57.3 mm
	(2.26 in.)
Displacement	246.4 cc
	(15.03 cu. in.)
Compression Ratio	9.2-9.6:1
Engine Lubrication	Wet Sump/Oil Pump
Transmission Lubrication	Common With Engine
Engine/Transmission Oil	SAE 10W-40
Forward Speeds	5
Reverse Speeds	1
Tire Size:	
Front	22 × 7-10
Rear	22 × 10-9
Tire Pressure:	
Front	30 kPa
	(4.4 psi)
Rear	20 kPa
	(2.9 psi)
Dry Weight (Approx.)	159 kg
	(351 lbs.)
Tune-Up	
Engine Idle Speed	1300-1500 rpm
Compression Pressure	1175-1375 kPa
	(170-199 psi)
Spark Plug:	
NGK	DR8ES-L
Nippon Denso	X24ESR-U
Electrode Gap	0.6-0.7 mm
	(0.024-0.028 in.)
Ignition:	
Type	Breakerless
Timing	10° BTDC
Carburetor:	
Make	Keihin
Model	See Text
Float Height	18.5 mm
	(0.73 in.)
Main Jet	See Text

Tune-Up (Cont.)
Carburetor: (Cont.)

Idle Jet	See Text
Clip Position	3rd Groove From Top
Idle Mixture Setting	See Text
Throttle Lever Free Play	3-8 mm
	(0.12-0.31 in.)

Sizes-Clearances
Valve Clearance (cold):

Intake & Exhaust	0.08 mm
	(0.003 in.)

Valve Face & Seat Angle:

Intake & Exhaust	45°

Valve Seat Width:

Intake & Exhaust	1.2 mm
	(0.05 in.)
Wear Limit	1.5 mm
	(0.06 in.)

Valve Stem Diameter:

Intake	5.480-5.490 mm
	(0.2157-0.2161 in.)
Wear Limit	5.45 mm
	(0.215 in.)
Exhaust	5.460-5.470 mm
	(0.2150-0.2154 in.)
Wear Limit	5.43 mm
	(0.214 in.)

Valve Guide Bore Diameter:

Intake & Exhaust	5.500-5.512 mm
	(0.2165-0.2170 in.)
Wear Limit	5.525 mm
	(0.2175 in.)

Valve Stem to Guide Clearance:

Intake	0.010-0.032 mm
	(0.0004-0.0013 in.)
Wear Limit	0.12 mm
	(0.005 in.)
Exhaust	0.030-0.052 mm
	(0.0012-0.0020 in.)
Wear Limit	0.14 mm
	(0.006 in.)

Valve Spring Free Length:

Inner	36.06 mm
	(1.42 in.)
Minimum Length	33.0 mm
	(1.30 in.)
Outer	40.97 mm
	(1.61 in.)
Minimum Length	37.9 mm
	(1.49 in.)

Rocker Arm Bore Diameter:

Intake & Exhaust	11.988-12.006 mm
	(0.4720-0.4727 in.)
Wear Limit	12.04 mm
	(0.474 in.)

Rocker Shaft Diameter:

Intake & Exhaust	11.966-11.984 mm
	(0.4711-0.4718 in.)

Sizes-Clearances (Cont.)

Rocker Shaft Diameter: (Cont.)

    Wear Limit . . . .   11.92 mm
    (0.469 in.)

Camshaft Lobe Height:

  Intake . . . .   35.751 mm
    (1.4075 in.)

    Wear Limit . . . .   35.571 mm
    (1.4004 in.)

  Exhaust . . . .   35.764 mm
    (1.4080 in.)

    Wear Limit . . . .   35.584 mm
    (1.4009 in.)

Cylinder Head Distortion (Max.) . . . .   0.10 mm
    (0.004 in.)

Cylinder Bore Diameter . . . .   74.00-74.01 mm
    (2.913-2.914 in.)

  Wear Limit . . . .   74.10 mm
    (2.917 in.)

Piston-to-Cylinder Wall Clearance . . . .   0.015-0.045 mm
    (0.0006-0.0018 in.)

  Wear Limit . . . .   0.10 mm
    (0.004 in.)

Piston Diameter—

Measured 10 mm (0.4 in.) From
Skirt Bottom & 90° to Pin Bore . . . .   73.965-73.985 mm
    (2.9120-2.9128 in.)

  Wear Limit . . . .   73.90 mm
    (2.909 in.)

Piston Pin Bore . . . .   17.002-17.008 mm
    (0.6694-0.6696 in.)

  Wear Limit . . . .   17.04 mm
    (0.671 in.)

Piston Pin Diameter . . . .   16.994-17.000 mm
    (0.6691-0.6693 in.)

  Wear Limit . . . .   16.96 mm
    (0.668 in.)

Piston-to-Pin Clearance . . . .   0.002-0.014 mm
    (0.0001-0.0006 in.)

  Wear Limit . . . .   0.02 mm
    (0.001 in.)

Piston Ring End Gap:

  Top & Second Ring . . . .   0.15-0.30 mm
    (0.006-0.012 in.)

    Wear Limit . . . .   0.50 mm
    (0.020 in.)

  Oil Ring . . . .   0.20-0.70 mm
    (0.008-0.028 in.)

Piston Ring Side Clearance:

  Top & Second Ring . . . .   0.025-0.040 mm
    (0.0010-0.0016 in.)

    Wear Limit . . . .   0.08 mm
    (0.003 in.)

  Second Ring . . . .   0.015-0.045 mm
    (0.0006-0.0018 in.)

    Wear Limit . . . .   0.09 mm
    (0.004 in.)

Sizes-Clearances (Cont.)

Connecting Rod Small End Bore Diameter	17.016-17.034 mm (0.6699-0.6706 in.)
Wear Limit	17.10 mm (0.6732 in.)
Connecting Rod Big End Side Clearance (Max.)	0.80 mm (0.031 in.)
Connecting Rod Big End Radial Clearance (Max.)	0.05 mm (0.002 in.)
Crankshaft Runout (Max.)	0.05 mm (0.002 in.)

Capacities

Fuel Tank	8.5 L (2.2 gal.)
Engine/Transmission Sump	See Text

Tightening Torques

Axle Nut	
Front	70 N•m (51 ft.-lbs.)
Rear	145 N•m (107 ft.-lbs.)
Camshaft Sprocket	20 N•m (15 ft.-lbs.)
Clutch Nut	110 N•m (81 ft.-lbs.)
Crankcase	12 N•m (106 in.-lbs.)
Cylinder Head Nut & Screw	40 N•m (29 ft.-lbs.)
Flywheel Cap Screw	110 N•m (81 ft.-lbs.)
Spark Plug	18 N•m (160 in.-lbs.)
Wheel Retaining Nut	65 N•m (48 ft.-lbs.)
Standard Screws:	
5 mm	3.5-5.0 N•m (31-44 in.-lbs.)
6 mm	7-11 N•m (62-97 in.-lbs.)
Standard Bolts & Nuts:	
5 mm	4.5-6.0 N•m (40-53 in.-lbs.)
6 mm	8-12 N•m (71-106 in.-lbs.)
8 mm	18-25 N•m (13-18 ft.-lbs.)
10 mm	30-40 N•m (22-29 ft.-lbs.)
12 mm	50-60 N•m (36-43 ft.-lbs.)
Flanged Bolts & Nuts:	
6 mm	10-14 N•m (89-124 in.-lbs.)

Tightening Torques (Cont.)
Flanged Bolts & Nuts: (Cont.)

8 mm	24-30 N•m (17-22 ft.-lbs.)
10 mm	35-45 N•m (25-32 ft.-lbs.)

LUBRICATION

ENGINE AND TRANSMISSION. The engine and transmission are lubricated by a trochoid-type pump located on the right side of the crankcase and driven by a gear on the right end of the crankshaft. The engine and transmission share a common sump. Recommended oil is SAE 10W-40 motor oil with an API classification of SF or SG.

The sump is filled through filler plug (F—Fig. H9-1) opening. Oil level should be maintained at upper mark on filler plug dipstick. Do not screw filler plug in when checking oil level. Oil is drained by removing plug in underside of crankcase. Crankcase capacity after changing oil is 1.6 L (1.69 qt.). Crankcase oil capacity after changing oil and oil filter is 1.7 L (1.80 qt.). Crankcase dry capacity is 2.0 L (2.11 qt.).

Fig. H9-1—Remove filler plug (F) to check crankcase oil level. The oil filter is located behind filter cover (C). Sump screen is accessible after removing right crankcase cover as outlined in text.

C.	Filter cover		
F.	Filler plug		
1.	Kick starter pedal	5.	Cover
2.	Banjo bolt	6.	Cap screw
3.	Clutch cable	7.	Brake pedal
4.	Reverse lock cable	8.	Cable mount
		9.	Reverse indicator wire

Manufacturer recommends changing the oil and oil filter after the first week of operation and then after every 30 days of operation. A sump filter screen located in a compartment in right crankcase half should be removed periodically and cleaned.

The old filter can be renewed after removing filter cover (C). The new filter is inserted with rubber seal side facing toward filter cover (C). Ensure filter spring is correctly positioned between filter and crankcase cover. Renew filter cover "O" ring and crankcase cover oil passage "O" ring if required and install cover. Sump filter screen is accessible after removing right crankcase cover. With oil drained from crankcase, remove kick starter pedal (1), banjo bolt (2), clutch cable (3), decompression cable cap screw (6) and brake pedal (7). Be careful not to lose the two sealing washers when removing banjo bolt (2). Detach reverse lock cable (4) at lever, then remove cable mount (8) and reverse lock lever. Remove cover (5) and disconnect wire (9) at reverse switch. Remove cap screws and carefully remove right crankcase cover. Withdraw sump screen from compartment at base of crankcase.

Reinstall by reversing removal procedure while noting the following: Make sure alignment dowels and gasket are fitted to crankcase and install crankcase cover. Tighten crankcase cover retaining cap screws to 10-14 N•m (7-10 ft.-lbs.). Install reverse lock cable (4) and adjust reverse lock lever free travel as outlined in REVERSE LOCK section. Install kick starter pedal (1) while aligning punch mark on pedal with corresponding mark on shaft. Connect reverse indicator wire (9) to switch. Adjust clutch as outlined in CLUTCH section. Fill engine/transmission sump with the appropriate amount of oil and check for leaks.

DRIVE CHAIN. The final drive chain should be lubricated with SAE 80-90 gear oil after the first week of operation and then after every 30 days of operation. An "O" ring-sealed drive chain is used. Incorrect chain lubricating oil can cause damage to "O" ring seals.

The drive chain should be removed and cleaned when excessive dirt is evident. Remove chain as outlined in DRIVE CHAIN AND SPROCKETS section. The chain should be thoroughly washed in kerosene and wiped dry. The use of any cleaning solution other than kerosene can result in drive chain "O" ring seal damage.

HONDA TRX250X

Lubricate chain with SAE 80-90 gear oil. Reinstall and adjust as described in DRIVE CHAIN AND SPROCKETS section.

CABLES AND LEVERS. All cables and levers should be inspected and lubricated after the first week of operation and every 30 days of operation thereafter.

AIR CLEANER ELEMENT

The air cleaner element should be removed and cleaned after every 30 days of operation. To remove air cleaner element, first remove seat. Release four cover spring clips and remove cover. Loosen air cleaner frame to inlet tube clamp, then withdraw element and frame from case. Separate foam element from frame.

Thoroughly clean the foam element in a nonflammable solvent. Compress element between hands to remove solvent. Saturate element in clean SAE 80-90

gear oil. Compress element to remove excess oil. Reinstall air cleaner element assembly by reversing removal procedure.

FUEL SYSTEM

CARBURETOR. Early models are equipped with a Keihin Model QB29 carburetor, while later models are equipped with a Keihin Model QB01A or QB01B. Carburetors are similar to carburetor shown in Figs. H9-3, H9-4 and H9-5. Initial setting of idle mixture screw

Fig. H9-4—View of carburetor with fuel bowl removed. Primary jet (13) is not used. Components are also shown in Fig. H9-3.

8. Needle jet
9. Main jet
10. Baffle
11. Pilot jet
13. Primary jet
14. Idle speed screw
15. Idle mixture screw

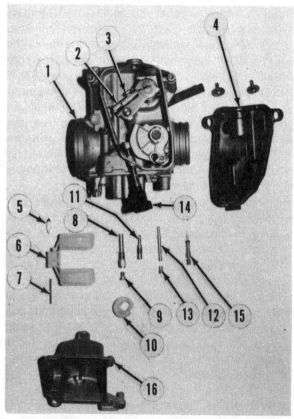

Fig. H9-3—View of partially disassembled carburetor similar to type used. Primary nozzle (12) and primary jet (13) are not used. Also refer to Fig. H9-4 and Fig. H9-5.

1. Carburetor body
2. Throttle link
3. Throttle slide lever & shaft
4. Cover
5. Fuel inlet valve
6. Float
7. Float pin
8. Needle jet
9. Main jet
10. Baffle
11. Pilot jet
12. Primary nozzle
13. Primary jet
14. Idle speed screw
15. Idle mixture screw
16. Fuel bowl

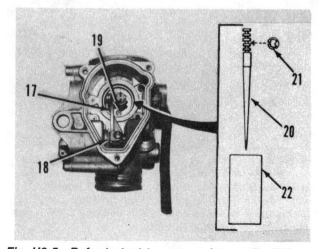

Fig. H9-5—Refer to text to remove jet needle (20) and throttle slide (22).

17. Throttle slide arm
18. Washer
19. Screw
20. Jet needle
21. Clip
22. Throttle slide

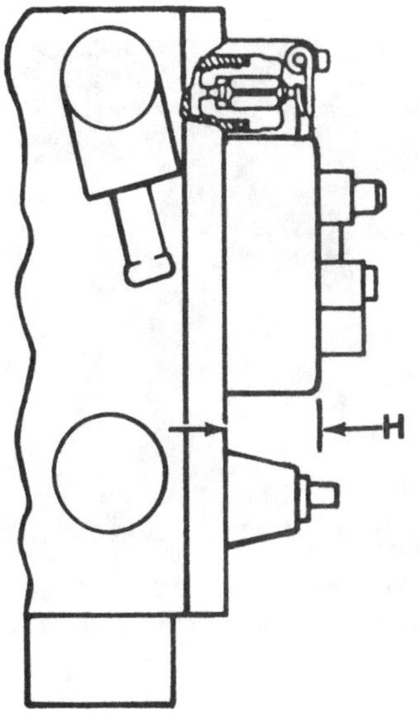

Fig. H9-6—Position carburetor so float rests lightly against fuel inlet valve and measure float height (H).

(15—Fig. H9-4) is 2½ turns out on Model QB29, 1¾ turns out on Model QB01A, and 2 turns out on Model QB01B. Rotating idle mixture screw clockwise will lean idle mixture. Final adjustment must be performed with engine at normal operating temperature. Adjust idle speed screw (14) so engine idles at 1300-1500 rpm. Slowly rotate idle mixture screw (15) clockwise, leaning idle mixture, until engine stalls, then turn idle mixture screw one turn counterclockwise. Readjust idle speed.

Standard main jet size is #125 for Models QB29 and QB01A, and #122 for Model QB01B. Standard slow jet size is #35 for Models QB29 and QB01A, and #38 for Model QB01B. Suggested main jet size for high altitudes of 3000-8000 feet is #120 for Models QB29 and QB01A and #118 for Model QB01B.

When servicing carburetor observe the following: Clip (21—Fig. H9-5) should be in third groove from top of jet needle (20). To obtain access to jet needle (20) and throttle slide (22) remove set screw in throttle slide arm (17) and withdraw throttle slide shaft (3—Fig. H9-3). Extract throttle slide assembly, but be careful not to lose washer (18—Fig. H9-5). Remove the two screws (19) and separate components. Check the throttle slide and throttle butterfly synchronization. With the throttle butterfly and throttle slide completely closed, the throttle slide lever (3—Fig. H9-3) should just contact throttle link (2). To synchronize the throttles, open or close the slot in throttle link (2). Float height should be 18.5 mm (0.73 in.) between bottom of float and carburetor body. Hold carburetor so float is vertical and resting lightly on fuel inlet needle when checking float height as shown in Fig. H9-6. Float height is not adjustable. Renew float and fuel inlet needle if required.

FUEL FILTER SCREEN AND STRAINER. A fuel filter screen located within the fuel control valve and a fuel strainer mounted on the fuel control valve pickup tube located within the fuel tank are used. The filter screen should be removed and cleaned after the first week of operation and every 30 days of operation thereafter. The fuel strainer should be removed and cleaned if reduced or restricted fuel flow is evident after cleaning fuel filter screen.

To remove the filter screen, set fuel control valve in "OFF" position and remove seat. Unscrew filter cup from bottom of fuel control valve assembly and withdraw cup, "O" ring and screen. Clean and inspect screen for damage. When reinstalling filter screen, align marks on filter screen and control valve body. Renew filter cup "O" ring and tighten cup to 3-5 N·m (24-48 in.-lbs.). Turn fuel control valve to "ON" position and check for leaks.

To remove the fuel strainer, disconnect fuel line and completely drain fuel from tank. Remove seat and unscrew fuel valve retaining nut and withdraw fuel control valve with strainer. Separate strainer from valve and clean strainer in a nonflammable solvent. Reinstall strainer by reversing removal procedure. Tighten fuel control valve retaining nut to 20-25 N·m (15-18 ft.-lbs.). After filling fuel tank check for leaks.

THROTTLE LEVER FREE PLAY. The throttle lever should have 3-8 mm (⅛-5⁄16 in.) of free play (F—Fig. H9-8) as measured at throttle lever end. Throttle lever free play is adjusted by first sliding rubber boot (B) down throttle cable. Loosen knurled locknut and rotate cable adjuster until recommended free play is obtained, then tighten locknut.

IGNITION AND ELECTRICAL

SPARK PLUG. Standard recommended spark plug is NGK DR8ES-L or Nippon Denso X24ESR-U. Spark plug electrode gap should be 0.6-0.7 mm (0.024-0.028 in.). Spark plug should be removed, cleaned and electrode gap set after every 30 days of operation. Renew spark plug if damage or excessive electrode wear is evident.

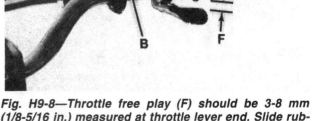

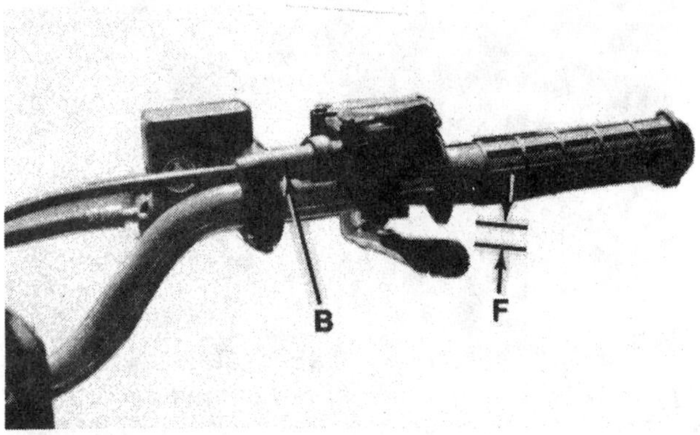

Fig. H9-8—Throttle free play (F) should be 3-8 mm (1/8-5/16 in.) measured at throttle lever end. Slide rubber boot (B) down cable to expose knurled locknut and cable adjuster.

IGNITION. The engine is equipped with a breaker-less, capacitor discharge ignition system. The electronic ignition circuit consists of the flywheel, exciter coil, CDI module, pulse generator, ignition coil, spark plug, engine stop switch and ignition switch. To check ignition timing, remove plug (I—Fig. H9-10) and attach a suitable timing light. Initial ignition (10° BTDC) should occur when "F" mark (F) on flywheel is aligned with notch (N) on case at 1300-1500 rpm on models prior to 1991, or at 1600-1800 rpm on models after 1990. Advanced ignition timing is 33° BTDC on models prior to 1991, or 23° BTDC on models after 1990. Advanced ignition should occur when "=" mark on flywheel is aligned with notch (N) on case at 2800-3200 rpm on all models. Ignition timing is not adjustable. If ignition timing is not as specified, check condition of CDI module and pulse generator as described in the following test procedures and renew faulty or questionable components.

If ignition malfunction occurs, check condition of spark plug, all wires and connections before troubleshooting the ignition circuit. Using Honda Digital Multi-Tester KS-AHM-32-003 or a suitable ohmmeter, refer to the following test specifications and procedures to aid troubleshooting.

To check condition of exciter coil, separate the black wire with red tracer from coil to CDI module at connector. Attach one tester lead to exciter coil wire and remaining tester lead to vehicle ground. Exciter coil can be considered satisfactory if resistance reading is within 100-300 ohms.

To check condition of pulse generator, separate blue wire with yellow tracer from pulse generator to CDI module at connector. Attach one tester lead to pulse

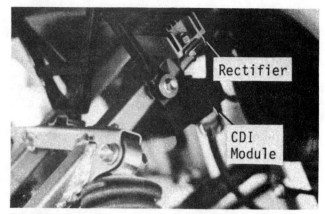

Fig. H9-11—CDI module and voltage rectifier are mounted on frame beneath front fender assembly.

generator wire and remaining tester lead to vehicle ground. Pulse generator can be considered satisfactory if resistance reading is within 290-360 ohms.

To check condition of ignition coil, remove black wire with yellow tracer and green wire from their respective terminals on coil. Disconnect high tension wire from spark plug. Attach one tester lead to black wire with yellow tracer terminal end on coil and remaining tester lead to green wire terminal end on coil. Primary coil resistance reading should be 0.1-0.2 ohms. Perform two secondary coil resistance tests, one with spark plug cap fitted to coil wire and one with cap removed. Attach one tester lead to spark plug cap and remaining lead to coil ground (green wire terminal). Secondary coil resistance through spark plug cap should be 8.8k-14k ohms. Remove spark plug cap from high tension wire. Attach one tester lead to high tension wire and remaining lead to coil ground. Secondary coil resistance reading with spark plug cap removed should be 5.8k-7.2k ohms. If secondary coil resistance is now within specification, then renew spark plug cap.

If no faulty component is found and ignition malfunction is still present, renew CDI module and recheck ignition operation. The CDI module is mounted on vehicle frame beneath front fender assembly as shown in Fig. H9-11.

NOTE: The lighting coil and exciter coil are contained within the magneto stator. If one coil tests defective, then the complete magneto stator assembly must be renewed.

LIGHTING CIRCUIT. The lighting coil is located in flywheel cover and should produce 12 volts-135 watts at 5000 rpm to provide current to the 12 volt-60/55 watt headlight and 12 volt-5 watt taillight.

The lighting coil can be checked statically using a suitable ohmmeter. Separate white wire with yellow tracer and green wire from lighting coil at connector. Lighting coil can be considered satisfactory if continuity is present between wires.

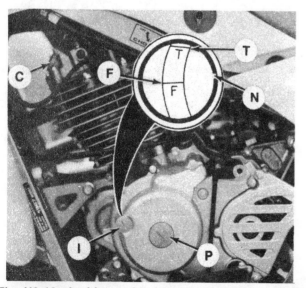

Fig. H9-10—Ignition at idle speed should occur when "F" mark (F) on flywheel aligns with notch (N). Remove plug (I) to view timing marks and plug (P) to expose flywheel retaining screw. Remove valve adjustment cap (C) at front and rear of cylinder head to expose intake and exhaust rocker arms.

NOTE: The lighting coil and exciter coil are contained within the magneto stator. If one coil tests defective, then the complete magneto stator assembly must be renewed.

FASTENERS

After the first week of operation and every 30 days of operation thereafter, the vehicle should receive an overall inspection. All cap screws, nuts and fasteners should be checked and tightened to proper torque specification shown in CONDENSED SERVICE DATA section or in the appropriate maintenance section.

VALVE SYSTEM

The valves are actuated via rocker arms by a single overhead camshaft. Two intake and two exhaust valves are used. A single rocker arm activates both intake valves and a single rocker arm activates both exhaust valves. Camshaft is driven by a roller chain attached to the right end of the crankshaft. Valve clearance should be adjusted after the first week of operation and then after 30 days of operation. Valve clearance should be adjusted with engine cold.

To adjust valve clearance, remove seat, fuel tank, rear fender, timing plug and valve adjustment cap (C—Fig. H9-10) at front and rear of cylinder head. Rotate crankshaft until "T" mark (T) (Top Dead Center) on flywheel aligns with notch (N) and piston is on compression stroke. Crankshaft can be rotated by removing center plug (P) and using a suitable tool to rotate flywheel retaining cap screw. To ensure piston is on compression stroke, rotate crankshaft approximately ¼ turn past TDC while observing intake valves. If valve movement is indicated, rotate crankshaft one complete revolution and align "T" mark (T) with notch (N) again.

Clearance between rocker arm adjusting screw and valve stem should be 0.10 mm (0.004 in.) for both the intake and exhaust valves. Measure clearance with a suitable feeler gauge and adjust by loosening adjusting screw locknut and turning adjusting screw. Be sure to recheck clearance after locknuts are tightened.

On models equipped with a decompression lever, check adjustment as outlined in following section.

DECOMPRESSION LEVER

Later models are equipped with a decompression lever that, when actuated, reduces starting effort. Actuating the lever holds the exhaust valve open slightly thereby reducing compression pressure.

To adjust the decompression lever, remove plug (I—Fig. H9-10). Rotate crankshaft so piston is on compression stroke and "T" mark (F) on flywheel is aligned with notch (N) on case. Free play at end of decompression lever (L—Fig. H9-12) should be 1-2 mm (0.04-0.08 in.).

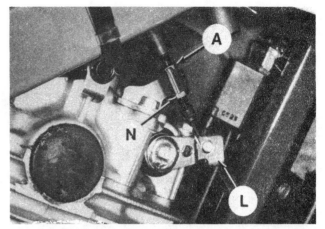

Fig. H9-12—Free play at end of decompression lever (L) should be 1-2 mm (0.04-0.08 in.). Loosen locknut (N) and rotate adjuster (A) to obtain desired free play.

Loosen locknut (N) and rotate adjuster (A) to obtain desired free play. Retighten locknut and check adjustment.

CLUTCH

A multiple-disc-type clutch manually actuated by left handlebar lever is used. The clutch lever should be adjusted after the first week of operation and then after every 30 days of operation.

The clutch lever should have 10-20 mm (⅜-¾ in.) of free play measured at clutch lever (L—Fig. H9-13) end as shown at (F). Clutch lever free play can be adjusted by sliding dust boot (D) down cables, then loosening knurled locknut on lower cable and rotating cable adjuster until recommended free play is obtained. If cable adjuster is near or has reached adjustment limit, loosen locknuts (N—Fig. H9-14) at lower adjuster bracket (B) and reposition cable in bracket to add or remove cable slack as needed. Complete adjustment at clutch lever cable adjuster and tighten knurled locknut.

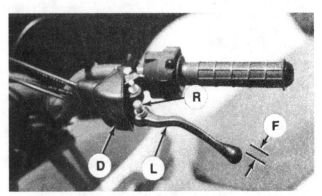

Fig. H9-13—Clutch lever (L) free play should be 10-20 mm (3/8-3/4 in.). To adjust free play, slide dust boot (D) down cables to expose knurled locknut and adjuster on lower cable. Button (R) is used to release reverse lock mechanism and engage parking brake. Refer to text.

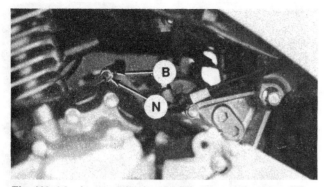

Fig. H9-14—Loosen locknuts (N) at lower bracket (B) to adjust clutch cable if handlebar adjuster is near or has reached adjustment limit. Refer to text.

Properly operated, the clutch should disengage and engage freely. Difficulty in shifting, clutch grabbing or slipping may indicate disassembly and repair of clutch unit is required.

REVERSE LOCK

The vehicle is equipped with a reverse lock mechanism designed to prevent accidental engagement of reverse gear. The reverse lock mechanism should have 2-4 mm (^{5}/$_{64}$-^{5}/$_{32}$ in.) of free travel measured between clutch lever (L—Fig. H9-13) and lever housing with reverse button (R) engaged. To adjust free travel, loosen locknut (L—Fig. H9-15) and turn adjuster nut (A). Tighten locknut (L) to secure adjustment after obtaining correct free travel.

FRONT BRAKE ASSEMBLY

A disc brake assembly is used on both front wheels. Front brake adjustment for disc pad wear is not required

Fig. H9-15—Adjust reverse lock free play by loosening locknut (L) and turning adjusting nut (A). Brake pedal (P) should be 10 mm (3/8 in.) below footpeg (G) in the released position when measured as shown. Adjust brake pedal height by loosening locknut (N) and rotating master cylinder actuator rod nut (T).

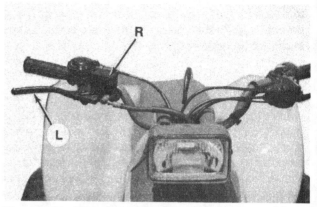

Fig. H9-17—View identifies front brake lever (L) and master cylinder reservoir (R).

due to the compensating action of the piston in the caliper.

Brake fluid must be rated DOT 3 or DOT 4 on models prior to 1992. DOT 4 rated brake fluid must be used on 1992 model. Maintain brake fluid level between marks on inner side of brake fluid reservoir. To avert spillage, be sure reservoir is horizontal before removing cover.

BLEEDING. Make sure reservoir (R—Fig. H9-17) is full. Connect a bleed hose to bleed valve (B—Fig. H9-18) on both front brake caliper assemblies. Route the bleed hoses into suitable containers. Operate brake lever (L—Fig. H9-17) until hard resistance is felt, then open bleed valve. Close bleed valve prior to releasing brake lever. Continue bleeding procedure on both wheels until no air bubbles are noted in discharged fluid from bleed valve.

NOTE: Make sure reservoir (R) remains full during bleeding procedure.

Fig. H9-18—Attach a hose to front wheel caliper bleed valve (B) and follow procedure in text to bleed front brakes.

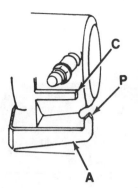

Fig. H9-19—Pointer (P) on wear indicator arm (A) of front brake caliper should not be in alignment with or below raised casting (C) on caliper or brake pad replacement is required.

When bleeding procedure is completed, add brake fluid to reservoir until fluid level is at upper level line in reservoir.

OVERHAUL. Brake pad thickness can be checked externally by viewing wear indicator arm (A—Fig. H9-19). If pointer (P) on wear indicator arm (A) aligns with or goes beyond raised casting (C) on caliper housing, then brake pads have reached wear limit and must be renewed.

WARNING: Inhaling asbestos brake dust is injurious to human health. Approved OSHA respiration equipment must be worn when working on or around brake calipers and pads. DO NOT use compressed air to clean brake calipers, pads or nearby components as brake dust will be blown into air. Only vacuum equipment designed to pick up brake dust should be used.

Brake components are accessible after removing wheel, caliper mounting screws and withdrawing caliper. Refer to Fig. H9-20 for an exploded view of caliper. Brake disc should be renewed if thickness is less than 3 mm (0.118 in.) or runout exceeds 0.3 mm (0.012 in.). Maximum allowable caliper bore diameter is 25.46 mm (1.002 in.). Minimum allowable piston diameter is 25.29 mm (0.996 in.). Tighten brake pad pins to 15-20 N·m (132-176 in.-lbs.). Push piston by hand back into caliper to allow clearance for new brake pads. Tighten brake caliper mounting screws to 24-30 N·m (18-22 ft.-lbs.). After reassembly, operate brake lever until brake lever will not pump up after continuous operation. Do not operate vehicle until brakes are tested and functioning properly.

MASTER CYLINDER. To remove front brake master cylinder (14—Fig. H9-21), detach brake line from master cylinder. Brake fluid will remove paint; be careful when removing master cylinder. Unscrew two retaining screws and remove master cylinder. Remove brake lever, reservoir cover (9) and diaphragm (11). Remove dust boot (1) and snap ring (2). Disassemble piston assembly while noting location and direction of components. Renew complete master cylinder if bore is scored, pitted or excessively worn. Maximum allowable bore diameter is 12.755 mm (0.5022 in.). Minimum allowable piston diameter is 12.645 mm (0.4978 in.). Superficial damage in master cylinder bore may be removed using a suitable cylinder hone. After honing, rinse bore with clean brake fluid. Shake out excess fluid but do not wipe dry. Using a shop towel or rag to dry cylinder will leave lint particles in bore. Renew boots and piston cups. During reassembly, lubricate components with clean brake fluid. Reassembly is reverse of disassembly. Install spring (5) so small end contacts piston (4). Bleed brakes as previously outlined. Do not operate vehicle until brakes are tested and functioning properly.

FRONT AXLE

The left and right front steering knuckle assemblies pivot on ball joint assemblies at the end of each upper and lower control arm. The control arms are bolted at the ends to the vehicle frame and a shock absorber is used to limit and cushion the up and down movement of the control arms. The shock absorbers are adjustable to alter absorber spring setting for different terrain and load conditions.

Remove the front wheel to service the ball joint assemblies. Note that removing the brake components will

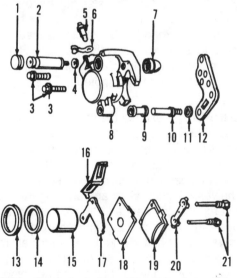

Fig. H9-20—Exploded view of front brake caliper.

1. Rubber plug	
2. Pin	
3. Screws	12. Mounting bracket
4. Spring washer	13. Piston seal
5. Bleed valve	14. Dust seal
6. Cap	15. Piston
7. Pin boot	16. Pad spring
8. Caliper body	17. Shim
9. Pin bushing	18. Outboard brake pad
10. Pin bolt	19. Inboard brake pad
11. Wave washer	20. Lockwasher
	21. Pad pin bolt

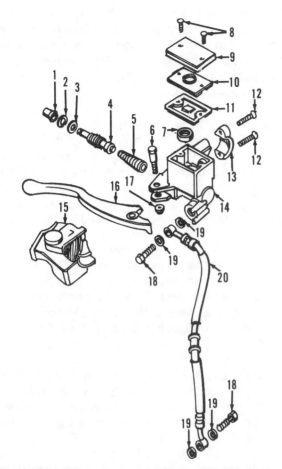

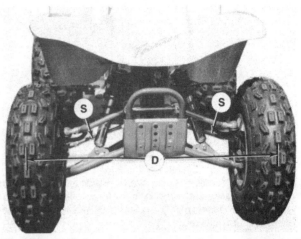

Fig. H9-22—Refer to text for procedure to check toe-in setting. Distance (D) is measured between centerline of wheel at axle height. Tie rod shafts (S) are rotated to adjust toe-in setting after loosening inside and outside tie rod end locknuts.

Fig. H9-21—Exploded view of front brake master cylinder.

1. Dust boot		11. Diaphragm
2. Snap ring		12. Screw
3. Washer		13. Clamp
4. Piston/primary cup		14. Body
5. Spring		15. Rubber boot
6. Bolt		16. Brake lever
7. Seal		17. Nut
8. Screw		18. Union bolt
9. Cover		19. Seal washer
10. Diaphragm plate		20. Brake hose

allow greater access to ball joint assemblies. If any ball joint or control arm is excessively worn or any other damage is noted, then ball joint or control arm must be renewed. Lower control arm and upper control arm retaining nuts should be tightened to 35-45 N•m (25-33 ft.-lbs.). Shock absorber retaining nuts should be tightened to 40-50 N•m (29-36 ft.-lbs). Upper ball joint to control arm retaining nut should be tightened to 60-80 N•m (43-58 ft.-lbs.). Tighten ball joint to steering knuckle retaining nuts to 50-60 N•m (36-43 ft.-lbs.).

STEERING

TOE-IN SETTING. Place the handlebar in a straight ahead position. Use a suitable measuring tool and measure distance (D—Fig. H9-22), at spindle height, between the center of the tires on the front and rear

sides. The measured distance (D) on the front side should be 0-20 mm (0.0-0.8 in.) shorter than the measured distance on the rear side. If not, loosen inside and outside locknuts on the left and right tie rod assemblies and rotate tie rod shaft (S) on each side equally until measured distance is within recommended range.

After obtaining the correct setting, securely tighten the locknuts to retain tie rod settings.

INSPECTION. Rotate the steering handlebar from one extreme to the other and note if any binding or roughness is felt. Periodically inspect the steering components for looseness or any other damage. Renew any damaged component. Clean and grease components if binding or excessive effort is noted.

OVERHAUL. To expose the steering shaft, the front fender assembly must be removed. Remove the four cap screws securing the upper clamp and withdraw the clamp halves. Withdraw steering shaft bushing and clean the old grease from the steering shaft. Inspect the clamp halves, steering shaft and bushing for damage. Renew components if needed. Grease inside of steering shaft bushing and install bushing and clamp halves. Make sure clamp half marked "IN" and half marked "OUT" are properly positioned. Markings are stamped on outside of clamp halves. Tighten the retaining clamp cap screws to 25-30 N•m (18-22 ft.-lbs.).

The tie rod assemblies, handlebar assembly and front skid plate must be removed to withdraw the steering shaft from the vehicle. Remove the lower bearing housing retaining cotter pin and nut to withdraw the steering shaft. Inspect the lower bearing assembly and seals and renew if needed. Bearing retaining snap ring must be removed prior to driving bearing out of housing. Tighten the lower bearing assembly retaining nut to 60-80 N•m

(43-58 ft.-lbs.). Tighten the tie rod assembly mounting nuts to 40-50 N·m (29-36 ft.-lbs.). Tighten handlebar clamp to steering shaft bracket nuts to 40-50 N·m (29-36 ft.-lbs.).

REAR BRAKE ASSEMBLY

A single disc brake assembly is used for both rear wheels. The running brake is operated hydraulically by a foot pedal on the lower right side. The parking brake is mechanically operated by a cable and handlebar components in conjunction with the clutch lever.

BRAKE PEDAL HEIGHT ADJUSTMENT. Brake pedal (P—Fig. H9-15) should be 10 mm (⅜ in.) below footpeg (G) in the released position when measured from the top of the footpeg to the top of the foot pad on the brake pedal as shown in Fig. H9-15. To adjust, loosen locknut (N) and rotate master cylinder actuator rod nut (T) until recommended pedal height is obtained, then tighten locknut (N) to retain adjustment.

PARKING BRAKE ADJUSTMENT. Make sure parking brake/clutch lever is in the released position. Loosen locknut (K—Fig. H9-23) and rotate adjuster screw (S) clockwise until resistance is felt, then rotate counterclockwise ⅛ turn and tighten locknut (K). Make sure screw (S) is not overtightened causing rear brake application. To adjust parking brake/clutch lever, apply button (R—Fig. H9-13) and actuate lever (L). Lever should travel 25-30 mm (1-1⅛ in.) as shown at (F). Slide dust boot (D) down cables, then loosen knurled locknut on upper cable and rotate cable adjuster to adjust travel distance.

BLEEDING. Make sure rear brake master cylinder reservoir is full. Connect a bleed hose to bleed valve (B—Fig. H9-23) on brake caliper assembly. Route the bleed hose into a suitable container. Operate foot pedal (P—Fig. H9-15) until firm resistance is felt, then open

bleed valve (B—Fig. H9-23). Close bleed valve prior to releasing foot pedal. Continue bleeding procedure until no air bubbles are noted in discharged fluid from bleed valve.

NOTE: Make sure rear brake master cylinder is kept full during bleeding procedure.

When bleeding procedure is completed, add brake fluid to rear brake master cylinder reservoir until fluid level is at "UPPER" level line on reservoir.

OVERHAUL. External determination of brake pad thickness is possible by viewing the brake pads. If brake pads are not worn down to service grooves, then brake pads do not require replacement because of excessive wear. If brake pad wear is down to service grooves or within service grooves, then both brake pads must be renewed.

WARNING: Inhaling asbestos brake dust is injurious to human health. Approved OSHA respiration equipment must be worn when working on or around brake calipers and pads. DO NOT use compressed air to clean brake calipers, pads or nearby components as brake dust will be blown into air. Only vacuum equipment designed to pick up brake dust should be used.

Brake components are accessible after removing caliper mounting screws and withdrawing caliper. Refer to Fig. H9-24 for an exploded view of brake caliper. Brake disc should be renewed if thickness is 3.0 mm (0.118 in.) or less or disc runout is 0.3 mm (0.012 in.) or more. Maximum allowable caliper bore diameter is 34.020 mm (1.3394 in.). Minimum allowable piston diameter is 33.870 mm (1.3335 in.). Push piston by hand back into caliper to allow clearance for new brake pads. Tighten brake pad pins to 15-20 N·m (132-176 in.-lbs.). Tighten brake caliper mounting screw to 24-30 N·m (18-22 ft.-lbs.). After reassembly, operate brake pedal (P—Fig. H9-15) until pedal will not pump up after continuous operation. Do not operate vehicle until brakes are tested and functioning properly.

MASTER CYLINDER. To remove rear brake master cylinder (5—Fig. H9-25), disconnect brake plunger from pedal. Detach brake lines from master cylinder and plug line to reservoir. Brake fluid will remove paint; be careful when removing master cylinder. Unscrew retaining screws and remove master cylinder. Remove dust boot (12) and snap ring (10). Disassemble piston assembly while noting location and direction of components. Renew complete master cylinder if bore is scored, pitted or excessively worn. Maximum allowable bore diameter is 12.755 mm (0.5022 in.). Minimum allowable piston diameter is 12.645 mm (0.4978 in.). Superficial damage in master cylinder bore may be removed using a suitable

Fig. H9-23—Adjust parking brake by loosening locknut (K) and turning adjuster screw (S).

Fig. H9-24—Exploded view of rear brake caliper.

9. Caliper mounting bracket
11. Boot
12. Caliper pin
13. Nut
14. Retainer clip
15. Bolt
16. Union bolt
17. Sealing washer
18. Flexible brake hose
19. Parking brake adjust screw
20. Locknut
21. Parking brake arm
22. Boot
23. Parking brake shaft
24. Parking brake base
25. Caliper mounting bolt
26. Caliper pivot collar
27. Collar
28. Caliper
29. Bleed valve
30. Bleed valve cap
31. Piston
32. Piston seal
33. Dust seal
34. Inboard brake pad
35. Outboard brake pad
36. Shim
37. Antirattle spring
38. Pad pin bolts
39. "O" ring
40. Piston

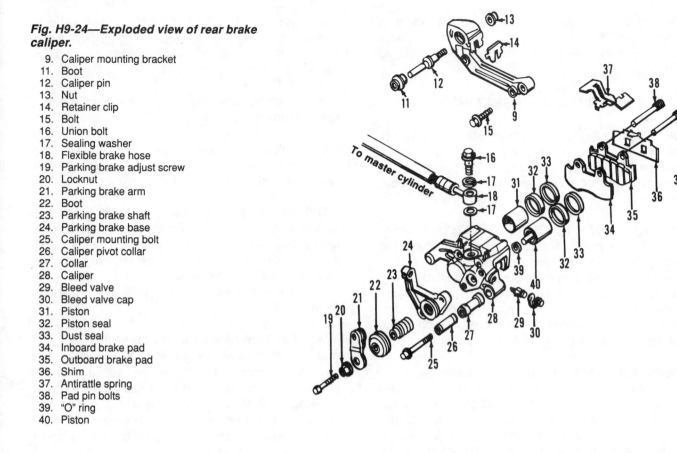

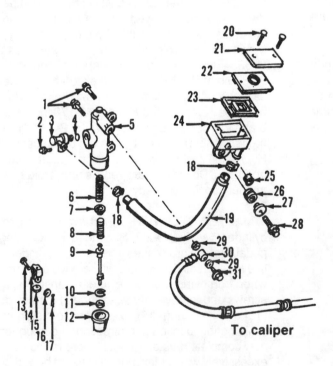

Fig. H9-25—Exploded view of rear brake master cylinder similar to type used on Model TRX250X.

1. Screw
2. Screw
3. Fitting
4. "O" ring
5. Master cylinder body
6. Spring
7. Primary cup
8. Piston
9. Push rod
10. Snap ring
11. Nut
12. Boot
13. Pin
14. Joint
15. Nut
16. Washer
17. Cotter pin
18. Hose clamp
19. Reservoir hose
20. Screw
21. Top cover
22. Diaphragm plate
23. Diaphragm
24. Reservoir
25. Collar
26. Rubber grommet
27. Collar
28. Bolt
29. Sealing washer
30. Flexible brake hose
31. Union bolt

cylinder hone. After honing, rinse bore with clean brake fluid. Shake out excess fluid but do not wipe dry. Using a shop towel or rag to dry cylinder will leave lint particles in bore. Renew boots and piston cups. During reassembly, lubricate components with clean brake fluid. Reassembly is reverse of disassembly. Install spring (6) so small end contacts primary cup (7). Bleed brakes as previously outlined. Do not operate vehicle until brakes are tested and functioning properly.

DRIVE CHAIN AND SPROCKETS

INSPECTION AND ADJUSTMENT. The drive chain should be inspected and adjusted after the first week of operation and every 30 days of operation thereafter. Improper maintenance and neglect can cause early failure of both drive chain and sprockets. Drive chain free play should be 35-45 mm (1⅜-1¾ in.) measured midway between sprockets.

Adjust chain tension by loosening screws (S—Fig. H9-26) and inserting a suitable tool into slot (T) to rotate axle housing toward front of vehicle to increase chain slack or toward rear of vehicle to decrease chain slack. Tighten screws (S) to 19-25 N·m (14-18 ft.-lbs.) to secure chain tension adjustment.

Inspect chain roller and pad near front end of swing arm. Remove ridges worn into roller or pad. Renew roller or pad if groove depth is more than 6 mm (¼ in.) below surface.

R&R AND OVERHAUL. Loosen two screws (S—Fig. H9-26) and insert a suitable tool into slot (T) and rotate axle housing toward front of vehicle to increase drive chain slack. Lift chain off rear sprocket toward left rear wheel. Use a location at rear of vehicle frame and lift rear wheels off the ground. Remove left rear wheel and shock absorber from lower mount. Remove clamps retaining brake hose and brake cable to swing arm. Remove nut securing swing arm pivot shaft. Support

Fig. H9-26—Loosen screws (S) and insert a suitable tool into slot (T) to adjust drive chain tension.

swing arm assembly and withdraw swing arm pivot shaft. Withdraw swing arm assembly far enough to provide clearance for drive chain removal. Remove front (engine) sprocket guard and withdraw drive chain. Remove front sprocket if needed.

Carefully examine sprockets for excessive wear. Worn sprockets will usually have a hooked tooth profile. A good test is to place a new chain on a used sprocket and check the fit. If sprockets require renewal due to wear, always renew drive chain. Sprockets should be renewed as a set. Renew drive chain if distance between 21 link pins exceeds 319.1 mm (12.6 in.) with chain straight and all slack removed.

Reassembly is reverse order of disassembly. Tighten rear sprocket nuts to 55-65 N·m (40-47 ft.-lbs.). Tighten lower shock absorber nut to 100-120 N·m (72-87 ft.-lbs.). Tighten swing arm pivot shaft nut to 70-110 N·m (51-80 ft.-lbs.). Tighten wheel retaining nuts to 65 N·m (48 ft.-lbs.). Refer to previous INSPECTION AND ADJUSTMENT paragraphs for recommended drive chain adjustment procedures.

HONDA

TRX300 AND TRX300FW

NOTE: Metric fasteners are used throughout vehicle.

CONDENSED SERVICE DATA

MODELS	TRX300, TRX300FW
General	
Engine Make	Honda
Engine Type	Four-Stroke/Air-Cooled
Number of Cylinders	1
Bore	74.0 mm
	(2.913 in.)
Stroke	65.5 mm
	(2.579 in.)
Displacement	281.7 cc
	(17.2 cu. in.)
Compression Ratio	9.0:1
Engine Lubrication	Wet Sump/Oil Pump
Transmission Lubrication	Common With Engine
Engine/Transmission Oil	SAE 10W-40
Forward Speeds	5
Reverse Speeds	1
Front Drive—FW Models	Shaft & Gears
Rear Drive	Shaft & Gears
Tire Size:	
Front	23 × 8-11
Rear—FW Models	24 × 9-11
Except FW Models	25 × 12-9
Tire Pressure:	
Front—FW Models	30 kPa
	(4.4 psi)
Except FW Models	20 kPa
	(2.9 psi)
Rear	20 kPa
	(2.9 psi)
Battery	12V-12AH
Dry Weight:	
FW Models	215 kg
	(473 lbs.)
Except FW Models	199 kg
	(438 lbs.)
Tune-Up	
Engine Idle Speed	1400-1600 rpm
Compression Pressure	1250-1450 kPa
	(181-210 psi)
Spark Plug:	
NGK	DPR8EA-9
Nippon Denso	X24EPR-U9
Electrode Gap	0.8-0.9 mm
	(0.031-0.035 in.)

Tune-Up (Cont.)
Ignition:

Type..........................	Breakerless
Timing	13° BTDC

Carburetor:

Make	Keihin
Model.........................	VE90A
Float Height	18.5 mm
	(0.73 in.)
Main Jet.......................	#120
Idle Jet.......................	#42
Clip Position...................	3rd Groove From Top
Idle Mixture Setting	1¾ Turns
Throttle Lever Free Play	3-8 mm
	(0.12-0.31 in.)

Sizes-Clearances
Valve Clearance (cold):

Intake & Exhaust	0.15 mm
	(0.006 in.)

Valve Face & Seat Angle:

Intake & Exhaust	45°

Valve Seat Width:

Intake & Exhaust	1.2 mm
	(0.05 in.)
Wear Limit	1.5 mm
	(0.06 in.)

Valve Stem Diameter:

Intake........................	5.475-5.490 mm
	(0.2156-0.2161 in.)
Wear Limit	5.45 mm
	(0.215 in.)
Exhaust	5.455-5.470 mm
	(0.2148-0.2154 in.)
Wear Limit	5.43 mm
	(0.214 in.)

Valve Guide Bore Diameter:

Intake & Exhaust	5.500-5.512 mm
	(0.2165-0.2170 in.)
Wear Limit	5.525 mm
	(0.2175 in.)

Valve Stem-to-Guide Clearance:

Intake........................	0.010-0.037 mm
	(0.0004-0.0015 in.)
Wear Limit	0.12 mm
	(0.005 in.)
Exhaust	0.030-0.057 mm
	(0.0012-0.0022 in.)
Wear Limit	0.14 mm
	(0.006 in.)

Valve Spring Free Length:

Inner.........................	38.31 mm
	(1.508 in.)
Minimum Length	35.3 mm
	(1.39 in.)
Outer	46.83 mm
	(1.84 in.)
Minimum Length	43.8 mm
	(1.72 in.)

Sizes-Clearances (Cont.)

Valve Spring Pressure:

Inner........................... 7.92-9.52 kg @ 31.6 mm
(17.4-20.9 lbs. @ 1.24 in.)

Outer .... 18.09-21.09 kg @ 35.1 mm
(39.8-46.4 lbs. @ 1.38 in.)

Rocker Arm Bore Diameter:

Intake & Exhaust .... 12.000-12.018 mm
(0.4724-0.4731 in.)

Wear Limit .... 12.05 mm
(0.474 in.)

Rocker Shaft Diameter:

Intake & Exhaust .... 11.966-11.984 mm
(0.4711-0.4718 in.)

Wear Limit .... 11.92 mm
(0.469 in.)

Camshaft Lobe Height:

Intake.......................... 36.133-36.143 mm
(1.4223-1.4229 in.)

Wear Limit .... 35.963 mm
(1.4159 in.)

Exhaust .... 36.003-36.013 mm
(1.4174-1.4178 in.)

Wear Limit .... 35.833 mm
(1.4107 in.)

Cylinder Head
Distortion (Max.)................. 0.10 mm
(0.004 in.)

Cylinder Bore Diameter .... 74.00-74.01 mm
(2.9134-2.9137 in.)

Wear Limit .... 74.10 mm
(2.917 in.)

Piston-to-Cylinder Clearance........... 0.015-0.050 mm
(0.0006-0.0020 in.)

Wear Limit .... 0.10 mm
(0.004 in.)

Piston Diameter—
Measured 10 mm (0.4 in.) From
Skirt Bottom & 90° to Pin Bore .... 73.960-73.985 mm
(2.9118-2.9128 in.)

Wear Limit .... 73.90 mm
(2.9094 in.)

Piston Pin Bore .... 17.002-17.008 mm
(0.6694-0.6696 in.)

Wear Limit .... 17.04 mm
(0.671 in.)

Piston Pin Diameter................. 16.994-17.000 mm
(0.6691-0.6693 in.)

Wear Limit .... 16.96 mm
(0.668 in.)

Piston-to-Pin Clearance.............. 0.002-0.014 mm
(0.0001-0.0006 in.)

Wear Limit .... 0.02 mm
(0.001 in.)

Piston Ring End Gap:

Top Ring........................ 0.15-0.30 mm
(0.006-0.012 in.)

Sizes-Clearances (Cont.)
Piston Ring End Gap: (Cont.)

Wear Limit	0.5 mm (0.020 in.)
Second Ring	0.25-0.40 mm (0.010-0.016 in.)
Wear Limit	0.6 mm (0.024 in.)
Oil Ring	0.2-0.7 mm (0.008-0.028 in.)

Piston Ring Side Clearance:

Top Ring.	0.02-0.05 mm (0.001-0.002 in.)
Wear Limit	0.09 mm (0.004 in.)
Second Ring	0.015-0.045 mm (0.0006-0.0018 in.)
Wear Limit	0.09 mm (0.004 in.)
Connecting Rod Small End Bore Diameter	17.016-17.034 mm (0.6699-0.6706 in.)
Wear Limit	17.10 mm (0.6732 in.)
Connecting Rod Big End Side Clearance (Max.)	0.80 mm (0.031 in.)
Connecting Rod Big End Radial Clearance (Max.)	0.006-0.018 mm (0.0002-0.0007 in.)
Crankshaft Runout (Max.)	0.05 mm (0.002 in.)

Capacities

Fuel Tank	12.5 L (3.3 gal.)
Engine/Transmission Sump.	See Text

Tightening Torques

Camshaft Sprocket	20 N•m (15 ft.-lbs.)
Clutch Nut: Centrifugal Clutch (L.H. Threads)	120 N•m (88 ft.-lbs.)
Shift Clutch	110 N•m (81 ft.-lbs.)
Crankcase	10 N•m (88 in.-lbs.)
Crankcase Cover.	10 N•m (88 in.-lbs.)
Cylinder Base Screw	10 N•m (88 in.-lbs.)
Cylinder Head: Nut.	40 N•m (29 ft.-lbs.)
Screw.	25 N•m (18 ft.-lbs.)
Flywheel Cap Screw	110 N•m (81 ft.-lbs.)

Tightening Torques (Cont.)

Output Gear Housing to Crankcase Screw	32 N·m (24 ft.-lbs.)
Spark Plug	18 N·m (159 in.-lbs.)
Wheel Retaining Nut	65 N·m (48 ft.-lbs.)
Standard Screws:	
5 mm	3.5-5.0 N·m (31-44 in.-lbs.)
6 mm	7-11 N·m (62-97 in.-lbs.)
Standard Bolts & Nuts:	
5 mm	4.5-6.0 N·m (40-53 in.-lbs.)
6 mm	8-12 N·m (71-106 in.-lbs.)
8 mm	18-25 N·m (13-18 ft.-lbs.)
10 mm	30-40 N·m (22-29 ft.-lbs.)
12 mm	50-60 N·m (36-43 ft.-lbs.)
Flanged Bolts & Nuts:	
6 mm	10-14 N·m (89-124 in.-lbs.)
8 mm	24-30 N·m (17-22 ft.-lbs.)
10 mm	35-45 N·m (25-32 ft.-lbs.)

LUBRICATION

All Models

ENGINE AND TRANSMISSION. The engine and transmission are lubricated by a gear-driven, trochoid-type pump located on the right side of the crankcase and driven by the crankshaft. The engine and transmission share a common sump. Recommended oil is SAE 10W-40 with an API classification of SF or SG.

Oil level should be maintained at upper mark on dipstick attached to fill plug (F—Fig. H11-1). Do not screw plug in when checking oil level. Fill sump through opening for fill plug (F). Drain oil by removing drain plug on underside of crankcase. Fill crankcase with 2.2 L (2.3 qt.) of oil if only oil is changed. Fill crankcase with 2.25 L (2.4 qt.) of oil if oil and oil filter are changed. Crankcase capacity totally dry is 2.5 L (2.6 qt.).

The manufacturer recommends changing the oil and oil filter after the first week of operation and then after every 30 days of operation. A sump filter screen, located in a compartment in the right crankcase half, should be removed periodically and cleaned.

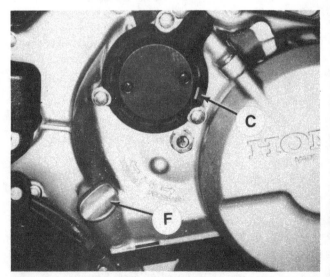

Fig. H11-1—The oil dipstick is attached to fill plug (F). Remove cover (C) for access to oil filter.

Fig. H11-2—Pour oil into rear drive housing through opening for fill plug (F). The drain screw is located on underside of housing. Front drive housing on Model TRX300FW is similar.

Remove oil filter cover (C) for access to oil filter. Before installing filter, be sure spring is against engine (crankcase cover) and "O" rings are in place. Install filter so rubber seal side and "OUTSIDE" are toward filter cover.

REAR DRIVE HOUSING. The oil in the rear drive housing should be changed every two years. Remove oil by unscrewing drain screw on underside of rear drive housing. Fill housing with oil through opening for fill plug (F—Fig. H11-2). Recommended oil is SAE 80 hypoid gear oil. Fill housing with 90 cc (3.0 oz.) of oil if oil is being changed. Housing capacity totally dry is 100 cc (3.4 oz.).

FRONT DRIVE HOUSING. Model TRX300FW. The oil in the front drive housing should be changed every two years. Remove oil by unscrewing drain screw on

Fig. H11-4—Pour oil into front gearcase on Model TRX300FW through opening for fill plug (F).

underside of housing. Fill housing with oil through opening for fill plug (F—Fig. H11-2). Recommended oil is SAE 80 hypoid gear oil. Fill housing with 180 cc (6.1 oz.) of oil if oil is being changed. Housing capacity totally dry is 200 cc (6.8 oz.).

FRONT GEARCASE. Model TRX300FW. A reduction gearcase is attached to the front of the engine on Model TRX300FW. The oil in the gearcase should be checked periodically and changed every two years. To check oil level remove check plug (G—Fig. H11-3). Oil should just flow from bottom of hole. Add oil as needed through opening for fill plug (F—Fig. H11-4). Recommended oil is SAE 10W-40 engine oil with an API classification of SF or SG. Remove oil by unscrewing drain screw (D—Fig. H11-3). Fill housing with 190 cc (6.4 oz.) of oil if oil is being changed. Housing capacity totally dry is 200 cc (6.8 oz.). Check oil level and add oil if necessary.

CABLES AND LEVERS. All cables and levers should be inspected and lubricated after the first week of operation and after every 30 days of operation thereafter.

AIR CLEANER ELEMENT

All Models

The air cleaner element should be removed and cleaned after every 30 days of operation. To remove the air cleaner element, remove the seat, release four cover clips (C—Fig. H11-5) and remove cover. Loosen air cleaner frame to inlet tube clamp, then withdraw element and frame from case. Remove nut and rear frame bracket, then carefully separate foam element from frame.

Thoroughly clean the foam element in a nonflammable solvent. Compress element between hands to remove solvent. Saturate element in clean SAE 10W-40

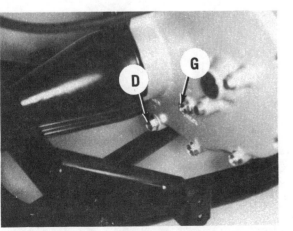

Fig. H11-3—On Model TRX300FW, oil in front gearcase should just flow from hole for check plug (G). Unscrew drain plug (D) to drain oil from gearcase.

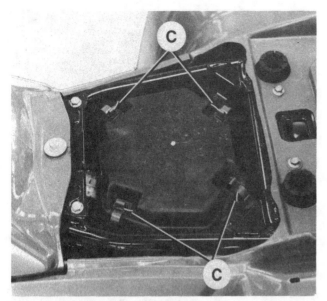

Fig. H11-5—Detach air cleaner cover clips (C) for access to air filter.

engine oil. Compress element to remove excess oil. Install element and reassemble air cleaner components.

FUEL SYSTEM

All Models

CARBURETOR. The engine is equipped with a Keihin constant-velocity-type carburetor (Fig. H11-6). Using a bellows attached to venturi piston (8) and an air chamber, the venturi piston is positioned according to vacuum present in the carburetor bore.

Recommended engine idle speed is 1400-1600 rpm. Adjust idle speed by turning idle speed knob (K—Fig. H11-7). Initial setting of idle mixture screw (I) is 1¾ turns out from a lightly seated position. To adjust idle mixture screw, engine must be running at idle speed at normal operating temperature. Slowly turn idle mixture screw in until engine speed starts to decrease and note position of screw. Slowly turn screw out until engine speed starts to decrease again and note screw position. Set idle

Fig. H11-6—Exploded view of Keihin VE90A carburetor.

1. Cover
2. Spring
3. Holder
4. Spring
5. Clip
6. Washer
7. Jet needle
8. Vacuum piston
9. Body
10. Spring
11. Choke valve
12. "O" ring
13. Cover
14. Screw
15. Idle speed knob
16. Washer
17. Spring
18. Starter jet
19. "O" ring
20. Washer
21. Spring
22. Idle mixture screw
23. Plug
24. Slow jet
25. Needle jet
26. Nozzle
27. Main jet
28. Baffle
29. Fuel inlet valve
30. Float
31. Pin
32. Gasket
33. Fuel bowl
34. "O" ring
35. Drain screw
36. Spring
37. Primer
38. Flange
39. Clips
40. Boot
41. Knob
42. Retainer

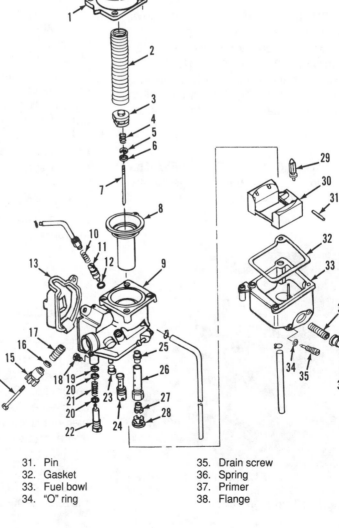

mixture screw halfway between positions that caused a decrease in engine speed. Readjust idle speed.

Refer to Fig. H11-6 when servicing carburetor and note the following: Retainer (3) must be rotated ¼ turn counterclockwise to release it from piston (8). Spring (2) must not be damaged or carburetor operation will be affected. Piston (8) must slide freely in carburetor and rubber bellows must be undamaged. Install jet needle clip (5) in middle groove on jet needle (7). Float height should be 18.5 mm (0.73 in.) between bottom of float and carburetor body. Hold carburetor so float is vertical and resting lightly against fuel inlet valve. See Fig. H11-8. Float height is not adjustable. Renew float and/or fuel inlet valve if float height is incorrect. Install piston (8—Fig. H11-6) so tab on edge of diaphragm is positioned in slot on top of carburetor body. Install cover (1) so tab is toward engine end of carburetor.

Recommended main jet size for operation above 3000 feet is #115.

FUEL FILTER SCREEN AND STRAINER. A fuel filter screen is located in the fuel control valve and a strainer that extends into the fuel tank is attached to the inlet of the fuel control valve. The filter screen should be cleaned after every 30 days of operation. Periodic cleaning of the fuel strainer should not be required.

To remove the filter screen, be sure fuel control valve is in "OFF" position and unscrew cup (C—Fig. H11-9) on bottom of valve. Remove and clean screen. Reassemble while making sure "O" ring is properly positioned. Tighten cup (do not overtighten), turn valve lever to "ON" and check for leaks.

To remove fuel strainer, disconnect fuel line and drain fuel from fuel tank. Unscrew nut (N—Fig. H11-9) to remove fuel control valve from fuel tank. Inspect and clean strainer attached to control valve. Reinstall components and tighten control valve nut to 28 N·m (21 ft.-lbs.). Turn control valve lever to "ON" and check for leaks.

THROTTLE LEVER FREE PLAY. Free play (F—Fig. H11-10) at the end of the throttle lever should be 3-8 mm (⅛-⁵⁄₁₆ in.). To adjust free play, slide back rubber boot (B), loosen the knurled nut and rotate cable adjuster. Retighten knurled nut.

IGNITION SYSTEM

All Models

SPARK PLUG. The recommended spark plug for normal operating conditions is a NGK DPR8EA-9 or Nippon Denso X24EPR-U9. Spark plug electrode gap should be 0.8-0.9 mm (0.031-0.035 in.). The spark plug should be removed, inspected, cleaned or renewed, and regapped after every 30 days of operation.

Fig. H11-7—Adjust idle mixture screw (I) and idle speed knob (K) as outlined in text.

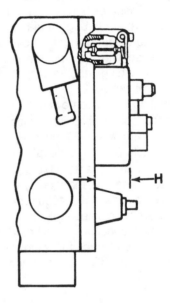

Fig. H11-8—Position carburetor so float rests lightly against fuel inlet valve and measure float height (H).

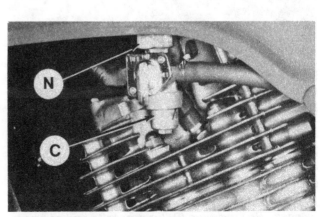

Fig. H11-9—The fuel filter screen is located in cup (C). Turn nut (N) on valve to unscrew valve from fuel tank.

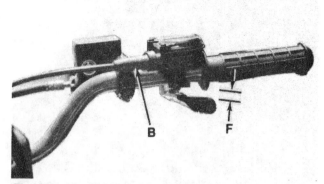

Fig. H11-10—Throttle free play (F) should be 3-8 mm (1/8-5/16 in.) measured at throttle lever end. Slide rubber boot (B) down cable to expose knurled locknut and cable adjuster.

IGNITION. The engine is equipped with a breakerless, capacitor discharge ignition system. Current is provided by the battery through a lead incorporating a 15 amp fuse. The electronic ignition circuit consists of the alternator sensor wire, CDI module, pulse generator, ignition coil, spark plug, engine stop switch, ignition switch and neutral switch.

To check ignition timing, remove plug (I—Fig. H11-11) and attach a suitable timing light. Initial ignition (13° BTDC) should occur when "F" mark (F) on flywheel is aligned with notch (N) on case at 1400-1600 rpm. Advanced ignition timing is 31° BTDC. Advanced ignition should occur when "=" mark on flywheel is aligned with notch (N) on case at 4400-4600 rpm on all models. Ignition timing is not adjustable. If ignition timing is not as specified, check condition of CDI module and pulse generator as described in the following test procedures and renew faulty or questionable components.

Fig. H11-11—Remove plug (I) to view timing marks on flywheel. Remove plug (P) for access to end of crankshaft.

If ignition malfunction occurs, check condition of spark plug, all wires and connections before troubleshooting the ignition circuit. Using Honda Digital Multi-Tester KS-AHM-32-003 or a suitable ohmmeter, refer to the following test procedures and specifications to aid troubleshooting.

To check condition of alternator sensor wire, disconnect connector at CDI module. Attach one ohmmeter lead to yellow/white sensor wire at connector and remaining ohmmeter lead to vehicle ground. Ohmmeter should read infinity (no continuity). Disconnect alternator connector at regulator/rectifier. Connect ohmmeter leads to yellow/white wire terminal of CDI connector and yellow wire terminal of alternator connector. Ohmmeter should show continuity. If meter readings are unsatisfactory, wiring or alternator is faulty.

To check condition of the pulse generator, disconnect the three-wire connector in loom running along middle frame upright. Connect an ohmmeter lead to blue/yellow wire going to engine and remaining ohmmeter lead to vehicle ground. Pulse generator is satisfactory if ohmmeter reading is 290-360 ohms. If reading is incorrect, remove left crankcase cover and repeat test at terminal of pulse generator.

To check condition of ignition coil, detach black/yellow wire and green wire from ignition coil. Disconnect high tension lead from spark plug. To check primary winding resistance, attach one ohmmeter lead to black/yellow wire terminal on ignition coil and remaining ohmmeter lead to green wire terminal. Ohmmeter should read 0.1-0.2 ohms. Perform two secondary winding tests, one with the spark plug cap attached to coil wire and one without spark plug cap attached. Attach one ohmmeter lead to spark plug cap and remaining ohmmeter lead to coil ground (green wire terminal). Secondary winding resistance through spark plug cap should be 8.1k-10k ohms. Remove spark plug cap from high tension wire. Attach an ohmmeter lead to high tension wire and remaining ohmmeter lead to coil ground. Secondary winding resistance reading with spark plug cap removed should be 3.6k-4.5k ohms. If secondary winding resistance is now within specification, renew spark plug cap.

The neutral switch is located in the right crankcase cover near the right footpeg and marked "N". Note that wire lead to switch is marked "N". To check neutral switch, remove the seat and disconnect the three-wire connector. Connect an ohmmeter lead to the terminal of the light green wire and connect the remaining ohmmeter lead to vehicle ground. With transmission in neutral the ohmmeter should show continuity. When transmission is in gear the ohmmeter should read infinity. Crankcase oil must be drained before removing neutral switch. Tightening torque for neutral switch is 13 N•m (115 in.-lbs.).

If no faulty component is found and ignition malfunction persists, renew CDI module and recheck ignition operation. The CDI module is attached to the vehicle frame under the front fender assembly.

ELECTRICAL SYSTEM

All Models

The vehicle is equipped with a charging system, battery and electric starter. The system is protected by a 15 amp fuse in the battery lead (Fig. H11-12, Fig. H11-12A and Fig. H11-12B).

BATTERY. Remove the seat for access to battery. The negative terminal is grounded. The battery is a sealed, maintenance-free, 12-volt unit with 12 amp-hour capacity.

CHARGING SYSTEM. The charging circuit consists of an alternator and a regulator/rectifier. The alternator rotor is attached to the left end of the crankshaft while the stator is mounted on the inside of the left crankcase cover. The regulator/rectifier module is mounted on the left rear of the vehicle frame.

The charging circuit should produce 13.5-15.5 VDC at 5000 rpm.

NOTE: Do not disconnect battery terminal wires while the engine is running as excessive alternator output will damage the regulator/rectifier.

To check the alternator stator coils, disconnect alternator connector (white with three yellow wires near middle frame upright). On connector leading to alternator, alternately check resistance between each terminal and the remaining two terminals. Resistance between any pair should be 0.09-0.11 ohms. Resistance between any terminal and vehicle ground must be infinity.

If previous tests prove satisfactory and fuse, wiring and connections are all good, replace regulator/rectifier with a good unit and recheck operation.

ELECTRIC STARTER. The starting circuit consists of the starter, starter relay, starter switch, diode, neutral switch and ignition switch. A 15 amp fuse protects the circuit.

The starter relay is located adjacent to the battery. To check relay, disconnect relay pigtail lead and wires from terminals on relay. Connect ohmmeter leads to terminals on top of relay. Ohmmeter should read infinity. Connect a 12-volt battery to each terminal of pigtail lead. Ohmmeter should show continuity, if not, renew relay.

The diode is located in wiring box attached to the frame under the front fender. Unplug diode and check for continuity between the diode terminals using an ohmmeter. After connecting the ohmmeter leads to the diode terminals, observe ohmmeter reading, then reverse ohmmeter leads and observe the second reading.

There should be continuity during one test and no continuity (infinity) during the other test. If not, renew diode.

To check the neutral switch, refer to procedure in IGNITION section.

To service starter motor, disconnect battery negative lead and starter motor lead. Remove cover (C—Fig. H11-11), slide gear off starter shaft, unscrew two screws securing starter motor and remove motor. Before disassembling motor, note alignment marks, or make alignment marks, on center housing and end caps so they can be reassembled in original positions. When disassembling motor, note location of all shims and washers. Minimum brush length is 9.0 mm (0.35 in.). Note tab on brush holder plate that must align with slot in rear end cap during assembly. Be sure "O" rings are correctly positioned during assembly.

OIL WARNING SYSTEM. The oil warning system provides a warning that indicates the engine may be damaged due to high oil temperature. The system obtains voltage through the ignition switch and consists of the alarm module, oil warning light and oil temperature sensor. During normal operation, the oil warning light should light for a few seconds when the ignition switch is turned on.

The oil temperature sensor is located on the right crankcase cover near the right footpeg. To check oil temperature sensor, remove the seat and disconnect the three-wire connector. Connect an ohmmeter lead to the terminal of the blue wire and connect the remaining ohmmeter lead to vehicle ground. When engine temperature is 25° C (77° F), ohmmeter should read approximately 10k ohms. Resistance should be less if engine is warm. If resistance reading is abnormal, remove oil temperature sensor (crankcase oil must be drained). Suspend sensor in heated oil so sensor does not touch sides of container and measure resistance at sensor leads. Resistance readings should be 9.5k-10k ohms at 25° C (77° F); 950-1050 ohms at 100° C (212° F); 209-231 ohms at 170° C (338° F). Tighten oil temperature sensor to 18 N•m (160 in.-lbs.).

The alarm module is attached to the front of the vehicle frame under the front fender. The alarm module cannot be tested, but must be replaced with a good module if suspected. Perform the following tests at connector before replacing module. With ignition switch in "ON" position, battery voltage should be present at brown/red wire terminal (oil warning light) and blue wire terminal (ignition switch). With ignition switch in "OFF" position, check oil temperature sensor line by connecting an ohmmeter lead to the terminal of the blue/red wire and the remaining ohmmeter lead to vehicle ground. When engine is cold, ohmmeter should read approximately 10k ohms. Resistance should be less if engine is warm. If tests are satisfactory, replace alarm unit.

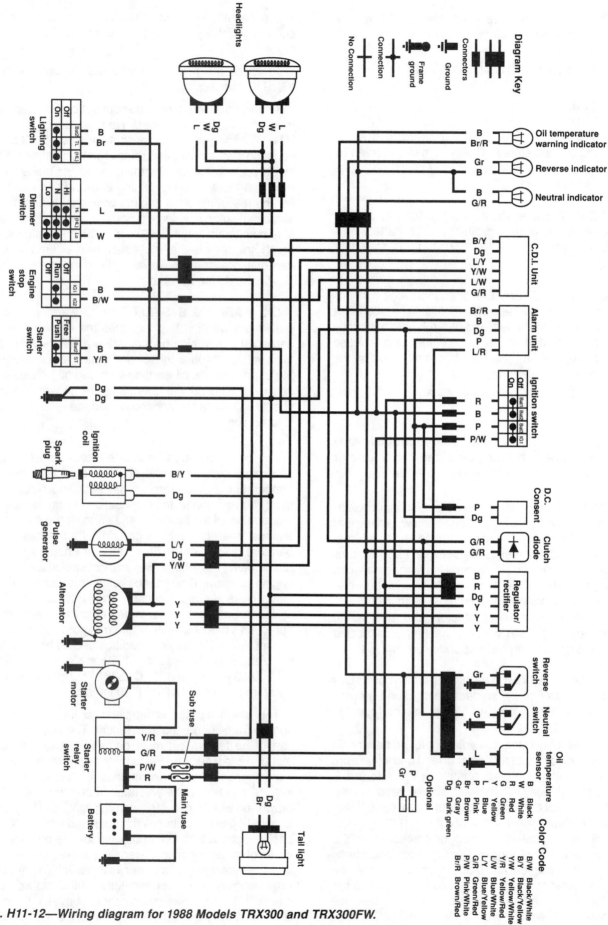

Fig. H11-12—Wiring diagram for 1988 Models TRX300 and TRX300FW.

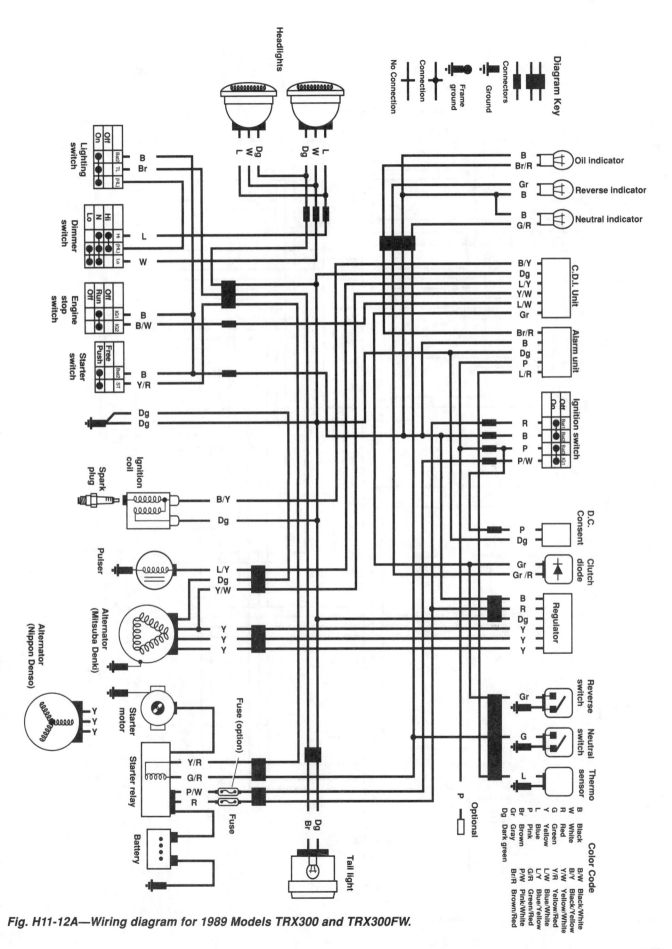

Fig. H11-12A—Wiring diagram for 1989 Models TRX300 and TRX300FW.

HONDA TRX300 AND TRX300FW

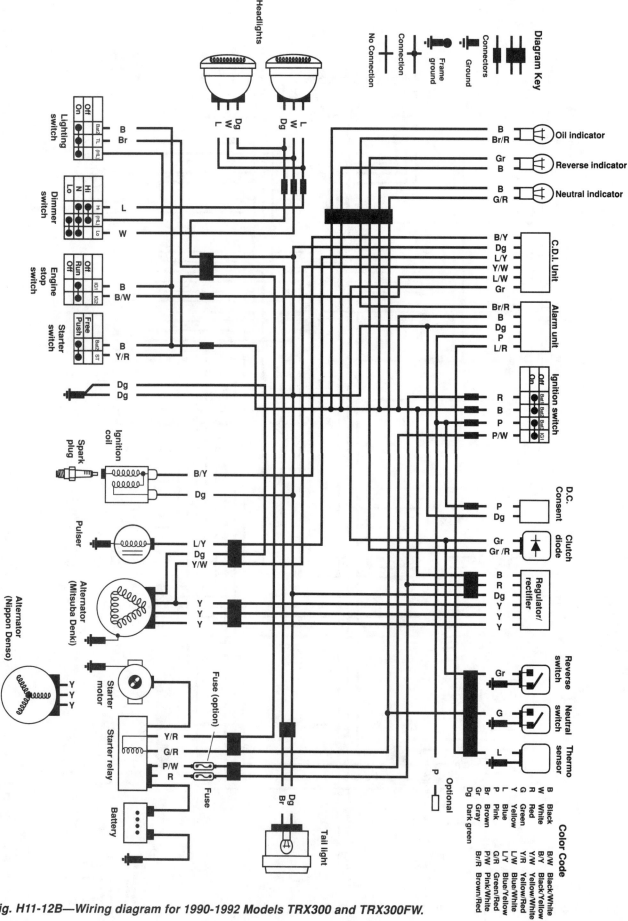

Fig. H11-12B—Wiring diagram for 1990-1992 Models TRX300 and TRX300FW.

REVERSE SWITCH. A reverse switch triggers a light to indicate when reverse gear is engaged. The reverse switch is located in the right crankcase cover near the right footpeg and marked "R". Note that wire lead to switch is marked "R". To check reverse switch, remove the seat and disconnect the three-wire connector. Connect an ohmmeter lead to the terminal of the green wire and connect the remaining ohmmeter lead to vehicle ground. With transmission in reverse, the ohmmeter should show continuity. When any other transmission gear is selected, the ohmmeter should read infinity. Crankcase oil must be drained before removing reverse switch. Tightening torque for reverse switch is 13 N·m (115 in.-lbs.).

LIGHTS. Headlight rating is 12V 25/25W. A dimmer switch is located in the switch module on the handlebar. Taillight rating is 12V 5W. Rating for neutral, reverse and oil temperature lights is 12V 3.4W.

WIRING. If wiring requires repair, always install wire that is the same gauge as original wire. Wires should be routed away from areas of extreme heat or sharp edges. Attach or hold wires in their original position using plastic tie straps to prevent short circuits.

FASTENERS

All Models

After the first week of operation and after every 30 days of operation thereafter, the vehicle should receive an overall inspection. All screws, nuts and other fasteners should be checked and tightened to proper torque specification shown in CONDENSED SERVICE DATA section or in the appropriate maintenance section.

VALVE SYSTEM

All Models

The valves are actuated via rocker arms by a single overhead camshaft. The camshaft is driven by a roller chain attached to the right end of the crankshaft. Valve clearance should be adjusted after the first week of operation and then after every 30 days of operation. Adjust valve clearance with engine cold.

To adjust valve clearance, remove seat, fuel tank, rear fender, timing plug (I—Fig. H11-11) and valve adjustment cap at front and rear of cylinder head. The "T" mark (T) on the flywheel indicates top dead center when aligned with notch (N) in plug hole. Remove plug (P) from Model TRX300 crankcase cover or plug (G) from Model TRX300FW starter gear cover. On Model TRX300, rotate the end of the crankshaft clockwise. On Model TRX300FW, rotate the starter reduction shaft counterclockwise. On both models, align top dead cen-

ter mark (T—Fig. H11-11) with notch (N) with piston on compression stroke. To ensure piston is on compression stroke, rotate crankshaft past top dead center and observe intake (rear) rocker arm. If intake rocker arm movement is observed, continue to rotate crankshaft until marks are again aligned.

Clearance between rocker arm adjusting screw and valve stem should be 0.10 mm (0.004 in.) for both valves. Measure clearance with a suitable feeler gauge. Adjust clearance by loosening the adjusting screw locknut and turning the adjusting screw. Be sure to recheck clearance after tightening locknut.

CLUTCH

All Models

The engine is equipped with two automatically actuated clutches. A five-shoe centrifugal clutch is mounted on the right end of the crankshaft. The centrifugal clutch is disengaged at idle speed and engages when crankshaft speed increases. A multiple-disc clutch is attached to the transmission mainshaft and is actuated by the gear shift mechanism. When the gear shift lever is operated, the multiple-disc clutch is disengaged to allow smooth transmission gear movement.

The clutch should be adjusted after the first week of operation and after every 30 days of operation. To adjust clutch, remove cover on right side of crankcase. Loosen locknut (L—Fig. H11-16). Turn adjusting screw (S) counterclockwise until internal resistance is felt, then turn screw 1/4 turn clockwise. Secure adjusting screw with locknut (L) and install cover.

The dual-clutch system should automatically disengage at engine idle speed. When selecting gears, clutch should engage and disengage freely without excess slippage. Difficult shifting, clutch grabbing or clutch slipping may indicate overhaul is necessary.

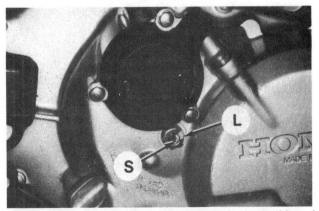

Fig. H11-16—To adjust clutch, loosen locknut (L) and turn adjusting screw (S) counterclockwise until internal resistance is felt. Then, turn screw 1/4 turn clockwise. Secure adjusting screw with locknut (L) and install cover.

REVERSE LOCK

All Models

A reverse lock mechanism prevents accidental engagement of reverse gear. There should be 2-4 mm ($5/64$-$5/32$ in.) free play at gap (G—Fig. H11-17). Adjust free play by loosening locknuts (N—Fig. H11-18) and repositioning cable. Retighten locknuts.

FRONT BRAKE SYSTEM

All Models

The front and rear brake systems are operated independently. The front brake system uses hydraulically actuated, drum-type brakes attached to each steering knuckle. Two brake shoes are contained behind each brake drum. A handlebar-mounted master cylinder with integral fluid reservoir supplies pressure to each wheel cylinder when the right handlebar lever is operated.

Only DOT 3 or DOT 4 rated brake fluid is recommended. Maintain brake fluid level between marks on inner side of brake fluid reservoir. To avert spillage, be sure reservoir is horizontal before removing cover.

Fig. H11-17—Reverse lock free play should be 2-4 mm (5/64-5/32 in.) at gap (G).

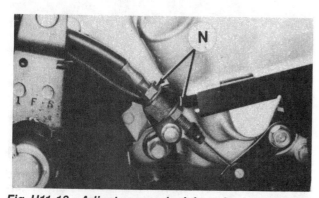

Fig. H11-18—Adjust reverse lock free play by loosening locknuts (N) and repositioning cable. Retighten locknuts.

INSPECTION. The brake system should be inspected after every 30 days of operation. Any indications of fluid leakage should be noted and corrected. Any worn, cracked or damaged brake lines or hoses should be renewed and the cause determined and corrected. Brake shoes should be adjusted to compensate for wear as needed.

To inspect the front brake drum components, support the front of the vehicle so the wheels are off the ground. Remove tire and wheel, unscrew axle nut and remove brake drum. Renew brake drum if inside diameter exceeds 131 mm (5.157 in.) on Model TRX300 or 161 mm (6.339 in.) on Model TRX300FW. Renew front brake shoes if lining thickness is less than 2.0 mm (0.08 in.). Wheel cylinders should be overhauled or renewed if brake fluid is observed within boots.

If either the brake shoes or wheel cylinders require servicing, then the complete drum brake assembly should be serviced as outlined in R&R AND OVERHAUL section. If brake components are satisfactory, reassemble brake and, if needed, perform adjustment. Apply multipurpose grease between lips of seal attached to drum edge. Tighten axle nut to 60-80 N•m (44-59 ft.-lbs.) on Model TRX300 or 80-100 N•m (59-74 ft.-lbs.) on Model TRX300FW. Tighten wheel nuts to 65 N•m (48 ft.-lbs.).

ADJUSTMENT. Free play (F—Fig. H11-19) at end of front brake lever should be 25-30 mm (1-1$3/16$ in.). If free play is excessive, adjust brake shoes using following procedure. Support front of vehicle so wheels are off ground. Remove plug (P—Fig. H11-20) from brake drum. Rotate wheel and locate notched adjuster wheel (there are two adjuster wheels, one for each brake shoe). Using a screwdriver or other tool, rotate adjuster wheel until brake shoe contacts brake drum, then back out adjuster three notches. Repeat procedure at other brake adjuster. Check brake lever free play. Repeat procedure if needed. Reinstall plug in brake drum. If brake lever free play cannot be adjusted by adjusting

Fig. H11-19—Free play (F) at end of front brake lever should be 25-30 mm (1 to 1-3/16 in.).

Fig. H11-20—Remove plug (P) from brake drum for access to brake adjusters.

brake shoes, there may be air in brake fluid. Perform bleeding procedure as outlined in BLEEDING section.

BLEEDING. The brake hydraulic system must be bled if any hydraulic brake components are disconnected or if the reservoir is drained. With reservoir horizontal, fill reservoir with DOT 3 or 4 brake fluid to full mark on inner side of reservoir. Do not allow reservoir to empty while performing bleeding operation. Reinstall cover to prevent entrance of dirt or foreign material. Attach a suitable hose, such as vacuum hose, to the bleed screw (B—Fig. H11-21) on brake backing plate. Submerge end of hose in a container of brake fluid to prevent air from reentering system. Actuate brake lever several times, then hold brake lever toward handlebar. Open brake bleed screw and allow fluid and air to flow into container. Continue holding brake lever and close

Fig. H11-21—Attach a hose to bleed valve (B) and follow procedure in text to bleed front brakes. Edge of pad (P) on the outside of the shock absorber cylinder must align with gap (G) between the clamp ends of the steering knuckle. Tighten the clamp screw to 55 N·m (40 ft.-lbs.).

bleed screw. Recheck reservoir level and refill if needed. Repeat procedure until air and/or old fluid is ejected from system.

R&R AND OVERHAUL. Support front of vehicle so wheel is off ground and remove wheel.

WARNING: Inhaling asbestos brake dust is injurious to human health. Approved OSHA respiration equipment must be worn when working on or around brake drum and shoes. DO NOT use compressed air to clean brake drum, shoes or nearby components as brake dust will be blown into air. Only vacuum equipment designed to pick up brake dust should be used.

Unscrew axle nut and remove brake drum and hub. While noting location of components, disassemble brake assembly. Note that wheel hub and brake drum are a unit on Model TRX300, while brake drum on Model TRX300FW may be separated from hub by unscrewing two screws. Detach brake line from wheel cylinder and plug line to reduce fluid loss. Two wheel cylinders are used on Model TRX300FW. The wheel cylinders are marked "L" or "R" to indicate position. Inspect components as outlined in INSPECTION section.

Disassemble and inspect wheel cylinder. Renew complete wheel cylinder if bore is scored, pitted or excessively worn. Maximum allowable bore diameter is 15.923 mm (0.6269 in.) on Model TRX300 and 17.515 mm (0.6896 in.) on Model TRX300FW. Minimum allowable piston diameter is 15.817 mm (0.6227 in.) on Model TRX300 and 17.405 mm (0.6852 in.) on Model TRX300FW. Superficial damage in wheel cylinder bore may be removed using a suitable cylinder hone. After honing, rinse bore with clean brake fluid. Shake out excess fluid but do not wipe dry. Using a shop towel or rag to dry cylinder will leave lint particles in bore. Renew boots and piston cups. During reassembly, lubricate components with clean brake fluid.

Backing plate retaining screws must be discarded. Tighten backing plate retaining screws to 30 N·m (22 ft.-lbs.). Apply a suitable sealer to wheel cylinder contact area on backing plate and install wheel cylinder. On Model TRX300FW, note "L" or "R" on wheel cylinder and install on indicated side of backing plate. Tighten 6 mm wheel cylinder retaining screws on Model TRX300FW to 6 N·m (53 in.-lbs.) and 8 mm screws on both models to 8 N·m (71 in.-lbs.). Attach brake line.

On Model TRX300 the brake shoe adjusters are contained in a housing at the bottom of the backing plate. Tighten housing retaining screws to 8 N·m (71 in.-lbs.). On Model TRX300FW the brake shoe adjuster fits in one end of the wheel cylinder. Clean adjuster and lubricate with silicone grease before installing in housing or wheel cylinder. Screw adjusters completely in to allow installation of new brake shoes. Apply a light coat of silicone grease to three points on backing plate that will contact edge of brake shoe. Install brake shoes so squared-off end contacts wheel cylinder piston and rounded end contacts adjuster. On Model TRX300, install top brake spring (near wheel cylinder) behind brake shoes, and install lower brake spring in front of brake shoes. On Model TRX300FW, install brake springs behind brake shoes with coiled end at same end as wheel cylinder piston. Secure brake shoes with pins and clips. Apply multipurpose grease between lips of seal attached to drum edge. Tighten axle nut to 60-80 N·m (44-59 ft.-lbs.) on Model TRX300 or 80-100 N·m (59-74 ft.-lbs.) on Model TRX300FW. Tighten wheel nuts to 65 N·m (48 ft.-lbs.).

Adjust and bleed brakes as previously outlined.

MASTER CYLINDER. To remove front brake master cylinder (14—Fig. H11-22), detach brake line from master cylinder. Brake fluid will remove paint; be careful when removing master cylinder. Unscrew two retaining screws and remove master cylinder. Remove brake lever, reservoir cover (9) and diaphragm (11). Remove dust boot (1) and snap ring (2). Disassemble piston assembly while noting location and direction of components. Renew complete master cylinder if bore is scored, pitted or excessively worn. Maximum allowable bore diameter is 12.755 mm (0.5022 in.) on Model TRX300 and 14.055 mm (0.5533 in.) on Model

TRX300FW. Minimum allowable piston diameter is 12.645 mm (0.4978 in.) on Model TRX300 and 13.945 mm (0.5490 in.) on Model TRX300FW. Superficial damage in master cylinder bore may be removed using a suitable cylinder hone. After honing, rinse bore with clean brake fluid. Shake out excess fluid but do not wipe dry. Using a shop towel or rag to dry cylinder will leave lint particles in bore. Renew boots and piston cups. During reassembly, lubricate components with clean brake fluid. Reassembly is reverse of disassembly. Install spring (5) so small end contacts piston (4). Bleed brakes as previously outlined.

FRONT AXLE

Model TRX300

A ball joint connects the lower control arm and steering knuckle. The shock absorber is attached to the steering knuckle that pivots on the shock absorber and the ball joint in the lower control arm. Lower control arm is bolted to the vehicle frame. The shock absorber limits and cushions vertical movement of the control arm. A spring on the shock absorber supports the vehicle.

The lower ball joint is available as a unit assembly with the lower control arm. If removed, tie rod and control arm retaining nuts should be discarded. Tighten control arm bolts to 45 N·m (33 ft.-lbs.). Tighten ball joint nut to 50-60 N·m (37-44 ft.-lbs.). Tighten tie rod end nut to 55 N·m (40 ft.-lbs.). Refer to SHOCK ABSORBERS section for installation of shock absorber.

Model TRX300FW

Both front steering knuckles pivot on ball joints at the end of the upper control arm and in the lower arm of the steering knuckle. The control arm ends are bolted to the vehicle frame. A shock absorber on each side limits and cushions vertical movement of the control arms. A spring on the shock absorber supports the vehicle. The axle shaft is supported by a ball bearing in the steering knuckle.

The control arms can be removed without separating axle shaft and steering knuckle. However, the steering knuckle must be removed for access to the lower ball joint as outlined in FRONT AXLE SHAFTS section. The ball joints are renewable using a suitable press or vise. To remove ball joint, remove snap ring and force ball joint out toward stud end. Install ball joint until bottomed against snap ring. Inspect, and if necessary, renew bearing in steering knuckle. Remove snap ring and drive out bearing. Pack bearing with grease before installation. Inspect, and if necessary, renew bearing seals. If removed, tie rod and control arm retaining nuts should be discarded. Tighten control arm bolts to 45 N·m (33 ft.-lbs.). Tighten ball joint nut to 30-36 N·m (22-26 ft.-lbs.). Tighten tie rod end nut to 55 N·m (40 ft.-lbs.).

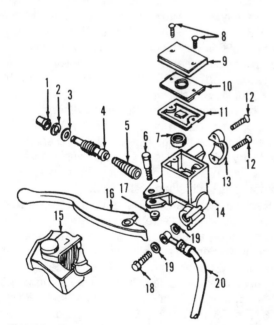

Fig. H11-22—Exploded view of front brake master cylinder.

1. Boot
2. Snap ring
3. Washer
4. Piston & cup
5. Spring
6. Bolt
7. Seal
8. Screw
9. Cover
10. Diaphragm plate
11. Diaphragm
12. Bolt
13. Clamp
14. Body
15. Rubber boot
16. Brake lever
17. Nut
18. Union bolt
19. Seal washer
20. Brake hose

STEERING

All Models

INSPECTION. Support front of vehicle so the wheels are off the ground. Rotate the handlebar to full left and right and check for excessive looseness, binding and roughness. Be sure cables do not prevent full movement. Clean and grease components if binding or excessive effort is noted. Renew any damaged components.

TOE-IN SETTING. Before checking toe-in setting, inspect front steering assembly and renew or repair any loose or damaged components.

To check toe-in, inflate tires to recommended pressure listed in CONDENSED SERVICE DATA. Position vehicle on a flat, smooth surface and set handlebar straight forward. Use a suitable measuring tool and measure distance (B—Fig. H11-23) at spindle height between the center of the tires on the rear sides. Locate the same tire centerline points on front side of tires and measure front distance (F). The toe-in distance on the front side (F) should be shorter than the measured distance on the rear side (B). Toe-in should be 2 mm (0.08 in.) on Model TRX300 and 8 mm (0.31 in.) on Model TRX300FW. Note that the distance from a projected vehicle centerline to left (L) and right (R) tire centerlines should also be equal. Loosen locknuts at both ends of tie rods (T) and rotate tie rod shaft to adjust toe-in. Retighten locknuts to 55 N.m (40 ft.-lbs.).

OVERHAUL. The steering shaft rides in a ball bearing at the lower end. The upper portion of the steering shaft rides in a bushing that is secured to the vehicle frame by a clamp. To remove the steering shaft, remove the front fender unit and detach the handlebar clamp blocks

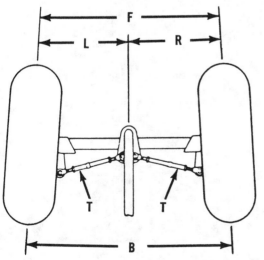

Fig. H11-23—Toe-in should be 2 mm (0.08 in.) on Model TRX300 and 8 mm (0.31 in.) on Model TRX300FW. Refer to text for measurement and adjustment procedures.

from the upper flange of the steering shaft. Detach tie rod ends from steering shaft arm. On Model TRX300, remove upper inner fender panel. Unscrew steering shaft nut at lower end. On Model TRX300, remove spacer at bottom end of shaft. On Model TRX300FW, detach steering arm from shaft. Remove steering shaft. Inspect shaft, bushing and bearing. To remove ball bearing, remove seal and snap ring, then drive bearing up and out of frame.

Note the following when installing components: New nuts should be installed on tie rod end and handlebar clamp blocks. Apply grease to ball bearing and install bearing so sealed side is up. Apply grease to cavities of bushing and install bushing so "UP" on bushing is up. Tighten bushing clamp screws to 33 N.m (24 ft.-lbs.). On Model TRX300FW be sure master splines on shaft and steering arm are aligned. Apply grease to splines. Tighten steering shaft nut to 70 N.m (52 ft.-lbs.). Tighten tie rod nut to 55 N.m (40 ft.-lbs.). Tighten nuts that secure handlebar clamp blocks to steering shaft flange to 40 N.m (29 ft.-lbs.).

FRONT AXLE SHAFTS

Model TRX300FW

Model TRX300FW is equipped with a front-wheel-drive system that uses an axle shaft between the final drive housing and steering knuckle. Each axle shaft is equipped with a ball joint at each end.

To remove axle shaft, first remove front brake drum as previously outlined. Using a suitable ball joint removal tool, separate steering knuckle from control arms. Move steering knuckle and brake assembly away from axle shaft. Support knuckle/brake assembly so brake line is not pulled or twisted; do not allow assembly to hang from brake line. Withdraw axle shaft while pulling inner shaft end straight out from drive housing so seal in housing is not distorted.

Move shaft in normal range of motion and check for excessive wear and damage. Note that outboard ball joint is not serviceable. If outboard joint is defective, then entire shaft assembly must be renewed. Boot bands should be renewed if removed. Boots should be renewed if cracked, torn or otherwise damaged. Boots are dissimilar and identified by number molded in boot at large end of boot. Number "BJ68L" indicates an outer boot while number "BJ68" indicates an inner boot. Note that inner ball joint must be disassembled to install a new outer boot. To inspect ball joints, detach boot bands and slide back boots. To disassemble inner joint, detach snap ring in periphery of joint housing and withdraw ball assembly. Detach snap ring on shaft end to separate ball race from shaft. Clean joint assembly and inspect for damage and excessive wear. Joint components should be renewed as a unit. When assembling ball joint, position splined end of bearing race and stepped ID of bearing cage toward end of shaft (see Fig. H11-24).

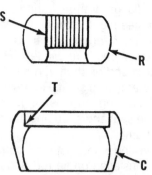

Fig. H11-24—When assembling inner ball joint on front axle, position splined end (S) of bearing race (R) and stepped end (T) of bearing cage (C) towards end of shaft.

Reassemble shaft by reversing disassembly procedure. Pack inner ball joint and boots with molybdenum disulfide grease.

Before installing shaft, be sure the snap ring is fitted in the circumferential groove around the end of the inner drive shaft. Install the axle in the drive housing while positioning the inner shaft so the snap ring fits into the groove of the gear inside the drive housing. Insert the axle in the knuckle and attach the knuckle to the control arm ball joints. Tighten ball joint nuts to 30-36 N·m (22-26 ft.-lbs.). Tighten axle nut to 80-100 N·m (59-74 ft.-lbs.). Tighten wheel nuts to 65 N·m (48 ft.-lbs.).

FRONT DRIVE ASSEMBLIES

Model TRX300FW

Service on front drive assemblies should be performed by a Honda service technician equipped with the special tools required for overhaul.

SHOCK ABSORBERS

All Models

FRONT. Spring tension is not adjustable. The front shock absorbers on Model TRX300 are secured to the frame at the upper end by a nut that should be tightened to 55 N·m (40 ft.-lbs.). The lower end of the shock absorber is clamped by the steering knuckle. The edge of pad (P—Fig. H11-21) on the outside of the shock absorber cylinder must align with gap (G) between the clamp ends of the steering knuckle. Tighten the clamp screw to 55 N·m (40 ft.-lbs.).

Both ends of the front shock absorbers on Model TRX300FW are secured by a bolt through the mounting eye. Tighten bolt to 25 N·m (18 ft.-lbs.).

REAR. Spring tension is not adjustable. Tighten upper mounting bolt to 45 N·m (33 ft.-lbs.) and lower mounting bolt to 35 N·m (26 ft.-lbs.).

REAR BRAKE SYSTEM

All Models

The front and rear brake systems are operated independently. The rear brake consists of a two-shoe, internally expanding drum brake mounted on the right end of the rear axle housing. The brake may be actuated by a brake lever attached to the left handlebar or a brake pedal near the right footpeg.

INSPECTION. The brake system should be inspected after every 30 days of operation. Service, repair or renew any components that are inoperable or damaged.

ADJUSTMENT. Actuate the rear brake pedal and measure free travel at end of pedal. Free travel should be 15-20 mm (⅝-¾ in.). Adjust pedal free travel by rotating adjuster (J—Fig. H11-26) at rear brake.

Rear brake lever free play measured at (F—Fig. H11-27) should be 15-20 (⅝-¾ in.). Rotate lever adjuster (R—Fig. H11-26) at rear brake to adjust lever free travel. Minor brake lever adjustment can be accomplished by turning cable adjuster (A—Fig. H11-27) on lever assembly.

A rear brake lining indicator (I—Fig. H11-26) is attached to the brake cam. To externally check brake lining wear, apply rear brake and note position of indicator (I) with mark (M) on backing plate. Brake shoes should be renewed if indicator aligns with or passes mark (M).

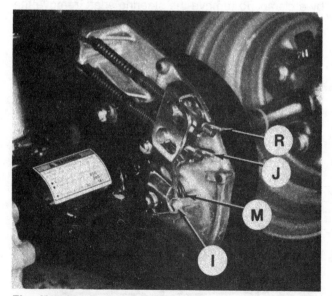

Fig. H11-26—To check brake lining wear, apply rear brake and note position of indicator (I) with mark (M) on backing plate. Brake shoes should be renewed if indicator aligns with or passes mark (M).

Fig. H11-27—Rear brake lever free play, measured at (F), should be 15-20 mm (5/8-3/4 in.). Minor brake lever adjustment can be accomplished by turning cable adjuster (A), otherwise, rotate lever adjuster (R—Fig. H11-26) at rear brake to adjust lever free travel.

R&R AND OVERHAUL. To remove rear brake shoes and drum, support rear of vehicle and remove right tire and wheel.

WARNING: Inhaling asbestos brake dust is injurious to human health. Approved OSHA respiration equipment must be worn when working on or around brake drum and shoes. DO NOT use compressed air to clean brake drum, shoes or nearby components as brake dust will be blown into air. Only vacuum equipment designed to pick up brake dust should be used.

Unscrew wheel hub retaining nut and remove wheel hub from axle. Unscrew locknuts on axle, remove the large flat washer, then unscrew and remove brake drum cover. Remove "O" ring around axle and brake drum.

Renew the brake shoes if thickness is less than 2.0 mm (0.08 in.). Renew the brake drum if inside diameter exceeds 161 mm (6.339 in.). Inspect "O" rings and seals and renew if deteriorated or damaged. Note that there is an "O" ring located between the backing plate and axle housing and a seal around the actuating camshaft.

Reassemble by reversing disassembly procedure and noting the following: Tighten backing plate retaining nuts to 35 N·m (26 ft.-lbs.). Apply a light coat of grease to brake shoe cam and anchor pin. Do not allow grease on brake shoe linings. Tighten inner axle nut to 40 N·m (29 ft.-lbs.) and outer axle nut to 130 N·m (96 ft.-lbs.). Tighten wheel hub retaining nut to 100-120 N·m (74-88 ft.-lbs.). Adjust rear brake as previously outlined.

SWING ARM AND REAR DRIVE ASSEMBLIES

All Models

Service on swing arm and rear drive assemblies should be performed by a Honda service technician equipped with the special tools required for overhaul.

HONDA
TRX350 AND TRX350D

NOTE: Metric fasteners are used throughout vehicle.

CONDENSED SERVICE DATA

MODELS	TRX350, TRX350D
General	
Engine Make	Honda
Engine Type	Four-Stroke; Air-Cooled
Number of Cylinders	1
Bore	81.0 mm (3.189 in.)
Stroke	68.0 mm (2.677 in.)
Displacement	350.4 cc (21.4 cu. in.)
Compression Ratio	8.5:1
Engine Lubrication	Wet Sump;Oil Pump
Transmission Lubrication	Common With Engine
Engine/Transmission Oil	SAE 10W-40
Forward Speeds	5
Reverse Speeds	1
Front Drive	Shaft & Gears
Rear Drive	Shaft & Gears
Tire Size:	
Front & Rear	24 × 9-11
Tire Pressure:	
Front & Rear	15 kPa (2.2 psi)
Battery	12V-12AH
Dry Weight:	
TRX350	259 kg (570 lbs.)
TRX350D	268 kg (590 lbs.)
Tune-Up	
Engine Idle Speed	1300-1500 rpm
Compression Pressure	1250-1450 kPa (181-210 psi)
Spark Plug:	
NGK	DR8ES-L
Nippon Denso	X24ESR-U
Electrode Gap	0.6-0.7 mm (0.024-0.028 in.)
Ignition:	
Type	Breakerless
Timing	10° BTDC
Carburetor:	
Make	Keihin
Model	QA03A

Tune-Up (Cont.)

Float Height	18.5 mm
	(0.73 in.)
Main Jet	#142
Idle Jet	#35
Clip Position.	3rd Groove From Top
Idle Mixture Setting	1½ Turns
Throttle Lever Free Play	3-8 mm
	(0.12-0.31 in.)

Sizes-Clearances

Valve Clearance (cold):	
Intake & Exhaust	0.08 mm
	(0.003 in.)
Valve Face & Seat Angle:	
Intake & Exhaust	45°
Valve Seat Width:	
Intake & Exhaust	1.2 mm
	(0.05 in.)
Wear Limit	1.5 mm
	(0.06 in.)
Valve Stem Diameter:	
Intake.	5.480-5.490 mm
	(0.2157-0.2161 in.)
Wear Limit	5.45 mm
	(0.215 in.)
Exhaust	5.460-5.470 mm
	(0.2150-0.2154 in.)
Wear Limit	5.43 mm
	(0.214 in.)
Valve Guide Bore Diameter:	
Intake & Exhaust	5.500-5.512 mm
	(0.2165-0.2170 in.)
Wear Limit	5.525 mm
	(0.2175 in.)
Valve Stem-to-Guide Clearance:	
Intake.	0.010-0.032 mm
	(0.0004-0.0013 in.)
Wear Limit	0.12 mm
	(0.005 in.)
Exhaust	0.030-0.052 mm
	(0.0012-0.0020 in.)
Wear Limit	0.14 mm
	(0.006 in.)
Valve Spring Free Length:	
Inner.	35.15 mm
	(1.384 in.)
Minimum Length	32.2 mm
	(1.27 in.)
Outer	45.75 mm
	(1.801 in.)
Minimum Length	42.7 mm
	(1.68 in.)
Valve Spring Pressure:	
Inner.	5.7-6.9 kg @ 26.8 mm
	(12.5-15.2 lbs. @ 1.05 in.)
Outer	14.4-17.6 kg @ 30.8 mm
	(31.7-38.7 lbs. @ 1.21 in.)

Sizes-Clearances (Cont.)

Rocker Arm Bore Diameter:

Intake & Exhaust . . . . 11.988-12.006 mm
(0.4720-0.4727 in.)

    Wear Limit . . . . 12.04 mm
(0.474 in.)

Rocker Shaft Diameter:

Intake & Exhaust . . . . 11.966-11.984 mm
(0.4711-0.4718 in.)

    Wear Limit . . . . 11.92 mm
(0.469 in.)

Camshaft Lobe Height
1986 Models:

Intake. . . . . 36.134-36.144 mm
(1.4226-1.4230 in.)

    Wear Limit . . . . 35.964 mm
(1.4159 in.)

Exhaust . . . . 35.926-35.936 mm
(1.4144-1.4148 in.)

    Wear Limit . . . . 35.756 mm
(1.4077 in.)

Models After 1986:

Intake & Exhaust . . . . 35.391-35.401 mm
(1.3933-1.3937 in.)

    Wear Limit . . . . 35.201 mm
(1.3859 in.)

Cylinder Head Distortion (Max.). . . . . 0.10 mm
(0.004 in.)

Cylinder Bore Diameter . . . . 81.00-81.01 mm
(3.1890-3.1894 in.)

    Wear Limit . . . . 81.10 mm
(3.193 in.)

Piston-to-Cylinder Clearance. . . . . 0.015-0.045 mm
(0.0006-0.0018 in.)

    Wear Limit . . . . 0.10 mm
(0.004 in.)

Piston Diameter—
Measured 10 mm (0.4 in.) From
Skirt Bottom & 90° to Pin Bore . . . . 80.965-80.985 mm
(3.1876-3.1884 in.)

    Wear Limit . . . . 80.90 mm
(3.185 in.)

Piston Pin Bore . . . . 21.002-21.008 mm
(0.8268-0.8271 in.)

    Wear Limit . . . . 21.04 mm
(0.828 in.)

Piston Pin Diameter. . . . . 20.994-21.000 mm
(0.8265-0.8268 in.)

    Wear Limit . . . . 20.96 mm
(0.826 in.)

Piston-to-Pin Clearance. . . . . 0.002-0.014 mm
(0.0001-0.0006 in.)

    Wear Limit . . . . 0.02 mm
(0.001 in.)

Piston Ring End Gap:
Top & Second Rings . . . . 0.20-0.35 mm
(0.008-0.014 in.)

Sizes-Clearances (Cont.)
Piston Ring End Gap: (Cont.)

Wear Limit	0.55 mm (0.022 in.)
Oil Ring	0.2-0.7 mm (0.008-0.028 in.)

Piston Ring Side Clearance:

Top & Second Rings	0.015-0.045 mm (0.0006-0.0018 in.)
Wear Limit	0.09 mm (0.004 in.)

Connecting Rod Small End Bore Diameter	21.020-21.041 mm (0.8275-0.8284 in.)
Wear Limit	21.10 mm (0.831 in.)
Connecting Rod Big End Side Clearance (Max.)	0.80 mm (0.031 in.)
Connecting Rod Big End Radial Clearance (Max.)	0.05 mm (0.002 in.)
Crankshaft Runout (Max.)	0.05 mm (0.002 in.)

Capacities

Fuel Tank	10.5 L (2.8 gal.)
Engine/Transmission Sump	See Text

Tightening Torques

Camshaft Sprocket	17-23 N•m (12-17 ft.-lbs.)

Clutch Nut:

Centrifugal Clutch (L.H. Threads)	120 N•m (88 ft.-lbs.)
Shift Clutch	110 N•m (81 ft.-lbs.)
Crankcase	10 N•m (88 in.-lbs.)
Crankcase Cover	10 N•m (88 in.-lbs.)
Cylinder Base Screw	10 N•m (88 in.-lbs.)
Cylinder Head Nut & Screw	40 N•m (29 ft.-lbs.)
Flywheel Cap Screw	110 N•m (81 ft.-lbs.)
Output Gear Housing to Crankcase Screw	32 N•m (24 ft.-lbs.)
Spark Plug	18 N•m (159 in.-lbs.)
Wheel Retaining Nut	65 N•m (48 ft.-lbs.)

Standard Screws:

5 mm	3.5-5.0 N•m (31-44 in.-lbs.)
6 mm	7-11 N•m (62-97 in.-lbs.)

Tightening Torques (Cont.)

Standard Bolts & Nuts:

5 mm	4.5-6.0 N•m (40-53 in.-lbs.)
6 mm	8-12 N•m (71-106 in.-lbs.)
8 mm	18-25 N•m (13-18 ft.-lbs.)
10 mm	30-40 N•m (22-29 ft.-lbs.)
12 mm	50-60 N•m (36-43 ft.-lbs.)

Flanged Bolts & Nuts:

6 mm	10-14 N•m (89-124 in.-lbs.)
8 mm	24-30 N•m (17-22 ft.-lbs.)
10 mm	35-45 N•m (25-32 ft.-lbs.)

LUBRICATION

ENGINE AND TRANSMISSION. The engine and transmission are lubricated by a gear-driven, trochoid-type pump located on the right side of the crankcase and driven by the crankshaft. The engine and transmission share a common sump. Recommended oil is SAE 10W-40 with an API classification of SF or SG.

Oil level should be maintained at upper mark on dipstick attached to fill plug. Do not screw plug in when checking oil level. Fill sump through opening for fill plug (F—Fig. H13-1). Drain oil by removing drain plug on underside of crankcase. Fill crankcase with 2.3 L (2.4 qt.) of oil if oil and oil filter are changed. Crankcase capacity totally dry is 2.8 L (3.0 qt.).

The manufacturer recommends changing the oil and oil filter after the first week of operation and then after every 30 days of operation. A sump filter screen, located in a compartment in the right crankcase half, should be removed periodically and cleaned.

Remove oil filter cover (C—Fig. H13-1) for access to oil filter. Before installing filter, be sure spring is against engine (crankcase cover) and "O" rings are in place. Install filter so rubber seal side and "OUTSIDE" are toward filter cover.

REAR DRIVE HOUSING. The oil in the rear drive housing should be changed every two years. With vehicle on level ground, oil in housing should be level with threads of hole for fill plug. Remove oil by unscrewing drain screw from underside of housing. Fill housing with oil through opening for fill plug (F—Fig. H13-2). Recom-mended oil is SAE 80 hypoid gear oil. If changing oil, fill housing with 110 cc (3.7 oz.) on 1986 models or 210 cc (7.1 oz.) on models after 1986. Housing capacity totally dry is 135 cc (4.6 oz.) for 1986 models or 225 cc (7.6 oz.) for models after 1986.

FRONT DRIVE HOUSING. The oil in the front drive housing should be changed every two years. With vehicle on level ground, oil in housing should be level with threads of hole for check plug (G—Fig. H13-3. Remove oil by unscrewing drain screw (D—Fig. H13-3). Fill housing with oil through opening for fill plug (F—Fig. H13-4). Recommended oil is SAE 80 hypoid gear oil.

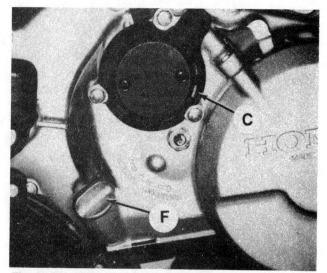

Fig. H13-1—The oil dipstick is attached to fill plug (F). Remove cover (C) for access to oil filter.

Fig. H13-2—Pour oil into rear drive housing through opening for fill plug (F). The drain screw is located on underside of housing.

Fill housing with 110 cc (3.7 oz.) of oil if oil is being changed. Housing capacity totally dry is 135 cc (4.6 oz.).

CABLES AND LEVERS. All cables and levers should be inspected and lubricated after the first week of operation and after every 30 days of operation thereafter.

AIR CLEANER ELEMENT

The air cleaner element should be removed and cleaned after every 30 days of operation. To remove the air cleaner element, remove the seat, unscrew center panel wing bolt, release four cover clips and remove cover. Loosen air cleaner frame to inlet tube clamp, then withdraw element and frame from case. Remove nut and rear frame bracket, then carefully separate foam element from frame.

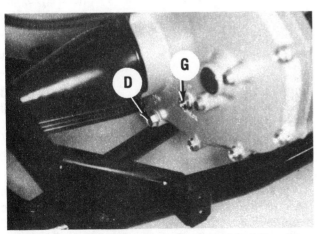

Fig. H13-3—Oil in front gearcase should just flow from hole for check plug (G). Unscrew drain plug (D) to drain oil from gearcase.

Fig. H13-4—Pour oil into front gearcase through opening for fill plug (F).

Thoroughly clean the foam element in a nonflammable solvent. Compress element between hands to remove solvent. Saturate element in clean SAE 10W-40 engine oil. Compress element to remove excess oil. Install element and reassemble air cleaner components.

FUEL SYSTEM

Fuel is contained in the fuel tank under the seat. A fuel gauge sender unit is attached to the side of the fuel tank on Model TRX350D to monitor fuel level. Fuel is routed from the tank through the control valve attached to the side of the fuel tank, to the fuel filter, to the electric fuel pump, then to the carburetor. A relay attached to the panel on the right rear portion of the frame controls the fuel pump. Refer to the following sections for service information on fuel system components.

CARBURETOR. The engine is equipped with a Keihin Model QA03A carburetor. Carburetor is similar to carburetor shown in Fig. H13-5. Initial setting of idle mixture screw (15—Fig. H13-6) is 1½ turns out. Rotating idle mixture screw clockwise will lean idle mixture. Final adjustment must be performed with engine at normal operating temperature. Adjust idle speed screw knob (14) so engine idles at 1300-1500 rpm. Slowly rotate idle mixture screw (15) clockwise, leaning idle mixture, until engine stalls, then turn idle mixture screw two turns counterclockwise. Readjust idle speed.

When servicing carburetor, note the following: Jet needle clip (21—Fig. H13-7) should be in third groove from top. To gain access to jet needle (20) and throttle slide (22), remove set screw in throttle slide arm (17) and withdraw throttle slide shaft (3—Fig. H13-5). Extract throttle slide assembly. Be careful not to lose washer (18—Fig. H13-7). Remove two screws (19) and separate components. Check synchronization of throttle slide and throttle plate. With throttle slide and throttle plate completely closed, throttle slide lever (3—Fig. H13-5) should just contact throttle link (2). To synchro-

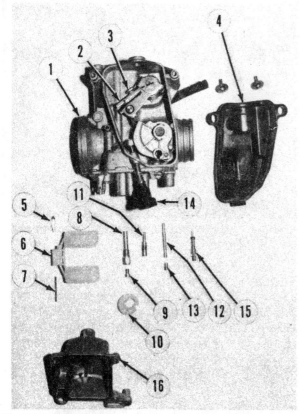

Fig. H13-5—*View of partially disassembled carburetor used on all models. Also refer to Figs. H13-6 and H13-7.*

1. Carburetor body
2. Throttle link
3. Throttle slide lever & shaft
4. Cover
5. Fuel inlet valve
6. Float
7. Float pin
8. Needle jet
9. Main jet
10. Baffle
11. Pilot jet
12. Primary nozzle
13. Primary jet
14. Idle speed screw
15. Idle mixture screw
16. Fuel bowl

nize the throttle slide and plate, open or close the slot in throttle link (2). Float height should be 18.5 mm (0.73 in.) between bottom of float and carburetor body. Hold carburetor so float is vertical and resting lightly against fuel inlet valve. See Fig. H13-8. Float height is not adjustable. Renew float and/or fuel inlet valve if float height is incorrect.

Recommended main jet size for operation above 3000 feet is #132.

FUEL PUMP. An electric fuel pump is attached to the frame near the carburetor. A relay attached to the panel on the right rear portion of the frame controls the fuel pump. The pump is protected by a 5 amp fuse (10 amp on Model TRX350D) located in the fuse box under the seat.

To check fuel pump, disconnect three-wire connector from fuel pump relay and connect a jumper wire between connector black/green wire terminal (black/brown wire on 1986 models) and black/blue wire terminal. Disconnect fuel line from fuel pump to carburetor and

Fig. H13-6—*View of carburetor with fuel bowl removed. Components are also shown in Fig. H13-1.*

8. Needle jet
9. Main jet
10. Baffle
11. Pilot jet
13. Primary jet
14. Idle speed screw
15. Idle mixture screw

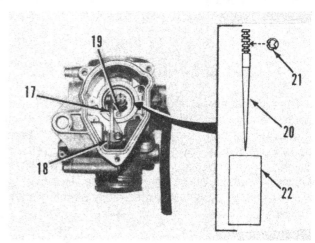

Fig. H13-7—*Refer to text to remove jet needle (20) and throttle slide (22).*

17. Throttle slide arm
18. Washer
19. Screw
20. Jet needle
21. Clip
22. Throttle slide

route fuel line into a container. Turn ignition switch to "ON" for 5 seconds and measure output of fuel pump. If fuel pump output is not 270-330 cc (9.1-11.1 oz.), renew pump. Fuel pump must be serviced as a unit assembly.

To check fuel pump relay, disconnect three-wire connector from relay and turn ignition switch "ON". Connect the positive lead of a voltmeter to connector black/green wire terminal (black/brown wire on 1986 models) and negative lead to green wire terminal. Voltmeter should indicate battery voltage. If not, check fuse. Reconnect positive voltmeter lead to black/blue wire terminal. Voltmeter should indicate zero voltage. Reinstall connector.

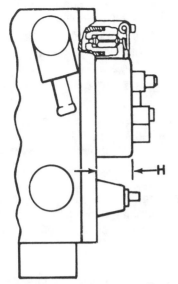

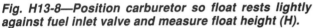

Fig. H13-8—Position carburetor so float rests lightly against fuel inlet valve and measure float height (H).

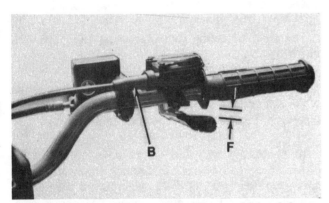

Fig. H13-9—Throttle free play (F) should be 3-8 mm (1/8-5/16 in.) measured at throttle lever end. Slide rubber boot (B) down cable to expose knurled locknut and cable adjuster.

Run engine. There should be voltage between connectors for black/blue and green wires leading to fuel pump.

Fuel pump relay control voltage is carried by the black/yellow wire between the relay and ignition module.

FUEL FILTER. A fuel filter is located in the line between the fuel tank and fuel pump. The fuel filter is a one-piece unit that should be renewed every six months.

FUEL LINES. Fuel hoses should be inspected periodically with particular attention directed to fuel hose between fuel pump and carburetor. Renew any hoses that are cracked, split, chaffed or hard.

THROTTLE LEVER FREE PLAY. Free play (F—Fig. H13-9) at the end of the throttle lever should be 3-8 mm (⅛-5/16 in.). To adjust free play, slide back rubber boot

(B), loosen the knurled nut and rotate cable adjuster. Retighten knurled nut.

IGNITION SYSTEM

SPARK PLUG. The recommended spark plug for normal operating conditions is a NGK DR8ES-L or Nippon Denso X24ESR-U. Spark plug electrode gap should be 0.6-0.7 mm (0.024-0.028 in.). The spark plug should be removed, inspected, cleaned or renewed, and regapped after every 30 days of operation.

IGNITION. All models are equipped with a breakerless, capacitor discharge ignition system. On Model TRX350, power for the ignition is obtained by an exciter coil located in the alternator. On Model TRX350D, power for the ignition is provided by the battery. The electronic ignition circuit consists of the CDI module, pulse generator, ignition coil, spark plug, engine stop switch, ignition switch and neutral switch. On models after 1987, an alternator sensor wire detects alternator charging current and prevents ignition if the engine is stopped.

To check ignition timing, remove timing hole plug in left engine side cover and attach a suitable timing light to engine. Initial ignition (10° BTDC) should occur when "F" mark on flywheel is aligned with mark (M—Fig. H13-10) on case at 1300-1500 rpm. Advanced ignition timing is 30° BTDC. Advanced ignition should occur when "=" mark on flywheel is aligned with mark (M) on case at 3400-3600 rpm on all models. Ignition timing is not adjustable. If ignition timing is not as specified, check condition of CDI module and pulse generator as described in the following test procedures and renew faulty or questionable components.

If ignition malfunction occurs, check condition of spark plug, all wires and connections before troubleshooting the ignition circuit. Using Honda Digital Multi-Tester KS-AHM-32-003 or a suitable ohmmeter, refer to the following test procedures and specifications to aid troubleshooting.

Fig. H13-10—Ignition at idle speed should occur when "F" mark on flywheel aligns with stationary mark (M). Piston is at TDC when "T" mark is aligned with mark (M).

To check condition of exciter coil on Model TRX350, remove right frame cover, locate connector cover near the fuel valve, and disconnect the black/red wire connector. Using an ohmmeter measure resistance between exciter coil wire and vehicle ground. Exciter coil is considered satisfactory if resistance is 50-200 ohms.

To check condition of alternator sensor wire on models after 1987, disconnect four-wire connector at CDI module (CDI module is attached to front upper portion of vehicle frame). Attach one ohmmeter lead to yellow sensor wire at connector and remaining ohmmeter lead to vehicle ground. Ohmmeter should read infinity (no continuity). Disconnect three-yellow-wire alternator connector at regulator/rectifier. Connect ohmmeter leads to yellow wire terminal of CDI connector and any yellow wire terminal of alternator connector. Ohmmeter should show continuity. If meter readings are unsatisfactory, wiring or alternator is faulty.

To check condition of the pulse generator, remove right frame cover, locate connector cover near the fuel valve, and disconnect the blue/yellow wire connector. Connect an ohmmeter lead to blue/yellow wire going to engine and remaining ohmmeter lead to vehicle ground. Pulse generator is satisfactory if ohmmeter reading is 300-360 ohms. If reading is incorrect, remove left crankcase cover and repeat test at terminal of pulse generator.

To check condition of ignition coil, detach black/yellow wire and green wire from ignition coil. Disconnect high tension lead from spark plug. To check primary winding resistance, attach one ohmmeter lead to black/yellow wire terminal on ignition coil and remaining ohmmeter lead to green wire terminal. Ohmmeter should read 0.1-0.2 ohms. Perform two secondary winding tests, one with the spark plug cap attached to coil wire and one without spark plug cap attached. Attach one ohmmeter lead to spark plug cap and remaining ohmmeter lead to coil ground (green wire terminal). Secondary winding resistance through spark plug cap should be 7.5k-10.8k ohms. Remove spark plug cap from high tension wire. Attach an ohmmeter lead to high tension wire and remaining ohmmeter lead to coil ground. Secondary winding resistance reading with spark plug cap removed should be 3.7k-4.5k ohms. If secondary winding resistance is now within specification, renew spark plug cap.

The neutral switch is located in the right crankcase cover near the right footpeg and marked "N". Note that wire lead to switch is marked "N". To check neutral switch, disconnect the light green wire from the switch. Connect an ohmmeter lead to the wire terminal of the switch and connect the remaining ohmmeter lead to vehicle ground. With transmission in neutral the ohmmeter should show continuity. When transmission is in gear the ohmmeter should read infinity. Crankcase oil must be drained before removing neutral switch. Tightening torque for neutral switch is 13 N·m (115 in.-lbs.).

If no faulty component is found and ignition malfunction persists, renew CDI module and recheck ignition operation. The CDI module is attached to the vehicle frame under the front fender assembly.

ELECTRICAL SYSTEM

The vehicle is equipped with a charging system, battery and electric starter. The system is protected by a 20 amp fuse on TRX350 models or 30 amp fuse on TRX350D models.

BATTERY. Remove the seat for access to battery. The negative terminal is grounded. The battery is a sealed, maintenance-free, 12-volt unit with 12 amp-hour capacity.

CHARGING SYSTEM. The charging circuit consists of an alternator and a regulator/rectifier. The alternator rotor is attached to the left end of the crankshaft while the stator is mounted on the inside of the left crankcase cover. The regulator/rectifier module is mounted on the right rear of the vehicle frame.

The charging circuit should produce 13.5-15.5 VDC at 5000 rpm.

NOTE: Do not disconnect battery terminal wires while the engine is running as excessive alternator output will damage the regulator/rectifier.

To check the alternator stator coils, remove right frame cover, locate and disconnect green three-wire connector near the fuel valve (all wires are yellow). On connector leading to alternator, alternately check resistance between each terminal and the remaining two terminals. Resistance between any pair should be 0.2-1.0 ohms. Resistance between any terminal and vehicle ground must be infinity.

If previous tests prove satisfactory and fuse, wiring and connections are all good, replace regulator/rectifier with a good unit and recheck operation.

ELECTRIC STARTER. The starting circuit consists of the starter, starter relay, starter switch, diode, neutral light, neutral switch and ignition switch. A fuse protects the circuit.

The starter relay is located adjacent to the battery. To check relay, disconnect relay pigtail lead and wires from terminals on relay. Connect ohmmeter leads to terminals on top of relay. Ohmmeter should read infinity. Connect a 12-volt battery to terminals of pigtail lead with positive battery lead connected to yellow/red wire terminal and negative battery lead connected to light green/red wire terminal. Ohmmeter should show continuity, if not, renew relay.

To check the neutral switch, refer to procedure in IGNITION section.

The diode is molded into the neutral light wire near neutral light. The neutral light must be on for the starter to operate. If the neutral light does not come on when the transmission is in neutral, renew neutral light. If new neutral light does not come on, disconnect wire from light. Disconnect wire marked "N" from the neutral switch located in the right crankcase cover near the right footpeg. Check for continuity between the wire ends at neutral light and neutral switch using an ohmmeter. After connecting the ohmmeter leads to the wire ends, observe ohmmeter reading, then reverse ohmmeter leads and observe the second reading. There should be continuity during one test and no continuity (infinity) during the other test. If not, renew neutral light wire.

To service starter motor, disconnect battery negative lead and remove the fuel pump. Remove starter gear cover, slide gear off starter shaft, unscrew two screws securing starter motor and remove motor. Disconnect starter motor cable. Before disassembling motor, note alignment marks, or make alignment marks, on center housing and end caps so they can be reassembled in original positions. When disassembling motor note location of all shims and washers. Minimum brush length is 5.5 mm (0.22 in.). Note pin on brush holder plate that must align with notch in frame during assembly. Install rear cap so slot engages pin on brush holder plate. Be sure "O" rings are correctly positioned during assembly.

OIL COOLING SYSTEM. An oil temperature sensor monitors oil temperature in the engine sump. Engine oil is routed through a radiator to cool the oil. If oil temperature reaches 110°-130° C (230°-266° F), the fan motor control module activates the electric fan. If oil temperature exceeds 170°-190° C (338°-374° F), the oil temperature warning light is energized.

The fan motor can be checked by disconnecting the blue wire lead and connecting a jumper wire from the positive terminal of the battery to the motor's blue wire terminal.

CAUTION: Exercise caution during this procedure. To prevent sparks at positive terminal, make connection at positive terminal first. Do not allow jumper wire to touch vehicle or engine after connection is made at positive terminal.

If fan motor operates, check fan control module. If fan motor does not operate, check wiring and ground, and if satisfactory, renew fan motor.

To check fan motor control module, disconnect module connectors located on left side of frame near upper end of front shock absorber. Connect a voltmeter to connectors of wires leading toward engine. Connect negative voltmeter lead to green wire during testing and turn ignition switch to "ON". Voltmeter should read battery voltage when positive lead is connected to white wire (ignition switch), black/brown wire (ignition switch) and blue/red wire (oil warning light). If zero voltage is indicated, check circuit. If voltmeter indicates battery voltage, renew fan motor control module.

The oil temperature sensor is located on the right crankcase cover near the right footpeg. To check oil temperature sensor, remove oil temperature sensor (crankcase oil must be drained). Suspend sensor in heated oil so sensor does not touch sides of container and measure resistance at sensor leads. On later models with a single lead, touch remaining ohmmeter lead to body of sensor. Resistance readings should be 9.5k-10k ohms at 25° C (77° F); 950-1050 ohms at 100° C (212° F); 209-231 ohms at 170° C (338° F). Tighten oil temperature sensor to 18 N·m (160 in.-lbs.).

REVERSE SWITCH. A reverse switch triggers a light to indicate when reverse gear is engaged. The reverse switch is located in the right crankcase cover near the right footpeg and marked "R". Note that wire lead to switch is marked "R". To check reverse switch, disconnect the black wire from the switch. Connect an ohmmeter lead to the wire terminal of the switch and connect the remaining ohmmeter lead to vehicle ground. With transmission in reverse the ohmmeter should show continuity. When any other transmission gear is selected the ohmmeter should read infinity. Crankcase oil must be drained before removing reverse switch. Tightening torque for reverse switch is 13 N·m (115 in.-lbs.).

LIGHTS. Headlight rating is 12V 60/50W. A dimmer switch is located in the switch module on the handlebar. Taillight rating is 12V 5W. Rating for neutral, reverse and oil temperature lights is 12V 3W.

WIRING. If wiring requires repair, always install wire that is the same gauge as original wire. Wires should be routed away from areas of extreme heat or sharp edges. Attach or hold wires in their original position using plastic tie straps to prevent short circuits.

FASTENERS

After the first week of operation and after every 30 days of operation thereafter, the vehicle should receive an overall inspection. All screws, nuts and other fasteners should be checked and tightened to proper torque specification shown in CONDENSED SERVICE DATA section or in the appropriate maintenance section.

VALVE SYSTEM

The engine is equipped with two exhaust valves and two intake valves that are actuated via rocker arms by a single overhead camshaft. The camshaft is driven by a roller chain attached to the right end of the crankshaft. Valve clearance should be adjusted after the first week of operation and then after every 30 days of operation. Adjust valve clearance with engine cold.

To adjust valve clearance, remove seat and air cleaner cover. Remove frame brace above intake tube, then remove intake tube and top fender cover. Detach inlet tubes and breather hose from air cleaner box, then remove air cleaner box. Unscrew timing hole plug in left engine side cover and valve adjustment hole covers at front and rear of cylinder head. The "T" mark on the flywheel indicates top dead center when aligned with mark (M—Fig. H13-10) in plug hole. Remove plug in center of cover and rotate the end of the crankshaft (Y) clockwise. Align top dead center mark "T" with mark (M) with piston on compression stroke. To ensure piston is on compression stroke, rotate crankshaft past top dead center and observe intake (rear) rocker arm. If intake rocker arm movement is observed, continue to rotate crankshaft until marks are again aligned.

Clearance between rocker arm adjusting screw and valve stem should be 0.08 mm (0.003 in.) for both valves. Measure clearance with a suitable feeler gauge. Adjust clearance by loosening the adjusting screw locknut and turning the adjusting screw. Be sure to recheck clearance after tightening locknut.

On models equipped with a decompression lever, check adjustment as outlined in following section.

DECOMPRESSION LEVER

Later models are equipped with a decompression lever that, when actuated, reduces starting effort. Actuating the lever holds the exhaust valve open slightly thereby reducing compression pressure.

To adjust the decompression lever, remove timing hole plug in left engine side cover. Rotate crankshaft so piston is on compression stroke and "T" mark on flywheel is aligned with mark (M) in plug hole. Free play at end of decompression lever (L—Fig. H13-11) should be 1-3 mm (0.04-0.12 in.). Loosen locknut (N) and rotate adjuster (A) to obtain desired free play. Retighten locknut and check adjustment.

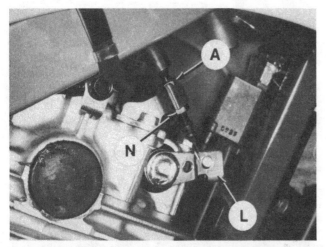

Fig. H13-11—Free play at end of decompression lever (L) should be 1-3 mm (0.04-0.12 in.). Loosen locknut (N) and rotate adjuster (A) to obtain desired free play.

Fig. H13-12—To adjust clutch, loosen locknut (L) and turn adjusting screw (S) counterclockwise until internal resistance is felt, then turn screw 1/4 turn clockwise. Secure adjusting screw with locknut (L) and install cover.

CLUTCH

The engine is equipped with two automatically actuated clutches. A five-shoe centrifugal clutch is mounted on the right end of the crankshaft. The centrifugal clutch is disengaged at idle speed and engages when crankshaft speed increases. A multiple-disc clutch is attached to the transmission mainshaft and is actuated by the gear shift mechanism. When the gear shift lever is operated, the multiple-disc clutch is disengaged to allow smooth transmission gear movement.

The clutch should be adjusted after the first week of operation and after every 30 days of operation. To adjust clutch, remove cover on right side of crankcase. Loosen locknut (L—Fig. H13-12). Turn adjusting screw (S) counterclockwise until internal resistance is felt, then turn screw 1/4 turn clockwise. Secure adjusting screw with locknut (L) and install cover.

The dual-clutch system should automatically disengage at engine idle speed. When selecting gears, clutch should engage and disengage freely without excess slippage. Difficult shifting, clutch grabbing or clutch slipping may indicate overhaul is necessary.

REVERSE LOCK

A reverse lock mechanism prevents accidental engagement of reverse gear. There should be 2-4 mm ($\frac{5}{64}$-$\frac{5}{32}$ in.) free play at gap (G—Fig. H13-13). Adjust free play at lower end of cable by loosening locknut and turning adjusting nut. Retighten locknut.

FRONT BRAKE SYSTEM

The front and rear brake systems are operated independently. The front brake system uses hydraulically actuated, drum-type brakes attached to each steering

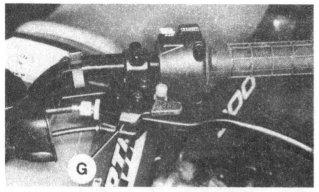

Fig. H13-13—Reverse lock free play should be 2-4 mm (5/64-5/32 in.) at gap (G).

Fig. H13-15—Free play (F) at end of front brake lever should be 25-30 mm (1 13/16 in.).

knuckle. Two brake shoes are contained behind each brake drum. A handlebar-mounted master cylinder with integral fluid reservoir supplies pressure to each wheel cylinder when the right handlebar lever is operated.

Only DOT 3 or DOT 4 rated brake fluid is recommended. Maintain brake fluid level between marks on inner side of brake fluid reservoir. To avert spillage, be sure reservoir is horizontal before removing cover.

INSPECTION. The brake system should be inspected after every 30 days of operation. Correct any occurrences of brake fluid leakage. Renew worn, cracked or damaged brake lines or hoses and determine and correct the cause. Brake shoes should be adjusted to compensate for wear as needed.

To inspect the front brake drum components, support the front of the vehicle so the wheels are off the ground. Remove tire and wheel, unscrew axle nut and remove brake drum. Renew brake drum if inside diameter exceeds 161 mm (6.339 in.). Renew front brake shoes if lining thickness is less than 1.0 mm (0.04 in.). Wheel cylinders should be overhauled or renewed if brake fluid is observed within boots.

If either the brake shoes or wheel cylinders require servicing, then the complete drum brake assembly should be serviced as outlined in R&R AND OVERHAUL section. If brake components are satisfactory, reassemble brake and, if needed, perform adjustment. On later models, apply multipurpose grease between lips of seal attached to drum edge. Tighten axle nut to 80-100 N·m (59-74 ft.-lbs.). Tighten wheel nuts to 65 N·m (48 ft.-lbs.).

ADJUSTMENT. Free play (F—Fig. H13-15) at end of front brake lever should be 25-30 mm (1-1³/₁₆ in.). If free play is excessive, adjust brake shoes using following procedure. Support front of vehicle so wheels are off ground. Remove plug (P—Fig. H13-16) from brake drum. Rotate wheel and locate notched adjuster wheel (there are two adjuster wheels, one for each brake shoe). Using a screwdriver or other tool, rotate adjuster wheel until brake shoe contacts brake drum, then back out adjuster three notches. Repeat procedure at other

Fig. H13-16—Remove plug (P) from brake drum for access to brake adjusters.

brake adjuster. Check brake lever free play. Repeat procedure if needed. Reinstall plug in brake drum. If brake lever free play cannot be adjusted by adjusting brake shoes, there may be air in brake fluid. Perform bleeding procedure as outlined in BLEEDING section.

BLEEDING. The brake hydraulic system must be bled if any hydraulic brake components are disconnected or if the reservoir is drained. With reservoir horizontal, fill reservoir with DOT 3 or 4 brake fluid to full mark on inner side of reservoir. Do not allow reservoir to empty while performing bleeding operation. Reinstall cover to prevent entrance of dirt or foreign material. Attach a suitable hose, such as vacuum hose, to the bleed screw on brake backing plate. Submerge end of hose in a container of brake fluid to prevent air from reentering system. Actuate brake lever several times, then hold brake lever toward handlebar. Open brake bleed screw and allow fluid and air to flow into container. Continue holding brake lever and close bleed screw. Recheck reservoir level and refill if needed. Repeat procedure until air and/or old fluid is ejected from system.

R&R AND OVERHAUL. Support front of vehicle so wheel is off ground and remove wheel.

WARNING: Inhaling asbestos brake dust is injurious to human health. Approved OSHA respiration equipment must be worn when working on or around brake drum and shoes. DO NOT use compressed air to clean brake drum, shoes or nearby components as brake dust will be blown into air. Only vacuum equipment designed to pick up brake dust should be used.

Unscrew axle nut and remove brake drum and wheel hub. While noting location of components, disassemble brake assembly. Detach brake line from wheel cylinder and plug line to reduce fluid loss. The wheel cylinders are marked "L" or "R" to indicate position. Inspect components as outlined in INSPECTION section.

Disassemble and inspect wheel cylinder. Renew complete wheel cylinder if bore is scored, pitted or excessively worn. Maximum allowable bore diameter is 19.12 mm (0.753 in.). Minimum allowable piston diameter is 18.81 mm (0.741 in.). Superficial damage in wheel cylinder bore may be removed using a suitable cylinder hone. After honing, rinse bore with clean brake fluid. Shake out excess fluid but do not wipe dry. Using a shop towel or rag to dry cylinder will leave lint particles in bore. Renew boots and piston cups. During reassembly, lubricate components with clean brake fluid.

Backing plate retaining screws on models after 1987 must be discarded. Tighten backing plate retaining screws to 27-33 N·m (20-24 ft.-lbs.). Apply a suitable sealer to wheel cylinder contact area on backing plate and install wheel cylinder. Note "L" or "R" on wheel cylinder and install on indicated side of backing plate. Attach brake line.

The brake shoe adjuster fits in one end of the wheel cylinder. Clean adjuster and lubricate with silicon grease before installing in housing or wheel cylinder. Screw adjusters completely in to allow installation of new brake shoes. Apply a light coat of silicone grease to three points on backing plate that will contact edge of brake shoe. Install brake springs behind brake shoes with coiled end at same end as wheel cylinder piston. Secure brake shoes with pins and clips. On later models, apply multipurpose grease between lips of seal attached to drum edge. Tighten axle nut to 80-100 N·m (59-74 ft.-lbs.). Tighten wheel nuts to 65 N·m (48 ft.-lbs.).

Adjust and bleed brakes as previously outlined.

MASTER CYLINDER. To remove front brake master cylinder (14—Fig. H13-18), detach brake line from master cylinder. Brake fluid will remove paint; be careful when removing master cylinder. Unscrew two retaining screws and remove master cylinder. Remove brake

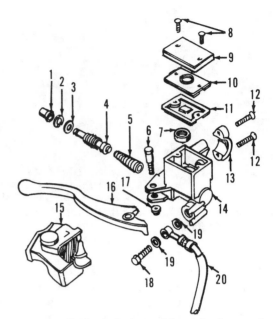

Fig. H13-18—Exploded view of front brake master cylinder.

1. Boot		11. Diaphragm	
2. Snap ring		12. Bolt	
3. Washer		13. Clamp	
4. Piston & cup		14. Body	
5. Spring		15. Rubber boot	
6. Bolt		16. Brake lever	
7. Seal		17. Nut	
8. Screw		18. Union bolt	
9. Cover		19. Seal washer	
10. Diaphragm plate		20. Brake hose	

lever, reservoir cover (9) and diaphragm (11). Remove dust boot (1) and snap ring (2). Disassemble piston assembly while noting location and direction of components. Renew complete master cylinder if bore is scored, pitted or excessively worn. Maximum allowable bore diameter is 12.75 mm (0.502 in.). Minimum allowable piston diameter is 12.64 mm (0.498 in.). Superficial damage in master cylinder bore may be removed using a suitable cylinder hone. After honing, rinse bore with clean brake fluid. Shake out excess fluid but do not wipe dry. Using a shop towel or rag to dry cylinder will leave lint particles in bore. Renew boots and piston cups. During reassembly, lubricate components with clean brake fluid. Reassembly is reverse of disassembly. Install spring (5) so small end contacts piston (4). Bleed brakes as previously outlined.

FRONT AXLE

The steering knuckles are supported by kingpins that ride in bearings located in the axle housing flanges. A ball bearing in each steering knuckle supports the axle shaft. The front drive and axle assembly is located in a swing arm similar to the rear swing arm. The shock absorbers attached to the swing arm limit and cushion vertical movement of the front drive unit. A spring on each shock absorber supports the vehicle.

To remove steering knuckle, support vehicle so wheel is off ground. Remove wheel and wheel hub. Detach tie rod from steering knuckle. Unscrew upper kingpin locknut, then unscrew upper kingpin. Unscrew lower kingpin bolt. Move steering knuckle and brake assembly away from axle shaft. Support knuckle/brake assembly so brake line is not pulled or twisted; do not allow assembly to hang from brake line. Inspect, and if necessary, renew kingpin bearings.

Steering knuckles are not identical. Knuckle is marked with an "L" or "R" to indicate side. Inspect, and if necessary, renew axle bearing in steering knuckle. Remove snap ring and drive out bearing. Pack bearing with grease before installation. Inspect, and if necessary, renew bearing seals.

Reassemble by reversing disassembly procedure while noting the following. Tighten the lower kingpin bolt first. Tighten lower kingpin bolt to 50-70 N·m (37-51 ft.-lbs.), then lock head of bolt in place with tab washer. Tighten upper kingpin bolt to 5-10 N·m (45-88 in.-lbs.), then while holding kingpin bolt, tighten locknut to 50-70 N·m (37-51 ft.-lbs.). There should be at least 2.0 mm (0.08 in.) clearance between axle boot and knuckle. Discard tie rod retaining nut on models after 1987. Tighten tie rod nut to 65-75 N·m (48-55 ft.-lbs.) on models prior to 1988 or to 35-45 N·m (26-33 ft.-lbs.) on models after 1987. Tighten axle nut to 80-100 N·m (59-74 ft.-lbs.). Tighten wheel nuts to 65 N·m (48 ft.-lbs.).

STEERING

INSPECTION. Support the front of the vehicle so the wheels are off the ground. Rotate the handlebar to full left and right and check for excessive looseness, binding and roughness. Be sure cables do not prevent full movement. Clean and grease components if binding or excessive effort is noted. Renew any damaged components.

TOE-IN SETTING. Before checking toe-in setting, inspect front steering assembly and renew or repair any loose or damaged components.

To check toe-in, inflate tires to recommended pressure listed in CONDENSED SERVICE DATA. Position vehicle on a flat, smooth surface and set handlebar straight forward. Use a suitable measuring tool and measure distance (B—Fig. H13-19) at spindle height between the center of the tires on the rear sides. Locate the same tire centerline points on front side of tires and measure front distance (F). The measured distance on the front side (F) should be equal to the measured distance on the rear side (B). Toe-in should be 0 mm (0.00 in.). Note that the distance from a projected vehicle centerline to left (L) and right (R) tire centerlines should also be equal. Loosen locknuts at both ends of tie rods (T) and rotate tie rod shaft to adjust toe-in. Retighten locknuts to 35-45 N·m (26-33 ft.-lbs.).

FRONT AXLE SHAFTS

The front-wheel-drive system is equipped with an axle shaft on each side between the final drive housing and steering knuckle. Each axle shaft is equipped with a ball joint at each end.

To remove axle shaft, first remove steering knuckle as outlined in FRONT AXLE section. Move steering knuckle and brake assembly away from axle shaft. Support knuckle/brake assembly so brake line is not pulled or twisted; do not allow assembly to hang from brake line. Withdraw axle shaft while pulling inner shaft end straight out from drive housing so seal in housing is not distorted.

Move shaft in normal range of motion and check for excessive wear and damage. Axle shaft is available only as a unit assembly. If any components are defective, excluding the boot, then entire shaft assembly must be renewed. The axle boot may be renewed. Boot should be renewed if cracked, torn or otherwise damaged. Boot bands should be renewed if removed. Pack boot with molybdenum disulfide grease before installation.

Reassemble by reversing disassembly procedure.

FRONT SWING ARM AND DRIVE ASSEMBLIES

Service on front swing arm and drive assemblies should be performed by a Honda service technician equipped with the special tools required for overhaul.

SHOCK ABSORBERS

Spring tension is not adjustable on front shock absorbers. Spring tension on rear shock absorbers can be

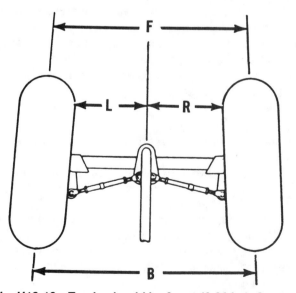

Fig. H13-19—Toe-in should be 0 mm (0.00 in.). See text for measurement procedure.

adjusted by rotating adjusting sleeve. Both ends of the shock absorbers are secured by a bolt through the mounting eye.

When installing front shock absorber tighten lower bolt to 60-80 N·m (44-59 ft.-lbs.). Tighten upper bolt to 60-80 N·m (44-59 ft.-lbs.) on models prior to 1988 or to 35-45 N·m (26-33 ft.-lbs.) on models after 1987. If removed, discard upper shock retaining nuts on models after 1987.

When installing rear shock absorber tighten upper retaining nut on 1986 and 1987 models to 40-50 N·m (29-37 ft.-lbs.) on models prior to 1988 or to 35-45 N·m (26-33 ft.-lbs.) on models after 1987. Tighten lower bolt to 60-80 N·m (44-59 ft.-lbs.) on models prior to 1988 or to 35-45 N·m (26-33 ft.-lbs.) on models after 1987. If removed, discard shock retaining nuts on models after 1987.

REAR BRAKE SYSTEM

The front and rear brake systems are operated independently. The rear brake consists of a two-shoe, internally expanding drum brake mounted on the right end of the rear axle housing. The brake may be actuated by a brake lever attached to the left handlebar or a brake pedal near the right footpeg.

INSPECTION. The brake system should be inspected after every 30 days of operation. Service, repair or renew any components that are inoperable or damaged.

ADJUSTMENT. Actuate the rear brake pedal and measure free travel at end of pedal. Free travel should

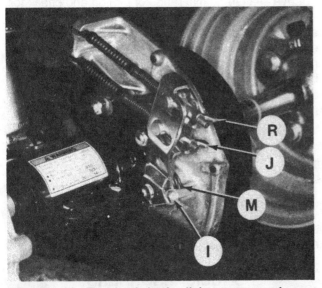

Fig. H13-20—To check brake lining wear, apply rear brake and note position of indicator (I) with mark (M) on backing plate. Brake shoes should be renewed if indicator aligns with or passes mark (M).

Fig. H13-21—Rear brake lever free play, measured at (F), should be 15-20 mm (5/8-3/4 in.). Minor brake lever adjustment can be accomplished by turning cable adjuster (A). Otherwise, rotate lever adjuster (R—Fig. H13-20) at rear brake to adjust lever free travel.

be 15-20 mm (5/8-3/4 in.). Adjust pedal free travel by rotating adjuster (J—Fig. H13-20) at rear brake.

Rear brake lever free play measured at (F—Fig. H13-21) should be 15-20 mm (5/8-3/4 in.). Rotate lever adjuster (R—Fig. H13-20) at rear brake to adjust lever free travel. Minor brake lever adjustment can be accomplished by turning cable adjuster (A—Fig. H13-21) on lever assembly.

A rear brake lining indicator (I—Fig. H13-20) is attached to the brake cam. To externally check brake lining wear, apply rear brake and note position of indicator (I) with mark (M) on backing plate. Brake shoes should be renewed if indicator aligns or passes mark (M).

R&R AND OVERHAUL. To remove rear brake shoes and drum, support rear of vehicle and remove right tire and wheel.

WARNING: Inhaling asbestos brake dust is injurious to human health. Approved OSHA respiration equipment must be worn when working on or around brake drum and shoes. DO NOT use compressed air to clean brake drum, shoes or nearby components as brake dust will be blown into air. Only vacuum equipment designed to pick up brake dust should be used.

Unscrew axle nut and remove wheel hub from axle. Unscrew and remove brake drum cover. Remove brake drum.

Renew the brake shoes if thickness is less than 2.0 mm (0.08 in.). Renew the brake drum if inside diameter exceeds 181 mm (7.1 in.). Inspect "O" rings and seals and renew if deteriorated or damaged. Note that there is an "O" ring located between the brake drum cover and backing plate and a seal around the actuating camshaft. If removed, discard backing plate retaining nuts on models after 1987.

Reassemble by reversing disassembly procedure and noting the following: Tighten backing plate retaining nuts to 50-60 N•m (37-44 ft.-lbs.) on models prior to 1988 or to 35-45 N•m (26-33 ft.-lbs.) on models after 1987. Apply a light coat of grease to brake shoe cam and anchor pin. Do not allow grease on brake shoe linings. Tighten wheel hub retaining nut to 120-160 N•m (88-117 ft.-lbs.). Adjust rear brake as previously outlined.

SWING ARM AND
REAR DRIVE ASSEMBLIES

Service on swing arm and rear drive assemblies should be performed by a Honda service technician equipped with the special tools required for overhaul.

KAWASAKI

KAWASAKI MOTORS CORPORATION, U.S.A.
P.O. Box 25252
9950 Jeronimo Road
Irvine, CA 92799-5252

KLF110

NOTE: Metric fasteners are used throughout vehicle.

CONDENSED SERVICE DATA

MODELS	KLF110-A2, B2
General	
Engine Make	Own
Engine Type.	Air-Cooled/Four-Stroke
Number of Cylinders	1
Bore	51 mm
	(2.0 in.)
Stroke.	50.6 mm
	(1.99 in.)
Displacement	103 cc
	(6.3 cu. in.)
Compression ratio	8.2:1
Engine Lubrication	Wet Sump; Oil Pump
Transmission Lubrication	Same as Engine
Engine/Transmission Oil	See Text
Forward Speeds.	5
Reverse Speeds	None
Tire Size—Front.	20 × 7-8
Tire Size—Rear	21 × 9-8
Tire Pressure (cold)—	
Front	21 kPa
	(3 psi)
Rear.	15 kPa
	(2.2 psi)
Dry Weight:	
KLF110-A2 Models	120 kg
	(264 lbs.)
KLF110-B2 Models	125 kg
	(275 lbs.)
Tune-Up	
Engine Idle Speed	See Text
Spark Plug.	NGK C6HA
Electrode Gap	0.6-0.7 mm
	(0.024-0.027 in.)
Ignition Type.	Capacitor Discharge
Point Gap.	Pointless
Timing	10° BTDC @ Less Than 1500 rpm
	35° BTDC @ Less Than 4000 rpm

Tune-Up (Cont.)

Carburetor:

Make	Keihin
Model	PC18
Float Height	18-22 mm
	(0.709-0.866 in.)
Main Jet	#88
Pilot Jet	#35
Jet Needle	N17B
Clip Position	Third Groove from Top
Throttle Valve Cutaway	3.0
Idle Mixture Setting	1-1½ Turns
Throttle Lever Free Play	2-3 mm
	(0.079-0.118 in.)

Sizes-Clearances

Valve Clearance (cold):

Intake & Exhaust	0.12-0.17 mm
	(0.005-0.006 in.)
Valve Face & Seat Angle	45°

Valve Seat Width:

Intake	0.80-1.15 mm
	(0.032-0.045 in.)
Exhaust	0.85-1.15 mm
	(0.034-0.045 in.)

Valve Stem Diameter:

Intake	5.495-5.510 mm
	(0.2163-0.2169 in.)
Exhaust	5.480-5.495 mm
	(0.2157-0.2163 in.)

Valve Guide Bore Diameter:

Intake & Exhaust	5.520-5.532 mm
	(0.2173-0.2178 in.)

Valve Stem-to-Guide Clearance:

Intake	0.010-0.037 mm
	(0.0004-0.0015 in.)
Exhaust	0.025-0.037 mm
	(0.0010-0.0015 in.)

Rocker Arm Bore Diameter:

Intake & Exhaust	10.000-10.015 mm
	(0.3937-0.3943 in.)

Rocker Shaft Diameter:

Intake & Exhaust	9.980-9.995 mm
	(0.3929-0.3935 in.)

Camshaft Lobe Height:

Intake & Exhaust	28.750-28.858 mm
	(1.1319-1.1361 in.)
Wear Limit	28.65 mm
	(1.128 in.)
Cylinder Head Distortion (Max.)	0.05 mm
	(0.002 in.)
Cylinder Bore Diameter	51.000-51.012 mm
	(2.0079-2.0083 in.)
Wear Limit	51.10 mm
	(2.012 in.)
Piston-to-Cylinder Wall Clearance	0.015-0.039 mm
	(0.0006-0.0015 in.)

Sizes-Clearances (Cont.)

Piston Diameter:
Measured 5 mm (0.2 in.) From
Skirt Bottom and 90° to Pin Bore . . . . 50.973-50.985 mm
(2.0068-2.0073 in.)

Piston Ring End Gap in
Standard Bore:
Top Ring. . . . . 0.15-0.35 mm
(0.006-0.014 in.)

Second Ring . . . . 0.15-0.35 mm
(0.006-0.014

Piston Ring Groove Width:
Top & Second Ring . . . . 1.00-1.02 mm
(0.039-0.040 in.)

Oil Ring . . . . 2.00-2.02 mm
(0.078-0.079 in.)

Piston Ring Width:
Top Ring. . . . . 0.97-0.99 mm
(0.0382-0.0390 in.)

Second Ring . . . . 0.97-0.99 mm
(0.0382-0.390 in.)

Piston Ring Side Clearance:
Top Ring. . . . . 0.01-0.05 mm
(0.0004-0.0020 in.)

Max.. . . . . 0.15 mm
(0.006 in.)

Second Ring . . . . 0.01-0.05 mm
(0.0004-0.0020 in.)

Max.. . . . . 0.15 mm
(0.006 in.)

Connecting Rod Big
End Side Clearance. . . . . 0.3-0.5 mm
(0.012-0.020 in.)

Maximum Allowable. . . . . 0.7 mm
(0.027 in.)

Connecting Rod Big
End Radial Clearance . . . . 0.007-0.022 mm
(0.0003-0.0009 in.)

Maximum Allowable. . . . . 0.7 mm
(0.003 in.)

Crankshaft Runout
(Max.). . . . . 0.1 mm
(0.004 in.)

Capacities

Fuel Tank . . . . 7.6 L
(2.0 gal.)

Engine/Transmission Sump. . . . . 1.1 L
(1.16 qt.)

Tightening Torques

Front Axle Nut . . . . 34 N•m
(25 ft.-lbs.)

Rear Axle Nut. 145 N•m
(110 ft.-lbs.)

Camshaft Sprocket Screws . . . . 12 N•m
(104 in.-lbs.)

Clutch Nut . . . . 62 N•m
(46 ft.-lbs.)

Tightening Torques (Cont.)

Cylinder Head Screws:

6 mm	9.8 N•m (87 in.-lbs.)

8 mm:

Initial	11 N•m (95 in.-lbs.)
Final.	22 N•m (16 ft.-lbs.)
Flywheel Nut	42 N•m (31 ft.-lbs.)
Secondary Drive Gear	72 N•m (53 ft.-lbs.)
Wheel Retaining Nut	41 N•m (30 ft.-lbs.)

Standard Fasteners:

5 mm	3.4-4.9 N•m (30-43 in.-lbs.)
6 mm	5.9-7.8 N•m (52-69 in.-lbs.)
8 mm	14-19 N•m (10-13.5 ft.-lbs.)
10 mm	25-39 N•m (19-25 ft.-lbs.)
12 mm	44-61 N•m (33-45 ft.-lbs.)
14 mm	73-98 N•m (54-72 ft.-lbs.)
16 mm	115-155 N•m (83-115 ft.-lbs.)
18 mm	165-225 N•m (125-165 ft.-lbs.)
20 mm	225-325 N•m (165-240 ft.-lbs.)

LUBRICATION

All Models

ENGINE AND TRANSMISSION. The engine is lubricated by pressurized oil from an oil pump attached to the right side of the crankcase. Oil is contained in a sump that is common to the engine and transmission.

Recommended oil is API grade SF or SG oil with an SAE viscosity rating of 10W-40, 10W-50, 20W-40 or 20W-50. Use an oil with a viscosity rating best suited for the ambient temperature.

An oil level window is located in the rear of the right side cover. The oil level should be between the two marks (M—Fig. K1-1) with the vehicle situated on a level surface. Add oil through the oil fill opening on top of the right side cover.

The manufacturer recommends that the engine/transmission oil be changed after the first 10 hours of use and after every 30 days of use thereafter, or more frequently if usage is severe. The drain plug is located on the underside of the crankcase directly behind the front frame tube. Check the oil level at the oil level window as previously described.

A flat filter screen is located in a compartment in the bottom of the right crankcase half. The filter screen should be removed and cleaned after the first 10 hours of use and after every 90 days of use thereafter, or more frequently if usage is severe. To remove the filter screen, drain the engine oil and detach the oil line from the right side cover. Unscrew the right side cover screws and remove the right side cover shown in Fig. K1-2. Remove the gasket if it remains on the engine. Pull out the filter screen and wash it in a suitable solvent. Insert the clean filter screen into the engine. Also remove the ball bear-

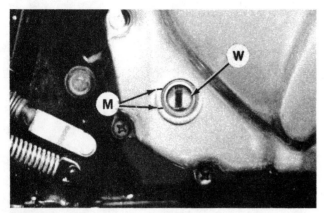

Fig. K1-1—Oil level should be between marks (M) of oil gauge window (W).

Fig. K1-2—View showing location of oil fill plug. The side cover must be removed for access to the filter screen.

ing in the clutch cover and clean the cavity behind the bearing. Reinstall the bearing so the open side is out (toward the side cover). Install a new gasket, then reinstall the right side cover whole, being sure the pin on the clutch arm indexes in the notch of the clutch release mechanism.

DRIVE CHAIN. The drive chain should be lubricated with a suitable chain lubricant or SAE 90 gear oil prior to vehicle operation. The drive chain uses "O" rings as a part of the chain assembly to retain lubricant in the inner components. The chain lubricant must be designed for use on "O" ring-type drive chains or the "O" rings may be damaged.

If the drive chain is dirty, wash the chain in diesel oil or kerosene. Do not use gasoline, cleaning solutions or solvents as the "O" rings may be damaged. Remove, install and adjust the chain as outlined in FINAL DRIVE CHAIN AND SPROCKET section.

CABLES, LEVERS AND SHAFTS. Depending on use and riding conditions, lubricate all cables with cable lubricant or light oil. Lubricate lever pivot pins and cable ends. Remove the brake pedal and apply grease to the shaft. Remove the brake assembly and lubricate the brake cam with multipurpose grease.

AIR CLEANER ELEMENT

All Models

The engine is equipped with a foam-type air cleaner filter located underneath the seat. The air cleaner element should be removed and cleaned after the first 10 hours of use and after every 10 days of use thereafter, or more frequently if usage is severe.

To remove the air cleaner element, remove the seat, remove the air cleaner cover and lift out the element. Carefully remove the foam filter element from its support frame and clean the element in a suitable nonflammable solvent. Squeeze the element dry but to prevent tearing, do not wring or twist it. Inspect the element for tears or other damage which may prevent proper filtration. Saturate the foam with SAE 30 oil or a good quality air cleaner oil, then squeeze out all excess oil. Carefully squeeze out as much oil as possible as too much oil in the filter will affect the fuel:air ratio.

Apply grease to the foam gasket end of the element and install the filter element by reversing the removal procedure.

FUEL SYSTEM

All Models

CARBURETOR. The Keihin PC18 sliding valve-type carburetor shown in Fig. K1-4 is used. Refer to CONDENSED SERVICE DATA for carburetor specifications.

Throttle lever free play should be 2-3 mm (0.079-0.118 in.) as measured at end of lever. To adjust lever free play, loosen locknut and rotate adjuster nut at throttle lever case or slide up the dust boot and turn adjusting nut (1—Fig. K1-4).

Initial setting of the idle mixture screw (12—Fig. K1-5) is 1-1½ turns out from a lightly seated position. Final adjustment should be performed with engine running at normal operating temperature. The idle mixture screw meters air and turning the screw counterclockwise will lean the idle mixture. Adjust the idle speed screw (11) to obtain the lowest smooth idle setting. After adjusting carburetor idle setting, check throttle lever free play as outlined in previous paragraph.

When servicing the carburetor, note the following: Jet needle clip (7—Fig. K1-4) should be located in third groove from top of jet needle (8). Float height (A—Fig. K1-6) should be 18-22 mm (0.709-0.866 in.) as measured from gasket surface of carburetor body to lowest edge of float. Hold carburetor at an angle that will allow the float assembly to close the inlet valve but not compress the spring in the valve. Adjust the float level by bending tang (B) on float arm.

FUEL STRAINERS. Two fuel strainers are located on the pickup tubes of the fuel valve assembly mounted on the fuel tank. To inspect the strainers the fuel in the fuel tank must be drained. Disconnect the fuel hoses from the fuel valve. Unscrew the two screws securing the fuel valve to the fuel tank and carefully remove the fuel valve from the tank. Clean and inspect the strainers. The strainers are not available separately, only as a part of the valve housing. Reinstall the valve assembly while noting that nylon washers are used on the two retaining screws to prevent fuel leakage.

IGNITION AND ELECTRICAL

All Models

IGNITION SYSTEM. The engine is equipped with a capacitor discharge, pointless ignition system. An exciter coil located behind the flywheel provides electrical power for the system. The pickup coil is located outside and just below the flywheel while the CDI unit and ignition coil are mounted underneath the fuel tank.

NOTE: Do not disconnect ignition system connectors while the engine is running as the CDI unit may be damaged.

Ignition timing can be checked after removing the inspection hole plug located adjacent to the starter. Using a suitable power timing light and tachometer, check alignment of timing marks with engine running at various engine speeds. With engine running at idle or less than 1500 rpm, the second flywheel timing mark should align with the index notch (see Fig. K1-7; note that the first timing mark is marked "T" and indicates top dead center). As engine rpm is increased, ignition timing should advance. At approximately 4000 rpm the third timing mark should align with the index mark and ignition timing should advance no farther as engine speed increases. Ignition timing is not adjustable. If ignition timing is incorrect, then the CDI unit is probably faulty.

Some components may be checked using an ohmmeter. Disconnect the connectors for the wires leading from the magneto.

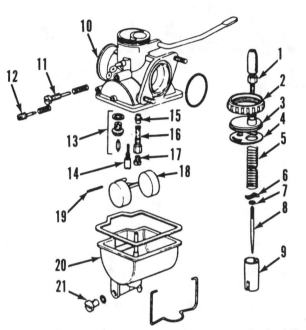

Fig. K1-4—Exploded view of carburetor typical of the type used on all models.

1. Cable adjuster
2. Cap nut
3. Cap
4. Gasket
5. Throttle return spring
6. Retainer
7. Jet needle clip
8. Jet needle
9. Throttle slide
10. Body
11. Idle speed screw
12. Idle mixture screw
13. Fuel inlet valve
14. Slow jet
15. Needle jet
16. Needle jet holder
17. Main jet
18. Float
19. Float pin
20. Fuel bowl
21. Drain plug

Fig. K1-5—View showing location of idle mixture screw (12) and idle speed screw (11).

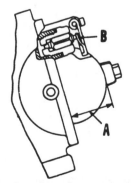

Fig. K1-6—Tilt carburetor when measuring float height (A) so spring in inlet valve is not compressed. Float height should be 18-22 mm (0.709-0.866 in.). Bend float tang (B) for adjustment.

Fig. K1-7—Piston is at TDC (top dead center) when "T" mark on flywheel is aligned with timing notch (N). The second flywheel mark is the ignition timing mark.

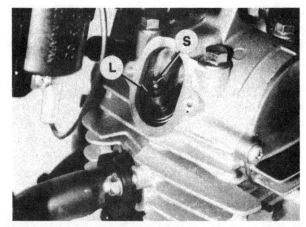

Fig. K1-8—Loosen locknut (L) and rotate adjusting screw (S) to adjust valve clearance. Valve clearance should be 0.12-0.17 mm (0.005-0.006 in.).

To check the exciter coil, connect one ohmmeter lead to the red lead from the magneto and ground the other ohmmeter lead. Exciter coil resistance should be 180-280 ohms. To check the pickup coil resistance, connect one ohmmeter lead to the black lead and the other ohmmeter lead to the black lead with yellow tracer from the magneto. Pickup coil resistance should be 80-150 ohms. Ignition coil primary winding resistance should be 0.14-0.22 ohm, while secondary winding resistance should be 3300-4900 ohms.

If the ignition system does not operate properly after checking all components but the CDI unit, replace the CDI unit with a new or known to be good unit and recheck the system. Be sure all wiring and connectors are good.

ELECTRICAL SYSTEM. On nonelectric start models, a lighting coil is located behind the flywheel to provide power for the lights. The lighting coil should produce at least 10 volts AC with engine running at 3000 rpm. Lighting coil resistance should be 0.56-0.84 ohm on KLT models and 0.9-1.6 ohms on KLF models.

On electric start models, maximum output of alternator is 7.5 amps. 14 volts. Charging coil resistance should be 0.1-0.8 ohm measured between the two yellow charging coil leads.

The headlight is 12 V 35 W unit on KLT models and a 12 V 25 W unit on KLF models while the taillight is a 12 V 8 W unit on all models.

VALVE SYSTEM

All Models

The valves are actuated via rocker arms by a single overhead camshaft. The camshaft is driven by a roller chain which is connected to the left end of the crankshaft.

Valve clearance should be checked after the first 10 hours of use and then after every 90 days of use thereafter. Valve clearance must be checked with the engine cold. To check valve clearance, remove the seat and fuel tank. Remove valve covers for access to valve adjusting screws. Rotate the crankshaft so the piston is on its compression stroke, then stop when the "T" mark on the flywheel is aligned with the index mark viewed through the inspection hole (see Fig. K1-7). To ensure piston is on the compression stroke, watch the rocker arms as the flywheel "T" mark approaches the index mark. If either rocker arm is moving then the piston is not on the compression stroke.

Valve clearance is adjusted by loosening locknut (L—Fig. K1-8) then turning adjusting screw (S) so the proper clearance between the valve stem and adjusting screw is obtained. Valve clearance for both valves should be 0.12-0.17 mm (0.005-0.006 in.). Recheck valve clearance after tightening the locknut.

CLUTCH

All Models

All models are equipped with a multiple-disc clutch that is actuated by the gear shift lever. As the gear shift lever is operated to change gears the clutch is disengaged through linkage connected to the shift shaft.

To adjust the clutch, remove the rubber cap in the right side cover. Loosen locknut (L—Fig. K1-9). Turn screw (S) clockwise until it is easy to turn, then turn the screw counterclockwise until resistance to turning is felt. Hold screw in position and tighten locknut (L). Check clutch adjustment by shifting gears with engine idling. Engine should not die when changing gears.

Fig. K1-9—View showing location of clutch adjusting screw (S). Refer to text for adjustment.

MANUAL STARTER

All Models

R&R AND OVERHAUL. Refer to Fig. K1-11 for a partially disassembled view of manual starter assembly. Manual starter can be removed from the vehicle as a complete unit after removing the three starter retaining screws. If starter rope remains under tension, pull starter rope and hold rope pulley (8—Fig. K1-11) with notch (N) in pulley adjacent to rope outlet. Pull a loop of rope back through outlet so rope engages notch in pulley and allow pulley (8) to slowly unwind.

Remove retaining nut (1) and disassemble unit. Be careful when removing rewind spring located behind

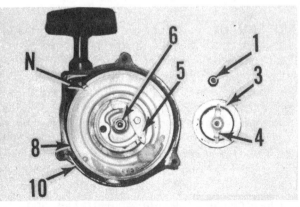

Fig. K1-11—Partially disassembled view of manual starter assembly typical of the type used on KLF models.

N. Notch	5. Starter pawl
1. Nut	6. Friction spring
3. Friction plate	8. Rope pulley
4. Pawl guide	10. Starter housing

pulley (8), a rapidly uncoiling starter spring can cause serious injury.

Rewind spring is wound into rope pulley (8) in a clockwise direction. Starter rope is wound on rope pulley (8) in a clockwise direction as viewed with rope pulley in starter housing. Reassemble starter by reversing disassembly procedure. Lightly grease pulley shaft and starter pawl.

To place tension on rewind spring after assembly, pass starter rope through rope outlet in starter housing and install rope handle. Pull a loop of rope back through outlet between notch (N) in pulley and housing. Rotate rope pulley (8) clockwise two or three complete revolutions, then release starter rope from pulley notch (N) and allow starter rope to wind onto pulley (8). Do not place any more tension on rewind spring than is necessary to draw starter rope handle up against housing.

ELECTRIC STARTER

KLF Models So Equipped

The starter assembly can be removed and disassembled to clean, inspect and lubricate individual parts. To remove electric starter, first disconnect battery. Disconnect wire at terminal on starter. Remove the three mounting screws and withdraw the starter motor. Note the location of all components during disassembly to aid in reassembly. The starter assembly should be renewed if starter brushes are worn to 3.5 mm (0.14 in.) or less.

During installation, make sure "O" ring is positioned around starter neck, then guide starter into position. Remainder of installation is the reverse of removal procedure.

FRONT AXLE

All Models

The left and right front spindle assemblies pivot on the knuckle assembly at the end of each control arm. The control arms are bolted at the ends to the vehicle frame and a shock absorber is used to limit and cushion the up and down movement of the control arm. A grease fitting is located on the side of each knuckle and should be used to grease the knuckle components during each periodic maintenance check.

Remove the front wheel to service the knuckle assembly. Note that removing the brake components will allow greater access to knuckle components. If knuckle bushings are excessively worn or any other damage is noted, then control arm assembly must be renewed. Control arm mounting screws should be tightened to 88 N·m (65 ft.-lbs.). Shock absorber retaining nuts should be tightened to 34 N·m (25 ft.-lbs.). Spindle assembly to control arm knuckle retaining nut should be tightened to 34 N·m (25 ft.-lbs.).

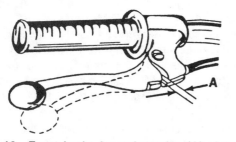

Fig. K1-13—Front brake lever free play (A) should be 3-4 mm (0.12-0.16 in.). Gap, measured at (A) when brake lever is applied, should be 10-12 mm (0.39-0.47 in.) on KLF models. Refer to text.

FRONT BRAKE

All Models

BRAKE LEVER FREE PLAY. Brake lever free play is adjusted by loosing brake cable locknut and rotating cable adjuster. Note that actuating lever at each front brake should be 3-4 mm (0.12-0.16 in.) free play. Rotate wing nut on cable end at each actuating lever until 3-4 mm (0.12-0.16 in.) free play is obtained. Then rotate brake cable adjuster until free play, measured at gap (A—Fig. K1-13), is 10-12 mm (0.39-0.47 in.) with front brake lever applied. Tighten brake cable locknut to retain adjustment.

OVERHAUL. External determination of lining thickness is possible by actuating brake and noting position of pointer attached to actuating lever at each front brake. There is sufficient brake lining if pointer falls in "USABLE RANGE" on brake backing plate.

WARNING: Inhaling asbestos brake dust is injurious to human health. Approved OSHA respiration equipment must be worn when working on or around brake components. DO NOT use compressed air to clean brake drums, shoes or nearby components as brake dust will be blown into air. Only vacuum equipment designed to pick up brake dust should be used.

Each front brake assembly is accessible after removing the respective brake drum. Renew the brake shoes if they are damaged or if the lining thickness is less than 1.6 mm (0.063 in.). Renew the brake drum assembly if the inside diameter is more than 110.70 mm (4.36 in.).

STEERING

All Models

TOE-IN SETTING. Raise the front wheels off the ground. Place the steering handlebars in a straight ahead position. Use a suitable measuring tool and

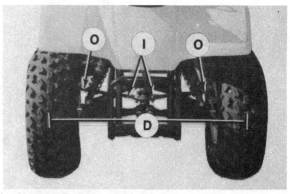

Fig. K1-16—Refer to text for toe-in setting procedures on KLF models. Inside (I) tie rod locknuts are right-hand threaded and outside (O) tie rod locknuts are left-hand threaded.

measure distance (D—Fig. K1-16), at spindle height, between the center of the tires on the front and rear sides. The measured distance (D) on the front side should be 15 mm (0.59 in.) shorter than the measured distance on the rear side. If not, loosen the inside (I) and outside (O) locknuts on the left and right tie rod assemblies and rotate the tie rod sleeves equally until a difference of 15 mm (0.59 in.) is noted.

NOTE: The outside (O) locknuts are left-hand threaded.

After obtaining the correct setting, securely tighten the locknuts to retain tie rod settings.

INSPECTION. Rotate the steering handlebars from one extreme to the other and note if any binding or roughness is felt. Periodically inspect the steering components for looseness or any other damage. Renew any damaged component. Clean and grease components if binding or excessive effort is noted.

OVERHAUL. To expose the steering tube, the front fender assembly must be removed. Remove the Allen head bolts and nuts securing the upper tube clamp and withdraw the clamp halves. Clean the old grease from the steering tube and bearing portions of the clamp halves. Inspect the clamp halves and the upper and lower grease seals for damage. Renew components if needed. Position the grease seals so slits are aligned and facing toward front. Grease components and install clamp halves. Tighten the retaining clamp Allen head bolts and nuts to 25 N·m (18 ft.-lbs.).

The tie rod assemblies, front brake cables, upper tube clamp and handlebar assembly must be removed to withdraw the steering tube from the vehicle. Remove the lower bearing housing mounting screws to withdraw the steering tube. Inspect the lower bearing assembly and renew if needed. Install the lower bearing assembly with the brass side facing down. Tighten the lower bearing assembly retaining nut to 29 N·m (22 ft.-lbs.). Tighten the tie rod assembly mounting nuts to 41 N·m (30 ft.-lbs.). When installing the handlebar assembly to the steering tube, the handlebar should be positioned so the handlebar and steering tube are set at the same angle. Tighten the rear handlebar mounting clamp screws first, then tighten the front screws. If properly tightened, there should be no gap at the rear of the clamp and an even gap at the front.

REAR BRAKE

All Models

ADJUSTMENT. The rear brake may be actuated either by a foot pedal or handlebar lever. Brake pedal free play should be 20-30 mm (0.787-1.181 in.) measured at the pedal pad. Adjust pedal free play by turning adjusting nut (P—Fig. K1-20). Brake lever free play measured at gap (G—Fig. K1-21) should be 4-5 mm (0.16-0.20 in.). Brake lever free play can be adjusted by rotating adjuster nut on brake cable at handlebar brake lever if beyond handlebar brake lever adjustment.

OVERHAUL. Brake lining thickness can be determined externally by actuating brake and noting position of pointer attached to actuating lever. There is sufficient brake lining if pointer falls in "USABLE RANGE" on brake backing plate.

On all models, use the following procedure for access to the rear brake assembly. Remove the cotter pin and axle nut at the right end of the rear axle. Remove the right rear wheel and hub. If so equipped, remove the cover surrounding the brake drum. Prevent axle rotation by applying the rear brake, then unscrew the two nuts holding the brake drum in place. Slide the brake drum off the axle.

Fig. K1-20—View showing location of rear brake adjusters for brake pedal (P) and handlebar lever (B).

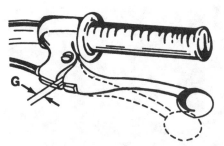

Fig. K1-21—Brake lever free play (G) should be 4-5 mm (0.16-0.20 in.).

WARNING: Inhaling asbestos brake dust is injurious to human health. Approved OSHA respiration equipment must be worn when working on or around brake components. DO NOT use compressed air to clean brake drums, shoes or nearby components as brake dust will be blown into air. Only vacuum equipment designed to pick up brake dust should be used.

Inspect brake components. Inspect the splines on the axle and brake drum. Minimum brake shoe lining thickness is 2 mm (0.079 in.). Maximum allowable inside diameter for the brake drum is 130.75 mm (5.147 in.).

Reassemble brake and axle components by reversing removal procedure. Tighten the two nuts securing the brake drum to 145 N·m (110 ft.-lbs.). Apply grease to axle splines. Tighten axle nut to 145 N·m (110 ft.-lbs.).

DRIVE CHAIN AND SPROCKETS

All Models

CHAIN ADJUSTMENT. Remove the inspection plug in the left side of the chain case. Rotate the rear wheels manually until chain tension is greatest. Measure chain free play. Chain free play should be 10-25 mm (0.39-0.98 in.).

To adjust chain free play, loosen chain adjusting nut (N—Fig. K1-24). Loosen rear axle housing retaining screws (S). Tighten adjusting nut (N) to reduce chain free play or loosen nut to increase chain free play. Note that if chain is excessively worn, adjustment may not be possible. Retighten axle housing screws to 54 N·m (40 ft.-lbs.). Recheck chain free play after all fasteners are tightened.

R&R AND OVERHAUL. To remove the drive chain, proceed as follows: Remove the seat, rear fenders, air filter and air filter box. Remove the chain cover attached to the left side of the engine. Detach the axle dust cover from the chain case then remove the upper chain case half. Remove the protection plate from underneath the rear of the vehicle. Remove the lower chain case half. Remove the left rear wheel. Remove the snap ring

Fig. K1-24—Loosen rear housing retaining screws (S) and rotate adjusting nut (N) to adjust chain tension.

retaining the engine sprocket then remove the sprocket. Remove the chain from the axle sprocket.

Inspect the drive chain and renew the chain if damaged or excessively worn. The distance between 21 chain pins should not exceed 260 mm (10.236 in.). The manufacturer recommends that only an endless-type drive chain be used.

Install engine sprocket so side stamped with tooth number is out. If removed, install a new "O" ring on output shaft and install spacer with beveled end toward engine.

The axle sprocket may be removed after removing the wheel hub on the end of the axle. New lockwashers should be used when assembling and installing sprocket. Tighten sprocket retaining nuts to 34 N·m (25 ft.-lbs.). Apply grease to axle splines. Tighten axle nut to 145 N·m (110 ft.-lbs.).

Reverse removal procedure to install drive chain. Adjust chain free play as outlined in previous section.

REAR AXLE, BEARINGS AND HOUSING

All Models

R&R AND OVERHAUL. To remove the rear axle assembly, support the rear of the vehicle so both wheels are off the ground. Remove the drive chain and axle sprocket as previously outlined. Remove the rear brake assembly as previously outlined. Disconnect the rear brake cables from the actuating lever. Remove the four screws securing the axle housing to the frame and remove the axle housing assembly. Withdraw the axle from the housing. Remove the brake shoes if still attached to housing. Using a suitable tool, drive bearings and spacer out of housing.

Inspect components and renew any which are damaged or excessively worn. Reverse disassembly procedure to install components.

KAWASAKI

KLF185 AND KLF220

NOTE: Metric fasteners are used throughout vehicle.

CONDENSED SERVICE DATA

MODELS	KLF185-A4	KLF220-A1, A2, A3, A4
General		
Engine Make	Own	Own
Engine Type.	Air-Cooled; Four-Stroke	Air-Cooled; Four-Stroke
Number of Cylinders	1	1
Bore.	66 mm (2.6 in.)	67 mm (2.64 in.)
Stroke	53.2 mm (2.1 in.)	61 mm (2.4 in.)
Displacement.	182 cc (11.1 cu. in.)	215 cc (13.1 cu. in.)
Compression Ratio	9.5:1	9.3:1
Engine Lubrication.	Wet Sump; Oil Pump	Wet Sump; Oil Pump
Transmission Lubrication.	Common With Engine	Common With Engine
Engine/Transmission Oil	See Text	See Text
Forward Speeds	5	5
Reverse Speeds	1	1
Tire Size:		
Front	21 × 9-8	21 × 8-9
Rear.	22 × 11-8	22 × 10-10
Tire Pressure (cold):		
Front	21 kPa (3 psi)	21 kPa (3 psi)
Rear.	14 kPa (2 psi)	21 kPa (3 psi)
Dry Weight.	163 kg (357 lbs.)	183 kg (403 lbs.)
Tune-Up		
Engine Idle Speed.	See Text	See Text
Spark Plug:		
Type.	NGKD8EA	NGKD8EA
Electrode Gap	0.6-0.7 mm (0.024-0.027 in.)	0.6-0.7 mm (0.024-0.027 in.)
Ignition:		
Type.	Capacitor Discharge Pointless	Capacitor Discharge Pointless
Point Gap.		
Timing	10° BTDC @ 1350 rpm 30° BTDC @ 4600 rpm	10° BTDC @ 1300 rpm 35° BTDC @ 4600 rpm
Carburetor:		
Make	Mikuni	Mikuni

MODELS	KLF185-A4	KLF220-A1, A2, A3, A4
Tune-Up (Cont.)		
Carburetor: (Cont.)		
Model	VM22SS	VM24SS
Float Height	28.1 mm	21.8 mm
	(1.11 in.)	(0.86 in.)
Main Jet	#100	#115
Pilot Jet	#22.5	#30
Jet Needle	5J14	5GN46
Clip Position.	Third Groove From Top	Second Groove From Top
Idle Mixture Setting	1 Turn	1½ Turns
Throttle Lever Free Play	2-3 mm	2-3 mm
	(0.079-0.118 in.)	(0.079-0.118 in.)
Sizes-Clearances		
Valve Clearance (cold):		
Intake.	0.12-0.17 mm	0.15-0.20 mm
	(0.005-0.006 in.)	(0.006-0.008 in.)
Exhaust	0.18-0.23 mm	0.18-0.23 mm
	(0.007-0.009 in.)	(0.007-0.009 in.)
Valve Face & Seat Angle.	45°	45°
Valve Seat Width:		
Intake.	0.5-1.0 mm	0.5-1.0 mm
	(0.020-0.039 in.)	(0.020-0.039 in.)
Exhaust	0.5-1.0 mm	0.5-1.0 mm
	(0.020-0.039 in.)	(0.020-0.039 in.)
Valve Stem Diameter:		
Intake.	5.495-5.510 mm	5.495-5.510 mm
	(0.2163-0.2169 in.)	(0.2163-0.2169 in.)
Exhaust	5.480-5.495 mm	5.480-5.495 mm
	(0.2157-0.2163 in.)	(0.2157-0.2163 in.)
Valve Guide Bore Diameter:		
Intake & Exhaust	5.520-5.532 mm	5.520-5.532 mm
	(0.2173-0.2178 in.)	(0.2173-0.2178 in.)
Valve Stem-to-Guide Clearance:		
Intake.	0.010-0.037 mm	0.010-0.037 mm
	(0.0004-0.0015 in.)	(0.0004-0.0015 in.)
Exhaust	0.025-0.037 mm	0.025-0.037 mm
	(0.0010-0.0015 in.)	(0.0010-0.0015 in.)
Rocker Arm Bore Diameter:		
Intake & Exhaust	13.000-13.018 mm	10.000-10.015 mm
	(0.5118-0.5125 in.)	(0.3937-0.3942 in.)
Rocker Shaft Diameter:		
Intake & Exhaust	12.967-12.994 mm	9.970-9.995 mm
	(0.5108-0.5116 in.)	(0.3925-0.3935 in.)
Camshaft Lobe Height:		
Intake.	40.281-40.389 mm	40.395-40.503 mm
	(1.5859-1.5901 in.)	(1.5904-1.5946 in.)
Exhaust	40.001-40.109 mm	39.720-39.828 mm
	(1.5748-1.5791 in.)	(1.5638-1.5680 in.)
Wear Limit:		
Intake.	40.18 mm	40.30 mm
	(1.5819 in.)	(1.5866 in.)
Exhaust	39.90 mm	39.62 mm
	(1.5709 in.)	(1.5598 in.)

MODELS	KLF185-A4	KLF220-A1, A2, A3, A4
Sizes-Clearances (Cont.)		
Cylinder Head Distortion (Max.).....................	0.05 mm (0.002 in.)	0.05 mm (0.002 in.)
Cylinder Bore Diameter................	66.000-66.012 mm (2.5984-2.5989 in.)	67.000-67.012 mm (2.6378-2.6383 in.)
Wear Limit	66.10 mm (2.6024 in.)	67.10 mm (2.6417 in.)
Piston-to-Cylinder Wall Clearance........	0.025-0.052 mm (0.0010-0.0020 in.)	0.025-0.052 mm (0.0010-0.0020 in.)
Piston Diameter: Measured 5 mm (0.2 in.) from Skirt Bottom & 90° to Pin Bore.........	65.960-65.975 mm (2.5968-2.5974 in.)	66.960-66.975 mm (2.6362-2.6368 in.)
Piston Ring End Gap in Standard Bore:		
Top Ring.......................	0.15-0.30 mm (0.006-0.012 in.)	0.15-0.35 mm (0.006-0.014 in.)
Second Ring	0.15-0.35 mm (0.006-0.014 in.)	0.30-0.45 mm (0.012-0.018 in.)
Piston Ring Groove Width:		
Top Ring........................	1.01-1.03 mm (0.039-0.040 in.)	0.81-0.83 mm (0.032-0.033 in.)
Second Ring	1.21-1.23 mm (0.047-0.048 in.)	1.21-1.23 mm (0.047-0.048 in.)
Oil Ring	2.51-2.53 mm (0.099-0.100 in.)	2.51-2.53 mm (0.099-0.100 in.)
Piston Ring Width:		
Top Ring........................	0.965-0.995 mm (0.038-0.039 in.)	0.77-0.79 mm (0.030-0.031 in.)
Second Ring	1.17-1.19 mm (0.046-0.047 in.)	1.17-1.19 mm (0.046-0.047 in.)
Piston Ring Side Clearance:		
Top Ring........................	0.015-0.065 mm (0.0006-0.0025 in.)	0.02-0.06mm (0.0008-0.0023 in.)
Max.........................	0.16 mm (0.006 in.)	0.16 mm (0.006 in.)
Second Ring	0.02-0.06 mm (0.0008-0.0023 in.)	0.02-0.06 mm (0.0008-0.0023 in.)
Max.........................	0.16 mm (0.006 in.)	0.16 mm (0.006 in.)
Connecting Rod Big End Side Clearance	0.4-0.5 mm (0.015-0.019 in.)	0.4-0.5 mm (0.015-0.019 in.)
Maximum Allowable................	0.7 mm (0.030 in.)	0.7 mm (0.030 in.)
Connecting Rod Big End Radial Clearance..................	0.008-0.019 mm (0.0003-0.00075 in.)	0.008-0.020 mm (0.0003-0.0008 in.)
Maximum Allowable..............	0.07 mm (0.003 in.)	0.07 mm (0.003 in.)
Crankshaft Runout (Max.)	0.1 mm (0.004 in.)	0.1 mm (0.004 in.)
Capacities		
Fuel Tank......................	9.0 L (2.3 gal.)	10.0 L (2.6 gal.)

MODELS	KLF185-A4	KLF220-A1, A2, A3, A4
Capacities (Cont.)		
Engine/Transmission Sump.	1.7 L (1.79 qt.)	2.0 L (2.1 qt.)
Differential Case	0.2 L (0.21 qt.)	0.2 L (0.21 qt.)
Tightening Torques		
Axle Nut or Screw:		
Front	34 N•m (25 ft.-lbs.)	34 N•m (25 ft.-lbs.)
Rear.	145 N•m (110 ft.-lbs.)	145 N•m (110 ft.-lbs.)
Camshaft Sprocket Screw.	29 N•m (22 ft.-lbs.)	34 N•m (25 ft.-lbs.)
Clutch Nut	78 N•m (58 ft.-lbs.)	78 N•m (58 ft.-lbs.)
Cylinder Head Screws:		
6 mm	9.8 N•m (87 in.-lbs.)	9.8 N•m (87 in.-lbs.)
8 mm:		
Initial.	11 N•m (95 in.-lbs.)	13 N•m (115 in.-lbs.)
Final	25 N•m (18 ft.-lbs.)	34 N•m (25 ft.-lbs.)
Wheel Retaining Nut	41 N•m (30 ft.-lbs.)	34 N•m (25 ft.-lbs.)
Standard Fasteners:		
5 mm	3.4-4-9 N•m (30-43 in.-lbs.)	
6 mm	5.9-7.8 N•m (52-69 in.-lbs.)	
8 mm	14-19 N•m (10-13.5 ft.-lbs.)	
10 mm	25-39 N•m (19-25 ft.-lbs.)	
12 mm	44-61 N•m (33-45 ft.-lbs.)	
14 mm	73-98 N•m (54-72 ft.-lbs.)	
16 mm	115-155 N•m (83-115 ft.-lbs.)	
18 mm	165-225 N•m (125-165 ft.-lbs.)	
20 mm	225-325 N•m (165-240 ft.-lbs.)	

LUBRICATION

ENGINE AND TRANSMISSION. The engine is lubricated by pressurized oil from an oil pump attached to the right side of the crankcase. Oil is contained in a sump that is common to the engine and transmission.

Recommended oil is API grade SF or SG oil with an SAE viscosity rating of 10W-40, 10W-50, 20W-40 or 20W-50. Use an oil with a viscosity rating best suited for the ambient temperature.

An oil level window (W—Fig. K4-1) is located in the rear of the right side cover. The oil level should be

Fig. K4-1—Engine/transmission sump is filled through fill plug (F) opening. Oil level should be maintained between the two marks (M) next to level window (W).

between the two marks (M) with the vehicle situated on a level surface. Add oil through fill plug (F) opening on top of the right side cover.

The manufacturer recommends that the engine/transmission oil be changed after the first 10 hours of use and after every 30 days of use thereafter, or more frequently if usage is severe. The drain plug is located on the underside of the right crankcase half. An oil filter assembly is located to the left of the drain plug in the left crankcase half. Check the oil level at the oil level window as previously described.

The oil filter plug should be removed and the filter screen cleaned after the first 10 hours of use and after every 90 days of use thereafter, or more frequently if usage is severe. Wash filter screen in a suitable solvent having a high flash-point. Renew oil filter assembly if any damage is noted.

DIFFERENTIAL UNIT. The differential oil should be changed after the first 10 hours of operation and annually thereafter. Check oil level periodically and renew

Fig. K4-3—View identifying differential case oil level plug (C) and fill plug (P). Drain plug is located at base of differential case.

more frequently if vehicle is operated under adverse conditions. Recommended differential lubricant is API GL-5 hypoid gear oil or a good quality SAE 90 hypoid gear oil when the ambient temperature is above 5° C (41° F) or SAE 80 hypoid gear oil when the ambient temperature is 5° C (41° F) or below. Differential case capacity is 0.2 L (0.21 qt.).

Differential case is checked at plug (C—Fig. K4-3) and filled through oil plug (P) opening. Oil is drained through plug at the base of the differential case. Oil should be maintained at level of oil plug (C) opening when vehicle is positioned on a flat level surface. When renewing oil, first operate vehicle to allow differential case oil to pick up any contaminates within the case and to allow oil to warm-up for easier drainage. Then remove drain plug at base of differential case and fill plug (P) and allow oil to drain into a suitable container.

CABLES, LEVERS AND LINKAGE. All cables, levers and linkage should be inspected and lubricated after every 30 days of operation.

AIR CLEANER ELEMENT

All models are equipped with a foam-type air cleaner element located underneath the seat. The air cleaner element should be removed and cleaned after the first 10 hours of use and after every 10 days of use thereafter, or more frequently if usage is severe.

To remove air cleaner element, first remove the seat. Then remove air cleaner cover and lift out the element. Carefully remove the foam filter element from its support frame and clean the element in a suitable nonflammable solvent. Squeeze the element dry, but to prevent tearing, do not wring or twist the element. Inspect the element for tears or other damage that may prevent proper filtration. Saturate the foam with SAE 30 oil or a good-quality air cleaner oil, then squeeze out excess oil. Squeeze out as much oil as possible because too much oil in the filter will affect the fuel:air ratio.

Apply grease to the foam gasket end of the element and install the filter element by reversing the removal procedure.

FUEL SYSTEM

CARBURETOR. A Mikuni sliding valve-type carburetor (Fig. K4-5) is used. Refer to CONDENSED SERVICE DATA for carburetor specifications.

Throttle lever free play should be 2-3 mm (0.079-0.118 in.) as measured at end of lever. Two methods can be used to adjust throttle lever free play. Either slide dust boot at throttle lever down throttle cable or slide dust boot at carburetor cap up throttle cable to expose locknut and adjuster nut. Loosen locknut and rotate adjuster nut until correct throttle lever free play is obtained, then tighten locknut and reinstall dust boot.

Initial setting of idle mixture screw (10—Fig. K4-5) is 1 turn out from a lightly seated position on KLF185 models and 1½ turns out on KLF220 models. Final adjustment should be performed with engine running at normal operating temperature. Adjust idle speed screw (9) to obtain the lowest smooth idle setting. After adjust-ing carburetor idle setting, check throttle lever free play as outlined in previous paragraph.

When servicing the carburetor, note the following: Jet needle clip (5) should be located in third groove from top of jet needle (6) on KLF185 models or second groove from top on KLF220 models. Float height (A—Fig. K4-6) should be 28.1 mm (1.11 in.) on KLF185 models and 21.8 mm (0.86 in.) on KLF220 models. Measure from gasket surface of carburetor body to lowest edge of float. Adjust float level by bending tang (B) on float arm.

The fuel level is checked with the carburetor installed and vehicle operational. To check fuel level, attach a suitable clear hose (H—Fig. K4-7) to fuel overflow fitting (F). Hose should be sufficient length to extend above the bottom edge of carburetor body without kinking the hose. Open the float bowl drain screw (19) approximately two turns. Run the engine at idle speed until fuel level in hose stabilizes, then stop engine. Measure the distance from the bottom edge of carburetor body (float bowl contact surface) to fuel level in hose to determine fuel level as shown at (L). Fuel level check will not be accurate if hose is raised or lowered after fuel level has stabilized. Fuel level (L) should be 5 mm (0.2 in.). To adjust fuel level, the float bowl must be removed. Carefully bend float arm tang (B—Fig. K4-6).

FUEL STRAINER. On KLF185 models, an inline fuel filter located between the fuel tank and fuel pump is used. On KLF220 models, a strainer is mounted on the end of the "ON" pickup tube and the "RES" (reserve) pickup tube of the fuel valve assembly mounted on the fuel tank. A strainer is also located behind the fuel valve control lever. To inspect the strainers, the fuel in the fuel

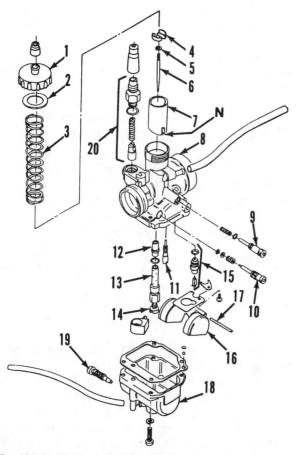

Fig. K4-5—Exploded view of Mikuni VM22SS carbure-tor. VM24SS carburetor is similar. However, idle mixture screw (10) is located on underside of carburetor.

N. Notch
1. Cap
2. Gasket
3. Spring
4. Retainer
5. Jet needle clip
6. Jet needle
7. Throttle slide
8. Body
9. Idle speed screw
10. Idle mixture screw
11. Pilot jet
12. Needle jet
13. Jet holder
14. Main jet
15. Inlet valve
16. Float
17. Pin
18. Float bowl
19. Drain screw
20. Starter valve assy.

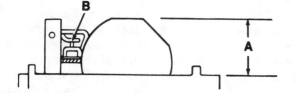

Fig. K4-6—Float height is measured at (A). Gently bend float arm tang (B) to adjust.

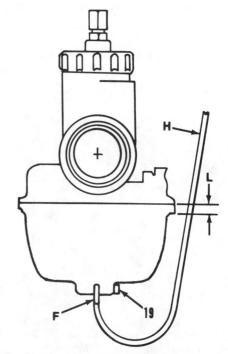

Fig. K4-7—The fuel level (L) is measured from the bot-tom edge of carburetor body. Refer to text.

tank must be drained. Disconnect the fuel hose from the fuel valve. Unscrew the two screws securing the fuel valve to the fuel tank and carefully remove the fuel valve from the tank. Clean and inspect the strainers. The strainers are not available separately, only as a part of the valve housing. Reinstall the valve assembly while noting that nylon washers are used on the two retaining screws to prevent fuel leakage.

FUEL PUMP. The KLF185 model is equipped with a diaphragm-type fuel pump located below the air cleaner assembly and adjacent to the front of the differential drive shaft. Fuel pump is electrically operated.

The fuel pump should produce 7-15 kPa (1.0-2.1 psi) of pressure when checked at the carburetor inlet. After the fuel pump is turned off, the pressure should stay within the specified range for at least one minute.

If fuel delivery to carburetor is interrupted, first eliminate other sources of difficulty such as insufficient fuel, clogged fuel filter, no electrical supply to fuel pump or damaged fuel hoses before renewing fuel pump. The fuel pump must be renewed as a complete unit. No service parts are available.

IGNITION AND ELECTRICAL

SPARK PLUG. Standard spark plug is NGK D8EA. Spark plug electrode gap should be 0.6-0.7 mm (0.024-0.027 in.). Spark plug should be removed, cleaned and electrode gap set after the first 10 hours of operation and every 90 days of operation thereafter. Renew spark plug if damage and excessive electrode wear is evident.

IGNITION. A breakerless Capacitor Discharge Ignition (CDI) system is used. The electronic ignition circuit consists of the CDI module, pickup coil, exciter coil, flywheel, ignition coil, spark plug, engine stop switch and ignition switch. Ignition timing at idle speed should occur when "F" mark (F—Fig. K4-10) on flywheel is aligned with pointer (P) as viewed through timing plug opening. Specified ignition timing is 10° BTDC ("F"

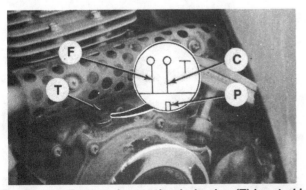

Fig. K4-10—Remove inspection hole plug (T) located in left side cover to check ignition timing. At idle speed, "F" mark (F) on flywheel should align with pointer (P) for correct ignition timing. Top Dead Center mark "T" is identified at (C).

mark) at 1300 rpm on all models, 30° BTDC (maximum advance) at 4600 rpm on KLF185 models and 35° BTDC (maximum advance) at 4600 rpm on KLF220 models. Ignition timing is checked with a power timing light and is not adjustable. If ignition timing is not as specified, check condition of CDI module and pickup coil as described in the following test procedures.

If ignition malfunction occurs, check condition of spark plug, all wires and connections before troubleshooting ignition circuit. Using Kawasaki tester 57001-983 or a suitable ohmmeter, refer to following test specifications and procedures to aid troubleshooting.

Disconnect the connectors for the wires leading from the magneto. To check the exciter coil, connect one ohmmeter lead to the red lead and the other ohmmeter lead to the black/red lead from the magneto. Exciter coil resistance should be 100-190 ohms.

NOTE: The exciter coil and charging coil are both contained within the magneto stator. If one coil tests defective, then the complete magneto stator assembly must be renewed.

To check the pickup coil resistance, connect one ohmmeter lead to the black lead and the other ohmmeter lead to the blue lead from the magneto. Pickup coil resistance should be 90-160 ohms on KLF185 models and 85-130 ohms on KLF220 models. Pickup coil air gap should be 0.45-0.95 mm (0.018-0.038 in.). Ignition coil primary winding resistance should be 0.18-0.28 ohm on KLF185 models and 0.09-0.13 ohms on KLF220 models. Secondary winding resistance should be 3200-4800 ohms on KLF185 models and 3800-5800 ohms in KLF220 models.

If the ignition system does not operate properly after checking all components except the CDI unit, replace the CDI unit with a new or known good unit and recheck the system. Be sure all wiring and connectors are good.

CHARGING CIRCUIT. The charging circuit consists of an alternator charge coil, a regulator/rectifier, battery and ignition switch. Standard battery has a 12 ampere hour, 12 volt rating.

The battery should be checked and filled to maximum level with distilled water, if required, after the first 10 hours of operation and then after every 30 days of operation. During periods of vehicle storage, the battery should be charged once a month to reduce sulfation and prolong battery life. The battery should always be removed from the vehicle prior to charging. Do not exceed maximum charging rate of 1.1 amperes.

The alternator charge coil can be statically tested using a suitable ohmmeter. There are two yellow wires from alternator charge coil to regulator/rectifier. Separate wires from alternator to regulator/rectifier at connector block and measure resistance between the wires. Resistance reading should be 0.2-0.8 ohm. Check for continuity between each of the alternator wires and ground. Tester should read infinite resistance at each wire.

NOTE: The exciter coil and alternator charging coil are both contained within the magneto stator. If one coil tests defective, then the complete magneto stator assembly must be renewed.

Test procedures for checking condition of regulator/rectifier are not reliable as unit may test satisfactory but still be defective. The recommended procedure is to test all associated charging circuit components and eliminate them as the source of defect prior to renewing regulator/rectifier or install a known good regulator/rectifier assembly and check charging circuit for proper operation. Regulator/rectifier output voltage should not be higher than 15 volts.

ELECTRICAL SYSTEM. The headlight on Model KLF185 is a 12 V 45 W unit. Model KLF220 is equipped with a 12 V-25/25W headlight. The taillight is a 12 V 8 W unit on all models.

FASTENERS

The vehicle should receive an overall inspection after the first 10 hours of operation and every 10 days of operation thereafter. All cap screws, nuts and fasteners should be checked and tightened to proper torque specification listed in CONDENSED SERVICE DATA section or in the appropriate MAINTENANCE section.

VALVE SYSTEM

The valves are actuated via rocker arms by a single overhead camshaft. The camshaft is driven by a roller chain connected to the left end of the crankshaft.

Valve clearance should be checked after the first 10 hours of use and then after every 90 days of use thereafter. Valve clearance must be checked with the engine cold. To check valve clearance, remove the seat

and front fender assembly. Remove valve covers for access to valve adjusting screws. Rotate the crankshaft so the piston is on compression stroke, then stop when the "T" mark (C—Fig. K4-10) on the flywheel is aligned with pointer (P) when viewed through inspection plug (T) hole. To ensure piston is on the compression stroke, watch the rocker arms as the flywheel "T" mark approaches pointer (P). If either rocker arm is moving, then the piston is not on the compression stroke.

Valve clearance is adjusted by loosening locknut (L—Fig. K4-12), then turning adjusting screw (S) until the proper clearance between the valve stem and adjusting screw is obtained. Intake valve clearance should be 0.12-0.17 mm (0.005-0.006 in.) on KLF185 and 0.15-0.20 mm (0.006-0.008 in.) on KLF220. Exhaust valve clearance should be 0.18-0.23 mm (0.007-0.009 in.) on all models. Recheck valve clearance after tightening locknut (L).

CLUTCH

Vehicles are equipped with a multiple-disc clutch that is actuated by the gear shift lever. As the gear shift lever is operated to change gears, the clutch is disengaged through linkage connected to the shift shaft.

To adjust the clutch remove two screws (S—Fig. K4-14) to allow removal of cover (C). Loosen the locknut located behind cover (C) and turn the adjusting screw clockwise until screw becomes hard to turn. Then turn the screw counterclockwise until resistance to turning is felt. Hold screw in position and tighten the locknut. Install cover (C) and check clutch adjustment by shifting gears with engine idling. Engine should not die when changing gears.

MANUAL STARTER

R&R AND OVERHAUL. Refer to Fig. K4-16 for a view of a partially disassembled manual starter assembly.

Fig. K4-12—Loosen locknut (L) and rotate adjusting screw (S) to adjust valve clearance.

Fig. K4-14—To gain access to clutch adjustment screw and locknut, remove two screws (S) and withdraw cover (C).

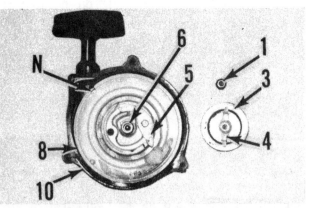

Fig. K4-16—View of a partially disassembled manual starter assembly typical of the type used on all models.

N. Notch	5. Starter pawl
1. Nut	6. Friction spring
3. Friction plate	8. Rope pulley
4. Pawl guide	10. Starter housing

Manual starter can be removed from the vehicle as a complete unit after removing the starter retaining screws. If starter rope remains under tension, pull starter rope and hold rope pulley (8—Fig. K4-16) with notch (N) in pulley adjacent to rope outlet. Pull a loop of rope back through outlet so rope engages notch in pulley and allow pulley (8) to slowly unwind.

Remove retaining nut (1) and disassemble unit. Be careful when removing rewind spring located behind pulley (8), a rapidly uncoiling starter spring can cause serious injury.

Rewind spring is wound in starter housing (10) in a clockwise direction. Starter rope is wound on rope pulley (8) in a clockwise direction as viewed with rope pulley in starter housing. Reassemble starter by reversing disassembly procedure. Lightly grease pulley shaft and starter pawl.

To replace tension on rewind spring after assembly, pass starter rope through rope outlet in starter housing and install rope handle. Pull a loop of rope back through outlet between notch (N) in pulley and housing. Rotate rope pulley (8) clockwise two or three complete revolutions, then release starter rope from pulley notch (N) and allow starter rope to wind onto pulley (8). Do not place any more tension on rewind spring than is necessary to draw starter rope handle up against housing.

ELECTRIC STARTER

The starter assembly can be removed and disassembled to clean, inspect and lubricate individual parts. To remove electric starter, first disconnect battery. Disconnect wire at terminal on starter. Remove the two mounting screws and withdraw the starter motor. Note the location of all components during disassembly to aid in reassembly. The starter assembly should be renewed if starter brushes are worn to 5.5 mm (0.22 in.) or less.

During installation, make sure "O" ring is positioned around starter neck, then guide starter into position. Remainder of installation is the reverse of removal procedure.

FRONT AXLE

The left and right front knuckle assemblies pivot on the outer bracket assembly at the end of each control arm. The control arms are bolted at the ends to the vehicle frame and a shock absorber is used to limit and cushion the up and down movement of the control arm.

Remove the front wheel to service the knuckle assembly. Note that removing the brake components will allow greater access to knuckle components. If knuckle bushings are excessively worn or any other damage is noted, then knuckle assembly must be renewed. Control arm mounting screws should be tightened to 88 N·m (65 ft.-lbs.). Shock absorber retaining nuts should be tightened to 34 N·m (25 ft.-lbs.). Knuckle assembly retaining bolt should be tightened to 34 N·m (25 ft.-lbs.).

FRONT BRAKE

BRAKE LEVER FREE PLAY. Brake lever free play is adjusted by loosening brake cable locknut and turning brake cable adjuster. On Model KLF185, rotate wing nut on each front brake cable at equalizer lever so cable movement is equal for both front brake cables. On Model KLF220, turn adjusting nut at brake end of each front brake cable so brake actuating lever has 2-3 mm (0.080-0.120 in.) free travel. On all models, turn adjuster at handlebar lever end of brake cable to adjust brake lever free play (A—Fig. K4-18). Free play should be 4-5 mm (0.16-0.20 in.) on KLF185 models or 1-2 mm (0.04-0.08 in.) on KLF220 models. Tighten brake cable locknut.

OVERHAUL. Brake lining thickness may be determined externally by actuating brake and noting position of pointer attached to actuating lever at each front brake. There is sufficient brake lining if pointer falls in "USABLE RANGE" on brake backing plate.

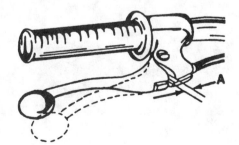

Fig. K4-18—Brake lever free play (A) should be 4-5 mm (0.16-0.20 in.) on KLF185 models and 1-2 mm (0.04-0.08 in.) on KLF220 models.

WARNING: Inhaling asbestos brake dust is injurious to human health. Approved OSHA respiration equipment must be worn when working on or around brake components. DO NOT use compressed air to clean brake drums, shoes or nearby components as brake dust will be blown into air. Only vacuum equipment designed to pick up brake dust should be used.

Each front brake assembly is accessible after removing the respective brake drum. Renew the brake shoes if they are damaged or if the lining thickness is less than 2 mm (0.08 in.). Renew the brake drum assembly if the inside diameter is more than 140. 75 mm (5.54 in.).

STEERING

TOE-IN SETTING. Place the handlebars in a straight ahead position. Use a suitable measuring tool and measure distance (D—Fig. K4-22), at spindle height, between the center of the tires on the front and rear

Fig. K4-22—Refer to text for correct procedures in measuring distance (D) for setting toe-in.

Fig. K4-23—Tie rod sleeves (S) are secured by inside (I) and outside (O) locknuts on each side.

sides. The measured distance (D) on the front side should be 32-37 mm (1.25-1.45 in.) shorter on KLF185 models or 30 mm (1.18 in.) on KLF220 models than the measured distance on the rear side. If not, loosen inside (I—Fig. K4-23) and outside (O) locknuts on the left and right tie rod assemblies and rotate tie rod sleeves (S) equally to obtain specified toe-in.

NOTE: If the handlebars are not positioned straight ahead when the front wheels are facing straight ahead, then rotate left and right tie rod sleeves the same direction in equal increments until handlebars are facing straight ahead. If tie rod sleeves are rotated equal amounts, then toe-in setting should not be affected.

After obtaining the correct setting, securely tighten the locknuts to retain tie rod setting.

INSPECTION. Rotate the handlebars from one extreme to the other and note if any binding or roughness is felt. Periodically inspect the steering components for looseness or any other damage. Renew any damaged component. Clean and grease components if binding or excessive effort is noted.

OVERHAUL. To expose the steering tube, the front fender assembly must be removed, as well as the fuel tank on KLF220 models. Remove the Allen head bolts and nuts securing the upper tube clamp and withdraw the clamp halves. Clean the old grease from the steering tube and bearing portions of the clamp halves. Inspect the clamp halves and the upper and lower grease seals for damage. Renew components if needed. Grease components and install clamp halves. Align marks on clamp halves on KLF220 models. Tighten the retaining clamp Allen head bolts and nuts to 20 N·m (14.5 ft.-lbs.) on KLF185 models and 26 N·m (19 ft.-lbs.) on KLF220 models.

The tie rod assemblies, upper tube clamp and handlebar assembly must be removed to withdraw the steering tube from the vehicle. Remove the lower bearing housing mounting screws to withdraw the steering tube. Inspect the lower bearing assembly and renew if needed.

Tighten the lower bearing assembly retaining nut to 29 N·m (22 ft.-lbs.). Tighten the tie rod assembly mounting nuts to 41 N·m (30 ft.-lbs.). When installing the handlebar assembly to the steering tube, the handlebar assembly should be positioned so the handlebars and steering tube are set at the same angle. First tighten the front handlebar mounting clamp screws to 20 N·m (14.5 ft.-lbs.), then tighten the rear screws to 20 N·m (14.5 ft.-lbs.). If properly tightened, there should be no gap at the front of the clamp and an even gap at the rear.

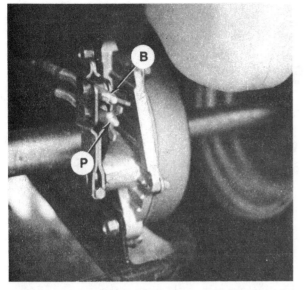

Fig. K4-24—View showing location of rear brake adjusters for brake pedal (P) and handlebar lever (B).

REAR BRAKE

ADJUSTMENT. The rear brake can be actuated either by a foot pedal or handlebar lever. Brake pedal free play should be 25-30 mm (0.984-1.181 in.) measured at the pedal pad. Adjust pedal free play by turning adjusting nut (P—Fig. K4-24). Brake lever free play measured at gap (G—Fig. K4-25) should be 4-5 mm (0.16-0.20 in.) on KLF185 models and 1-2 mm (0.04-0.08 in.) on KLF220 models. Adjust brake lever free play by rotating adjuster nut on brake cable at handlebar brake lever. If handlebar brake lever adjustment limit is reached, turn adjusting nut (B—Fig. K4-24).

OVERHAUL. Brake lining thickness may be determined externally by actuating brake and noting position of pointer attached to actuating lever. There is sufficient brake lining if pointer falls in "USABLE RANGE" on brake backing plate.

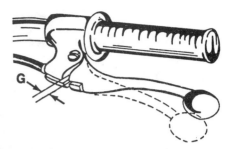

Fig. K4-25—Brake lever free play (G) should be 4-5 mm (0.16-0.20 in.) on KLF185 models and 1-2 mm (0.04-0.08 in.) on KLF220 models.

WARNING: Inhaling asbestos brake dust is injurious to human health. Approved OSHA respiration equipment must be worn when working on or around brake components. DO NOT use compressed air to clean brake drums, shoes or nearby components as brake dust will be blown into air. Only vacuum equipment designed to pick up brake dust should be used.

Use the following procedure for access to the rear brake assembly. Remove the cotter pin and axle nut at the right end of the rear axle. Remove the right rear wheel. On Model KLF220, remove brake drum. On Model KLF185, remove hub. Prevent axle rotation by applying the rear brake then unscrew the two nuts holding the brake drum in place. Slide the brake drum off the axle.

Inspect brake components. Inspect the splines on the axle and brake drum. Minimum brake shoe lining thickness is 2 mm (0.079 in.). Maximum allowable inside diameter for the brake drum is 160.65 mm (6.32 in.).

Reassemble brake and axle components by reversing removal procedure. On KLF185 models, tighten the two nuts securing the brake drum to 83 N.m (61 ft.-lbs.). Apply grease to axle splines. Tighten axle nut on all models to 145 N.m (110 ft.-lbs.).

KAWASAKI

KSF250

Metric fasteners are used throughout vehicle.

CONDENSED SERVICE DATA

MODELS	KSF250-A2, A3, A4, A5
General	
Engine Make	Own
Engine Type	Liquid-Cooled; Four Stroke
Number of Cylinders	1
Bore	74 mm
	(2.9 in.)
Stroke	58 mm
	(2.28 in.)
Displacement	249 cc
	(15.2 cu. in.)
Compression Ratio	11:1
Engine Lubrication	Wet Sump; Oil Pump
Transmission Lubrication	Common With Engine
Engine/Transmission Oil	See Text
Forward Speeds	5
Reverse Speeds	1
Tire Size:	
Front	21 × 7-10
Rear	22 × 10-10
Tire Pressure:	
Front (cold)	25 kPa
	(3.6 psi)
Rear (cold)	21 kPa
	(3 psi)
Dry Weight	165 kg
	(363 lbs.)
Tune-Up	
Engine Idle Speed	See Text
Spark Plug:	
Type	NGK DP8EA-9
Electrode Gap	0.8-0.9 mm
	(0.031-0.035 in.)
Ignition:	
Type	Capacitor Discharge
Point Gap	Pointless
Timing	10° BTDC @ 1300 rpm
	35° BTDC @ 3000 rpm
Carburetor:	
Make	Keihin
Model	CVK34
Float Height	15-19 mm
	(0.59-0.75 in.)
Main Jet	#132

Tune-Up (Cont.)
Carburetor: (Cont.)
Main Air Jet . . . . #125
Pilot Jet . . . . #35
Pilot Air Jet. . . . . #135
Jet Needle N54C
Needle Jet 6
Idle Mixture Setting . . . . 1¾ Turns
Throttle Lever Free Play . . . . 2-3 mm
(0.079-0.118 in.)

Sizes-Clearances
Valve Clearance (cold):
Intake & Exhaust . . . . 0.20-0.24 mm
(0.008-0.009 in.)
Valve Face & Seat Angle . . . . 45°
Valve Seat Width:
Intake & Exhaust . . . . 0.5-1.0 mm
(0.020-0.039 in.)
Valve Stem Diameter:
Intake. . . . . 5.475-5.490 mm
(0.2155-0.2161 in.)
Exhaust . . . . 5.455-5.470 mm
(0.2147-0.2153 in.)
Valve Guide Bore Diameter:
Intake & Exhaust . . . . 5.500-5.512 mm
(0.2165-0.2170 in.)
Valve Stem-to-Guide Clearance:
Intake. . . . . 0.010-0.037 mm
(0.0004-0.0015 in.)
Exhaust . . . . 0.030-0.057 mm
(0.012-0.022 in.)
Rocker Arm Bore Diameter:
Intake & Exhaust . . . . 12.500-12.518 mm
(0.4921-0.4928 in.)
Rocker Shaft Diameter:
Intake & Exhaust . . . . 12.466-12.484 mm
(0.4908-0.4915 in.)
Camshaft Lobe Height:
Intake & Exhaust . . . . 35.106-35.248 mm
(1.3821-1.3877 in.)
Wear Limit
Intake & Exhaust . . . . 35.01 mm
(1.3783 in.)
Cylinder Head Distortion (Max.). . . . . 0.05 mm
(0.002 in.)
Cylinder Bore Diameter . . . . 74.000-74.012 mm
(2.9134-2.9138 in.)
Wear Limit . . . . 74.10 mm
(2.9173 in.)
Piston-to-Cylinder Wall Clearance . . . . . . 0.035-0.062 mm
(0.0014-0.0024 in.)
Piston Diameter—
Measured 5 mm (0.02 in.) from
Skirt Bottom & 90° to Pin Bore . . . . 73.950-73.965 mm
(2.9114-2.9120 in.)

Sizes-Clearances (Cont.)

Piston Ring End Gap in
  Standard Bore:
    Top & Second Ring . . . .   0.20-0.35 mm
                                                       (0.007-0.014 in.)

Piston Ring Groove Width:
    Oil Ring . . . .   2.51-2.53 mm
                                                   (0.099-0.100 in.)

Piston Ring Width:
    Top & Second Ring . . . .   0.97-0.99 mm
                                                    (0.038-0.039 in.)

Piston Ring Side Clearance:
    Top & Second Ring . . . .   Semi-Keystone
Connecting Rod Big End
    Side Clearance . . . .   0.25-0.35 mm
                                                     (0.010-0.014 in.)

    Maximum Allowable . . . .   0.6 mm
                                                      (0.023 in.)

Connecting Rod Big End Radial Clearance   0.008-0.020 mm
                                                 (0.0003-0.0008 in.)

    Maximum Allowable . . . .   0.07 mm
                                                      (0.003 in.)

Crankshaft Runout (Max.):
    LH . . . .   0.08 mm
                                                     (0.003 in.)

    RH . . . .   0.1 mm
                                                     (0.004 in.)

Capacities

Fuel Tank . . . .   8.3 L
                                                      (2.16 gal.)
Cooling Systems . . . .   1.45 L
                                                      (1.54 qt.)
Engine/Transmission Sump . . . .   2.0 L
                                                   (2.12 qt.)

Tightening Torques

Axle Nut:
    Front . . . .   34 N•m
                                                     (25 ft.-lbs.)

    Rear . . . .   145 N•m
                                                      (110 ft.-lbs.)

Camshaft Sprocket Screw . . . .   39 N•m
                                                    (29 ft.-lbs.)

Clutch Screws . . . .   9.8 N•m
                                                     (87 in.-lbs.)

Cylinder Head Screws & Nuts:
    6 mm Screws . . . .   9.8 N•m
                                                     (87 in.-lbs.)

    8 mm Nuts . . . .   25 N•m
                                                     (18 ft.-lbs.)

    10 mm Screws:
        Initial . . . .   23 N•m
                                                     (17 ft.-lbs.)

        Final . . . .   45 N•m
                                                     (33 ft.-lbs.)

Wheel Retaining Nut . . . .   34 N•m
                                                   (25 ft.-lbs.)

Tightening Torques (Cont.)
Standard Fasteners:

5 mm	3.4-4.9 N·m (30-43 in.-lbs.)
6 mm	5.9-7.8 N·m (52-69 in.-lbs.)
8 mm	14-19 N·m (10-13.5 ft.-lbs.)
10 mm	25-39 N·m (19-25 ft.-lbs.)
12 mm	44-61 N·m (33-45 ft.-lbs.)
14 mm	73-98 N·m (54-72 ft.-lbs.)
16 mm	115-155 N·m (83-115 ft.-lbs.)
18 mm	165-225 N·m (125-165 ft.-lbs.)
20 mm	225-325 N·m (165-240 ft.-lbs.)

LUBRICATION

ENGINE AND TRANSMISSION. The engine is lubricated by a trochoid-type pump located on the right side of the crankcase and driven by a gear on the right end of the crankshaft. The engine and transmission share a common sump. Recommended oil is a multigrade SAE 10W-40, 10W-50, 20W-40 or 20W-50 motor oil with an API classification of SF or SG.

Sump is filled through filler cap opening (F—Fig. K7-1). Oil level should be maintained between oil level lines adjacent to sight glass. Sump is drained by removing plug in underside of crankcase and oil passage plug (P—Fig. K7-1). Crankcase capacity after changing oil and oil filter is 2.0 L (2.12 qt.).

Manufacturer recommends changing oil and oil filter after the first 10 hours of operation. Thereafter, the oil and oil filter should be changed after every 90 days of operation. In conjunction with oil filter change, the oil pressure relief valve (located within the oil filter mounting pin) should be disassembled, cleaned and inspected. The sump screen, located in the right crankcase half and to the left of the oil pump, should also be removed and cleaned.

The oil filter and oil pressure relief valve are accessible after removing cover (C). To disassemble oil pressure relief valve, drive out cross-pin (1—Fig. K7-2) and separate components. Renew the complete assembly if excessive wear or damage is evident. During reassembly, insert piston (3) with open end toward spring (2). Insert and compress spring (2) just beyond cross-

pin hole and install cross-pin (1). Install the oil filter ensuring "O" ring seals are located on both sides of filter. Renew filter cover (C—Fig. K7-1) "O" ring seal if required and install cover with arrow (A) pointing up.

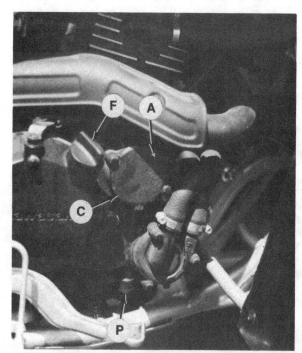

Fig. K7-1—Engine/transmission sump is filled through filler plug opening (F). The oil filter is located behind cover (C). Install cover (C) with arrow (A) pointing up. Sump is drained by removing plug in underside of crankcase and oil passage plug (P).

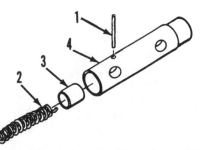

Fig. K7-2—Exploded view of oil pressure relief valve.

1. Cross-pin
2. Spring
3. Piston
4. Filter mount sleeve

Sump screen is accessible after removing right crankcase cover. Drain oil from crankcase. Unbolt and carefully remove the right crankcase cover. Withdraw the sump screen from crankcase half. Reinstall by reversing removal procedure while noting the following: Make sure alignment dowels and gasket are fitted to crankcase and install cover. Adjust clutch as outlined in CLUTCH section. Fill engine/transmission sump with the appropriate amount of oil and check for leaks.

CABLES, LEVERS AND LINKAGE. All cables, levers and linkage should be inspected and lubricated after every 30 days of operation.

AIR CLEANER ELEMENT

The air cleaner element should be removed and cleaned after the first 10 hours of operation and every 10 days of operation thereafter. To remove air cleaner element, first remove plugs (P—Fig. K7-4), then remove four screws (S). Two screws are located behind plugs

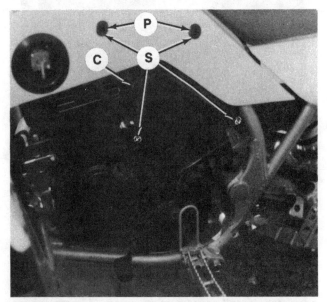

Fig. K7-4—Remove plugs (P) and four screws (S), then withdraw cover (C) to gain access to foam air filter element.

(P). Withdraw cover (C) and foam element located behind cover.

Thoroughly clean element in a nonflammable solvent. Compress element between hands to remove solvent. Saturate element in clean SAE 30 motor oil and compress element to remove excess oil. Reinstall foam element and complete reassembly by reversing removal procedures.

NOTE: Manufacturer recommends renewing foam element if damage is noted, or after cleaning five times.

FUEL SYSTEM

CARBURETOR. A Keihin CVK34-type carburetor is used. Refer to CONDENSED SERVICE DATA for carburetor specifications.

Adjust idle speed screw (I—Fig. K7-6) to obtain the lowest smooth idle setting. After adjusting carburetor idle setting, check throttle lever free play as outlined in THROTTLE LEVER FREE PLAY section.

When servicing the carburetor, note the following: Float height (A—Fig. K7-7) should be 15-19 mm (0.59-0.75 in.) as measured from gasket surface of carburetor

Fig. K7-6—Installed view of carburetor identifying idle speed screw (I) and fuel drain screw (S).

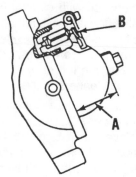

Fig. K7-7—Float height (A) should be 15-19 mm (0.59-0.75 in.). Bend float arm tang (B) to adjust.

body to bottom of float. Hold carburetor so float is vertical and resting lightly against fuel inlet valve when checking float height as shown in Fig. K7-7. Adjust the float level by bending tang (B) on float arm.

The fuel level is checked with the carburetor installed and vehicle operational. To check fuel level, attach Kawasaki fuel level gauge 57001-1017 to open end of carburetor overflow hose and position gauge so zero line is even with bottom edge of carburetor body (float bowl contact surface). Turn fuel valve to "ON" position and open fuel drain screw (S—Fig. K7-6) to allow fuel drainage. After fuel in hose has stabilized, measure the distance from the bottom edge of carburetor body to fuel level in hose. Fuel level check will not be accurate if hose is raised or lowered after fuel level has stabilized. Fuel level should be 0.5 mm (0.02 in.) below bottom edge of carburetor body to 1.5 mm (0.06 in.) above bottom edge of carburetor body. To adjust fuel level, the float bowl must be removed to carefully bend float arm tang (B—Fig. K7-7).

FUEL STRAINER. A strainer is mounted on the end of the "ON" pickup tube and the "RES" (reserve) pickup tube of the fuel valve assembly mounted on the fuel tank. A strainer is also located behind the fuel valve control lever. To inspect the strainers, the fuel in the fuel tank must be drained. Disconnect the fuel hose from the fuel valve. Unscrew the two screws securing the fuel valve to the fuel tank and carefully remove the fuel valve from the tank. Clean and inspect the strainers. The strainers are not available separately, only as a part of the valve housing. Reinstall the valve assembly while noting that nylon washers are used on the two retaining screws to prevent fuel leakage.

THROTTLE LEVER FREE PLAY. The throttle lever should have 2-3 mm (0.079-0.118 in.) of free play measured at throttle lever end as shown at (F—Fig. K7-12).

Throttle lever free play can be adjusted by sliding boot (B) down cable to expose outer adjuster nut and inner locknut. Loosen locknut and rotate adjuster nut until 2-3 mm (0.079-0.118 in.) free play is obtained. Secure adjustment with locknut and reinstall boot (B).

COOLING SYSTEM

INSPECTION. The engine assembly is liquid-cooled. A one-piece radiator assembly is used. Renew any hoses that are cracked, split or show any other damage. Inspect all other cooling system components and renew if leakage or damage is noted.

CHANGING COOLANT. The manufacturer recommends using a 50 percent water to 50 percent antifreeze mixture in cooling system. Cooling system capacity with reservoir tank at full level is 1.45 L (1.54 qt.).

To drain coolant, remove radiator cap (C—Fig. K7-14) and drain plug (D) in water pump housing and allow coolant to drain into a suitable container. Remove reservoir tank (R—Fig. K7-15) and empty all coolant from tank.

Before refilling cooling system, install and tighten drain plug (D—Fig. K7-14). Pour recommended coolant mixture into radiator cap (C) opening until coolant level is at base of filler neck and install radiator cap (C). Remove reservoir tank cap (P—Fig. K7-15), and fill reservoir tank with recommended coolant mixture until coolant level is even with "FULL" line on tank.

NOTE: **Vehicle may need to be operated and allowed to cool in order to remove any air pockets within system. After system has cooled, remove radiator cap (C—Fig. K7-14) and reservoir tank cap (P—Fig. K7-15) and complete cooling system filling.**

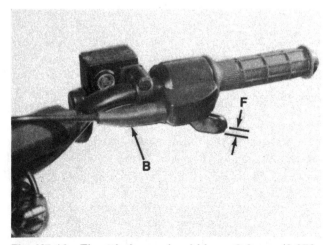

Fig. K7-12—Throttle lever should have 2-3 mm (0.079-0.118 in.) of free play (F) measured at end of lever. To adjust, slide boot (B) down cable to expose adjuster nut and locknut.

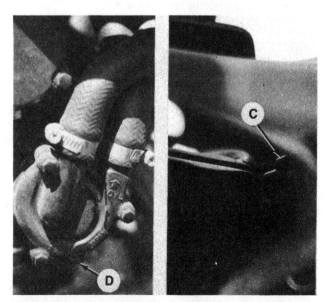

Fig. K7-14—View identifying radiator cap (C) and drain plug (D) located in water pump housing.

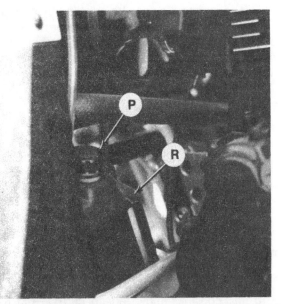

Fig. K7-15—Coolant level in reservoir tank (R) should be kept at "FULL" line. Remove cap (P) to add coolant.

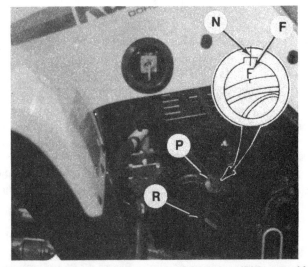

Fig. K7-17—Remove inspection hole plug (P) located in left side cover to check ignition timing. At idle speed, "F" mark (F) on flywheel should align with notch (N) for correct ignition timing. Remove plug (R) to expose flywheel retaining screw.

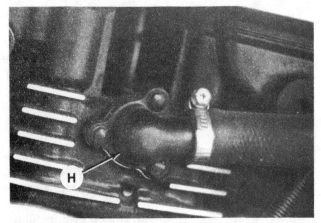

Fig. K7-16—Thermostat assembly is located behind housing (H) on right-side of cylinder.

RADIATOR CAP. Radiator cap (C—Fig. K7-14) should have a relief opening pressure of 73.5-103 kPa (11-15 psi).

THERMOSTAT. A thermostat assembly is located behind thermostat housing (H—Fig. K7-16) located on right-side of cylinder. Thermostat valve should start to open when engine coolant temperature reaches 69.5°-72.5° C (157°-163° F) and be fully open at 85° C (185° F). Thermostat valve should open at least 3 mm (0.118 in.). When installing thermostat in cylinder, position air bleed hole on the top.

IGNITION AND ELECTRICAL

SPARK PLUG. Standard spark plug is NGK BP8EA-9. Spark plug electrode gap should be 0.8-0.9 mm (0.031-0.035 in.). Spark plug should be removed, cleaned and electrode gap set after the first 10 hours of operation and every 90 days of operation thereafter. Renew spark plug if damage and excessive electrode wear is evident.

IGNITION SYSTEM. A breakerless Capacitor Discharge Ignition (CDI) system is used. An exciter coil located behind the flywheel provides electrical power for the system. The pickup coil is located outside and just above the flywheel. The CDI unit is located behind the air cleaner and underneath the seat. The ignition coil is mounted underneath the fuel tank.

NOTE: Do not disconnect ignition system connectors while the engine is running as the CDI unit may be damaged.

Ignition timing can be checked after removing inspection hole plug (P—Fig. K7-17) located in left side cover. Ignition timing at idle speed should occur when "F" mark (F) on flywheel is aligned with notch (N) as viewed through timing plug opening. Specified ignition timing is 10° BTDC ("F" mark) at 1300 rpm and 35° (maximum advance) at 3000 rpm.

Ignition timing is checked with a power timing light and is not adjustable. If ignition timing is not as specified, check condition of CDI unit and pickup coil as described in the following test procedures.

Some components can be checked using an ohmmeter. Disconnect the connectors for the wires leading from the magneto. To check the exciter coil, connect one ohmmeter lead to the black/red lead and the other ohmmeter lead to the black/white lead from the magneto. Exciter coil resistance should be 60-120 ohms.

NOTE: The exciter coil, fan motor power coil and lighting coil are all contained within the magneto stator. If one coil tests defective, then the complete magneto stator assembly must be renewed.

To check the pickup coil resistance, connect one ohmmeter lead to the black lead and the other ohmmeter lead to the black/yellow lead from the magneto. Pickup coil resistance should be 100-150 ohms. Ignition coil primary winding resistance should be 0.14-0.22 ohm while secondary winding resistance should be 3300-4900 ohms.

If the ignition system does not operate properly after checking all components except the CDI unit, replace the CDI unit with a new or known good unit and recheck the system. Be sure all wiring and connectors are good.

ELECTRICAL SYSTEM. A lighting coil is located behind the flywheel to provide power for the lights. The lighting coil should produce at least 9.5 volts AC with the engine running at 3000 rpm. Lighting coil resistance should be 0.6-1.3 ohms checked between the black/yellow lead from the magneto and a good engine ground. The headlight is a 12 V 45/45 W unit while the taillight is a 12 V 8 W unit.

A fan motor power coil is located behind the flywheel to provide power for the cooling fan. On 1990 and 1991 models, a voltage regulator is included in the cooling fan circuit. On 1988 and 1989 models, the fan motor power coil should produce at least 25 volts AC with the engine running at 3000 rpm. On 1990 and 1991 models, the coil output is regulated to 12.3-13.7 volts at 5000 rpm. To test, connect a suitable voltmeter to the green/black lead and green lead from the fan motor power coil to the rectifier. If voltage is excessive on 1990 and 1991 models, the voltage regulator is faulty. The fan motor power coil resistance should be 0.6-1.3 ohms checked between the two brown leads from the magneto.

NOTE: The exciter coil, fan motor power coil and lighting coil are all contained within the magneto stator. If one coil tests defective, then the complete magneto stator assembly must be renewed.

The fan "ON/OFF" switch (located on side of radiator, underneath filler neck) should switch from "OFF" to "ON" when coolant temperature reaches 84°-90° C (183°-194° F) and from "ON" to "OFF" when coolant temperature reaches 71°-77° C (160°-170° F).

FASTENERS

The vehicle should receive an overall inspection after the first 10 hours of operation and every 10 days of operation thereafter. All cap screws, nuts and fasteners should be checked and tightened to proper torque speci-

fication listed in CONDENSED SERVICE DATA section or in the appropriate MAINTENANCE section.

VALVE SYSTEM

The valves are actuated via rocker arms by dual overhead camshafts. Two intake and two exhaust valves are used. A single rocker arm activates both intake valves and a single rocker arm activates both exhaust valves. Camshafts are driven by a roller chain attached to the left end of the crankshaft. Valve clearance on all models should be adjusted after the first 10 hours of operation and then after every 90 days of operation. Valve clearance should be adjusted with engine cold.

To adjust valve clearance, remove seat, fuel tank, air filter assembly, interfering fender assemblies, cylinder head cover, plug (P—Fig. K7-17) and plug (R) to expose flywheel retaining screw. Attach a suitable tool to flywheel screw and rotate crankshaft until "T" mark (Top Dead Center) on flywheel aligns with notch (N) with piston on compression stroke. To ensure piston is on compression stroke, rotate crankshaft ¼ turn past "T" mark while observing intake valves. If valve movement is indicated, rotate crankshaft one complete revolution and align "T" mark with stationary mark again.

Clearance between rocker arm adjusting screw and valve stem should be 0.20-0.24 mm (0.008-0.009 in.) for both intake and exhaust valves. Measure clearance with a suitable feeler gauge and adjust by loosening adjusting screw locknut and turning adjusting screw. Be sure to recheck clearance after locknuts are tightened.

CLUTCH

All models are equipped with a multiple-disc-type clutch manually actuated by left handlebar lever. The clutch should be adjusted after the first 10 hours of operation and then after every 10 days of operation.

The clutch lever should have 2-3 mm (0.079-0.118 in.) of free play measured at clutch lever end as shown at (F—Fig. K7-18). Clutch lever free play can be adjusted by sliding dust boot down cable to expose adjuster nut

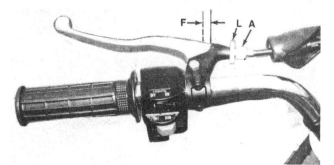

Fig. K7-18—Measure clutch lever free play at (F) and make adjustment with adjuster nut (A). Secure free play adjustment with locknut (L).

Fig. K7-19—Loosen locknuts (N) and slide cable (C) in mounting bracket if clutch lever adjuster nut (A—Fig. K7-18) is near or has reached adjustment limit. View identifies location of engine/transmission sump sight glass (G) and level lines (L).

(A) and locknut (L). Loosen locknut (L) and rotate adjuster nut (A) until 2-3 mm (0.079-0.118 in.) free play is obtained. If adjuster nut (A) is near or has reached adjustment limit, then loosen locknuts (N—Fig. K7-19) and slide cable (C) in direction required to add or remove cable slack as needed. Secure adjuster nut (A—Fig. K7-18) setting with locknut (L) and reinstall dust boot.

Properly operated, the clutch should disengage and engage freely. Difficulty in shifting, clutch grabbing or slipping may indicate disassembly and repair of clutch unit is required.

REVERSE KNOB FREE PLAY

The reverse knob should have 2-3 mm (0.079-0.118 in.) of free play measured at outer circumference of knob. Reverse knob free play can be adjusted by loosening jam nut on cable adjuster located in front of cylinder head and rotating adjuster nut until 2-3 mm (0.079-0.118 in.) free play is obtained. Secure adjustment with jam nut.

FRONT BRAKE ASSEMBLY

A disc brake assembly is used on both front wheels. As the disc or disc pads wear, the piston within the brake caliper assembly will move out to automatically compensate for the wear, so adjustment on the front brakes is not required.

BLEEDING. Make sure reservoir (R—Fig. K7-20) is full. Connect a bleed hose to bleed valve (B—Fig.

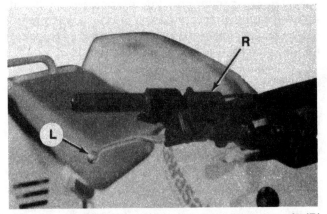

Fig. K7-20—View identifying front brake reservoir (R) and operational lever (L).

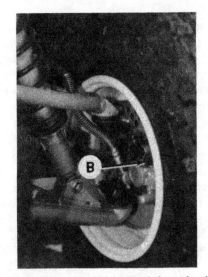

Fig. K7-21—Bleed valve (B) on both front brake calipers is used to bleed front brake system.

K7-21) on both front brake caliper assemblies. Route the bleed hoses into suitable containers. Operate brake lever (L—Fig. K7-20) until a hardness (fluid resistance) is felt, then open one bleed valve (rotate counterclockwise). Close bleed valve prior to releasing brake lever. Continue bleeding procedure on both wheels until no air bubbles are noted in discharged fluid from bleed valve.

NOTE: Make sure reservoir (R) is kept full during bleeding procedure.

When bleeding procedure is completed, add brake fluid to reservoir until fluid level is at upper level line in reservoir. Approximately ¾ full as viewed through reservoir sight glass.

OVERHAUL. Brake pad thickness may be determined externally by viewing the brake pads. If brake pad is 1 mm (0.039 in.) or less in thickness, then brake pads must be renewed.

WARNING: Inhaling asbestos brake dust is injurious to human health. Approved OSHA respiration equipment must be worn when working on or around brake calipers and pads. DO NOT use compressed air to clean brake calipers, pads or nearby components as brake dust will be blown into air. Only vacuum equipment designed to pick up brake dust should be used.

Brake components are accessible after removing wheel, caliper mounting screws and withdrawing caliper. Push piston by hand back into caliper to allow clearance for new brake pads. Brake disc should be renewed if thickness is 3 mm (0.118 in.) or less or disc runout is 0.3 mm (0.012 in.) or more. After reassembly, operate brake lever until brake lever will not pump up after continuous operation. Do not operate vehicle until correct brake operation is noted.

FRONT AXLE

The left and right front steering knuckle assemblies pivot on ball joint assemblies at the end of each upper and lower control arm. The control arms are bolted at the ends of the vehicle frame and a shock absorber is used to limit and cushion the up and down movement of the control arms. The shock absorbers are adjustable to alter absorber spring setting for different terrain and load conditions.

Remove the front wheel to service the ball joint assemblies. Note that removing the brake components will allow greater access to ball joint assemblies. If any ball joint or control arm is excessively worn or any other damage is noted, then ball joint or control arm must be renewed. Shock absorber, lower control arm and upper control arm retaining nuts should be tightened to 34 N·m (25 ft.-lbs.). Ball joints should be tightened to 44 N·m (33 ft.-lbs.) and retained with a clip. Tighten ball joint to steering knuckle retaining nuts to 41 N·m (30 ft.-lbs.).

STEERING

TOE-IN SETTING. Raise the front wheels off the ground until the front spindle nuts are at the same height of the rear axle nuts. Place the handlebars in a straight ahead position. Use a suitable measuring tool and measure distance (D—Fig. K7-22), at spindle height, between the center of the tires on the front and rear sides. The measured distance (D) on the front side should be 20 mm (0.79 in.) shorter than the measured distance on the rear side. If not, loosen the inside and outside locknuts on the left and right tie rod assemblies and rotate tie rod sleeves (S) equally until a difference of 20 mm (0.79 in.) is noted.

NOTE: If the handlebars are not positioned straight ahead when the front wheels are facing

Fig. K7-22—Refer to text for correct procedures in measuring distance (D) for setting toe-in. Tie rod sleeves (S) are secured by inside and outside locknuts.

straight ahead, then rotate left and right tie rod sleeves the same direction in equal increments until handlebars are facing straight ahead. If tie rod sleeves are rotated equal amounts, then toe-in setting should not be affected.

After obtaining the correct setting, securely tighten the locknuts to retain tie rod settings.

INSPECTION. Rotate the handlebars from one extreme to the other and note if any binding or roughness is felt. Periodically inspect the steering components for looseness or any other damage. Renew any damaged component. Clean and grease components if binding or excessive effort is noted.

OVERHAUL. To expose the steering tube, the front fender assembly must be removed. Remove the Allen head bolts and nuts securing the upper tube clamp and withdraw the clamp halves. Clean the old grease from the steering tube and bearing portions of the clamp halves. Inspect the clamp halves and the upper and lower grease seals for damage. Renew components if needed. Position the grease seals so slits are aligned and facing toward front. Grease components and install clamp halves so match marks on sides of halves are aligned. Tighten the retaining clamp Allen head bolts and nuts to 20 N·m (15 ft.-lbs.)

The tie rod assemblies, handlebar assembly, reverse knob assembly, handlebar clamp for cables and hoses and upper tube clamp must be removed to withdraw the steering tube from the vehicle. Remove the lower bearing housing mounting screws to withdraw the steering tube. Inspect the lower bearing assembly and seals and renew if needed. Tighten the lower bearing assembly retaining nut to 29 N·m (22 ft.-lbs.). Tighten the tie rod assembly mounting nuts to 41 N·m (30 ft.-lbs.).

When installing the handlebar assembly to the steering tube, the handlebar should be positioned so the handlebar and steering tube are set at the same angle. Tighten the front handlebar mounting clamp screws first, then tighten the rear screws. If properly tightened, there should be no gap at the front of the clamp and an even gap at the rear.

REAR BRAKE ASSEMBLY

A single disc brake assembly is used for both rear wheels. The running brake is operated hydraulically by a foot pedal on the lower right side. The parking brake is mechanically operated by a cable and handlebar components in conjunction with the clutch lever.

BLEEDING. Make sure reservoir (R—Fig. K7-23) is full. Connect a bleed hose to bleed valve (B) on brake caliper assembly. Route the bleed hose into a suitable container. Operate foot pedal until a hardness (fluid resistance) is felt, then open bleed valve (B) (rotate counterclockwise). Close bleed valve prior to releasing foot pedal. Continue bleeding procedure until no air bubbles are noted in discharged fluid from bleed valve.

NOTE: Make sure reservoir (R) is kept full during bleeding procedure.

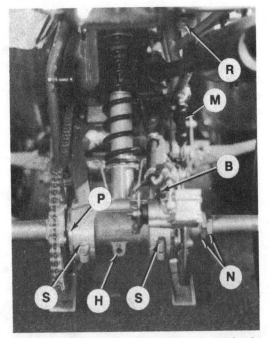

Fig. K7-23—View identifying location of rear brake reservoir (R), master cylinder (M), caliper bleed valve (B), bearing housing snap ring (P) and rear axle retaining nuts (N). Drive chain tension is adjusted by loosening clamp screws (S) and rotating rear axle housing by using a suitable size bar inserted in hole (H).

Fig. K7-24—Refer to text for adjusting rear parking brake.

A. Actuator lever
B. Mounting bracket
D. Measured distance
L. Locknut
N. Locknuts
S. Adjusting screw

When bleeding procedure is completed, add brake fluid to reservoir (R) until fluid level is at upper level line on reservoir.

PARKING BRAKE ADJUSTMENT. Loosen cable locknuts (N—Fig. K7-24) to allow cable to slide freely. Loosen locknut (L) and rotate screw (S) clockwise until seated, then turn out (counterclockwise) ¼ turn and tighten locknut (L). Adjust actuator lever (A) until a distance (D) of 42-44 mm (1.65-1.73 in.) is between mounting bracket (B) and center of actuator lever (A) as shown in Fig. K7-24. After obtaining correct distance (D), tighten locknuts (N).

OVERHAUL. Brake pad thickness may be determined externally by viewing the brake pads. If brake pad thickness is 1 mm (0.039 in.) or less, then both brake pads must be renewed.

WARNING: Inhaling asbestos brake dust is injurious to human health. Approved OSHA respiration equipment must be worn when working on or around brake calipers and pads. DO NOT use compressed air to clean brake calipers, pads or nearby components as brake dust will be blown into air. Only vacuum equipment designed to pick up brake dust should be used.

Brake components are accessible after removing caliper mounting screws and withdrawing caliper. Remove the brake pad mounting screws and withdraw the brake pads. Loosen parking brake locknut (L—Fig. K7-24) and turn adjusting screw (S) out to provide a clearance between screw and piston. Push piston by hand back into caliper to allow clearance for new brake pads. Brake disc should be renewed if thickness is 3.5 mm (0.138

in.) or less or disc runout is 0.3 mm (0.012 in.) or more. After reassembly, operate brake foot pedal until pedal will not pump up after continuous operation. Adjust parking brake as outlined in previous PARKING BRAKE ADJUSTMENT section. Do not operate vehicle until correct brake operation is noted.

DRIVE CHAIN AND SPROCKETS

INSPECTION AND ADJUSTMENT. The final drive chain should be inspected and adjusted after every 90 days of operation. Improper maintenance and neglect can cause early failure of both drive chain and sprockets. An endless-type drive chain is used. Distance between 20 chain links should not exceed 324 mm (12.7 in.). Drive chain free play should be 40-50 mm (1.57-1.97 in.) measured midway between sprockets. Drive chain free play can be checked by pulling firmly up on chain. Chain tension is adjusted by loosening clamp screws (S—Fig. K7-23) and inserting a suitable size bar into hole (H) and rotating rear axle housing up or down as needed. Tighten screws (S) and recheck drive chain free play.

R&R AND OVERHAUL. Loosen screws (S—Fig. K7-23) and rotate rear axle housing to loosen chain. Remove chain guard and front and rear sprocket guards. Lift chain off rear sprocket toward left rear wheel. Use a location at rear of vehicle frame and lift rear wheels off the ground. Detach the rear shock absorber at the lower mounting bracket. Remove parking brake cable, at caliper, if needed. Remove the swing arm caps and remove one swing arm shaft nut. Support swing arm and withdraw swing arm shaft toward end with nut still attached. Remove left rear wheel and withdraw drive chain.

Reassemble by reversing disassembly procedure while noting the following: Install engine sprocket (front sprocket) with raised shoulder side toward engine. Tighten sprocket retaining nut to 98 N·m (72 ft.-lbs.) and secure with lockplate. Install final drive sprocket (rear sprocket) with stamped tooth (number) side facing outward toward wheel. Tighten rear sprocket retaining nuts to 34 N·m (25 ft.-lbs.). Adjust chain tension as previously outlined in INSPECTION AND ADJUSTMENT section and parking brake cable as outlined in PARKING BRAKE ADJUSTMENT.

FINAL DRIVE ASSEMBLY

R&R AND OVERHAUL. Removal of final drive assembly is accomplished by removing rear brake caliper assembly as outlined under OVERHAUL in the REAR BRAKE ASSEMBLY section and by removing final drive assembly as outlined under R&R AND OVERHAUL in the DRIVE CHAIN AND SPROCKETS section. To complete disassembly, remove right-side rear wheel and left and right rear hub assemblies. Remove rear axle retaining locknuts (N—Fig. K7-23), brake disc and holder and push rear axle out toward left side. Remove snap ring (P) to separate final drive bearing housing from swing arm clamp brackets.

Renew any seals or bearings as needed. Reassembly is reverse order of disassembly. Tighten rear axle retaining nuts (N) to 145 N·m (110 ft.-lbs.). Refer to appropriate sections for reassembly procedures and to TIGHTENING TORQUES in the CONDENSED SERVICE DATA section for torque values not listed in maintenance sections.

KAWASAKI
KXF250

NOTE: Metric fasteners are used throughout vehicle.

CONDENSED SERVICE DATA

MODELS	KXF250-A1, A2
General	
Engine Make	Kawasaki
Engine Type	Two-Stroke; Liquid-Cooled
Number of Cylinders	1
Bore	67.4 mm
	(2.65 in.)
Stroke	70.0 mm
	(2.76 in.)
Displacement	250 cc
	(15.25 cu. in.)
Compression Ratio	8.9:1
Engine Lubrication	Fuel:Oil Premix
Transmission Lubrication	Oil Sump
Forward Speeds	6
Reverse Speeds	N/A
Tire Size	
Front	20 × 7-10
Rear	20 × 10-10
Tire Pressure	
Front	32 kPa
	(4.5 psi)
Rear	28 kPa
	(4.0 psi)
Dry Weight	149 kg
	(328 lbs.)
Tune-Up	
Engine Idle Speed	See Text
Spark Plug:	
Type	NGK B8ES
Electrode Gap	0.7-0.8 mm
	(0.028-0.031 in.)
Ignition:	
Type	Capacitor Discharge
Timing:	
A1 Models	18° BTDC @ 6000 rpm
A2 Models	20° BTDC @ 6000 rpm
Carburetor:	
Make & Model:	
A1	Mikuni VM34SS
A2	Keihin PWK35
Float Height	See Text
Main Jet:	
A1	#260
A2	#140

Tune-Up (Cont.)

Carburetor: (Cont.)

Pilot Jet:
- A1 .... #30
- A2 .... #65*

Jet Needle:
- A1 .... 6FL61
- A2 .... R1472J*

Clip Position:
- A1 .... 3rd Groove From Top
- A2 .... 2nd Groove From Top*

Throttle Valve Cutaway:
- A1 .... 3.0
- A2 .... #6

Idle Mixture Setting .... See Text

Throttle Lever Free Play .... 2-3 mm
(0.08-0.12 in.)

*On A2 models with engine numbers higher than XF250AE004205, pilot jet is #50, jet needle is R1469J and clip position is third groove from top.

Sizes-Clearances

Reed Petal Stand Open
(Max.).......................... 0.7 mm
(0.028 in.)

Cylinder Head Distortion (Max.)......... 0.05 mm
(0.002 in.)

Cylinder Bore Diameter .... 67.400-67.415 mm
(2.6535-2.6541 in.)

  Wear Limit .... 67.51 mm
(2.6579 in.)

Piston-to-Cylinder Wall Clearance....... 0.054-0.064 mm
(0.0021-0.0025 in.)

Piston Diameter:
Measured 5 mm (0.020 in.) From
Skirt Bottom & 90° to Pin Bore......... 67.341-67.356 mm
(2.6512-2.6518 in.)

Piston Ring End Gap:
Top & Second Ring .... 0.15-0.35 mm
(0.006-0.014 in.)

Piston Ring Side Clearance:
Top & Second Ring .... 0.04-0.08 mm
(0.0016-0.0031 in.)

Connecting Rod Big End
Side Clearance .... 0.45-0.55 mm
(0.018-0.022 in.)

  Maximum Allowable............... 0.8 mm
(0.031 in.)

Connecting Rod Big End
Radial Clearance.................. 0.037-0.049 mm
(0.0014-0.0019 in.)

  Maximum Allowable............... 0.1 mm
(0.004 in.)

Crankshaft Runout
(Max.).......................... 0.08 mm
(0.003 in.)

Capacities

Cooling System .... 1.5 L
(1.6 qt.)

Capacities (Cont.)

Fuel Tank	9.0 L (2.4 gal.)
Transmission Sump	1.15 L (1.2 qt.)

Tightening Torques

Axle Nut:	
Front	34 N·m (25 ft.-lbs.)
Rear.	145 N·m (107 ft.-lbs.)
Balancer Gear	9.8 N·m (87 in.-lbs.)
Clutch Nut	88 N·m (65 ft.-lbs.)
Cylinder Head:	
6 mm Screws.	9.8 N·m (87 in.-lbs.)
8 mm Nuts:	
Initial	11 N·m (95 in.-lbs.)
Final.	25 N·m (18 ft.-lbs.)
Cylinder Nuts	34 N·m (25 ft.-lbs.)
Flywheel.	27 N·m (20 ft.-lbs.)
Primary Drive Gear	78 N·m (57 ft.-lbs.)
Spark Plug	27 N·m (20 ft.-lbs.)
Water Pump Impeller	6.9 N·m (61 in.-lbs.)
Wheel Retaining Nuts	34 N·m (25 ft.-lbs.)
Standard Fasteners:	
5 mm	3.4-4.9 N·m (30-43 in.-lbs.)
6 mm	5.9-7.8 N·m (52-69 in.-lbs.)
8 mm	14-19 N·m (10-13.5 ft.-lbs.)
10 mm	25-39 N·m 19-25 ft.-lbs.)
12 mm	44-61 N·m (33-45 ft.-lbs.)
14 mm	73-98 N·m (54-72 ft.-lbs.)
16 mm	115-155 N·m (83-115 ft.-lbs.)
18 mm	165-225 N·m (125-165 ft.-lbs.)
20 mm	225-325 N·m (165-240 ft.-lbs.)

Fig. K9-1—Oil level in transmission sump must be maintained at middle of sight glass (G). Add oil through opening for fill plug (F).

LUBRICATION

ENGINE. The engine is lubricated by oil mixed with the fuel. Recommended oil is a good quality two-stroke racing oil designed for use in motorcycles. Specified fuel:oil ratio is 20:1.

TRANSMISSION. Recommended transmission oil is SAE 10W-30 or 10W-40 oil with API classification SE or SF. The manufacturer recommends changing the transmission oil after every 20 days of operation.

Transmission oil level must be maintained at middle of sight glass (G—Fig. K9-1) on right side of engine. Oil can be poured into transmission through opening for fill plug (F). Oil can be drained by unscrewing drain plug on underside of engine. Tighten sump drain plug to 20 N·m (14.5 ft.-lbs.). Capacity of transmission sump is 1.15 L (1.2 qt.). After refilling transmission, check oil level at sight glass (G).

DRIVE CHAIN. The drive chain should be lubricated daily with SAE 90 gear oil. The chain utilizes "O" rings to seal the chain rollers and pins. Incorrect lubrication may damage the "O" rings resulting in premature chain failure.

Remove and clean the drive chain when excessive dirt is evident. Remove chain as outlined in DRIVE CHAIN AND SPROCKETS section. The chain should be thoroughly washed in kerosene and wiped dry. The use of any cleaning solution other than kerosene may damage "O" rings. Lubricate chain with SAE 90 gear oil, then install and adjust chain as outlined in DRIVE CHAIN AND SPROCKETS section.

AIR CLEANER ELEMENT

The air cleaner element should be removed and cleaned after every 10 hours of operation. To remove the air cleaner element, remove the rear fender and seat. Remove air cleaner cover and filter element. Carefully separate foam element from frame.

Thoroughly clean the foam element in a nonflammable solvent. Compress element between hands to remove solvent. Saturate element with clean engine oil, then rub element so oil is distributed throughout. Squeeze out as much oil as possible. Apply grease to sealing end of filter element and reassemble air cleaner components.

Air cleaner element should be discarded after fifth cleaning.

FUEL SYSTEM

CARBURETOR. Model A1 is equipped with a Mikuni VM34SS carburetor while Model A2 is equipped with a Keihin PWK35 carburetor. Refer to CONDENSED SERVICE DATA and following paragraphs for service information.

Mikuni VM34SS Carburetor. Set idle speed to desired engine speed by turning idle speed screw (19—Fig. K9-3). Refer to Fig. K9-3 for an exploded view of carburetor. Jet needle clip (9) should be installed in third groove from top of jet needle (10). Installing clip in a lower groove on jet needle will richen mid-range fuel mixture. Groove in side of needle jet (22) must index with pin in carburetor. To obtain correct float height, height (H—Fig. K9-4) of float arm (R) must be 15.1-19.1 mm (0.60-0.75 in.) above carburetor fuel bowl mating surface with carburetor inverted. Bend float arm tang (T) to adjust float arm height. Make sure groove in side of throttle slide is aligned with pin in carburetor body when inserting slide in carburetor.

With the carburetor installed, the fuel level should be checked. Attach Kawasaki fuel level gauge 57001-202 or a suitable clear hose (T—Fig. K9-5) and plug in place of fuel bowl drain screw. Hose should be long enough to extend above the bottom edge of carburetor body without kinking. Run the engine at idle speed until fuel level in hose stabilizes, then stop engine. Measure distance from the bottom edge of carburetor body (fuel bowl contact surface) to fuel level in hose to determine fuel level (L). Fuel level check will not be accurate if hose is moved after fuel level is stabilized. Fuel level (L) should be 0.0-2.0 mm (0.0-0.08 in.) below carburetor body edge. To adjust fuel level, remove the fuel bowl and carefully bend float arm tang (T—Fig. K9-4).

Keihin PWK35 Carburetor. Initial setting of idle mixture screw (13—Fig. K9-7) is 1½ turns out. Rotating idle mixture screw clockwise will richen idle mixture. Final adjustment must be performed with engine at normal operating temperature. Adjust idle speed screw (26) so engine idles at desired engine speed.

When servicing carburetor, refer to Fig. K9-7 for an exploded view of carburetor. Jet needle clip (7) should be installed in second groove from top of jet needle on A2 models with engine number prior to

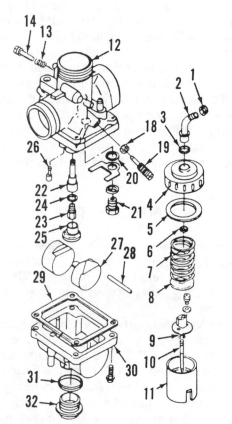

Fig. K9-3—Exploded view of typical Mikuni VM-type carburetor.

1. Nut
2. Cable guide
3. Washer
4. Cap
5. Washer
6. "E" ring
7. Spring
8. Washer
9. Jet needle clip
10. Jet needle
11. Throttle slide
12. Body
13. Spring
14. Idle mixture screw
18. Locknut
19. Idle speed screw
20. Washer
21. Inlet valve
22. Needle jet
23. Main jet
24. Spacer
25. Cover
26. Pilot jet
27. Float
28. Float pin
29. Gasket
30. Fuel bowl
31. Gasket
32. Plug

XF250AE004205 or third groove from top on A2 models with later engine numbers. Float height (H—Fig. K9-8) should be 14.0-18.0 mm (0.55-0.71 in.) between bottom of float and carburetor body. Hold carburetor so float is vertical and resting lightly against fuel inlet valve. Gently bend float arm tang (T) to adjust float height. When inserting slide (9—Fig. K9-7) in carburetor, insert slide so cutaway is toward air cleaner end of carburetor.

With the carburetor installed, the fuel level should be checked. Attach a suitable clear hose (H—Fig. K9-9) to fuel bowl nozzle. Hose should be long enough to extend above the bottom edge of carburetor body without kinking. Open fuel bowl drain screw (D). Run the engine at idle speed until fuel level in hose stabilizes, then stop engine. Measure distance from the bottom edge of carburetor body (fuel bowl contact surface) to fuel level in hose to determine fuel level (L). Fuel level check will not be accurate if hose is moved after fuel level is stabilized. Fuel level (L) should be 0.0-2.0 mm (0.0-0.08 in.) above carburetor body edge. To adjust fuel level, remove the fuel bowl and carefully bend float arm tang (T—Fig. K9-8).

THROTTLE LEVER FREE PLAY. Free play at the end of the throttle lever should be 2-3 mm (0.08-0.12 in.). Throttle lever free play may be adjusted by turning adjusters at either end of throttle cable.

REED VALVE. A "V" type reed valve assembly is located between the intake manifold and engine. The reed valve assembly is accessible after removing the carburetor and intake manifold.

Reed petal seats must be smooth and flat. Renew reed petals if bent, broken or otherwise damaged. Do not attempt to straighten reed petals.

Reed valve petals may stand open (S—Fig. K9-11) a maximum of 0.7 mm (0.028 in.). Install reed housing so arrow on flange points down.

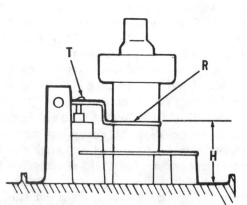

Fig. K9-4—Float arm (R) height (H) must be 15.1-19.1 mm (0.60-0.75 in.) with carburetor inverted. Bend float arm tang (T) to adjust float arm height.

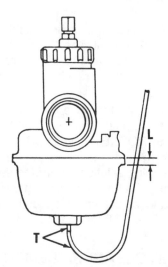

Fig. K9-5—The fuel level is measured from the bottom edge of the carburetor body. Fuel level (L) should be 0.0-2.0 mm (0.0-0.08 in.) below carburetor body edge.

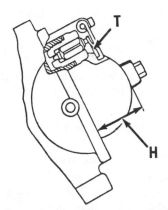

Fig. K9-8—Tilt carburetor when measuring float height so tang (T) just touches inlet valve and valve spring is not compressed. Float height (H) should be 14.0-18.0 mm (0.55-0.71 in.). Bend tang (T) to adjust float height.

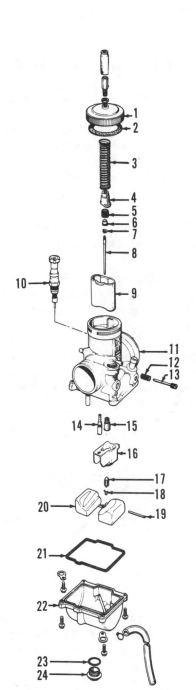

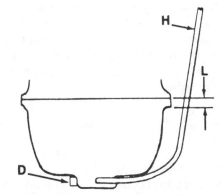

Fig. K9-9—The fuel level is measured from the bottom edge of the carburetor body. Fuel level (L) should be 0.0-2.0 mm (0.0-0.08 in.) above carburetor body edge.

Fig. K9-7—Exploded view of Keihin carburetor used on A2 models.

1. Cap
2. Gasket
3. Spring
4. Cable holder
5. Spring
6. Collar
7. Clip
8. Jet needle
9. Throttle slide
10. Idle/choke assy.
11. Body
12. Spring
13. Idle mixture screw
14. Slow jet
15. Main jet
16. Baffle
17. Fuel inlet valve
18. Clip
19. Float pin
20. Float
21. Gasket
22. Fuel bowl
23. Gasket
24. Drain screw

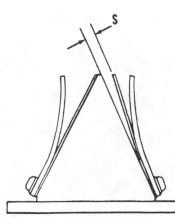

Fig. K9-11—Reed valve petals may stand open (S) a maximum of 0.7 mm (0.028 in.).

FUEL STRAINER. A strainer is mounted on the end of each pickup tube that extends into the fuel tank from the fuel valve. To inspect the strainers, the fuel in the fuel tank must be drained. Disconnect the fuel hose from the fuel valve. Unscrew fuel valve retaining screws and remove fuel valve. Clean and inspect the strainers.

COOLING SYSTEM

INSPECTION. The engine is liquid-cooled by a pressurized cooling system that consists of a radiator, water pump and hoses. System components should be inspected periodically. Replace hoses if cracked, split or otherwise damaged. Inspect radiator for signs of leakage and remove any obstructions.

CHANGING COOLANT. The coolant should be changed annually. The manufacturer recommends a mixture of 50 percent distilled water and 50 percent antifreeze. Cooling system capacity is 1.5 L (1.6 qt.).

NOTE: Distilled water must be used to prevent corrosion and clogging in the radiator. Only antifreeze designed for aluminum engines and radiators may be used. A mixture of antifreeze and distilled water must be present at all times. Use of only distilled water will cause corrosion and subsequent damage.

To drain coolant, remove radiator cap and unscrew drain plug (P—Fig. K9-12) at bottom right of cylinder. Catch coolant in a suitable container and dispose of according to prevailing ordinances. Tip vehicle side-to-side to drain trapped coolant. Detach reserve tank and pour out coolant.

To refill cooling system, pour coolant into radiator until full and reserve tank to full mark. Unscrew air bleed screw on hose fitting on the cylinder head. Tip vehicle side-to-side to release trapped air bubbles. Install air bleed screw and refill radiator. Start and run engine at fast idle, then stop engine. Refill radiator, if necessary, and fill reserve tank to full mark. Install radiator cap and run engine until warm, then stop engine, check for leaks

and allow engine to cool. Refill radiator, if necessary, and fill reserve tank to full mark.

RADIATOR CAP. The radiator cap should have a relief opening pressure of 93-123 kPa (13.5-18 psi).

IGNITION AND ELECTRICAL

IGNITION SYSTEM. All models are equipped with a breakerless, capacitor discharge ignition system.

Ignition timing can be checked after removing magneto cover located on left side of engine. Connect a suitable timing light to engine. Start and run engine until at normal operating temperature. Accelerate engine to 6000 rpm.

NOTE: Engine should not be run at excessive rpm any longer than necessary to check ignition timing.

The center timing mark (C—Fig. K9-13) on the flywheel should align with crankcase pointer (P). If not, remove flywheel retaining cap screw and use a suitable puller to withdraw flywheel. Note timing marks on magneto base plate. The center mark (T—Fig. K9-14) should align with crankcase pointer (P). If not, loosen magneto plate mounting screws (S) and rotate plate. Tighten screws and install flywheel. Tighten flywheel screw to 27 N·m (20 ft.-lbs.).

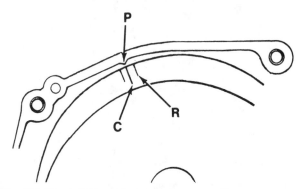

Fig. K9-13—Ignition timing is correct if center timing mark (C) on flywheel aligns with crankcase pointer (P).

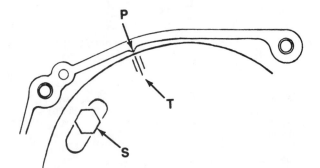

Fig. K9-14—To adjust ignition timing, loosen magneto plate mounting screws (S) and rotate plate so timing mark (T) aligns with crankcase pointer (P).

Fig. K9-12—Unscrew drain plug (P) to drain coolant from cylinder.

The ignition system may be checked using an ohmmeter. To check the exciter coil, disconnect the lead to the magneto and measure resistance between black wire and white/red lead to magneto. Resistance should be 50-75 ohms. Ignition coil primary winding resistance should be 0.25-0.35 ohm. Ignition coil secondary winding resistance should be 5k-7.5k ohms.

If the ignition system malfunctions and all components test satisfactory, replace CDI module with a new or good unit and recheck ignition system.

ELECTRICAL SYSTEM. A lighting coil is located behind the flywheel to provide electrical power for the lights. The lighting coil can be checked using an ohmmeter. Connect an ohmmeter to yellow wire and black wire leads to engine. Resistance should be 0.4-0.7 ohms.

To check lighting coil output, connect a voltmeter to red wire and black/yellow wire leads at headlight. Run engine at 2500 rpm. Voltmeter should indicate at least 10.2 VAC.

Headlight is a 12V 60W unit and the taillight is a 12V 8W unit.

FASTENERS

All screws, nuts and other fasteners should be checked daily and tightened to proper torque specification shown in CONDENSED SERVICE DATA section or in the appropriate maintenance section.

CLUTCH

The engine is equipped with a multiple-disc type clutch that is actuated by the left handlebar lever. The clutch lever free play should be checked daily and adjusted as necessary.

To adjust clutch lever free play, loosen locknut (L—Fig. K9-15) and turn cable adjuster (A) so there is a 2-3 mm (0.08-0.12 in.) gap (G—Fig. K9-15) between lever and housing. Additional adjustment is provided by turning adjuster in cable.

Fig. K9-15—Clutch lever free play is correct if there is a 2-3 mm (0.08-0.12 in.) gap (G) between lever and housing with cable slack removed. Loosen locknut (L) and turn adjuster (A) to adjust free play.

Properly operated, the clutch should disengage and engage freely. Difficult shifting, clutch grabbing or clutch slipping may indicate overhaul is necessary.

FRONT BRAKE ASSEMBLY

A disc brake assembly is used on both front wheels. Front brake adjustment for disc pad wear is not required due to the compensating action of the piston in the caliper.

Brake fluid must be rated DOT 3. Maintain brake fluid level above low mark adjacent to sight glass on side of brake fluid reservoir. Do not overfill. To avert spillage, be sure reservoir is horizontal before removing cover.

BRAKE LEVER FREE PLAY. Front brake lever free play is not adjustable. If brake lever operation is spongy or abnormal lever travel occurs, check brake fluid level and bleed system as outlined in following section.

BLEEDING. Make sure reservoir is full. Connect a bleed hose to bleed valve (B—Fig. K9-16) on both front brake caliper assemblies. Route the bleed hoses into suitable containers. Operate the brake lever until hard resistance is felt, then open one bleed valve. Close bleed valve prior to releasing brake lever. Continue bleeding procedure on both wheels until no air bubbles are noted in discharged fluid from bleed valve.

NOTE: Make sure reservoir remains full during bleeding procedure.

When bleeding procedure is completed, add brake fluid to reservoir until fluid level is at upper level line in reservoir.

OVERHAUL. Brake pads should be renewed if pad thickness is 1.0 mm (0.039 in.) or less.

Fig. K9-16—Connect bleed hose to bleed valve (B) and bleed front brakes as outlined in text.

WARNING: Inhaling asbestos brake dust is injurious to human health. Approved OSHA respiration equipment must be worn when working on or around brake calipers and pads. DO NOT use compressed air to clean brake calipers, pads or nearby components as brake dust will be blown into air. Only vacuum equipment designed to pick up brake dust should be used.

Brake components are accessible after removing wheel, caliper mounting screws and withdrawing caliper. Brake disc should be renewed if thickness is less than 3 mm (0.118 in.) or runout exceeds 0.3 mm (0.012 in.). Tighten brake disc mounting bolts to 36 N·m (26 ft.-lbs.). Push piston by hand back into caliper to allow clearance for new brake pads. Tighten brake caliper mounting screws to 25 N·m (18 ft.-lbs.). After reassembly, operate brake lever until brake lever will not pump up after continuous operation. Do not operate vehicle until brakes are tested and functioning properly.

MASTER CYLINDER. To remove front brake master cylinder (9—Fig. K9-17), detach brake line from master cylinder. Brake fluid will remove paint; be careful when removing master cylinder. Unscrew two retaining screws and remove master cylinder. Remove brake lever, reservoir cover (7) and diaphragm (8). Remove dust boot (1) and snap ring (2). Disassemble piston assembly while noting location and direction of components. Renew complete master cylinder if bore is scored, pitted or excessively worn. Superficial damage in master cylinder bore may be removed using a suitable cylinder hone. After honing, rinse bore with clean brake fluid. Shake out excess fluid but do not wipe dry. Using a shop towel or rag to dry cylinder will leave lint particles in bore. Renew boots and piston cups. During reassembly, lubricate components with clean brake fluid. Reassembly is reverse of disassembly. Install spring (6) so small end contacts primary cup (5). Bleed brakes as

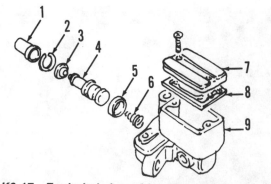

Fig. K9-17—Exploded view of front brake master cylinder.

1. Dust boot
2. Snap ring
3. Secondary cup
4. Piston
5. Primary cup
6. Spring
7. Cover
8. Diaphragm
9. Body

previously outlined. Do not operate vehicle until brakes are tested and functioning properly.

FRONT AXLE

Both front steering knuckle assemblies pivot on ball joint assemblies at the end of each upper and lower control arm. The control arms are bolted at the ends to the vehicle frame and a shock absorber is used to limit and cushion the up and down movement of the control arms. The shock absorbers are adjustable to alter shock absorber spring setting for different terrain and load conditions.

Remove front wheel for access to hub and spindle. Unscrew hub nut to remove wheel hub. Renew bearings if rough or otherwise damaged. Be sure to install spacer between bearings when reassembling components. Tapered end of spacer must be toward wheel side of hub. Tighten hub retaining nut to 34 N·m (25 ft.-lbs.). Tighten wheel retaining nuts to 34 N·m (25 ft.-lbs.).

Remove the front wheel to service the ball joint assemblies. Note that removing the brake components will allow greater access to ball joint assemblies. Ball joints are threaded into control arms and should be tightened to 44 N·m (32 ft.-lbs.). Lower control arm and upper control arm retaining nuts should be tightened to 34 N·m (25 ft. lbs.). Tighten upper ball joint to steering knuckle nut to 41 N·m (30 ft.-lbs.). Tighten lower ball joint to steering knuckle clamp bolt to 41 N·m (30 ft.-lbs.). Tighten shock absorber retaining nuts to 34 N·m (25 ft.-lbs.).

STEERING

INSPECTION. Rotate the handlebar from one extreme to the other and note if any binding or roughness is felt. Periodically inspect the steering components for looseness or any other damage. Renew any damaged component. Clean and grease components if binding or excessive effort is noted.

TOE-IN SETTING. Place the handlebar in a straight ahead position. Use a suitable measuring tool and measure distance (B—Fig. K9-18) at spindle height between the center of the tires on the rear sides. Locate the same tire centerline points on front side of tires and measure front distance (F). On A1 models, the distance on the front side (F) should be 20 mm (0.80 in.) shorter than the measured distance on the rear side (B). On A2 models, distance (F) should be 40 mm (1.60 in.) shorter than distance (B). Note that the distance from a projected vehicle centerline to left (L) and right (R) tire centerlines should also be equal.

To adjust, loosen inside and outside locknuts on the left and right tie rod assemblies and rotate tie rod shaft on each side equally until distance is within recommended range. Note that inner locknuts have left-hand

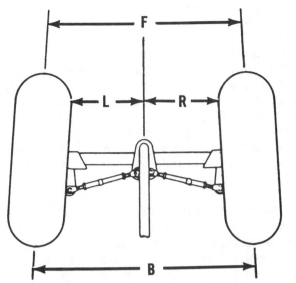

Fig. K9-18—Toe-in should be 20 mm (0.80 in.) on A1 models and 40 mm (1.60 in.) on A2 models. Refer to text for adjustment procedure.

Fig. K9-19—Loosen locknut and rotate adjusting screw (A) to adjust brake pedal height. Loosen locknuts and rotate brake push rod (R) to adjust brake pedal free play.

threads. After obtaining the correct setting, tighten locknuts to 27 N·m (20 ft.-lbs.).

OVERHAUL. To expose the steering shaft, remove rear fender, front fender cover, front fender, fuel tank, handlebar, wire clamp and headlight stay. Mark clamp halves so they can be reinstalled in original position. Unscrew the two cap screws securing the steering shaft clamp halves. Clean the old grease from the steering shaft. Inspect the clamp halves and steering shaft for damage. Renew components if needed. Grease inside of steering shaft clamp halves with a lithium base grease and install. Tighten the retaining clamp cap screws to 20 N·m (15 ft.-lbs.).

To remove steering shaft, remove steering shaft clamps as outlined in previous paragraph. Remove the lower steering shaft retaining cotter pin and nut. Detach inner tie rod ends from steering shaft and withdraw the steering shaft. Inspect the lower bearing and renew if needed. Apply a molybdenum disulfide grease to bearing before installation. Tighten the lower steering shaft retaining nut to 29 N·m (21 ft.-lbs.). Tighten retaining nuts for tie rod ends to 41 N·m (30 ft.-lbs.).

Tighten handlebar clamp screws to 21 N·m (15 ft.-lbs.). Tighten front screw on handlebar clamps first, then tighten the rear clamp screws. If properly tightened, there should be no gaps at the front of the clamps and even gaps at the rear of the clamps.

REAR BRAKE ASSEMBLY

A single disc brake assembly is used for both rear wheels. The running brake is operated hydraulically by a foot pedal on the lower right side. The parking brake is mechanically operated by a cable and handlebar components in conjunction with the clutch lever.

BRAKE PEDAL HEIGHT AND FREE PLAY. Brake pedal height can be adjusted using adjuster screw (A—Fig. K9-19) located next to brake pedal pivot shaft. Brake pedal free play is adjusted by loosening locknuts, then rotating brake master cylinder push rod (R).

PARKING BRAKE ADJUSTMENT. Make sure parking brake/clutch lever is in the released position. Loosen locknut (N—Fig. K9-20) so cable slides freely. Loosen locknut (L) and rotate adjuster screw (S) clockwise until resistance is felt, then rotate counterclockwise ¼ turn and tighten locknut (L). Adjust actuator lever (A) so distance (D) between mounting bracket (B) and center

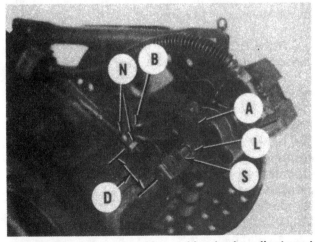

Fig. K9-20—Refer to text for parking brake adjustment.

A. Actuator lever
B. Mounting bracket
D. Measure distance
L. Locknut
N. Locknuts
S. Adjusting screw

Fig. K9-21—View of final drive assembly.
B. Caliper bleed valve
N. Rear axle retaining nuts
P. Snap ring
S. Clamp screws

of actuator lever (A) is 42-44 mm (1.65-1.73 in.). Tighten locknuts (N).

BLEEDING. Make sure rear brake master cylinder reservoir is full. Connect a bleed hose to bleed valve (B—Fig. K9-21) on brake caliper assembly. Route the bleed hose into a suitable container. Operate foot pedal until firm resistance is felt, then open bleed valve (B). Close bleed valve prior to releasing foot pedal. Continue bleeding procedure until no air bubbles are noted in discharged fluid from bleed valve.

NOTE: Make sure rear brake master cylinder remains full during bleeding procedure.

When bleeding procedure is completed, add brake fluid to rear brake master cylinder reservoir until fluid level is above line on reservoir.

OVERHAUL. Brake pad thickness may be determined by viewing the brake pads. If brake pad thickness is less than 1 mm (0.039 in.), both brake pads must be renewed.

WARNING: Inhaling asbestos brake dust is injurious to human health. Approved OSHA respiration equipment must be worn when working on or around brake calipers and pads. DO NOT use compressed air to clean brake calipers, pads or nearby components as brake dust will be blown into air. Only vacuum equipment designed to pick up brake dust should be used.

Brake components are accessible after removing caliper mounting screws and withdrawing caliper. Loosen

parking brake locknut (L—Fig. K9-20) and turn adjusting screw (S) out so there is space between the screw and piston. Push back piston by hand into caliper to provide room for new brake pads. Brake disc should be renewed if thickness is 3.5 mm (0.138 in.) or less or disc runout is 0.3 mm (0.012 in.) or more. Tighten brake disc mounting screws to 23 N·m (17 ft.-lbs.). Tighten brake pad pins to 18 N·m (160 in.-lbs.). Tighten brake caliper mounting screws to 25 N·m (18 ft.-lbs.). After reassembly, operate brake pedal until pedal will not pump up after continuous operation. Do not operate vehicle until brakes are tested and functioning properly.

MASTER CYLINDER. To remove rear brake master cylinder, disconnect brake plunger from pedal. Detach brake lines from master cylinder and plug line to reservoir. Brake fluid will remove paint; be careful when removing master cylinder. Unscrew retaining screws and remove master cylinder. Remove dust boot and snap ring. Disassemble piston assembly while noting location and direction of components. Renew complete master cylinder if bore is scored, pitted or excessively worn. Superficial damage in master cylinder bore may be removed using a suitable cylinder hone. After honing, rinse bore with clean brake fluid. Shake out excess fluid but do not wipe dry. Using a shop towel or rag to dry cylinder will leave lint particles in bore. Renew boots and piston cups. During reassembly, lubricate components with clean brake fluid. Reassembly is reverse of disassembly. Bleed brakes as previously outlined. Do not operate vehicle until brakes are tested and functioning properly.

DRIVE CHAIN AND SPROCKETS

INSPECTION AND ADJUSTMENT. The drive chain should be inspected and adjusted daily. Improper maintenance and neglect can cause early failure of both drive chain and sprockets. To measure drive chain free play, support rear of frame near swing arm pivot so rear wheels are off ground. Measure drive chain travel at a point midway between rub block at swing arm and rear sprocket. Drive chain free play should be 45-55 mm (1.77-2.16 in.). To adjust chain free play, loosen clamp screws (S—Fig. K9-21) and use a suitable tool to engage lugs on rear axle housing and rotate rear axle housing. Rotate rear axle housing as needed to obtain desired chain free play. Tighten screws (S) and recheck chain free play.

R&R AND OVERHAUL. Loosen screws (S—Fig. K9-21) and rotate rear axle housing to loosen chain. Remove chain guard and front and rear sprocket guards. Lift chain off rear sprocket toward left rear wheel. Use a location at rear of vehicle frame and lift rear wheels off the ground. Detach the rear shock absorber at the lower mounting bracket. Remove parking brake cable at caliper, if needed. Remove the swing arm caps and remove one swing arm shaft nut. Support swing arm and withdraw swing arm pivot shaft toward end with nut still attached. Remove left rear wheel and detach drive chain.

Carefully examine sprockets for excessive wear. Worn sprockets will usually have a hooked tooth profile. A good test is to place a new chain on a used sprocket and check the fit. If sprockets require renewal due to wear, always renew drive chain. Sprockets should be renewed as a set. Renew drive chain if distance between 20 link pins exceeds 324 mm (12.76 in.) with chain straight and all slack removed.

Reassemble by reversing disassembly procedure. Tighten rear sprocket retaining nuts to 25 N·m (18 ft.-lbs.). Tighten wheel retaining nuts to 34 N·m (25 ft.-lbs.). Refer to previous INSPECTION AND ADJUST-MENT paragraphs for recommended drive chain adjustment procedure.

FINAL DRIVE ASSEMBLY

R&R AND OVERHAUL. To remove final drive assembly, remove drive chain and brake caliper as previously outlined. Remove right rear wheel and both wheel hubs. Remove rear axle retaining locknuts (N—Fig. K9-21), brake disc and holder and push rear axle out toward left side. Remove snap ring (P) to separate final drive bearing housing from swing arm clamp brackets.

Renew seals and bearings as needed. With axle supported at ends, maximum allowable runout measured at bearing journals is 0.2 mm (0.008 in.). Reassembly is reverse of disassembly. Tighten rear axle retaining nuts (N) to 145 N·m (110 ft.-lbs.).

KAWASAKI
KLF300

NOTE: Metric fasteners are used throughout vehicle.

CONDENSED SERVICE DATA

MODELS	KLF300-B1, B2, B3, B4
General	
Engine Make	Own
Engine Type	Air-Cooled; Four-Stroke
Number of Cylinders	1
Bore	76 mm
	(3.0 in.)
Stroke	64 mm
	(2.52 in.)
Displacement	290 cc
	(17.7 cu. in.)
Compression Ratio	8.6:1
Engine Lubrication	Wet Sump; Oil Pump
Transmission Lubrication	Common With Engine
Engine/Transmission Oil	See Text
Forward Speeds	5
Reverse Speeds	1
Tire Size:	
Front	22 × 9-10
Rear	24 × 11-10
Tire Pressure:	
Front & Rear (cold)	21 kPa
	(3 psi)
Dry Weight	223 kg
	(491 lbs.)
Tune-Up	
Engine Idle Speed	See Text
Spark Plug:	
Type	NGK B8ES
Electrode Gap	0.7-0.8 mm
	(0.027-0.031 in.)
Ignition:	
Type	Capacitor Discharge
Point Gap	Pointless
Timing	10° BTDC @ 1300 rpm
	40° BTDC @ 4000 rpm
Carburetor:	
Make	Keihin
Model	CVK32
Float Height	17 mm
	(0.67 in.)
Main Jet	#128
Main Air Jet	#100
Pilot Jet	#38

Tune-Up (Cont.)
Carburetor: (Cont.)
Pilot Air Jet........................	#140
Jet Needle........................	N27Q
Needle Jet........................	#6
Idle Mixture Setting................	2$\frac{1}{8}$ Turn
Throttle Lever Free Play.............	2-3 mm
	(0.079-0.118 in.)

Sizes-Clearances
Valve Clearance (cold):	
Intake........................	0.10-0.15 mm
	(0.004-0.006 in.)
Exhaust........................	0.15-0.20 mm
	(0.006-0.008 in.)
Valve Face & Seat Angle.............	45°
Valve Seat Width:	
Intake & Exhaust...................	0.5-1.0 mm
	(0.020-0.039 in.)
Valve Stem Diameter:	
Intake........................	6.965-6.980 mm
	(0.2742-0.2748 in.)
Exhaust........................	6.950-6.970 mm
	(0.2736-0.2744 in.)
Valve Guide Bore Diameter:	
Intake & Exhaust...................	7.000-7.015 mm
	(0.2756-0.2762 in.)
Valve Stem-to-Guide Clearance:	
Intake........................	0.020-0.050 mm
	(0.0008-0.0020 in.)
Exhaust........................	0.030-0.065 mm
	(0.0012-0.0025 in.)
Rocker Arm Bore Diameter:	
Intake & Exhaust...................	13.000-13.018 mm
	(0.5118-0.5125 in.)
Rocker Shaft Diameter:	
Intake & Exhaust...................	12.976-12.994 mm
	(0.5108-0.5116 in.)
Camshaft Lobe Height:	
Intake & Exhaust...................	40.876-40.984 mm
	(1.6093-1.6135 in.)
Wear Limit...................	40.78 mm
	(1.6055 in.)
Cylinder Head Distortion (Max.)........	0.05 mm
	(0.002 in.)
Cylinder Bore Diameter..............	76.000-76.012 mm
	(2.9921-2.9926 in.)
Wear Limit........................	76.10 mm
	(2.9961 in.)
Piston-to-Cylinder Wall	
Clearance........................	0.035-0.062 mm
	(0.0014-0.0024 in.)
Piston Diameter:	
Measured 5 mm (0.2 in.) From	
Skirt Bottom & 90° to Pin Bore........	75.950-75.965 mm
	(2.9901-2.9907 in.)

Sizes-Clearances (Cont.)

Piston Ring End Gap
  in Standard Bore:
    Top & Second Ring . . . . 0.20-0.35 mm
(0.008-0.014 in.)

Piston Ring Groove Width:
  Top Ring. . . . . 1.22-1.24 mm
(0.048-0.049 in.)

  Second Ring . . . . 1.21-1.23 mm
(0.047-0.048 in.)

  Oil Ring . . . . 2.51-2.53 mm
(0.099-0.100 in.)

Piston Ring Width:
  Top & Second Ring . . . . 1.170-1.90 mm
(0.046-0.047 in.)

Piston Ring Side Clearance:
  Top Ring. . . . . 0.03-0.07 mm
(0.0012-0.0027 in.)

    Max.. . . . . 0.17 mm
(0.007 in.)

  Second Ring . . . . 0.02-0.06 mm
(0.0007-0.0023 in.)

    Max.. . . . . 0.16 mm
(0.006 in.)

Connecting Rod Big End
  Side Clearance . . . . 0.25-0.35 mm
(0.010-0.014 in.)

  Maximum Allowable. . . . . 0.6 mm
(0.023 in.)

Connecting Rod Big End
  Radial Clearance. . . . . 0.008-0.020 mm
(0.0003-0.0008 in.)

  Maximum Allowable. . . . . 0.07 mm
(0.003 in.)

Crankshaft Runout:
  LH . . . . 0.08 mm
(0.003 in.)

  RH . . . . 0.1 mm
(0.004 in.)

Capacities

Fuel Tank . . . . 9 L
(2.38 gal.)

Engine/Transmission Sump. . . . . 1.7 L
(1.79 qt.)

Differential Case . . . . 0.3 L
(0.32 qt.)

Tightening Torques

Axle Nut:
  Front . . . . 34 N•m
(25 ft.-lbs.)

  Rear. . . . . 145 N•m
(110 ft.-lbs.)

Camshaft Sprocket Screw . . . . 41 N•m
(30 ft.-lbs.)

Primary Clutch Nut. . . . . 83 N•m
(61 ft.-lbs.)

Tightening Torques (Cont.)

Secondary Clutch Nut . . . . 78 N·m
(58 ft.-lbs.)

Cylinder Head Screws:

6 mm . . . . 12 N·m
(104 in.-lbs.)

8 mm:

    Initial . . . . 14 N·m
(124 in.-lbs.)

    Final: Used Screws . . . . 29 N·m
(22 ft.-lbs.)

    New Screws . . . . 34 N·m
(25 ft.-lbs.)

Starter Cup (Flywheel) . . . . 59 N·m
(43 ft.-lbs.)

Wheel Retaining Nut . . . . 34 N·m
(25 ft.-lbs.)

Standard Fasteners:

5 mm . . . . 3.4-4.9 N·m
(30-42 in.-lbs.)

6 mm . . . . 5.9-7.8 N·m
(52-69 in.-lbs.)

8 mm . . . . 14-19 N·m
(10-13.5 ft.-lbs.)

10 mm . . . . 25-39 N·m
(19-25 ft.-lbs.)

12 mm . . . . 44-61 N·m
(33-45 ft.-lbs.)

14 mm . . . . 73-98 N·m
(54-72 ft.-lbs.)

16 mm . . . . 115-155 N·m
(83-115 ft.-lbs.)

18 mm . . . . 165-225 N·m
(125-165 ft.-lbs.)

20 mm . . . . 225-325 N·m
(165-240 ft.-lbs.)

LUBRICATION

ENGINE AND TRANSMISSION. The engine is lubricated by a trochoid-type pump located on the right side of the crankcase and driven by a gear on the right end of the crankshaft. The engine and transmission share a common sump. Recommended oil is a multigrade SAE 10W-40, 10W-50, 20W-40 or 20W-50 motor oil with an API classification of SE or SF.

Sump is filled through filler cap opening (F—Fig. K11-1). Oil level should be maintained between oil level lines (L) adjacent to sight glass (G). Sump is drained by removing plug in underside of crankcase. Crankcase capacity after changing oil and oil filter is 1.7 L (1.79 qt.).

Manufacturer recommends changing oil and oil filter after the first 10 hours of operation. Thereafter, the oil and oil filter should be changed after every 90 days of operation. In conjunction with oil filter change, the oil pressure relief valve, located within the oil filter mounting pin, should be disassembled, cleaned and inspected. The sump screen, located in the right crankcase half and below and to the left of the oil pump, should also be removed and cleaned.

The oil filter and oil pressure relief valve are accessible after removing cover (C). To disassemble oil pressure relief valve, drive out cross-pin (1—Fig. K11-2) and separate components. Renew the complete assembly if excessive wear or damage is evident. During reassembly, insert piston (3) with open end toward spring (2). Insert and compress spring (2) just beyond cross-

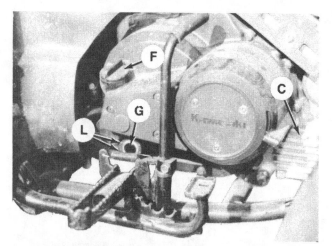

Fig. K11-1—Engine/transmission sump is filled through filler plug opening (F). Oil level should be maintained between lines (L) next to sight glass (G). The oil filter is located behind cover (C).

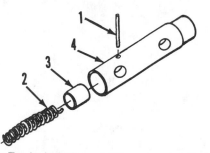

Fig. K11-2—Exploded view of oil pressure relief valve.

1. Cross-pin
2. Spring
3. Piston
4. Filter mount sleeve

pin hole and install cross-pin (1). Install the oil filter ensuring "O" ring seals are located on both sides of filter. Renew filter cover "O" ring seal if required and install cover.

Sump screen is accessible after removing right crankcase cover. Drain oil from crankcase. Unbolt and carefully remove the right crankcase cover. Withdraw the sump screen from crankcase half. Reinstall by reversing removal procedure while noting the following: Make sure alignment dowels and gasket are fitted to crankcase and install cover. Adjust clutch as outlined in CLUTCH section. Fill engine/transmission sump with the appropriate amount of oil and check for leaks.

DIFFERENTIAL UNIT. The differential oil should be changed after the first 10 hours of operation and annually thereafter. Check oil level periodically and renew more frequently if vehicle is operated under adverse conditions. Recommended differential lubricant is API GL-5 hypoid gear oil or a good quality SAE 90 hypoid gear oil when the ambient temperature is above 5° C (41° F) or SAE 80 hypoid gear oil when the ambient temperature is 5° C (41° F) or below. Differential case capacity is 0.3 L (0.32 qt.)

Fig. K11-4—View identifying differential case oil level plug (P). Drain plug is located at base of differential case.

Differential case is checked and filled through oil plug (P—Fig. K11-4) opening. Oil is drained through plug at the base of the differential case. Oil should be maintained at level of oil plug (P) opening when vehicle is positioned on a flat level surface. When renewing oil, first operate vehicle to allow differential case oil to pick up any contaminates within the case and to allow oil to warm-up for easier drainage. Then, remove drain plug at base of differential case and level plug (P) and allow oil to drain into a suitable container.

CABLES, LEVERS AND LINKAGE. All cables, levers and linkage should be inspected and lubricated after every 30 days of operation.

AIR CLEANER ELEMENT

The air cleaner element should be removed and cleaned after the first 10 hours of operation and every 10 days of operation thereafter. To remove air cleaner element, first remove seat and air cleaner cover (C—Fig. K11-5). Unscrew and remove element and frame from case. Carefully separate foam element from frame.

Thoroughly clean element in a nonflammable solvent. Compress element between hands to remove solvent. Saturate element in clean SAE 30 motor oil and compress element to remove excess oil. Reinstall element by reversing removal procedure.

FUEL SYSTEM

CARBURETOR. A Keihin CVK32-type carburetor is used. Refer to CONDENSED SERVICE DATA for carburetor specifications.

Adjust idle speed knob (K—Fig. K11-7) to obtain the lowest smooth idle setting. After adjusting carburetor

Fig. K11-5—Remove air cleaner cover (C) for access to filter element.

Fig. K11-7—View of carburetor identifying idle speed knob (K).

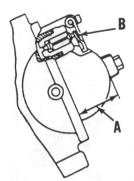

Fig. K11-8—Float height (A) should be 17 mm (0.67 in.). Bend float arm tang (B) to adjust.

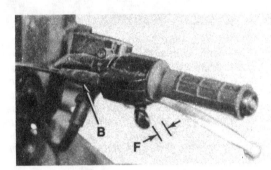

Fig. K11-12—Throttle lever should have 2-3 mm (0.079-0.118 in.) of free play measured at (F). To adjust, slide boot (B) down cable to expose adjuster nut and locknut.

idle setting, check throttle lever free play as outlined in THROTTLE LEVER FREE PLAY section.

When servicing the carburetor, note the following: Float height (A—Fig. K11-8) should be 17 mm (0.67 in.) as measured from gasket surface of carburetor body to lowest edge of float. Hold carburetor so float is vertical and resting lightly against fuel inlet valve when checking float height as shown in Fig. K11-8. Adjust the float level by bending tang (B) on float arm.

The fuel level is checked with the carburetor installed and vehicle operational. To check fuel level, attach Kawasaki fuel level gauge 57001-1017 to open end of carburetor overflow hose and position gauge so zero line is even with bottom edge of carburetor body (float bowl contact surface). Turn fuel valve to "ON" position and open fuel drain screw to allow fuel drainage. After fuel in hose has stabilized, measure the distance from the bottom edge of carburetor body to fuel level in hose. Fuel level check will not be accurate if hose is raised or lowered after fuel level has stabilized. Fuel level should be 0.5 mm (0.02 in.) below bottom edge of carburetor body to 1.5 mm (0.06 in.) above bottom edge of carburetor body. To adjust fuel level, the float bowl must be removed to carefully bend float arm tang (B—Fig. 11-8).

FUEL STRAINER. A strainer is mounted on the end of the "ON" pickup tube and the "RES" (reserve) pickup tube of the fuel valve assembly mounted on the fuel tank. A strainer is also located behind the fuel valve control lever. To inspect the strainers, the fuel in the fuel tank must be drained. Disconnect the fuel hose from the fuel valve. Unscrew the two screws securing the fuel valve to the fuel tank and carefully remove the fuel valve from the tank. Clean and inspect the strainers. The strainers are not available separately, only as a part of the valve housing. Reinstall the valve assembly while noting that nylon washers are used on the two retaining screws to prevent fuel leakage.

THROTTLE LEVER FREE PLAY. The throttle lever should have 2-3 mm (0.079-0.118 in.) of free play measured at throttle lever end as shown at (F—Fig. K11-12). Throttle lever free play can be adjusted by sliding boot (B) down cable to expose outer adjuster nut and inner locknut. Loosen locknut and rotate adjuster nut until 2-3 mm (0.079-0.118 in.) free play is obtained. Secure adjustment with locknut and reinstall boot (B).

IGNITION AND ELECTRICAL

SPARK PLUG. Standard spark plug is NGK B8ES. Spark plug electrode gap should be 0.7-0.8 mm(0.027-0.031 in.). Spark plug should be removed, cleaned and

Fig. K11-14—Remove plug (P) to check ignition timing. "F" mark (F) should align with notch (N) when engine is operated at idle speed. To adjust reverse knob free play, loosen jam nuts on cable at mounting bracket (B) and rotate adjuster (A) until 2-3 mm (0.079-0.118 in.) free play is obtained at reverse knob. Reverse lever (L) must be installed with lever slot and case mark aligned as shown at (M) when reverse knob and shift linkage are in disengaged position. Differential lock shifter is identified at (D).

electrode gap set after the first 10 hours of operation and every 90 days of operation thereafter. Renew spark plug if damage and excessive electrode wear is evident.

IGNITION. A breakerless Capacitor Discharge Ignition (CDI) system is used. The electronic ignition circuit consists of the battery, CDI module, pickup coil, flywheel, ignition coil, spark plug, engine stop switch and ignition switch. Ignition timing at idle speed should occur

when "F" mark (F—Fig. K11-14) on flywheel is aligned with notch (N) as viewed through timing plug (P) opening. Specified ignition timing is 10° BTDC ("F" mark) at 1300 rpm and 40° BTDC (maximum advance) at 4000 rpm. Ignition timing is checked with a power timing light and is not adjustable. If ignition timing is not as specified, check condition of CDI module and pick up coil as described in following test procedures.

If ignition malfunction occurs, check condition of battery, spark plug, all wires and connections before troubleshooting the ignition circuit. Using Kawasaki tester 57001-983 or a suitable ohmmeter, refer to following test specifications and procedures to aid troubleshooting.

To check condition of CDI module, first remove module from vehicle. Use tester or ohmmeter in conjunction with the test chart in Fig. K11-15. Renew CDI module if module fails to meet test specificatiions.

To check condition of pickup coil, separate blue and black wires leading from pulse generator to CDI module at connector. Attach one lead to blue wire and remaining tester lead to black wire from pulse coil. Pickup coil can be considered satisfactory if resistance reading is within 390-590 ohms.

To check condition of ignition coil, remove green/white wire and yellow/red wire from their respective terminals on coil and high tension wire from spark plug. Attach one tester lead to green/white wire terminal and remaining tester lead to yellow/red wire terminal on ignition coil. Primary coil resistance reading should be 1.8-2.8 ohms. Attach one tester lead to green/white wire terminal on ignition coil and remaining tester lead to high tension wire. Secondary coil resistance reading should be 10k-16k ohms. Renew ignition coil if coil fails to meet either test specification.

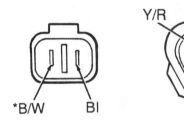

Fig. K11-15—Use the test chart and values listed below to test condition of CDI module.

A. Infinite resistance.
B. 3k-30k ohms
C. 800-8000 ohms
D. 50k-500k ohms
E. 1.2k-12k ohms
F. 70k-550k ohms
G. 2k-15k ohms
H. 30k-300k ohms
I. 60k-500k
J. Zero resistance

		+Test Lead				
		Y/R	G/W	B/W	*B/W	BI
−Test Lead	Y/R		B	G	G	I
	G/W	A		A	A	A
	B/W	E	C		J	H
	*B/W	E	C	J		H
	BI	F	D	H	H	

CHARGING CIRCUIT. The charging circuit consists of an alternator charge coil, a regulator/rectifier, battery and ignition switch. Standard battery has a 14 ampere hour, 12-volt rating.

The battery should be checked and filled to maximum level with distilled water, if required, after the first 10 hours of operation and then after every 30 days of operation. During periods of vehicle storage, the battery should be charged once a month to reduce sulfation and prolong battery life. The battery should always be removed from the vehicle prior to charging. Do not exceed maximum charging rate of 1.9 amperes.

The alternator charge coil can be statically tested using a suitable ohmmeter. There are three yellow wires from alternator charge coil to regulator/rectifier. Separate wires from alternator to regulator/rectifier at connector block and measure resistance between the wires. Resistance reading should be 0.1-0.7 ohm. Check for continuity between each of the alternator wires and ground. Tester should read infinite resistance at each wire.

Test procedures for checking condition of regulator/rectifier are not reliable as unit may test satisfactory but still be defective. The recommended procedure is to test all associated charging circuit components and eliminate them as the source of defect prior to renewing regulator/rectifier or install a known good regulator/rectifier assembly and check charging circuit for proper operation. Regulator/rectifier output voltage should not be higher than 15 volts.

ELECTRIC STARTER. The starter can be removed and disassembled to clean, inspect and lubricate individual parts. The starter brushes should be renewed if worn to 6 mm (0.24 in.) or less. Starter brushes are available from the manufacturer in kit form with springs, brush plate and associated components. Starter armature and gear set are not available separately and the complete assembly should be renewed if defective.

To remove electric starter, first disconnect battery. Disconnect wire at terminal on starter. Unbolt and withdraw starter motor. Note the location of all components during disassembly to aid in reassembly.

During installation, make sure "O" ring is positioned around starter neck, then guide starter into position while aligning starter shaft with starter sprocket splines. Remainder of installation is the reverse of removal procedure.

FASTENERS

The vehicle should receive an overall inspection after the first 10 hours of operation and every 10 days of operation thereafter. All cap screws, nuts and fasteners should be checked and tightened to proper torque specification listed in CONDENSED SERVICE DATA section or in the appropriate MAINTENANCE section.

Fig. K11-16—Valve clearance should be 0.10-0.15 mm (0.004-0.006 in.) for intake valve and 0.15-0.20 mm (0.006-0.008 in.) for exhaust valve. Loosen locknut (L) and turn adjuster screw (A) to adjust clearance.

VALVE SYSTEM

The valves are actuated via rocker arms by a single overhead camshaft. Camshaft is driven by a roller chain attached to the left end of crankshaft. Valve clearance on all models should be adjusted after the first 10 hours of operation and then after every 90 days of operation. Valve clearance should be adjusted with engine cold.

To adjust valve clearance, remove seat, fuel tank, valve adjustment caps, rewind starter and plug (P—Fig. K11-14). Attach a suitable tool to flywheel screw and rotate crankshaft until "T" mark (Top Dead Center) on flywheel aligns with notch (N) with piston on compression stroke. To ensure piston is on compression stroke, rotate crankshaft 1/4 turn past "T" mark while observing intake valve. If valve movement is indicated, rotate crankshaft one complete revolution and align "T" mark with stationary mark again.

Clearance between rocker arm adjusting screw (A—Fig. K11-16) and valve stem should be 0.10-0.15 mm (0.004-0.006 in.) for the intake valve and 0.15-0.20 mm (0.006-0.008 in.) for the exhaust valve. Measure clearance with a suitable feeler gauge and adjust by loosening locknut (L) and turning adjusting screw (A). Be sure to recheck clearance after locknuts are tightened.

CLUTCH

Vehicles are equipped with a multiple-disc clutch that is actuated by the gear shift lever. As the gear shift lever is operated to change gears, the clutch is disengaged through linkage connected to the shift shaft.

To adjust the clutch, remove three screws (S—Fig. K11-17) to allow removal of right side cover (C). Loosen the locknut located behind cover (C) and turn the adjusting screw clockwise until screw becomes hard to turn. Then turn the screw counterclockwise until resistance to turning is felt. Hold screw in position and tighten the locknut. Install cover (C) and check clutch adjustment

Fig. K11-17—To gain access to clutch adjustment screw and locknut, remove three screws (S) and withdraw cover (C).

by shifting gears with engine idling. Engine should not die when changing gears.

MANUAL STARTER

R&R AND OVERHAUL. Refer to Fig. K11-18 for view of a partially disassembled manual starter assembly. Manual starter can be removed from the vehicle as a complete unit after removing the four starter retaining screws. If starter rope remains under tension, pull starter rope and hold rope pulley (8—Fig. K11-18) with notch (N) in pulley adjacent to rope outlet. Pull a loop of rope back through outlet so rope engages notch in pulley and allow pulley (8) to slowly unwind.

Remove retaining nut (1) and disassemble unit. Be careful when removing rewind spring. A rapidly uncoiling starter spring can cause serious injury.

Rewind spring is wound into starter housing (10) in a clockwise direction. Starter rope is wound on rope pulley (8) in a clockwise direction as viewed with rope pulley in starter housing. Reassemble starter by reversing disassembly procedure. Lightly grease pulley shaft, starter pawl and inside face of friction plate (3).

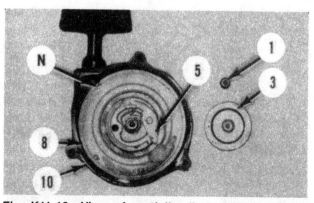

Fig. K11-18—View of partially disassembled manual starter typical of starter used on all models.

N. Notch	5. Starter pawl
1. Nut	8. Rope pulley
3. Friction plate	10. Starter housing

To place tension on rewind spring after reassembly, pass starter rope through rope outlet in starter housing and install rope handle. Pull a loop of rope back through outlet between notch (N) in pulley and housing. Rotate rope pulley (8) clockwise four complete revolutions, then release starter rope from pulley notch (N) and allow starter rope to wind onto pulley (8). Do not place any more tension on rewind spring than is necessary to draw starter rope handle up against housing.

REVERSE KNOB FREE PLAY

The reverse knob should have 2-3 mm (0.079-0.118 in.) of free play measured at outer circumference of knob. Reverse knob free play can be adjusted by loosening jam nuts on cable at mounting bracket (B—Fig. K11-14) and rotating adjuster (A) until 2-3 mm (0.079-0.118 in.) free play is obtained. Secure adjustment with jam nuts.

When reverse lever (L) is removed, make sure lever is installed with lever slot and case mark aligned as shown at (M) when reverse knob and shift linkage are in disengaged position.

FRONT BRAKE ASSEMBLY

A disc brake assembly is used on both front wheels. As the disc or disc pads wear, the piston within the brake caliper assembly will move out to automatically compensate for the wear, so adjustment on the front brakes is not required.

BLEEDING. Make sure reservoir (R—Fig. K11-19) is full. Connect a bleed hose to bleed valve (B—Fig. K11-20) on both front brake caliper assemblies. Route the bleed hoses into suitable containers. Operate brake lever (L—Fig. K11-19) until a hardness (fluid resistance) is felt, then open one bleed valve (rotate counterclockwise). Close bleed valve prior to releasing brake lever.

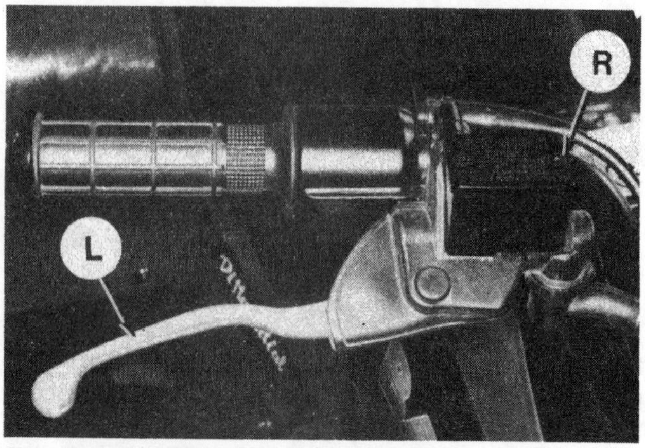

Fig. K11-19—View identifying front brake operating lever (L) and brake fluid reservoir (R).

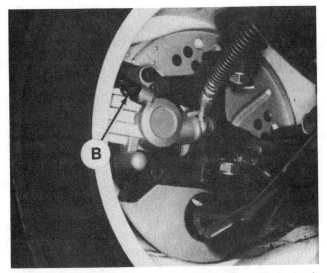

Fig. K11-20—Attach a hose to bleed valve (B) on both front brake calipers to bleed front brake system. See text.

Continue bleeding procedure on both wheels until no air bubbles are noted in discharged fluid from bleed valve.

NOTE: Make sure reservoir (R) is kept full during bleeding procedure.

When bleeding procedure is completed, add brake fluid to reservoir until fluid level is at upper level line in reservoir.

OVERHAUL. Brake pad thickness may be determined externally by viewing the brake pads. If brake pad thickness is 1 mm (0.039 in.) or less, then brake pads must be renewed.

WARNING: Inhaling asbestos brake dust is injurious to human health. Approved OSHA respiration equipment must be worn when working on or around brake calipers and pads. DO NOT use compressed air to clean brake calipers, pads or nearby components as brake dust will be blown into air. Only vacuum equipment designed to pick up brake dust should be used.

Brake components are accessible after removing wheel, caliper mounting screws and withdrawing caliper. Push piston by hand back into caliper to allow clearance for new brake pads. Brake disc should be renewed if thickness is 3 mm (0.118 in.) or less or disc runout is 0.3 mm (0.012 in.) or more. After reassembly, operate brake lever until brake lever will not pump up after continuous operation. Do not operate vehicle until brakes operate properly.

FRONT AXLE

The left and right front steering knuckle assemblies pivot on ball joint assemblies at the end of each upper and lower control arm. The control arms are bolted at the ends to the vehicle frame and a shock absorber is used to limit and cushion the up and down movement of the control arms. The shock absorbers are adjustable to alter absorber spring setting for different terrain and load conditions.

Remove the front wheel to service the ball joint assemblies. Note that removing the brake components will allow greater access to ball joint assemblies. If any ball joint or control arm is excessively worn or any other damage is noted, then ball joint or control arm must be renewed. Note that ball joints are threaded in control arms and can be unscrewed after detaching snap ring. Lower and upper control arm mounting screws should be tightened to 88 N•m (65 ft.-lbs). Tighten ball joint nuts to 41 N•m (30 ft.-lbs.). Tighten shock absorber bolts to 34 N•m (25 ft.-lbs.).

STEERING

TOE-IN SETTING. Place the handlebars in a straight ahead position. Use a suitable measuring tool and measure distance (D—Fig. K11-22), at spindle height, between the center of the tires on the front and rear sides. The measured distance (D) on the front side should be 27 mm (1.06 in.) shorter than the measured distance on the rear side. If not, loosen the inside (I) and outside (O) locknuts on the left and right tie rod assemblies and rotate the tie rods sleeves equally until a difference of 27 mm (1.06 in.) is noted.

NOTE: If the handlebars are not positioned straight ahead when the front wheels are facing straight ahead, then rotate left and right tie rod sleeves the same direction in equal increments until

Fig. K11-22—Refer to text for correct procedures in measuring distance (D) for setting toe-in. Tie rod sleeves are secured by inside (I) and outside (O) locknuts.

handlebars are facing straight ahead. The toe-in setting should not be affected if tie rod sleeves are rotated equal amounts.

After obtaining the correct setting, securely tighten the locknuts to retain tie rod settings.

INSPECTION. Rotate the handlebars from one extreme to the other and note if any binding or roughness is felt. Periodically inspect the steering components for looseness or any other damage. Renew any damaged component. Clean and grease components if binding or excessive effort is noted.

OVERHAUL. To expose the steering tube, the front fender assembly, seat and gas tank must be removed. Remove the Allen head bolts and nuts securing the upper tube clamp and withdraw the clamp halves. Clean the old grease from the steering tube and bearing portions of the clamp halves. Inspect the clamp halves and the upper and lower grease seals for damage. Renew components if needed. Grease components and install clamp halves so match marks on sides of halves are aligned. Tighten the retaining clamp Allen head bolts and nuts to 20 N·m (15 ft.-lbs.).

The tie rod assemblies, handlebar assembly, control panel components on handlebar holder, headlight and upper tube clamp must be removed to withdraw the steering tube from the vehicle. Remove the lower bearing housing mounting screws to withdraw the steering tube. Inspect the lower bearing assembly and seals and renew if needed. Tighten the lower bearing assembly retaining nut to 29 N·m (22 ft.-lbs.). Tighten the tie rod assembly mounting nuts to 41 N·m (30 ft.-lbs.).

When installing the handlebar assembly to the steering tube, the handlebar should be positioned so the handlebar and steering tube are set at the same angle. Tighten the rear handlebar mounting clamp screws first, then tighten the front screws. If properly tightened, there should be no gap at the rear of the clamp and an even gap at the front.

REAR BRAKE ASSEMBLY

ADJUSTMENT. The rear brake is actuated by a foot pedal. Brake pedal free play should be 20-30 mm (0.787-1.181 in.) measured at the pedal pad. Adjust pedal free play by turning adjusting nut (N—Fig. K11-24) equally on each rear wheel. Additional adjustment is possible by loosening nuts (N—Fig. K11-25) on front end of each cable and turning adjuster (A).

OVERHAUL. Brake lining thickness may be determined externally by actuating brake and noting position of pointer (P—Fig. K11-24) mounted on actuating lever. There is sufficient brake lining if pointer falls in "USABLE RANGE" on brake backing plate.

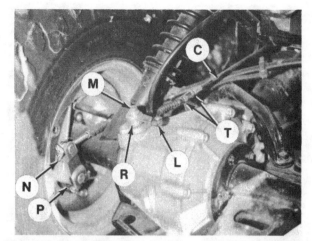

Fig. K11-24—Adjusting nut (N) on each rear wheel is used to adjust rear brake pedal free play and pointer (P) on each rear wheel is used to externally identify brake lining wear. Refer to text for adjustment of differential lock components.

C. Cable
L. Lever
M. Nut

R. Return spring
T. Nuts

WARNING: Inhaling asbestos brake dust is injurious to human health. Approved OSHA respiration equipment must be worn when working on or around brake components. DO NOT use compressed air to clean brake drums, shoes or nearby components as brake dust will be blown into air. Only vacuum equipment designed to pick up brake dust should be used.

Brake components are accessible after removing wheel and brake drum. Renew brake drum assembly if the inside diameter is more than 160.55 mm (6.32 in.).

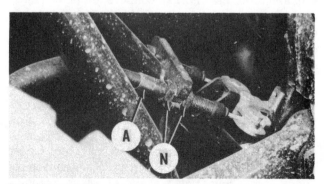

Fig. K11-25—Rear brake may be adjusted by loosening locknuts (N) and rotating adjuster (A) at front end of cable.

DIFFERENTIAL LOCK

In the unlocked position, the rear wheels are free to rotate at different speeds improving slow speed handling characteristics on hard terrain. In the locked position, the rear wheels rotate simultaneously providing maximum traction on adverse or soft terrain. The differential lock shifter (D—Fig. K11-14) is located on the left side of the engine.

ADJUSTMENT. Place differential lock shifter (D—Fig. K11-14) in "LOCKED" position. Remove nut (M—Fig. K11-24), disconnect return spring (R) and lift lever (L) off shift shaft. Loosen nuts (T) and slide cable (C) housing forward until seated in holder, then tighten nuts (T). Turn differential lock shaft clockwise to position differential in locked mode. Pull cable inner wire taut and install lever (L) on cable end, then slide lever on differential lock shaft. Connect return spring (R) and install nut (M) and securely tighten.

DIFFERENTIAL ASSEMBLY

REMOVE AND REINSTALL. Lift vehicle frame so the rear of the vehicle is off the ground. Drain differential gearcase oil. Remove the rear wheels, rear brake drums and rear brake backing plates with brake components. Loosen worm clamp screw at front of drive shaft dust cover. Detach differential lock cable and differential case vent hose. Remove left and right shock absorber lower mounting screws and left and right pivot arm outer screws, then withdraw differential assembly.

NOTE: Differential assembly service should be performed by a factory trained service technician as Kawasaki special tools are required.

Reverse removal procedures to install differential assembly. Tighten shock absorber and lower pivot arm screws to 34 N·m (25 ft.-lbs.).

KAWASAKI

KLF300 4X4

NOTE: Metric fasteners are used throughout vehicle.

CONDENSED SERVICE DATA

MODELS	KLF300-C1, C2, C3, C4
General	
Engine Make	Own
Engine Type	Air-Cooled; Four-Stroke
Number of Cylinders	1
Bore	76 mm
	(3.0 in.)
Stroke	64 mm
	(2.52 in.)
Displacement	290 cc
	(17.7 cu. in.)
Compression Ratio	8.6:1
Engine Lubrication	Wet Sump; Oil Pump
Transmission Lubrication	Common With Engine
Engine/Transmission Oil	See Text
Forward Speeds	5
Reverse Speeds	1
Tire Size:	
Front	24 × 8-10
Rear	24 × 10-10
Tire Pressure:	
Front (cold)	35 kPa
	(5 psi)
Rear (cold)	28 kPa
	(4 psi)
Dry Weight	257 kg
	(565 lbs.)
Tune-Up	
Engine Idle Speed	See Text
Spark Plug:	
Type	NGK DR8EA
Electrode Gap	0.6-0.7 mm
	(0.024-0.027 in.)
Ignition:	
Type	Capacitor Discharge
Point Gap	Pointless
Timing	10° BTDC @ 2000 rpm*
	30° BTDC @ 3200 rpm
Carburetor:	
Make	Keihin
Model	CVK32
Float Height	17 mm
	(0.67 in.)
Main Jet	#125
Main Air Jet	#50

Tune-Up (Cont.)

Carburetor: (Cont.)

Pilot Jet	#38
Pilot Air Jet.	#140
Jet Needle	N36W
Needle Jet	#6
Idle Mixture Setting	$2\frac{1}{8}$ Turn
Throttle Lever Free Play	2-3 mm
	(0.079-0.118 in.)

*Initial timing of 10° BTDC should be checked at 1300 rpm on -C3 and -C4 models.

Sizes-Clearances

Valve Clearance (cold):	
Intake.	0.10-0.15 mm
	(0.004-0.006 in.)
Exhaust	0.15-0.20 mm
	(0.006-0.008 in.)
Valve Face & Seat Angle	45°
Valve Seat Width:	
Intake & Exhaust	0.5-1.0 mm
	(0.020-0.039 in.)
Valve Stem Diameter:	
Intake.	6.965-6.980 mm
	(0.2742-0.2748 in.)
Exhaust	6.950-6.970 mm
	(0.2736-0.2744 in.)
Valve Guide Bore Diameter:	
Intake & Exhaust	7.000-7.015 mm
	(0.2756-0.2762 in.)
Valve Stem-To-Guide Clearance:	
Intake.	0.020-0.050 mm
	(0.0008-0.0020 in.)
Exhaust	0.030-0.065 mm
	(0.0012-0.0025 in.)
Rocker Arm Bore Diameter:	
Intake & Exhaust	13.000-13.018 mm
	(0.5118-0.5125 in.)
Rocker Shaft Diameter:	
Intake & Exhaust	12.976-12.994 mm
	(0.5108-0.5116 in.)
Camshaft Lobe Height:	
Intake & Exhaust	40.642-40.782 mm
	(1.6001-1.6056 in.)
Wear Limit	40.54 mm
	(1.5961 in.)
Cylinder Head Distortion (Max.).	0.05 mm
	(0.002 in.)
Cylinder Bore Diameter	76.000-76.012 mm
	(2.9921-2.9926 in.)
Wear Limit	76.10 mm
	(2.9961 in.)
Piston-to-Cylinder Wall Clearance	0.035-0.062 mm
	(0.0014-0.0024 in.)

Sizes-Clearances (Cont.)

Piston Diameter:
  Measured 5 mm (0.2 in.) From
  Skirt Bottom & 90° to Pin Bore . . . .   75.950-75.965 mm
                                                     (2.9901-2.9907 in.)

Piston Ring End Gap in
  Standard Bore:
     Top & Second Ring . . . .   0.20-0.35 mm
                                                     (0.008-0.014 in.)

Piston Ring Groove Width:
  Top Ring. . . . .   1.02-1.04 mm
                                                     (0.040-0.041 in.)

  Second Ring . . . .   1.01-1.03 mm
                                                     (0.0398-0.0406 in.)

  Oil Ring . . . .   2.51-2.53 mm
                                                     (0.099-0.100 in.)

Piston Ring Width:
  Top & Second Ring . . . .   0.97-0.99 mm
                                                     (0.0382-0.0390 in.)

Piston Ring Side Clearance:
  Top Ring. . . . .   0.03-0.07 mm
                                                     (0.0012-0.0027 in.)

     Max. . . . .   0.17 mm
                                                     (0.007 in.)

  Second Ring . . . .   0.02-0.06 mm
                                                     (0.0007-0.0023 in.)

     Max. . . . .   0.16 mm
                                                     (0.006 in.)

Connecting Rod Big End
  Side Clearance . . . .   0.25-0.35 mm
                                                     (0.010-0.014 in.)

  Maximum Allowable. . . . .   0.6 mm
                                                     (0.023 in.)

Connecting Rod Big End
  Radial Clearance . . . .   0.008-0.020 mm
                                                     (0.0003-0.0008 in.)

  Maximum Allowable. . . . .   0.07 mm
                                                     (0.003 in.)

Crankshaft Runout:
  LH . . . .   0.08 mm
                                                     (0.003 in.)

  RH . . . .   0.1 mm
                                                     (0.004 in.)

Capacities

Fuel Tank . . . .   11 L
                                                     (2.9 gal.)

Engine/Transmission Sump . . . .   2.2 L*
                                                     (2.32 qt.)

Differential Case:
  Front . . . .   0.25 L
                                                     (0.26 qt.)

  Rear. . . . .   0.2 L
                                                     (0.21 qt.)

*Engine/transmission sump capacity on -C4 models is 2.4 L (2.5 qt.).

Tightening Torques

Axle Nut:

Front	145 N·m (110 ft.-lbs.)
Rear	145 N·m (110 ft.-lbs.)
Camshaft Sprocket Screw	41 N·m (30 ft.-lbs.)
Primary Clutch Nut	125 N·m (92 ft.-lbs.)
Secondary Clutch Nut	78 N·m (58 ft.-lbs.)

Cylinder Head Screws:

6 mm	12 N·m (104 in.-lbs.)

8 mm:

Initial	14 N·m (124 in.-lbs.)
Final—Used Screws	29 N·m (22 ft.-lbs.)
New Screws	34 N·m (25 ft.-lbs.)
Starter Cup (Flywheel)	59 N·m (43 ft.-lbs.)
Wheel Retaining Nut	34 N·m (25 ft.-lbs.)

Standard Fasteners:

5 mm	3.4-4.9 N·m (30-43 in.-lbs.)
6 mm	5.9-7.8 N·m (52-69 in.-lbs.)
8 mm	14-19 N·m (10-13.5 ft.-lbs.)
10 mm	25-39 N·m (19-25 ft.-lbs.)
12 mm	44-61 N·m (33-45 ft.-lbs.)
14 mm	73-98 N·m (54-72 ft.-lbs.)
16 mm	115-155 N·m (83-115 ft.-lbs.)
18 mm	165-225 N·m (125-165 ft.-lbs.)
20 mm	225-325 N·m (165-240 ft.-lbs.)

LUBRICATION

ENGINE AND TRANSMISSION. The engine is lubricated by a trochoid-type pump located on the right side of the crankcase and driven by a gear on the right end of the crankshaft. The engine and transmission share a common sump. Recommended oil is a multigrade SAE 10W-40, 10W-50, 20W-40 or 20W-50 motor oil with an API classification of SE or SF.

Sump is filled through filler cap opening (F—Fig. K13-1). Oil level should be maintained between oil level lines (L) adjacent to sight glass (G). Sump is drained by

Fig. K13-1—Engine/transmission sump is filled through filler plug opening (F). Oil level should be maintained between lines (L) next to sight glass (G). The oil filter is located behind cover (C).

removing plug in underside of crankcase. Crankcase capacity after changing oil and oil filter is 2.2 L (2.32 qt.).

Manufacturer recommends changing oil and oil filter after the first 10 hours of operation. Thereafter, the oil and oil filter should be changed after every 90 days of operation. In conjunction with oil filter change, the oil pressure relief valve, located within the oil filter mounting pin, should be disassembled, cleaned and inspected. the sump screen, located in the right crankcase half and below and to the left of the oil pump, should also be removed and cleaned.

The oil filter and oil pressure relief valve are accessible after removing cover (C). To disassemble oil pressure relief valve, drive out cross-pin (1—Fig. K13-2) and separate components. Renew the complete assembly if excessive wear or damage is evident. During reassembly, insert piston (3) with open end toward spring (2). Insert and compress spring (2) just beyond cross-pin hole and install cross-pin (1). Install the oil filter ensuring "O" ring seals are located on both sides of filter. Renew filter cover "O" ring seal if required and install cover.

Sump screen is accessible after removing right crankcase cover. Drain oil from crankcase. Unbolt and carefully remove the right crankcase cover. Withdraw the sump screen from crankcase half. Reinstall by reversing removal procedure while noting the following: Make sure alignment dowels and gasket are fitted to crankcase and install cover. Adjust clutch as outlined in CLUTCH section. Fill engine/transmission sump with the appropriate amount of oil and check for leaks.

DIFFERENTIAL UNITS. The differential oil for front and rear units should be changed after the first 10 hours of operation and annually thereafter. Check oil level periodically and renew more frequently if vehicle is operated under adverse conditions. Recommended differential lubricant is API GL-5 hypoid gear oil. (Oil in front differential must be designed for limited slip differentials). Use a good quality SAE 90 hypoid gear oil in the rear differential when the ambient temperature is above 5° C (41° F) or SAE 80 hypoid gear oil when the ambient temperature is 5° C (41° F) or below. Recommended viscosity for the front differential is SAE 85W-140. Differential case capacity is 0.25 L (0.26 qt.) for front differential and 0.2 L (0.21 qt.) for rear differential.

Differential case is checked and filled through oil plug (P—Fig. K13-4) opening. Unscrew plug at the base of the differential case to drain oil. Oil should be maintained at level of oil plug (P) opening when vehicle is positioned on a flat level surface. When renewing oil, first operate vehicle to allow differential case oil to pick up any contaminates within the case and to allow oil to warm-up for easier drainage. Then, remove drain plug at base of differential case and level plug (P) and allow oil to drain into a suitable container.

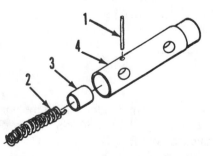

Fig. K13-2—Exploded view of oil pressure relief valve.

1. Cross-pin
2. Spring
3. Piston
4. Filter mount sleeve

Fig. K13-4—View identifying differential case oil level plug (P). Drain plug is located at base of differential case.

Fig. K13-5—Remove air cleaner cover (C) for access to filter element.

CABLES, LEVERS AND LINKAGE. All cables, levers and linkage should be inspected and lubricated after every 30 days of operation.

AIR CLEANER ELEMENT

The air cleaner element should be removed and cleaned after the first 10 hours of operation and every 10 days of operation thereafter. To remove air cleaner element, first remove seat and air cleaner cover (C—Fig. K13-5). Unscrew and remove element and frame from case. Carefully separate foam element from frame.

Thoroughly clean element in a nonflammable solvent. Compress element between hands to remove solvent. Saturate element in clean SAE 30 motor oil and compress element to remove excess oil. Reinstall element by reversing removal procedure.

FUEL SYSTEM

CARBURETOR. A Keihin CVK32-type carburetor is used. Refer to CONDENSED SERVICE DATA for carburetor specifications.

Adjust idle speed knob (K—Fig. 13-7) to obtain the lowest smooth idle setting. After adjusting carburetor idle setting, check throttle lever free play as outlined in THROTTLE LEVER FREE PLAY section.

Fig. K13-7—View of carburetor identifying idle speed knob (K).

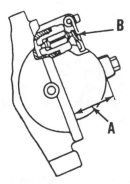

Fig. K13-8—Float height (A) should be 17 mm (0.67 in.). Bend float arm tang (B) to adjust.

When servicing the carburetor, note the following: Float height (A—Fig. K13-8) should be 17 mm (0.67 in.) as measured from gasket surface of carburetor body to lowest edge of float. Hold carburetor so float is vertical and resting lightly against fuel inlet valve when checking float height as shown in Fig. K13-8. Adjust the float level by bending tang (B) on float arm.

The fuel level is checked with the carburetor installed and vehicle operational. To check fuel level, attach Kawasaki fuel level gauge 57001-1017 to open end of carburetor overflow hose and position gauge so zero line is even with bottom edge of carburetor body (float bowl contact surface). Turn fuel valve to "ON" position and open fuel drain screw to allow fuel drainage. After fuel in hose has stabilized, measure the distance from the bottom edge of carburetor body to fuel level in hose. Fuel level check will not be accurate if hose is raised or lowered after fuel level has stabilized. Fuel level should be 0.5 mm (0.02 in.) below bottom edge of carburetor body to 1.5 mm (0.06 in.) above bottom edge of carburetor body. To adjust fuel level, the float bowl must be removed to carefully bend float arm tang (B—Fig. K13-8).

FUEL STRAINER. A strainer is mounted on the end of the "ON" pickup tube and the "RES" (reserve) pickup tube of the fuel valve assembly mounted on the fuel tank. A strainer is also located behind the fuel valve control lever. To inspect the strainers, the fuel in the fuel tank must be drained. Disconnect the fuel hose from the fuel valve. Unscrew the two screws securing the fuel valve to the fuel tank and carefully remove the fuel valve from the tank. Clean and inspect the strainers. The strainers are not available separately, only as a part of the valve housing. Reinstall the valve assembly while noting that nylon washers are used on the two retaining screws to prevent fuel leakage.

THROTTLE LEVER FREE PLAY. The throttle lever should have 2-3 mm (0.079-0.118 in.) of free play measured at throttle lever end as shown at (F—Fig. K13-12). Throttle lever free play can be adjusted by sliding boot (B) down cable to expose outer adjuster nut and inner

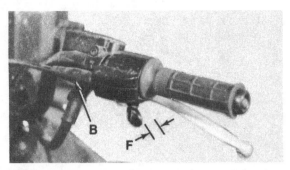

Fig. K13-12—Throttle lever should have 2-3 mm (0.079-0.118 in.) of free play measured at (F). To adjust, slide boot (B) down cable to expose adjuster nut and locknut.

locknut. Loosen locknut and rotate adjuster nut until 2-3 mm (0.079-0.118 in.) free play is obtained. Secure adjustment with locknut and reinstall boot (B).

IGNITION AND ELECTRICAL

SPARK PLUG. Standard spark plug is NGK B8ES. Spark plug electrode gap should be 0.7-0.8 mm (0.027-0.031 in.). Spark plug should be removed, cleaned and electrode gap set after the first 10 hours of operation and every 90 days of operation thereafter. Renew spark plug if damage and excessive electrode wear is evident.

IGNITION. A breakerless Capacitor Discharge Ignition (CDI) system is used. The electronic ignition circuit consists of the battery, CDI module, pickup coil, flywheel, ignition coil, spark plug, engine stop switch and ignition switch. Ignition timing at idle speed should occur when "F" mark (F—Fig. 13-14) on flywheel is aligned with notch (N) as viewed through timing plug (P) opening. Specified ignition timing is 10° BTDC ("F" mark) at 2000 rpm and 30° BTDC (maximum advance) at 3200 rpm. Ignition timing is checked with a power timing light

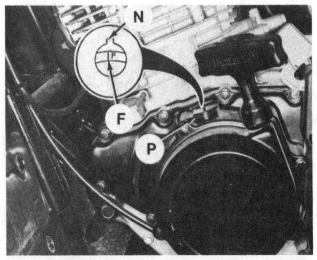

Fig. K13-14—Remove plug (P) to check ignition timing. "F" mark (F) should align with notch (N) when engine is operated at idle speed.

and is not adjustable. If ignition timing is not as specified, check condition of CDI module and pick up coil as described in the following test procedures.

If ignition malfunction occurs, check condition of battery, spark plug, all wires and connections before troubleshooting the ignition circuit. Using Kawasaki tester 57001-983 or a suitable ohmmeter, refer to the following test specifications and procedures to aid troubleshooting.

To check condition of CDI module, first remove module from vehicle. Use tester or ohmmeter in conjunction with the test chart in Fig. K13-15. Renew CDI module if module fails to meet test specifications.

To check condition of pickup coil, separate blue and black wires leading from pulse generator to CDI module at connector. Attach one lead to blue wire and remaining tester lead to black wire from pulse coil. Pickup coil can be considered satisfactory if resistance reading is within 390-590 ohms.

To check condition of ignition coil, remove green/white wire and yellow/red wire from their respective terminals on coil and high tension wire from spark plug. Attach one tester lead to green/white wire terminal and remaining tester lead to yellow/red wire terminal on ignition coil. Primary coil resistance reading should be 1.8-2.8 ohms. Attach one tester lead to green/white wire terminal and ignition coil and remaining tester lead to high tension wire. Secondary coil resistance reading should be 10k-16k ohms. Renew ignition coil if coil fails to meet eithe test specification.

CHARGING CIRCUIT. The charging circuit consists of an alternator charge coil, a regulator/rectifier, battery and ignition switch. Standard battery has a 14 ampere hour, 12-volt rating.

The battery should be checked and filled to maximum level with distilled water, if required, after the first 10 hours of operation and then after every 30 days of operation. During periods of vehicle storage, the battery should be charged once a month to reduce sulfation and prolong battery life. The battery should always be removed from the vehicle prior to charging. Do not exceed maximum charging rate of 1.9 amperes.

The alternator charge coil can be statically tested using a suitable ohmmeter. There are three yellow wires from alternator charge coil to regulator/rectifier. Separate wires from alternator to regulator/rectifier at connector block and measure resistance between the wires. Resistance reading should be 0.1-0.7 ohm. Check for continuity between each of the alternator wires and ground. Tester should read infinite resistance at each wire.

Test procedures for checking condition of regulator/rectifier are not reliable as unit may test satisfactory but still be defective. The recommended procedure is to test all associated charging circuit components and eliminate them as the source of defect prior to renewing regulator/rectifier or install a known good regulator/rec-

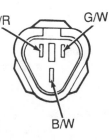

Fig. K13-15—Use chart shown and values listed below to test condition of CDI module.

A. Infinity
B. 5k-15k ohms
C. 1k-10k ohms
D. 1k-5k ohms
E. 50k-150k ohms
F. Zero ohms

		+Test Lead				
		Y/R	G/W	B/W	*B/W	Bl
−Test Lead	Y/R		B	G	G	I
	G/W	A		A	A	A
	B/W	E	C		J	H
	*B/W	E	C	J		H
	Bl	F	D	H	H	

tifier assembly and check charging circuit for proper operation. Regulator/rectifier output voltage should not be higher than 15 volts.

ELECTRIC STARTER. The starter can be removed and disassembled to clean, inspect and lubricate individual parts. The starter brushes should be renewed if worn to 6 mm (0.24 in.) or less. Starter brushes available from the manufacturer in kit form with springs, brush plate and associated components. Starter armature and gear set are not available separately and the complete assembly should be renewed if defective.

To remove electric starter, first disconnect battery. Disconnect wire at terminal on starter. Unbolt and withdraw starter motor. Note the location of all components during disassembly to aid in reassembly.

During installation, make sure "O" ring is positioned around starter neck, then guide starter into position while aligning starter shaft with starter sprocket splines. Remainder of installation is the reverse of removal procedure.

FASTENERS

The vehicle should receive an overall inspection after the first 10 hours of operation and every 10 days of operation thereafter. All cap screws, nuts and fasteners should be checked and tightened to proper torque specification listed in CONDENSED SERVICE DATA section or in the appropriate MAINTENANCE section.

VALVE SYSTEM

The valves are actuated via rocker arms by a single overhead camshaft. Camshaft is driven by a roller chain attached to the left end of crankshaft. Valve clearance on all models should be adjusted after the first 10 hours of operation and then after every 90 days of operation. Valve clearance should be adjusted with engine cold.

To adjust valve clearance, remove seat, fuel tank, valve adjustment caps, rewind starter and plug (P—Fig. K13-14). Attach a suitable tool to flywheel screw and rotate crankshaft until "T" mark (Top Dead Center) on flywheel aligns with notch (N) with piston on compression stroke. To ensure piston is on compression stroke, rotate crankshaft 1/4 turn past "T" mark while observing intake valve. If valve movement is indicated, rotate crankshaft one complete revolution and align "T" mark with stationary mark again.

Clearance between rocker arm adjusting screw (A—Fig. K13-16) and valve stem should be 0.10-0.15 mm (0.004-0.006 in.) for the intake valve and 0.15-0.20 mm (0.006-0.008 in.) for the exhaust valve. Measure clearance with a suitable feeler gauge and adjust by loosen-

Fig. K13-16—Valve clearance should be 0.10-0.15 mm (0.004-0.006 in.) for intake valve and 0.15-0.20 mm (0.006-0.008 in.) for exhaust valve. Loosen locknut (L) and turn adjuster screw (A) to adjust clearance.

Fig. K13-17—To gain access to clutch adjustment screw and locknut, remove screws (S) and withdraw cover (C).

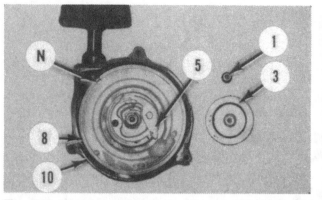

Fig. K13-18—View of partially disassembled manual starter typical of starter used on all models.

N. Notch
1. Nut
3. Friction plate

5. Starter pawl
8. Rope pulley
10. Starter housing

ing locknut (L) and turning adjusting screw (A). Be sure to recheck clearance after locknuts are tightened.

CLUTCH

Vehicles are equipped with a multiple-disc clutch that is actuated by the gear shift lever. As the gear shift lever is operated to change gears, the clutch is disengaged through linkage connected to the shift shaft.

To adjust clutch, remove cover (C—Fig. K13-17). Loosen locknut on upper adjusting screw. Turn upper adjusting screw counterclockwise until resistance is felt, then continue turning one-half to one turn more. Loosen locknut on lower adjusting screw. Turn lower adjusting screw in both directions until screw is hard to turn, then position screw midway between hard-to-turn positions. Hold screw and tighten locknut. Rotate upper adjusting screw clockwise two or three turns clockwise, then turn screw counterclockwise until resistance is felt. Hold screw and tighten locknut. Reinstall cover.

MANUAL STARTER

R&R AND OVERHAUL. Refer to Fig. K13-18 for view of a partially disassembled manual starter assembly. Manual starter can be removed from the vehicle as a complete unit after removing the four starter retaining screws. If starter rope remains under tension, pull starter rope and hold rope pulley (8—Fig. K13-18) with notch (N) in pulley adjacent to rope outlet. Pull a loop of rope back through outlet so rope engages notch in pulley and allow pulley (8) to slowly unwind.

Remove retaining nut (1) and disassemble unit. Be careful when removing rewind spring. A rapidly uncoiling starter spring can cause serious injury.

Rewind spring is wound into starter housing (10) in a clockwise direction. Starter rope is wound on rope pulley (8) in a clockwise direction as viewed with rope pulley in starter housing. Reassemble starter by reversing disassembly procedure. Lightly grease pulley shaft, starter pawl and inside face of friction plate (3).

To place tension on rewind spring after assembly, pass starter rope through rope outlet in starter housing and install rope handle. Pull a loop of rope back through outlet between notch (N) in pulley and housing. Rotate rope pulley (8) clockwise four complete revolutions, then release starter rope from pulley notch (N) and allow starter rope to wind onto pulley (8). Do not place any more tension on rewind spring than is necessary to draw starter rope handle up against housing.

REVERSE KNOB FREE PLAY

The reverse knob should have 3-4 mm (0.12-0.16 in.) of free play measured at outer circumference of knob. Reverse knob free play can be adjusted by loosening jam nuts on cable at lower mounting bracket and rotating adjuster until desired free play is obtained. Secure adjustment with jam nuts.

FRONT BRAKE ASSEMBLY

A disc brake assembly is used on both front wheels. As the disc or disc pads wear, the piston within the brake caliper assembly will move out to automatically compensate for wear, so adjustment on the front brakes is not required.

BLEEDING. Make sure reservoir (R—Fig. K13-19) full. Connect a bleed hose to bleed valve (B—Fig. K13-20) on both front brake caliper assemblies. Route the bleed hoses into suitable containers. Operate brake lever (L—Fig. K13-19) until a hardness (fluid resistance) is felt, then open one bleed valve (rotate counterclockwise). Close bleed valve prior to releasing brake lever. Continue bleeding procedure on both wheels until no air bubbles are noted in discharged fluid from bleed valve.

NOTE: Make sure reservoir (R) is kept full during bleeding procedure.

Fig. K13-19—View identifying front brake operating lever (L) and brake fluid reservoir (R).

Fig. K13-20—Attach a hose to bleed valve (B) on both front brake calipers to bleed front brake system. See text.

When bleeding procedure is completed, add brake fluid to reservoir until fluid level is at upper level line in reservoir.

OVERHAUL. Brake pad thickness may be determined externally by viewing the brake pads. If brake pad thickness is 1 mm (0.039 in.) or less, then brake pads must be renewed.

WARNING: Inhaling asbestos brake dust is injurious to human health. Approved OSHA respiration equipment must be worn when working on or around brake calipers and pads. DO NOT use compressed air to clean brake calipers, pads or nearby components as brake dust will be blown into air. Only vacuum equipment designed to pick up brake dust should be used.

Brake components are accessible after removing wheel, caliper mounting screws and withdrawing caliper. Push piston by hand back into caliper to allow clearance for new brake pads. Brake disc should be renewed if thickness is 3 mm (0.118 in.) or less or disc runout is 0.3 mm (0.012 in.) or more. After reassembly, operate brake lever until brake lever will not pump up after continuous operation. Do not operate vehicle until brakes operate properly.

FRONT AXLE

The left and right front steering knuckle assemblies pivot on ball joint assemblies at the end of each upper and lower control arm. The control arms are bolted at the ends to the vehicle frame and a shock absorber is used to limit and cushion the up and down movement of the control arms. The shock absorbers are adjustable to alter absorber spring setting for different terrain and load conditions.

Remove the front wheel to service the ball joint assemblies. Note that removing the brake components will allow greater access to ball joint assemblies. If any ball joint or control arm is excessively worn or any other damage is noted, then ball joint or control arm must be renewed. Note that ball joints are threaded in control arms and can be unscrewed after detaching snap ring. Lower and upper control arm mounting screws should be tightened to 88 N·m (65 ft.-lbs.). Tighten ball joints to 49 N·m (36 ft.-lbs.). Tighten ball joint/retaining nuts to 52 N·m (38 ft.-lbs.). Tighten shock absorber bolts to 34 N·m (25 ft.-lbs.).

STEERING

TOE-IN SETTING. Place the handlebars in a straight ahead position. Use a suitable measuring tool and measure distance (F—Fig. K13-22), at spindle height, between the center of the tires on the front and rear

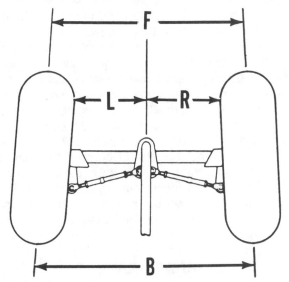

Fig. K13-22—Refer to text for correct procedures in measuring distances (F and B) for setting toe-in. Tie rod sleeves are secured by inside and outside locknuts.

sides. The measured distance (F) on the front side should be 20 mm (0.787 in.) shorter than the measured distance (B) on the rear side. If not, loosen the inside and outside locknuts on the left and right tie rod assemblies and rotate the tie rod sleeves equally until a difference of 20 mm (0.787 in.) is noted and distances (L and R) to centerline are equal.

NOTE: If the handlebars are not positioned straight ahead when the front wheels are facing straight ahead, then rotate left and right tie rod sleeves the same direction in equal increments until handlebars are facing straight ahead. The toe-in setting should not be affected if tie rod sleeves are rotated equal amounts.

After obtaining the correct setting, securely tighten the locknuts to retain tie rod settings.

INSPECTION. Rotate the handlebars from one extreme to the other and note if any binding or roughness is felt. Periodically inspect the steering components for looseness or any other damage. Renew any damaged component. Clean and grease components if binding or excessive effort is noted.

OVERHAUL. To expose the steering tube, the front fender assembly, seat and gas tank must be removed. Remove the Allen head bolts and nuts securing the upper tube clamp and withdraw the clamp halves. Clean the old grease from the steering tube and bearing portions of the clamp halves. Inspect the clamp halves and the upper and lower grease seals for damage. Renew components if needed. Grease components and install clamp halves so match marks on sides of halves are aligned. Tighten the retaining clamp Allen head bolts and nuts to 25 N·m (18 ft.-lbs.).

The tie rod assemblies, handlebar assembly, control panel components on handlebar holder, headlight and upper tube clamp must be removed to withdraw the steering tube from the vehicle. Remove the lower bearing housing mounting screws to withdraw the steering tube. Inspect the lower bearing assembly and seals and renew if needed. Tighten the lower bearing assembly retaining nut to 29 N·m (22 ft.-lbs.). Tighten the tie rod assembly mounting nuts to 41 N·m (30 ft.-lbs.).

When installing the handlebar assembly to the steering tube, the handlebar should be positioned so the handlebar and steering tube are set at the same angle. Tighten the rear handlebar mounting clamp screws first, then tighten the front screws. If properly tightened, there should be no gap at the rear of the clamp and an even gap at the front.

REAR BRAKE

ADJUSTMENT. The rear brake can be actuated either by a foot pedal or handlebar lever. Brake pedal

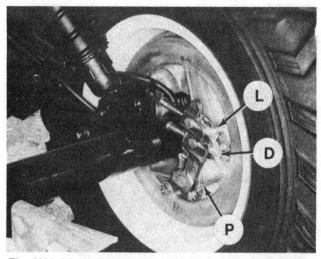

Fig. K13-24—Adjust brake pedal height by turning adjusting nut (D). Adjust brake lever gap (G—Fig. K13-25) by turning adjusting nut (L). Pointer (P) indicates brake lining wear.

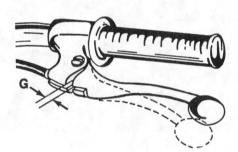

Fig. K13-25—Brake lever free play (G) should be 4-5 mm (0.16-0.20 in.).

free play should be 15-25 mm (0.59-0.98 in.) measured at the pedal pad. Adjust pedal free play by turning adjusting nut (D—Fig. K13-24). Brake lever free play measured at gap (G—Fig. K13-25) should be 1-2 mm (0.04-0.08 in.). Brake lever free play can be adjusted by rotating adjuster nut on brake cable at handlebar brake lever, or can be adjusted by turning adjusting nut (L—Fig. K13-24) if beyond handlebar brake lever adjustment.

OVERHAUL. Brake lining thickness may be determined externally by actuating brake and noting position of pointer (P—Fig. K13-24) mounted on actuating lever. There is sufficient brake lining if pointer falls in "USABLE RANGE" on brake backing plate.

WARNING: Inhaling asbestos brake dust is injurious to human health. Approved OSHA respiration equipment must be worn when working on or around brake components. DO NOT use compressed air to clean brake drums, shoes or nearby components as brake dust will be blown into air.

Only vacuum equipment designed to pick up brake dust should be used.

Brake components are accessible after removing wheel and brake drum. Renew the brake drum assembly if the inside diameter is more than 180.75 mm (7.116 in.).

DIFFERENTIAL ASSEMBLIES

The vehicle is equipped with differential assemblies in front and rear drive trains. Service on differential assemblies should be performed by a Kawasaki service technician equipped with the special tools required for overhaul.

POLARIS

POLARIS INDUSTRIES INC.
Highway 89 South
Roseau, MN 56751

BIG BOSS, TRAIL BLAZER AND TRAIL BOSS

CONDENSED SERVICE DATA

MODELS	Big Boss, Trail Blazer & Trail Boss (Except 350L)	Trail Boss 350L
General		
Engine Make	Polaris	Polaris
Engine Type	Two-Stroke Air-Cooled	Two-Stroke; Liquid-Cooled
Number of Cylinders	1	1
Bore	2.756 in. (72 mm)	3.150 in. (80 mm)
Stroke	2.362 in. (60 mm)	2.756 in. (70 mm)
Displacement	14.9 cu. in. (244 cc)	21.47 cu. in. (352 cc)
Engine Lubrication	Oil Injection	Oil Injection
Transmission Positions	Forward, Neutral & Reverse	Forward, Neutral & Reverse
Transmission Speeds	Variable	Variable
Tire Size		
Front	22 × 8-10	25 × 8-12
Rear:		
Big Boss	22 × 11-10	....
Trail Blazer	22 × 11-10	....
Trail Boss 2x4, 4x4	24 × 11-10*	....
Trail Boss 250	22 × 11-10	....
Trail Boss 350L 2x4	....	24 × 11-10
Trail Boss 350L 4x4	....	25 × 12-10
Tire Pressure		
Front:		
Big Boss	5 psi (34.5 kPa)	....
Trail Blazer, Trail Boss 250, Trail Boss 2x4	3 psi (20.7 kPa)	....
Trail Boss 4x4	4 psi (27.6 kPa)	....
Trail Boss 350L 2x4, 4x4	....	4 psi (27.6 kPa)
Rear:		
All Except Big Boss	3 psi (20.7 kPa)	3 psi (20.7 kPa)
Big Boss	5 psi (34.5 kPa)	....

MODELS	Big Boss, Trail Blazer & Trail Boss (Except 350L)	Trail Boss 350L
General (Cont.)		
Battery	12V-14AH	12V-14AH
Dry Weight (Approx.):		
Big Boss 4x6	650 lbs. (295.5 kg)	....
Big Boss 6x6	750 lbs. (340.9 kg)	....
Trail Blazer	390 lbs. (177.3 kg)	....
Trail Boss 2x4	440 lbs. (200 kg)	....
Trail Boss 4x4	490 lbs. (220.5 kg)	....
Trail Boss 250	425 lbs. (193.2 kg)	....
Trail Boss 350L 2x4	....	490 lbs. (220.5 kg)
Trail Boss 350L 4x4	....	560 lbs. (254.5 kg)

*Early Trail Boss 2x4 was equipped with 22x11-10 rear tires.

Tune-Up

	Big Boss, Trail Blazer & Trail Boss (Except 350L)	Trail Boss 350L
Engine Idle Speed:		
1988 & 1989	800 rpm	....
After 1989	700 rpm	700 rpm
Spark Plug:		
Champion	RN4YC	RN4YC
NGK	BR8ES	BR8ES
Electrode Gap:		
Before 1989	0.025 in. (0.63 mm)	....
After 1988	0.028 in. (0.7 mm)	0.028 in. (0.7 mm)
Ignition:		
Type	Breakerless	Breakerless
Ignition Timing:		
Before 1990	25° BTDC @ 3000 rpm 19.5° BTDC @ 6000 rpm	....
After 1989	25° BTDC @ 3000 rpm 20° BTDC @ 6000 rpm	23° BTDC @ 3000 rpm 18° BTDC @ 6000 rpm
Carburetor:		
Make	Mikuni	Mikuni
Model	VM30SS	VM34SS
Float Height	See Text	See Text
Main Jet	#145	#200**
Idle Jet:		
Before 1989	#35	....
After 1988	#40	#30
Clip Position	3rd Groove From Top	2nd Groove From Top
Idle Mixture Setting	1 Turn Out	¾ Turn Out**
Throttle Cable Free Play	0.25 in. (6.35 mm)	0.25 in. (6.35 mm)

**Main jet size is #220 and idle mixture screw setting is 1½ turns out on 1990 Trail Boss 350L models.

MODELS	Big Boss, Trail Blazer & Trail Boss (Except 350L)	Trail Boss 350L
Sizes-Clearances		
Piston-to-Cylinder Wall Clearance:		
Before 1991	0.0014-0.0028 in. (0.035-0.070 mm)	0.0024-0.0037 in. (0.060-0.095 mm)
Wear Limit	0.006 in. (0.15 mm)	0.006 in. (0.15 mm)
After 1990	0.0011-0.0021 in. (0.028-0.053 mm)	0.0024-0.0037 in. (0.060-0.095 mm)
Wear Limit	0.006 in. (0.15 mm)	0.006 in. (0.15 mm)
Piston Ring End Gap (New):		
Before 1991	0.008-0.016 in. (0.20-0.40 mm)	0.008-0.016 in. (0.20-0.40 mm)
After 1990	0.009-0.018 in. (0.23-0.46 mm)	0.010-0.021 in. (0.26-0.53 mm)
Crankshaft End Play	0.008-0.016 in. (0.20-0.40 mm)	0.008-0.016 in. (0.20-0.40 mm)
Crankshaft Runout (Max.)	0.010 in. (0.25 mm)	0.010 in. (0.25 mm)
Capacities		
Cooling System	....	2 qt. (1.9 L)
Engine Oil Tank	2 qt. (1.9 L)	2 qt. (1.9 L)
Fuel Tank	4 gal. (15.2 L)	4 gal. (15.2 L)
Transmission	16.9 oz. (500 cc)	16.9 oz. (500 cc)
Tightening Torques		
Clutch Screw	40 ft.-lbs. (54 N•m)	40 ft.-lbs. (54 N•m)
Crankcase:		
6 mm	72-96 in.-lbs. (8-11 N•m)	72-96 in.-lbs. (8-11 N•m)
8 mm	17-18 ft.-lbs. (23-24 N•m)	17-18 ft.-lbs. (23-24 N•m)
Crankshaft Slotted Nut (L.H.)	....	30-44 ft.-lbs. (41-60 N•m)
Cylinder Base	24-28 ft.-lbs. (33-38 N•m)	24-28 ft.-lbs. (33-38 N•m)
Cylinder Head	18-20 ft.-lbs. (24-27 N•m)	18-20 ft.-lbs. (24-27 N•m)
Flywheel	38-40 ft.-lbs. (52-54 N•m)	30-44 ft.-lbs. (41-60 N•m)
Wheel Retaining Nut:		
Plain Nut	20 ft.-lbs. (27 N•m)	20 ft.-lbs. (27 N•m)
Flanged Nut	15 ft.-lbs. (20.4 N•m)	15 ft.-lbs. (20.4 N•m)

LUBRICATION

All Models

ENGINE. The engine is lubricated by oil injected into intake manifold by an oil injection pump. Oil is metered according to engine speed and throttle position.

Recommended oil is Polaris Injection Oil. Oil tank capacity is 2 qt. (1.9 L).

Refer to OIL PUMP section if pump control cable adjustment or bleeding of the oil system is required. Note that bleeding of the oil system is necessary if the oil tank runs dry, lines are disconnected or vehicle lies on its side.

TRANSMISSION. The transmission oil should be checked after the first 25 hours of operation and after every 100 hours of operation thereafter, or more frequently if required. On early models with shifter knob on side of transmission, recommended oil is Polaris Chain Lubricant. Oil level should be maintained at hole for level plug (L—Fig. P1-1). Add oil through hole for fill plug (F). On later models, fill transmission with SAE 30 engine oil to full mark on dipstick (see Fig. P1-2).

COUNTERBALANCER. Model 350L. The engine on 350L models is equipped with a counterbalancer that is gear-driven by the crankshaft. The gears and shafts are lubricated by an oil bath. The oil should be changed annually, or anytime water contaminates oil.

To change oil, remove bottom chain guard and unscrew drain plug (Fig. P1-3). Install drain plug and unscrew fill plug (Fig. P1-4). Fill compartment with SAE 10W-30 engine oil and install fill plug.

DRIVE CHAIN. The chain utilizes "O" rings to seal the chain rollers and pins. The drive chain should be lubricated periodically with chain lubricant designed for chains with "O" rings. Incorrect lubrication may damage the "O" rings resulting in premature chain failure. The chain should be thoroughly washed in kerosene and wiped dry. The use of any cleaning solution other than kerosene may damage "O" rings.

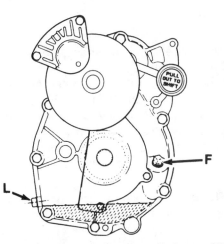

Fig. P1-1—On early model transmissions with shifter knob on side of transmission, oil level should be maintained at hole for level plug (L). Add oil through hole for fill plug (F).

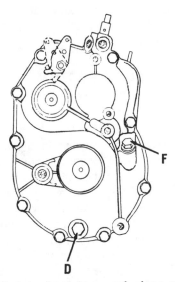

Fig. P1-2—On later model transmissions, unscrew plug (D) to drain oil. Add oil through hole for fill plug (F).

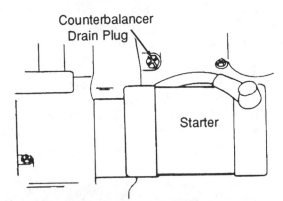

Fig. P1-3—Unscrew plug to drain oil from counterbalancer compartment on 350L models.

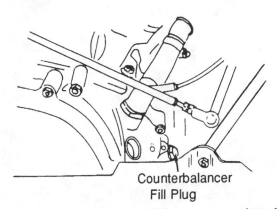

Fig. P1-4—Add oil to counterbalancer compartment on 350L models through hole for fill plug.

Fig. P1-5—Inject grease into rear axle housing through grease fitting (G).

CABLES AND LEVERS. All cables and levers should be inspected and lubricated after every 50 hours of operation. Recommended lubricant is Polaris Cable Lube.

REAR AXLE HOUSING. Inject grease into grease fitting (G—Fig. P1-5) on rear axle housing semi-annually or after every 50 hours of operation, whichever occurs first. Grease should meet specification NLG1NO.2, such as Conoco Superlube M or Mobilgrease Special.

FRONT HUB. Trail Boss 4x4. Check front hub lubricant level after every 50 hours of operation. Recommended oil level in hub is one-half full. To check oil level, rotate wheel so plug (P—Fig. P1-6) is at three o'clock or nine o'clock position. With plug removed, oil should

Fig. P1-6—Remove plug (P) and refer to text to lubricate front hub.

be level with plug hole. Add oil as needed through plug hole.

SUSPENSION. Grease fittings are provided on some suspension components. Inject grease into grease fittings semi-annually or after every 50 hours of operation, whichever occurs first. Grease should meet specification NLG1NO.2, such as Conoco Superlube M or Mobilgrease Special.

STEERING. Steering shaft bushings and tie rod ends sould be lubricated semi-annually or after every 50 hours of operation, whichever occurs first. Grease should meet specification NLG1NO.2, such as Conoco Superlube M or Mobilgrease Special.

AIR CLEANER ELEMENT

All Models

The air cleaner element should be removed and cleaned after the first 25 hours of operation and after every 25 hours of operation thereafter. Air cleaner element should be renewed after every 50 hours of operation or more frequently in severe operating conditions.

To remove air cleaner element, remove seat and support bracket, if needed, then remove air cleaner element cover and remove element.

CAUTION: Wear proper eye protection when cleaning air cleaner element using compressed air.

Tap element lightly on a solid surface to dislodge debris. Direct low-pressure compressed air (approximately 40 psi [5.8 kPa]) at outside of element toward inside to blow away dirt. Renew element if it remains dirty after air-cleaning, or if element is torn or otherwise damaged. Lightly grease top and bottom sealing surfaces of element and reinstall element by reversing removal procedure.

FUEL SYSTEM

All Models

CARBURETOR. The engine is equipped with a Mikuni carburetor. Initial setting of idle mixture screw (I—Fig. P1-7) is ¾ turn out on 350L models and 1 turn out on all other models. Rotating idle mixture screw clockwise will richen idle mixture. Final adjustment must be performed with engine at normal operating temperature. Adjust idle speed screw (S) so engine idles at 800 rpm on 1988 and 1989 models or 700 rpm on later models. Rotate idle mixture screw (I) so engine runs at highest idle speed, then readjust idle speed screw (S) so engine idles at specified rpm.

When servicing carburetor, refer to Fig. P1-8 for an exploded view of carburetor and to carburetor specifications in CONDENSED SERVICE DATA section while noting the following: Jet needle clip (4) should be installed in second groove from top of jet needle on 350L models or third groove from top on all other models. To obtain correct float height, float arm (17—Fig. P1-9) must be parallel with carburetor fuel bowl mating surface. Bend float arm tang that contacts fuel inlet valve to adjust float arm position. Make sure groove in side of throttle slide is aligned with pin in carburetor body when inserting slide in carburetor.

THROTTLE CABLE FREE PLAY. The throttle cable should be adjusted to provide 0.25 inch (6.35 mm) free play at idle position. Before adjusting throttle cable free play, adjust engine idle speed as outlined in CARBURE-TOR section. With engine stopped, detach oil pump cable. Slide dust boot (B—Fig. P1-11) down cable and dust boots (D) away from cable adjuster assembly. Pull throttle cable housing away from housing (H) and measure free play between stop on throttle cable housing and throttle lever housing (H). Loosen locknut (L) and rotate adjuster nut (A) to obtain desired free play. Retighten locknut, install dust boots and reattach oil pump cable. Adjust oil pump cable as described in the following section.

OIL PUMP CABLE ADJUSTMENT. Model 350L. Before adjusting the oil pump cable, check and, if necessary, adjust throttle cable free play as outlined in previous section. Remove oil pump cover on left front of engine. Push throttle lever until throttle cable free play is removed, then note position of oil pump lever mark (M—Fig. P1-12) in relation to fixed mark (F) on pump housing. If the marks are not aligned, loosen oil pump cable locknuts (N) and turn cable adjuster (A) so marks are aligned. Retighten locknuts (N).

All Other Models. Before adjusting the oil pump cable, check and, if necessary, adjust throttle cable free play as outlined in previous section. Push throttle lever until throttle cable free play is removed, then note position of oil pump lever mark (M—Fig. P1-13) in relation to fixed mark (F) on pump housing. If the marks are not aligned, loosen oil pump cable locknuts (N) and turn

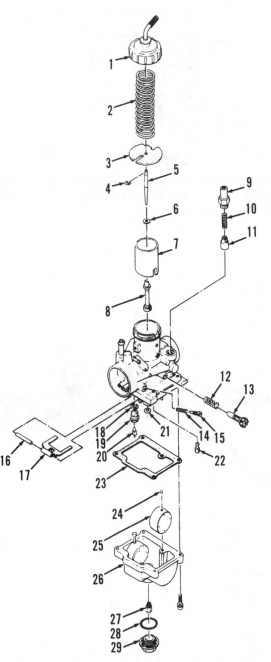

Fig. P1-8—Exploded view of Mikuni carburetor used on all models.

1.	Cap	16.	Float pin
2.	Spring	17.	Float arm
3.	Retainer	18.	Washer
4.	Clip	19.	Fuel inlet valve seat
5.	Jet needle	20.	Fuel inlet valve
6.	Washer	21.	Washer
7.	Throttle slide	22.	Slow jet
8.	Needle jet	23.	Gasket
9.	Starter plunger retainer	24.	Float retainer
10.	Spring	25.	Float
11.	Starter plunger	26.	Fuel bowl
12.	Spring	27.	Main jet
13.	Idle speed screw	28.	"O" ring
14.	Spring	29.	Plug
15.	Idle mixture screw		

Fig. P1-7—Adjust idle mixture screw (I) and idle speed screw (S) as outlined in text.

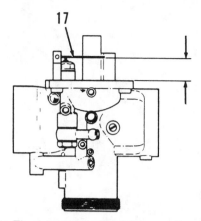

Fig. P1-9—Float arm (17) should be parallel to fuel bowl mating surface of carburetor body. Bend tang on float arm to adjust height.

cable adjuster (A) so marks are aligned. Retighten locknuts (N).

CHOKE LEVER. The control panel mounted choke lever should have 0.125-0.250 inch (3.17-6.35 mm) free play when choke lever is in the off position. To adjust free play, first loosen locknut (L—Fig. P1-14) on choke valve and turn adjuster (T) clockwise until 0.250 inch (6.35 mm) free play is exceeded at choke lever. Rotate adjuster (T) counterclockwise so free play is zero, then rotate adjuster clockwise until desired free play is obtained. Tighten locknut (L).

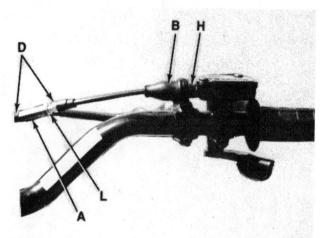

Fig. P1-11—Refer to text for adjustment of throttle cable free play.

A. Adjuster nut
B. Dust boot
D. Dust boots

H. Housing
L. Locknut

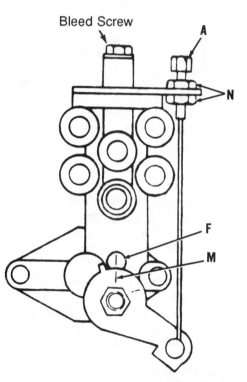

Fig. P1-13—On all models except 350L, mark (M) on oil pump arm should align with fixed mark (F) when free play is removed from throttle cable. Loosen locknuts (N) and rotate adjuster (A) to align marks.

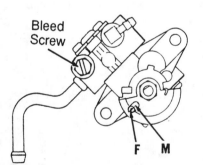

Fig. P1-12—On 350L models, mark (M) on oil pump arm should align with fixed mark (F) when throttle slide just begins to open.

Fig. P1-14—Free play on control-panel-mounted choke lever is adjusted by loosening locknut (L) and rotating adjuster (T). Refer to text for adjustment procedure.

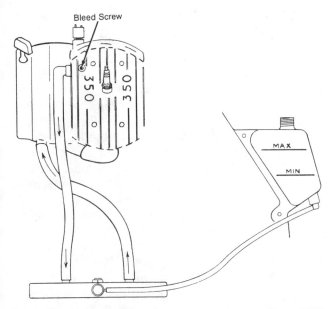

Fig. P1-15—Diagram of cooling system used on 350L models. Trapped air in system can be vented through bleed screw opening.

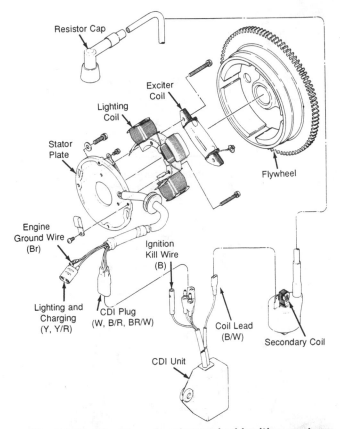

Fig. P1-16—Drawing showing typical ignition system.

COOLING SYSTEM

Model 350L

INSPECTION. The engine is liquid-cooled by a pressurized cooling system that consists of a radiator, water pump and hoses. System components should be inspected periodically. Replace hoses if cracked, split or otherwise damaged. Inspect radiator for signs of leakage and remove any obstructions. Refer to Fig. P1-15 for diagram of cooling system. Note location of bleed plug (B) that allows purging of trapped air in system.

CHANGING COOLANT. The manufacturer recommends a mixture of 50 percent distilled water and 50 percent antifreeze. Only antifreeze designed for aluminum engines and radiators should be used. Cooling system capacity is 2.0 qt. (1.9 L).

IGNITION SYSTEM

All Models

SPARK PLUG. The recommended spark plug for normal operating conditions is a NGK BR8ES or Champion RN4YC. Spark plug electrode gap should be 0.025 inch (0.63 mm) on models prior to 1989 or 0.028 inch (0.7 mm) on models after 1988. The spark plug should be removed, inspected, cleaned or renewed, and regapped after every 100 hours of operation.

IGNITION. The engine is equipped with a capacitor-discharge ignition system. See Fig. P1-16 Refer to CONDENSED SERVICE DATA for ignition timing speci-

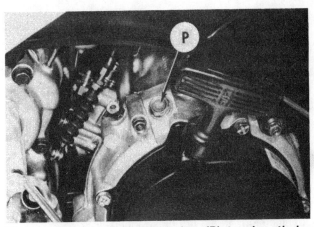

Fig. P1-17—Remove timing plug (P) to view timing marks (Fig. P1-18) on flywheel.

fications. To check ignition timing, unscrew timing plug (P—Fig. P1-17) and connect a power timing light to engine. Ignition timing must be checked when engine is cold, otherwise timing will retard approximately two degrees. Appropriate timing mark on flywheel should align with timing pointer shown in Fig. P1-18.

To adjust ignition timing, remove the right crankcase side cover (removal of manual starter housing is not required). Unscrew the flywheel retaining screw and use a suitable puller to detach the flywheel from the crankshaft. Ignition timing is adjusted by loosening stator

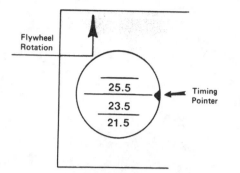

Fig. P1-18—View of flywheel timing marks. Refer to text for ignition timing procedure and specifications.

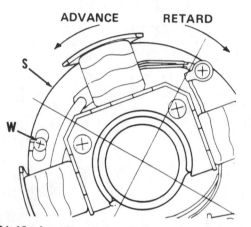

Fig. P1-19—Loosen stator plate retaining screws and rotate stator plate in direction shown to adjust ignition timing.

plate retaining screws (W—Fig. P1-19) and rotating stator plate (S). Rotate stator plate counterclockwise to advance ignition timing. When reassembling components, tighten flywheel retaining screw to 30-44 ft.-lbs. (41-60 N.m) on 350L models or to 38-40 ft.-lbs. (52-54 N.m) on all other models. Apply liquid gasket compound to mating surface of side cover before installation.

If ignition malfunction occurs, check condition of spark plug, all wires and connections before troubleshooting the ignition circuit. Using a suitable ohmmeter, refer to the following test procedures and specifications to aid troubleshooting.

To check condition of exciter coil, disconnect the three-wire connector leading to the alternator. Using an ohmmeter measure resistance between terminals for black/red wire and brown/white wire. Exciter coil is considered satisfactory if resistance is 108-132 ohms. If reading is incorrect, remove left crankcase cover and repeat test at terminal of pulse generator.

To check condition of ignition coil, disconnect wire leads to ignition coil. Primary winding resistance should be 0.3-0.5 ohms. Secondary winding resistance with spark plug cap removed should be 5.7k-6.9k ohms. If available, the ignition coil should be dynamically tested on an ignition coil tester.

A test procedure is not available for the CDI module. If preceding tests were satisfactory, replace CDI module with a good module and recheck engine operation.

The vehicle is equipped with a reverse speed limiter module (located near the front of the fuel tank under the splash guard). When the reverse light switch is actuated, the module senses engine speed from the alternator and grounds the ignition above approximately 3200 rpm. If the override switch on the handlebar is depressed, ignition grounding occurs at approximately 4800 rpm, in any gear. Note that if the reverse indicator light is faulty or the circuit is open that the reverse speed limiter module will limit engine speed to approximately 4800 rpm in any gear. To isolate the limiter module for testing purposes, disconnect black wire lead from module. Ignition should operate normally at all engine speeds with black wire disconnected from module.

Models after 1988 are equipped with an electronic throttle control switch as part of the reverse speed limiter circuit. If the engine overspeeds, the throttle lever must be returned to idle speed position to reset the switch. There should be continuity between white wire and red/white wire when throttle is closed and infinity when throttle is open. On models with a third wire (gray/white), there should be continuity between gray/white wire and red/white wire when throttle is open and infinity with throttle closed.

LIGHTING CIRCUIT. The lighting coil is a part of the magneto stator, which is attached on the right crankcase half behind the flywheel. To check condition of lighting coil, disconnect the white/yellow wire connector leading to alternator on left frame rail near the fuel tank. Using an ohmmeter measure resistance between white/yellow wire and vehicle ground. Lighting coil is considered satisfactory if resistance is 0.1-1.0 ohms. See previous NOTE.

Headlight rating is 12 volts-55/60 watts. Taillight rating is 12 volt-8 watt for 1986 models and 12 volt-5 watts for models after 1986.

ELECTRICAL SYSTEM

All Models

Trail Blazer models are equipped with a lighting circuit (Fig. P1-20) while all other models are equipped with a battery to provide electrical power for lights and accessories (Fig. P1-21). Systems using a battery are protected by a 10 amp circuit breaker except for the electric starter.

BATTERY. The negative terminal is grounded. The battery is a 12-volt unit with 14 amp-hour capacity.

CHARGING SYSTEM. All Models Except Trail Blazer. The charging circuit consists of an alternator and a regulator/rectifier. The alternator rotor (flywheel) is attached to the right end of the crankshaft while the stator is mounted on the right crankcase half.

The charging circuit should produce 13-14.6 VDC.

NOTE: Do not disconnect battery terminal wires while the engine is running as excessive alternator output will damage the regulator/rectifier.

To check the alternator stator coils, disconnect yellow/red and yellow wires leading from alternator. Check resistance between yellow/red and yellow wires. Ohmmeter should indicate 0.45-0.6 ohm on 1988 models or 0.25-0.35 ohm on models after 1988. There should be infinite resistance between either wire and engine ground. Connect a voltmeter between both wires. With engine running at 3000 rpm, voltmeter should indicate 25-50 volts.

If previous tests prove satisfactory and fuse, wiring and connections are all good, replace regulator/rectifier with a good unit and recheck operation.

ELECTRIC STARTER. All Models Except Trail Blazer. To check the starter relay, disconnect wires from terminals on relay. Connect ohmmeter leads to ground wire and red wire terminals on relay. Ohmmeter should read 3.4 ohms.

To service starter motor, refer to exploded view in Fig. P1-23. Before disassembling motor, note alignment marks, or make alignment marks, on center housing and end caps so they can be reassembled in original positions. When disassembling motor note location of all shims and washers. Minimum brush length is 5/16 inch (8.0 mm). Note tab on brush holder plate that must align with slot in rear end cap during assembly. Be sure "O" rings are correctly positioned during assembly.

LIGHTING CIRCUIT. Trail Blazer. Trail Blazers are equipped with lighting coils that are mounted on the stator plate behind the flywheel. The flywheel is attached to the right end of the crankshaft while the stator is mounted on the right crankcase half.

The light coils should produce 11-15 VAC if coils and voltage regulator are operating properly.

To check the lighting coils, disconnect yellow/red and yellow wires leading from stator. Check resistance between yellow/red and yellow wires. Ohmmeter should indicate 0.45-0.6 ohm on 1988 models or 0.25-0.35 ohm on models after 1988. There should be infinite resistance between either wire and engine ground. Connect

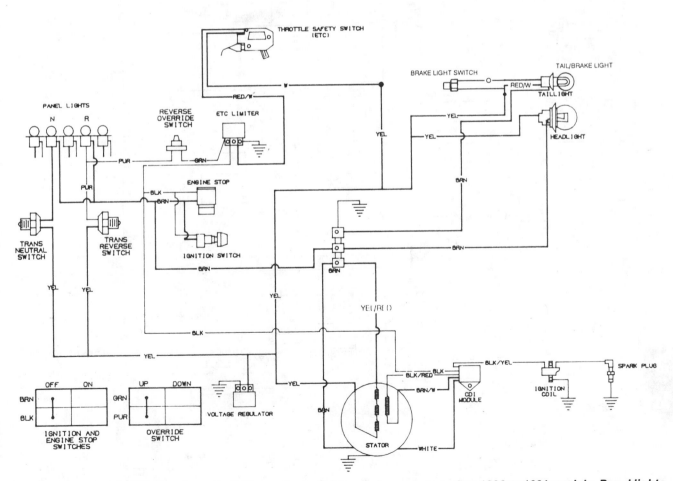

Fig. P1-20—Wiring diagram for 1992 Trail Blazer. Brake light switch was not used on 1990 or 1991 models. Panel lights were not used on 1990 models.

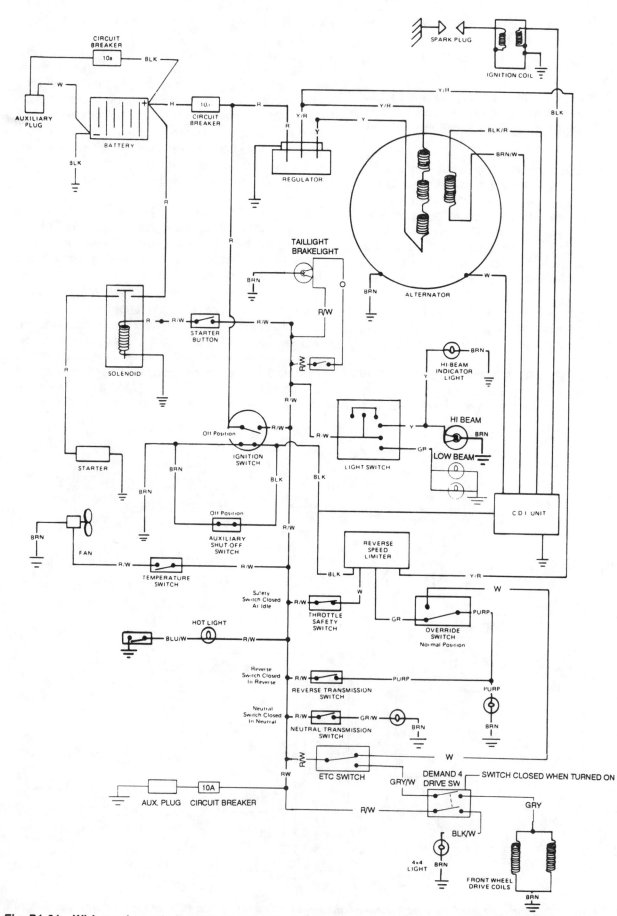

Fig. P1-21—Wiring schematic for 1992 Model 350L 4x4. Other models, except Trail Blazer, are similar.

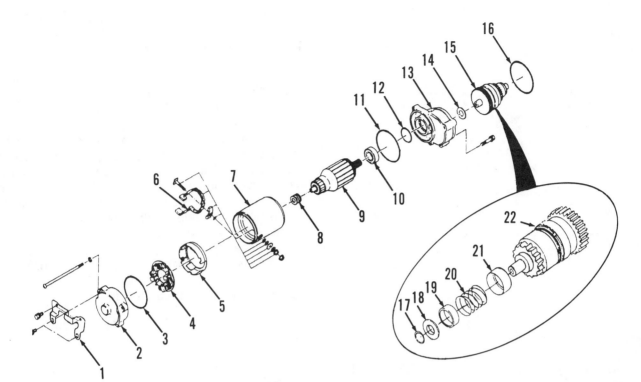

Fig. P1-23—Exploded view of typical electric starter motor with four brushes. Motor with two brushes is similar.

1. Bracket
2. End cap
3. "O" ring
4. Brush plate
5. Insulator
6. Brushes
7. Frame
8. Thrust washer
9. Armature
10. Bearing
11. "O" ring
12. "O" ring
13. Drive housing
14. Thrust washer
15. Pinion gear assy.
16. "O" ring
17. Snap ring
18. Washer
19. Collar
20. Spring
21. Spring case
22. Garter spring

a voltmeter between both wires. With engine running at 3000 rpm, voltmeter should indicate 25-50 volts.

If previous tests prove satisfactory and wiring and connections are all good, replace voltage regulator with a good unit and recheck operation.

LIGHTS. Headlight rating is 12 volts-45/45 watts on 1988 Trail Boss 2x4 and 4x4, 12 volts-60 watts on Trail Blazer, and 12 volts-60/60 watts on all other models. Taillight rating is 12 volt-5 watts for all models.

WIRING. If wiring requires repair, always install wire that is the same gauge as original wire. Wires should be routed away from areas of extreme heat or sharp edges. Attach or hold wires in their original position using plastic tie straps to prevent short circuits.

FASTENERS

All Models

After the first 25 hours of operation and after every 25 hours of operation thereafter, the vehicle should receive an overall inspection. All screws, nuts and other fasteners should be checked and tightened to proper torque

specification shown in CONDENSED SERVICE DATA section or in the appropriate maintenance section.

TRANSMISSION

All Models

ADJUSTMENT. 1988 Models. To adjust transmission shift rod (R—Fig. P1-24) on models equipped with a high-low transmission, detach rod end from transmis-

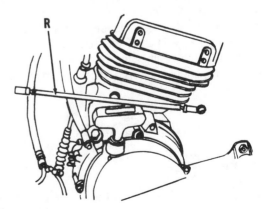

Fig. P1-24—Adjust length of transmission shift rod (R) as outlined in text.

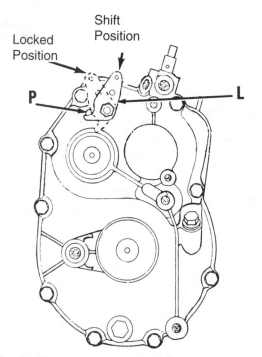

Fig. P1-25—Locking lever (L), on models so equipped, should contact lock pin (P). See text for adjustment procedure.

sion shift arm. Turn transmission shift arm so transmission is in neutral. Place shift control in neutral position. Adjust length of shift rod (R) by turning rod ends so shift rod end will reattach to transmission shift arm without disturbing position of transmission shift arm. Install jam nuts.

Models After 1988. To adjust transmission shift rod (R—Fig. P1-24) on models equipped with a high-low transmission, run engine and shift transmission from neutral to low and note where gear engagement begins. Shift transmission from neutral to reverse and note where gear engagement begins. The midpoint between the gear engagement points should be centered on neutral slot on gear shifter quadrant. If not, adjust length of shift rod (R—Fig. P1-24).

SHIFT LOCK ADJUSTMENT. On models with a locking transmission, the cable should be adjusted for proper operation. With shift lever button depressed, locking lever (L—Fig. P1-25) should contact lock pin (P). If not, adjust cable. With shift lever button released, locking lever (L) should again contact lock pin (P). If not, adjust cable.

MANUAL STARTER

All Models

R&R AND OVERHAUL. Refer to Fig. P1-26 for an exploded view of manual starter. Removing pulley housing (17) permits access to rope pulley (15) while side

cover (13) must be removed from engine for access to rewind spring (10) and starter pawl mechanism. Before disassembling starter, release rewind spring tension by removing rope handle (16) and allow rope to wind into pulley housing. Detach pawl spring (2), then unscrew pulley (15) from stud on pawl carrier (4). Be careful when removing rewind spring (10); a rapidly uncoiling starter spring can cause serious injury.

Before assembly, apply grease to side of rewind spring and spring retainer (9). Apply grease to spring hook (6) and install so it properly engages rewind spring end. Install friction spring (8) on friction ring (7) then install on starter so closed end of spring (8) surrounds bent tab on spring retainer (9). Install pawl (3) and pin (5) on carrier (4), then install carrier. Pin on carrier (4) must engage hole in spring hook (6). Screw rope pulley onto threads of carrier (4) and firmly hand tighten. Attach rope to rope pulley then pass rope through pulley housing rope outlet. Attach rope handle to rope end. Hold

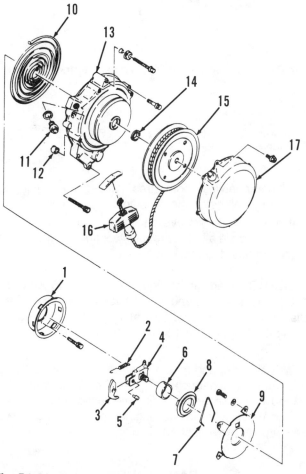

Fig. P1-26—Exploded view of manual starter.

1. Starter cup
2. Pawl spring
3. Pawl
4. Pawl carrier
5. Pin
6. Spring hook
7. Friction ring
8. Friction spring
9. Spring retainer
10. Rewind spring
11. Timing plug
12. Dowel
13. Side cover
14. Seal
15. Rope pulley
16. Rope handle
17. Pulley housing

pawl carrier (4) and rotate pulley housing (17) clockwise until rope is wrapped on rope pulley and rope handle is snug against rope outlet of pulley housing. Rotate pulley housing an additional three revolutions to apply tension to rewind spring and attach pulley housing to side cover. Install pawl spring (2) and check starter action. Apply liquid gasket compound to mating surface of side cover and install on engine.

FRONT BRAKE

All Models

The front and rear brake systems are operated by the same brake lever. The front brake system uses hydraulically actuated, disc-type brakes attached to each steering knuckle. A handlebar-mounted master cylinder with integral fluid reservoir supplies pressure to each wheel caliper when the left handlebar lever is operated.

Only DOT 3 rated brake fluid is recommended. On 1988 models, maintain brake fluid level at ⅛ inch (3.2 mm) below top of reservoir. On models after 1988, maintain brake fluid level at ¼ inch (6.35 mm) below top of reservoir. To avert spillage, be sure reservoir is horizontal before removing cover.

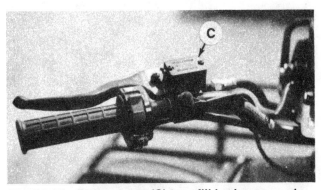

Fig. P1-27—Remove cap (C) to refill brake reservoir.

Fig. P1-28—Remove cap (P) to connect bleed hose to bleed screw (S).

BLEEDING. Any operation that required draining or repair of hydraulic brake components will make it necessary to fill and bleed brake system. Check reservoir fluid level. On 1988 models, brake fluid level must be ⅛ inch (3.2 mm) below top of reservoir. On models after 1988, brake fluid level must be ¼ inch (6.35 mm) below top of reservoir. Remove cap (C—Fig. P1-27) and fill reservoir. Reinstall cap. Remove cap (P—Fig. P1-28) and attach a suitable hose to either bleed screw (S). Submerge lower hose end in a container partially filled with brake fluid so air cannot reenter system. Operate brake lever until hard resistance is felt, then open bleed valve. Close bleed valve prior to releasing brake lever. Continue bleeding procedure on both front wheels until no air bubbles are noted in discharged fluid from bleed valve. Repeat bleeding procedure at rear caliper using bleed screw (B—Fig. P1-29). Do not allow reservoir to run dry while bleeding. When bleeding procedure is completed, fill reservoir to correct fluid level.

INSPECTION. The brake system should be inspected periodically. Renew brake pads if worn beyond service limit groove. Renew brake pads if remaining lining is less than 0.075 inch (1.9 mm) thick. Correct any occurrences of brake fluid leakage. Renew any worn, cracked or damaged brake lines or hoses and determine and correct the cause.

WARNING: Inhaling asbestos brake dust is injurious to human health. Approved OSHA respiration equipment must be worn when working on or around brake calipers and pads. DO NOT use compressed air to clean brake calipers, pads or nearby components as brake dust will be blown into air. Only vacuum equipment designed to pick up brake dust should be used.

OVERHAUL. Brake components are accessible after removing wheel, caliper mounting screws and withdrawing caliper. Refer to Fig. P1-30 for an exploded view of caliper. Push piston by hand back into caliper to allow clearance for new brake pads. Tighten brake caliper mounting screws to 18 ft.-lbs. (24 N·m). With caliper

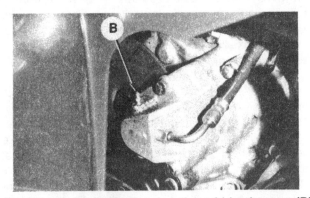

Fig. P1-29—View showing location of bleed screw (B) on rear brake caliper.

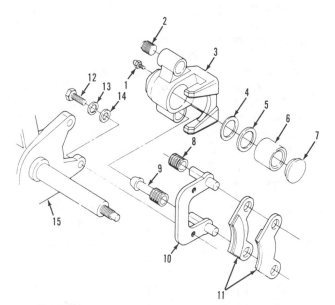

Fig. P1-30—Exploded view of front brake caliper. Caliper may be used as rear caliper on Big Boss 4x6 models.

1. Bleed screw
2. Socket screw
3. Caliper
4. Square ring
5. Square ring
6. Piston
7. Insulator
8. Seal
9. Bushing
10. Mounting bracket
11. Brake pads
12. Cap screw
13. Lockwasher
14. Washer
15. Knuckle

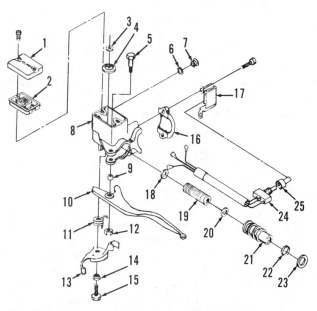

Fig. P1-31—Exploded view of brake master cylinder.

1. Cap
2. Diaphragm
3. Washer
4. Baffle
5. Shoulder bolt
6. Seal
7. Sight glass
8. Reservoir
9. Bushing
10. Brake lever
11. Spring
12. Nut
13. Parking brake lever
14. Bushing
15. Screw
16. Clamp
17. Override switch
18. Washer
19. Spring
20. Seal
21. Piston
22. "O" ring
23. Seal
24. Override switch
25. Boot

mounted on knuckle, turn set screw (2) in until brake pads contact disc. Rotate wheel hub and adjust set screw so pads barely drag against disc, then back out set screw approximately one-half turn so disc rotates freely. If the brake line is disconnected or the caliper is disassembled, bleed brakes as previously outlined. After reassembly, operate brake lever until brake lever will not pump up after continuous operation. Do not operate vehicle until brakes are tested and functioning properly.

MASTER CYLINDER. To remove front brake master cylinder (Fig. P1-31), detach brake line from master cylinder. Brake fluid will remove paint; be careful when removing master cylinder. Unscrew two retaining screws and remove master cylinder. Remove brake lever, reservoir cover (1) and diaphragm (2). Insert a tool through brake line hole in body and push or drive piston assembly out of body. Disassemble piston assembly while noting location and direction of components. Renew complete master cylinder if bore is scored, pitted or excessively worn. Superficial damage in master cylinder bore may be removed using a suitable cylinder hone. After honing, rinse bore with clean brake fluid. Shake out excess fluid but do not wipe dry. Using a shop towel or rag to dry cylinder will leave lint particles in bore. Renew boots and piston cups. During reassembly, lubricate components with clean brake fluid. Reassembly is reverse of disassembly. Bleed brakes as previously outlined. Do not operate vehicle until brakes are tested and functioning properly.

STEERING

All Models

TOE-IN SETTING. The toe-in should be checked and adjusted, if needed, periodically. Prior to toe-in adjustment, inspect steering assembly for damaged or excessively worn parts and renew if required.

To check toe-in, inflate tires to specified tire pressure. Position vehicle on a flat, smooth surface and set handlebar straight forward. Using a suitable tape measure, measure distance (D—Fig. P1-33) between right left tire centerlines on back side of tires and record measurement. Locate the same tire centerline points on front side of tires and measure distance (D). The front measurement should be 0.125-0.250 inch (3.18-6.35 mm) greater that rear measurement.

To adjust, loosen inner tie rod locknuts (N—Fig. P1-34) and outer tie rod locknuts (L—Fig. P1-35) on left and right tie rod assemblies. Rotate tie rod adjuster rods (R—Fig. P1-33) in equal increments to maintain equal vehicle centerline to left and right tire centerline distances. Securely tighten tie rod locknuts.

Fig. P1-33—Refer to text for toe-in checking procedure. Toe-in is adjusted by rotating tie rod shafts (R).

Fig. P1-34—View showing location of inner tie rod locknut (N).

Fig. P1-35—View showing location of outer tie rod locknut (L).

REAR BRAKE

All Models

The front and rear brake systems are operated by the same brake lever. A single caliper assembly attached to the transmission stops rotation of the transmission output shaft. A handlebar-mounted master cylinder with integral fluid reservoir supplies pressure to each wheel caliper an the rear brake caliper when the left handlebar lever is operated. Refer to BLEEDING paragraphs under FRONT BRAKE section for recommended bleeding procedure.

NOTE: When transmission is in neutral, rear brake has no stopping effect.

INSPECTION. The brake system should be inspected periodically. Renew brake pads if worn beyond service limit groove. Renew brake pads if remaining lining is less than 0.075 inch (1.9 mm) thick. Correct any occurrences of brake fluid leakage. Renew any worn, cracked or damaged brake lines or hoses and determine and correct the cause.

WARNING: Inhaling asbestos brake dust is injurious to human health. Approved OSHA respiration equipment must be worn when working on or around brake calipers and pads. DO NOT use compressed air to clean brake calipers, pads or nearby components as brake dust will be blown into air. Only vacuum equipment designed to pick up brake dust should be used.

OVERHAUL. 1988 Models. To remove caliper, unscrew caliper retaining screws and detach caliper from transmission and disc. Unscrew pad retaining pins and remove pads. Push piston by hand back into caliper to allow clearance for new brake pads. Tighten brake caliper mounting screws to 15 ft.-lbs. (20 N•m). If the brake line is disconnected or the caliper is disassembled, bleed brakes as previously outlined. After reassembly, operate brake lever until brake lever will not pump up after continuous operation. Do not operate vehicle until brakes are tested and functioning properly.

Models After 1988. To remove caliper, disconnect foot pedal linkage and unscrew caliper retaining screws. Separate caliper from disc. Loosen jam nut (2—Fig. P1-37) and unscrew adjuster screw (1). Remove pin retaining plate (3) and extract pins (9). Remove pads. Push piston by hand back into caliper to allow clearance for new brake pads. If further caliper disassembly is required, note the following during assembly: Apply a thin coat of grease on ramps of brake ramp (15). When assembling ramp (15) and collar (17), turn ramp so that when the ramp surfaces on the ramp and collar are meshed fully, the flats on the ramp end will be 90° from

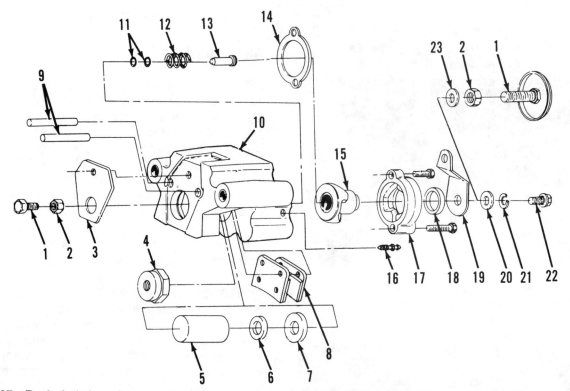

Fig. P1-37—Exploded view of rear brake caliper. Location of mechanical brake adjusting screw (1) will depend on type of transmission used.

1. Adjusting screw
2. Locknut
3. Pin retainer plate
4. Nut
5. Piston
6. Seal
7. Seal
8. Brake pads
9. Brake pad pins
10. Caliper
11. "O" rings
12. Spring
13. Brake apply pin
14. Gasket
15. Movable ramp
16. Bleed screw
17. Collar
18. Seal
19. Actuating arm
20. Washer
21. Lockwasher
22. Screw
23. Washer

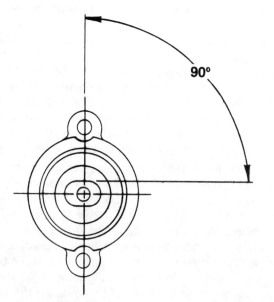

Fig. P1-38—When the ramp surfaces on the ramp and collar are meshed fully, the flats on the ramp end will be 90° from screw holes in collar.

screw holes in collar as shown in Fig. P1-38. Install piston (5—Fig. P1-37) by inserting beveled end first. Tighten brake caliper mounting screws to 15 ft.-lbs. (20 N·m). If the brake line is disconnected or the caliper is disassembled, bleed brakes as previously outlined. After reassembly, operate brake lever until brake lever will not pump up after continuous operation. On models so equipped, place transmission in neutral and turn adjuster screw (1) in until brake pads contact disc. Rotate disc and turn screw so pads barely drag against disc, then back out screw approximately one-half turn so disc rotates freely.

REAR DRIVE CHAIN

All Models

The rear drive chain should be inspected and adjusted periodically depending on vehicle usage. Improper maintenance and neglect can cause premature failure of chain and sprockets. Refer to LUBRICATION section for drive chain lubrication information.

Rear drive chain free travel should be 1½ inches (38 mm) on Big Boss models and ¼ inch (6.35 mm) on all

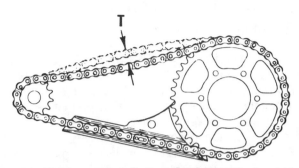

Fig. P1-39—Rear drive chain free travel (T) should be measured midway between sprockets.

Fig. P1-40—To adjust rear drive chain free play on all models except Big Boss, loosen rear axle housing clamp bolts (B) and insert a pin through the rear sprocket (R) into the rear axle housing. Rock vehicle backward or forward to increase or decrease chain free travel.

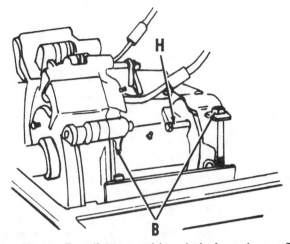

Fig. P1-41—To adjust rear drive chain free play on Big Boss models, loosen rear axle housing clamp bolts (B) and insert a 5/16 inch pin through hole (H) in top of the rear axle housing. Move vehicle so the pin engages a hole in the sprocket hub. Move vehicle so the rear axle housing is forced to rotate in its retaining clamps, thereby, loosening or tightening drive chain.

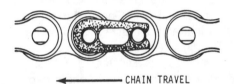

Fig. P1-42—Install drive chain master link clip with closed end of clip toward normal direction of chain travel.

other models. Measure chain free travel midway between sprockets as shown in Fig. P1-39.

To adjust rear drive chain free play on all models except Big Boss, the suspension must be loaded so chain is at tightest point in suspension travel. Loosen rear axle housing clamp bolts (B—Fig. P1-40). Insert a pin through the rear sprocket (R) into the rear axle housing. Move vehicle so the pin forces the rear axle housing to rotate in its retaining clamps thereby loosening or tightening drive chain. After obtaining desired chain travel tighten axle housing clamp bolts to 48 ft.-lbs. (65 N•m). Remove pin and recheck chain free travel.

To adjust rear drive chain free play on Big Boss models the vehicle must be unloaded. Loosen rear axle housing clamp bolts (B—Fig. P1-41). Insert a 5/16 inch

pin through hole (H) in top of the rear axle housing. Move vehicle so the pin engages a hole in the sprocket hub. Move vehicle so the rear axle housing is forced to rotate in its retaining clamps thereby loosening or tightening drive chain. Note that chain free travel can be measured on top strand just forward of chain case. Chain free travel at this point should be 1 inch (25.4 mm), which will equal 1½ inches (38 mm) at midway point. After obtaining desired chain travel tighten axle housing clamp bolts to 48 ft.-lbs. (65 N•m). Remove pin and recheck chain free travel. Note that changing rear drive chain free play will affect rear axle drive chain free play. Refer to REAR AXLE DRIVE CHAIN section.

When assembling chain, install master link clip as shown in Fig. P1-42.

CENTER AND FRONT DRIVE CHAIN

1988 Four-Wheel-Drive Models

INSPECTION AND ADJUSTMENT. The center and front drive chains should be inspected and adjusted periodically depending on vehicle usage. Improper maintenance and neglect can cause premature failure

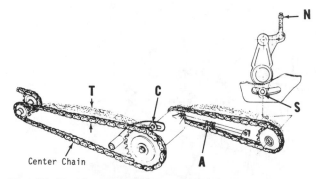

Fig. P1-43—On 1988 four-wheel-drive models, loosen cap screw (C) and alter length of adjuster assembly (A) to adjust tension on center drive chain. Loosen cap screw (S) and rotate adjuster nut (N) to adjust tension on front drive chain. The center drive chain must be adjusted prior to adjusting front drive chain.

of chain and sprockets. Refer to LUBRICATION section for drive chain lubrication information.

Free travel of center and front drive chains should be ¼ inch (6.35 mm) measured midway between sprockets as shown in Fig. P1-43. The center drive chain must be adjusted first as front drive chain free travel will be affected. To adjust center drive chain, loosen cap screw (C) and adjust length of adjuster (A) so chain free travel (T) is ¼ inch (6.35 mm), then tighten cap screw. To adjust front drive chain free travel, loosen cap screw (S) and rotate adjuster nut (N) so chain free travel is ¼ inch (6.35 mm), then tighten cap screw.

Four- And Six-Wheel-Drive Models After 1988

INSPECTION AND ADJUSTMENT. The center and front drive chains should be inspected and adjusted periodically depending on vehicle usage. Improper maintenance and neglect can cause premature failure of chain and sprockets. Refer to LUBRICATION section for drive chain lubrication information.

Free travel of center and front drive chains should be ¼ inch (6.35 mm) measured midway between sprockets. The center drive chain must be adjusted first as front drive chain free travel will be affected. To adjust chain free travel, disconnect and remove brake pedal linkage. Detach right front fender mud flap from foot board. Remove center chain guard and front chain guard. Loosen clamp bolts (CB—Fig. P1-44) that secure chain drive eccentric. Rock vehicle forward or rearward so hole in case aligns with hole in gear. Insert a pin in the holes. Move vehicle so the center chain drive case is forced to rotate in its retaining clamps thereby loosening or tightening drive chain. Move vehicle rearward to tighten chain. After obtaining desired chain travel tighten clamp bolts to 48 ft.-lbs. (65 N·m). Remove pin and recheck chain free travel.

To adjust free play of front drive chain, loosen clamp bolt (FB—Fig. P1-44) on front drive chain case. Rock vehicle forward or rearward so hole in case aligns with hole in gear. Insert a pin in the holes. Move vehicle so the front drive case is forced to rotate in its retaining clamp thereby loosening or tightening front drive chain.

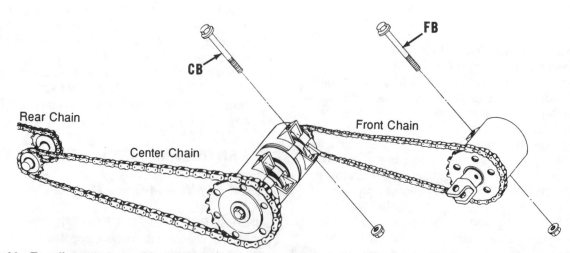

Fig. P1-44—To adjust center and front drive chain free travel on four- and six-wheel drive models after 1988, clamp bolts (CB and FB) must be loosened so their respective eccentric cases can be rotated. Refer to text.

Move vehicle rearward to tighten chain. Tighten clamp bolt (FB) to 48 ft.-lbs. (65 N•m). Remove pin and recheck chain free travel.

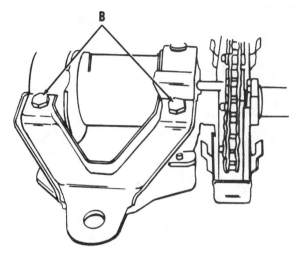

Fig. P1-45—To adjust rear axle chain drive free travel on Big Boss models, loosen clamp bolts (B) and rotate eccentric axle case as outlined in text.

REAR AXLE DRIVE CHAIN

Big Boss Models

INSPECTION AND ADJUSTMENT. The axle-to-axle drive chain should be inspected and adjusted periodically depending on vehicle usage. Improper maintenance and neglect can cause premature failure of chain and sprockets. Refer to LUBRICATION section for drive chain lubrication information.

Free travel of rear axle drive chain should be ¼ inch (6.35 mm) measured midway between sprockets. Final drive chain free travel must be adjusted first as rear axle drive chain free travel will be affected. To adjust free play of rear axle drive chain, loosen clamp bolts (B—Fig. P1-45) on rear axle case. Rock vehicle forward or rearward so hole in case aligns with hole in gear. Insert a pin in the holes. Move vehicle so the axle case is forced to rotate in its retaining clamps thereby loosening or tightening rear axle drive chain. Move vehicle rearward to tighten chain. Tighten clamp bolt (FB) to 48 ft.-lbs. (65 N•m). Remove pin and recheck chain free travel.

SUZUKI
LT80

NOTE: Metric fasteners are used throughout vehicle.

CONDENSED SERVICE DATA

MODEL	LT80
General	
Engine Make	Suzuki
Engine Type	Two-Stroke; Air-Cooled
Number of Cylinders	1
Bore	50 mm
	(1.969 in.)
Stroke	42 mm
	(1.654 in.)
Displacement	82.5 cc
	(5.03 cu. in.)
Compression Ratio	7.4:1
Fuel Recommendation	Unleaded or Low-Lead
Pump Octane Rating	85-95
Engine Lubrication	Oil Injection
Forward Speeds	Variable
Reverse Speeds	N/A
Tire Size:	
Front	19 × 7.00-8
Rear	19 × 7.00-8
Tire Pressure (cold):	
Front	15 kPa
	(2.2 psi)
Rear	20 kPa
	(2.8 psi)
Dry Weight	99.5 kg
	(219 lbs.)
Tune-Up	
Engine Idle Speed	1450-1750 rpm
Spark Plug:	
NGK	BP7HS
Nippon Denso	W22FP-U
Electrode Gap	0.6-0.8 mm
	(0.024-0.031 in.)
Ignition:	
Type	Breakerless
Timing	19°-25° BTDC @ 4000 rpm
Carburetor:	
Make	Mikuni
Model	VM16SH
Bore Size	16 mm
	(0.63 in.)
Float Height	17.5-19.5 mm
	(0.69-0.77 in.)
Jet Needle	3J17

Tune-Up (Cont.)
Carburetor: (Cont.)
Clip Position.	2nd Groove From Top
Pilot Jet	#20
Needle Jet	E-O
Main Jet	#92.5
Throttle Cut-Away	2.5
Throttle Cable Free Play	0.5-1.0 mm (0.02-0.04 in.)

Sizes-Clearances
Reed Petal Stand Open (Max.)	0.2 mm (0.008 in.)
Cylinder Head Distortion (Max.).	0.05 mm (0.002 in.)
Piston-to-Cylinder Wall Clearance	0.080-0.090 mm (0.0031-0.0035 in.)
Wear Limit	0.120 mm (0.0047 in.)
Cylinder Bore Diameter	50.000-50.015 mm (1.9685-1.9691 in.)
Wear Limit	50.050 mm (1.9705 in.)
Cylinder Bore Distortion (Max.)	0.05 mm (0.002 in.)
Piston Diameter Measured 20 mm (0.8 in.) from Skirt Bottom	49.915-49.930 mm (1.9652-1.9657 in.)
Wear Limit	49.880 mm (1.9638 in.)
Piston Pin Bore Diameter	12.002-12.010 mm (0.4725-0.4728 in.)
Wear Limit	12.030 mm (0.4736 in.)
Piston Pin Diameter	11.994-12.000 mm (0.4722-0.4724 in.)
Wear Limit	11.980 mm (0.4717 in.)
Piston Ring End Gap	0.15-0.35 mm (0.006-0.014 in.)
Wear Limit	0.80 mm (0.031 in.)
Piston Ring Side Clearance	0.020-0.060 mm (0.0008-0.0024 in.)
Connecting Rod Small End Bore Diameter	16.000-16.008 mm (0.6299-0.6302 in.)
Wear Limit	16.040 mm (0.6315 in.)
Crankshaft Runout (Max.)	0.05 mm (0.002 in.)

Capacities
Fuel Tank	6.0 L (1.58 gal.)
Transmission	See Text

Tightening Torques

Clutch Drum Nut	40-60 N·m (29.0-43.5 ft.-lbs.)
Crankcase Cap Screws	8-12 N·m (6.0-8.5 ft.-lbs.)
Cylinder Head Nut	8-12 N·m (6.0-8.5 ft.-lbs.)
Engine Pivot Bolt	110-160 N·m (81-117 ft.-lbs.)
Fixed Drive Face Nut	40-60 N·m (29.0-43.5 ft.-lbs.)
Flywheel Bolt	35-43 N·m (25.5-31.0 ft.-lbs.)
Front Axle Nuts	50-80 N·m (36-58 ft.-lbs.)
Rear Axle Nuts	60-90 N·m (43.5-66 ft.-lbs.)
Transmission-to-Rear Axle Bolts	18-28 N·m (13-20 ft.-lbs.)

Wheel Retaining Nuts:

Front	45-65 N·m (32.5-47.0 ft.-lbs.)
Rear	45-65 N·m (32.5-47.0 ft.-lbs.)

Standard Screws:
Unmarked or Marked "4"

4 mm	1.0-2.0 N·m (8.9-18 in.-lbs.)
5 mm	2.0-4.0 N·m (18-36 in.-lbs.)
6 mm	4.0-7.0 N·m (36-62 in.-lbs.)
8 mm	10-16 N·m (88.5-142 in.-lbs.)
10 mm	22-35 N·m (16-26 ft.-lbs.)
12 mm	36-55 N·m (26-40 ft.-lbs.)
14 mm	50-80 N·m (37-59 ft.-lbs.)
16 mm	80-130 N·m (59-96 ft.-lbs.)
18 mm	130-190 N·m (96-140 ft.-lbs.)

Marked "7"

4 mm	1.5-3.0 N·m (13-27 in.-lbs.)
5 mm	3.0-6.0 N·m (27-53 in.-lbs.)
6 mm	8.0-12.0 N·m (71-106 in.-lbs.)
8 mm	18-28 N·m (13-21 ft.-lbs.)
10 mm	40-60 N·m (29-44 ft.-lbs.)
12 mm	70-100 N·m (52-74 ft.-lbs.)

Tightening Torques (Cont.)

14 mm	110-160 N·m (81-118 ft.-lbs.)
16 mm	170-250 N·m (125-184 ft.-lbs.)
18 mm	200-280 N·m (147-206 ft.-lbs.)

LUBRICATION

ENGINE. The engine is lubricated by an automatic oil metering system. Recommended oil is Suzuki CCI or CCI Super Oil. If neither of the previous listed oils are available, then a good quality oil designed for use in a two-stroke air-cooled engine can be used. Ensure all dirt and debris is removed from around oil reservoir filler cap before adding oil.

TRANSMISSION. The reduction gears, countershaft and drive shaft are lubricated by oil contained within the transmission housing. The transmission oil should be changed after the first month of operation and every six months thereafter. Recommended oil is a good quality multigrade SAE 20W-40 motor oil. Pour oil through fill plug (F—Fig. S1-1) opening and maintain oil level at plug (L) opening. Remove plug in underside of housing to drain. Dry capacity of housing is 80-90 mL (2.7-2.8 oz.) Refilling housing after a routine oil change requires only 80 mL (2.7 oz.) of oil because some oil will be retained in case castings.

DRIVE CHAIN. The final drive chain should be lubricated with heavy weight motor oil prior to each operating interval. Incorrect chain lubricating oil may cause damage to "O" ring seals in drive chain. Drive chain should be removed periodically and thoroughly washed in kerosene and lubricated. Any cleaning solutions other than kerosene may result in "O" ring seal damage. To obtain access to drive chain, remove the four cap screws securing chain cover, then slide chain cover outward.

Refer to DRIVE CHAIN AND SPROCKETS section for chain renewal information.

CABLES, LEVERS, SHAFTS AND BEARINGS. The throttle cable and front brake cable should be lubricated with motor oil every three months. The front wheel bearings, steering shaft, rear brake lever and rear wheel bearings should be greased every three months. Do not excessively grease the brake camshaft as grease may contact brake linings reducing braking ability.

AIR CLEANER ELEMENT

The air cleaner element should be removed and cleaned after every three months of operation or more frequently if vehicle is operated under adverse conditions. To remove air cleaner element, remove the two air cleaner housing retaining screws and the element mounting screw, then withdraw element assembly. Carefully separate the two foam elements from frame.

Thoroughly clean each element in a suitable nonflammable solvent. Saturate each element in a clean recommended motor oil. Compress elements to remove excess oil. Reinstall elements by reversing removal procedure.

FUEL SYSTEM

CARBURETOR. A Mikuni VM16SH-type carburetor is used. Refer to CONDENSED SERVICE DATA for carburetor specifications.

Before performing carburetor adjustments, throttle cable should be carefully adjusted to provide 0.5-1.0 mm (0.02-0.04 in.) free play (P—Fig. S1-3) at idle position. Cable adjustment is accomplished by first sliding dust boot (1) up cable. Loosen locknut (3) and rotate adjuster (2) as required. Adjust idle speed screw (26—Fig. S1-4) so engine idles at 1450-1750 rpm. After adjusting carburetor, check throttle cable adjustment as

Fig. S1-1—View identifying transmission fill plug (F) and oil level plug (L).

previously described, then tighten locknut (3—Fig. S1-3) and reinstall boot (1).

The carburetor should be removed, disassembled and cleaned if carburetor malfunction is determined. Disassembly of the carburetor is evident after inspection of unit and referral to exploded view in Fig. S1-5. Carefully inspect jet needle (9), inlet valve (17) and idle speed screw (26) for excessive wear or damage.

During reassembly, renew all gaskets. Clip (7) should be in second groove from top on jet needle (9). To check float height, remove float bowl (24) and invert carburetor. Distance (A—Fig. S1-6) between bottom of float and carburetor body with gasket removed should be 17.5-19.5 mm (0.69-0.77 in.). If float height is incorrect, renew inlet valve (17—Fig. S1-5) and/or float (22) as needed to obtain correct float height.

FUEL COCK. A fuel cock assembly is located on the lower right side of the fuel tank. A fuel strainer located at fuel pickup area of fuel cock is used to filter the fuel. The fuel cock assembly should be removed and the strainer cleaned periodically to prevent fuel starvation because of strainer restriction.

The fuel cock uses a vacuum operated diaphragm to open and close fuel delivery outlet to carburetor. When vacuum is applied to vacuum nipple on fuel cock, the diaphragm is pulled downward to allow fuel flow. When vacuum is removed, the diaphragm spring will force the

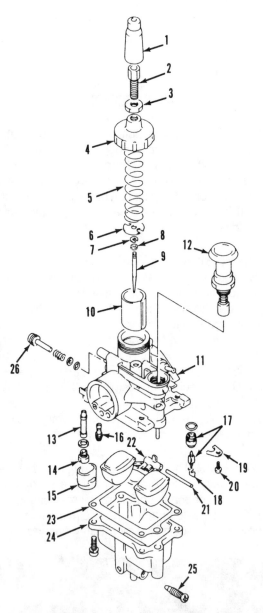

Fig. S1-5—Exploded view of Mikuni VM16SH type carburetor.

1.	Boot	14.	Main jet
2.	Adjuster	15.	Cap
3.	Locknut	16.	Pilot jet
4.	Cap	17.	Inlet valve
5.	Spring	18.	Needle clip
6.	Retainer	19.	Inlet valve retainer
7.	Clip	20.	Screw
8.	Washer	21.	Float pin
9.	Jet needle	22.	Float
10.	Throttle slide	23.	Gasket
11.	Body	24.	Float bowl
12.	Starter valve	25.	Drain screw
13.	Needle jet	26.	Idle speed screw

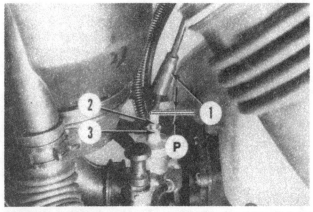

Fig. S1-3—Throttle cable free play (P) should be 0.5-1.0 mm (0.02-0.04 in.). Slide dust boot (1) up cable, loosen locknut (3) and rotate adjuster (2) to adjust throttle cable free play.

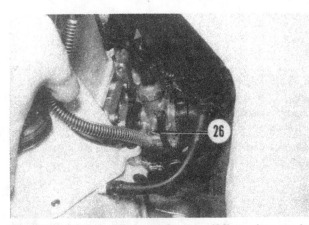

Fig. S1-4—Rotate idle speed screw (26) to alter engine idle speed.

222

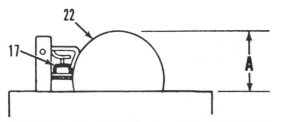

Fig. S1-6—Float height (A) should be 17.5-19.5 mm (0.69-0.77 in.). Inlet valve (17) and/or float (22) must be renewed if float height is incorrect.

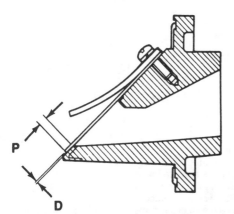

Fig. S1-8—Reed valve petals may stand open (D) a maximum of 0.2 mm (0.008 in.) at the tip. The reed valve petals should overlap (P) at the petal tip a minimum of 1 mm (0.04 in.).

diaphragm upward to close off the fuel delivery port, thus stopping fuel flow.

REED VALVE.

A reed valve assembly is located between the carburetor and engine crankcase. Reed valve assembly is accessible after removing the carburetor and the four screws retaining the reed plate.

Reed petal seats must be smooth and flat. Renew reed petals if bent, broken or otherwise damaged. DO NOT attempt to straighten bent petals.

Reed valve petals may stand open (D—Fig. S1-8) a maximum of 0.2 mm (0.008 in.) at the tip. The reed valve petals should overlap (P) at the petal tip a minimum of 1 mm (0.04 in.). Renew components as needed.

OIL PUMP

BLEEDING. If air has been allowed to enter the transfer hose between the oil reservoir and the oil pump, the air must be bled out prior to operation. To bleed system, first fill oil reservoir, then open screw (S—Fig. S1-10) and allow oil to drain from around screw threads until no air bubbles are noted. Tighten screw (S) and refill oil reservoir.

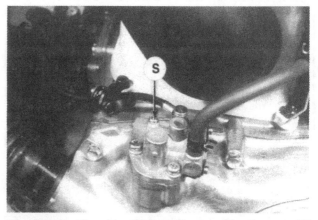

Fig. S1-10—View identifying oil pump bleed screw (S). Refer to text for bleeding procedure.

IGNITION AND ELECTRICAL

SPARK PLUG. Standard recommended spark plug is NGK BP7HS or Nippon Denso W22FP-U. Spark plug electrode gap should be 0.6-0.8 mm (0.024-0.031 in.).

Spark plug should be removed and inspected at three-month operating intervals, or more often depending on vehicle operation. Spark plug should be renewed after every six months of operation, or more often if necessary.

IGNITION. A capacitor discharge ignition (CDI) system is used. The ignition system consists of the flywheel, a magneto coil located under flywheel, CDI module and ignition coil unit attached to frame under fuel tank, a spark plug, an engine stop switch and an ignition switch. Ignition timing should be 19-25° BTDC and is not adjustable.

If ignition malfunction occurs, check condition of spark plug, all wires and connections before troubleshooting ignition circuit. Using Suzuki pocket tester 09900-25002 or a suitable ohmmeter, refer to the following test specifications and procedures to aid troubleshooting.

To check condition of CDI module, first remove module from vehicle. Attach tester positive lead to spark plug high tension wire and negative lead to module ground. Resistance between high tension wire and ground should be 12k-17.5k ohms.

To check condition of magneto coil, disconnect connector leading from magneto coil. Attach tester positive lead to black wire with red tracer leading from magneto coil and negative tester lead to a good engine ground or magneto base plate if assembly is removed. Magneto coil can be considered satisfactory if resistance reading is 139-207 ohms.

Renew either assembly if test results are not within the recommended standards.

		+Tester Lead		
		Red	White/Red	Ground
−Tester Lead	Red		B	B
	White/Red	A		B
	Ground	B	B	

Fig. S1-12—Use chart shown above and Suzuki pocket tester 09900-25002 to test regulator/rectifier assembly. "A" indicates continuity reading on meter and "B" indicates infinite reading on meter.

CHARGING CIRCUIT. The charging circuit consists of an alternator charge coil located under the flywheel, a regulator/rectifier, battery and ignition switch.

Standard battery is a YTH5L-12B. Standard battery is maintenance-free and has a 4 ampere hour, 12-volt rating. The manufacturer does not recommend using any other battery. The battery should never require periodic maintenance other than cleaning terminal posts, if needed, and charging battery if voltage tests low. If battery tests below 12 volts, charge battery at the rate of 5 amperes for a period of 30 minutes or 0.4 ampere for a period of 5 hours. Do not exceed maximum charging rate of 5 amperes.

NOTE: The battery should always be removed from the vehicle prior to charging.

During periods of vehicle storage, the battery should be charged once a month at the rate previously outlined to reduce sulfation and prolong battery life.

The alternator charge coil can be tested using Suzuki pocket tester 09900-25002. Disconnect connector leading from alternator charge coil. Attach tester positive lead to white wire with red tracer leading from alternator charge coil and negative tester lead to a good engine ground or magneto base plate if assembly is removed. Alternator charge coil can be considered satisfactory if resistance reading is 0.51-0.75 ohm.

To test regulator/rectifier, use Suzuki pocket tester 09900-25002 and refer to chart shown in Fig. S1-12. If tester readings are not as shown, then renewal of regulator/rectifier is required.

ELECTRIC STARTER. The starter can be removed and disassembled to clean, inspect and lubricate individual parts. The starter brushes should be renewed if worn to 6 mm (0.24 in.) or less. Commutator undercut should be a minimum of 0.2 mm (0.008 in.).

To remove electric starter, first disconnect battery. Disconnect wire at connector or starter motor lead. Unbolt and withdraw starter motor. Note location of all components during disassembly to aid in reassembly.

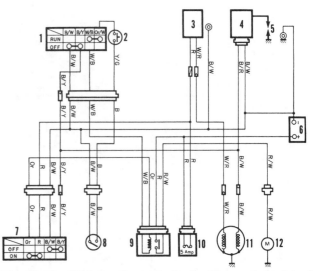

Fig. S1-13—Wiring schematic for ignition and electrical circuits.

B. Black	2. Starter switch
R. Red	3. Regulator/rectifier
Or. Orange	4. CDI module &
B/R. Black with red tracer	ignition coil unit
B/W. Black with white tracer	5. Spark plug
B/Y. Black with yellow tracer	6. Battery
R/W. Red with white tracer	7. Ignition switch
W/B. White with black tracer	8. Starter interlock switch
W/R. White with red tracer	9. Starter relay
Y/G. Yellow with green tracer	10. Fuse
Or/W. Orange with white tracer	11. Magneto
1. Stop switch	12. Starter motor

During installation, make sure "O" ring is positioned around neck of pinion cover, then guide starter into position. Remainder of installation is the reverse of removal procedure.

WIRING. If wiring requires repair, always use replacement wire of the same gauge. Wires should be routed away from areas of extreme heat or sharp edges. Plastic tie straps should be used to retain wires in their original positions to prevent short circuiting. Refer to Fig. S1-13 for schematic wiring diagram.

FASTENERS

The vehicle should receive an overall inspection after the first one month of operation and every three months of operation thereafter. All cap screws, nuts and fasteners should be checked and tightened to proper torque specification listed in CONDENSED SERVICE DATA section or in the appropriate MAINTENANCE section.

DRIVE BELT AND VARIABLE RATIO DRIVE

R&R AND OVERHAUL. A variable ratio drive unit is mounted on the left end of the crankshaft. As the engine speed varies, the centrifugal rollers within the movable

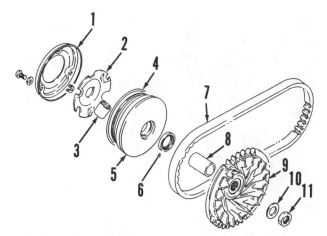

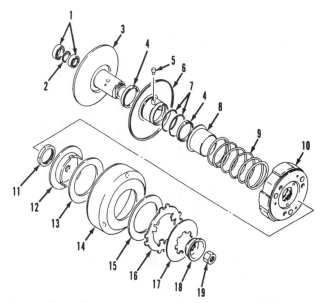

Fig. S1-15—Exploded view of variable ratio drive assembly and drive belt.

1. Cover
2. Plate
3. Roller
4. "O" ring
5. Movable drive face
6. Seal
7. Drive belt
8. Spacer
9. Fixed drive face
10. Washer
11. Nut

Fig. S1-16—Exploded view of clutch assembly.

1. Seals
2. Snap ring
3. Fixed face
4. Seals
5. Pin
6. Movable face
7. "O" rings
8. Bushing
9. Spring
10. Clutch shoe assy.
11. Nut
12. Limiter hub
13. Friction plate
14. Clutch drum
15. Friction plate
16. Pressure plate
17. Spring
18. Stopper
19. Nut

drive face assembly will force the movable drive face closer to or allow contraction from the fixed drive face, thus raising or lowering the drive belt position between face halves.

The movable drive face assembly is serviceable after removing the left crankcase half cover nut (11—Fig. S1-15) and withdrawing fixed drive face (9). Inspect drive faces and centrifugal rollers for excessive wear or any other damage. Drive belt (7) must be renewed if belt width is less than 16.7 mm (0.66 in.).

Note the following during reassembly: Apply Suzuki Super Grease "A" to centrifugal rollers (3) and install a new "O" ring (4).

NOTE: Make sure no grease is applied to the drive faces or the drive belt.

Install the drive belt with the directional arrows pointing in the direction of crankshaft rotation.

CLUTCH

R&R AND OVERHAUL. The three-shoe centrifugal clutch is mounted on the transmission countershaft. Clutch should begin engagement at 2700-3100 rpm with complete lockup at 4300-4900 rpm. To remove clutch assembly for inspection or renewal of individual components, first remove the left crankcase half cover. Remove mounting nut (19—Fig. S1-16) and withdraw clutch components in order after referring to Fig. S1-16.

NOTE: Nut (11) has left-hand threads.

Clean, inspect and renew any components that are excessively worn or show any other damage. Renew clutch shoes (10) if thickness is less than 2.5 mm (0.10 in.). Renew clutch springs if free length is more than 34.2 mm (1.35 in.).

NOTE: Clutch shoes and clutch springs must be renewed as a complete set if either group of components requires renewal.

Renew clutch drum (14) if inside diameter is greater than 110.50 mm (4.350 in.).

Reassembly is reverse order of disassembly. Tighten clutch drum retaining nut (19) to 40-60 N.m (29.0-43.5 ft.-lbs.).

FRONT BRAKE

BRAKE LEVER ADJUSTMENT. Adjust each brake cable adjuster screw at lever (2—Fig. S1-19) until equalizer lever (E—Fig. S1-20) is parallel with cable bracket (B). Raise the front wheels off the ground and slowly rotate each front wheel while lightly applying the brake lever. An even amount of brake drag should be noted on each wheel. If not, loosen the appropriate cable locknut (N) and rotate adjuster (A) until equal brake drag is felt. Note that no brake drag should be felt when brake lever is released.

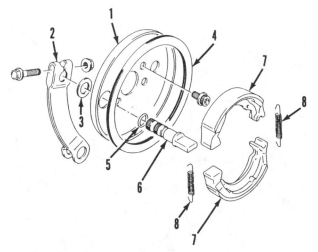

Fig. S1-19—Exploded view of front brake components.

1. Backing plate
2. Lever
3. Washer
4. Dust seal
5. "O" ring
6. Camshaft
7. Brake shoes
8. Springs

Fig. S1-20—Refer to text for adjustment of front brake lever components.

A. Adjuster
B. Cable bracket
E. Equalizer lever
N. Locknut

OVERHAUL. Brake lining thickness may be determined externally by actuating brake and noting position of scribed line (L—Fig.S1-21) on brake camshaft. If scribed line falls within range (R) shown on backing plate, then lining thickness is acceptable and brake shoes do not require renewal.

WARNING: Inhaling asbestos brake dust is injurious to human health. Approved OSHA respiration equipment must be worn when working on or around brake components. DO NOT use compressed air to clean brake drums, shoes or nearby components as brake dust will be blown into air. Only vacuum equipment designed to pick up brake dust should be used.

The front brake assembly is accessible after removing brake drum and hub assembly (40—Fig. S1-22). Renew

Fig. S1-21—When lower brake lever (2) actuates camshaft (6), scribed line (L) should be within range (R). Otherwise, brake shoe linings are excessively worn and should be renewed.

the brake shoes if shoe lining thickness is less than 1.5 mm (0.06 in.) or any other damage is noted. Renew the brake drum assembly if the inside diameter is more than 80.7 mm (3.18 in.).

FRONT AXLE ASSEMBLY

R&R AND OVERHAUL. Refer to Fig. S1-22 for exploded view of front axle assembly. To remove either wheel hub (40), remove front wheel, cap (45), cotter pin (44) and castle nut (43). Pull wheel hub (40) off spindle (26). Do not lose spacer (41). Drive seals (37), bearings (38) and spacer (39) from hub (40) if necessary.

To reassemble, reverse disassembly procedure. Bearings (38) should be packed with Suzuki Super Grease "A" or a good quality wheel bearing grease. Seals (37) are installed with open sides toward bearings (38). Tighten castle nut (43) to 50-80 N·m (36-58 ft.-lbs.) and wheel nuts to 45-65 N·m (32.5-47.0 ft.-lbs.).

STEERING

ADJUSTMENT. The toe-in should be checked and adjusted after the first month of operation and every three months thereafter. Prior to toe-in adjustment, inspect steering assembly for damaged or excessively worn components. If service to steering assembly is required, refer to R&R AND OVERHAUL section.

To check toe-in, inflate tires to recommended pressure listed in CONDENSED SERVICE DATA. Position vehicle on a flat smooth surface and set handlebars straight forward. Using a suitable tape measure, measure the distance between right and left tire centerlines on back side of tires (B—Fig. S1-23) and record measurement. Locate the same tire centerline points on front side of tires (F) and record measurement. The front measurement should be 8 mm (0.31 in.) less than rear measurement; note that the distance from a projected vehicle centerline to left (L) and right (R) tire centerlines should also be equal.

To adjust, loosen tie rod locknuts (21—Fig. S1-22) on both left and right tie rods. Tie rod end locknuts (21) color-coded yellow have left-hand threads. Rotate tie rod sleeves (22) in equal increments to maintain equal left and right tire centerline distances. Tighten tie rod locknuts to 22-35 N·m (16.0-25.5 ft.-lbs.).

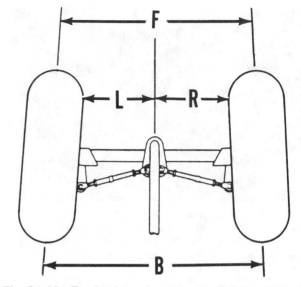

Fig. S1-23—To check toe-in, measure distance between front side (F) and back side (B) of tire centerlines while maintaining equal distances between front left (L) and right (R) tire to vehicle centerlines. Toe-in measurement should be 8 mm (0.31 in.).

R&R AND OVERHAUL. Removal and disassembly of steering components is evident after inspection of unit and referral to exploded view in Fig. S1-22. During reassembly, renew all cotter pins. Lubricate all friction points with Suzuki Super Grease "A" or a good quality grease. Tighten steering shaft clamp cap screws (7) to 18-28 N·m (13-20 ft.-lbs.). Tighten steering shaft lower nut (18) and tie rod end retaining nuts (35) to 22-35 N·m (16-25.5 ft.-lbs.). Tighten spindle nuts (31) to 40-60 N·m (29.0-43.5 ft.-lbs.).

REAR BRAKE

ADJUSTMENT. A single two-shoe internal expanding drum brake mounted on the rear axle and actuated by a foot brake pedal on the vehicle right side is used. The brake adjustment should be checked after the first month of operation and every three months thereafter.

The brake pedal should have 15-25 mm (0.59-0.98 in.) free travel. To adjust brake pedal free travel, rotate adjuster nut (N—Fig. S1-25) at rear axle housing until correct free travel is obtained.

R&R AND OVERHAUL. Brake lining thickness may be determined externally by actuating brake and noting position of pointer on lining wear indicator (13—Fig. S1-25). There is sufficient brake lining if pointer falls in range (R) on rear axle housing.

WARNING: Inhaling asbestos brake dust is injurious to human health. Approved OSHA respiration equipment must be worn when working on or around brake components. DO NOT use com-

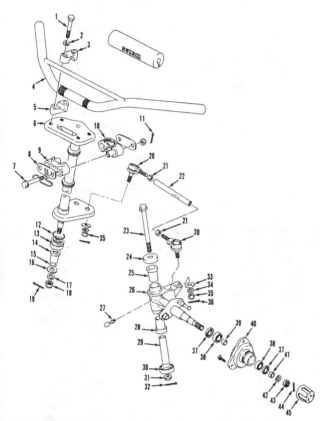

Fig. S1-22—Exploded view of steering and front axle assembly. Refer to Fig. S1-19 for front brake components.

1. Cap screw
2. Lockwasher
3. Clamp half
4. Handlebar
5. Clamp half
6. Steering shaft
7. Cap screw
8. Washer plate
9. Shaft retainer
10. Shaft retainer
11. Cotter pin
12. "O" ring
13. Dust seal
14. Bushing
15. "O" ring
16. Flat washer
17. Lockwasher
18. Nut
19. Cotter pin
20. Tie rod end
21. Locknut
22. Tie rod sleeve
23. Spindle cap screw
24. Dust seal
25. Upper bushing
26. Spindle
27. Grease fitting
28. Lower bushing
29. Spacer
30. Dust seal
21. Spindle nut
32. Cotter pin
33. Flat washer
34. Lockwasher
35. Nut
36. Cotter pin
37. Seal
38. Bearing
39. Spacer
40. Brake drum & hub assy.
41. Spacer
42. Flat washer
43. Castle nut
44. Cotter pin
45. Cap

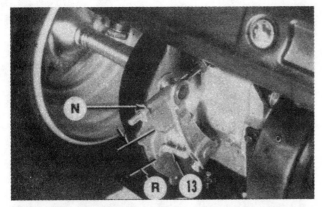

Fig. S1-25—Brake pedal free travel is adjusted by rotating adjuster nut (N) at rear axle housing. Brake shoe linings are acceptable if pointer on lining wear indicator (13) falls within range (R) on rear axle housing when brake pedal is applied.

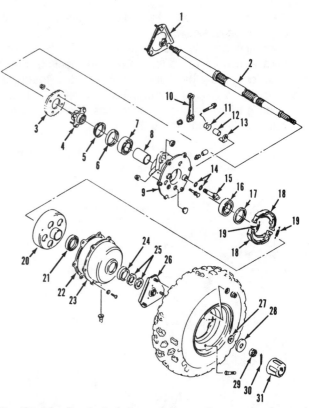

Fig. S1-26—Exploded view of rear axle, rear brake and related components.

1. Hub	
2. Axle shaft	17. Seal
3. Rear sprocket	18. Brake shoes
4. Sprocket mount	19. Springs
5. Dust seal	20. Brake drum
6. Seal	21. Dust seal
7. Bearing	22. Gasket
8. Spacer	23. Drum cover
9. Axle housing	24. Dust seal
10. Cam lever	25. Nuts
11. Spring	26. Hub
12. Spacer	27. Washer
13. Lining wear indicator	28. Cap retainer
14. "O" rings	29. Castle nut
15. Camshaft	30. Cotter pin
16. Bearing	31. Cap

pressed air to clean brake drums, shoes or nearby components as brake dust will be blown into air. Only vacuum equipment designed to pick up brake dust should be used.

To remove rear brake shoes for inspection or renewal, first support rear of vehicle and remove left rear axle nut. Pull tire, wheel and hub off axle as an assembly. Unbolt and remove brake drum cover (23—Fig. S1-26). Remove drum retaining nuts (25). Slide brake drum (20) off axle. Carefully extract brake shoes (18) and springs (19) from backing plate.

Brake shoes should be renewed if linings are worn to 1.5 mm (0.06 in.) or less. Brake drum should be renewed if inside diameter exceeds 130.7 mm (5.15 in.).

Reinstall brake shoes by reversing removal procedure while noting the following: Lightly coat brake camshaft and anchor pin with grease. Lightly coat splined portion of axle for brake drum with grease. Apply Thread Lock Super "1303" or a suitable equivalent to threads of drum retaining nuts and tighten both nuts to 100-160 N·m (72.5-115.5 ft.-lbs.). Tighten axle nut to 50-80 N·m (36-58 ft.-lbs.). Adjust rear brake as outlined in ADJUSTMENT paragraphs.

DRIVE CHAIN AND SPROCKETS

INSPECTION. The drive chain should be inspected after the first month of operation and every six months thereafter. Renew drive chain and sprockets if excessive wear or any other damage is noted. Refer to DRIVE CHAIN in LUBRICATION section for drive chain maintenance information.

REMOVE AND REINSTALL. To remove the drive chain and sprockets, suitably support rear of vehicle and remove right rear wheel assembly. Remove the four cap screws securing the chain cover and withdraw chain cover. Remove the snap ring retaining the engine

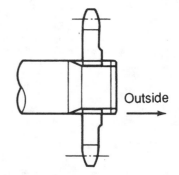

Fig. S1-27—Install engine sprocket on later models so stepped side is toward end of shaft.

sprocket and withdraw engine sprocket with drive chain. Remove the four nuts to remove the rear sprocket.

Carefully examine sprockets for excessive wear. Worn sprockets will usually have a hooked tooth profile. A good test is to place a new chain on a used sprocket and check the fit. Wear on sprocket sides indicates misalignment. If sprockets require renewal due to wear, always renew drive chain.

Standard chain size on 1988 models is 428 with 44 links. Later models are equipped with 520 chain with 36 links. Engine sprocket on later models must be installed so stepped side is toward end of shaft as shown in Fig. S1-27. On later models, be sure there is a washer between rear sprocket retaining nut and sprocket. Tighten rear sprocket retaining nuts to 18-28 N•m (13-20 ft.-lbs.).

SUZUKI
LT160E

NOTE: Metric fasteners are used throughout vehicle.

CONDENSED SERVICE DATA

MODEL	LT160E
General	
Engine Make	Suzuki
Engine Type	Four-Stroke; Air-Cooled
Number of Cylinders	1
Bore	58.0 mm
	(2.283 in.)
Stroke	60.0 mm
	(2.362 in.)
Displacement	158 cc
	(9.6 cu. in.)
Compression Ratio	9.2:1
Fuel Recommended	Unleaded or Low-Lead
Pump Octane Rating	85-95
Engine Lubrication	Wet Sump; Pump
Engine/Transmission Oil	
Recommendation	SAE 10W-40
Forward Speeds	5
Reverse Speeds	1
Tire Size:	
Front	20 × 7.00-8
Rear	22 × 11.00-8
Tire Pressures (cold):	
Front	17.5 kPa
	(2.4 psi)
Rear	15 kPa
	(2.2 psi)
Dry Weight	152 kg
	(334 lbs.)
Tune-Up	
Engine Idle Speed	1450-1550 rpm
Spark Plug:	
NGK	D7EA
Champion	A8YC
Electrode Gap	0.6-0.7 mm
	(0.024-0.028 in.)
Ignition:	
Type	Breakerless
Timing	10° BTDC @ 1000 rpm
Carburetor:	
Make	Mikuni
Model	VM20SS
Float Height	24.8-26.8 mm
	(0.98-1.06 in.)
Jet Needle	5FU96

Tune-Up (Cont.)
Carburetor: (Cont.)
Clip Position......................	3rd Groove From Top
Throttle Cutaway....................	2.5
Pilot Jet..........................	#17.5
Needle Jet........................	O-1
Main Jet..........................	#82.5
Throttle Cable Free Play..............	0.5-1.0 mm
	(0.02-0.04 in.)

Sizes-Clearances
Valve Clearance (cold):
Intake............................	0.03-0.08 mm
	(0.001-0.003 in.)
Exhaust..........................	0.08-0.13 mm
	(0.003-0.005 in.)
Valve Face Angle....................	45°
Valve Seat Angle....................	15° & 45°
Valve Seat Width....................	0.9-1.1 mm
	(0.035-0.043 in.)

Valve Stem Diameter:
Intake............................	5.475-5.490 mm
	(0.2156-0.2161 in.)
Exhaust..........................	5.455-5.470 mm
	(0.2148-0.2153 in.)

Valve Guide Bore Diameter:
Intake & Exhaust..................	5.500-5.512 mm
	(0.2165-0.2170 in.)

Valve Stem-to-Guide Clearance:
Intake............................	0.010-0.037 mm
	(0.0004-0.0015 in.)
Exhaust..........................	0.030-0.057 mm
	(0.0012-0.0022 in.)
Valve Spring Free Length (Min.)........	39.5 mm
	(1.56 in.)

Rocker Arm Bore Diameter:
Intake & Exhaust..................	12.000-12.018 mm
	(0.4724-0.4731 in.)

Rocker Shaft Diameter:
Intake & Exhaust..................	11.977-11.995 mm
	(0.4715-0.4722 in.)

Camshaft Lobe Height:
Intake............................	33.768-33.808 mm
	(1.3294-1.3310 in.)
Wear Limit.....................	33.470 mm
	(1.3177 in.)
Exhaust..........................	33.390-33.430 mm
	(1.3146-1.3161 in.)
Wear Limit.....................	33.090 mm
	(1.3028 in.)
Camshaft Journal Diameter...........	21.959-21.980 mm
	(0.8645-0.8654 in.)
Camshaft Journal Clearance..........	0.032-0.066 mm
	(0.0013-0.0026 in.)
Wear Limit.....................	0.150 mm
	(0.0059 in.)
Camshaft Runout (Max.)..............	0.10 mm
	(0.004 in.)

Sizes-Clearances (Cont.)

Cylinder Head Cover Distortion (Max.) . . .	0.05 mm (0.002 in.)
Cylinder Head Distortion (Max.).	0.05 mm (0.002 in.)
Piston-to-Cylinder Wall Clearance	0.030-0.040 mm (0.0012-0.0016 in.)
Cylinder Bore Diameter	58.000-58.015 mm (2.2835-2.2840 in.)
Wear Limit	58.100 mm (2.2874 in.)
Cylinder Bore Distortion (Max.)	0.05 mm (0.002 in.)
Piston Diameter: Measured 15 mm (0.59 in.) from Skirt Bottom	57.965-57.980 mm (2.2821-2.2827 in.)
Wear Limit	57.880 mm (2.2787 in.)
Piston Pin Bore Diameter in Piston	14.002-14.008 mm (0.5513-0.5514 in.)
Wear Limit	14.030 mm (0.5524 in.)
Piston Pin Diameter	13.995-14.000 mm (0.5510-0.5512 in.)
Wear Limit	13.980 mm (0.5504 in.)
Piston Ring End Gap in Standard Bore . . .	0.10-0.25 mm (0.004-0.010 in.)
Wear Limit	0.70 mm (0.028 in.)
Piston Ring Side Clearance in Piston (Max.): Top	0.180 mm (0.0071 in.)
Second.	0.150 mm (0.0059 in.)
Connecting Rod Small End Bore Diameter	14.004-14.012 mm (0.5513-0.5516 in.)
Wear Limit	14.040 mm (0.5528 in.)
Connecting Rod Small End Side Shake (Max.)	3.0 mm (0.12 in.)
Crankshaft Runout at Main Bearing Journal (Max.).	0.05 mm (0.002 in.)

Capacities

Fuel Tank	8.5 L (2.2 gal.)
Engine/Transmission Oil	See Text

Tightening Torques

Camshaft Sprocket Bolt	10-12 N•m (88-106 in.-lbs.)
Clutch Hub Nut	60-80 N•m (44-59 ft.-lbs.)
Cylinder Base Nut	7-11 N•m (62-97 in.-lbs.)
Cylinder Head Cover Bolt	9-11 N•m (80-97 in.-lbs.)

Tightening Torques (Cont.)

Cylinder Head Nut	21-25 N·m (15-18 ft.-lbs.)
Engine Mounting Nut	60-72 N·m (44-53 ft.-lbs.)
Engine Sprocket Nut	80-100 N·m (59-73 ft.-lbs.)
Flywheel Nut	145-175 N·m (107-129 ft.-lbs.)
Front Axle Nut	50-80 N·m (37-59 ft.-lbs.)
Rear Axle Nut.	85-115 N·m (63-83 ft.-lbs.)

Wheel Retaining Nuts:

Front	20-31 N·m (15-23 ft.-lbs.)
Rear.	44-66 N·m (32-48 ft.-lbs.)

Standard Screws:
Unmarked or Marked "4"

4 mm	1.0-2.0 N·m (8.9-18 in.-lbs.)
5 mm	2.0-4.0 N·m (18-36 in.-lbs.)
6 mm	4.0-7.0 N·m (36-62 in.-lbs.)
8 mm	10-16 N·m (88.5-142 in.-lbs.)
10 mm	22-35 N·m (16-26 ft.-lbs.)
12 mm	35-55 N·m (26-40 ft.-lbs.)
14 mm	50-80 N·m (37-59 ft.-lbs.)
16 mm	80-130 N·m (59-96 ft.-lbs.)
18 mm	130-190 N·m (96-140 ft.-lbs.)

Marked "7"

4 mm	1.5-3.0 N·m (13-27 in.-lbs.)
5 mm	3.0-6.0 N·m (27-53 in.-lbs.)
6 mm	8.0-12.0 N·m (71-105 in.-lbs.)
8 mm	18-28 N·m (13-21 ft.-lbs.)
10 mm	40-60 N·m (29-44 ft.-lbs.)
12 mm	70-100 N·m (52-74 ft.-lbs.)
14 mm	110-160 N·m (81-118 ft.-lbs.)
16 mm	170-250 N·m (125-184 ft.-lbs.)
18 mm	200-280 N·m (147-206 ft.-lbs.)

LUBRICATION

ENGINE AND TRANSMISSION. The engine and transmission have a common sump and are lubricated by a crankshaft driven oil pump. Recommended oil is a multigrade SAE 10W-40 motor oil with an API classification of SE or SF.

The sump is filled through filler plug opening (F—Fig. S3-1). Oil level should be maintained at level indicated on sight glass (G). Oil is drained by removing plug in underside of crankcase. Dry capacity of crankcase is 1.9 L (2.0 qt.) after an engine or transmission overhaul. Refilling after changing oil and oil filter requires only 1.7 L (1.8 qt.) as some oil will be retained in crankcase castings.

Manufacturer recommends oil and oil filter be changed after the first month of operation and every three months thereafter.

The oil filter may be renewed after removing filter cap (C). Insert new filter with closed end toward filter cap. Renew filter cap "O" ring and ensure filter retaining spring is properly located when installing cap.

DRIVE CHAIN. The final drive chain should be lubricated with a suitable chain lube or SAE 90 gear oil prior to each operating interval. Select chain lube designed for use on "O" ring-type drive chains; incorrect chain lubricating oil may cause damage to "O" ring seals.

After every month of operation, the chain should be thoroughly washed in kerosene then lubricated with SAE 90 gear oil. The use of any cleaning solutions other than kerosene may result in "O" ring seal damage. Adjust drive chain as outlined in DRIVE CHAIN AND SPROCKETS section.

Fig. S-1—Engine/transmission sump is filled through filler plug opening (F). Oil level should be maintained at level on sight glass (G). Oil filter is located behind side cover (C).

CABLES, LEVERS AND SHAFTS. The brake, choke and throttle cables should be lubricated with motor oil every three months. Brake pedal shaft, throttle lever rear axle housing, front wheel bearings, king pins and steering shaft should be greased every 2000 km (1200 miles).

AIR CLEANER ELEMENT

The air cleaner element should be removed and cleaned every three months. To remove air cleaner element, first remove seat and element cover. Remove element retaining pin and withdraw element. Carefully separate foam element from frame.

Thoroughly clean element in a suitable nonflammable solvent. Compress element between hands to remove solvent. Saturate element in clean motor oil. Compress element to remove excess oil. Reinstall element by reversing removal procedure.

FUEL SYSTEM

CARBURETOR. All models are equipped with a Mikuni VM20SS carburetor. Refer to CONDENSED SERVICE DATA for carburetor specifications.

Before performing carburetor adjustments, the throttle cable should be adjusted to provide 0.5-1.0 mm (0.02-0.04 in.) free play at idle position. To adjust, push back dust boot on throttle cable, loosen locknut (L—Fig. S3-2) and rotate adjuster (A) as required.

Initial setting of idle mixture screw (18—Fig. S3-3) is two turns out from a lightly seated position. Rotating idle mixture screw counterclockwise will richen mixture while clockwise rotation will lean mixture. Final adjustment should be made with engine at normal operating temperature and running. Adjust idle speed screw (17) so engine idles at 1450-1550 rpm. Adjust idle mixture screw so highest idle is achieved and readjust idle speed screw to recommended rpm. After adjusting car-

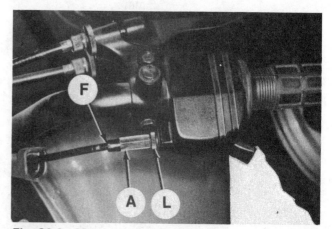

Fig. S3-2—Measure throttle cable free play (F) at cable guide as shown. Loosen locknut (L) and turn adjuster (A) to adjust free play.

buretor, check throttle cable adjustment as previously described.

When servicing carburetor, observe the following: Clip (6—Fig. S3-4) should be in third groove from top of jet needle (9). Float height should be 24.8-26.8 mm (0.98-1.06 in.). To check float height, remove float bowl and invert carburetor. Measure the distance (A—Fig. S3-5) between bottom of float and gasket surface on carburetor body. Adjust float by bending float arm tang.

FUEL STRAINER. All models are equipped with a fuel strainer located in each fuel tank outlet. The strainer should be removed and cleaned periodically.

IGNITION AND ELECTRICAL

SPARK PLUG. Standard recommended spark plug is NGK D7EA or Nippon Denso X22ES-U. Spark plug electrode gap should be 0.6-0.7 mm (0.024-0.028 in.).

Spark plug should be removed, cleaned and electrode gap set every three months and renewed annually.

IGNITION. All models are equipped with a capacitor discharge, pointless electronic ignition system. The ignition system consists of the flywheel, a magneto coil located underneath flywheel, an externally mounted pickup coil, a CDI module attached to front frame bracket, an ignition coil located on front frame bracket, a spark plug and an engine stop switch. Ignition timing should occur at 10° BTDC with engine operating at 1000 rpm and below and at 30° BTDC at 5000 rpm and above. Ignition timing is fixed and not adjustable. The flywheel has a single mark "T" (Fig. S3-6) to indicate Top Dead Center and which is used during valve clearance adjustment or when setting camshaft timing.

If ignition malfunction occurs, check condition of spark plug, all wires and connections before troubleshooting ignition circuit. Using Suzuki pocket tester 09900-25002 or a suitable ohmmeter, refer to the following test specifications and procedures to aid troubleshooting.

To check condition of CDI module, first remove module from vehicle. Use tester or ohmmeter in conjunction

with test chart shown in Fig. S3-7. Renew CDI module if required.

To check condition of magneto coil and pickup coil, remove rear fender and disconnect leads to CDI module. To check pickup coil, attach one tester lead to pickup coil end of blue wire and remaining tester lead to green wire. Resistance reading should be approximately 200-400 ohms. Attach one tester lead to magneto coil end of black/white wire and remaining tester lead to brown wire. Resistance reading should be approximately 350-550 ohms.

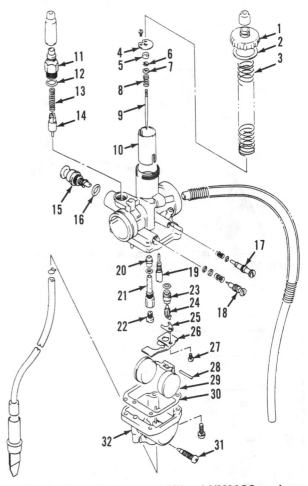

Fig. S3-4—Exploded view of Mikuni VM20SS carburetor.

1. Cap	17. Idle speed screw
2. Gasket	18. Idle mixture screw
3. Spring	19. Pilot jet
4. Retainer	20. Needle jet
5. Spacer	21. Nozzle
6. Jet needle clip	22. Main jet
7. Packing	23. Fuel inlet seat
8. Spring	24. Fuel inlet valve
9. Jet needle	25. Inlet seat retainer
10. Throttle slide	26. Baffle plate
11. Cable guide	27. Screw
12. Washer	28. Float pin
13. Spring	29. Float
14. Starter valve	30. Gasket
15. Starter limiter	31. Drain screw
16. "O" ring	32. Fuel bowl

Fig. S3-3—View of carburetor showing location of idle speed screw (17) and idle mixture screw (18).

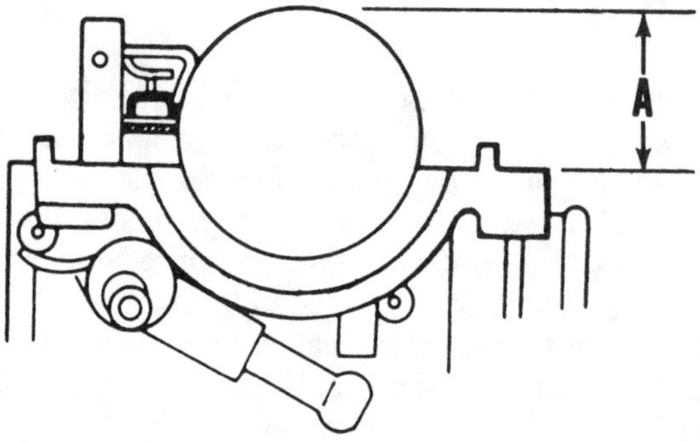

Fig. S3-5—Float level (A) should be 24.8-26.8 mm (0.98-1.06 in.). Bend float arm tang to adjust float level.

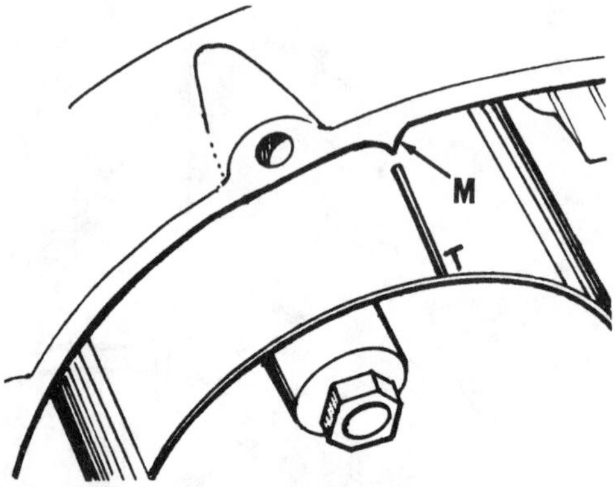

Fig. S3-6—View of top dead center mark (T) on flywheel and reference mark (M) on crankcase.

−Tester Lead	+Tester Lead					
	Green	Blue	White/ Blue	Black/ Blue	Black/ Yellow	Brown
Green		A	A	D	F	A
Blue	E		A	B	F	A
White/ Blue	E	A		B	F	A
Black/ White	C	A	A		D	A
Black/ Yellow	A	A	A	A		A
Brown	H	J	A	G	K	

Fig. S3-7—Use chart shown above and values listed below to test condition of CD ignition module. All values are approximations.

A. Infinite resistance
B. 1.5k-5k ohms
C. 6k-15k ohms
D. 6k-16k ohms
E. 10k-25k ohms
F. 20k-40k ohms
G. 25k-50k ohms
H. 30k-100k ohms
J. 80k-250k ohms
K. 100k-500k ohms

To check condition of ignition coil, separate white/blue wire connector from coil to CDI module and remove high tension wire from spark plug. Attach one tester lead to white/blue wire and remaining lead to coil ground. Primary coil resistance reading should be approximately 0.1-1.0 ohms. Attach one tester lead to high tension wire and remaining lead to coil ground. Secondary coil resistance reading should be approximately 10-25 ohms.

CHARGING CIRCUIT. A charging circuit which consists of an AC generator located underneath the flywheel, a regulator/rectifier and a battery is used. Standard battery is YB9A-A with 9 ampere hour, 12-volt rating. Under load, the AC generator should produce 13.5-15.5 volts DC at 5000 rpm. No-load voltage of AC generator should be 55 volts AC at 5000 rpm.

The battery should be checked and filled to maximum level with distilled water, if required, after the first month and every three months thereafter. During periods of vehicle storage, the battery should be charged once a month to reduce sulfation and prolong battery life. When charging battery, always disconnect battery from charging circuit to prevent damage to regulator/rectifier or other components. Do not exceed maximum charging rate of 0.9 amperes.

The AC generator can be statically checked using Suzuki pocket tester 09900-25002 or a suitable ohmmeter. Separate wire connector block from AC generator to regulator/rectifier and attach tester leads between each yellow stator lead. Tester reading should indicate continuity between each lead. Attach one tester lead to ground and remaining tester lead to each yellow wire individually. Tester reading should indicate infinite resistance at each lead.

An operational check can be performed using Suzuki pocket tester 09900-25002 or a suitable voltmeter as follows: Set lighting switch to on position and dimmer switch to high beam position. Remove front fender cover and attach voltmeter leads to battery noting correct polarity. Start and run engine at 5000 rpm. With a fully charged battery, AC generator and regulator/rectifier may be considered satisfactory if voltage reading is within the limits of 13.5-15.5 volts. If voltage is not within required limits the AC generator may be eliminated as cause of difficulty by performing a no-load test. Separate AC generator to regulator/rectifier wire connector block. Start and run engine at 5000 rpm. Attach voltmeter leads between each yellow stator lead. The AC generator may be considered satisfactory if no-load voltage is not less than 55 volts AC.

STARTER. An electric starter is used. Starter should draw 80 amperes at engine starting speed. Removal and disassembly of starter is evident after inspection of unit. Starter brushes should be renewed if worn to 9 mm (0.4 in.) or less.

WIRING. If wiring requires repair, always use replacement wire of the same gauge. Wires should be routed away from areas of extreme heat or sharp edges. Plastic tie straps should be used to retain wires in their original positions to prevent short circuiting. Refer to Fig.S3-9 for schematic wiring diagram.

FASTENERS

After the first month of operation and every three months thereafter the cylinder head, cylinder, exhaust system, engine mounts and all chassis nuts or bolts should be retightened. Refer to TIGHTENING TORQUES section of CONDENSED SERVICE DATA for torque specifications.

VALVE SYSTEM

The valves are actuated via rocker arms by a single overhead camshaft. Camshaft is timed and driven by a roller drive chain from left end of crankshaft. Valve clearance should be adjusted after the first month of operation and every three months thereafter. Valve clearance should be adjusted with engine cold.

To adjust valve clearance, first drain engine oil then remove seat, front fender, spark plug, valve adjustment caps and left side cover. Rotate crankshaft until "T" mark (TDC—Fig. S3-6) on flywheel aligns with stationary mark (M) on crankcase and piston is on compression stroke. To ensure piston is on compression stroke, rotate crankshaft 1/4 turn past TDC while observing intake valve. If valve movement is indicated, rotate crankshaft one full revolution and align timing marks again.

Clearance between rocker arm adjusting screw and valve stem should be 0.03-0.08 mm (0.001-0.003 in.) for intake valve and 0.08-0.13 mm (0.003-0.005 in.) for exhaust valve. Adjust clearance by loosening locknut (L—Fig. S3-13) and turning screw (A). Be sure to recheck adjustment after locknuts have been tightened.

CAM CHAIN

Cam chain should be adjusted after the first month of operation and every three months thereafter. Cam chain tension is adjusted with piston at TDC on compression stroke. Align timing marks as previously described in VALVE SYSTEM section to set piston at TDC on compression stroke; however for cam chain tension adjust-

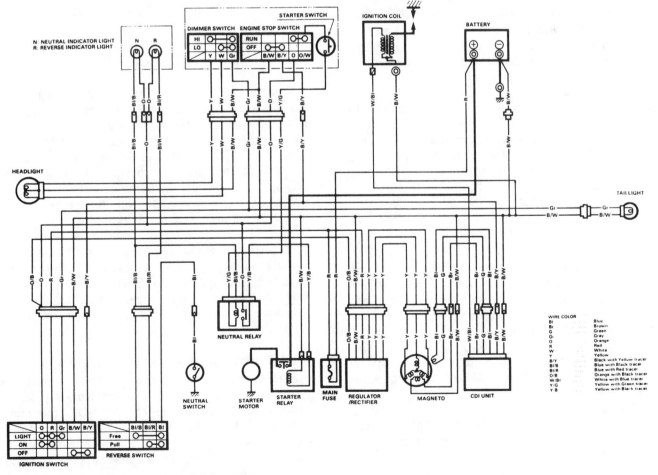

Fig. S3-9—Wiring diagram for Model LT106E.

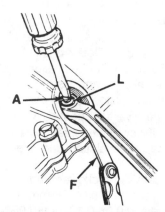

Fig. S3-13—Measure valve clearance with feeler gauge (F). Loosen locknut (L) and rotate screw (A) to adjust.

Fig. S3-15—Following procedure outlined in text, loosen locknut (L) and set screw (S) to adjust cam chain tension.

ment, make sure flywheel is rotated in normal operation direction (counterclockwise) only. Loosen locknut (L—Fig. S3-15) and back out set screw (S) one complete revolution to release tensioner push rod. Spring in tensioner mechanism automatically adjusts cam chain tension. Tighten set screw and secure with locknut.

Cam chain noise after adjustment may be caused by a stuck tensioner push rod. Remove tensioner retaining cam screws (C) and withdraw the unit. Loosen set screw and clean tensioner with a suitable solvent. Lubricate tensioner push rod with clean motor oil. Actuate push rod several times to ensure smooth movement. Reinstall tensioner and adjust as previously described.

CLUTCH

All models are equipped with two types of automatically actuated clutches. One type is a three-shoe centrifugal clutch attached to right end of crankshaft and actuated by engine rpm. The other type is a multiple-disc clutch attached to right end of transmission countershaft and actuated by the gear shift lever. During gear selection, a lever attached to end of gear shift shaft simultaneously disengages the multiple-disc clutch to permit smooth transmission operation.

The clutch should be adjusted after the first month of operation and every six months thereafter. To adjust clutch, drain engine/transmission sump and remove the three screws securing engine/transmission sump sight glass cover and withdraw cover. Loosen locknut (L—

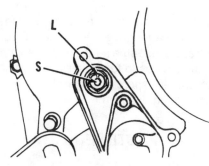

Fig. S3-17—To adjust clutch, loosen locknut (L) and rotate screw (S) as outlined in text.

Fig. S3-17), turn adjusting screw (S) clockwise one-half turn, then rotate screw (S) counterclockwise stopping just as internal resistance is felt. Rotate screw (S) clockwise 1/8 turn and retain adjusting screw position while tightening locknut (L).

To check clutch operation, first adjust clutch as previously described. Ensure oil level is correct and engine is at operation temperature. Attach a suitable tachometer. Select low gear and slowly accelerate engine while observing meter. Initial engagement should begin at 2000-2400 rpm. Next, with transmission still in low gear, lock up brakes and momentarily open the throttle. Do not maintain open throttle longer than 10 seconds. Engine speed should be held to 3250-3750 rpm. Any results other than specified may indicate disassembly and repair of clutch unit is required.

FRONT BRAKE

BRAKE LEVER ADJUSTMENT. Adjust each brake cable adjuster (J—Fig. S3-19) until equalizer lever (E) is parallel with cable bracket (B). Raise the front wheels off the ground and slowly rotate each front wheel while lightly applying the brake lever. An even amount of brake drag should be noted on each wheel. If not, loosen the appropriate cable locknut (N) and rotate adjuster (A) until equal brake drag is felt. Note that no brake drag should be felt when brake lever is released.

OVERHAUL. Brake lining thickness may be determined externally by actuating brake and noting position of pointer (P—Fig. S3-20) on brake camshaft. If pointer falls within limit mark (L) on backing plate, then lining thickness is acceptable and brake shoes do not require renewal.

WARNING: Inhaling asbestos brake dust is injurious to human health. Approved OSHA respiration equipment must be worn when working on or around brake components. DO NOT use compressed air to clean brake drums, shoes or nearby components as brake dust will be blown into air. Only vacuum equipment designed to pick up brake dust should be used.

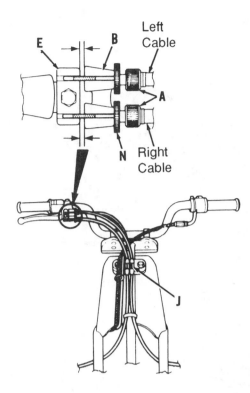

Fig. S3-19—Braking action at the two front brakes is equalized by adjusting front brake cables. Refer to text for procedure.

Fig. S3-20—If pointer (P) attached to brake camshaft does not pass line (L), brake lining thickness is within wear limit.

The front brake assembly is accessible after removing brake drum and hub assembly (14—Fig. S3-21). Renew the brake shoes if shoe lining thickness is less than 1.5 mm (0.06 in.) or any other damage is noted. Renew the brake drum assembly if the inside diameter is more than 20.7 mm (4.75 in.). During reassembly note that marks (M—Fig. S3-22) on lever (1) and pointer (2) must align with groove (G) in camshaft (7).

FRONT AXLE ASSEMBLY

R&R AND OVERHAUL. Refer to Fig. S3-21 for an exploded view of front axle assembly. To remove either

wheel hub (14), remove front wheel and axle nut (20). Pull wheel hub from spindle. Do not lose spacer (17). Drive seals (10 and 16), bearings (11 and 15) and spacer (12) from hub if necessary.

To reassemble, reverse disassembly procedure while noting the following: Install the inner bearing (11) into hub first. Seals (10 and 16) are installed with open sides toward bearings. Tighten axle nut (20) to 50-80 N•m (37-59 ft.-lbs.) torque. Tighten wheel retaining nuts to 20-31 N•m (15-22 ft.-lbs.).

STEERING

ADJUSTMENT. The toe-in should be checked and adjusted after the first month of operation and every three months thereafter. Prior to toe-in adjustment, inspect steering assembly for damaged or excessively worn components. If service to steering assembly is required, refer to R&R AND OVERHAUL section.

To check toe-in, inflate tires to recommended pressure in CONDENSED SERVICE DATA. Position vehicle on a flat smooth surface and set handlebars straight forward. Using a suitable tape measure, measure the distance between right and left tire centerlines on back side of tires (B—Fig. S3-23) and record measurement. Locate the same tie centerline points on front side of tires (F) and record measurement. The front measurement should be 3-11 mm (0.1-0.4 in.) less than rear measurement. Note that the distance from a projected vehicle centerline to left (L) and right (R) tire centerlines should also be equal.

To adjust toe-in, loosen tie rod locknuts (17 and 19—Fig. S3-24) on both left and right tie rods. Inner tie rod ends (16) and locknuts (17) are color coded yellow and have left-hand threads. Rotate tie rods (18) in equal increments to maintain equal vehicle centerline to left and right tire centerline distances. Tighten tie rod locknuts to 22-35 N•m (16-25 ft.-lbs.) torque.

R&R AND OVERHAUL. Refer to Fig. S3-24 for an exploded view of steering assembly. Removal and disassembly of steering components is evident after inspection of unit and referral to exploded view. During reassembly, renew all cotter pins. Lubricate all friction points with a good quality grease. Tighten steering shaft clamp cap screws to 18-28 N•m (13-20 ft.-lbs.). Tighten steering shaft lower nut and tie rod retaining nuts to 22-35 N•m (16-25 ft.-lbs.). Tighten king pin bolt to 40-60 N•m (30-44 ft.-lbs.).

SUSPENSION

The vehicle is equipped with a single wishbone-type front suspension and oil dampened shock absorbers. Shock absorber load setting is not adjustable. Refer to Fig. S3-24 for an exploded view of suspension components. The suspension components should be periodically inspected for excessive wear or damage.

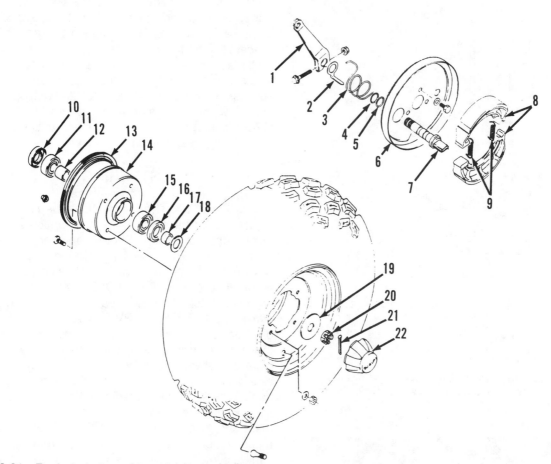

Fig. S3-21—Exploded view of front brake and hub assembly.

1. Brake lever
2. Pointer
3. Spring
4. "O" ring
5. "O" ring
6. Backing plate

7. Camshaft
8. Brake shoes
9. Springs
10. Seal
11. Bearing

12. Spacer
13. Seal
14. Brake drum
15. Bearing
16. Seal

17. Spacer
18. Washer
19. Washer
20. Nut
21. Cotter pin
22. Cap

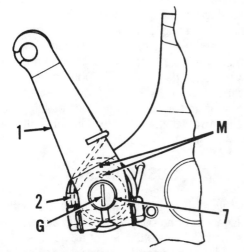

Fig. S3-22—Install brake lever and pointer so marks (M) on lever (1) and pointer (2) are aligned with groove (G) in end of camshaft (7).

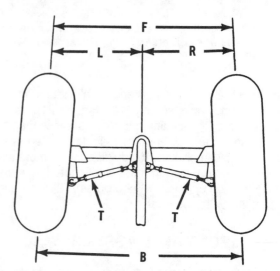

Fig. S3-23—Toe-in should be 3-11 mm (0.1-0.4 in.). Refer to text for measuring procedure.

Tighten control arm retaining bolts to 55-77 N·m (40-56 ft.-lbs.). Tighten shock absorber retaining cap screws to 40-60 N·m (30-44 ft.-lbs.).

REAR BRAKE

ADJUSTMENT. All models are equipped with a two-shoe internal expanding drum brake mounted on rear axle and actuated by the brake pedal. The brake should be checked and adjusted after the first month and every three months thereafter.

To properly check and adjust brake system, first actuate brake pedal and measure free travel at end of pedal. Free travel should be 20-30 mm (0.8-1.2 in.) and

is adjusted by rotating brake cable adjuster nut (A—Fig. S3-25) at rear brake actuating lever.

OVERHAUL. Brake lining thickness may be determined externally by actuating brake and noting position of pointer (P—Fig. S3-25) on brake camshaft. If pointer falls within limit mark (L) on backing plate, then lining thickness is acceptable and brake shoes do not require renewal.

WARNING: Inhaling asbestos brake dust is injurious to human health. Approved OSHA respiration equipment must be worn when working on or around brake components. DO NOT use com-

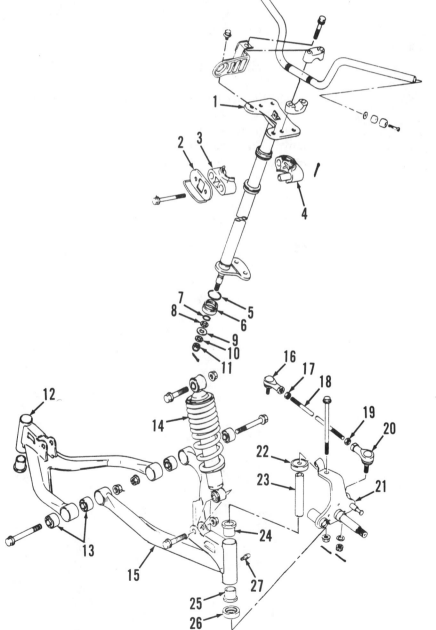

Fig. S3-24—Exploded view of steering and suspension components.

1. Steering shaft
2. Plate
3. Clamp half
4. Clamp half
5. Snap ring
6. Seal
7. "O" ring
8. Packing
9. Washer
10. Lockwasher
11. Nut
12. Right control arm
13. Bushings
14. Shock absorber
15. Left control arm
16. Inner tie rod end
17. Locknut (L.H.)
18. Tie rod
19. Locknut
20. Outer tie rod end
21. Steering knuckle
22. Seal
23. King pin
24. Bushing
25. Bushing
26. Seal
27. Grease fitting

pressed air to clean brake drums, shoes or nearby components as brake dust will be blown into air. Only vacuum equipment designed to pick up brake dust should be used.

To remove rear brake shoes for inspection or renewal, first support rear of vehicle and remove right rear axle

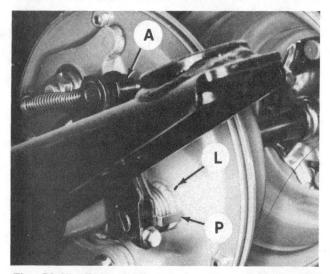

Fig. S3-25—Rotate adjuster nut (A) to adjust brake pedal free travel. If pointer (P) attached to brake camshaft does not pass line (L), brake lining thickness is within wear limit.

nut. Pull tire, wheel and hub off axle as an assembly. Unscrew drum retaining nuts (1—Fig. S3-26). Unbolt and withdraw brake drum cover (5). Remove "O" ring (3) then slide brake drum (7) off axle. Carefully extract brake shoes (8) and springs (9) from backing plate.

Brake shoes should be renewed if linings are worn to 1.5 mm (0.06 in.) or less. Brake drum should be renewed if inside diameter exceeds (150.7 mm (5.93 in.).

Reinstall brake shoes by reversing removal procedure while noting the following: Lightly coat brake camshaft and pin with grease. Note that marks (M—Fig. S3-27) on lever (18) and pointer (17) must align with groove (G) in camshaft (14). Apply grease to seal (4—Fig. S3-26). Install brake cover with drain opening down and tighten cap screws to 5-8 N·m (44-71 in.-lbs.). Apply Thread Lock "1303" or "1324" to threads of nuts (1). Install and tighten drum nuts (2) to 160-200 N·m (118-147 ft.-lbs.). Tighten axle nut to 85-115 N·m (63-85 ft.-lbs.) and secure with a new cotter pin. Adjust brake as outlined in ADJUSTMENT paragraph.

DRIVE CHAIN AND SPROCKETS

INSPECTION AND ADJUSTMENT. The final drive chain should be inspected and adjusted, if needed, each month. Improper maintenance and neglect can cause early failure of both drive chain and sprockets. Distance between 20 chain links should not exceed 319.4 mm

Fig. S3-26—Exploded view of rear brake and axle housing assembly.

1. Nuts
2. Spacer
3. "O" ring
4. Seal
5. Cover
6. Gasket
7. Brake drum
8. Brake shoes
9. Springs
10. Seal
11. Bearing
12. Spacer
13. Axle housing
14. Camshaft
15. "O" rings
16. Spring
17. Pointer
18. Brake lever
19. Bearing
20. Seal
21. Axle
22. Sprocket
23. Nut

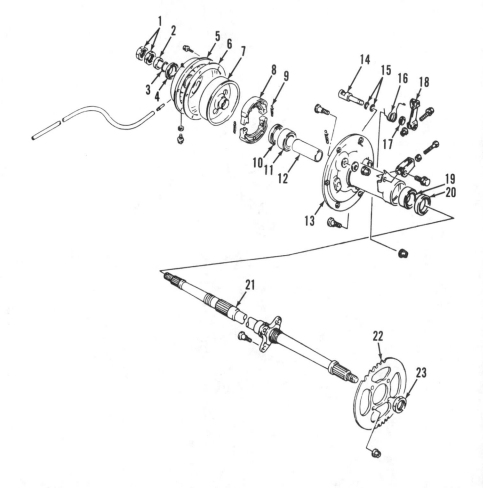

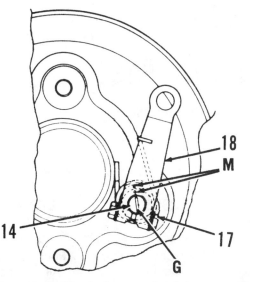

Fig. S3-27—Install brake lever and pointer so marks (M) on lever (18) and pointer (17) are aligned with groove (G) in end of camshaft (14).

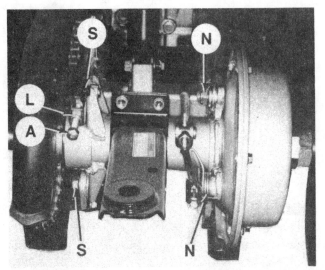

Fig. S3-28—Loosen axle housing retaining screws (S) and nuts (N), loosen locknut (L) and rotate adjusting screw (A) to adjust chain tension.

(12.57 in.). Drive chain free travel should be 20-30 mm (0.8-1.2 in.) measured midway between sprockets. To adjust chain tension, loosen axle housing retaining nuts (N—Fig. S3-28) and screws (S). Loosen locknut (L) and rotate adjuster screw (A) until the correct drive chain free travel is obtained, then securely tighten all fasteners and recheck drive chain free travel. Tighten axle housing retaining nuts and screws to 70-100 N·m (51-74 ft.-lbs.).

R&R AND OVERHAUL. Carefully examine sprockets for excessive wear. Worn sprockets will usually have a hooked tooth profile. A good test is to place a new chain on a used sprocket and check the fit. If sprockets require renewal due to wear, always renew drive chain. Sprockets should be renewed as a set. Standard drive chain on all models is either D.I.D. 520V or Takasago RK520SM with 84 links.

Disassembly is evident after inspection of unit and referral to Fig. S3-26. During assembly note the following: Tighten front sprocket retaining nut to 80-100 N·m (59-74 ft.-lbs.), tighten rear sprocket nuts to 48-73 N·m (35-54 ft.-lbs.), tighten shock absorber mounting cap screw to 40-60 N·m (30-44 ft.-lbs.), tighten swing arm pivot shaft nut to 50-80 N·m (37-59 ft.-lbs.) and tighten wheel retaining nuts to 44-66 N·m (32-48 ft.-lbs.). Refer to INSPECTION AND ADJUSTMENT paragraphs for recommended drive chain adjustment procedures.

SUZUKI

LT230E, LT230S AND LT250S

NOTE: Metric fasteners are used throughout vehicle.

CONDENSED SERVICE DATA

MODELS	LT230E	LT230S	LT250S
General			
Engine Make	Suzuki	Suzuki	Suzuki
Engine Type	Four-Stroke; Air-Cooled	Four-Stroke; Air-Cooled	Four-Stroke; Air-Cooled
Number of Cylinders	1	1	1
Bore	66.0 mm (2.598 in.)	66.0 mm (2.598 in.)	68.5 mm (2.697 in.)
Stroke	67.0 mm (2.638 in.)	67.0 mm (2.638 in.)	67.0 mm (2.638 in.)
Displacement	229 cc (14.0 cu. in.)	229 cc (14.0 cu. in.)	246 cc (15.0 cu. in.)
Compression Ratio	9.0:1	9.0:1	9.2:1
Fuel Recommendation	Unleaded or Low-Lead	Unleaded or Low-Lead	Unleaded or Low-Lead
Engine Lubrication	Wet Sump; Pump	Wet Sump; Pump	Wet Sump; Pump
Engine/Transmission Oil	SAE 10W-40	SAE 10W-40	SAE 10W-40
Forward Speeds	5	5	5
Reverse Speeds	1	1	1
Tire Size:			
Front	21 × 7.00-10	21 × 7.00-10	21 × 7.00-10
Rear	22 × 11.00-9	22 × 11.00-9	21 × 11.00-9
Tire Pressure (cold):			
0-80 kg (0-175 lbs.) Load:			
Front	20 kPa (2.9 psi)	20 kPa (2.9 psi)	25 kPa (3.6 psi)
Rear	20 kPa (2.9 psi)	20 kPa (2.9 psi)	20 kPa (2.9 psi)
Above 80 kg (175 lbs.) Load:			
Front	30 kPa (4.4 psi)	35 kPa* (5.0 psi)	25 kPa (3.6 psi)
Rear	25 kPa (3.6 psi)	20 kPa (2.9 psi)	22.5 kPa (3.3 psi)
Dry Weight	172 kg (379 lbs.)	153 kg (337 lbs.)	159 kg (350 lbs.)

*Tire pressure for front tire on Model LT230S should be 35 kPa (5.0 psi) when load is above 70 kg (155 lbs.)

Tune-Up

	LT230E	LT230S	LT250S
Engine Idle Speed	1350-1450 rpm	1350-1450 rpm	1400-1600 rpm
Spark Plug:			
NGK	D7EA	D7EA	DP7EA-9
Nippon Denso	X22ES-U	X22ES-U	X22EP-U9
Electrode Gap	0.6-0.7 mm (0.024-0.028 in.)	0.6-0.7 mm (0.024-0.028 in.)	0.8-0.9 mm (0.031-0.035 in.)

MODELS	LT230E	LT230S	LT250S
Tune-Up (Cont.)			
Carburetor:			
Make	Mikuni	Mikuni	Mikuni
Model.	VM24SS	VM26SS	VM26SS
Bore Size.	24 mm	26 mm	26 mm
	(0.94 in.)	(1.02 in.)	(1.02 in.)
Float Height.	23.5-25.5 mm	20.8-22.8 mm	23.5-25.5 mm
	(0.92-1.00 in.	(0.82-0.90 in.)	(0.92-1.00 in.)
Jet Needle.	4JR45	5HN23	5HN31
Clip Position	4th Groove	3rd Groove	3rd Groove
	From Top	From Top	From Top
Pilot Jet	#20†	#20	#17.5
Needle Jet	0-4†	0-0	0-3
Main Jet.	#115	#112.5	#110
Throttle Cut-Away	1.5	1.5	1.5
Throttle Cable Free Play	0.5-1.0 mm	0.5-1.0 mm	0.5-1.0 mm
	(0.02-0.04 in.)	(0.02-0.04 in.)	(0.02-0.04 in.)

†On Model LT230EJ, carburetor needle jet is 0-2 and pilot jet is #17.5.

Sizes-Clearances

	LT230E	LT230S	LT250S
Valve Clearance (cold):			
Intake.	0.03-0.08 mm	0.03-0.08 mm	0.03-0.08 mm
	(0.001-0.003 in.)	(0.001-0.003 in.)	(0.001-0.003 in.)
Exhaust	0.08-0.13 mm	0.08-0.13 mm	0.08-0.13 mm
	(0.003-0.005 in.)	(0.003-0.005 in.)	(0.003-0.005 in.)
Valve Face Angle	45°	45°	45°
Valve Seat Angle.	15° & 45°	15° & 45°	15° & 45°
Valve Seat Width.	0.9-1.1 mm	0.9-1.1 mm	0.9-1.1 mm
	(0.035-0.043 in.)	(0.035-0.043 in.)	(0.035-0.043 in.)
Valve Stem Diameter:			
Intake.	5.475-5.490 mm	5.475-5.490 mm	5.475-5.490 mm
	(0.2156-0.2161 in.)	(0.2156-0.2161 in.)	(0.2156-0.2161 in.)
Exhaust	5.455-5.470 mm	5.455-5.470 mm	5.455-5.470 mm
	(0.2148-0.2153 in.)	(0.2148-0.2153 in.)	(0.2148-0.2153 in.)
Valve Guide Bore Diameter:			
Intake & Exhaust.	5.500-5.512 mm	5.500-5.512 mm	5.500-5.512 mm
	(0.2165-0.2170 in.)	(0.2165-0.2170 in.)	(0.2165-0.2170 in.)
Valve Stem-to-Guide Clearance:			
Intake.	0.010-0.037 mm	0.010-0.037 mm	0.010-0.037 mm
	(0.0004-0.0015 in.)	(0.0004-0.0015 in.)	(0.0004-0.0015 in.)
Exhaust	0.030-0.057 mm	0.030-0.057 mm	0.030-0.057 mm
	(0.0012-0.0022 in.)	(0.0012-0.0022 in.)	(0.0012-0.0022 in.)
Wear Limit (Intake & Exhaust)	0.35 mm	0.35 mm	0.35 mm
	(0.014 in.)	(0.014 in.)	(0.014 in.)
Valve Spring Free Length (Min.):			
Inner	36.4 mm	35.1 mm	35.1 mm
	(1.43 in.)	(1.38 in.)	(1.38 in.)
Outer	39.9 mm	39.9 mm	39.9 mm
	(1.57 in.)	(1.57 in.)	(1.57 in.)
Rocker Arm Bore Diameter:			
Intake & Exhaust.	12.000-12.018 mm	12.000-12.018 mm	12.000-12.018 mm
	(0.4724-0.4731 in.)	(0.4724-0.4731 in.)	(0.4724-0.4731 in.)
Rocker Shaft Diameter	11.977-11.995 mm	11.977-11.995 mm	11.977-11.995 mm
	(0.4715-0.4722 in.)	(0.4715-0.4722 in.)	(0.4715-0.4722 in.)
Camshaft Lobe Height:			
Intake.	33.780-33.820 mm	34.166-34.206 mm	34.17-34.21 mm
	(1.3299-1.3315 in.)	(1.3451-1.3467 in.)	(1.345-1.347 in.)

MODELS **Sizes-Clearances (Cont.)**	LT230E	LT230S	LT250S
Camshaft Lobe Height: (Cont.)			
Wear Limit	33.48 mm (1.318 in.)	33.87 mm (1.333 in.)	33.87 mm (1.333 in.)
Exhaust	32.990-33.030 mm (1.2988-1.3004 in.)	33.464-33.504 mm (1.3175-1.3191 in.)	34.13-34.17 mm (1.344-1.345 in.)
Wear Limit	32.69 mm (1.287 in.	33.16 mm (1.306 in.)	33.83 mm (1.332 in.)
Camshaft Journal Diameter:			
Intake & Exhaust	21.959-21.980 mm (0.8645-0.8654 in.)	21.959-21.980 mm (0.8645-0.8654 in.)	21.959-21.980 mm (0.8645-0.8654 in.)
Camshaft Journal Clearance:			
Intake & Exhaust	0.032-0.066 mm (0.0013-0.0026 in.)	0.032-0.066 mm (0.0013-0.0026 in.)	0.032-0.066 mm (0.0013-0.0026 in.)
Wear Limit	0.150 mm (0.0059 in.)	0.150 mm (0.0059 in.)	0.150 mm (0.0059 in.)
Camshaft Runout (Max.)	0.10 mm (0.004 in.)	0.10 mm (0.004 in.)	0.10 mm (0.004 in.)
Cylinder Head Cover Distortion (Max.) . .	0.05 mm (0.002 in.)	0.05 mm (0.002 in.)	0.05 mm (0.002 in.)
Cylinder Head Distortion (Max.)	0.05 mm (0.002 in.)	0.05 mm (0.002 in.)	0.05 mm (0.002 in.)
Piston-to-Cylinder Wall Clearance	0.040-0.050 mm (0.0016-0.0020 in.)	0.040-0.050 mm (0.0016-0.0020 in.)	0.050-0.060 mm (0.0020-0.0024 in.)
Wear Limit	0.120 mm (0.0047 in.)	0.120 mm (0.0047 in.)	0.120 mm (0.0047 in.)
Cylinder Bore Diameter	66.000-66.015 mm (2.5984-2.5990 in.)	66.000-66.015 mm (2.5984-2.5990 in.)	68.500-68.515 mm (2.6968-2.6974 in.)
Wear Limit	66.090 mm (2.6020 in.)	66.090 mm (2.6020 in.)	68.580 mm (2.7000 in.)
Cylinder Bore Distortion (Max.)	0.05 mm (0.002 in.)	0.05 mm (0.002 in.)	0.05 mm (0.002 in.)
Piston Diameter Measured 18 mm (0.71 in.) from Skirt Bottom	65.955-65.970 mm (2.5966-2.5972 in.)	65.955-65.970 mm (2.5966-2.5972 in.)	68.445-68.460 mm (2.6947-2.6953 in.)
Wear Limit	65.880 mm (2.5937 in.)	65.880 mm (2.5937 in.)	68.380 mm (2.6921 in.)
Piston Pin Bore Diameter	16.002-16.008 mm (0.6300-0.6302 in.)	16.002-16.008 mm (0.6300-0.6302 in.)	17.002-17.008 mm (0.6694-0.6696 in.)
Wear Limit	16.030 mm (0.6311 in.)	16.030 mm (0.6311 in.)	17.030 mm (0.6705 in.)
Piston Pin Diameter	15.996-16.000 mm (0.6298-0.6299 in.)	15.996-16.000 mm (0.6298-0.6299 in.)	16.996-17.000 mm (0.6691-0.6693 in.)
Wear Limit	15.980 mm (0.6291 in.)	15.980 mm (0.6291 in.)	16.980 mm (0.6685 in.)
Piston Ring End Gap	0.10-0.25 mm (0.004-0.010 in.)	0.10-0.25 mm (0.004-0.010 in.)	0.20-0.40 mm (0.008-0.016 in.)
Wear Limit	0.70 mm (0.028 in.)	0.70 mm (0.028 in.)	0.70 mm (0.028 in.)
Piston Ring Side Clearance (Max.):			
Top	0.180 mm (0.0071 in.)	0.180 mm (0.0071 in.)	0.180 mm (0.0071 in.)
Second	0.150 mm (0.0059 in.)	0.150 mm (0.0059 in.)	0.150 mm (0.0059 in.)
Connecting Rod Small End Bore Diameter	16.006-16.014 mm (0.6302-0.6305 in.)	16.006-16.014 mm (0.6302-0.6305 in.)	17.006-17.014 mm (0.6695-0.6698 in.)

MODELS	LT230E	LT230S	LT250S
Sizes-Clearances (Cont.)			
Connecting Rod Small End Bore (Cont.)			
Wear Limit	16.040 mm (0.6315 in.)	16.040 mm (0.6315 in.)	17.040 mm (0.6710 in.)
Capacities			
Fuel Tank.	9.5 L (2.4 gal.)	9.5 L (2.4 gal.)	9.5 L (2.4 gal.)
Engine/Transmission Sump	See Text	See Text	See Text
Tightening Torques			
Camshaft Sprocket Bolt	10-12 N·m (7.5-8.5 ft.-lbs.)	10-12 N·m (7.5-8.5 ft.-lbs.)	10-12 N·m (7.5-8.5 ft.-lbs.)
Clutch Shoe Nut	90-110 N·m (66-81 ft.-lbs.)	....	....
Clutch Sleeve Hub Nut	60-80 N·m (44-59 ft.-lbs.)	40-60 N·m (30-44 ft.-lbs.)	40-60 N·m (30-44 ft.-lbs.)
Cylinder Base Nut.	7-11 N·m (5.0-8.0 ft.-lbs.)	7-11 N·m (5.0-8.0 ft.-lbs.)	7-11 N·m (5.0-8.0 ft.-lbs.
Cylinder Head Cover Bolt	9-11 N·m (6.5-8.0 ft.-lbs.)	9-11 N·m (6.5-8.0 ft.-lbs.)	9-11 N·m (6.5-8.0 ft.-lbs.)
Cylinder Head Nut:			
6 mm	7-11 N·m (5.0-8.0 ft.-lbs.)	7-11 N·m (5.0-8.0 ft.-lbs.)	7-11 N·m (5.0-8.0 ft.-lbs.)
8 mm	21-25 N·m (16-18 ft.-lbs.)	21-25 N·m (16-18 ft.-lbs.)	21-25 N·m (16-18 ft.-lbs.)
Flywheel Bolt.	150-170 N·m (110-125 ft.-lbs.)	50-60 N·m (37-44 ft.-lbs.)	50-60 N·m (37-44 ft.-lbs.)
Front Axle Nuts	50-80 N·m (37-59 ft.-lbs.)	50-80 N·m (37-59 ft.-lbs.)	50-80 N·m (37-59 ft.-lbs.)
Rear Axle Nuts	85-115 N·m (63-85 ft.-lbs.)	85-115 N·m (63-85 ft.-lbs.)	85-115 N·m (63-85 ft.-lbs.)
Wheel Retaining Nuts:			
Front	20-31 N·m (15-23 ft.-lbs.)	20-31 N·m (15-23 ft.-lbs.)	20-31 N·m (15-23 ft.-lbs.)
Rear.	45-65 N·m (33-48 ft.-lbs.)	45-65 N·m (33-48 ft.-lbs.)	45-65 N·m (33-48 ft.-lbs.)
Standard Screws:			
Unmarked or Marked "4"			
4 mm	1.0-2.0 N·m (8.9-18 in.-lbs.)	1.0-2.0 N·m (8.9-18 in.-lbs.)	1.0-2.0 N·m (8.9-18 in.-lbs.)
5 mm	2.0-4.0 N·m (18-36 in.-lbs.)	2.0-4.0 N·m (18-36 in.-lbs.)	2.0-4.0 N·m (18-36 in.-lbs.)
6 mm	4.0-7.0 N·m (36-62 in.-lbs.)	4.0-7.0 N·m 36-62 in.-lbs.)	4.0-7.0 N·m 36-62 in.-lbs.)
8 mm	10-16 N·m (88.5-142 in.-lbs.)	10-16 N·m (88.5-142 in.-lbs.)	10-16 N·m (88.5-142 in.-lbs.)
10 mm	22-35 N·m (16-26 ft.-lbs.)	22-35 N·m (16-26 ft.-lbs.)	22-35 N·m (16-26 ft.-lbs.)
12 mm	35-55 N·m (26-40 ft.-lbs.)	35-55 N·m (26-40 ft.-lbs.)	35-55 N·m (26-40 ft.-lbs.)
14 mm	50-80 N·m (37-59 ft.-lbs.)	50-80 N·m (37-59 ft.-lbs.)	50-80 N·m (37-59 ft.-lbs.)
16 mm	80-130 N·m (59-96 ft.-lbs.)	80-130 N·m (59-96 ft.-lbs.)	80-130 N·m (59-96 ft.-lbs.)
18 mm	130-190 N·m (96-140 ft.-lbs.)	130-190 N·m (96-140 ft.-lbs.)	130-190 N·m (96-140 ft.-lbs.)

MODELS	LT230E	LT230S	LT250S
Tightening Torques (Cont.)			
Standard Screws: (Cont.)			
Marked "7"			
4 mm	1.5-3.0 N·m (13-27 in.-lbs.)	1.5-3.0 N·m (13-27 in.-lbs.)	1.5-3.0 N·m (13-27 in.-lbs.)
5 mm	3.0-6.0 N·m (27-53 in.-lbs.)	3.0-6.0 N·m (27-53 in.-lbs.)	3.0-6.0 N·m (27-53 in.-lbs.)
6 mm	8.0-12.0 N·m (71-106 in.-lbs.)	8.0-12.0 N·m (71-106 in.-lbs.)	8.0-12.0 N·m (71-106 in.-lbs.)
8 mm	18-28 N·m (13-21 ft.-lbs.)	18-28 N·m (13-21 ft.-lbs.)	18-28 N·m (13-21 ft.-lbs.)
10 mm	40-60 N·m (29-44 ft.-lbs.)	40-60 N·m (29-44 ft.-lbs.)	40-60 N·m (29-44 ft.-lbs.)
12 mm	70-100 N·m (52-74 ft.-lbs.)	70-100 N·m (52-74 ft.-lbs.)	70-100 N·m (52-74 ft.-lbs.)
14 mm	110-160 N·m (81-118 ft.-lbs.)	110-160 N·m (81-118 ft.-lbs.)	110-160 N·m (81-118 ft.-lbs.)
16 mm	170-250 N·m (125-184 ft.-lbs.)	170-250 N·m (125-184 ft.-lbs.)	170-250 N·m (125-184 ft.-lbs.)
18 mm	200-280 N·m (147-206 ft.-lbs.)	200-280 N·m (147-206 ft.-lbs.)	200-280 N·m (147-206 ft.-lbs.)

LUBRICATION

All Models

ENGINE AND TRANSMISSION. The engine and transmission are lubricated by a crankshaft-driven oil pump. Recommended oil is a multigrade SAE 10W-40 motor oil with an API classification of SE or SF.

Fill the sump by pouring oil through opening for filler plug (F—Fig. S5-1 or S5-2). Oil level should be maintained at level indicated on sight glass (G). Drain oil by removing plug in underside of crankcase. Dry capacity of crankcase is 1.9 L (2.0 qt.) on LT230E models and 2.3 L (2.4 qt.) on LT230S and LT250S models after an engine or transmission overhaul. Refilling after changing oil and oil filter requires only 1.7 L (1.8 qt.) on LT230E models and 2.2 L (2.3 qt.) on LT230S and LT250S models as some oil is retained by crankcase castings. Oil quantity after only changing oil is 1.5 L (1.6 qt.) on LT230E models and 2.0 L (2.1 qt.) on LT230S and LT250S models.

Manufacturer recommends changing the oil and oil filter after the first month or 200 km (125 miles) of operation and every three months or 1000 km (600 miles) thereafter.

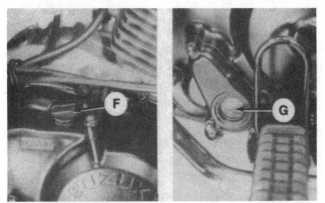

Fig. S5-1—On Model LT230E, pour engine and transmission oil through filler plug (F) opening. Oil level is visible on sight glass (G).

Fig. S5-2—On Models LT230S and LT250S, pour engine and transmission oil through filler plug (F) opening. Oil level is visible on sight glass (G). Filter cap (C) location is typical of all models.

The oil filter may be renewed after removing filter cap (C—Fig. S5-2). Make certain inner "O" ring is properly installed before inserting filter. Insert new filter with open end toward engine and closed end toward filter cap. Renew filter cap "O" ring and ensure filter retaining spring is properly located when installing cap.

DRIVE CHAIN. The final drive chain should be inspected and lubricated with SAE 90 gear oil at least once each month. Incorrect chain lubricating oil may cause damage to "O" ring seals in drive chain. Periodically the drive chain should be thoroughly washed in kerosene and lubricated. Any cleaning solutions other than kerosene may result in "O" ring seal damage.

Refer to DRIVE CHAIN AND SPROCKETS section for chain renewal and adjustment information.

CABLES, LEVERS, BEARINGS AND SHAFTS. As equipped, the choke cable, throttle cable, reverse cable, and throttle lever should be lubricated with motor oil every three months or 1000 km (600 miles). The front wheel bearings, steering shaft, gearshift lever, rear brake lever and brake camshaft should be greased every three months or 1000 km (600 miles). Do not excessively grease the brake camshaft as grease may contact brake linings reducing braking ability.

AIR CLEANER ELEMENT

All Models

The air cleaner element should be removed and cleaned after every three months or 1000 km (600 miles) of operation. To remove air cleaner element, first remove seat and element cover. Remove element retaining screw and withdraw element. Carefully separate foam element from frame.

Thoroughly clean element in a suitable nonflammable solvent. Saturate element in clean motor oil. Compress element to remove excess oil. Reinstall element by reversing removal procedure.

Fig. S5-7—On Models LT230S and LT250S, slide dust boot (B) down throttle cable and loosen locknut (L) and rotate adjuster (A) to adjust throttle cable free play (P).

FUEL SYSTEM

All Models

CARBURETOR. All models are equipped with a Mikuni-type carburetor. Refer to CONDENSED SERVICE DATA for carburetor model and specifications.

Before performing carburetor adjustments, throttle cable should be adjusted to provide 0.5-1.0 mm (0.02-0.04 in.) free play at idle position. To adjust throttle cable free play on LT230E models, remove front fender cover and slide dust boot down cable. Loosen locknut (N—Fig. S5-5) and rotate adjuster (R) to obtain correct free play (F). Tighten locknut (N) to retain adjustment and install dust boot. On LT230S and LT250S models, slide dust boot (B—Fig. S5-7) away from adjuster assembly. Loosen locknut (L) and rotate adjuster (A) to obtain correct free play (P). Tighten locknut (L) to retain adjustment, and install dust boot.

Initial setting of idle mixture screw (18—Fig. S5-10) is $2\frac{3}{4}$ turns out from a lightly seated position on Model LT230EJ, $1\frac{7}{8}$ turns out on LT230S models and $2\frac{3}{8}$

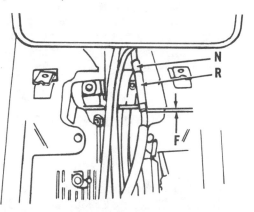

Fig. S5-5—On Model LT230E, slide dust boots away from adjuster assembly and loosen locknut (N) and rotate adjuster (R) as required to obtain correct free play (F).

Fig. S5-10—Installed view of carburetor showing location of idle speed screw (17) and idle mixture screw (18).

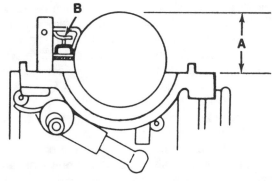

Fig. S5-12—Bend float arm tang (B) to adjust float height (A).

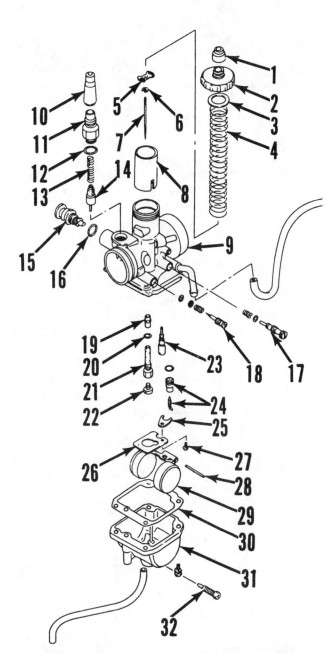

Fig. S5-11—Exploded view typical of Mikuni carburetor used on all models.

1. Grommet
2. Cap
3. Gasket
4. Spring
5. Retainer
6. Jet needle clip
7. Jet needle
8. Throttle slide
9. Body
10. Grommet
11. Cable guide
12. Washer
13. Spring
14. Starter valve
15. Starter valve limiter
16. Washer
17. Idle speed screw
18. Idle mixture screw
19. Needle jet
20. Washer
21. Air bleed
22. Main jet
23. Pilot jet
24. Inlet valve
25. Inlet valve retainer
26. Baffle plate
27. Screw
28. Float pin
29. Float
30. Gasket
31. Float bowl
32. Drain screw

turns out on LT250S models. Rotating idle mixture screw clockwise will lean mixture while rotating screw counterclockwise will richen mixture. Final adjustment should be made with engine running at normal operating temperature. Adjust idle speed screw (17) so engine idles at 1350-1450 rpm on LT230E and LT230S models and 1400-1600 rpm on LT250S models. Adjust idle mixture screw (18) so highest idle speed is achieved and readjust idle speed screw to recommended rpm. After adjusting carburetor, check throttle cable adjustment as previously outlined.

Refer to Fig. S5-11 for an exploded view of the carburetor if complete disassembly is required. Note location of components during disassembly. Float height should be 23.5-25.5 mm (0.92-1.00 in.) on LT230E and LT250S models and 20.8-22.8 mm (0.82-0.90 in.) on LT230S models. To check float height, remove float bowl and invert carburetor. Measure distance (A—Fig. S5-12) between bottom of float and gasket surface on carburetor body. Adjust float by bending float arm tang (B).

FUEL STRAINER. A strainer is mounted on the end of the "ON" pickup tube and the "RES" (reserve) pickup tube of the fuel valve assembly mounted on the fuel tank. The strainers should be cleaned periodically to prevent fuel starvation. To gain access to strainers, drain fuel tank and detach fuel hose. Remove cap screws and withdraw fuel valve assembly with strainers from fuel tank. Reinstall by reversing removal procedure.

IGNITION AND ELECTRICAL

All Models

SPARK PLUG. Standard spark plug is NGK D7EA or Nippon Denso X22ES-U for LT230E and LT230S models, and NGK D7EA-9 or Nippon Denso X22EP-U9 for LT250S models. Electrode gap should be 0.6-0.7 mm (0.024-0.028 in.) on LT230E and LT230S models and 0.8-0.9 mm (0.032-0.035 in.) on LT250S models.

Fig. S5-14—Piston is at Top Dead Center when "T" mark (TDC) on flywheel is aligned with stationary mark (M). On LT230S models, the flywheel cover must be removed to view "T" mark (TDC). Piston must also be on compression stroke as outlined in text for valve clearance adjustment.

Spark plug should be removed, cleaned and electrode gap set every three months or 1000 km (600 miles) and renewed every 18 months or 6000 km (4000 miles).

IGNITION. All models are equipped with a capacitor discharge pointless electronic ignition system. The ignition system consists of the flywheel, a power source coil located underneath the flywheel, an externally mounted pickup coil, a CD ignition module, an ignition coil, an engine stop switch and an ignition switch.

At approximately 1800 rpm and below, ignition timing should be 5° BTDC on LT230E and LT230S models, and 2° BTDC on LT250S models. At approximately 3800 rpm and above, ignition timing should be 35° BTDC on Model LT230EN, 30° BTDC on all other LT230E models, 35° on LT230S models, and 32° BTDC on LT250S models. Ignition timing is fixed and not adjustable. The flywheel has a single mark "T" (Fig. S5-14) to indicate top dead center (TDC). The mark is used when adjusting valve clearance or when setting camshaft timing.

If ignition malfunction occurs, check condition of spark plug, all wires and connections before troubleshooting ignition circuit. Using Suzuki pocket tester 09900-25002 or a suitable ohmmeter, refer to the following test specifications and procedures to aid troubleshooting.

To check power source coil, separate wire connectors leading from power source coil to CDI module and attach one tester lead to coil end of brown wire. Attach remaining tester lead to pink wire. Power source coil can be considered satisfactory if resistance reading is within the limits of 160-240 ohms on LT230E models or 150-350 ohms on LT230S and LT250S models.

To check pickup coil, proceed as follows: Separate blue wire with yellow tracer at connector and green wire with white tracer at connector from pickup coil to CDI module. Attach one tester lead to each wire leading from pickup coil. Pickup coil can be considered satisfactory if resistance reading is within the limits of 96-144 ohms

on LT230E models and 100-200 ohms on LT230S and LT250S models.

To check condition of ignition coil, separate wire connectors from terminal ends on ignition coil. Identify wire location for correct reassembly. Attach one tester lead to negative terminal on coil and remaining tester lead to positive terminal on coil. Primary coil resistance should be approximately 0-1 ohm on LT230E models and 0.1-2 ohms on LT230S and LT250S models. Attach one tester lead to high tension wire and remaining tester lead to positive terminal on coil. Secondary coil resistance reading should be approximately 10,000-25,000 ohms.

LIGHT CIRCUIT. Models LT230S and LT250S. A lighting coil located underneath the flywheel is used. The lighting coil on LT230S models should produce above 10.5 volts at 2500 rpm and below 16 volts at 8000 rpm. Lighting coil on LT250S models should produce above 45 volts at 5000 rpm. A 12V 45/45W headlight and a 12V 5W taillight are used.

CHARGING CIRCUIT. Model LT230E. The charging circuit consists of an AC generator located beneath the flywheel, a regulator/rectifier and a battery. Standard battery is a YT12-12 with a 10-ampere hour, 12-volt rating. Under load, the AC generator should produce 13.5-15.5 volts DC at 5000 rpm. No-load voltage of AC generator should be 60 volts AC at 5000 rpm.

The battery should be checked and filled to maximum level with distilled water, if required, after the first month or 200 km (125 miles) and every three months or 1000 km (600 miles) thereafter. During periods of vehicle storage, the battery should be charged once a month to reduce sulfation and prolong battery life. When charging battery, always disconnect battery from charging circuit to prevent damage to regulator/rectifier or other components. Do not exceed maximum charging rate of 1.2 amperes.

The AC generator can be statically checked using Suzuki pocket tester 09900-25002 or a suitable ohmmeter. Separate wire connector block from AC generator to regulator/rectifier and attach tester leads between each yellow stator lead. Tester reading should indicate continuity between each lead. Attach one tester lead to ground and remaining tester lead to each yellow wire individually. Tester reading should indicate infinite resistance at each lead.

An operational check can be performed using Suzuki pocket tester 09900-25002 or a suitable voltmeter as follows: Set ignition switch to light position. Remove seat and attach voltmeter leads noting correct polarity. Start and run engine at 5000 rpm. With a fully charged battery, AC generator and regulator/rectifier can be considered satisfactory if voltage reading is within the limits of approximately 13.5-15.5 volts. If voltage is not within required limits, then the AC generator can be eliminated as cause of difficulty by performing a no-load test. Separate AC generator to regulator/rectifier wire con-

SUZUKI LT230E, LT230S AND LT250S

nector block. Start and run engine at 5000 rpm. Attach voltmeter leads between each yellow stator lead. The AC generator can be considered satisfactory if no-load voltage is not less than 60 volts AC.

ELECTRIC STARTER. Model LT230E. Starter should draw 80 amperes at engine starting speed. Removal and disassembly of starter is evident after inspection of unit. Starter brushes should be renewed if worn to 6 mm (0.24 in.) or less. Service limit of commutator on all models is 0.2 mm (0.008 in.).

WIRING. If wiring requires repair, always use replacement wire of the same gauge. Wires should be routed away from areas of extreme heat or sharp edges. Plastic tie straps should be used to retain wires in their original positions to prevent short circuiting. Refer to Fig. S5-17 and Fig. S5-18 for a schematic wiring diagram.

FASTENERS

All Models

After the first month or 200 km (125 miles) of operation and every three months or 1000 km (600 miles) there-

after, retighten the cylinder head, cylinder, exhaust system, engine mounts, and all chassis nuts and bolts. Refer to TIGHTENING TORQUES section of CONDENSED SERVICE DATA for torque specifications.

VALVE SYSTEM

All Models

The valves are actuated via rocker arms by a single overhead camshaft. Camshaft is timed and driven by a roller drive chain from left end of crankshaft. Valve clearance should be adjusted after the first month or 200 km (125 miles) of operation and every six months or 1000 km (600 miles) thereafter. Valve clearance should be adjusted with engine cold.

To adjust valve clearance, first remove seat, front fender, spark plug, valve adjustment caps and timing inspection plug. On Model LT230E, remove fuel tank, manual starter and timing inspection plug. On Models LT230S and LT250S, remove the flywheel cover. Rotate crankshaft until "T" mark (TDC—Fig. S5-14) on flywheel aligns with stationary mark (M) on crankcase and piston is on compression stroke. To ensure piston is on com-

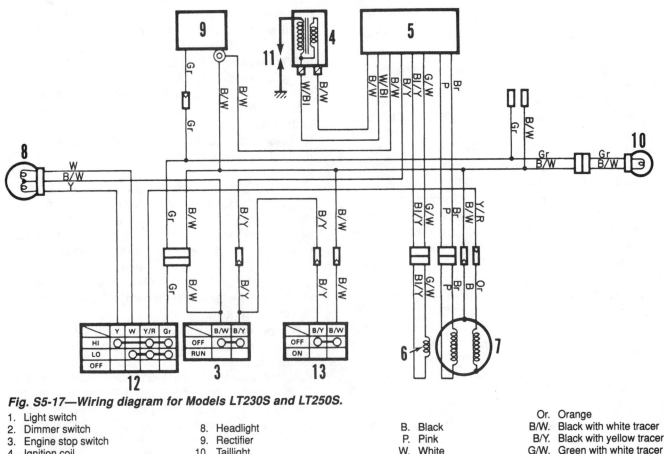

Fig. S5-17—Wiring diagram for Models LT230S and LT250S.

1. Light switch	8. Headlight	B. Black
2. Dimmer switch	9. Rectifier	P. Pink
3. Engine stop switch	10. Taillight	W. White
4. Ignition coil	11. Spark plug	Y. Yellow
5. CDI module	12. Light/dimmer switch	Br. Brown
6. Pickup coil	13. Ignition switch	Gr. Gray
7. Magneto		

Or. Orange
B/W. Black with white tracer
B/Y. Black with yellow tracer
G/W. Green with white tracer
Y/R. Yellow with red tracer
W/Bl. White with blue tracer
Bl/Y. Blue with yellow tracer

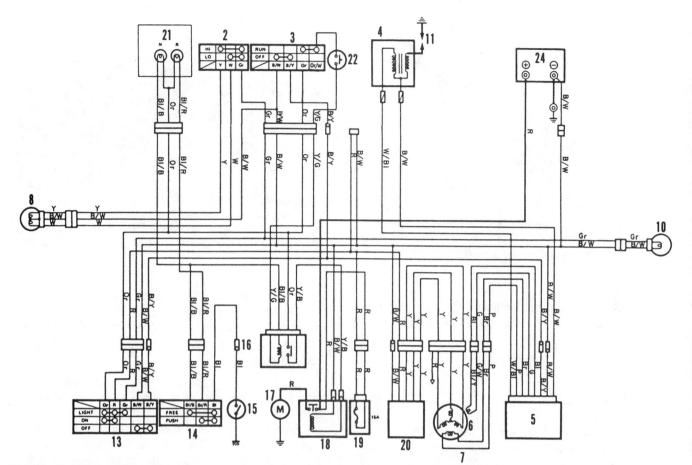

Fig. S5-18—Wiring diagram for Model LT230E. Refer to legend in Fig. S5-17 for identification of components and wiring color codes except the following.

14. Reverse switch
15. Neutral switch
16. Neutral relay
17. Starter motor
18. Starter relay

19. Fuse
20. Regulator/rectifier
21. Neutral & reverse indicator lights
22. Starter button

24. Battery
R. Red
Bl. Blue
Y/B. Yellow with black tracer

Y/G. Yellow with green tracer
Bl/B. Blue with black tracer
Bl/R. Blue with red tracer
Or/W. Orange with white tracer

pression stroke, rotate crankshaft ¼ turn past TDC while observing intake valve. If valve movement is indicated, rotate crankshaft one full revolution and align timing marks again.

Clearance between rocker arm adjusting screw and valve stem should be 0.03-0.08 mm (0.001-0.003 in.) for intake valve and 0.08-0.13 mm (0.003-0.005 in.) for exhaust valve. Clearance is checked with feeler gauge (F—Fig. S5-21) and adjusted by loosening locknut (L) and turning screw (A). Be sure to recheck clearance after locknut is tightened.

DECOMPRESSION LEVER

All Models So Equipped

Some models are equipped with a cable-actuated decompression lever. Cable length should be adjusted for proper decompression lever operation.

Before adjusting decompression lever cable, adjust valve clearance as previously outlined. To adjust the decompression lever cable, pull decompression hand lever to engaged position. Lever (L—Fig. S5-22) should just contact cylinder head cover (C). If not, loosen

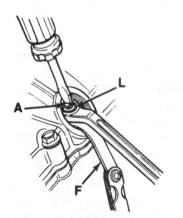

Fig. S5-21—Measure valve clearance with feeler gauge (F). Loosen locknut (L) and rotate screw (A) to adjust.

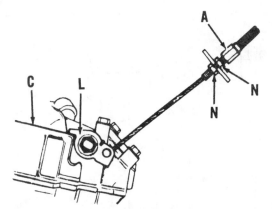

Fig. S5-22—*Decompression lever (L) should just contact cylinder head cover (C) on models with a cable-actuated decompression lever. See text for adjustment procedure.*

locknut (N) and rotate cable adjuster (A), then retighten locknuts. Operate lever and check adjustment.

CLUTCH

Model LT230E

Model LT230E is equipped with two types of automatically actuated clutches. One type is a three-shoe centrifugal clutch attached to right end of crankshaft and actuated by engine rpm. The other type is a multiple-disc clutch attached to right end of transmission countershaft and actuated by the gear shift lever. During gear selection, a lever attached to end of gear shift shaft simultaneously disengages the multiple-disc clutch to permit smooth transmission operation.

The clutch should be adjusted after the first month or 200 km (125 miles) of operation and every six months or 2000 km (1200 miles) thereafter. To adjust clutch, drain engine/transmission sump and remove the three screws securing engine/transmission sump sight glass

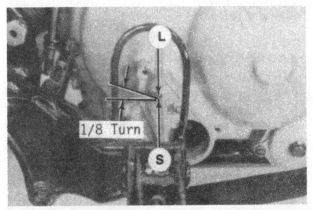

Fig. S5-23—*View identifying clutch adjusting screw (S) and locknut (L) used on Model LT230E. Refer to text for adjustment procedures.*

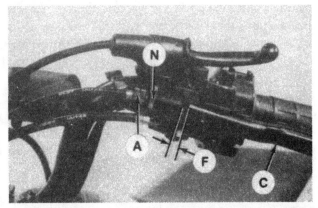

Fig. S5-24—*Clutch lever (C) should have 2-3 mm (0.079-0.118 in.) free play (F) at idle position. Refer to text for locknut (N) and adjuster nut (A) adjustment procedures.*

cover and withdraw cover. Loosen locknut (L—Fig. S5-23). Turn adjusting screw (S) clockwise stopping just as internal resistance is felt. Rotate screw (S) clockwise 1/8 turn and retain adjusting screw position while tightening locknut (L).

To check clutch operation, first adjust clutch as previously outlined. Ensure oil level is correct and engine is at operating temperature. Attach a suitable tachometer. Select low gear and slowly accelerate engine while observing meter. Initial engagement should occur at 2000-2400 rpm. With transmission still in low gear, lock up brakes and momentarily open throttle. Do not maintain full throttle longer than 10 seconds. Engine speed should be held to 3300-3700 rpm. Any results other than specified may indicate disassembly and repair of clutch assemblies is required.

Models LT230S And LT250S

ADJUSTMENT. All models are equipped with a multiple-disc-type clutch manually actuated by left handlebar lever. The clutch lever adjustment should be checked after the first month or 200 km (125 miles) of operation and every six months or 2000 km (1200 miles) thereafter.

The clutch lever should have 2-3 mm (0.079-0.118 in.) of free play measured at clutch lever (C—Fig. S5-24) as shown at (F). Clutch lever free play (F) can be adjusted by first loosening locknut (N) and rotating adjuster nut (A) completely inward. Then, loosen locknuts (L—Fig. S5-25) and rotate adjuster (R) until 2-3 mm (0.079-0.118 in.) free play (F—Fig. S5-24) is obtained at handlebar clutch lever (C). Tighten the cable securing locknuts (L—Fig. S5-25) to retain clutch cable adjustment.

Properly operated, the clutch should disengage and engage freely. Difficulty in shifting, clutch grabbing or slipping may indicate disassembly and repair of clutch unit is required.

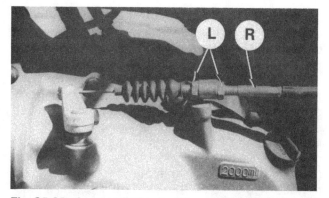

Fig. S5-25—Loosen locknuts (L) and rotate adjuster (R) as outlined in text to adjust clutch lever (C—Fig. S5-24) free play.

MANUAL STARTER

Model LT230E

R&R AND OVERHAUL. Refer to Fig. S5-27 for exploded view of manual starter used on all models. Starter may be removed as a complete unit from vehicle after removing four starter housing retaining cap screws. Refer to exploded view and disassemble starter as follows: If starter spring remains under tension, pull starter rope and hold rope pulley (9) with notch in pulley adjacent to rope outlet. Pull rope back through outlet so it engages notch in pulley and allow pulley to slowly

unwind. Remove retaining nut (1) and disassemble unit. Be careful when removing rewind spring (10); a rapidly uncoiling starter spring could cause serious injury.

Rewind spring is wound in a clockwise direction in starter housing. Rope is wound on rope pulley in a clockwise direction as viewed with pulley in housing. Reassemble starter assembly by reversing disassembly procedure. To place tension on rewind spring, pass rope through rope outlet in housing and install rope handle. Pull rope out and hold pulley so notch in pulley is adjacent to rope outlet. Pull a loop of rope back through outlet between notch in pulley and housing. Turn rope pulley clockwise three or four complete revolutions to place tension on spring. Do not place more tension on rewind spring than is necessary to draw rope handle up against housing.

FRONT BRAKE

All Models

Independently operated front and rear brakes are used. The front brake system has hydraulically actuated disc brake assemblies mounted on each front spindle. A handlebar mounted master cylinder with fluid reservoir supplies pressure to each wheel caliper assembly when actuated by right handlebar lever. Information on rear brake system is outlined in REAR BRAKE ASSEMBLY section.

Only DOT 3 or DOT 4 glycol-based brake fluid should be used in front brake system. The use of other types of brake fluids such as petroleum-based or silicone-based fluids may damage hydraulic components resulting in brake system failure. Under normal operating conditions, brake fluid will absorb small amounts of moisture which can cause pitting to caliper bore surface resulting in early brake caliper failure. Drain and refill hydraulic system with new brake fluid every two years to reduce corrosion damage.

BLEEDING. Any operation that required draining or repair of hydraulic brake components will make it necessary to fill and bleed brake system. Check reservoir fluid level before proceeding. Remove cap (7—Fig. S5-28) diaphragm (8) and fill reservoir with DOT 3 or DOT 4 glycol-based fluid only. Reinstall cap to prevent entrance of dirt or foreign materials. Remove cap (19) and attach a suitable hose such as vacuum hose to either bleeder screw (20) and submerge other end in a container filled with a small amount of brake fluid to prevent air from reentering system. Actuate brake lever several times, then hold brake lever toward handlebar. Open brake bleeder to relieve line pressure allowing fluid and air to flow into container. Close bleed screw before releasing brake lever. Do not permit reservoir to run dry while bleeding. Repeat procedure while periodically refilling fluid reservoir until all air or old fluid is removed.

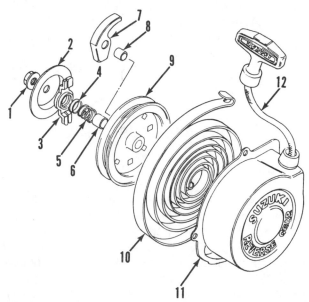

Fig. S5-27—Exploded view of manual starter used on Model LT230E.

1. Nut
2. Friction plate
3. Pawl guide
4. Spring guide
5. Spring
6. Spacer
7. Starter pawl
8. Pin
9. Rope pulley
10. Rewind spring
11. Starter housing
12. Rope

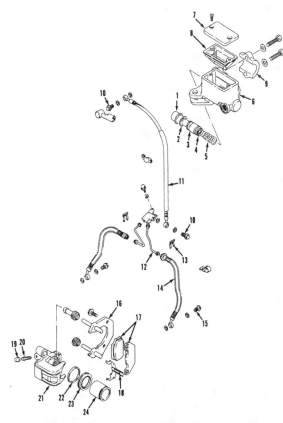

Fig. S5-28—Exploded view of front brake system.

1. Boot	13. Hose retainer
2. Snap ring	14. Brake hose
3. Piston & cup	15. Union cap screw
4. Primary cup	16. Caliper holder
5. Spring	17. Brake pads
6. Reservoir & housing	18. Spring
7. Cap	19. Cap
8. Diaphragm	20. Bleed screw
9. Clamp	21. Caliper
10. Union cap screw	22. Piston seal
11. Brake hose	23. Dust seal
12. Brake line	24. Piston

Attach bleeder hose to remaining bleeder screw and repeat bleeding procedure to complete brake bleeding operation.

OVERHAUL. Brake pad thickness may be determined externally by viewing the brake pads. If more than 1 mm (0.039 in.) of brake pad is measured, then brake pads do not require replacement because of excessive wear. If brake pad is 1 mm (0.039 in.) or less in thickness, then both brake pads on the side being serviced must be renewed.

WARNING: Inhaling asbestos brake dust is injurious to human health. Approved OSHA respiration equipment must be worn when working on or around brake calipers and pads. DO NOT use compressed air to clean brake calipers, pads or nearby components as brake dust will be blown into air. Only vacuum equipment designed to pick up brake dust should be used.

Brake components are accessible after removing caliper mounting screws and withdrawing caliper. Push piston by hand back into caliper to allow clearance for new brake pads. Brake disc should be renewed if thickness is 3.0 mm (0.12 in.) or less or disc runout is 0.3 mm (0.012 in.) or more. Tighten screws securing brake disc to wheel hub to 15-25 N·m (11-18 ft.-lbs.). After reassembly, operate brake lever until brake lever will not pump up after continuous operation. Do not operate vehicle until correct brake operation is noted.

MASTER CYLINDER. To remove front brake master cylinder (6—Fig. S5-28), remove union cap screw (10) at master cylinder. Brake fluid will remove paint; be careful when removing master cylinder. Remove the two retaining cap screws and withdraw master cylinder. Remove brake lever, reservoir cap (7) and diaphragm (8). Remove dust boot (1) and snap ring (2). Disassemble plunger assembly while noting location and direction of components. Inspect cylinder bore for damage due to corrosion or scoring. Renew complete master cylinder if excessive damage is evident. Superficial damage can be removed using a suitable cylinder hone. After honing, rinse cylinder with clean brake fluid. Shake out excess fluid but do not wipe dry. Using a shop towel or rag to dry cylinder will leave lint particles in bore. Renew boot (1) and primary and secondary cups (3 and 4). During reassembly, lubricate components with clean brake fluid. Reassembly is the reverse of disassembly. Tighten union cap screw (10) to 20-25 N·m (15-18 ft.-lbs.). Bleed brakes as outlined in BLEEDING section.

FRONT AXLE ASSEMBLY

All Models

R&R AND OVERHAUL. Refer to Fig. S5-29 for an exploded view of front axle assembly. To remove either wheel hub (47), remove front wheel, brake caliper assembly, cotter pin (53) and castle nut (52). Pull wheel hub (47) from spindle end of knuckle (40). Do not lose spacer (50). Remove seals (44 and 49) and drive bearings (45 and 48) and spacer (46) from hub if necessary.

To reassemble, reverse disassembly procedure while noting the following: Install inner bearing (45) into hub first. Tighten castle nut (52) to 50-80 N·m (37-59 ft.-lbs.) and install a new cotter pin (53). Tighten brake caliper mounting cap screws to 15-25 N·m (11-18 ft.-lbs.) and wheel retaining nuts to 20-31 N·m (15-23 ft.-lbs.) torque.

STEERING

All Models

ADJUSTMENT. The toe-in should be checked and adjusted after the first month or 200 km (125 miles) of operation and every three months or 1000 km (600 miles) thereafter. Prior to toe-in adjustment, inspect steering assembly for damaged or excessively worn components. If service to steering assembly is required, refer to R&R AND OVERHAUL section.

To check toe-in, inflate tires to recommended pressure listed in CONDENSED SERVICE DATA. Position vehicle on a flat smooth surface and set handlebars straight forward. Position a load of 75 kg (165 lbs.) on the vehicle's seat. Using a suitable tape measure, measure distance between right and left tire centerlines on back side of tires (B—Fig. S5-31) and record measurement. Locate the same tie centerline points on front side of tires (F) and record measurement. The front measurement should be 11-19 mm (0.04-0.07 in.) less than rear measurement. Note the distance from a pro-

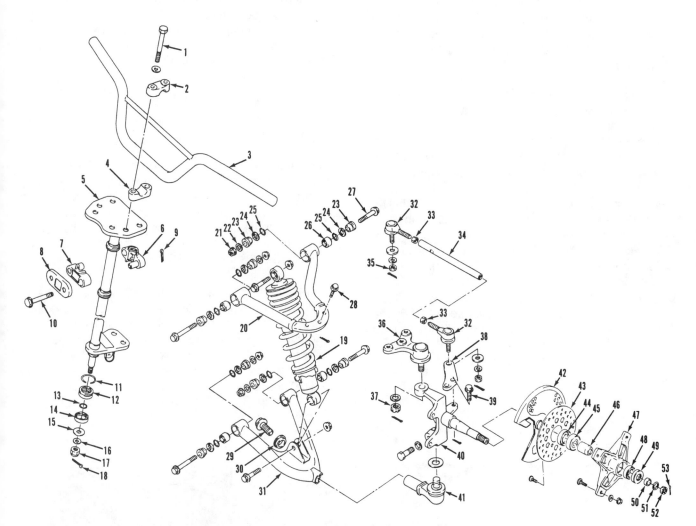

Fig. S5-29—Exploded view of steering, suspension and front axle assembly.

1. Cap screw	15. Flat washer	28. Cap screw	41. Lower ball joint
2. Upper clamp half	16. Lockwasher	29. Cap screw	42. Backing plate
3. Handlebar	17. Nut	30. Stopper	43. Brake disc
4. Lower clamp half	18. Cotter pin	31. Lower control arm	44. Seal
5. Steering shaft	19. Shock absorber	32. Tie rod end	45. Bearing
6. Inner shaft holder	20. Upper control arm	33. Locknut	46. Spacer
7. Outer shaft holder	21. Nut	34. Sleeve	47. Hub
8. Plate	22. Washer	35. Nut	48. Bearing
9. Cotter pin	23. Spacer	36. Upper ball joint	49. Seal
10. Cap screw	24. Dust seal	37. Nut	50. Spacer
11. Clip	25. "O" ring	38. Knuckle arm	51. Washer
12. Dust seal	26. Bushing	39. Cap screw	52. Castle nut
13. "O" ring	27. Bolt	40. Knuckle	53. Cotter pin
14. Dust seal			

jected vehicle centerline to left (L) and right (R) tire centerlines should also be equal.

To adjust, loosen tie rod locknuts (33—Fig. S5-29) on both left and right tie rods. The tie rod ends and locknuts color-coded yellow have left-hand threads. Rotate tie rod sleeves (34) in equal increments to maintain equal vehicle centerline to left and right tire centerline distances. Tighten tie rod locknuts (33) to 22-35 N·m (16-26 ft.-lbs.).

R&R AND OVERHAUL. Refer to Fig. S5-29 for an exploded view of steering assembly. To remove either knuckle (40), first remove wheel hub (47) as outlined in FRONT AXLE ASSEMBLY section. Remainder of steering component disassembly is evident after inspection of unit and referral to Fig. S5-29.

During reassembly, renew all cotter pins. Lubricate all friction points with Suzuki Super Grease "A" or a good quality grease. Tighten steering shaft holder cap screws (10) to 18-28 N·m (13-20 ft.-lbs.); steering shaft lower nut (17) to 38-60 N·m (28-44 ft.-lbs.); ball joint cap screws (29) to 120-170 N·m (89-125 ft.-lbs.); ball joint (36) knuckle retaining nut (37) to 40-60 N·m (30-44 ft.-lbs.); knuckle arm cap screws (39) to 35-45 N·m (26-33 ft.-lbs.); ball joint (41) spindle retaining cap screw to 44-66 N·m (32-48 ft.-lbs.); upper ball joint cap screws (28) to 35-45 N·m (26-33 ft.-lbs.) and tie rod end nut (35) to 22-35 N·m (16-26 ft.-lbs.) on LT230E and LT250S models or 35-50 N·m (26-37 ft.-lbs.) on Model LT230S. Coat threads on knuckle arm cap screws (39), ball joint cap screws (29) and upper ball joint screws (28) with Thread Lock "1333B" or equivalent prior to installation.

FRONT SUSPENSION

All Models

All models are equipped with a double wishbone-type front suspension and oil dampened shock absorbers. Shock absorbers have five load settings. Refer to Fig. S5-29 for exploded view of suspension components. The suspension components should be periodically inspected for excessive wear and damage. Removal and disassembly is evident after inspection of unit and referral to appropriate exploded view.

During reassembly, upper and lower control arm bolts (27) should be tightened to 50-70 N·m (37-51 ft.-lbs.) while ball joint cap screws (29) should be tightened to 120-170 N·m (89-125 ft.-lbs.). Tighten shock absorber retaining bolts to 40-60 N·m (30-44 ft.-lbs.).

REAR BRAKE ASSEMBLY

All Models

A single disc brake assembly is used for both rear wheels. The running brake is operated hydraulically by a foot pedal on the lower right side. The parking brake is mechanically operated by a cable and a handlebar lever on Model LT230E, and by a cable and handlebar components in conjunction with the clutch lever on Models LT230S and LT250S.

BRAKE PEDAL HEIGHT ADJUSTMENT. The top of brake pedal foot pad should be 5 mm (0.2 in.) lower than top of footpeg. To adjust, loosen locknut (N—Fig. S5-36) and turn stop screw (S) out to create a clearance between pedal stop and head of stop screw. Loosen locknut (L) on master cylinder actuator rod and rotate rod (R) until brake pedal foot pad is 5 mm (0.2 in.) lower than footpeg. Tighten locknut (L), then adjust head of stop screw (S) to touch pedal stop. Tighten locknut (N) to retain adjustment.

Fig. S5-36—Refer to text for brake pedal height adjustment.

L. Locknut
N. Locknut
R. Master cylinder actuator rod
S. Stop screw

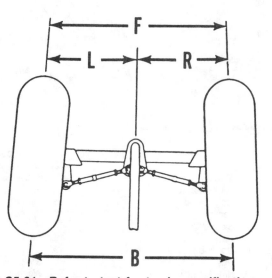

Fig. S5-31—Refer to text for toe-in specifications and procedures.

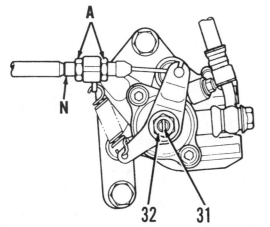

Fig. S5-37—Refer to text for parking brake adjustment procedure.

A. Locknuts
N. Adjuster

31. Screw
32. Locknut

PARKING BRAKE ADJUSTMENT. Loosen cable locknuts (A—Fig. S5-37) and adjust cable adjuster (N) until zero or near zero free play is obtained at handlebar lever when actuating parking brake, then tighten locknuts (A). Loosen locknut (32) and rotate screw (31) until seated, then turn out ¼ turn on Models LT230E and ½ turn on Models LT230S and LT250S and tighten locknut (32).

BLEEDING. Make sure reservoir (3—Fig. S5-38) is full. Connect a bleed hose to bleed valve (21) on brake caliper assembly. Route the bleed hose into a suitable container. Operate rear brake foot pedal until a hardness (fluid resistance) is felt, then open bleed valve (21). Close bleed valve prior to releasing foot pedal. Continue bleeding procedure until no air bubbles are noted in discharged fluid from bleed valve.

Fig. S5-38—Exploded view of rear brake caliper assembly. Parking brake assembly shown is used on Model LT230S. Refer to Fig. S5-37 for parking brake assembly used on Model LT230E.

1. Cap
2. Diaphragm
3. Reservoir
4. Union cap screw
5. Master cylinder housing
6. Spring
7. Piston & cup
8. Actuator rod
9. Snap ring
10. Piston seal
11. Dust seal
12. Piston
13. "O" ring
14. Bracket
15. Cap
16. Tab plate
17. Caliper guide pin
18. Dust seal
19. Caliper
20. Cap
21. Bleed screw
22. Dust seal
23. Gasket
24. Parking brake housing
25. Washer
26. Caliper guide pin
27. Dust seal
28. Dust seal
29. Lever
30. Spring
31. Screw
32. Locknut
33. Shim
34. Brake pads
35. Spring

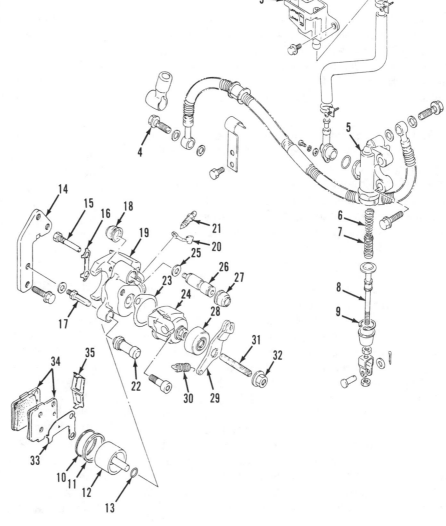

Fig. S5-40—Loosen axle housing retaining nuts (N) and two locknuts (L) and rotate adjuster screws (S) in equal increments to adjust drive chain free play.

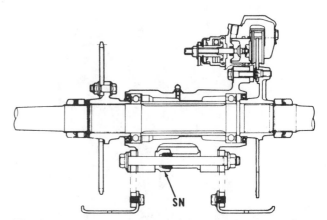

Fig. S5-41—Cross-sectional view of rear axle housing on early models showing location of spacer nuts (SN) between axle housing mounting lugs.

NOTE: Make sure reservoir (3) is kept full during bleeding procedure.

When bleeding procedure is completed, add brake fluid to reservoir (3) until fluid level is at upper level line on reservoir.

OVERHAUL. Brake pad thickness may be determined externally by viewing the brake pads. If more than 1 mm (0.039 in.) of brake pad is measured, then brake pads do not require replacement because of excessive wear. If brake pad is 1 mm (0.039 in.) or less in thickness, then both brake pads must be renewed.

WARNING: Inhaling asbestos brake dust is injurious to human health. Approved OSHA respiration equipment must be worn when working on or around brake calipers and pads. DO NOT use compressed air to clean brake calipers, pads or nearby components as brake dust will be blown into air. Only vacuum equipment designed to pick up brake dust should be used.

Brake components are accessible after removing caliper mounting screws and withdrawing caliper. Loosen parking brake locknut (32—Fig. S5-38) and rotate screw (31) outward. Push piston by hand back into caliper to allow clearance for new brake pads (34). Refer to Fig. S5-38 for an exploded view of brake caliper components if complete overhaul is required. Brake disc should be renewed if thickness is 3.0 mm (0.12 in.) or less or disc runout is 0.3 mm (0.012 in.) or more. After reassembly, operate brake foot pedal until pedal will not pump up after continuous operation or refer to previous BLEEDING paragraphs if caliper assembly was overhauled. Do not operate vehicle until correct brake operation is noted. Adjust parking brake as outlined in previous PARKING BRAKE ADJUSTMENT paragraph.

DRIVE CHAIN AND SPROCKETS

All Models

INSPECTION AND ADJUSTMENT. The final drive chain should be inspected and adjusted, if needed, each month. Improper maintenance and neglect can cause early failure of both drive chain and sprockets. An endless-type drive chain is used on all models. Distance between 20 chain links should not exceed 319.4 mm (12.57 in.) on all models. Drive chain free travel should be 45 mm (1.8 in.) measured midway between rear sprocket and chain buffer on swing arm. Chain tension is adjusted by loosening axle housing retaining nuts (N—Fig. S5-40) and two locknuts (L). Rotate each adjuster screw (S) in equal increments until the correct drive chain free travel is obtained. On LT230EM and LT230EN, drive chain adjusters are also provided on upper axle housing bolt. Standard position is middle notch. Securely tighten locknuts (L) and recheck drive chain free travel. Tighten axle housing retaining nuts (N) to 85-120 N·m (63-88 ft.-lbs.).

R&R AND OVERHAUL. Loosen axle housing retaining nuts (N—Fig. S5-40) and two locknuts (L) and rotate adjuster screws (S) outward. Push axle housing inward to increase drive chain free travel. Lift chain off rear sprocket toward left rear wheel. Use a location at rear of vehicle frame and lift rear wheels off the ground. Remove both rear wheels. Remove seat and rear fender assembly. Remove shock absorber upper mounting cap screw. Remove nut securing swing arm pivot shaft. Support swing arm assembly and withdraw swing arm pivot shaft. Withdraw swing arm with shock absorber assembly. Remove front (engine) sprocket guard and withdraw drive chain. Remove front sprocket if needed.

Carefully examine sprockets for excessive wear. Worn sprockets will usually have a hooked tooth profile.

SUZUKI LT230E, LT230S AND LT250S

A good test is to place a new chain on a used sprocket and check the fit. If sprockets require renewal due to wear, always renew drive chain. Sprockets should be renewed as a set. Standard drive chain on all models is either D.I.D. 520V or Takasago RK520SM with 84 links.

Reassembly is reverse order of disassembly. On early models, note location of spacer nuts (SN—Fig. S5-41) between mounting lugs on axle housing. Tighten spacer nuts to 20-30 N•m (15-22 ft.-lbs.) before tightening axle housing retaining nuts to 85-120 N•m (63-88 ft.-lbs.). On later models, tighten axle housing retaining nuts to 85-120 N•m (63-88 ft.-lbs.). Tighten front sprocket retaining nut to 80-100 N•m (59-74 ft.-lbs.). Tighten rear sprocket nuts to 50-70 N•m (37-51 ft.-lbs.). Tighten shock absorber mounting cap screw to 77-110 N•m (57-81 ft.-lbs.) on Model LT230E and to 40-50 N•m (30-37 ft.-lbs.) on Models LT230S and LT250S. Tighten swing arm pivot shaft nut to 50-80 N•m (37-59 ft.-lbs.). Tighten wheel retaining nuts to 45-65 N•m (33-48 ft.-lbs.). Refer to previous INSPECTION AND ADJUSTMENT paragraphs for recommended drive chain adjustment procedures.

SUZUKI

LT250R

NOTE: Metric fasteners are used throughout vehicle.

CONDENSED SERVICE DATA

MODEL	LT250R
General	
Engine Make	Suzuki
Engine Type	Two-Stroke; Water-Cooled
Number of Cylinders	1
Bore	67 mm
	(2.638 in.)
Stroke	70 mm
	(2.756 in.)
Displacement	246 cc
	(15.0 cu. in.)
Compression Ratio	8:1
Fuel Recommendation	Unleaded or Low-Lead
Pump Octane Rating	85-95
Engine Lubrication	Fuel:Oil Premix
Fuel:Oil Ratio	20:1
Forward Speeds	6
Reverse Speeds	N/A
Tire Size:	
Front	21 × 7.00-10
Rear	21 × 10.00-10
Tire Pressure (cold):	
0-80 kg (0-175 lbs.):	
Front	25 kPa
	(3.6 psi)
Rear	20 kPa
	(2.9 psi)
Above 80 kg (175 lbs.):	
Front	30 kPa
	(4.4 psi)
Rear	25 kPa
	(3.6 psi)
Dry Weight	147 kg
	(323 lbs.)
Tune-Up	
Engine Idle Speed	1350-1450 rpm
Spark Plug:	
NGK	B8EGV
Electrode Gap	0.6-0.8 mm
	(0.024-0.031 in.)
Ignition:	
Type	Breakerless
Timing	6° BTDC @ 1000 rpm
	11° BTDC @ 9000 rpm

Tune-Up (Cont.)

Carburetor:

Make	Mikuni
Model	TM34SS
Bore Size:	34 mm
	(1.3 in.)
Float Height	10.9-12.9 mm
	(0.43-0.51 in.)
Jet Needle	6FP63
Clip Position	3rd Groove From Top
Pilot Jet	#30
Needle Jet	R-O*
Main Jet	#240*
Throttle Cut-Away	4.0
Throttle Cable Free Play	0.5-1.0 mm
	(0.02-0.04 in.)

*LT250RM models may be equipped with a #270 main jet and Q-8 needle jet, or with a #260 main jet and Q-7 needle jet.

Sizes-Clearances

Reed Petal Stand Open (Max.)	0.2 mm
	(0.008 in.)
Cylinder Head Distortion (Max.)	0.05 mm
	(0.002 in.)
Piston-to-Cylinder Wall Clearance	0.080-0.090 mm
	(0.0031-0.0035 in.)
Wear Limit	0.120 mm
	(0.0047 in.)
Cylinder Bore Diameter	67.000-67.015 mm
	(2.6378-2.6384 in.)
Wear Limit	67.050 mm
	(2.6398 in.)
Cylinder Bore Distortion (Max.)	0.05 mm
	(0.002 in.)
Piston Diameter Measured 26 mm (1.02 in.) from Skirt Bottom	66.915-66.930 mm
	(2.6344-2.6350 in.)
Wear Limit	66.880 mm
	(2.6331 in.)
Piston Pin Bore Diameter	18.002-18.012 mm
	(0.7087-0.7091 in.)
Wear Limit	18.030 mm
	(0.7098 in.)
Piston Pin Diameter	17.994-18.000 mm
	(0.7084-0.7087 in.)
Wear Limit	17.980 mm
	(0.7079 in.)
Piston Ring End Gap	0.2-0.4 mm
	(0.008-0.016 in.)
Wear Limit	0.85 mm
	(0.033 in.)
Connecting Rod Small End Bore Diameter	23.003-23.011 mm
	(0.9056-0.9059 in.)
Wear Limit	23.040 mm
	(0.9071 in.)

Capacities

Fuel Tank	11.5 L
	(3.0 gal.)

Capacities (Cont.)
Cooling System . . . .   880 mL
(0.9 qt.)

Transmission Sump . . . .   See Text

Tightening Torques
Clutch Sleeve Hub Nut . . . .   40-60 N•m
(29.0-43.5 ft.-lbs.)

Cylinder Nut:
  6 mm . . . .   8-12 N•m
(71-106 in.-lbs.)

  8 mm . . . .   23-27 N•m
(16.5-19.5 ft.-lbs.)

Engine Mounting Bolts . . . .   37-45 N•m
(27.0-32.5 ft.-lbs.)

Engine Mounting Bracket Bolts . . . .   22-33 N•m
(16-24 ft.-lbs.)

Flywheel Nut . . . .   90-100 N•m
(66-74 ft.-lbs.)

Front Axle Nuts . . . .   50-80 N•m
(36-58 ft.-lbs.)

Impeller Cap Screw . . . .   8-12 N•m
(71-106 in.-lbs.)

Rear Axle Nuts . . . .   85-115 N•m
(61.5-83.0 ft.-lbs.)

Wheel Retaining Nuts:
  Front . . . .   20-31 N•m
(14.5-22.5 ft.-lbs.)

  Rear . . . .   45-65 N•m
(32.5-47.0 ft.-lbs.)

Standard Screws:
Unmarked or Marked "4"
  4 mm . . . .   1.0-2.0 N•m
(8.9-18 in.-lbs.)

  5 mm . . . .   2.0-4.0 N•m
(18-36 in.-lbs.)

  6 mm . . . .   4.0-7.0 N•m
(36-62 in.-lbs.)

  8 mm . . . .   10-16 N•m
(88.5-142 in.-lbs.)

  10 mm . . . .   22-35 N•m
(16-26 ft.-lbs.)

  12 mm . . . .   35-55 N•m
(26-40 ft.-lbs.)

  14 mm . . . .   50-80 N•m
(37-59 ft.-lbs.)

  16 mm . . . .   80-130 N•m
(59-96 ft.-lbs.)

  18 mm . . . .   130-190 N•m
(96-140 ft.-lbs.)

Marked "7"
  4 mm . . . .   1.5-3.0 N•m
(13-27 in.-lbs.)

  5 mm . . . .   3.0-6.0 N•m
(27-53 in.-lbs.)

  6 mm . . . .   8.0-12.0 N•m
(71-106 in.-lbs.)

  8 mm . . . .   18-28 N•m
(13-21 ft.-lbs.)

Tightening Torques (Cont.)

Marked "7" (Cont.)

10 mm	40-60 N·m (29-44 ft.-lbs.)
12 mm	70-100 N·m (52-74 ft.-lbs.)
14 mm	110-160 N·m (81-118 ft.-lbs.)
16 mm	170-250 N·m (125-184 ft.-lbs.)
18 mm	200-280 N·m (147-206 ft.-lbs.)

LUBRICATION

ENGINE. The engine is lubricated by oil mixed with the fuel. Recommended oil is Suzuki CCI Super 2-Cycle Motor Lubricant mixed at a fuel:oil ratio of 20:1.

TRANSMISSION. Recommended transmission oil is SAE 20W-40 motor oil. The manufacturer recommends changing transmission oil after the first month of operation and every six months thereafter.

Fill transmission sump through filler cap (F—Fig. S7-1) opening. Drain sump by removing plug in underside of sump. Dry capacity of sump is 950 mL (32.3 oz.). Refilling sump after a routine oil change requires only 900 mL (30.6 oz.) of oil as some oil will be retained by case castings.

DRIVE CHAIN. The final drive chain should be inspected and lubricated with SAE 90 gear oil prior to each operating interval. Periodically the drive chain should be thoroughly washed in kerosene and lubricated.

Refer to DRIVE CHAIN AND SPROCKETS section for chain renewal and adjustment information.

CABLES, LEVERS, SHAFTS AND BEARINGS. The choke cable, throttle cable and throttle lever should be lubricated periodically with motor oil. The front wheel bearings, steering shaft and rear wheel bearings should be greased periodically to ensure component longevity.

AIR CLEANER ELEMENT

The air cleaner element should be removed and cleaned after every six months of operation. To remove air cleaner element, first remove seat and element cover. Remove element retaining nut and withdraw element. Carefully separate foam element from frame.

Thoroughly clean element in a suitable nonflammable solvent. Saturate element in clean motor oil. Compress element to remove excess oil. Reinstall element by reversing removal procedure.

FUEL SYSTEM

CARBURETOR. A Mikuni-type carburetor is used on all models. Refer to CONDENSED SERVICE DATA for carburetor model used and carburetor specifications.

Before performing carburetor adjustments, throttle cable should be carefully adjusted to provide 0.5-1.0 mm (0.02-0.04 in.) free play (P—Fig. S7-3) at idle position. Cable adjustment is accomplished by first sliding dust boot down throttle cable at handlebar lever. Loosen cable locknut and rotate cable adjuster inward. Loosen locknut (3) and rotate adjuster (2) as required.

Initial setting of idle mixture screw (B—Fig. S7-4) for Models LT250RM E-01, E-02, E-03 (above frame number 100434) and E-28 is 1¾ turns out. Initial setting for all other models is 2 turns out. Start engine and allow to

Fig. S7-1—Pour transmission oil through filler plug opening (F).

Fig. S7-3—Throttle cable should have 0.5-1.0 mm (0.02-0.04 in.) free play (P) at idle position. Refer to text for adjustment procedures on adjuster (2) and locknut (3).

Fig. S7-4—View of carburetor showing location of idle speed screw (A) and idle mixture screw (B).

FUEL STRAINER. A strainer is mounted on the end of the "ON" pickup tube and the "RES" (reserve) pickup tube of the fuel valve assembly mounted on the fuel tank. The strainers should be cleaned periodically to prevent fuel starvation. To gain access to strainers, drain fuel tank and detach fuel hose. Remove cap screws and withdraw fuel valve assembly with strainers from fuel tank. Reinstall by reversing removal procedure.

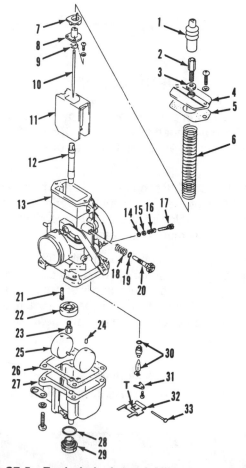

Fig. S7-5—Exploded view of Mikuni-type carburetor used on all models.

T.	Tang	17.	Idle mixture screw
1.	Boot	18.	Spring
2.	Adjuster	19.	"O" ring
3.	Locknut	20.	Idle speed screw
4.	Plate	21.	Pilot jet
5.	Gasket	22.	Baffle ring
6.	Spring	23.	Main jet
7.	Cable stopper ring	24.	Pin
8.	Cable stopper plate	25.	Float
9.	Clip	26.	Gasket
10.	Jet needle	27.	Float bowl
11.	Throttle valve	28.	"O" ring
12.	Needle jet	29.	Drain plug
13.	Body	30.	Inlet valve
14.	"O" ring	31.	Inlet valve retainer
15.	Washer	32.	Float arm
16.	Spring	33.	Float pin

warm up to normal operating temperature, then adjust idle speed screw (A) so engine idles at 1350-1450 rpm. Rotate idle mixture screw (B) until engine idles at highest rpm, then adjust idle speed screw (A) until the recommended idle speed is obtained. After adjusting carburetor, check throttle cable adjustment as previously described, then tighten locknut (3—Fig. S7-3). Tighten throttle cable locknut at handlebar lever and reinstall dust boot.

The carburetor should be removed, disassembled and cleaned if carburetor malfunction is determined. Disassembly of the removed carburetor is evident after inspection of unit and referral to exploded view in Fig. S7-5. Carefully inspect jet needle (10), inlet valve (30) and idle mixture screw (17) for excessive wear and damage.

During reassembly, renew all gaskets. Clip (9) should be in third groove from top on jet needle (10). To check float height, remove float bowl (27) and invert carburetor. Distance (A—Fig. S7-6) between bottom of carburetor body and float arm, measured as shown in Fig. S7-6, should be 9.9-11.9 mm (0.39-0.47 in.). If float height (A) is incorrect, bend tang (T—Fig. S7-5) on float arm as needed to obtain correct float height.

Fig. S7-6—Distance (A) for setting correct float height should be 9.9-11.9 mm (0.39-0.47 in.) when measured between bottom of carburetor body and float arm. Bend float arm tang (T—Fig. S7-5) to adjust.

COOLING SYSTEM

INSPECTION. The engine assembly is liquid-cooled. A one-piece radiator is used. Renew either radiator hose if it is cracked, split or shows any other damage. The radiator hoses should be renewed at least every four years. Inspect all other cooling system components and renew if leakage or damage is noted.

CHANGING COOLANT. The manufacturer recommends using a 50 percent distilled water to 50 percent antifreeze mixture in the cooling system.

NOTE: Distilled water must be used to prevent corroding and clogging of the aluminum radiator. An antifreeze that is designed for a cooling system with aluminum components must be used.

Cooling system capacity is 880 mL (0.9 qt.).

To drain coolant, remove the radiator cover and remove radiator cap and loosen drain plug (D—Fig. S7-8) in water pump housing. Raise front of vehicle and allow coolant to drain into a suitable container.

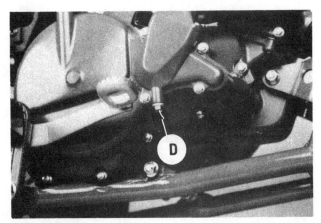

Fig. S7-8—View showing location of cooling system drain plug (D).

Before refilling cooling system, tighten drain plug (D). Pour the recommended coolant mixture into radiator cap opening.

NOTE: The vehicle may need to be operated and allowed to cool in order to remove any air pockets within system. After system has cooled, remove radiator cap and complete filling of cooling system.

RADIATOR CAP. Radiator cap relief opening pressure of 95-125 kPa (13.7-18.1 psi).

IGNITION AND ELECTRICAL

SPARK PLUG. Standard spark plug is NGK B8EGV. Spark plug electrode gap should be 0.6-0.8 mm (0.024-0.031 in.).

Spark plug should be removed, cleaned and electrode gap set every three months and renewed every six months.

IGNITION. All models are equipped with a capacitor discharge, pointless electronic ignition system. The ignition system consists of the flywheel, a power source coil located underneath the flywheel, an externally mounted pickup coil, a CD ignition module, an ignition coil and an engine stop switch. Ignition timing should occur at 6° BTDC with engine operating at 1000 rpm and at 11° BTDC with engine operating at 9000 rpm. Ignition timing is fixed and not adjustable.

If ignition malfunction occurs, check condition of spark plug, all wires and connections before troubleshooting ignition circuit. Using Suzuki pocket tester 09900-25002 or a suitable ohmmeter, refer to the following test specifications and procedures to aid in troubleshooting.

To check power source coil, separate wire connectors leading from power source coil to CDI module and attach one tester lead to coil end of brown wire with red tracer. Attach remaining tester lead to black wire with white tracer. Power source coil can be considered satisfactory if resistance reading is within the limits of 315-475 ohms.

To check pickup coil, separate wire connectors leading from pickup coil to CDI module and attach one tester lead to coil end of blue wire. Attach remaining tester lead to black wire with white tracer. Pickup coil can be considered satisfactory if resistance reading is within the limits of 175-165 ohms.

To check condition of ignition coil, separate black wire connector from coil to CD ignition module and remove high-tension wire from spark plug. Attach one tester lead to black wire terminal on coil and remaining tester lead to coil ground. Primary coil resistance reading should be approximately 0-1.0 ohm. Attach one tester lead to high-tension wire and remaining tester lead to coil ground. Secondary coil resistance reading should be approximately 3k-5k ohms.

LIGHT CIRCUIT. All models are equipped with a lighting coil located underneath the flywheel. The lighting coil should produce above 12 volts at 3000 rpm and below 18 volts at 8000 rpm.

To statically check lighting coil, separate wire connectors leading from lighting coil to light switch and attach one tester lead to coil end of yellow wire with red tracer. Attach remaining tester lead to black wire with white tracer. Lighting coil can be considered satisfactory if resistance reading is within the limits of 0.5-1.0 ohm.

WIRING. If wiring requires repair, always use replacement wire of the same gauge. Wires should be routed away from areas of extreme heat or sharp edges. Plastic tie straps should be used to retain wires in their original positions to prevent short circuiting. Refer to Fig. S7-10 for schematic wiring diagram.

FASTENERS

After the first month of operation and every three months thereafter, the cylinder head, cylinder, exhaust system, engine mounts and all chassis nuts or bolts

should be retightened. Refer to TIGHTENING TORQUES section of CONDENSED SERVICE DATA for torque specifications.

CLUTCH

ADJUSTMENT. All models are equipped with a multiple-disc-type clutch manually actuated by a left handlebar lever. The clutch lever adjustment should be checked after the first month of operation and every six months thereafter.

The clutch lever should have 2-3 mm (0.079-0.118 in.) free play measured at clutch lever (C—Fig. S7-12) as shown at (F). Clutch lever free play can be adjusted by first loosening locknut (N) and rotating adjuster nut (A) completely inward. Then, loosen locknut (L—Fig. S7-13) and rotate adjuster (R) until 2-3 mm (0.079-0.118 in.) free play is obtained at handlebar clutch lever (C—Fig. S7-12). Tighten the cable securing locknuts to retain clutch cable adjustment.

Properly operated, the clutch should disengage and engage freely. Difficulty in shifting, clutch grabbing or

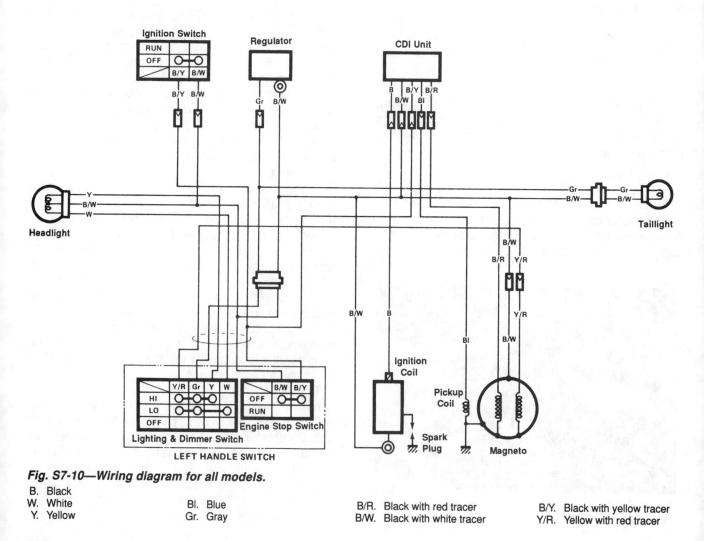

Fig. S7-10—Wiring diagram for all models.

B. Black
W. White
Y. Yellow

Bl. Blue
Gr. Gray

B/R. Black with red tracer
B/W. Black with white tracer

B/Y. Black with yellow tracer
Y/R. Yellow with red tracer

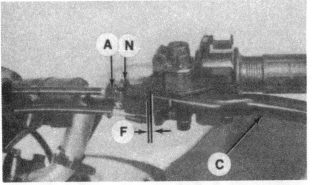

Fig. S7-12—Clutch lever (C) should have 2-3 mm (0.079-0.118 in.) free play (F) at idle position. Refer to text for locknut (N) and adjuster nut (A) adjustment procedures.

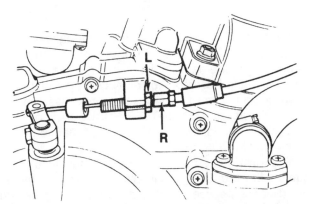

Fig. S7-13—Loosen locknut (L) and rotate adjuster nut (R) as outlined in text to adjust clutch lever (C—Fig. S7-12) free play.

slipping may indicate that disassembly and repair of clutch unit is required.

FRONT BRAKE ASSEMBLY

All models are equipped with independently operated front and rear brakes. The front brake system has hydraulically actuated disc brake assemblies mounted on each front spindle. A handlebar mounted master cylinder with fluid reservoir supplies pressure to each wheel caliper assembly when actuated by right handlebar lever. Information on rear brake system is outlined in REAR BRAKE ASSEMBLY section.

Only DOT 3 or DOT 4 glycol-based brake fluid should be used in front brake system. The use of other types of brake fluids such as petroleum-based or silicone-based fluids may damage hydraulic components resulting in brake system failure. Under normal operation conditions, brake fluid will absorb small amounts of moisture which can cause pitting to caliper bore surface resulting in early brake caliper failure. Drain and refill hydraulic system with new brake fluid every two years to reduce corrosion damage.

BLEEDING. Any operation that required draining or repair of hydraulic brake components will make it necessary to fill and bleed brake system. Check reservoir fluid level before proceeding. Remove cap (1—Fig. S7-14), diaphragm (2) and fill reservoir with DOT 3 or DOT 4 glycol-based fluid only. Reinstall cap to prevent entrance of dirt or foreign materials. Remove cap (14) and attach a suitable hose such as vacuum hose to either bleeder screw (15) and submerge other end in a container filled with a small amount of brake fluid to prevent air from reentering system. Actuate brake lever several times, then hold brake lever toward handlebar.

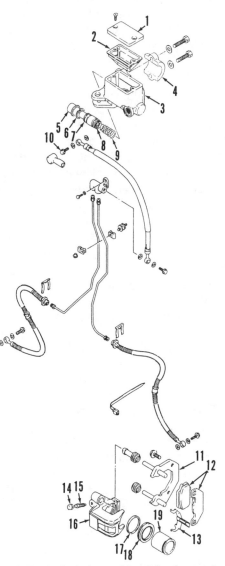

Fig. S7-14—Exploded view of front brake system used on all models.

1. Cap
2. Diaphragm
3. Reservoir & housing
4. Clamp
5. Dust boot
6. Snap ring
7. Piston & cup
8. Primary cup
9. Spring
10. Union cap screw
11. Caliper holder
12. Brake pads
13. Spring
14. Cap
15. Bleed screw
16. Caliper
17. Piston seal
18. Dust seal
19. Piston

Open brake bleeder to relieve line pressure allowing fluid and air to flow into container. Close bleed screw before releasing brake lever. Do not permit reservoir to run dry while bleeding. Repeat procedure while periodically refilling fluid reservoir until all air or old fluid is removed.

Attach bleeder hose to remaining bleeder screw and repeat bleeding procedure to complete brake bleeding operation.

OVERHAUL. Brake pad thickness may be determined externally by viewing the brake pads. If neither of the brake pads are worn below the grooved limit line around the outside of the pads, then the brake pads do not require renewal because of excessive wear. If either of the brake pads is worn down to or below the grooved limit line, then both brake pads must be renewed.

WARNING: Inhaling asbestos brake dust is injurious to human health. Approved OSHA respiration equipment must be worn when working on or around brake calipers and pads. DO NOT use compressed air to clean brake calipers, pads or nearby components as brake dust will be blown into air. Only vacuum equipment designed to pick up brake dust should be used.

Brake components are accessible after removing caliper mounting screws and withdrawing caliper. Push piston by hand back into caliper to allow clearance for new brake pads. Brake disc should be renewed if thickness is 3.0 mm (0.12 in.) or less or disc runout is 0.3 mm (0.012 in.) or more. Tighten screws securing brake disc to wheel hub to 15-25 N•m (11-18 ft.-lbs.). After reassembly, operate brake lever until brake lever will not pump up after continuous operation. Do not operate vehicle until correct brake operation is noted.

MASTER CYLINDER. To remove front brake master cylinder (3—Fig. S7-14), remove union cap screw (10) at master cylinder. Brake fluid will remove paint; be careful when removing master cylinder. Remove the two retaining cap screws and withdraw master cylinder. Remove brake lever, reservoir cap (1) and diaphragm (2). Remove dust boot (5) and snap ring (6). Disassemble plunger assembly while noting location and direction of components. Inspect cylinder bore for damage due to corrosion or scoring. Renew complete master cylinder if excessive damage is evident. Superficial damage may be removed using a suitable cylinder hone. After honing, rinse cylinder with clean brake fluid. Shake out excess fluid but do not wipe dry. Using a shop towel or rag to dry cylinder will leave lint particles in bore. Renew boot (5) and primary and secondary cups (7 and 8). During reassembly, lubricate components with clean brake fluid. Reassembly is the reverse of disassembly. Tighten union cap screw (10) to 20-25 N•m (14.5-18.0 ft.-lbs.). Bleed brakes as outlined in bleeding section.

FRONT AXLE ASSEMBLY

R&R AND OVERHAUL. Refer to Fig. S7-15 for an exploded view of front axle assembly used on all models. To remove either wheel hub (42), remove front wheel, brake caliper assembly, cotter pin (48) and castle nut (47). Pull wheel hub (42) from spindle end of knuckle (35). Do not lose spacer (45). Remove seals (39 and 44) and drive bearings (40 and 43) and spacer (41) from hub if necessary.

To reassemble, reverse disassembly procedure while noting the following: Install inner bearing (40) into hub first. Tighten castle nut (47) to 50-80 N•m (36-58 ft.-lbs.) and install a new cotter pin (48). Tighten brake caliper mounting cap screws to 15-35 N•m (11-18 ft.-lbs.) and wheel retaining nuts to 20-31 N•m (14.5-22.5 ft.-lbs.).

STEERING

ADJUSTMENT. The toe-in should be checked and adjusted after the first month of operation and every three months thereafter. Prior to toe-in adjustment, inspect steering assembly for damaged or excessively worn components. If service to steering assembly is required, refer to R&R AND OVERHAUL section.

To check toe-in, inflate tires to recommended pressure listed in CONDENSED SERVICE DATA. Position vehicle on a flat smooth surface and set handlebars straight forward. Using a suitable tape measure, measure distance between right and left tire centerlines on back side of tires (B—Fig. S7-16) and record measurement. Locate the same tire centerline points on front side of tires (F) and record measurement. The front measurement should be 11-19 mm (0.43-0.75 in.) less than rear measurement. Note that the distance from a projected vehicle centerline to left (L) and right (R) tire centerlines should also be equal.

To adjust, loosen tie rod locknuts (31—Fig. S7-15) on both left and right tie-rods. The tie rod ends and locknuts color coded yellow have left-hand threads. Rotate tie rod sleeves (32) in equal increments to maintain equal vehicle centerline to left and right tire centerline distances. Tighten tie rod locknuts (31) to 22-35 N•m (16.0-25.5 ft.-lbs.).

R&R AND OVERHAUL. Refer to Fig. S7-15 for an exploded view of steering assembly. To remove either knuckle (35), first remove wheel hub (42) as outlined in FRONT AXLE ASSEMBLY section. Remainder of steering component disassembly is evident after inspection of unit and referral to Fig. S7-15.

During reassembly, renew all cotter pins. Lubricate all friction points with Suzuki Super Grease "A" or a good quality grease. Tighten steering shaft holder cap screws (10) to 18-28 N•m (13-20 ft.-lbs.); steering shaft lower nut (17) to 38-60 N•m (27.5-43.5 ft.-lbs.); ball joint cap screws (28) to 120-170 N•m (87-123 ft.-lbs.); ball joint (34) knuckle retaining nut to 35-50 N•m (26-37 ft.-lbs.);

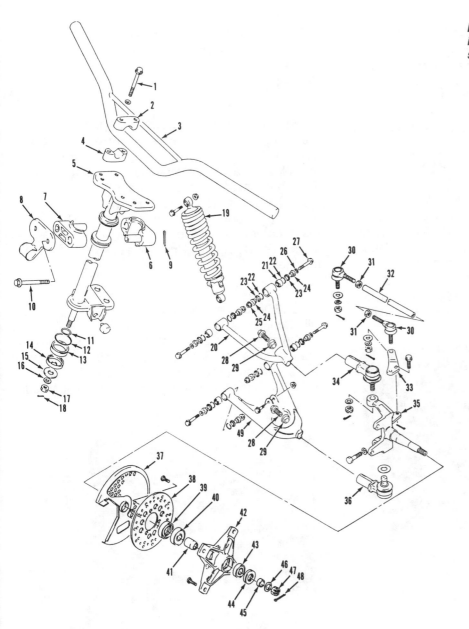

Fig. S7-15—Exploded view of steering, suspension and front axle assembly used on all models.

1. Cap screw
2. Upper clamp half
3. Handlebar
4. Lower clamp half
5. Steering shaft
6. Inner shaft holder
7. Outer shaft holder
8. Plate
9. Cotter pin
10. Cap screw
11. "O" ring
12. Seal snap ring
13. Dust seal
14. Dust seal
15. Flat washer
16. Lockwasher
17. Nut
18. Cotter pin
19. Shock absorber
20. Upper control arm
21. Bushing
22. "O" ring
23. Dust seal
24. Spacer
25. Nut
26. Lockwasher
27. Bolt
28. Cap screw
29. Stopper
30. Tie rod end
31. Locknut
32. Sleeve
33. Knuckle arm
34. Upper ball joint
35. Knuckle
36. Lower ball joint
37. Backing plate
38. Brake disc
39. Seal
40. Bearing
41. Spacer
42. Hub
43. Bearing
44. Seal
45. Spacer
46. Washer
47. Castle nut
48. Cotter pin
49. Lower control arm

knuckle arm (33) cap screws to 42.5-47.5 N•m (31-35 ft.-lbs.); ball joint (36) knuckle retaining cap screw to 40-60 N•m (29-43.5 ft.-lbs.) and tie rod end nut to 22-35 N•m (16-26 ft.-lbs.). Coat threads on knuckle arm (33) cap screws and ball joint cap screws (28) with Thread Lock "1303" or equivalent prior to installation.

FRONT SUSPENSION

R&R AND OVERHAUL. All models are equipped with a double wishbone-type front suspension and oil dampened shock absorbers. Shock absorber load settings are adjustable. Refer to Fig. S7-15 for exploded view of suspension components. The suspension components should be inspected periodically for excessive wear and

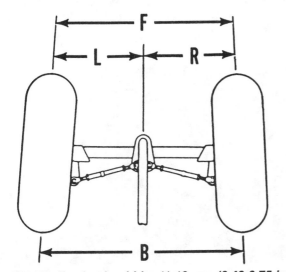

Fig. S7-16—Toe-in should be 11-19 mm (0.43-0.75 in.). Refer to text for measuring procedures.

damage. Removal and disassembly is evident after inspection of unit and referral to exploded view.

During reassembly, upper and lower control arm bolts (27) should be tightened to 40-60 N·m (29-43.5 ft.-lbs.) while ball joint cap screws (28) should be tightened to 120-170 N·m (87-123 ft.-lbs.). Tighten shock absorber (19) retaining bolts to 40-60 N·m (29-43.5 ft.-lbs.).

REAR BRAKE ASSEMBLY

A single disc brake assembly is used for both rear wheels. The running brake is operated hydraulically by a foot pedal on the lower right side. The parking brake is mechanically operated by a cable and handlebar components in conjunction with the clutch lever.

BRAKE PEDAL HEIGHT ADJUSTMENT. The top of brake pedal (P—Fig. S7-20) foot pad should be 5 mm

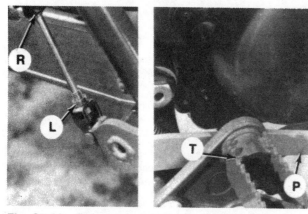

Fig. S7-20—Refer to text for brake pedal height adjustment procedures.

L. Locknut
P. Brake pedal
R. Master cylinder actuator rod
T. Footpeg

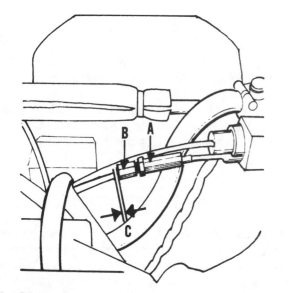

Fig. S7-21—Refer to text for parking brake adjustment procedures.

(0.2 in.) lower than top of footpeg (T). Loosen locknut (L) on master cylinder actuator rod and rotate rod (R) until brake pedal (P) foot pad is 5 mm (0.2 in.) lower than footpeg (T). Tighten locknut (L).

PARKING BRAKE ADJUSTMENT. With parking brake released, loosen parking brake cable locknut (A—Fig. S7-21). Turn adjuster (B) so there is little or no free play at cable (C) when actuating parking brake. Tighten locknut (A). Loosen locknut (9—Fig. S7-22) at brake lever arm so locknut does not contact caliper mounting bracket. Rotate adjuster screw (10) in until resistance is felt, then back out screw ¼ turn and tighten locknut (9). Be sure parking brake does not drag when released.

BLEEDING. Make sure reservoir (R—Fig. S7-23) is full. Connect a bleed hose to bleed valve (S—Fig. S7-22) on brake caliper assembly. Route the bleed hose into a suitable container. Operate rear brake foot pedal until a hardness (fluid resistance) is felt, then open bleed valve (S). Close bleed valve prior to releasing foot pedal.

Fig. S7-22—View of rear brake caliper showing location of bleed screw (S).

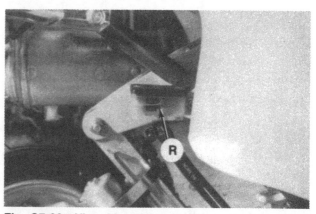

Fig. S7-23—View identifying location of reservoir (R) for rear brake master cylinder.

Continue bleeding procedure until no air bubbles are noted in discharged fluid from bleed valve.

NOTE: Make sure reservoir (R—Fig. S7-23) is kept full during bleeding procedure.

When bleeding procedure is completed, add brake fluid to reservoir (R) until fluid level is at upper level line on reservoir.

OVERHAUL. Brake pad thickness may be determined externally by viewing the brake pads. If neither of the brake pads are worn below the grooved limit line around the outside of the pads, then the brake pads do not require renewal because of excessive wear. If either of the brake pads is worn down to or below the grooved limit line, then both brake pads must be renewed.

WARNING: Inhaling asbestos brake dust is injurious to human health. Approved OSHA respiration equipment must be worn when working on or around brake calipers and pads. DO NOT use compressed air to clean brake calipers, pads or nearby components as brake dust will be blown into air. Only vacuum equipment designed to pick up brake dust should be used.

Brake components are accessible after removing caliper mounting screws and withdrawing caliper. Loosen parking brake locknut (9—Fig. S7-22) and rotate screw (10) outward. Push piston by hand back into caliper to allow clearance for new brake pads. Refer to Fig. S7-24 for an exploded view of brake caliper components if complete overhaul is required. Brake disc should be renewed if thickness is 3.0 mm (0.12 in.) or less or disc runout is 0.3 mm (0.012 in.) or more. After reassembly, operate brake foot pedal until pedal will not pump up after continuous operation or refer to previous BLEEDING paragraphs if caliper assembly was overhauled. Do not operate vehicle until correct brake operation is noted. Adjust parking brake as outlined in previous PARKING BRAKE ADJUSTMENT paragraph.

DRIVE CHAIN AND SPROCKETS

INSPECTION AND ADJUSTMENT. The final drive chain should be inspected and adjusted, if needed, prior to each operating interval. Improper maintenance and neglect can cause early failure of both drive chain and sprockets. An endless-type drive chain is used. Distance between 20 chain links should not exceed 323.9 mm (12.75 in.). Drive chain free play should be 35-40 mm (1.4-1.6 in.) measured midway between sprockets. Chain tension is adjusted by loosening four bolts (10 and 13—Fig. S7-25) and locknuts (17). Rotate adjuster nuts (16) until correct drive chain free play is obtained. The notch (H) on each side of adjuster plate must be aligned with corresponding scale marks on each side to ensure proper rear wheel tracking and drive chain-to-rear

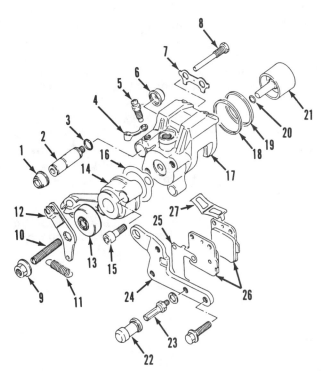

Fig. S7-24—Exploded view of rear brake caliper and parking brake assembly.

1. Dust seal	15. Screw
2. Caliper guide pin	16. Gasket
3. Washer	17. Caliper
4. Cap	18. Piston seal
5. Bleed screw	19. Dust seal
6. Dust seal	20. "O" ring
7. Lock tab	21. Piston
8. Brake pad screw	22. Dust cap
9. Locknut	23. Caliper guide pin
10. Screw	24. Bracket
11. Spring	25. Shim
12. Lever	26. Brake pads
13. Dust seal	27. Spring
14. Parking brake housing	

Fig. S7-25—Loosen bolts (10 and 13) and locknuts (17) and rotate adjuster nuts (16) to adjust drive chain free play. Drive chain free play should be 35-40 mm (1.4-1.6 in.) measured midway between sprockets. Notch (H) on adjuster plate must align with corresponding scale marks on each side.

sprocket alignment. Tighten sprocket side bolts (13) to 70-90 N·m (52-66 ft.-lbs.) torque and brake disc side bolts (10) to 40-60 N·m (29-43.5 ft.-lbs.) torque. Securely tighten locknuts (17).

R&R AND OVERHAUL. Loosen four bolts (10 and 13—Fig. S7-25) and locknuts (17). Rotate adjuster nuts (16) outward and push rear axle housing toward vehicle's front to increase drive chain free play. Lift chain off rear sprocket toward left rear wheel. Use a location at rear of vehicle frame and lift rear wheels off the ground. Remove both rear wheels. Remove seat and rear fender assembly. Remove shock absorber upper and lower mounting bolts and nuts. Remove cushion lever center shaft and nut. Remove clamps securing brake hose to swing arm. Remove screws securing shock absorber reservoir to frame and withdraw shock absorber assembly. Remove nut securing swing arm pivot shaft. Support swing arm assembly and withdraw swing arm pivot shaft. Withdraw swing arm assembly far enough to provide adequate clearance for drive chain renewal. Remove front (engine) sprocket guard and withdraw drive chain. Remove front sprocket if needed.

Carefully examine sprockets for excessive wear. Worn sprockets will usually have a hooked tooth profile. A good test is to place a new chain on a used sprocket and check the fit. If sprockets require renewal due to wear, always renew drive chain. Sprockets should be renewed as a set. Standard drive chain is a DID 520VS or Takasago RK520SMO-Z9 with 102 links.

Reassembly is reverse order of disassembly. Tighten rear sprocket cap screws (25—Fig. S7-27) to 50-60 N·m (36-43.5 ft.-lbs.). Tighten cushion lever center shaft securing nut to 70-100 N·m (52-74 ft.-lbs.). Tighten

swing arm pivot shaft nut to 50-80 N·m (36-58 ft.-lbs.). Tighten shock absorber mounting bolts to 40-60 N·m (29-43.5 ft.-lbs.). Tighten wheel retaining nuts to 45-65 N·m (32.5-47 ft.-lbs.). Refer to previous INSPECTION AND ADJUSTMENT paragraphs for recommended drive chain adjustment procedures.

FINAL DRIVE ASSEMBLY

R&R AND OVERHAUL. Remove two cap screws securing rear brake caliper assembly and withdraw caliper with parking brake assembly. Remove brake disc guard. Remove drive chain as outlined under R&R AND OVERHAUL in the DRIVE CHAIN AND SPROCKETS section. To complete disassembly, remove left and right rear hub assemblies. Remove brake disc retaining nuts (1—Fig. S7-27), then withdraw brake disc (3) and push axle shaft (4) out of axle housing (9) toward brake side. Remove bolts (10 and 13) and adjustment studs (15) to withdraw housing (9) from swing arm casing.

Renew any component that is excessively worn or damaged in any other way. Reassembly is reverse order of disassembly. Install Belleville washers (23) so concave sides are together. If sprocket side nuts (24) were removed, then apply Suzuki Bond No. 1207B to outside surface of flange (21) and Thread Lock "1303" to threads of nuts (24) and tighten to 160-200 N·m (115.5-144.5 ft.-lbs.). On brake disc (3) side, apply Suzuki Bond No. 1207B to outside surface of flange (27) and Thread Lock "1303" to threads of nuts (1) and tighten to 160-200 N·m (115.5-144.5 ft.-lbs.). Tighten axle hub nuts to 85-115 N·m (61.5-83 ft.-lbs.) and install new cotter pins.

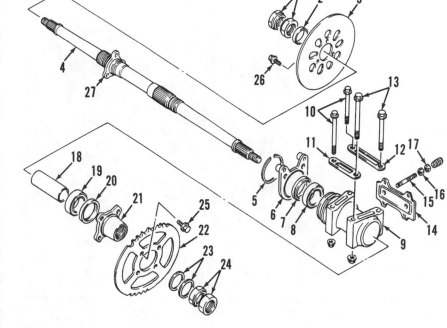

Fig. S7-27—Exploded view of axle housing and related components.

1. Nuts
2. Spacer
3. Brake disc
4. Axle
5. Snap ring
6. Caliper mounting bracket
7. Seal
8. Bearing
9. Housing
10. Bolts
11. Plate
12. Plate
13. Bolts
14. Adjustment plate
15. Stud
16. Adjuster nut
17. Locknut
18. Spacer
19. Bearing
20. Dust seal
21. Flange
22. Sprocket
23. Belleville washers
24. Nuts
25. Cap screw
26. Cap screw
27. Flange

SUZUKI

LT300E AND LT-F300

NOTE: Metric fasteners are used throughout vehicle.

CONDENSED SERVICE DATA

MODELS	**LT300E, LT-F300**
General	
Engine Make	Suzuki
Engine Type	Four-Stroke; Air-Cooled
Number of Cylinders	1
Bore	72.0 mm
	(2.835 in.)
Stroke	72.0 mm
	(2.835 in.)
Displacement	293 cc
	(17.9 cu. in.)
Compression Ratio	8.5:1
Fuel Recommendation	Unleaded or Low-Lead
Pump Octane Rating	85-95
Engine Lubrication	Wet Sump; Pump
Engine/Transmission	
Oil Recommendation	SAE 10W-40
Forward Speeds	5
Reverse Speeds	1
Tire Size:	
Front	21 × 8.00-9
Rear	25 × 12.00-9
Tire Pressure (cold):	
Front	20 kPa*
	(2.8 psi)
Rear	20 kPa*
	(2.8 psi)
Dry Weight	203 kg
	(447 lbs.)

*When load capacity is below 80 kg (175 lbs.), cold tire pressure should be 17.5 kPa (2.5 psi) on front tires and 15 kPa (2.2 psi) on rear tires.

Tune-Up	
Engine Idle Speed	1350-1450 rpm
Spark Plug:	
NGK	DR8ES-L
Nippon Denso	X24ESR-U
Electrode Gap	0.6-0.7 mm
	(0.024-0.028 in.)
Ignition:	
Type	Breakerless
Timing	See Text
Carburetor:	
Make	Mikuni
Model	VM26SS
Bore Size	26 mm
	(1.02 in.)

Tune-Up (Cont.)

Carburetor: (Cont.)

Float Height	20.8-22.8 mm (0.82-0.90 in.)
Jet Needle	5DM1
Clip Position.	3rd Groove From Top
Pilot Jet	#20
Needle Jet	N-5
Main Jet	#112.5
Throttle Cut-Away	1.5
Throttle Cable Free Play	0.5-1.0 mm (0.02-0.04 in.)

Sizes-Clearances

Valve Clearance (cold):

Intake.	0.03-0.08 mm (0.001-0.003 in.)
Exhaust	0.08-0.13 mm (0.003-0.005 in.)
Valve Face & Seat Angle	45°
Valve Seat Width	0.9-1.1 mm (0.035-0.043 in.)

Valve Stem Diameter:

Intake.	5.460-5.475 mm (0.2150-0.2156 in.)
Exhaust	5.445-5.460 mm (0.2144-0.2150 in.)

Valve Guide Bore Diameter:

Intake & Exhaust	5.500-5.512 mm (0.2150-0.2156 in.)

Valve Stem-to-Guide Clearance:

Intake.	0.025-0.052 mm (0.001-0.002 in.)
Exhaust	0.040-0.067 mm (0.0016-0.0026 in.)
Wear Limit (Intake & Exhaust).	0.35 mm (0.014 in.)

Valve Spring Free Length (Min.):

Inner.	35.4 mm (1.39 in.)
Outer	39.4 mm (1.55 in.)

Rocker Arm Bore Diameter:

Intake & Exhaust	11.990-12.008 mm (0.4720-0.4728 in.)
Rocker Shaft Diameter	11.966-11.984 mm (0.4711-0.4718 in.)

Camshaft Lobe Height:

Intake.	35.022-35.062 mm (1.3788-1.3804 in.)
Wear Limit	34.730 mm (1.3673 in.)
Exhaust	35.036-35.076 mm (1.3794-1.3809 in.)
Wear Limit	34.740 mm (1.3677 in.)

Camshaft Journal Diameter:

Intake.	19.959-19.980 mm (0.7858-0.7866 in.)

Sizes-Clearances (Cont.)

Camshaft Journal Diameter: (Cont.)
Exhaust . . . . 24.959-24.980 mm
(0.9826-0.9835 in.)

Camshaft Journal Clearance:
Intake & Exhaust . . . . 0.032-0.066 mm
(0.0013-0.0026 in.)
Wear Limit . . . . 0.150 mm
(0.0059 in.)

Camshaft Runout (Max.) . . . . 0.10 mm
(0.004 in.)

Cylinder Head Cover Distortion (Max.) . . . 0.05 mm
(0.002 in.)

Cylinder Head Distortion (Max.). . . . . 0.05 mm
(0.002 in.)

Piston-to-Cylinder Wall Clearance . . . . 0.040-0.050 mm
(0.0016-0.0020 in.)
Wear Limit . . . . 0.120 mm
(0.0047 in.)

Cylinder Bore Diameter . . . . 72.000-72.015 mm
(2.8346-2.8352 in.)
Wear Limit . . . . 72.090 mm
(2.8382 in.)

Cylinder Bore Distortion (Max.) . . . . 0.05 mm
(0.002 in.)

Piston Diameter—Measured 15 mm
(0.59 in.) from Skirt Bottom . . . . 71.955-71.970 mm
(2.8329-2.8335 in.)
Wear Limit . . . . 71.880 mm
(2.8299 in.)

Piston Pin Bore Diameter . . . . 18.002-18.008 mm
(0.7087-0.7090 in.)
Wear Limit . . . . 18.030 mm
(0.7098 in.)

Piston Pin Diameter. . . . . 17.996-18.000 mm
(0.7085-0.7087 in.)
Wear Limit . . . . 17.980 mm
(0.7079 in.)

Piston Ring End Gap
Top. . . . . 0.10-0.30 mm
(0.004-0.012 in.)
Wear Limit . . . . 0.70 mm
(0.028 in.)
Second. . . . . 0.15-0.35 mm
(0.006-0.014 in.)
Wear Limit . . . . 0.70 mm
(0.028 in.)

Piston Ring Side Clearance (Max.):
Top. . . . . 0.180 mm
(0.0071 in.)
Second. . . . . 0.150 mm
(0.0059 in.)

Connecting Rod Small
End Bore Diameter . . . . 18.006-18.014 mm
(0.7089-0.7092 in.)
Wear Limit . . . . 18.040 mm
(0.7102 in.)

Capacities

Fuel Tank . . . .   9.5 L
    (2.5 gal.)

Engine/Transmission
  Sump . . . .   See Text

Tightening Torques

Balancer Bolt . . . .   34-45 N•m
    (24.5-32.5 ft.-lbs.)

Camshaft Sprocket Bolt . . . .   14-16 N•m
    (10.0-11.5 ft.-lbs.)

Clutch Shoe Nut . . . .   90-110 N•m
    (65.0-79.5 ft.-lbs.)

Clutch Sleeve Hub Nut . . . .   60-80 N•m
    (43.5-58.0 ft.-lbs.)

Cylinder Base Nut . . . .   9-11 N•m
    (6.5-8.0 ft.-lbs.)

Cylinder Head
  Cover Bolt . . . .   9-11 N•m
    (6.5-8.0 ft.-lbs.

Cylinder Head Nut:
  6 mm . . . .   8-12 N•m
    (6.0-8.5 ft.-lbs.)
  10 mm . . . .   35-40 N•m
    (25.5-29.0 ft.-lbs.)

Engine Mounting Bolts:
  8 mm . . . .   37-45 N•m
    (27.0-32.5 ft.-lbs.)
  10 mm . . . .   80-95 N•m
    (58.0-68.5 ft.-lbs.)

Flywheel Bolt . . . .   120-140 N•m
    (87.0-101.5 ft.-lbs.)

Front Axle Nuts . . . .   50-80 N•m
    (36-58 ft.-lbs.)

Rear Axle Nuts . . . .   85-115 N•m
    (61.5-83.0 ft.-lbs.)

Wheel Retaining Nuts:
  Front . . . .   20-31 N•m
    (14.5-22.5 ft.-lbs.)
  Rear . . . .   44-66 N•m
    (32-48 ft.-lbs.)

Standard Screws:
  Unmarked or Marked "4"
  4 mm . . . .   1.0-2.0 N•m
    (8.9-18 in.-lbs.)
  5 mm . . . .   2.0-4.0 N•m
    (18-36 in.-lbs.)
  6 mm . . . .   4.0-7.0 N•m
    (36-62 in.-lbs.)
  8 mm . . . .   10-16 N•m
    (88.5-142 in.-lbs.)
  10 mm . . . .   22-35 N•m
    (16-26 ft.-lbs.)
  12 mm . . . .   35-55 N•m
    (26-40 ft.-lbs.)
  14 mm . . . .   50-80 N•m
    (37-59 ft.-lbs.)
  16 mm . . . .   80-130 N•m
    (59-96 ft.-lbs.)

Tightening Torques (Cont.)
Standard Screws: (Cont.)
  Unmarked or Marked "4" (Cont.)

18 mm	130-190 N·m (96-140 ft.-lbs.)
Marked "7"	
4 mm	1.5-3.0 N·m (13-27 in.-lbs.)
5 mm	3.0-6.0 N·m (27-53 in.-lbs.)
6 mm	8.0-12.0 N·m (71-106 in.-lbs.)
8 mm	18-28 N·m (13-21 ft.-lbs.)
10 mm	40-60 N·m (29-44 ft.-lbs.)
12 mm	70-100 N·m (52-74 ft.-lbs.)
14 mm	110-160 N·m (81-118 ft.-lbs.)
16 mm	170-250 N·m (125-184 ft.-lbs.)
18 mm	200-280 N·m (147-206 ft.-lbs.)

LUBRICATION

ENGINE AND TRANSMISSION. The engine and transmission are lubricated by a crankshaft-driven oil pump. Recommended oil is a multigrade SAE 10W-40 motor oil with an API classification of SE or SF.

The sump is filled through filler plug opening (F—Fig. S9-1). Oil level should be maintained at level indicated on sight glass (G). Oil is drained by removing plug in underside of crankcase. Dry capacity of crankcase is 2100 mL (2.2 qt.) after an engine or transmission over-

Fig. S9-1—Engine and transmission oil is poured through filler plug opening (F) and maintained at level on sight glass (G).

haul. Refilling after changing oil and oil filter requires only 1800 mL (1.9 qt.) as approximately 300 mL (0.3 qt.) of oil will be retained by crankcase castings. Oil requirement after only changing oil is 1600 mL (1.7 qt.).

Manufacturer recommends changing the oil and oil filter after the first 200 km (125 miles) of operation and every 1000 km (600 miles) thereafter. A sump filter screen is located above the oil drain plug and is accessible after removing guard pan and cover which houses the oil drain plug. The sump filter screen should be removed and cleaned at least every 2000 km (1200 miles) or during every other oil and oil filter change. Install a new "O" ring in cover during reinstallation.

The oil filter may be renewed after removing filter cap (C—Fig. S9-2). Make certain inner "O" ring is properly installed before inserting filter. Insert new filter with open end toward engine and closed end toward filter cap. Renew filter cap "O" ring and ensure filter retaining spring is properly located when installing cap.

REAR AXLE HOUSING. Grease should be injected into the rear axle housing after every 1000 km (600 miles) of use. Inject grease through the grease fitting located on the rear side of the rear axle housing. Recommended grease is Suzuki Super Grease "A".

DRIVE CHAIN. The final drive chain should be lubricated with SAE 90 gear oil prior to each operating

Fig. S9-2—Oil filter is located behind side cover (C).

Fig. S9-4—Throttle cable should have 0.5-1.0 mm (0.02-0.04 in.) free play (P). To adjust, slide dust boot (B) down cable and loosen locknut (L) and rotate adjuster (A) as required.

interval. Incorrect chain lubricating oil may cause damage to "O" ring seals in drive chain. After every 1000 km (600 miles) of operation, the chain should be thoroughly washed in kerosene and lubricated. Any cleaning solutions other than kerosene may result in "O" ring seal damage. To obtain access to drive chain, remove seat, rear fender, gearshift lever and bottom guard plate. Release the three chain case clamps and remove the one cap screw, then slide chain case outward.

Refer to DRIVE CHAIN AND SPROCKETS section for chain renewal and adjustment information.

CABLES, LEVERS AND SHAFTS. The choke cable, throttle cable, reverse cable, speedometer cable and throttle lever should be lubricated with motor oil every 1000 km (600 miles). The front wheel bearings, steering shaft, gearshift lever, rear brake lever and brake camshaft should be greased every 1000 km (600 miles). Do not excessively grease the brake camshaft as grease may contact brake linings reducing braking ability.

AIR CLEANER ELEMENT

The air cleaner element should be cleaned after every 1000 km (600 miles) of operation. To remove air cleaner element, first remove seat and element cover. Remove element retaining pin and withdraw element. Carefully separate foam element from frame.

Thoroughly clean element in a suitable nonflammable solvent. Saturate element in clean motor oil. Compress element to remove excess oil. Reinstall element by reversing removal procedure.

FUEL SYSTEM

CARBURETOR. A Mikuni VM26SS carburetor is used. Refer to CONDENSED SERVICE DATA for carburetor specifications.

Before performing carburetor adjustments, throttle cable should be adjusted to provide 0.5-1.0 mm (0.02-0.04 in.) free play (P—Fig. S9-4) at idle position. To adjust, slide dust boot (B) down cable and loosen

locknut (L) and rotate adjuster (A) as required. Tighten locknut (L) and reinstall dust boot.

Initial setting of idle mixture screw (18—Fig. S9-5) is 2 turns out from a lightly seated position. Rotating idle mixture screw clockwise will lean mixture while rotating screw counterclockwise will richen mixture. Final adjustment should be made with engine at normal operating temperature and running. Adjust idle speed screw (17) so engine idles at 1350-1450 rpm. Adjust idle mixture screw (18) so highest idle speed is achieved and readjust idle speed screw to recommended rpm. After adjusting carburetor, check throttle cable adjustment as previously described.

When servicing carburetor observe the following: Clip (6—Fig. S9-6) should be in third groove from top of jet needle (7). Float height should be 20.8-22.8 mm (0.82-0.90 in.). To check float height, remove float bowl and invert carburetor. Measure distance (A—Fig. S9-7) between bottom of float and gasket surface on carburetor body. Adjust float by bending float arm tang (B).

FUEL PUMP. A diaphragm-type fuel pump located adjacent to fuel tank is used. Alternating pressure and vacuum inside intake manifold is directed to one side of

Fig. S9-5—Installed view of carburetor showing location of idle speed screw (17) and idle mixture screw (18).

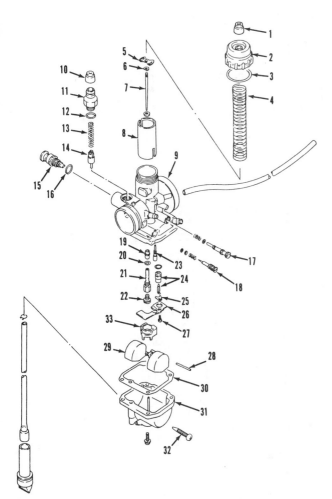

Fig. S9-6—Exploded view of Mikuni VM26SS carburetor.

1. Grommet
2. Cap
3. Gasket
4. Spring
5. Retainer
6. Jet needle clip
7. Jet needle
8. Throttle slide
9. Body
10. Grommet
11. Cable guide
12. Washer
13. Spring
14. Starter valve
15. Starter valve limiter
16. Washer
17. Idle speed screw
18. Idle mixture screw
19. Needle jet
20. Washer
21. Air bleed
22. Main jet
23. Pilot jet
24. Inlet valve
25. Inlet valve retainer
26. Baffle plate
27. Screw
28. Float pin
29. Float
30. Gasket
31. Float bowl
32. Drain screw
33. Fuel guide

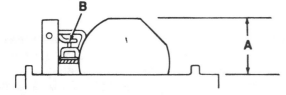

Fig. S9-7—Float level (A) should be 20.8-22.8 mm (0.82-0.90 in.). Bend float arm tang (B) to adjust.

fuel pump diaphragm via a hose. During vacuum pulse, diaphragm draws fuel through inlet check valve into fuel chamber. During pressure pulse, diaphragm reduces fuel chamber volume moving fuel through outlet check valve.

If fuel delivery to carburetor is interrupted, first eliminate other sources of difficulty such as insufficient fuel, clogged fuel strainers, cracked or split hoses or loose pump housing retaining screws before servicing fuel pump. When servicing pump, defective or questionable parts should be renewed. Diaphragm should be renewed if deterioration is evident.

FUEL STRAINER. Fuel strainers located in each fuel tank outlet are used. The strainers should be removed and cleaned periodically to prevent fuel starvation. To gain access to strainers, remove rear fender and carrier assembly. Drain fuel tank and detach fuel hoses. Unbolt and remove fuel tank from vehicle. Withdraw strainers from tank. Reinstall by reversing removal procedure.

IGNITION AND ELECTRICAL

SPARK PLUG. Standard spark plug is NGK DR8ES-L or Nippon Denso X24ESR-U. Spark plug electrode gap should be 0.6-0.7 mm (0.024-0.028 in.).

Spark plug should be removed, cleaned and electrode gap set every 1000 km (600 miles) and renewed every 6000 km (4000 miles).

IGNITION. A capacitor discharge, pointless electronic ignition system is used. The ignition system consists of the flywheel, a power source coil located underneath flywheel, an externally mounted pickup coil, a CD ignition module, an ignition coil, engine stop switch and ignition switch. Ignition timing should occur at 5° BTDC with engine operating at 1700 rpm and below, and at 30° BTDC at 3800 rpm and above. Ignition timing is fixed and not adjustable. The flywheel has a single mark "T" (Fig. S9-10) to indicate Top Dead Center, which is used during valve clearance adjustment or when setting camshaft timing.

If ignition malfunction occurs, check condition of spark plug, all wires and connections before troubleshooting ignition circuit. Using Suzuki pocket tester 09900-25002 or a suitable ohmmeter, refer to the following test specifications and procedures to aid troubleshooting.

To check power source coil, separate wire connectors leading from power source coil to CDI module and attach one tester lead to coil end of brown wire. Attach remaining tester lead to black wire. Power source coil may be considered satisfactory if resistance reading is within the limits of 180-350 ohms.

To check pickup coil, separate blue wire connector and green wire connector from pickup coil to CDI module. Attach one tester lead to blue wire and remaining lead to green wire. Pickup coil may be considered

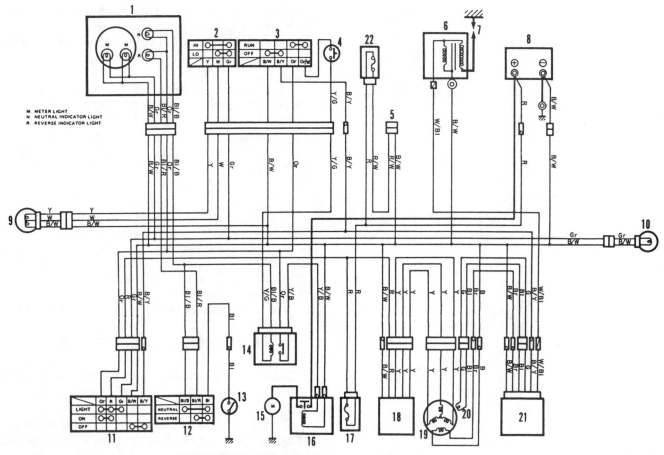

Fig. S9-9—Wiring diagram for Model LT300E. Model LT-F300 is similar.

B. Black	B/Y. Black with yellow tracer	3. Engine stop switch	13. Neutral light switch
Bl. Blue	Bl/B. Blue with black tracer	4. Starter switch	14. Neutral relay
Br. Brown	Bl/R. Blue with red tracer	5. Accessory terminal	15. Starter motor
G. Green	Or/W. Orange with white tracer	6. Ignition coil	16. Starter relay
Gr. Gray	R/W. Red with white tracer	7. Spark plug	17. Fuse
Or. Orange	W/Bl. White with blue tracer	8. Battery	18. Regulator/rectifier
R. Red	Y/B. Yellow with black tracer	9. Headlight	19. Magneto
W. White	Y/G. Yellow with green tracer	10. Taillight	20. Pickup coil
Y. Yellow	1. Speedometer assy.	11. Ignition switch	21. CDI module
B/W. Black with white tracer	2. Dimmer switch	12. Reverse switch	22. Accessory terminal fuse

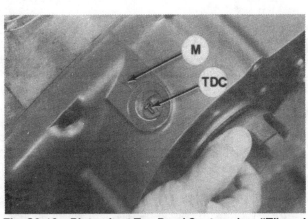

Fig. S9-10—Piston is at Top Dead Center when "T" mark (TDC) is aligned with stationary mark (M). Piston must also be on compression stroke as outlined in text for valve clearance adjustment.

satisfactory if resistance reading is within the limits of 450-650 ohms.

To check condition of ignition coil, separate black wire with white tracer connector from coil to CD ignition module and remove high-tension wire from spark plug. Attach one tester lead to black wire with white tracer terminal on coil and remaining tester lead to coil ground. Primary coil resistance reading should be approximately 0-2.2.0 ohms. Attach one tester lead to high-tension wire and remaining tester lead to positive terminal on coil. Secondary coil resistance reading should be approximately 12k-20k ohms.

CHARGING CIRCUIT. A charging circuit which consists of an AC generator located underneath the flywheel, a regulator/rectifier and a battery is used. Standard battery on Model LT300E is YB14A-A2 with a 14 ampere hour, 12-volt rating. Standard battery on Model LT-F300 is Y50-N18A-A with a 20 ampere hour,

12-volt rating. Under load, the AC generator should produce 14-15 volts DC at 5000 rpm. No-load voltage of AC generator should be 60 volts AC at 5000 rpm.

The battery should be checked and filled to maximum level with distilled water, if required, after the first 200 km (125 miles) and every 1000 km (600 miles) thereafter. During periods of vehicle storage, the battery should be charged once a month to reduce sulfation and prolong battery life. When charging battery, always disconnect battery from charging circuit to prevent damage to regulator/rectifier or other components. Do not exceed maximum charging rate of 1.2 amperes.

The AC generator can be statically checked using Suzuki pocket tester 09900-25002 or a suitable ohmmeter. Separate wire connector block from AC generator to regulator/rectifier and attach tester leads between each yellow stator lead. Tester reading should indicate continuity between each lead. Attach one tester lead to ground and remaining tester lead to each yellow wire individually. Tester reading should indicate infinite resistance at each lead.

An operational check can be performed using Suzuki pocket tester 09900-25002 or a suitable voltmeter as follows: Set lighting switch to on position and dimmer switch to high-beam position. Remove seat and attach voltmeter leads noting correct polarity. Start and run engine at 5000 rpm. With a fully charged battery, AC generator and regulator/rectifier may be considered satisfactory if voltage reading is within the limits of 14-15 volts. If voltage is not within required limits of 14-15 volts, the AC generator may be eliminated as cause of difficulty by performing a no-load test. Separate AC generator to regulator/rectifier wire connector block. Start and run engine at 5000 rpm. Attach voltmeter leads between each yellow stator lead. The AC generator may be considered satisfactory if no-load voltage is not less than 60 volts AC.

STARTER. An electric starter is used. Starter should draw 80 amperes at engine starting speed. Removal and disassembly of starter is evident after inspection of unit. Starter brushes should be renewed if worn to 9 mm (0.4 in.) or less.

WIRING. If wiring requires repair, always use replacement wire of the same gauge. Wires should be routed away from areas of extreme heat or sharp edges. Plastic tie straps should be used to retain wires in their original positions to prevent short circuiting. Refer to Fig. S9-9 for schematic wiring diagram.

FASTENERS

After the first 200 km (125 miles) of operation and every 1000 km (600 miles) thereafter, the cylinder head, cylinder, exhaust system, engine mounts and all chassis nuts or bolts should be retightened. Refer to TIGHTEN-ING TORQUES section of CONDENSED SERVICE DATA for torque specifications.

VALVE SYSTEM

The valves are actuated via rocker arms by a single overhead camshaft. Camshaft is timed and driven by a roller drive chain from right end of crankshaft. Valve clearance should be adjusted after the first 200 km (125 miles) of operation and every 1000 km (600 miles) thereafter. Valve clearance should be adjusted with engine cold.

To adjust valve clearance, first remove seat, front fender, spark plug, valve adjustment caps and timing inspection plug. Rotate crankshaft until "T" mark (TDC—Fig. S9-10) on flywheel aligns with stationary mark (M) on crankcase and piston is on compression stroke. To ensure piston is on compression stroke, rotate crankshaft 1/4 turn past TDC while observing intake valves. If valve movement is indicated, rotate crankshaft one full revolution and align timing marks again.

Two intake valves and two exhaust valves are used. Make certain each set of valves is adjusted equally. Clearance between rocker arm adjusting screw and valve stem should be 0.03-0.08 mm (0.001-0.003 in.) for intake valves and 0.08-0.13 mm (0.003-0.005 in.) for exhaust valves. Clearance is checked with feeler gauge (F—Fig. S9-12) and adjusted by loosening locknut (L) and turning screw (A). Be sure to recheck clearance after locknuts are tightened.

CLUTCH

Two types of automatically actuated clutches are used. One type is a three-shoe centrifugal clutch attached to right end of crankshaft and actuated by engine rpm. The other type is a multiple-disc clutch attached to right end of transmission countershaft and actuated by

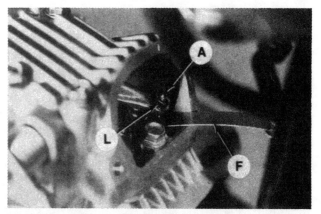

Fig. S9-12—Clearance between valve stem and adjusting screw (A) should be 0.03-0.08 mm (0.001-0.003 in.) for both intake valves and 0.08-0.13 mm (0.003-0.005 in.) for both exhaust valves. Measure clearance with suitable feeler gauge (F) and loosen locknut (L) prior to turning screw (A).

Fig. S9-14—View of clutch adjusting screw (S) and locknut (L). Refer to text for adjustment procedure.

the gear shift lever. During gear selection, a lever attached to end of gear shift shaft simultaneously disengages the multiple-disc clutch to permit smooth transmission operation.

The clutch should be adjusted after the first 200 km (125 miles) of operation and every 2000 km (1200 miles) thereafter. To adjust clutch, remove rear cover on right side of crankcase. Loosen locknut (L—Fig. S9-14). Turn adjusting screw (S) in, stopping just as internal resistance is felt, then back screw out 1/8 turn. Secure adjusting screw while tightening locknut.

To check clutch operation, first adjust clutch as previously described. Ensure oil level is correct and engine is at operating temperature. Attach a suitable tachometer. Select low gear and slowly accelerate engine while observing meter. Initial engagement should occur at 1800-2200 rpm. Next, with transmission still in low gear, lockup brakes and momentarily open throttle. Do not maintain full throttle longer than 10 seconds. Engine speed should be held to 3500-3900 rpm. Any results other than specified may indicate disassembly and repair of clutch assemblies is required.

MANUAL STARTER

R&R AND OVERHAUL. Refer to Fig. S9-16 for exploded view of manual starter used. Starter may be removed as a complete unit from vehicle after removing four starter housing retaining cap screws. Refer to exploded view and disassemble starter as follows: If starter spring remains under tension, pull starter rope and hold rope pulley (9) with notch in pulley adjacent to rope outlet. Pull rope back through outlet so it engages notch in pulley and allow pulley to slowly unwind. Remove retaining nut (1) and disassemble unit. Be careful when removing rewind spring (10); a rapidly uncoiling starter spring could cause serious injury.

Rewind spring is wound in a clockwise direction in starter housing. Rope is wound on rope pulley in a clockwise direction as viewed with pulley in housing. Reassemble starter assembly by reversing disassembly

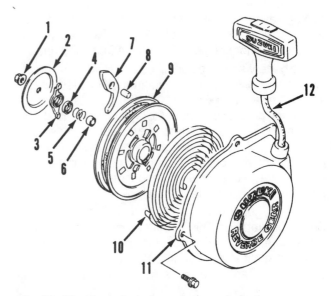

Fig. S9-16—Exploded view of manual starter.

1. Nut	7. Starter pawl
2. Friction plate	8. Pin
3. Pawl guide	9. Rope pulley
4. Spring guide	10. Rewind spring
5. Spring	11. Starter housing
6. Spacer	12. Rope

procedure. To place tension on rewind spring, pass rope through rope outlet in housing and install rope handle. Pull rope out and hold pulley so notch in pulley is adjacent to rope outlet. Pull a loop of rope back through outlet between notch in pulley and housing. Turn rope pulley clockwise three or four complete revolutions to place tension on spring. Do not place more tension on rewind spring than is necessary to draw rope handle up against housing.

FRONT BRAKE ASSEMBLY

Independently operated front and rear brakes are used. The front brake system has hydraulically actuated two-shoe internal expanding drum brakes mounted on each front spindle. A handlebar mounted master cylinder with fluid reservoir supplies pressure to each wheel cylinder when actuated by right handlebar lever. Information on rear brake system is outlined in REAR BRAKE ASSEMBLY section.

Only DOT 3 or DOT 4 glycol-based brake fluid should be used in front brake system. The use of other types of brake fluids such as petroleum-based or silicone-based fluids may damage hydraulic components resulting in brake system failure. Under normal operating conditions, brake fluid will absorb small amounts of moisture which can cause pitting to cylinder bore surface and early brake cylinder failure. Drain and refill hydraulic system with new brake fluid every two years to reduce corrosion damage.

BLEEDING. Any operation that required draining or repair of hydraulic brake components will make it necessary to fill and bleed brake system. Check reservoir fluid level before proceeding. Remove cap (7—Fig. S9-17), diaphragm (8) and fill reservoir with DOT 3 or DOT 4 glycol-based fluid only. Reinstall cap to prevent entrance of dirt or foreign materials. Attach a suitable hose such as vacuum hose to either bleeder screw (B—Fig. S9-18) and submerge other end in a container filled with small amount of brake fluid to prevent air from reentering system. Actuate brake lever several times, then hold brake lever toward handlebar. Open brake bleeder to relieve line pressure allowing fluid and air to

flow into container. Close bleed screw before releasing brake lever. Do not permit reservoir to run dry while bleeding. Repeat procedure while periodically refilling fluid reservoir until all air or old fluid is removed.

Attach bleeder hose to remaining bleeder screw and repeat bleeding procedure to complete brake bleeding operation.

INSPECTION AND ADJUSTMENT. The brake system should be inspected and adjusted after the first 200 km (125 miles) of operation and every 1000 km (600 miles) thereafter. To inspect front brake drums, shoes and wheel cylinders, suitably support front of vehicle and remove front axle nuts. Pull tire, wheel and drum off axle as an assembly. Remove wheel retaining nuts and separate brake drum from wheel. Brake drum should be renewed if inside diameter exceeds 142.7 mm (5.62 in.). Front brake shoes (20—Fig. S9-17) should be renewed if linings are worn to 1.5 mm (0.06 in.) or less. Wheel cylinders (27) should be overhauled or renewed if brake fluid is observed within boots (25) indicating defective cups or cylinder.

If either the brake shoes or wheel cylinders require servicing, then the complete drum brake assembly should be serviced as outlined in R&R AND OVERHAUL section. If brake components are considered satisfactory, reinstall the brake drum and wheel then continue with adjustment procedure. Tighten front axle nut to 50-80 N.m (36-58 ft.-lbs.) and wheel nuts to 20-31 N.m (14.5-22.5 ft.-lbs.) torque.

To adjust front brakes, support front of vehicle so tires clear the ground. Remove rubber plug from hole (H) in brake drum and align hole with one of the adjuster wheels in brake shoe anchor (22). Using a suitable screwdriver through hole (H), rotate adjuster in the direction required to lock brake shoe against drum. With brake shoe fully expanded, slowly back off adjuster one notch at a time until wheel can be rotated without brake shoe dragging on drum. Repeat adjustment procedure for remaining brake shoe. Actuate front brake lever several times then check for brake shoe drag. Readjust

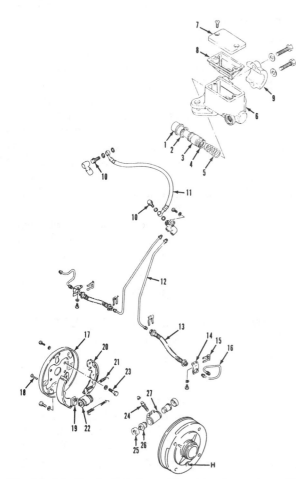

Fig. S9-17—Exploded view of front brake system. When assembled, access to brake shoe adjusters is through hole (H) in brake drum.

1. Boot	
2. Snap ring	15. Hose retainer
3. Piston & cup	16. Brake line
4. Primary cup	17. Backing plate
5. Spring	18. Pin
6. Reservoir & housing	19. Spring clip
7. Cap	20. Shoe
8. Diaphragm	21. Spring
9. Clamp	22. Shoe anchor
10. Union cap screw	23. Cap screw
11. Brake hose	24. Bleed screw
12. Brake line	25. Boot
13. Brake hose	26. Piston & cup
14. Bracket	27. Slave cylinder

Fig. S9-18—Front brake bleeder screw is located at (B) on each front wheel cylinder.

if required. Adjust brake shoes in opposite brake assembly as just described.

R&R AND OVERHAUL. Refer to Fig. S9-17 for an exploded view of front brake system. To remove drum brake components (17 through 27), first remove brake drums as outlined in INSPECTION AND ADJUSTMENT section.

WARNING: Inhaling asbestos brake dust is injurious to human health. Approved OSHA respiration equipment must be worn when working on or around brake components. DO NOT use compressed air to clean brake drums, shoes or nearby components as brake dust will be blown into air. Only vacuum equipment designed to pick up brake dust should be used.

Rotate pins (18) 90° to release clips (19). Carefully expand brake shoes (20) to clear shoe locating slots in wheel cylinder pistons (26) and brake shoe anchor (22). Withdraw brake shoes and springs (21). Detach brake line (16) from wheel cylinder (27) and plug line to reduce fluid loss. Unbolt and remove wheel cylinder assembly (24 through 27) and shoe anchor with adjuster assembly (22) from backing plate (17).

Inspect and renew any components that are damaged or worn excessively. The flexible brake hoses (11 and 13) should be renewed if cracks, splits or chaffing is evident or if hoses have been in service for four years.

To overhaul wheel cylinders (24 through 27), disassemble cylinder noting location and direction of components. Inspect cylinder bore for damage due to corrosion or scoring. Renew complete wheel cylinder if excessive damage is evident. Superficial damage may be removed using a suitable cylinder hone. After honing, rinse cylinder with clean brake fluid. Shake out excess fluid but do not wipe dry. Using a shop towel or rag to dry cylinder will leave lint particles in bore. Renew boots (25) and piston cups (26). During reassembly, lubricate components with clean brake fluid. Apply a suitable sealer to wheel cylinder contact area on backing plate and install wheel cylinder. Tighten wheel cylinder retaining cap screws to 6-9 N·m (54-78 in.-lbs.) torque and attach brake line (16).

Disassemble and clean brake shoe anchor and adjuster (22). Lubricate adjuster threads with oil and ensure adjusters will rotate freely. Lightly coat anchor bores with grease and insert adjusters. Screw adjusters completely in to allow installation of new brake shoes. Apply a suitable sealer to brake shoe anchor contact area on backing plate and install anchor. Tighten anchor retaining cap screws to 15-22 N·m (11-16 ft.-lbs.) torque.

Apply a light coat of grease to brake shoe locating slots in wheel cylinder and shoe anchor. Apply a light coat of silicone grease to three brake shoe-to-backing plate contact points on each shoe. Install the brake shoes and springs with spring intermediate sections opposing each other. Secure brake shoes with pins (18) and clips (19). Install brake drum and tighten axle nut to 50-80 N·m (36-58 ft.-lbs.) torque. Install tire and wheel and tighten wheel retaining nuts to 20-31 N·m (15-22 ft.-lbs.) torque.

Adjust front brakes as outlined in INSPECTION AND ADJUSTMENT section. If master cylinder overhaul is necessary, proceed to MASTER CYLINDER section. Fill and bleed brake system as outlined in BLEEDING section.

MASTER CYLINDER. To remove front brake master cylinder (6—Fig. S9-17), remove union cap screw (10) at master cylinder. Brake fluid will remove paint; be careful when removing master cylinder. Remove the two retaining cap screws and withdraw master cylinder. Remove brake lever, reservoir cap (7) and diaphragm (8). Remove dust boot (1) and snap ring (2). Disassemble plunger assembly while noting location and direction of components. Inspect cylinder bore for damage due to corrosion or scoring. Renew complete master cylinder if excessive damage is evident. Superficial damage may be removed using a suitable cylinder hone. After honing, rinse cylinder with clean brake fluid. Shake out excess fluid but do not wipe dry. Using a shop towel or rag to dry cylinder will leave lint particles in bore. Renew boot (1) and primary and secondary cups (3 and 4). During reassembly, lubricate components with clean brake fluid. Reassembly is the reverse of disassembly. Bleed brakes as outlined in BLEEDING section.

FRONT AXLE ASSEMBLY

R&R AND OVERHAUL. Refer to Fig. S9-20 for an exploded view of front axle assembly used. To remove either wheel hub (32), remove front wheel and castle nut (38). Pull wheel hub (32) from spindle (26). Do not lose spacer (36). Remove seal (35) and drive bearings (28 and 33) and spacer (29) from hub if necessary.

To reassemble, reverse disassembly procedure while noting the following: Install inner bearing (28) into hub first. Tighten nut (38) to 50-80 N·m (36-58 ft.-lbs.) and wheel retaining nuts (42) to 20-31 N·m (15-22 ft.-lbs.) torque.

STEERING

ADJUSTMENT. The toe-in should be checked and adjusted after the first 200 km (125 miles) of operation and every 1000 km (600 miles) thereafter. Prior to toe-in adjustment, inspect steering assembly for damaged or excessively worn components. If service to steering assembly is required, refer to R&R AND OVERHAUL section.

To check toe-in, inflate tires to recommended pressure listed in CONDENSED SERVICE DATA. Position vehicle on a flat smooth surface and set handlebars straight forward. Using a suitable tape measure, measure distance between right and left tire centerlines on back side of tires (B—Fig. S9-21) and record measurement. Locate the same tire centerline points on front side of tires (F) and record measurement. The front measurement should be 11-19 mm (0.43-0.75 in.) less than rear measurement. Note that the distance from a projected vehicle centerline to left (L) and right (R) tire centerlines should also be equal.

To adjust, loosen tie rod locknuts (17—Fig. S9-20) on both left and right tie rods. The tie rod ends and locknuts color coded yellow have left-hand threads. Rotate tie rod sleeves (18) in equal increments to maintain equal vehicle centerline to left and right tire centerline distances. Tighten tie rod locknuts (17) to 22-35 N·m (16.0-25.5 ft.-lbs.) torque.

R&R AND OVERHAUL. Refer to Fig. S9-20 for an exploded view of steering assembly. To remove either

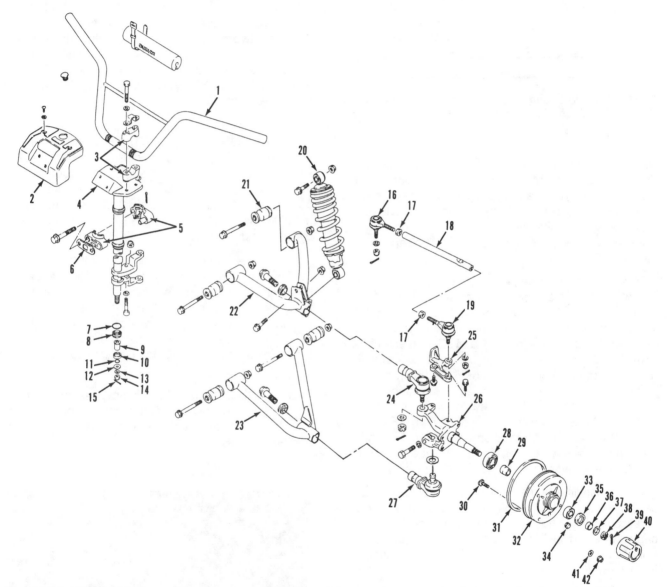

Fig. S9-20—Exploded view of steering, suspension and front axle assembly. Refer to Fig. S9-17 for front brake components.

1. Handlebar assy.	12. Flat washer	22. Upper control arm	32. Brake drum & hub
2. Cover	13. Lockwasher	23. Lower control arm	33. Bearing
3. Handlebar mounting clamps	14. Nut	24. Upper ball joint	34. Plug
4. Steering shaft	15. Cotter pin	25. Steering spindle arm	35. Seal
5. Shaft holders	16. Inner tie rod end	26. Spindle assy.	36. Spacer
6. Washer plate	17. Locknut	27. Lower ball joint	37. Washer
7. Seal circlip	18. Tie rod sleeve	28. Bearing	38. Castle nut
8. Dust seal	19. Outer tie rod end	29. Bearing spacer	39. Cotter pin
9. Lower bushing	20. Shock absorber	30. Wheel stud	40. Cap
10. Dust seal	21. Bushing	31. Dust seal	41. Washer
11. "O" ring			42. Wheel nut

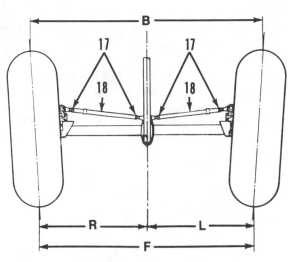

Fig. S9-21—Toe-in should be 11-19 mm (0.43-0.75 in.). Refer to text for measuring procedure.

spindle (26), first remove wheel hub (32) as outlined in FRONT AXLE ASSEMBLY section. Remove brake lines (16—Fig. S9-17) and backing plate retaining cap screws (23). Withdraw backing plate, brake shoes and cylinders as an assembly. Remainder of steering component disassembly is evident after inspection of unit and referral to Fig. S9-20.

During reassembly, renew all cotter pins. Lubricate all friction points with a good quality grease. Tighten steering shaft holder (5) cap screws to 18-28 N•m (13-20 ft.-lbs.); steering shaft lower nut (14) to 38-60 N•m (27.5-43.5 ft.-lbs.); ball joint (24 and 27) cap screws to 120-170 N•m (87-123 ft.-lbs.); ball joint (24) spindle retaining nut to 35-50 N•m (25.5-36.0 ft.-lbs.); spindle arm (25) cap screw to 35-45 N•m (25.5-32.5 ft.-lbs.); ball joint (27) spindle retaining screw to 44-68 N•m (32.0-47.5 ft.-lbs.) and tie rod end nut to 22-35 N•m (16.0-25.5 ft.-lbs.) torque. Coat threads on ball joint (27) spindle retaining cap screw and spindle arm (25) cap screw with Loctite or equivalent prior to installation.

When installing brake assemblies, apply a suitable sealer around holes for backing plate retaining cap screws on brake shoe side plate. Tighten backing plate cap screws to 18-28 N•m (13-20 ft.-lbs.) torque. Bleed front brakes as outlined in BLEEDING paragraphs of FRONT BRAKES section.

FRONT SUSPENSION

A double wishbone-type front suspension and oil dampened shock absorbers are used. Shock absorbers have five load settings. Refer to Fig. S9-20 for exploded view of suspension components. The suspension components should be periodically inspected for excessive wear and damage. Removal and disassembly is evident after inspection of unit and referral to exploded view.

During reassembly, upper and lower control arm (22 and 23) cap screws should be tightened to 48-72 N•m (34.5-52.0 ft.-lbs.) while ball joint (24 and 27) cap screws should be tightened to 120-170 N•m (87-123 ft.-lbs.) torque. Tighten shock absorber (20) retaining cap screws to 44-66 N•m (32-48 ft.-lbs.) torque.

REAR BRAKE ASSEMBLY

Independently operated front and rear brakes are used. The rear brake system has one mechanically actuated two-shoe internal expanding drum brake mounted on rear axle housing. The right foot pedal operates the rear brake via a brake cable. Refer to FRONT BRAKE ASSEMBLY section for information on front brake system.

INSPECTION AND ADJUSTMENT. The brake system should be inspected and adjusted after the first 200 km (125 miles) of operation and every 1000 km (600 miles) thereafter. To adjust rear brake, actuate brake pedal and measure free travel at end of pedal. Free travel should be 20-30 mm (0.8-1.2 in.) and is adjusted by rotating pedal adjuster (P—S9-25).

A rear brake lining wear indicator mark (I) scribed on rear brake shoe cam is used to externally determine brake lining wear limit. To externally check rear brake lining wear, apply rear brake and note the bottom edge location of indicator (I) with stationary mark (M). If indicator (I) does not rotate beyond wear mark (M), brake linings may be considered satisfactory.

R&R AND OVERHAUL. To remove rear brake shoes for inspection or renewal, first suitably support rear of vehicle and remove right rear axle nut. Pull tire, wheel and hub off axle as an assembly.

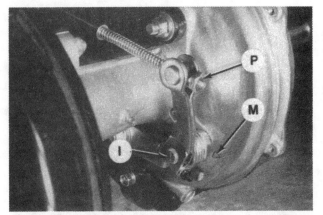

Fig. S9-25—Adjust rear brake pedal free travel by rotating adjuster (P). Use indicator mark (I) on brake shoe cam and stationary mark (M) on axle housing to determine rear brake lining wear. Refer to text.

WARNING: Inhaling asbestos brake dust is injurious to human health. Approved OSHA respiration equipment must be worn when working on or around brake components. DO NOT use compressed air to clean brake drums, shoes or nearby components as brake dust will be blown into air. Only vacuum equipment designed to pick up brake dust should be used.

Unbolt and remove brake drum cover (3—Fig. S9-26). Remove drum retaining nuts (4). Drum retaining nuts (4) have left-hand threads. Slide brake drum (5) off axle. Carefully extract brake shoes (7) and springs (6) from backing plate.

Brake shoes should be renewed if linings are worn to 1.5 mm (0.06 in.) or less. Brake drum should be renewed if inside diameter exceeds 180.7 mm (7.11 in.).

Reinstall brake shoes by reversing removal procedure while noting the following: Lightly coat brake camshaft and anchor pin with grease. Lightly coat splined portion of axle for brake drum with grease. Apply Loctite or equivalent to threads of drum retaining nuts and tighten both nuts to 160-220 N·m (115.5-144.5 ft.-lbs.) torque. Tighten axle nut to 85-115 N·m (61.5-83.0 ft.-lbs.) torque. Adjust rear brake as outlined in ADJUSTMENT paragraphs.

Fig. S9-28—View of rear axle showing location of axle housing retaining nuts (N), chain adjuster locknuts (L) and chain adjuster cap screws (S).

DRIVE CHAIN AND SPROCKETS

INSPECTION AND ADJUSTMENT. The drive chain should be inspected every month and adjusted if needed. Improper maintenance and neglect can cause early failure of both drive chain and sprockets. To determine drive chain wear, remove seat, rear fender, gearshift lever and engine sprocket cover. Release chain case clamps and remove the one retaining screw. Slide chain case toward left wheel. Loosen the four axle housing retaining nuts (N—Fig. S9-28) and two chain adjuster locknuts (L). Tighten chain adjuster cap screws (S) so all slack is removed from chain. The drive chain should be renewed if the distance measured in a straight line between 21 chain link pins exceeds 319.4 mm (12.57 in.). Refer to R&R AND OVERHAUL paragraphs for chain renewal information. If chain is considered satisfactory, continue with adjustment procedure.

Drive chain free play should be 20-30 mm (0.8-1.2 in.) measured midway between sprockets. To adjust chain fee play, loosen the four axle housing retaining nuts and two chain adjuster locknuts as previously described. Rotate right and left adjuster cap screws (S) equally in the direction required for specified chain free play. Tighten axle housing retaining nuts to 48-72 N·m (34.5-52.0 ft.-lbs.) torque.

R&R AND OVERHAUL. To remove drive chain and sprockets, remove seat, rear fender, gear shift lever, engine sprocket cover and chain case cover clamps and screw. Suitably support rear of vehicle and remove left axle nut (27—Fig. S9-29). Slide tire, wheel and hub from axle as an assembly. Remove chain case cover. Loosen the four axle housing retaining nuts and two chain adjuster locknuts. Rotate chain adjuster screws to slacken chain and remove the engine sprocket retaining snap ring. Withdraw engine sprocket and drive chain. Bend back tabs on rear sprocket lock plates (23) and remove nuts (30). Slide rear sprocket (22) off axle.

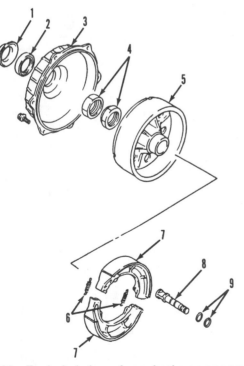

Fig. S9-26—Exploded view of rear brake components.

1. Outer dust seal
2. Dust seal
3. Drum cover
4. Nuts
5. Drum
6. Springs
7. Brake shoes
8. Brake shoe cam
9. "O" rings

Carefully examine engine and rear sprockets for excessive wear. Worn sprockets will usually have a hooked profile. A good test is to place a new chain on a used sprocket and check the fit. Wear on sprocket sides indicates misalignment. If sprockets require renewal due to wear, always renew drive chain.

Standard chain on Model LT300E has 92 links while chain on Model LT-F300 has 90 links. Standard engine sprocket has 11 teeth on Model LT300E and nine teeth on Model LT-F300. Standard rear sprocket has 41 teeth on all models.

Reinstall by reversing removal procedure while noting the following: Renew all lock plates and cotter pins. Tighten nuts (30) to 50-70 N·m (36.0-50.5 ft.-lbs.) torque. Bend tabs on lock plates around flats on nuts. Adjust chain free play as outlined in INSPECTION AND ADJUSTMENT section.

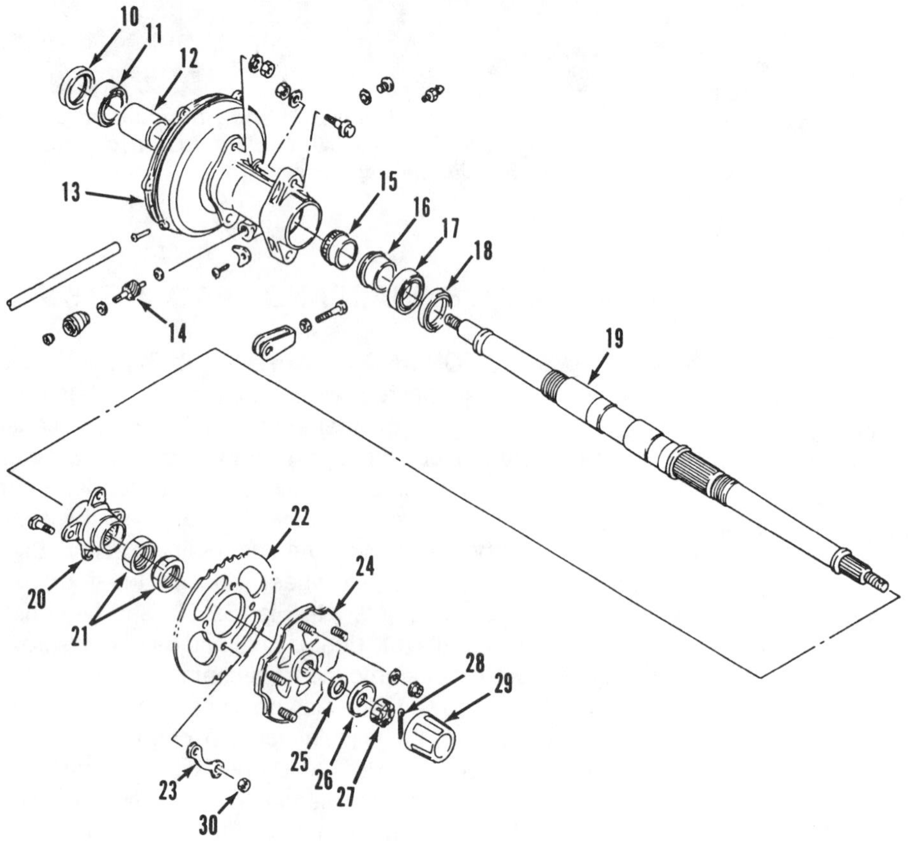

Fig. S9-29—Exploded view of axle housing and related components.

10. Seal
11. Bearing
12. Spacer
13. Axle housing
14. Speedometer driven gear
15. Speedometer drive gear
16. Spacer
17. Bearing
18. Seal
19. Axle shaft
20. Sprocket mounting flange
21. Axle nuts
22. Sprocket
23. Lock plate
24. Hub
25. Washer
26. Cap retainer
27. Axle nut
28. Cotter pin
29. Cap
30. Nut

SUZUKI

LT500R

NOTE: Metric fasteners are used throughout vehicle.

CONDENSED SERVICE DATA

MODEL	LT500R
General	
Engine Make	Suzuki
Engine Type	Two-Stroke; Water-Cooled
Number of Cylinders	1
Bore	86 mm
	(3.4 in.)
Stroke	86 mm
	(3.4 in.)
Displacement	499 cc
	(30.4 cu. in.)
Compression Ratio	6.3:1
Fuel Recommendation	Unleaded or Low-Lead
Pump Octane Rating	85-95
Engine Lubrication	Fuel:Oil Premix
Fuel:Oil Ratio	20:1
Forward Speeds	5
Reverse Speeds	N/A
Tire Size:	
Front	21 × 7.00-10
Rear	20 × 11.00-10
Tire Pressure (cold):	
Front	30 kPa*
	(4.4 psi)
Rear	25 kPa*
	(3.6 psi)
Dry Weight	133 kg
	(293 lbs.)

*Increase front and rear tire pressure to 35 kPa (5.0 psi) when load exceeds 80 kg (175 lbs.).

Tune-Up	
Engine Idle Speed	1350-1450 rpm
Spark Plug:	
NGK	B8EGV
Electrode Gap	0.55-0.65 mm
	(0.022-0.026 in.)
Ignition:	
Type	Breakerless
Timing	4° BTDC @ 1000 rpm
	12° BTDC @ 9000 rpm
Carburetor:	
Make	Mikuni
Model	TM38SS
Bore Size	38 mm
	(1.5 in.)
Float Height	10.4-12.4 mm
	(0.41-0.49 in.)

Tune-Up (Cont.)
Carburetor: (Cont.)

Jet Needle	6DK3
Clip Position.	3rd Groove From Top
Pilot Jet	#22.5
Needle Jet	R-2
Main Jet	#350
Throttle Cut-Away	4.0
Throttle Cable Free Play	0.5-1.0 mm
	(0.02-0.04 in.)

Sizes-Clearances

Reed Petal Stand Open (Max.)	0.2 mm
	(0.008 in.)
Cylinder Head Distortion (Max.).	0.05 mm
	(0.002 in.)
Piston-to-Cylinder Wall Clearance	0.080-0.090 mm
	(0.0031-0.0035 in.)
Wear Limit	0.120 mm
	(0.0047 in.)
Cylinder Bore Diameter	86.000-86.015 mm
	(3.3858-3.3864 in.)
Wear Limit	86.050 mm
	(3.3882 in.)
Cylinder Bore Distortion (Max.)	0.05 mm
	(0.002 in.)
Piston Diameter Measured 33 mm	
(1.3 in.) from Skirt Bottom	85.915-85.930 mm
	(3.3825-3.3831 in.)
Wear Limit	85.880 mm
	(3.3811 in.)
Piston Pin Bore Diameter	18.002-18.012 mm
	(0.7087-0.7091 in.)
Wear Limit	18.030 mm
	(0.7098 in.)
Piston Pin Bore Diameter	17.994-18.000 mm
	(0.7084-0.7087 in.)
Wear Limit	17.980 mm
	(0.7079 in.)
Piston Ring End Gap	0.3-0.5 mm
	(0.01-0.02 in.)
Wear Limit	0.85 mm
	(0.033 in.)
Piston Ring Side Clearance.	0.01-0.07 mm
	(0.0004-0.0028 in.)
Connecting Rod Small	
End Bore Diameter	23.000-23.011 mm
	(0.9055-0.9059 in.)
Wear Limit	23.040 mm
	(0.9071 in.)

Capacities

Fuel Tank	13 L
	(3.43 gal.)
Cooling System	1700 mL
	(1.8 qt.)
Transmission Sump	See Text

Tightening Torques

Clutch Sleeve Hub Nut	40-60 N·m (29.0-43.5 ft.-lbs.)

Cylinder Nut:

6 mm	8-12 N·m (6.0-8.5 ft.-lbs.)
10 mm	36-40 N·m (26-29 ft.-lbs.)
Cylinder Head Nut	26-30 N·m (19.0-21.5 ft.-lbs.)

Engine Mounting Bolts:

265 mm (1.04 in.) long.	37-45 N·m (27.0-32.5 ft.-lbs.)
All Other Bolts	28-34 N·m (20.0-24.5 ft.-lbs.)
Engine Mounting Bracket Bolts	28-34 N·m (20.0-24.5 ft.-lbs.)
Engine Sprocket Nut	80-100 N·m (58.0-72.5 ft.-lbs.)
Flywheel Nut	90-100 N·m (65.0-72.5 ft.-lbs.)
Front Axle Nuts	50-80 N·m (36-58 ft.-lbs.)
Impeller Cap Screw	8-12 N·m (6.0-8.5 ft.-lbs.)
Rear Axle Nuts.	85-115 N·m (61.5-83.0 ft.-lbs.)

Wheel Retaining Nuts:

Front	20-31 N·m (14.5-22.5 ft.-lbs.)
Rear.	45-65 N·m (32.5-47.0 ft.-lbs.)

Standard Screws:
Unmarked or Marked "4"

4 mm	1.0-2.0 N·m (8.9-18 in.-lbs.)
5 mm	2.0-4.0 N·m (18-36 in.-lbs.)
6 mm	4.0-7.0 N·m (36-62 in.-lbs.)
8 mm	10-16 N·m (88.5-142 in.-lbs.)
10 mm	22-35 N·m (16-26 ft.-lbs.)
12 mm	35-55 N·m (26-40 ft.-lbs.)
14 mm	50-80 N·m (37-59 ft.-lbs.)
16 mm	80-130 N·m (59-96 ft.-lbs.)
18 mm	130-190 N·m (96-140 ft.-lbs.)

Marked "7"

4 mm	1.5-3.0 N·m (13-27 in.-lbs.)
5 mm	3.0-6.0 N·m (27-53 in.-lbs.)

Tightening Torques (Cont.)
Standard Screws: (Cont.)
  Marked "7" (Cont.)

6 mm	8.0-12.0 N·m
	(71-106 in.-lbs.)
8 mm	18-28 N·m
	(13-21 ft.-lbs.)
10 mm	40-60 N·m
	(29-44 ft.-lbs.)
12 mm	70-100 N·m
	(52-74 ft.-lbs.)
14 mm	110-160 N·m
	(81-118 ft.-lbs.)
16 mm	170-250 N·m
	(125-184 ft.-lbs.)
18 mm	200-280 N·m
	(147-206 ft.-lbs.)

LUBRICATION

ENGINE. The engine is lubricated by oil mixed with fuel. Recommended oil is Suzuki CCI Super 2-Cycle Motor Lubricant mixed at a fuel:oil ratio of 20:1.

TRANSMISSION. Recommended transmission lubricant is SAE 20W-40 motor oil. The manufacturer recommends changing transmission oil after the first month or 200 km (125 miles) of operation and every six months or 2000 km (1200 miles) thereafter.

Fill the transmission sump through filler cap (F—Fig. S11-1) opening. Oil level should be maintained at level plug (L) opening. Drain sump by removing plug in underside of sump. Dry capacity of sump is 1100 mL (1.16 qt.). Refilling sump after a routine oil change requires only 1000 mL (1.06 qt.) of oil as some oil will be retained by case castings.

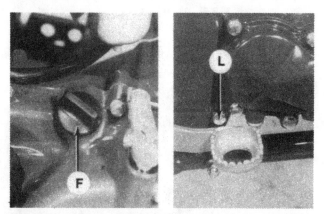

Fig. S11-1—Transmission oil is poured through filler plug opening (F) and maintained at level of oil level plug (L) opening.

DRIVE CHAIN. The final drive chain should be inspected and lubricated with SAE 90 gear oil prior to each operating interval. Periodically the drive chain should be thoroughly washed in kerosene and lubricated.

Refer to DRIVE CHAIN AND SPROCKETS section for chain renewal and adjustment information.

CABLES, LEVERS, SHAFTS AND BEARINGS. The choke cable, throttle cable and throttle lever should be lubricated every three months or 1000 km (600 miles) with motor oil. The front wheel bearings, steering shaft and rear wheel bearings should be greased every three months or 1000 km (600 miles) to ensure component longevity.

AIR CLEANER ELEMENT

The air cleaner element should be removed and cleaned after every three months or 1000 km (600 miles) of operation. To remove air cleaner element, first remove seat and element cover. Remove element retaining clip and withdraw element. Carefully separate the two foam elements from the frame.

Thoroughly clean element in a suitable nonflammable solvent. Saturate element in clean motor oil. Compress element to remove excess oil. Reinstall element by reversing removal procedure.

FUEL SYSTEM

CARBURETOR. A Mikuni TM38SS-type carburetor is used. Refer to CONDENSED SERVICE DATA for carburetor specifications.

Before performing carburetor adjustments, throttle cable should be carefully adjusted to provide 0.5-1.0 mm (0.02-0.04 in.) free play (P—Fig. S11-3) at idle position. Cable adjustment is accomplished by first sliding dust boot (B) down throttle cable at handlebar lever. Loosen cable locknut (N) and rotate cable adjuster (A) as required. Tighten locknut (N) to secure adjustment and reinstall dust boot (B).

Initially adjust idle mixture screw (16—Fig. S11-4) 1½ turns out from a lightly seated position. Start engine and allow the engine to warm-up to normal operating temperature, then adjust idle speed screw (12) so engine idles at 1350-1450 rpm. Rotate idle mixture screw (16) until engine idles at highest rpm, then adjust idle speed screw (12) until the recommended idle speed is obtained. After adjusting carburetor, check throttle cable adjustment as previously described.

The carburetor should be removed, disassembled and cleaned if carburetor malfunction is determined. Disassembly of the removed carburetor is evident after inspection of unit and referral to exploded view in Fig.

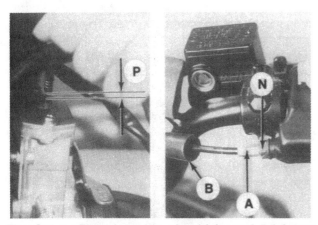

Fig. S11-3—Throttle cable should have 0.5-1.0 mm (0.02-0.04 in.) free play (P) at idle position. To adjust, slide dust boot (B) down throttle cable and loosen cable locknut (N) and rotate cable adjuster (A) as required.

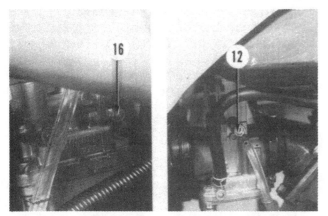

Fig. S11-4—View of installed carburetor showing location of idle speed screw (12) and idle mixture screw (16).

S11-5. Carefully inspect jet needle (8), inlet valve (20) and idle speed screw (12) for excessive wear and damage.

During reassembly, renew all gaskets. Clip (7) should be in third groove from top on jet needle (8). To check float height, remove float bowl (27) and invert carburetor. Distance (A—Fig. S11-6) between bottom of carburetor body (11) and float arm (24) should be 10.4-12.4 mm (0.41-0.49 in.). If float height (A) is incorrect, bend

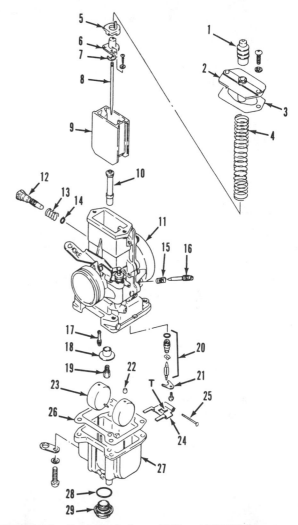

Fig. S11-5—Exploded view of Mikuni TM38SS type carburetor.

T. Tang
1. Boot
2. Plate
3. Gasket
4. Spring
5. Cable stopper ring
6. Cable stopper plate
7. Clip
8. Jet needle
9. Throttle valve
10. Needle jet
11. Body
12. Idle speed screw
13. Spring
14. "O" ring
16. Idle mixture screw
17. Pilot jet
18. Baffle ring
19. Main jet
20. Inlet valve
21. Inlet valve retainer
22. Pin
23. Float
24. Float arm
25. Float pin
26. Gasket
27. Float bowl
28. "O" ring
29. Drain plug

Fig. S11-6—Float height (A) should be 10.4-12.4 mm (0.41-0.49 in.) when measured between bottom of carburetor body (11) and float arm (24). Bend float arm tang (T—Fig. S11-5) to adjust.

tang (T—Fig. S11-5) on float arm as needed to obtain correct float height.

FUEL STRAINER. A strainer is mounted on the end of the "ON" pickup tube and the "RES" (reserve) pickup tube of the fuel valve assembly mounted on the fuel tank. The strainers should be cleaned periodically to prevent fuel starvation. To gain access to strainers, drain fuel tank and detach fuel hose. Remove cap screws and withdraw fuel valve assembly with strainers from fuel tank. Reinstall by reversing removal procedure.

COOLING SYSTEM

INSPECTION. The engine is liquid-cooled. A one-piece radiator is used. Renew either radiator hose if cracked, split or any other damage is evident. The radiator hoses should be renewed at least every two years. Inspect all other cooling system components and renew if leakage or damage is noted.

Fig. S11-8—View of radiator cap (C) and cooling system drain plug (D).

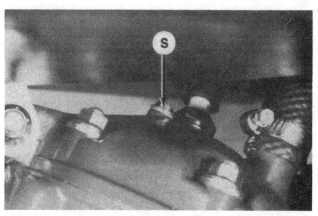

Fig. S11-9—View of cooling system air bleed screw (S) in cylinder head.

CHANGING COOLANT. The manufacturer recommends using a 50 percent distilled water to 50 percent antifreeze mixture in the cooling system.

NOTE: Distilled water must be used to prevent corroding and clogging of the aluminum radiator. An antifreeze that is designed for a cooling system with aluminum components must be used.

Cooling system capacity is 1700 mL (1.8 qt.). The closed engine system holds 1500 mL (1.59 qt.) and the reserve tank holds 200 mL (0.21 qt.).

To drain coolant, remove the radiator cover and remove radiator cap (C—Fig. S11-8) and drain plug (D) in water pump housing. Allow coolant to drain into a suitable container.

Before refilling cooling system, install and tighten drain plug (D). Loosen air bleed screw (S—Fig. S11-9) in cylinder head. Pour the recommended coolant mixture into radiator cap (C—Fig. S11-8) opening. Tighten air bleed screw (S—Fig. S11-9) when coolant mixture begins to flow from around screw threads.

NOTE: The vehicle may need to be operated and allowed to cool in order to remove any air pockets within system. After system has cooled, remove radiator cap (C) and complete filling of cooling system.

Fill the cooling system reserve tank to the recommended level.

RADIATOR CAP. Radiator cap (C—Fig. S11-8) should have a relief opening pressure of 95-125 kPa (13.7-18.1 psi).

IGNITION AND ELECTRICAL

SPARK PLUG. Standard spark plug is NGK B8EGV. Spark plug electrode gap should be 0.55-0.65 mm (0.022-0.026 in.)

Spark plug should be removed, cleaned and electrode gap set every three months or 1000 km (600 miles) and renewed every six months or 2000 km (1200 miles).

IGNITION. All models are equipped with a capacitor discharge, pointless electronic ignition system. The ignition system consists of the flywheel, a power source coil located underneath the flywheel, an externally mounted pickup coil, a CD ignition module, an ignition coil, an ignition switch and an engine stop switch. Ignition timing should occur at 4° BTDC with engine operating at 1000 rpm and at 12° BTDC with engine operating at 9000 rpm. Ignition timing is fixed and not adjustable.

If ignition malfunctions, check condition of spark plug, all wires and connections before troubleshooting ignition circuit. Using Suzuki pocket tester 09900-25002 or a suitable ohmmeter, refer to the following test specifications and procedures to aid in troubleshooting.

To check power source coil, separate wire connectors leading from power source coil to CDI module and attach one tester lead to coil end of black wire with red tracer. Attach remaining tester lead to black wire with white tracer. Power source coil can be considered satisfactory if resistance reading is within the limits of 315-475 ohms.

To check pickup coil, separate wire connectors leading from pickup coil to CDI module and attach one tester lead to coil end of blue wire. Attach remaining tester lead to black wire with white tracer. Pickup coil can be considered satisfactory if resistance reading is within the limits of 175-265 ohms.

To check condition of ignition coil, separate black wire connector from coil to CD ignition module and remove high-tension wire from spark plug. Attach one tester lead to black wire terminal on coil and remaining tester lead to coil ground. Primary coil resistance reading should be approximately 0-1.0 ohm. Attach one tester lead to high-tension wire and remaining tester lead to coil ground. Secondary coil resistance reading should be approximately 3k-5k ohms.

LIGHT CIRCUIT. All models are equipped with a lighting coil located underneath the flywheel. The lighting coil should produce above 12 volts at 3000 rpm and below 18 volts at 8000 rpm.

To statically check lighting coil, separate wire connectors leading from lighting coil to light switch and attach one tester lead to coil end of yellow wire with red tracer. Attach remaining tester lead to black wire with white tracer. Lighting coil can be considered satisfactory if resistance reading is within the limits of 0.5-1.0 ohm.

WIRING. If wiring requires repair, always use replacement wire of the same gauge. Wires should be routed away from areas of extreme heat or sharp edges. Plastic tie straps should be used to retain wires in their original positions to prevent short circuiting. Refer to Fig. S11-11 for schematic wiring diagram.

FASTENERS

After the first 200 km (125 miles) of operation and every 1000 km (600 miles) thereafter, the cylinder head, cylinder, exhaust system, engine mounts and all chassis

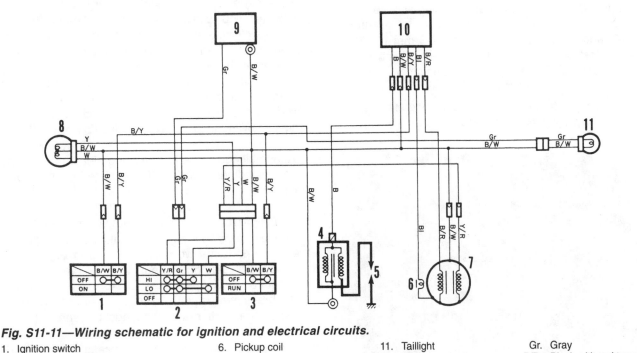

Fig. S11-11—Wiring schematic for ignition and electrical circuits.

1. Ignition switch
2. Lighting/dimmer switch
3. Engine stop switch
4. Ignition coil
5. Spark plug
6. Pickup coil
7. Magneto
8. Headlight
9. Regulator
10. CDI module
11. Taillight
B. Black
W. White
Y. Yellow
Bl. Blue
Gr. Gray
B/R. Black with red tracer
B/W. Black with white tracer
B/Y. Black with yellow tracer
Y/R. Yellow with red tracer

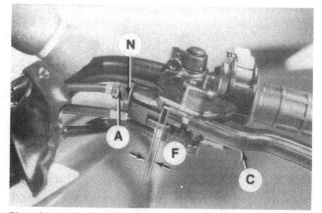

Fig. S11-13—Clutch lever (C) should have 2-3 mm (0.079-0.118 in.) free play (F) at idle position. Refer to text for adjustment procedures.

nuts or bolts should be retightened. Refer to TIGHTENING TORQUES section of CONDENSED SERVICE DATA for torque specifications.

CLUTCH

ADJUSTMENT. A multiple-disc-type clutch manually actuated by left handlebar lever is used. The clutch lever adjustment should be checked after the first month or 200 km (125 miles) of operation and every six months or 2000 km (1200 miles) thereafter.

The clutch lever should have 2-3 mm (0.079-0.118 in.) of free play measured at clutch lever (C—Fig. S11-13) as shown at (F). Clutch lever free play can be adjusted by first loosening locknut (N) and rotating adjuster nut (A) completely inward. Then, loosen locknut (L—Fig. S11-14) and rotate adjuster (R) until 2-3 mm (0.079-0.118 in.) free play is obtained at handlebar clutch lever (C—Fig. S11-13). Tighten the cable securing locknuts to retain clutch cable adjustment.

Properly operated, the clutch should disengage and engage freely. Difficulty in shifting, clutch grabbing or

Fig. S11-14—Loosen locknut (L) and rotate adjuster nut (R) as outlined in text to adjust clutch lever (C—Fig. S11-13) free play.

slipping may indicate disassembly and repair of clutch unit is required.

FRONT BRAKE ASSEMBLY

Independently operated front and rear brakes are used. The front brake system has hydraulically actuated disc brake assemblies mounted on each front spindle. A handlebar mounted master cylinder with fluid reservoir supplies pressure to each wheel caliper assembly when actuated by right handlebar lever. Information on rear brake system is outlined in REAR BRAKE ASSEMBLY section.

Only DOT 3 or DOT 4 glycol-based brake fluid should be used in front brake system. The use of other types of brake fluids such as petroleum-based or silicone-based fluids may damage hydraulic components resulting in brake system failure. Under normal operating conditions, brake fluid will absorb small amounts of moisture which can cause pitting to caliper bore surface resulting in early brake caliper failure. Drain and refill hydraulic system with new brake fluid every two years to reduce corrosion damage.

BLEEDING. Any operation that required draining or repair of hydraulic brake components will make it necessary to fill and bleed brake system. Check reservoir fluid level before proceeding. Remove cap (1—Fig. S11-15), diaphragm (2) and fill reservoir with DOT 3 or DOT 4 glycol-based fluid only. Reinstall cap to prevent entrance of dirt or foreign materials. Remove cap (14) and attach a suitable hose such as vacuum hose to either bleeder screw (15) and submerge other end in a container filled with a small mount of brake fluid to prevent air from reentering system. Actuate brake lever several times, then hold brake lever toward handlebar. Open brake bleeder to relieve line pressure allowing fluid and air to flow into container. Close bleed screw before releasing brake lever. Do not permit reservoir to run dry while bleeding. Repeat procedure while periodically refilling fluid reservoir until all air or old fluid is removed.

Attach bleeder hose to remaining bleeder screw and repeat bleeding procedure to complete brake bleeding operation.

OVERHAUL. Brake pad thickness may be determined externally by viewing the brake pads. If neither of the brake pads are worn below the grooved limit line around the outside of the pads, then the brake pads do not require renewal because of excessive wear. If either of the brake pads is worn down to or below the grooved limit line, then both brake pads must be renewed.

WARNING: Inhaling asbestos brake dust is injurious to human health. Approved OSHA respiration equipment must be worn when working on or around brake calipers and pads. DO NOT use com-

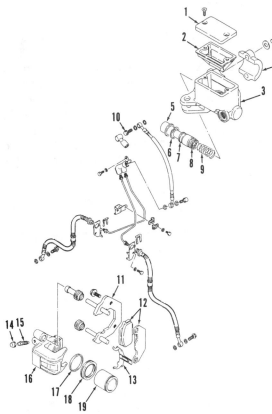

Fig. S11-15—Exploded view of front brake system.

1. Cap
2. Diaphragm
3. Reservoir & housing
4. Clamp
5. Dust boot
6. Snap ring
7. Piston & cup
8. Primary cup
9. Spring
10. Union cap screw
11. Caliper holder
12. Brake pads
13. Spring
14. Cap
15. Bleed screw
16. Caliper
17. Piston seal
18. Dust seal
19. Piston

pressed air to clean brake calipers, pads or nearby components as brake dust will be blown into air. Only vacuum equipment designed to pick up brake dust should be used.

Brake components are accessible after removing caliper mounting screws and withdrawing caliper. Push piston by hand back into caliper to allow clearance for new brake pads. Brake disc should be renewed if thickness is 3.0 mm (0.12 in.) or less or disc runout is 0.3 mm (0.012 in.) or more. Tighten screws securing brake disc to wheel hub to 15-25 N·m (11-18 ft.-lbs.). After reassembly, operate brake lever until brake lever will not pump up after continuous operation. Do not operate vehicle until correct brake operation is noted.

MASTER CYLINDER. To remove front brake master cylinder (3—Fig. S11-15), remove union cap screw (10) at master cylinder. Brake fluid will remove paint; be careful when removing master cylinder. Remove the two retaining cap screws and withdraw master cylinder.

Remove brake lever, reservoir cap (1) and diaphragm (2). Remove dust boot (5) and snap ring (6). Disassemble plunger assembly while noting location and direction of components. Inspect cylinder bore for damage due to corrosion or scoring. Renew complete master cylinder if excessive damage is evident. Superficial damage can be removed using a suitable cylinder hone. After honing, rinse cylinder with clean brake fluid. Shake out excess fluid but do not wipe dry. Using a shop towel or rag to dry cylinder will leave lint particles in bore. Renew boot (5) and primary and secondary cups (7 and 8). During reassembly, lubricate components with clean brake fluid. Reassembly is the reverse of disassembly. Tighten union cap screw (10) to 15-20 N·m (11-14.5 ft.-lbs.). Bleed brakes as outlined in BLEEDING section.

FRONT AXLE ASSEMBLY

R&R AND OVERHAUL. Refer to Fig. S11-16 for an exploded view of front axle assembly. To remove either wheel hub (42), remove front wheel, brake caliper assembly, cotter pin (48) and castle nut (47). Pull wheel hub (42) from spindle end of knuckle (35). Do not lose spacer (45). Remove seals (39 and 44) and drive bearings (40 and 43) and spacer (41) from hub if necessary.

To reassemble, reverse disassembly procedure while noting the following: Install inner bearing (40) into hub first. Tighten castle nut (47) to 50-80 N·m (36-58 ft.-lbs.) and install a new cotter pin (48). Tighten brake caliper mounting cap screws to 15-25 N·m (11-18 ft.-lbs.) and wheel retaining nuts to 20-31 N·m (14.5-22.5 ft.-lbs.).

STEERING

ADJUSTMENT. The toe-in should be checked and adjusted after the first month of 200 km (125 miles) of operation and every six months or 1000 km (600 miles) thereafter. Prior to toe-in adjustment, inspect steering assembly for damaged or excessively worn components. If service to steering assembly is required, refer to R&R AND OVERHAUL section.

To check toe-in, inflate tires to recommended pressure listed in CONDENSED SERVICE DATA. Position vehicle on a flat smooth surface and set handlebars straight forward. Position a load of 75 kg (165 lbs.) on the vehicle's seat.

Using a suitable tape measure, measure distance between right and left tire centerlines on back side of tires (B—Fig. S11-17) and record measurement. Locate the same tire centerline points on front side of tires (F) and record measurement. The front measurement should be 32-40 mm (1.3-1.6 in.) less than rear measurement. Note that the distance from a projected vehicle centerline to left (L) and right (R) tire centerlines should also be equal.

To adjust, loosen tie rod locknuts (31—Fig. S11-16) on both left and right tie rods. The tie rod ends and locknuts color coded yellow have left-hand threads.

Rotate tie rod sleeves (32) in equal increments to maintain equal vehicle centerline to left and right tire centerline distances. Tighten tie rod locknuts (31) to 35-55 N·m (25.5-40.0 ft.-lbs.).

R&R AND OVERHAUL. Refer to Fig. S11-16 for an exploded view of steering assembly. To remove either spindle (35), first remove wheel hub (42) as outlined in FRONT AXLE ASSEMBLY section. Remainder of steering component disassembly is evident after inspection of unit and referral to Fig. S11-16.

During reassembly, renew all cotter pins. Lubricate all friction points with Suzuki Super Grease "A" or a good quality grease. Tighten steering shaft holder cap screws (10) to 18-28 N·m (13-20 ft.-lbs.); steering shaft lower nut (17) to 38-60 N·m (27.5-43.5 ft.-lbs.); ball joint cap screws (27) to 120-170 N·m (87-123 ft.-lbs.); ball joint (34) knuckle retaining nut to 35-50 N·m (25.5-36.0 ft.-lbs.); knuckle arm (33) cap screws to 42.5-47.5 N·m ((30.5-34.5 ft.-lbs.); ball joint (36) knuckle retaining cap screw to 40-60 N·m (29.0-43.5 ft.-lbs.) and tie rod end nut to 27-42 N·m (20-31 ft.-lbs.). Coat threads on spindle

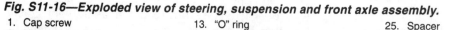

Fig. S11-16—Exploded view of steering, suspension and front axle assembly.

1. Cap screw	13. "O" ring	25. Spacer	37. Backing plate
2. Upper clamp half	14. Dust seal	26. Nut	38. Brake disc
3. Handlebar	15. Flat washer	27. Cap screw	39. Seal
4. Lower clamp half	16. Lockwasher	28. Stopper	40. Bearing
5. Steering shaft	17. Nut	29. Lower control arm	41. Spacer
6. Inner shaft holder	18. Cotter pin	30. Tie rod end	42. Hub
7. Outer shaft holder	19. Shock absorber	31. Locknut	43. Bearing
8. Plate	20. Upper control arm	32. Sleeve	44. Seal
9. Cotter pin	21. Bolt	33. Knuckle arm	45. Spacer
10. Cap screw	22. Dust seal	34. Upper ball joint	46. Washer
11. Dust seal	23. Washer	35. Lower ball joint	47. Castle nut
12. Bushing	24. Bearing	36. Lower ball joint	48. Cotter pin

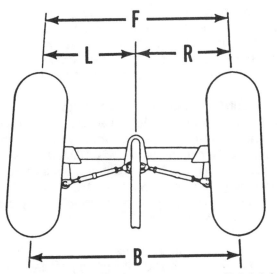

Fig. S11-17—Toe-in should be 32-40 mm (1.3-1.6 in.). Refer to text for measuring procedures.

arm (33) cap screws and ball joint cap screws (27) with Thread Lock "1303" or equivalent prior to installation.

FRONT SUSPENSION

R&R AND OVERHAUL. A double wishbone-type front suspension and oil dampened shock absorbers are used. The stiffness of the front suspension can be adjusted by varying the shock absorbers spring length and damping position. The standard spring length is 257 mm (10.1 in.) and damping position 2nd/4th. For a softer ride, leave spring length at standard setting and adjust damping position to 1st/4th. For a stiffer ride, adjust spring length to 254 mm (10 in.) and dampening position to 2nd or 3rd/4th or spring length to 247-254 mm (9.7-10.0 in.) and dampening position to 4th/4th.

Refer to Fig. S11-16 for exploded view of suspension components. The suspension components should be periodically inspected for excessive wear and damage. Removal and disassembly is evident after inspection of unit and referral to exploded view.

During reassembly, upper and lower control arm bolts (21) should be tightened to 50-70 N•m (36.0-50.5 ft.-lbs.) while ball joint cap screws (27) should be tightened to 120-170 N•m (87-123 ft.-lbs.). Tighten shock absorber retaining bolts to 40-60 N•m (29.0-43.5 ft.-lbs.).

REAR BRAKE ASSEMBLY

A single disc brake assembly is used for both rear wheels. The running brake is operated hydraulically by a foot pedal on the lower right side. The parking brake is mechanically operated by a cable and handlebar components in conjunction with the clutch lever.

BRAKE PEDAL HEIGHT ADJUSTMENT. The top of brake pedal foot pad (P—Fig. S11-21) should be 5 mm

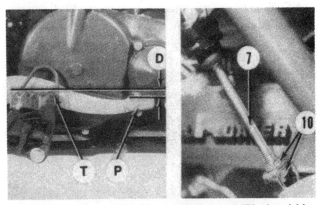

Fig. S11-21—Top of brake pedal foot pad (P) should be 5 mm (0.2 in.) lower than top of footpeg (T) measured as shown at (D). Loosen locknuts (10) and rotate master cylinder actuator rod (7) to adjust.

(0.2 in.) lower than top of footpeg (T) measured as shown at (D). To adjust, loosen locknuts (10) and rotate master cylinder actuator (7) until brake pedal foot pad (P) is 5 mm (0.2 in.) lower than footpeg (T). Tighten locknuts (10) to retain adjustment.

PARKING BRAKE ADJUSTMENT. Loosen cable locknuts (N—Fig. S11-22) and adjust cable adjuster (A) until zero or near zero free play is obtained at clutch lever when actuating parking brake, then tighten locknuts (N). Loosen locknut (21) and rotate screw (22) until seated, then turn out ¼ turn and tighten locknut (21).

BLEEDING. Make sure reservoir (3—Fig. S11-23) is full. Connect a bleed hose to bleed valve (17) on brake caliper assembly. Route the bleed hose into a suitable container. Operate rear brake foot pedal until a hardness (fluid resistance) is felt, then open bleed valve (17). Close bleed valve prior to releasing foot pedal. Continue bleeding procedure until no air bubbles are noted in discharged fluid from bleed valve.

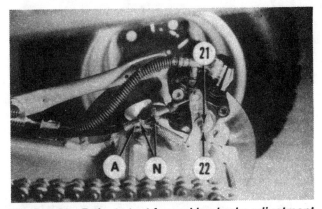

Fig. S11-22—Refer to text for parking brake adjustment procedures.

A. Adjuster	21. Locknut
N. Locknuts	22. Screw

NOTE: Make sure reservoir (3) is kept full during bleeding procedure.

When bleeding procedure is completed, add brake fluid to reservoir (3) until fluid level is at upper level line on reservoir.

OVERHAUL. Brake pad thickness may be determined externally by viewing the brake pads. If neither of the brake pads are worn below the grooved limit line around the outside of the pads, then the brake pads do not require renewal because of excessive wear. If either of the brake pads is worn down to or below the grooved limit line, then both brake pads must be renewed.

WARNING: Inhaling asbestos brake dust is injurious to human health. Approved OSHA respiration equipment must be worn when working on or around brake calipers and pads. DO NOT use compressed air to clean brake calipers, pads or nearby components as brake dust will be blown into air. Only vacuum equipment designed to pick up brake dust should be used.

Brake components are accessible after removing caliper mounting screws and withdrawing caliper. Loosen parking brake locknut (21—Fig. S11-23) and rotate screw (22) outward. Push piston by hand back into caliper to allow clearance for new brake pads. Refer to Fig. S11-23 for an exploded view of brake caliper components if complete overhaul is required. Brake disc should be renewed if thickness is 4.0 mm (0.16 in.) or less or disc runout is 0.30 mm (0.012 in.) or more. After reassembly, operate brake foot pedal until pedal will not pump up after continuous operation or refer to previous BLEEDING paragraphs if caliper assembly was overhauled. Do not operate vehicle until correct brake operation is noted. Adjust parking brake as outlined in previous PARKING BRAKE ADJUSTMENT paragraph.

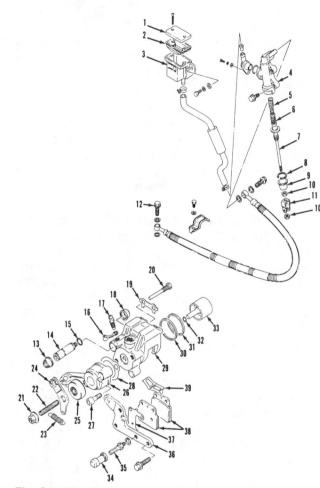

Fig. S11-23—Exploded view of rear brake system.

1. Cap
2. Diaphragm
3. Reservoir
4. Master cylinder housing
5. Spring
6. Piston assy.
7. Actuator rod
8. Snap ring
9. Dust cap
10. Locknuts
11. Clevis
12. Union cap screw
13. Dust seal
14. Caliper guide pin
15. Washer
16. Cap
17. Bleed screw
18. Dust seal
19. Lock tab
20. Brake pad screw
21. Locknut
22. Screw
23. Spring
24. Lever
25. Dust seal
26. Parking brake housing
27. Screw
28. Gasket
29. Caliper
30. Piston seal
31. Dust seal
32. "O" ring
33. Piston
34. Dust cap
35. Caliper guide pin
36. Bracket
37. Shim
38. Brake pads
39. Spring

DRIVE CHAIN AND SPROCKETS

INSPECTION AND ADJUSTMENT. The final drive chain should be inspected and adjusted, if needed, prior to each operating interval. Improper maintenance and neglect can cause early failure of both drive chain and sprockets. An endless-type drive chain is used. Distance between 20 chain links should not exceed 319.4 mm (12.57 in.). Drive chain free play should be 25-30 mm (1.0-1.2 in.) measured midway between sprockets. Chain tension is adjusted by loosening four bolts (10 and 13—Fig. 11-25) and locknuts (17). Rotate adjuster nuts (16) until correct drive chain free play is obtained. The notch (H) on each side of adjuster plate must be aligned with corresponding scale marks on each side to assure proper tracking of rear wheels and drive chain to rear sprocket alignment. Tighten sprocket side bolts (13) to 100-120 N•m (72.5-87.0 ft.-lbs.) and brake disc side bolts (10) to 70-85 N•m (50.5-61.5 ft.-lbs.). Securely tighten locknuts (17).

R&R AND OVERHAUL. Loosen four bolts (10 and 13—Fig. S11-25) and locknuts (17). Rotate adjuster nuts (16) outward and push rear axle housing toward vehicle's front to increase drive chain free play. Lift chain off rear sprocket toward left rear wheel. Use a location at rear of vehicle frame and lift rear wheels off the

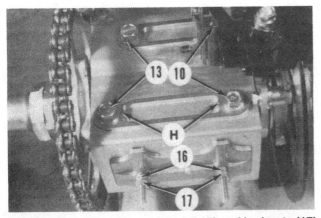

Fig. S11-25—Loosen bolts (10 and 13) and locknuts (17) and rotate adjuster nuts (16) to adjust drive chain free play. Drive chain free play should be 25-30 mm (1.0-1.2 in.) measured midway between sprockets. Notch (H) on adjuster plate must align with corresponding scale marks on each side.

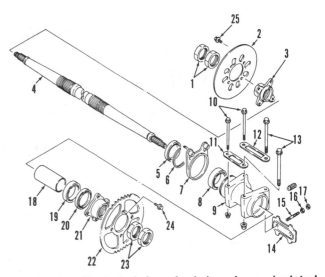

Fig. S11-27—Exploded view of axle housing and related components.

1. Nuts		14. Adjustment plate
2. Brake disc		15. Stud
3. Flange		16. Adjuster nut
4. Axle shaft		17. Locknut
5. Dust seal		18. Spacer
6. Snap ring		19. Bearing
7. Caliper mounting bracket		20. Dust seal
8. Bearing		21. Flange
9. Housing		22. Sprocket
10. Bolts		23. Nuts
11. Plate		24. Cap screw
12. Plate		25. Cap screw

ground. Remove both rear wheels. Remove seat and rear fender assembly. Remove shock absorber upper and lower mounting bolts and nuts. Remove cushion lever center shaft and nut. Remove clamps securing brake hose to swing arm. Remove screws securing shock absorber reservoir to frame and withdraw shock absorber assembly. Remove nut securing swing arm pivot shaft. Support swing arm assembly and withdraw swing arm pivot shaft. Withdraw swing arm assembly far enough to provide adequate clearance for drive chain renewal. Remove front (engine) sprocket guard and withdraw drive chain. Remove front sprocket if needed.

Carefully examine sprockets for excessive wear. Worn sprockets will usually have a hooked tooth profile. A good test is to place a new chain on a used sprocket and check the fit. If sprockets require renewal due to wear, always renew drive chain. Sprockets should be renewed as a set. Standard drive chain is a Takasago RK520SMO-Z10 with 96 links.

Reassembly is reverse order of disassembly. Tighten front sprocket retaining nut to 80-100 N·m (58.0-72.5 ft.-lbs.). Tighten rear sprocket cap screws (24—Fig. S11-27) to 40-60 N·m (29.0-43.5 ft.-lbs.). Tighten cushion lever center shaft securing nut to 80-120 N·m (58-87 ft.-lbs.). Tighten swing arm pivot shaft nut to 50-80 N·m (36.0-58.0 ft.-lbs.). Tighten shock absorber mounting bolts to 40-60 N·m (29.0-43.5 ft.-lbs.). Tighten wheel retaining nuts to 45-65 N·m (32.5-47.0 ft.-lbs.). Refer to previous INSPECTION AND ADJUSTMENT paragraphs for recommended chain adjustment procedures.

FINAL DRIVE ASSEMBLY

R&R AND OVERHAUL. Remove two cap screws securing rear brake caliper assembly and withdraw caliper with parking brake assembly. Remove brake disc guard. Remove drive chain as outlined under R&R AND OVERHAUL in the DRIVE CHAIN AND SPROCKETS section. To complete disassembly, remove left and right rear hub assemblies. Remove brake disc retaining nuts (1—Fig. S11-27), then withdraw brake disc (2) with flange (3) and push axle shaft (4) out of axle housing (9) toward sprocket (22) side. Remove bolts (10 and 13) and adjustment studs (15) to withdraw housing (9) from swing arm casing.

Renew any component that is excessively worn or damage. Reassembly is reverse of disassembly. Tighten right side axle nuts (1) before tightening left side axle nuts (23). Apply Suzuki Bond No. 1207B to end surface of flange (3) that contacts nut (1). Apply Thread Lock "1303" to threads of nuts (1). Tighten inner nut (1) to 15-25 N·m (11-18 ft.-lbs.), then hold inner nut and tighten outer nut (1) to 160-200 N·m (115.5-144.5 ft.-lbs.). If sprocket side nuts (23) were removed, apply Suzuki Bond No. 1207B to end surface of flange (21) that contacts nut (23). Apply Thread Lock "1303" to threads of nuts (23) and tighten both nuts to 160-200 N·m (115.5-144.5 ft.-lbs.). Tighten axle hub nuts to 85-115 N·m (61.5-83 ft.-lbs.) and install new cotter pins.

SUZUKI

LT-4WD, LT-F4WD, LT-F4WDX AND LT-F250

NOTE: Metric fasteners are used throughout vehicle.

CONDENSED SERVICE DATA

MODELS	LT-4WD, LT-F4WD, LT-F250	LT-F4WDX
General		
Engine Make	Suzuki	Suzuki
Engine Type	Four-Stroke; Air-Cooled	Four-Stroke; Air-Cooled
Number of Cylinders	1	1
Bore	66.0 mm (2.598 in.)	68.5 mm (2.697 in.)
Stroke	72.0 mm (2.835 in.)	76.0 mm (2.992 in.)
Displacement	246 cc (15.0 cu. in.)	280 cc (17.1 cu. in.)
Compression Ratio	8.5:1	8.9:1
Fuel Recommendation	Unleaded or Low-Lead	Unleaded or Low-Lead
Pump Octane Rating	85-95	85-95
Engine Lubrication	Wet Sump; Pump	Wet Sump; Pump
Engine/Transmission Oil	SAE 10W-40	SAE 10W-40
Forward Speeds	5	5
Reverse Speeds	1	1
Tire Size:		
Front	22 × 8.00-10	24 × 8.00-10
Rear	25 × 12.00-10*	25 × 10.00-12
Tire Pressure (cold):**		
Front	35 kPa*** (5.1 psi)	30 kPa (4.4 psi)
Rear	20 kPa (2.8 psi)	27.5 kPa (4.0 psi)

*On Model LT-F250, rear tire size is 24x11.00-10.
**On Model LT-F250, tire pressure for all tires is 25 kPa (3.6 psi).
***On Model LT-4WD, decrease front tire pressure to 30 kPa (4.4 psi) when load is less than 80 kg (175 lbs.).

Tune-Up		
Engine Idle Speed	1350-1450 rpm*	1400-1600 rpm
Spark Plug:		
NGK	D7EA	D7EA
Nippon Denso	X22ES-U	X22ES-U
Electrode Gap	0.6-0.7 mm (0.024-0.028 in.)	0.6-0.7 mm (0.024-0.028 in.)
Ignition:		
Type	Breakerless	Breakerless
Timing	See Text	See Text
Carburetor:		
Make	Mikuni	Mikuni

MODELS	LT-4WD, LT-F4WD, LT-F250	LT-F4WDX

Tune-Up (Cont.)
Carburetor: (Cont.)

	LT-4WD, LT-F4WD, LT-F250	LT-F4WDX
Model:		
Before 1990	VM24SS	....
After 1989	BST31SS	BST31SS
Bore Size:		
Before 1990	24 mm (0.94 in.)	....
After 1989	31 mm (1.22 in.)	31 mm (1.22 in.)
Float Height:		
Before 1990	23.5-25.5 mm (0.92-1.00 in.)	....
After 1989	12.5-13.5 mm (0.49-0.53 in.)	12.5-13.5 mm (0.49-0.53 in.)
Jet Needle:		
Before 1990	5L21	....
After 1989	5D40	5D40
Clip Position:		
Before 1990	3rd Groove From Top	....
After 1989	4th Groove From Top	4th Groove From Top
Pilot Jet:		
Before 1990	#22.5	....
After 1989	#40	#37.5
Needle Jet:		
Before 1990	O-1	....
After 1989	P-4	P-2
Main Jet:		
Before 1990	#100	....
After 1989	#122.5	#122.5
Throttle Cut-Away:		
Before 1990	1.5	....
After 1989	#125	#130
Idle Mixture Setting:		
Before 1990	1¾ Turns Out	....
After 1989	See Text	2⅝ Turns Out
Throttle Cable Free Play	0.5-1.0 mm (0.02-0.04 in.)	0.5-1.0 mm (0.02-0.04 in.)

*Idle speed on models after 1989 should be 1400-1600 rpm.

Sizes-Clearances

	LT-4WD, LT-F4WD, LT-F250	LT-F4WDX
Valve Clearance (cold):		
Intake	0.03-0.08 mm (0.001-0.003 in.)	0.03-0.08 mm (0.001-0.003 in.)
Exhaust	0.08-0.13 mm (0.003-0.005 in.)	0.08-0.13 mm (0.003-0.005 in.)
Valve Face Angle	45°	45°
Valve Seat Angle	15° & 45°	15° & 45°
Valve Seat Width	0.9-1.1 mm (0.035-0.043 in.)	0.9-1.1 mm (0.035-0.043 in.)
Valve Stem Diameter:		
Intake	5.475-5.490 mm (0.2156-0.2161 in.)	5.475-5.490 mm (0.2156-0.2161 in.)
Exhaust	5.455-5.470 mm (0.2148-0.2154 in.)	5.455-5.470 mm (0.2148-0.2154 in.)

MODELS	LT-4WD, LT-F4WD, LT-F250	LT-F4WDX
Sizes-Clearances (Cont.)		
Valve Guide Bore Diameter:		
Intake & Exhaust	5.500-5.512 mm (0.2165-0.2170 in.)	5.500-5.512 mm (0.2165-0.2170 in.)
Valve Stem-to-Guide Clearance:		
Intake	0.010-0.037 mm (0.0004-0.0015 in.)	0.010-0.037 mm (0.0004-0.0015 in.)
Exhaust	0.030-0.057 mm (0.0012-0.0022 in.)	0.030-0.057 mm (0.0012-0.0022 in.)
Wear Limit	0.35 mm (0.014 in.)	0.35 mm (0.014 in.)
Valve Spring Free Length (Min.):		
Inner	35.1 mm (1.38 in.)	35.1 mm (1.38 in.)
Outer	39.9 mm (1.57 in.)	39.9 mm (1.57 in.)
Rocker Arm Bore Diameter:		
Intake & Exhaust	12.000-12.018 mm (0.4724-0.4731 in.)	12.000-12.018 mm (0.4724-0.4731 in.)
Rocker Shaft Diameter	11.977-11.995 mm (0.4715-0.4722 in.)	11.977-11.995 mm (0.4715-0.4722 in.)
Camshaft Lobe Height:		
Intake	33.780-33.820 mm (1.3299-1.3315 in.)	34.112-34.152 mm (1.3430-1.3446 in.)
Wear Limit	33.480 mm (1.3181 in.)	33.820 mm (1.3315 in.)
Exhaust	32.990-33.030 mm (1.2988-1.3004 in.)	33.790-33.830 mm (1.3303-1.3319 in.)
Wear Limit	32.690 mm (1.2870 in.)	33.490 mm (1.3185 in.)
Camshaft Journal Diameter	21.959-21.980 mm (0.8645-0.8653 in.)	21.959-21.980 mm (0.8645-0.8653 in.)
Camshaft Journal Clearance	0.032-0.066 mm (0.0013-0.0026 in.)	0.032-0.066 mm (0.0013-0.0026 in.)
Wear Limit	0.150 mm (0.0059 in.)	0.150 mm (0.0059 in.)
Camshaft Runout (Max.)	0.10 mm (0.004 in.)	0.10 mm (0.004 in.)
Cylinder Head Cover Distortion (Max.)	0.05 mm (0.002 in.)	0.05 mm (0.002 in.)
Cylinder Head Distortion (Max.)	0.05 mm (0.002 in.)	0.05 mm (0.002 in.)
Piston-to-Cylinder Wall Clearance	0.040-0.060 mm (0.0016-0.0020 in.)	0.060-0.070 mm (0.0024-0.0028 in.)
Wear Limit	0.120 mm (0.0047 in.)	0.120 mm (0.0047 in.)
Cylinder Bore Diameter	66.000-66.015 mm (2.5984-2.5990 in.)	68.500-68.515 mm (2.6968-2.6974 in.)
Wear Limit	66.090 mm (2.6020 in.)	68.580 mm (2.7000 in.)
Cylinder Bore Distortion (Max.)	0.05 mm (0.002 in.)	0.05 mm (0.002 in.)
Piston Diameter Measured 18 mm (0.71 in.) from Skirt Bottom	65.955-69.970 mm (1.5966-2.5972 in.)	68.445-68.460 mm (2.6947-2.6953 in.)

MODELS	LT-4WD, LT-F4WD, LT-F250	LT-F4WDX
Sizes-Clearances (Cont.)		
Piston Diameter Measured 18 mm (0.71 in.) from Skirt Bottom		
Wear Limit	65.880 mm (2.5937 in.)	68.380 mm (2.6921 in.)
Piston Pin Bore Diameter	16.002-16.008 mm (0.6300-0.6302 in.)	17.002-17.008 mm (0.6694-0.6696 in.)
Wear Limit	16.030 mm (0.6311 in.)	17.030 mm (0.6705 in.)
Piston Pin Diameter	15.996-16.000 mm (0.6298-0.6299 in.)	16.996-17000 mm (0.6691-0.6693 in.)
Wear Limit	15.980 mm (0.6291 in.)	16.980 mm (0.6685 in.)
Piston Ring End Gap:		
Top Ring	0.10-0.25 mm (0.004-0.010 in.)	0.15-0.30 mm (0.006-0.012 in.)
Wear Limit	0.70 mm (0.028 in.)	0.70 mm (0.028 in.)
Second Ring	0.10-0.25 mm (0.004-0.010 in.)	0.50-0.65 mm (0.020-0.026 in.)
Wear Limit	0.70 mm (0.028 in.)	1.00 mm (0.039 in.)
Piston Ring Side Clearance (Max.):		
Top	0.180 mm (0.0071 in.)	0.180 mm (0.0071 in.)
Second	0.150 mm (0.0059 in.)	0.150 mm (0.0059 in.)
Connecting Rod Small End Bore Diameter	16.006-16.014 mm (0.6302-0.6305 in.)	17.006-17.014 mm (0.6695-0.6698 in.)
Wear Limit	16.040 mm (0.6315 in.)	17.040 mm (0.6709 in.)
Capacities		
Fuel Tank	12 L (3.2 gal.)	12 L (3.2 gal.)
Engine/Transmission/ Final Drive Sump	See Text	See Text
Front Differential	150 mL (5.1 oz.)	150 mL (5.1 oz.)
Tightening Torques		
Camshaft Sprocket Bolt	10-12 N·m (88-106 in.-lbs.)	10-12 N·m (88-106 in.-lbs.)
Clutch Shoe Nut	90-100 N·m (65-79.5 ft.-lbs.)	110-130 N·m (79.5-95.5 ft.-lbs.)
Clutch Sleeve Hub Nut	60-80 N·m (43.5-58 ft.-lbs.)	60-80 N·m (43.5-58 ft.-lbs.)
Cylinder Base Nut	7-11 N·m (62-97 in.-lbs.)	7-11 N·m (62-97 in.-lbs.)
Cylinder Head Cover Bolt	8-10 N·m (71-88 in.-lbs.)	9-11 N·m (80-97 in.-lbs.)
Cylinder Head Nut:		
6 mm	7-11 N·m (62-97 in.-lbs.)	7-11 N·m (62-97 in.-lbs.)

SUZUKI LT-4WD, LT-F4WD, LT-F4WDX AND LT-F250

MODELS	LT-4WD, LT-F4WD, LT-F250	LT-F4WDX
Tightening Torques (Cont.)		
Cylinder Head Nut: (Cont.)		
8 mm	21-25 N•m (15-18 ft.-lbs.)	21-25 N•m (15-18 ft.-lbs.)
Engine Mounting Bolts:		
10 mm:		
Prior to 1990	80-95 N•m (58-68.5 ft.-lbs.)	....
After 1989	64-76 N•m (47-56 ft.-lbs.)	64-76 N•m (47-56 ft.-lbs.)
12 mm:		
Prior to 1990	80-95 N•m (58-68.5 ft.-lbs.)	....
After 1989	60-72 N•m (43.5-52 ft.-lbs.)	60-72 N•m (43.5-52 ft.-lbs.)
Flywheel Nut	145-175 N•m (105-126.5 ft.-lbs.)	145-175 N•m (105-126.5 ft.-lbs.)
Front Axle Nuts	85-115 N•m (61.5-83 ft.-lbs.)	85-115 N•m (61.5-83 ft.-lbs.)
Rear Axle Nuts	85-115 N•m (61.5-83 ft.-lbs.)	85-115 N•m (61.5-83 ft.-lbs.)
Wheel Retaining Nuts:		
Front	45-65 N•m (32.5-47 ft.-lbs.)	45-65 N•m (32.5-47 ft.-lbs.)
Rear	45-65 N•m (32.5-47 ft.-lbs.)	45-65 N•m (32.5-47 ft.-lbs.)
Standard Screws:		
Unmarked or Marked "4"		
4 mm	1.0-2.0 N•m (8.9-18 in.-lbs.)	1.0-2.0 N•m (8.9-18 in.-lbs.)
25 mm	2.0-4.0 N•m (18-36 in.-lbs.)	2.0-4.0 N•m (18-36 in.-lbs.)
6 mm	4.0-7.0 N•m (36-62 in.-lbs.)	4.0-7.0 N•m (36-62 in.-lbs.)
8 mm	10-16 N•m (88.5-142 in.-lbs.)	10-16 N•m (88.5-142 in.-lbs.)
10 mm	22-35 N•m (16-26 ft.-lbs.)	22-35 N•m (16-26 ft.-lbs.)
12 mm	35-55 N•m (26-40 ft.-lbs.)	35-55 N•m (26-40 ft.-lbs.)
14 mm	50-80 N•m (37-59 ft.-lbs.)	50-80 N•m (37-59 ft.-lbs.)
16 mm	80-130 N•m (59-96 ft.-lbs.)	80-130 N•m (59-96 ft.-lbs.)
18 mm	130-190 N•m (96-140 ft.-lbs.)	130-190 N•m (96-140 ft.-lbs.)
Marked "7"		
4 mm	1.5-3.0 N•m (13-27 in.-lbs.)	1.5-3.0 N•m (13-27 in.-lbs.)
5 mm	3.0-6.0 N•m (27-53 in.-lbs.)	3.0-6.0 N•m (27-53 in.-lbs.)
6 mm	8.0-12.0 N•m (71-106 in.-lbs.)	8.0-12.0 N•m (71-106 in.-lbs.)
8 mm	18-28 N•m (13-21 ft.-lbs.)	18-28 N•m (13-21 ft.-lbs.)

MODELS	LT-4WD, LT-F4WD, LT-F250	LT-F4WDX
Tightening Torques (Cont.)		
Marked "7" (Cont.)		
10 mm	40-60 N·m (29-44 ft.-lbs.)	40-60 N·m (29-44 ft.-lbs.)
12 mm	70-100 N·m (52-74 ft.-lbs.)	70-100 N·m (52-74 ft.-lbs.)
14 mm	110-160 N·m (81-118 ft.-lbs.)	110-160 N·m (81-118 ft.-lbs.)
16 mm	170-250 N·m (125-184 ft.-lbs.)	170-250 N·m (125-184 ft.-lbs.)
18 mm	200-280 N·m (147-206 ft.-lbs.)	200-280 N·m (147-206 ft.-lbs.)

LUBRICATION

All Models

ENGINE, TRANSMISSION AND FINAL DRIVE. The engine and transmission are lubricated by a crankshaft-driven oil pump. The final drive assembly is lubricated by the commonly shared sump. Recommended oil is a multigrade SAE 10W-40 motor oil with an API classification of SE or SF.

Fill the sump through filler plug (F—Fig. S13-1) opening. Oil level should be maintained at level indicated on sight glass (G). Oil is drained by removing plug in underside of housing. Dry capacity of sump is 3860 mL (4.1 qt.). Refilling after changing oil and oil filter requires only 3600 mL (3.8 qt.) as some oil will be retained in housing. Oil requirement after only changing oil is 3500 mL (3.7 qt.).

Manufacturer recommends changing the oil and oil filter after the first month of 200 km (125 miles) of operation and every three months or 1000 km (600 miles) thereafter.

The oil filter may be renewed after removing side cover (C). Make certain inner "O" ring is properly installed before inserting filter. Insert new filter with open end toward engine and closed end toward side cover. Renew side cover "O" ring and ensure filter retaining spring is properly located when installing cover.

FRONT DIFFERENTIAL UNIT. The differential oil level on models equipped with front-wheel drive should be checked after the first month or 200 km (125 miles) of operation and every six months of 2000 km (1200 miles) of operation thereafter. The differential oil should be changed on an annual basis. Recommended lubricant is a good quality SAE 90 hypoid gear oil. Differential capacity is 150 mL (5.1 oz.).

Check differential oil level through oil level plug (G—Fig. S13-3) opening with vehicle on a level surface. Oil is drained by removing drain plug (P) and level plug (G). To fill, install drain plug (P) and add recommended oil through level plug (G) opening until oil starts to run out plug opening, then install level plug (G) and securely tighten.

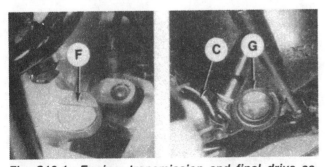

Fig. S13-1—Engine, transmission and final drive assembly oil is poured through filler plug opening (F) and maintained at level on sight glass (G). Oil filter is located behind side cover (C).

Fig. S13-3—On four-wheel-drive models, the front differential unit oil is checked and filled through plug (G) opening and drained through drain plug (P) opening.

CABLES, LEVERS AND SHAFTS. The choke cable, throttle cable, range cable, reverse cable, speedometer cable, shifting cable and throttle lever should be lubricated with motor oil every three months or 1000 km (600 miles). The front wheel bearings, steering shaft, rear brake lever and brake camshaft should be greased every three months or 1000 km (600 miles). Do not excessively grease the brake camshaft as grease may contact brake linings reducing braking ability.

AIR CLEANER ELEMENT

All Models

The air cleaner element should be removed and cleaned after every three months or 1000 km (600 miles) of operation. To remove air cleaner element, first remove seat and element cover. Remove element retainer and withdraw element. Remove screw and carefully separate foam element from frame.

Thoroughly clean element in a suitable nonflammable solvent. Saturate element in clean motor oil. Compress element to remove excess oil. Reinstall element by reversing removal procedure.

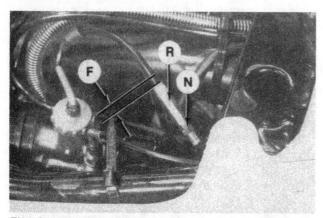

Fig. S13-5—Slide dust boots away from adjuster assembly and loosen locknut (N) and rotate adjuster (R) as required to obtain correct free play (F).

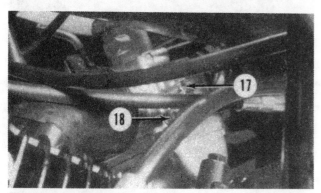

Fig. S13-6—View of installed carburetor showing location of idle speed screw (17) and idle mixture screw (18).

FUEL SYSTEM

All Models Prior to 1990

CARBURETOR. A Mikuni VM24SS-type carburetor is used. Refer to CONDENSED SERVICE DATA for carburetor specifications.

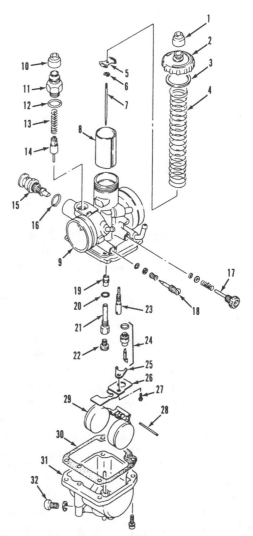

Fig. S13-7—Exploded view of Mikuni VM24SS carburetor.

1. Grommet	17. Idle speed screw
2. Cap	18. Idle mixture screw
3. Gasket	19. Needle jet
4. Spring	20. Washer
5. Retainer	21. Air bleed
6. Jet needle clip	22. Main jet
7. Jet needle	23. Pilot jet
8. Throttle slide	24. Inlet valve
9. Body	25. Inlet valve retainer
10. Grommet	26. Baffle plate
11. Cable guide	27. Screw
12. Washer	28. Float pin
13. Spring	29. Float
14. Starter valve	30. Gasket
15. Starter valve limiter	31. Float bowl
16. Washer	32. Drain screw

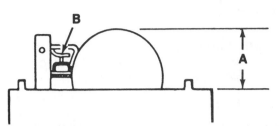

Fig. S13-8—Float level (A) on Mikuni VM24SS should be 23.5-25.5 mm (0.92-1.00 in.). Bend float arm tang (B) to adjust.

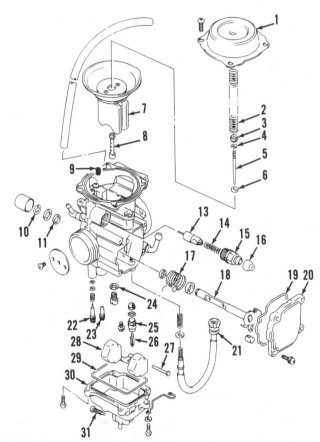

Fig. S13-9—Exploded view of Mikuni BST31SS carburetor.

1. Cover	17. Spring
2. Spring	18. Throttle shaft
3. Spring seat	19. Gasket
4. Clip	20. Cover
5. Jet needle	21. Idle speed screw
6. Washer	22. Idle mixture screw
7. Throttle slide	23. Pilot jet
8. Needle jet	24. Main jet
9. Pilot air jet	25. Fuel inlet valve seat
10. "E" ring	26. Fuel inlet valve
11. Seal	27. Float pin
12. Throttle plate	28. Float
13. Starter valve	29. Gasket
14. Spring	30. Fuel bowl
15. Cable guide	31. Drain screw
16. Grommet	

Before performing carburetor adjustments, throttle cable should be adjusted to provide 0.5-1.0 mm (0.02-0.04 in.) free play at idle position. To adjust throttle cable free play, the seat must be removed to expose throttle cable adjuster assembly. Slide dust boots away from adjuster assembly. Loosen locknut (N—Fig. S13-5) and rotate adjuster (R) as required to obtain correct free play (F). Tighten locknut (N) to retain adjustment and install dust boots and seat.

Initial setting of idle mixture screw (18—Fig. S13-6) is $1\frac{3}{4}$ turns out from a lightly seated position. Rotating idle mixture screw clockwise will lean mixture while rotating screw counterclockwise will richen mixture. Final adjustment should be made with engine running at normal operating temperature. Adjust idle speed screw (17) so engine idles at 1350-1450 rpm. Adjust idle mixture screw (18) so highest idle speed is achieved and readjust idle speed screw to recommended rpm. After adjusting carburetor, check throttle cable adjustment as previously described.

Refer to Fig. S13-7 for an exploded view of the carburetor if complete disassembly is required. Note location of components during disassembly. Float height should be 23.5-25.5 mm (0.92-1.00 in.). To check float height, remove float bowl and invert carburetor. Measure distance (A—Fig. S13-8) between bottom float and gasket surface on carburetor body. Adjust float by bending float arm tang (B).

All Other Models. All models after 1989 are equipped with a Mikuni BST31SS. Before making carburetor adjustments, adjust throttle cable free play as outlined in previous section for Mikuni VM24SS carburetor. Refer to CONDENSED SERVICE DATA for carburetor specifications.

Initial setting of idle mixture screw (22—Fig. S13-9) is $2\frac{7}{8}$ turns out on LT-4WD and LT-F4WD models, $2\frac{5}{8}$ turns out on LT-F4WDX models and $2\frac{3}{4}$ turns out on LT-F250 models. Make final adjustment with engine at normal operating temperature. Adjust idle speed screw (21) so engine idles at 1400-1600 rpm.

Refer to Fig. S13-9 for an exploded view of carburetor. Note location of components during disassembly. Inspect components for damage and excessive wear. Rubber bellows attached to throttle slide (7) must be free of tears and holes. Note the following during assembly: Install needle jet (8) so flat side matches flat in body. Be sure throttle slide (7) bellows fits groove in body properly. To check float height, hold carburetor so float is hanging down as shown in Fig. S13-10 and float arm is lightly pressing against float valve. Float height (H) should be 12.5-13.5 mm (0.49-0.53 in.). Adjust float height by carefully bending float arm tang.

FUEL PUMP. A diaphragm-type fuel pump located adjacent to the fuel tank is used. Alternating pressure and vacuum inside intake manifold is directed to one side of fuel pump diaphragm via a hose. During vacuum pulse, diaphragm draws fuel through inlet check valve

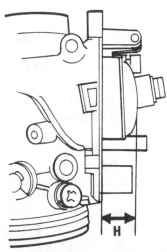

Fig. S13-10—Hold fuel bowl of Mikuni BST31SS carburetor as shown when measuring float height (H).

into fuel chamber. During pressure pulse, diaphragm reduces fuel chamber volume, thus moving fuel through outlet check valve.

If fuel delivery to carburetor is interrupted, first eliminate other sources of difficulty such as insufficient fuel, clogged fuel strainers, cracked or split hoses or loose pump housing retaining screws before servicing fuel pump. When servicing pump, defective or questionable parts should be renewed. Diaphragm should be renewed if deterioration is evident.

FUEL STRAINER. Strainers are mounted on the end of the "ON" pickup tube and the "RES" (reserve) pickup tube of the fuel valve assembly mounted on the fuel tank. The strainers should be cleaned periodically to prevent fuel starvation. For access to strainers, drain fuel tank and detach fuel hose. Remove cap screws and withdraw fuel valve assembly with strainers from fuel tank. Reinstall by reversing removal procedure.

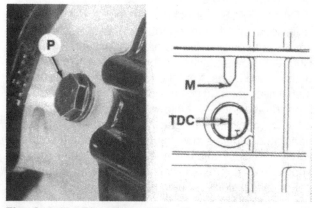

Fig. S13-11—Piston is at Top Dead Center when "T" mark (TDC) on flywheel is aligned with stationary mark (M). Remove inspection plug (P) in left crankcase half to view timing mark. Piston must also be on compression stroke as outlined in test for valve clearance adjustment.

IGNITION AND ELECTRICAL

All Models

SPARK PLUG. Standard spark plug is NGK D7EA or Nippon Denso X22ES-U. Spark plug electrode gap should be 0.6-0.7 mm (0.024-0.028 in.).

Spark plug should be removed, cleaned and electrode gap set every three months or 1000 km (600 miles) and renewed every 18 months or 6000 km (4000 miles).

IGNITION. A capacitor discharge, pointless electronic ignition system is used. The ignition system consists of the flywheel, a power source coil located underneath the flywheel, an externally mounted pickup coil, a CD ignition module, an ignition coil, an engine stop switch and an ignition switch. On later models, the battery provides current for the ignition and the power source coil is not used. Ignition timing should occur at 5° BTDC with engine operating at approximately 1800 rpm and below on all models. Ignition timing at approximately 3800 rpm should occur at 35° BTDC on LT-4WD, LT-F4WD and LT-F250 models and 30° BTDC on LT-F4WDX models. Ignition timing is fixed and not adjustable. The flywheel has a single mark "T" (Fig. S13-11) to indicate Top Dead Center (TDC) and which is used during valve clearance adjustment or when setting camshaft timing.

If ignition malfunction occurs, check condition of spark plug, all wires and connections before troubleshooting ignition circuit. Using Suzuki pocket tester 09900-25002 or a suitable ohmmeter, refer to the following test specifications and procedures to aid troubleshooting.

To check power source coil on Models LT-4WDJ, LT-4WDK, LT-F4WDJ, LT-F4WDK, LT-F250J and LT-F250K, separate wire connectors leading from power source coil to CDI module and attach one tester lead to coil end of black wire. Attach remaining tester lead to blue wire with yellow tracer. Power source coil can be considered satisfactory if resistance reading is within the limits of 105-160 ohms.

To check pickup coil, separate black wire with yellow tracer at connector and green wire with white tracer at connector leading from pickup coil to CDI module. Attach one tester lead to black wire with yellow tracer and remaining tester lead to green wire with white tracer. Pickup coil can be considered satisfactory if resistance reading is within the limits of 90-140 ohms.

To check condition of ignition coil, separate wire connectors from terminal ends on ignition coil. Identify wire location for correct reassembly. Attach one tester lead to negative terminal on coil and remaining tester lead to positive terminal on coil. Primary coil resistance should be approximately 0-0.5 ohms. Attach one tester lead to high tension wire and remaining tester lead to positive terminal on coil. Secondary coil resistance reading should be approximately 10k-16k on Models LT-4WDJ,

LT-4WDK, LT-F4WDJ, LT-F4WDK, LT-F250J and LT-F250K, and 12k-20k ohms on all other models.

CHARGING CIRCUIT. The charging circuit consists of an AC generator located underneath the flywheel, a regulator/rectifier and a battery. The standard battery is a FB14A-A2 on LT-4WD, LT-F4WD and LT-F250 models and YB14A-A2 on LT-F4WDX models. The battery has a 14 ampere hour, 12 volt rating. Under load the AC generator should produce approximately 14-15.5 volts DC at 5000 rpm on Models LT-4WDJ, LT-4WDK, LT-F4WDJ, LT-F4WDK, LT-F250J and LT-F250K, and 13-15 volts on all other models. No-load voltage of the AC generator should be 55 volts AC at 5000 rpm on Models LT-4WDJ, LT-4WDK, LT-F4WDJ, LT-F4WDK, LT-F250J and LT-F250K, and 60 volts on all other models.

The battery should be checked and filled to maximum level with distilled water, if required, after the first month or 200 km (125 miles) and every three months or 1000 km (600 miles) thereafter. During periods of vehicle storage, the battery should be charged once a month to reduce sulfation and prolong battery life. When charging battery, always disconnect battery from charging circuit to prevent damage to regulator/rectifier or other components. Do not exceed maximum charging rate of 1.4 amperes.

NOTE: A "spill retarded"-type battery is used. Prior to charging battery, remove all battery caps. Make sure battery is charged in a well-ventilated area.

The AC generator can be statically checked using Suzuki pocket tester 09900-25002 or a suitable ohmmeter. Separate wire connector block from AC generator to regulator/rectifier and attach tester leads between each yellow stator lead. Tester reading should indicate continuity between each lead. Attach one tester lead to ground and remaining tester lead to each yellow wire individually. Tester reading should indicate infinite resistance at each lead.

An operational check can be performed using Suzuki pocket tester 09900-25002 or a suitable voltmeter as follows: Set ignition switch to light position. Remove seat and attach voltmeter leads noting correct polarity. Start and run engine at 5000 rpm. With a fully charged battery, AC generator and regulator/rectifier can be considered satisfactory if voltage reading is within the limits of approximately 14-15.5 volts DC at 5000 rpm on Models LT-4WDJ, LT-4WDK, LT-F4WDJ, LT-F4WDK, LT-F250J and LT-F250K, and 13-15 volts on all other models. If voltage is not within required limits, then the AC generator may be eliminated as cause of difficulty by performing a no-load test. Separate AC generator to regulator/rectifier wire connector block. Start and run engine at 5000 rpm. Attach voltmeter leads between each yellow stator lead. The AC generator can be considered satisfactory if no-load voltage is not less than 55

volts AC on Models LT-4WDJ, LT-4WDK, LT-F4WDJ, LT-F4WDK, LT-F250J and LT-F250K, and 60 volts on all other models.

ELECTRIC STARTER. Starter should draw 80 amperes at engine starting speed. Removal and disassembly of starter is evident after inspection of unit. Starter brushes should be renewed if worn to 6 mm (0.24 in.) or less. Service limit of commutator under cut is 0.2 mm (0.008 in.)

WIRING. If wiring requires repair, always use replacement wire of the same gauge. Wires should be routed away from areas of extreme heat or sharp edges. Plastic tie straps should be used to retain wires in their original positions to prevent short circuiting. Refer to Fig. S13-12 for schematic wiring diagram.

FASTENERS

All Models

After the first month or 200 km (125 miles) of operation and every three months or 1000 km (600 miles) thereafter, retighten the cylinder head, cylinder, exhaust system, engine mounts, and all chassis nuts and bolts. Refer to TIGHTENING TORQUES section of CONDENSED SERVICE DATA for torque specifications.

VALVE SYSTEM

All Models

The valves are actuated via rocker arms by a single overhead camshaft. Camshaft is timed and driven by a roller drive chain from left end of crankshaft. Valve clearance should be adjusted after the first month or 200 km (125 miles) of operation and every three months or 1000 km (600 miles) thereafter. Valve clearance should be adjusted with engine cold.

To adjust valve clearance, first remove seat, rear carrier, rear fender, spark plug and valve adjustment caps. Remove manual starter and timing inspection plug. Rotate crankshaft until "T" mark (TDC—Fig. S13-11) on flywheel aligns with stationary mark (M) on crankcase and piston is on compression stroke. To ensure piston is on compression stroke, rotate crankshaft $\frac{1}{4}$ turn past TDC while observing intake valve. If valve movement is indicated, rotate crankshaft one full revolution and align timing marks again.

Clearance between rocker arm adjusting screw and valve stem should be 0.03-0.08 mm (0.001-0.003 in.) for intake valve and 0.08-0.13 mm (0.003-0.005 in.) for exhaust valve. Check clearance with feeler gauge (F—Fig. S13-13). Adjust clearance by loosening locknut (L) and turning screw (A). Be sure to recheck clearance after locknut is tightened.

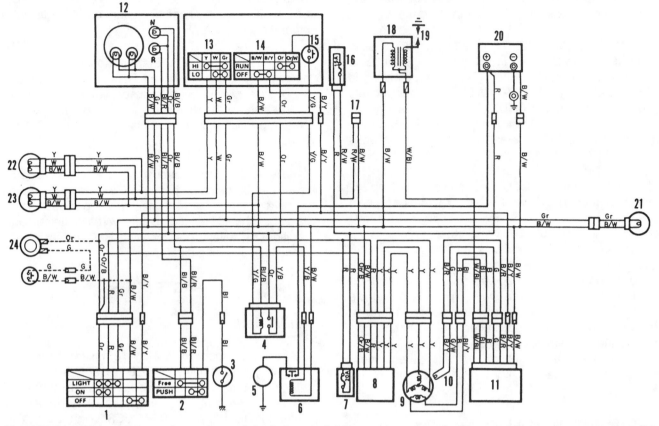

Fig. S13-12—Wiring diagram for early models. Later models are not equipped with an ignition power source coil in magneto.

1.	Ignition switch	13.	Dimmer switch
2.	Reverse switch	14.	Engine stop switch
3.	Neutral switch	15.	Starter button
4.	Neutral relay	16.	Accessory fuse
5.	Starter motor	17.	Accessory terminal
6.	Starter relay	18.	Ignition coil
7.	Fuse	19.	Spark plug
8.	Regulator/rectifier	20.	Battery
9.	Magneto	21.	Taillight
10.	Pickup coil	22.	Headlight
11.	CDI module	23.	Horn
12.	Speedometer		

24.	Horn button	G/W.	Green with white tracer
B.	Black	R/W.	Red with white tracer
G.	Green	Y/B.	Yellow with black tracer
R.	Red	Y/G.	Yellow with green tracer
W.	White	Y/R.	Yellow with red tracer
Y.	Yellow	W/Bl.	White with blue tracer
Bl.	Blue	Bl/B.	Blue with black tracer
Gr.	Gray	Bl/R.	Blue with red tracer
Or.	Orange	Bl/Y.	Blue with yellow tracer
B/W.	Black with white tracer	Or/B.	Orange with black tracer
B/Y.	Black with yellow tracer	Or/W.	Orange with white tracer

CLUTCH

All Models

Two types of automatically actuated clutches are used. One type is a three-shoe centrifugal clutch attached to right end of crankshaft and actuated by engine rpm. The other type is a multiple-disc clutch attached to right end of transmission countershaft and actuated by the gear shift lever. During gear selection, a lever attached to end of gear shift shaft simultaneously disengages the multiple-disc clutch to permit smooth transmission operation.

The clutch should be adjusted after the first month or 200 km (125 miles) of operation and every six months or 2000 km (1200 miles) thereafter. To adjust clutch, remove right rear tire and threaded plug in right crank-

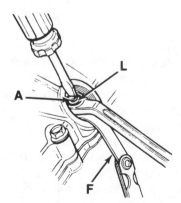

Fig. S13-13—Measure valve clearance with feeler gauge (F). Loosen locknut (L) and rotate screw (A) to adjust.

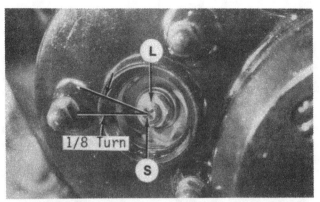

Fig. S13-15—View of clutch adjuster screw (S) and locknut (L). Refer to text for adjustment procedures.

case cover to expose adjuster screw (S—Fig. S13-15) and locknut (L). Loosen locknut (L) and turn adjuster screw (S) clockwise until internal resistance is felt. Then rotate screw (S) counterclockwise ⅛ turn and retain adjusting screw position while tightening locknut (L).

To check clutch operation, first adjust clutch as previously outlined. Ensure oil level is correct and engine is at operating temperature. Attach a suitable tachometer. Shift transfer lever to "2WD" position and sub-trans-

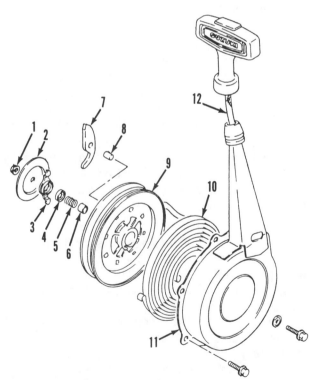

Fig. S13-17—Exploded view of manual starter.

1. Nut	7. Starter pawl
2. Friction plate	8. Pin
3. Pawl guide	9. Rope pulley
4. Spring guide	10. Rewind spring
5. Spring	11. Housing
6. Spacer	12. Rope

mission lever to "High" position, then select low gear and slowly accelerate engine while observing meter. Initial engagement should occur at 1800-2200 rpm. Next, with transmission still in low gear, lockup brakes and momentarily open throttle. Do not maintain full throttle longer than 10 seconds. Engine speed should be held to 3100-3700 rpm. Any results other than specified may indicate disassembly and repair of clutch assemblies is required.

MANUAL STARTER

All Models

R&R AND OVERHAUL. Refer to Fig. S13-17 for exploded view of manual starter used on all models. Starter may be removed as a complete unit from vehicle after removing six starter housing retaining cap screws. Refer to exploded view and disassemble starter as follows: If starter spring remains under tension, pull starter rope and hold rope pulley (9) with notch in pulley adjacent to rope outlet. Pull rope back through outlet so it engages notch in pulley and allow pulley to slowly unwind. Remove retaining nut (1) and disassemble unit. Be careful when removing rewind spring (10); a rapidly uncoiling starter spring could cause serious injury.

Rewind spring is wound in a clockwise direction in starter housing. Rope is wound on rope pulley in a clockwise direction as viewed with pulley in housing. Reassemble starter assembly by reversing disassembly procedure. To place tension on rewind spring, pass rope through rope outlet in housing and install rope handle. Pull rope out and hold pulley so notch in pulley is adjacent to rope outlet. Pull a loop of rope back through outlet between notch in pulley and housing. Turn rope pulley clockwise three or four complete revolutions to place tension on spring. Do not place more tension on rewind spring than is necessary to draw rope handle up against housing.

FRONT BRAKE ASSEMBLY

All Models

Independently operated front and rear brakes are used. The front brake system has hydraulically actuated two-shoe internal expanding drum brakes mounted on each front knuckle. A self-adjuster strut assembly is used to automatically adjust brake shoes as brake linings wear. A handlebar mounted master cylinder with fluid reservoir supplies pressure to each wheel cylinder when actuated by right handlebar lever. Information on rear brake system is outlined in REAR BRAKE ASSEMBLY section.

Only DOT 3 or DOT 4 glycol-based brake fluid should be used in front brake system. The use of other types of brake fluids such as petroleum-based or silicone-based fluids may damage hydraulic components resulting in brake system failure. Under normal operating conditions, brake fluid will absorb small amounts of moisture which can cause pitting to cylinder bore surface resulting in early brake cylinder failure. Drain and refill hydraulic system with new brake fluid every two years to reduce corrosion damage.

BLEEDING. Any operation that required draining or repair of hydraulic brake components will make it necessary to fill and bleed brake system. Check reservoir fluid level before proceeding. Remove cap (7—Fig. S13-18), diaphragm (8) and fill reservoir with DOT 3 or DOT 4 glycol-based fluid only. Reinstall cap to prevent entrance of dirt or foreign materials. Attach a suitable hose such as vacuum hose to either bleeder screw (10) and submerge other end in a container filled with small amount of brake fluid to prevent air from reentering system. Actuate brake lever several times, then hold brake lever toward handlebar. Open brake bleeder to relieve line pressure allowing fluid and air to flow into container. Close bleed screw before releasing brake

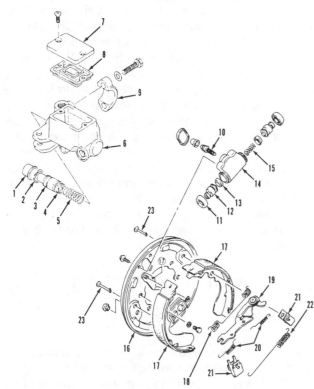

Fig. S13-18—Exploded view of front brake system.

1. Boot	
2. Snap ring	13. Cup
3. Piston & cup	14. Cylinder housing
4. Primary cup	15. Spring
5. Spring	16. Backing plate
6. Reservoir & housing	17. Brake shoes
7. Cap	18. Spring
8. Diaphragm	19. Self-adjuster strut
9. Clamp	20. Springs
10. Bleed screw	21. Clips
11. Boot	22. Spring
12. Piston	23. Pins

lever. Do not permit reservoir to run dry while bleeding. Repeat procedure while periodically refilling fluid reservoir until all air or old fluid is removed.

Attach bleeder hose to remaining bleeder screw and repeat bleeding procedure to complete brake bleeding operation.

INSPECTION. The brake system should be inspected after the first month or 200 km (125 miles) of operation and every three months or 1000 km (600 miles) thereafter. To inspect front brake drums, shoes and wheel cylinders, suitable support front of vehicle and remove front wheel. Pull brake drum (39—Fig. 13-20) off hub (37). Remove hub (37), if needed, for greater access to brake components. Brake drum should be renewed if inside diameter exceeds 165.7 mm (6.52 in.) on LT-4WD, LT-F4WD and LT-250 models or 180.7 mm (7.11 in.) on LT-F4WDX models. Front brake shoes (17—Fig. S13-18) should be renewed if linings are worn to 1.5 mm (0.06 in.) or less. Wheel cylinders (14) should be overhauled or renewed if brake fluid is observed within boots (11) indicating defective cups or cylinder.

If either the brake shoes or wheel cylinders require servicing, then the complete drum brake assembly should be serviced as outlined in R&R AND OVERHAUL section. If brake components are considered satisfactory, then reinstall the hub, brake drum and wheel. Tighten front axle nut to 85-115 N·m (61.5-83.0 ft.-lbs.) and wheel nuts to 45-65 N·m (32.5-47.0 ft.-lbs.)

R&R AND OVERHAUL. Refer to Fig. S13-18 for an exploded view of front brake system.

WARNING: Inhaling asbestos brake dust is injurious to human health. Approved OSHA respiration equipment must be worn when working on or around brake components. DO NOT use compressed air to clean brake drums, shoes or nearby components as brake dust will be blown into air. Only vacuum equipment designed to pick up brake dust should be used.

To remove drum brake components (10 through 23), first remove brake drums as outlined in INSPECTION AND ADJUSTMENT section. Rotate pins (23) 90° to release clips (21). Carefully expand brake shoes (17) to clear shoe locating slots in wheel cylinder pistons (12) and lower pivot bracket. Withdraw brake shoes (17), springs (18, 20 and 22) and self-adjuster strut (19) as an assembly. Detach brake line from wheel cylinder (14) and plug line to reduce fluid loss. Unbolt and remove wheel cylinder assembly (10 through 15) from backing plate (16).

Inspect and renew any components that are damaged or worn excessively. The flexible brake hoses should be renewed if cracks, splits or chaffing is evident or if hoses have been in service for four years.

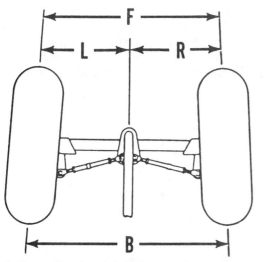

Fig. S13-19—Toe-in should be 11-19 mm (0.4-0.7 in.). Refer to text for measuring procedures.

To overhaul wheel cylinders (14), disassemble cylinder noting location and direction of components. Inspect cylinder bore for damage due to corrosion or scoring. Renew complete wheel cylinder if excessive damage is evident. Superficial damage may be removed using a suitable cylinder hone. After honing, rinse cylinder with clean brake fluid. Shake out excess fluid but do not wipe dry. Using a shop towel or rag to dry cylinder will leave lint particles in bore. Renew boots (11) and piston cups (13). During reassembly, lubricate components with clean brake fluid. Apply a suitable sealer to wheel cylinder contact area on backing plate and install wheel cylinder. Tighten wheel cylinder retaining cap screws to 10-13 N•m (7.0-9.5 ft.-lbs.) and attach brake line.

Apply a light coat of grease to brake shoe locating slots in pistons (12) and lower pivot bracket. Apply a light coat of silicone grease to three brake shoe-to-backing plate contact points on each shoe. With reference to Fig. S13-18, install the brake shoes, self-adjuster strut and springs. Secure brake shoes with pins (23) and clips (21). Install the hub, brake drum and wheel. Tighten front axle nut to 85-115 N•m (61.5-83.0 ft.-lbs.) and wheel nut to 45-65 N•m (32.5-47.0 ft.-lbs.).

MASTER CYLINDER. To remove front brake master cylinder (6—Fig. S13-18), remove union cap screw at master cylinder. Brake fluid will remove paint; be careful when removing master cylinder. Remove the two retaining cap screws and withdraw master cylinder. Remove brake lever, reservoir cap (7) and diaphragm (8). Remove dust boot (1) and snap ring (2). Disassemble plunger assembly while noting location and direction of components. Inspect cylinder bore for damage due to corrosion or scoring. Renew complete master cylinder if excessive damage is evident. Superficial damage may be removed using a suitable cylinder hone. After honing, rinse cylinder with clean brake fluid. Shake out excess fluid but do not wipe dry. Using a shop towel or rag to

dry cylinder will leave lint particles in bore. Renew boot (1) and primary and secondary cups (3 and 4). During reassembly, lubricate components with clean brake fluid. Reassembly is the reverse of disassembly. Bleed brakes as outlined in BLEEDING section.

STEERING

All Models

ADJUSTMENT. The toe-in should be checked and adjusted after the first month or 200 km (125 miles) of operation and every three months of 1000 km (600 miles) thereafter. Prior to toe-in adjustment, inspect steering assembly for damaged or excessively worn components. If service to steering assembly is required refer to R&R AND OVERHAUL section.

To check toe-in, inflate tires to recommended pressure listed in CONDENSED SERVICE DATA. Position vehicle on a flat smooth surface and set handlebars straight forward. Position a load of 75 kg (165 lbs.) on vehicle's seat. Using a suitable tape measure, measure distance between right and left tire centerlines on back side of tires (B—Fig. S13-19) and record measurement. Locate the same tire centerline points on front side of tires (F) and record measurement. The front measurement should be 11-19 mm (0.4-0.7 in.) less than rear measurement. Note that the distance from a projected vehicle centerline to left (L) and right (R) tire centerlines should be equal.

To adjust, loosen tie rod locknuts (21—Fig. S13-20) on both left and right tie rods. The tie rod ends and locknuts color coded yellow have left-hand threads. Rotate tie rod sleeves (22) in equal increments to maintain equal vehicle centerline to left and right tire centerline distances. Tighten tie rod locknuts (21) to 22-35 N•m (16.0-25.5 ft.-lbs.).

R&R AND OVERHAUL. Refer to Fig. S13-20 for an exploded view of steering assembly. To remove either knuckle (36), first remove wheel and components (37 through 44). Remove brake line from wheel cylinder and remove four cap screws securing backing plate to knuckle (36). Withdraw backing plate with brake components. Remove cotter pins and cap screws (25) retaining steering arm (24). Remove shock absorber (26) upper mounting bolt and remove upper control arm (29) and lower control arm (45) mounting bolts. Withdraw components as an assembly. Remainder of steering component disassembly is evident after inspection of unit and referral to Fig. S13-20.

During reassembly, renew all cotter pins. Lubricate all friction points with Suzuki Super Grease "A" or a good quality grease. Install knuckle (36) outer bearing first if inner and outer bearings were removed. Tighten steering shaft holder cap screws (9) to 18-28 N•m (13k-20 ft.-lbs.); steering shaft lower nut (17) to 38-60 N•m (27.5-43.5 ft.-lbs.); ball joint cap screws (27) to 120-170

N•m (87-123 ft.-lbs.); ball joint to knuckle retaining cap screw (34) to 44-66 N•m (32.0-47.5 ft.-lbs.); steering arm cap screws (25) to 40-60 N•m (29.0-43.5 ft.-lbs.); tie rod cap screw (23) to 40-60 N•m (29.0-43.5 ft.-lbs.); tie rod end nut (19) to 22-35 N•m (16.0-25.5 ft.-lbs.); brake backing plate cap screws to 18-28 N•m (13-20 ft.-lbs.) and front axle nut (42) to 85-115 N•m (61.5-83.0 ft.-lbs.). Coat threads on spindle arm cap screws (34) and ball joint cap screws (27) with Thread Lock Super "1303" or equivalent prior to installation. Brake system

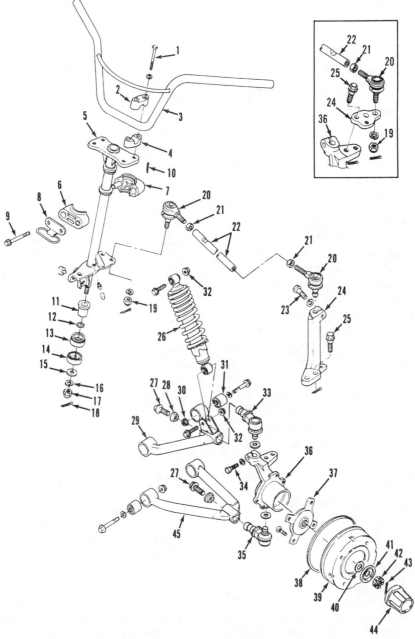

Fig. S13-20—Exploded view of steering and front suspension assembly. Components in box are used on LT-F250 models.

1. Cap screw
2. Handlebar clamp half
3. Handlebar
4. Handlebar clamp half
5. Steering shaft
6. Outer shaft holder
7. Inner shaft holder
8. Plate
9. Cap screw
10. Cotter pin
11. Bushing
12. Clip
13. Dust seal
14. Dust seal
15. Flat washer
16. Lockwasher
17. Nut
18. Cotter pin
19. Nut
20. Tie rod end
21. Locknut
22. Sleeve
23. Cap screw
24. Steering arm
25. Cap screw
26. Shock absorber
27. Cap screw
28. Stopper
29. Upper control arm
30. Nut
31. Bushing
32. Nut
33. Ball joint
34. Cap screw
35. Ball joint
36. Knuckle
37. Hub
38. Dust seal
39. Drum
40. Washer
41. Cap holder
42. Castle nut
43. Cotter pin
44. Cap
45. Lower control arm

must be bled as outlined under BLEEDING in FRONT BRAKE ASSEMBLY section.

FRONT SUSPENSION

All Models

A double wishbone-type front suspension and oil dampened shock absorbers are used. Shock absorbers have five load settings. Refer to Fig. S13-20 for exploded view of suspension components. The suspension components should be periodically inspected for excessive wear and damage. Removal and disassembly is evident after inspection of unit and referral to exploded view.

During reassembly, upper and lower control arm nuts (30) should be tightened to 50-70 N·m (36.0-50.5 ft.-lbs.) while ball joint cap screws (27) should be tightened to 120-170 N·m (87-123 ft.-lbs.). Tighten shock absorber retaining nuts to 48-60 N·m (35-43.5 ft.-lbs.).

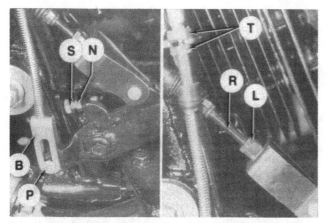

Fig. S13-24—Refer to text for adjustment procedures on rear brake pedal and related components.

B. Bracket
L. Locknut
N. Locknut
P. Pin
R. Rod
S. Screw
T. Nuts

REAR BRAKE ASSEMBLY

All Models

The rear brake system has a mechanically actuated two-shoe internal expanding drum brake mounted on each rear axle knuckle. The left handlebar lever and right foot pedal individually operate the rear brakes via brake cables. Refer to FRONT BRAKE ASSEMBLY section for information on front brake system.

INSPECTION AND ADJUSTMENT. The brake system should be inspected and adjusted after the first month or 200 km (125 miles) of operation and every three months or 1000 km (600 miles) thereafter. To adjust rear brake, first adjust brake pedal then adjust brake lever. Actuate brake pedal and measure free travel at end of pedal. Free travel should be 20-30 mm (0.8-1.2 in.).

To adjust brake pedal and brake lever, first loosen locknut (N—Fig. S13-24) and rotate screw (S) until top of brake pedal pad is level with footpeg, then tighten locknut (N). Loosen locknut (L) and rotate rod (R) until correct brake pedal free travel is obtained, then tighten locknut. After adjusting brake pedal, loosen nuts (T) and adjust cable length until lower end of slot in cable bracket (b) just contacts brake pedal pin (P). Then slide protective cover down brake lever cable and measure brake lever free travel. Lever should have 3-7 mm (0.1-0.3 in.) of free travel between lever base and bracket as measured at (F—Fig. S13-25). To adjust, loosen locknut (C), turn adjuster (A) on brake lever until correct free travel is obtained, then tighten locknut (C).

All models are equipped with a rear brake lining wear indicator mark (I—Fig. S13-26) scribed on rear brake shoe cam to externally determine brake lining wear limit. To externally check rear brake lining wear, apply rear brake and note location of indicator mark (I) in relation to range (R) on brake backing plate. If indicator mark (I)

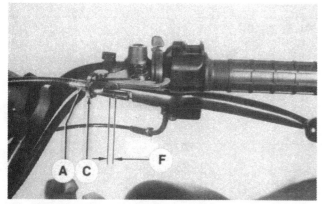

Fig. S13-25—Rear brake lever should have 3-7 mm (0.1-0.3 in.) free travel (F), and is adjusted by loosening locknut (C) and rotating adjuster (A). Refer to text.

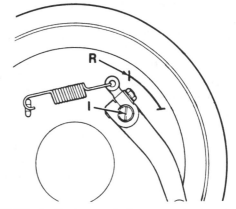

Fig. S13-26—Indicator mark (I) on rear brake shoe cam should be within range (R) when brakes are applied for brake linings to be considered satisfactory.

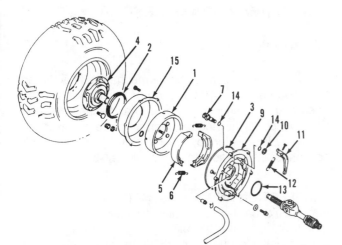

Fig. S13-27—Exploded view of rear brake and hub assembly used on LT-F4WDX models.

1. Brake drum	9. Backing plate
2. Dust seal	10. Washer
3. "O" ring	11. Lever
4. Axle hub	12. Spring
5. Brake shoes	13. "O" ring
6. Springs	14. "O" rings
7. Camshaft	15. Brake drum cover

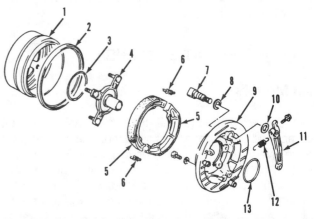

Fig. S13-28—Exploded view of rear brake components used on all models except LT-F4WDX.

1. Drum		
2. Dust seal	8.	"O" ring
3. "O" ring	9.	Backing plate
4. Hub	10.	Dust seal
5. Brake shoes	11.	Lever
6. Springs	12.	Spring
7. Camshaft	13.	"O" ring

stays within range (R), then brake linings can be considered satisfactory.

R&R AND OVERHAUL. To remove rear brake shoes for inspection or renewal, first support rear of vehicle and remove rear wheels. Unscrew axle nut.

WARNING: Inhaling asbestos brake dust is injurious to human health. Approved OSHA respiration equipment must be worn when working on or around brake components. DO NOT use compressed air to clean brake drums, shoes or nearby components as brake dust will be blown into air. Only vacuum equipment designed to pick up brake dust should be used.

On LT-F4WDX models, unscrew brake drum nuts securing brake drum to axle hub, then use a suitable puller and remove axle hub. Remove brake drum cover (15—Fig. S13-27). Disassemble remainder of brake components as required.

On all other models, remove brake drum (1—Fig. S13-28) and, using a suitable puller, remove axle hub. Disassemble other brake components as required.

Brake shoes should be renewed if linings are worn to 1.5 mm (0.06 in.) or less. Brake drum should be renewed if inside diameter exceeds 165.7 mm (6.52 in.) on LT-4WD, LT-F4WD and LT-F250 models or 180.7 mm (7.11 in.) on LT-F4WDX models.

Reinstall brake shoes by reversing removal procedure while noting the following: Lightly coat brake camshaft and anchor pin with grease. Lightly coat splined portion of axle with grease. Apply Suzuki Bond 1216 to surface of hub where brake drum and hub flanges meet. On LT-F4WDX models, tighten brake drum to axle hub retaining nuts to 48-72 N·m (34.5-72 ft.-lbs.). Apply rear brake, then tighten rear axle nuts to 85-115 N·m (61.5-83.0 ft.-lbs.). Tighten wheel retaining nuts to 45-65 N·m (32.5-47.0 ft.-lbs.).

FRONT AND REAR FINAL DRIVE ASSEMBLIES

All Models

Service on front and rear final drive assemblies should be performed by a factory-trained service technician as Suzuki special tools are required.

YAMAHA

YAMAHA MOTOR CORP.
6555 Katella Ave.
Cypress, California 90630

YFM80 AND YFM100

NOTE: Metric fasteners are used throughout vehicle.

CONDENSED SERVICE DATA

MODELS	YFM80, YFM100
General	
Engine Make	Yamaha
Engine Type	Four-Stroke; Air-Cooled
Number of Cylinders	1
Bore:	
YFM80	47.0 mm
	(1.85 in.)
YFM100	49.0 mm
	(1.93 in.)
Stroke:	
YFM80	45.6 mm
	(1.795 in.)
YFM100	52.0 mm
	(2.05 in.)
Displacement:	
YFM80	79 cc
	(4.82 cu. in.)
YFM100	98 cc
	(5.98 cu. in.)
Compression Ratio:	
YFM80	9.0:1
YFM100	9.4:1
Engine Lubrication	Wet Sump; Oil Pump
Transmission Lubrication	Common With Engine
Engine/Transmission Oil	SAE 10W-40
Forward Speeds	4
Tire Size:	
Front: YFM80	17 × 7-7
YFM100	18 × 7-7
Rear: YFM80	18 × 9-7
YFM100	20 × 9-8
Tire Pressure	19.6 kPa
	(2.8 psi)
Dry Weight (Approx.)	99 kg
	(218 lbs.)
Tune-Up	
Engine Idle Speed:	
YFM80	1750-1850 rpm
YFM100	1400-1600 rpm

Tune-Up (Cont.)

Spark Plug:
NGK	C7HSA
Electrode Gap	0.6-0.7 mm
	(0.024-0.028 in.)

Ignition Type	Breakerless

Carburetor:
Make	Mikuni
Model	VM16SH
Bore Size	16 mm
	(0.63 in.)
Float Height	21 mm
	(0.827 in.)

Jet Needle:
YFM80	3HP9
YFM100	3PZ5
Clip Position	3rd Groove From Top

Throttle Cut-Away:
YFM80	3.0
YFM100	3.5
Pilot Jet	#12.5

Needle Jet:
YFM80	E-2
YFM100	D-8

Main Jet:
YFM80	#80
YFM100	#77.5
Throttle Lever Free Play	3-5 mm
	(0.12-0.20 in.)

Sizes-Clearances

Valve Clearance (cold):
Intake	0.05-0.10 mm
	(0.002-0.004 in.)
Exhaust	0.075-0.125 mm
	(0.003-0.005 in.)

Valve Face & Seat Angle:
Intake & Exhaust	45°
Valve Seat Width	0.9-1.1 mm
	(0.035-0.043 in.)

Valve Margin (Min.):
Intake	0.4 mm
	(0.016 in.)
Exhaust	0.8 mm
	(0.031 in.)

Valve Stem Diameter:
Intake	4.975-4.990 mm
	(0.1960-0.1965 in.)
Exhaust	4.960-4.975 mm
	(0.1953-0.1960 in.)

Valve Guide Bore Diameter:
Intake & Exhaust	5.000-5.012 mm
	(0.1969-0.1973 in.)

Valve Stem-to-Guide Clearance:
Intake	0.010-0.037 mm
	(0.0004-0.0015 in.)
Exhaust	0.025-0.052 mm
	(0.0010-0.0020 in.)

Sizes-Clearances (Cont.)

Valve Spring Free Length (Min.):
Intake & Exhaust . . . .
25.4 mm
(1.00 in.)

Rocker Arm Bore Wear Limit . . . .
10.05 mm
(0.3957 in.)

Rocker Shaft Diameter
Wear Limit . . . .
9.95 mm
(0.3917 in.)

Rocker Arm Bore-to-Shaft
Clearance . . . .
0.009-0.034 mm
(0.0004-0.0013 in.)

Camshaft Lobe Height
Wear Limit:
Intake & Exhaust . . . .
25.227 mm
(0.993 in.)

Camshaft Journal Wear
Limit:
Intake . . . .
20.971 mm
(0.826 in.)

Exhaust . . . .
20.995 mm
(0.827 in.)

Camshaft Runout (Max.) . . . .
0.03 mm
(0.0012 in.)

Piston Diameter:
Measured 4 mm (0.16 in.) From
Skirt Bottom & 90° to Pin Bore:
YFM80 . . . .
46.960-46.975 mm
(1.8488-1.8494 in.)

YFM100 . . . .
48.960-48.975 mm
(1.9276-1.9281 in.)

Piston-to-Cylinder Clearance . . . .
0.025-0.045 mm
(0.0010-0.0018 in.)

Cylinder Bore Taper (Max.) . . . .
0.05 mm
(0.002 in.)

Cylinder Bore Out-of-Round (Max.) . . . . . .
0.01 mm
(0.0004 in.)

Piston Ring End Gap:
Top:
YFM80 . . . .
0.10-0.25 mm
(0.004-0.010 in.)

YFM100 . . . .
0.15-0.30 mm
(0.006-0.012 in.)

Second:
YFM80 . . . .
0.10-0.25 mm
(0.004-0.010 in.)

YFM100 . . . .
0.15-0.30 mm
(0.006-0.012 in.)

Piston Ring Side Clearance:
Top:
YFM80 . . . .
0.030-0.065 mm
(0.0012-0.0026 in.)

YFM100 . . . .
0.030-0.060 mm
(0.0012-0.0024 in.)

Sizes-Clearances (Cont.)
Piston Ring Side Clearance: (Cont.)
 Second:
  YFM80. . . . . 0.020-0.055 mm
  (0.0008-0.0022 in.)
  YFM100. . . . . 0.020-0.060 mm
  (0.0008-0.0024 in.)

Connecting Rod Big End
 Side Clearance . . . . 0.10-0.40 mm
 (0.004-0.016 in.)

Connecting Rod Small End
 Side Shake . . . . 0.8-1.0 mm
 (0.03-0.04 in.)

Crankshaft Runout at Main
 Bearing Journal . . . . 0.05 mm
 (0.002 in.)

Capacities
Fuel Tank:
 YFM80. . . . . 5.4 L
 (1.4 gal.)
 YFM100. . . . . 6.8 L
 (1.8 gal.)
Engine/Transmission Sump. . . . . See Text
Final Drive . . . . 0.1 L
 (3.3 oz.)

Tightening Torques
Axle Nut:
 Front . . . . 65 N·m
 (47 ft.-lbs.)
 Rear. . . . . See Text
Clutch Boss Nut. . . . . 60 N·m
 (43 ft.-lbs.)

Cylinder Head:
 6 mm . . . . 10 N·m
 (88 in.-lbs.)
 7 mm . . . . 16 N·m
 (142 in.-lbs.)

Engine Mounting
 Screws. . . . . 33 N·m
 (24 ft.-lbs.)
Flywheel Nut . . . . 40 N·m
 (29 ft.-lbs.)

Wheel Nuts:
 Front & Rear . . . . 28 N·m
 (20 ft.-lbs.)

Standard Screws:
 6 mm . . . . 6 N·m
 (53 in.-lbs.)
 8 mm . . . . 15 N·m
 (133 in.-lbs.)
 10 mm . . . . 30 N·m
 (22 ft.-lbs.)
 12 mm . . . . 55 N·m
 (40 ft.-lbs.)
 14 mm . . . . 85 N·m
 (61 ft.-lbs.)
 16 mm . . . . 130 N·m
 (94 ft.-lbs.)

LUBRICATION

ENGINE AND TRANSMISSION. The engine and transmission are lubricated by a crankshaft-driven oil pump. Recommended oil is SAE 10W-40 with an API classification of SE or SF. The oil should be changed and the oil strainer should be cleaned after the first month of operation and every six months thereafter.

The oil sump is filled through fill plug (F—Fig. Y1-1) opening. The oil level must be maintained between the two marks on the oil plug dipstick. When checking the oil level, do not screw plug (F) into cover.

Drain oil by removing oil drain plug (D—Fig. Y1-2) located on the underside of crankcase. The oil strainer is located behind right crankcase cover (C—Fig. Y1-1). With oil drained from crankcase, remove the nine screws securing right crankcase cover and withdraw cover. Remove strainer located at base of crankcase. Clean strainer in a suitable solvent and renew if damage is noted. Install strainer, then install crankcase cover

with a new gasket. Tighten crankcase cover screws to 7 N·m (62 in.-lbs.).

Dry capacity of crankcase is 0.95 L (1.0 qt.) after an engine or transmission overhaul. Refilling after changing oil requires only 0.8 L (0.85 qt.) as approximately 0.15 L (0.158 qt.) of oil will be retained by crankcase castings.

CABLES AND LEVERS. Depending on use and riding conditions, periodically lubricate all cables with cable lubricant or SAE 10W-30 motor oil. Lubricate lever pivot pins and cable ends.

AIR CLEANER ELEMENT

All models are equipped with a foam-type air cleaner element located behind the panel on front of the front fender assembly. The air cleaner element should be removed and cleaned after the first three months of vehicle operation and every six months thereafter.

Remove the four screws retaining the air cleaner cover and withdraw the cover. Separate foam element from frame assembly. Clean the foam element in a nonflammable solvent. Carefully squeeze solvent out of element. Inspect the filter element for tears, holes or other damage. Allow the element to dry, then pour SAE 10W-30 oil into element. Squeeze out any excess oil. Too much oil in the foam element may affect the fuel:air ratio. Reinstall the foam element and reassemble frame. Apply a light film of grease around frame and install cover and securely tighten screws.

FUEL SYSTEM

CARBURETOR. The carburetor is connected to the throttle lever by a cable. Throttle lever free play (F—Fig. Y1-4) must be adjusted for proper operation. Throttle lever free play (F) should be 3-5 mm (0.12-0.20 in.) as measured at end of lever. Throttle free play is adjusted

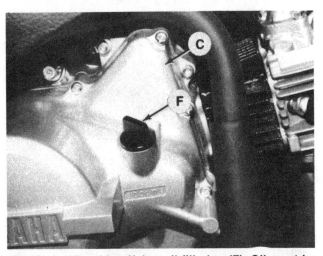

Fig. Y1-1—View identifying oil fill plug (F). Oil must be maintained between the two marks on the oil plug dipstick with the plug just resting on crankcase cover (C) opening.

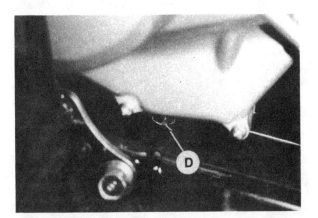

Fig. Y1-2—View identifies oil drain plug (D) located in underside of crankcase.

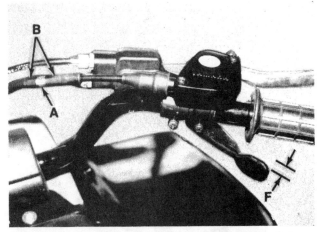

Fig. Y1-4—Throttle lever free play (F) should be 3-5 mm (0.12-0.20 in.). Slide dust boots (B) away from adjuster (A) and refer to text for adjustment procedures.

at lever on early models or at carburetor on later models. On early models, adjust free play by first sliding dust boots (B) away from adjuster assembly. Loosen locknut at end of adjuster and rotate adjuster (A) until recommended free play is obtained. Tighten locknut to retain

Fig. Y1-5—View identifies idle speed screw (2) and float bowl drain screw (3). Idle mixture screw is accessible after removing rubber plug (1).

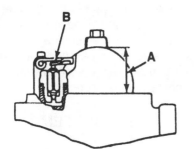

Fig. Y1-6—Float height (A) should be 21.0 mm (0.827 in.). Bend float arm tang (B) to adjust.

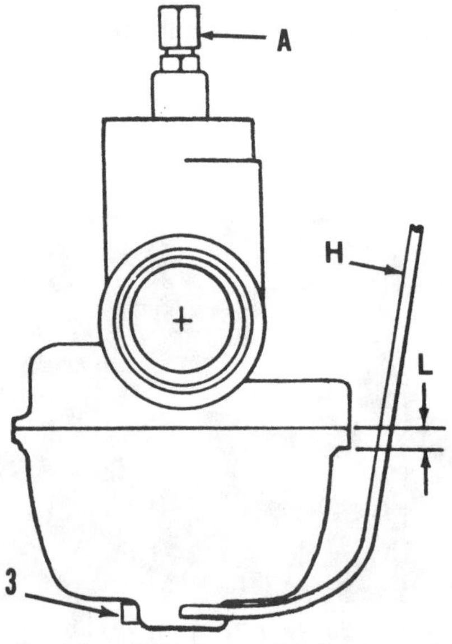

Fig. Y1-7—Fuel level (L) is measured from the bottom edge of carburetor body. Refer to text.

adjustment. On later models, perform same procedure using adjuster (A—Fig. Y1-7) on carburetor.

A Mikuni VM16SH sliding valve-type carburetor is used. Refer to CONDENSED SERVICE DATA for carburetor specifications. Initial setting of idle mixture screw is $1\frac{1}{2}$-$2\frac{1}{2}$ turns out from a lightly seated position on YFM80 models and $1\frac{1}{8}$ turns out on YFM100 models. Idle mixture screw is located behind rubber plug (1—Fig. Y1-5). Final adjustment should be performed with engine running at normal operating temperature. Adjust idle speed screw (2) to obtain recommended idle speed of 1750-1850 rpm on YFM80 models and 1400-1600 rpm on YFM100 models. After adjusting carburetor idle setting, check throttle lever free play as outlined in previous paragraph.

When servicing the carburetor, note the following: Jet needle clip should be located in third groove from the top. Float height (A—Fig. Y1-6) should be 21.0 mm (0.827 in.) as measured from gasket surface of carburetor body to lowest edge of float. Adjust the float level by bending tang (B) on float arm.

The fuel level is checked with the carburetor installed and vehicle operational. To check fuel level, attach Yamaha fuel level gauge YM-01312 or a suitable clear hose (H—Fig. Y1-7) to float bowl nozzle. Hose should be of sufficient length to extend above the bottom edge of carburetor body without kinking the hose. Open float bowl drain screw (3). Run engine at idle speed until fuel level in hose stabilizes, then stop engine. Measure the distance from the bottom edge of carburetor body (float bowl contact surface) to fuel level in hose to determine fuel level as shown at (L). Fuel level check will not be accurate if hose is raised or lowered after fuel level has stabilized. Fuel level (L) should be 2.5-4.5 mm (0.10-0.18 in.). To adjust fuel level, the float bowl must be removed to carefully bend float arm tang (B—Fig. Y1-6).

FUEL STRAINER. A strainer is mounted on the end of the "ON" pickup tube and the "RES" (reserve) pickup tube of the fuel valve assembly mounted on the fuel tank. To inspect the strainers, the fuel in the fuel tank must be drained. Disconnect the fuel hose from the fuel valve. Unscrew the two screws securing the fuel valve to the fuel tank and carefully remove the fuel valve from the tank. Clean and inspect the strainers. Reinstall valve assembly while noting that sealing washers are used on the two retaining screws to prevent fuel leakage.

IGNITION AND ELECTRICAL

SPARK PLUG. Standard spark plug is NGK C7HSA. Spark plug electrode gap should be 0.6-0.7 mm (0.024-0.027 in.). Spark plug should be removed, cleaned and electrode gap set after the first month of operation and every six months of operation thereafter. Renew spark plug if damage or excessive electrode wear is evident.

IGNITION SYSTEM. All models are equipped with a pointless, capacitor discharge ignition system. A source coil located behind the flywheel provides electrical power for the ignition system. The pickup coil is located on the outside and adjacent to the flywheel. The CDI unit and ignition coil are attached to the frame assembly below the fuel tank.

Ignition timing is not adjustable. Ignition timing should be correct if all components are in good working order.

Some ignition components can be checked using an ohmmeter. To check pickup coil, disconnect connector from CDI module that has green/white wire and white/red wire on YFM80 models and early YFM100 models. On later YFM100 models, disconnect connector with white/blue wire and white/red wire. Measure resistance between wires leading to pickup coil. Ohmmeter reading should be 297-363 ohms.

To check source coil, disconnect connector from CDI module that has white/black wire and black/red wire on YFM80 models and early YFM100 models. On later YFM100 models, disconnect connector with green/white wire and black/red wire. Measure resistance between wires leading to pickup coil. Ohmmeter reading should be 342-418 ohms.

Ignition coil resistance readings should be 1.44-1.76 ohms for the primary windings and 5280-7920 ohms for the secondary windings.

If the ignition system malfunctions and all components test satisfactory, replace CDI unit with a new or known to be good unit and recheck the ignition system.

ELECTRICAL SYSTEM

BATTERY. The battery is accessible after removing the seat. The negative battery terminal is grounded. The battery is 12 volt unit with 7 amp-hour capacity. Battery size is a 12N7D-3B.

The battery should be checked and filled to maximum level with distilled water, if required, after the first month of operation and then after every three months of operation. During periods of vehicle storage, the battery should be charged once a month to reduce sulfation and prolong battery life. The battery should always be removed from the vehicle prior to charging. Do not exceed maximum charging rate of 0.7 amperes for a period of 10 hours.

CHARGING SYSTEM. The charging system consists of a charge coil located behind the flywheel and a rectifier/regulator located just ahead of the taillight.

The charging system should produce 0.5 amps or more at 3000 rpm and 2.0 amps or more at 8000 rpm.

NOTE: Do not disconnect battery terminal wires while the engine is running as excessive charge coil output will damage the rectifier/regulator.

To check charge coil, disconnect the four-wire connector from magneto. Connect one ohmmeter lead to the white wire terminal and remaining tester lead to vehicle ground. The ohmmeter reading should be 0.81-0.99 ohm.

If the DC voltage produced by the charging system is less than or more than the previous recommended voltage range and the battery, charge coil and wiring is believed good, then the rectifier/regulator may be faulty and should be replaced with a new or good unit.

LIGHTING CIRCUIT. The lighting coil is located behind flywheel as a part of the charge coil. The lighting coil should produce 11 VAC or more at 3000 rpm and 15.5 VAC or less at 8000 rpm. The lighting coil produces current for the 12 volt-25/25 watt headlight and 12 volt-3.8 watt taillight.

Lighting coil can be checked statically using a suitable ohmmeter. Disconnect four-wire connector from magneto and check resistance between yellow/red wire and black wire terminals. Lighting coil can be considered satisfactory if resistance is approximately 0.4 ohm.

ELECTRIC STARTER. The starting circuit consists of the battery, main fuse, starter, starter relay, starter switch, cutoff relay and neutral switch. The cutoff relay and neutral switch prevent actuation of the starter relay unless the transmission is in neutral position. The starter relay and cutoff relay are located to the left of the battery.

The starter motor can be removed after first detaching battery cables and then detaching cable on starter motor. Unscrew the two screws securing the motor and withdraw starter motor. Note the "O" ring on the front of the motor. Minimum brush length is 3.5 mm (0.14 in.). Minimum commutator diameter is 15.5 mm (0.61 in.). Armature coil resistance should be 0.043 ohm.

WIRING. If wiring requires repair, always use replacement wire of the same gauge. Wires should be routed away from areas of extreme heat or sharp edges. Plastic tie straps should be used to retain wires in their original positions to prevent short circuiting.

FASTENERS

After the first month and every three months of operation thereafter, all fasteners should be checked and retightened if needed. Refer to TIGHTENING TORQUES section of CONDENSED SERVICE DATA for torque specifications.

VALVE SYSTEM

The valves are actuated via rocker arms by a single overhead camshaft. Camshaft is timed and driven by a roller drive chain from left end of crankshaft. Valve clearance should be adjusted after the first month of operation and every six months of operation thereafter. Valve clearance should be adjusted with engine cold.

To adjust valve clearance, first remove seat, battery, rear fender, shift pedal, left crankcase cover, spark plug and upper and lower valve adjustment caps (C—Fig. Y1-9). Rotate crankshaft until "T" mark (T—Fig. Y1-10) on flywheel aligns with stationary mark (M) on crankcase and piston is on compression stroke. To ensure

Fig. Y1-9—Remove valve adjustment cap (C) on top and bottom of cylinder head to expose intake and exhaust rocker arms.

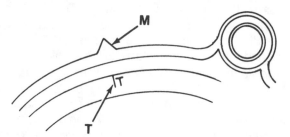

Fig. Y1-10—Align mark (T) on flywheel with stationary mark (M) on crankcase to position piston at top dead center (TDC).

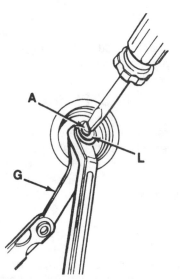

Fig. Y1-11—Measure valve clearance with a suitable feeler gauge (G). Loosen locknut (L) and rotate screw (A) to adjust valve clearance.

piston is on compression stroke, rotate crankshaft ¼ turn past top dead center (TDC) while observing intake valve. If valve movement is indicated, rotate crankshaft one full revolution and align timing marks again.

Clearance between rocker arm adjusting screw and valve stem should be 0.05-0.10 mm (0.002-0.004 in.) for intake valve and 0.075-0.125 mm (0.003-0.005 in.) for exhaust valve. Measure clearance using a suitable feeler gauge (G—Fig. Y1-11) then adjust clearance by loosening locknut (L) and turning screw (A). Be sure to recheck adjustment after locknuts have been tightened.

CAM CHAIN

ADJUSTMENT. Cam chain tension should be adjusted after the first month of operation and every six months of operation thereafter. Cam chain tension is adjusted with piston at top dead center (TDC) on compression stroke. Align timing marks as previously described in VALVE SYSTEM section to set piston at TDC on compression stroke; however, for cam chain tension adjustment, make sure flywheel is rotated in normal operation direction (counterclockwise) only. Remove crown nut (N—Fig. Y1-13) to expose adjuster screw. Loosen locknut (L) and lightly tighten adjuster screw. Tighten locknut (L) to 7 N·m (5.1 ft.-lbs.) to secure adjustment. Install and tighten crown nut (N) to 5 N·m (3.6 ft.-lbs.).

CLUTCH

ADJUSTMENT. An automatic multiple-disc clutch that is located behind the right side cover is used. The clutch should engage at approximately 2100 rpm. The clutch is actuated by centrifugal force, but is disengaged whenever the gear shift lever is operated.

To adjust clutch, remove cap in left crankcase cover to expose locknut (L—Fig. Y1-15) and adjuster screw (S). Loosen locknut (L) and rotate adjuster screw (S)

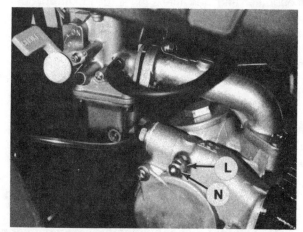

Fig. Y1-13—Remove crown nut (N) to expose cam chain adjuster screw. Loosen locknut (L) and rotate adjuster screw to adjust cam chain tension.

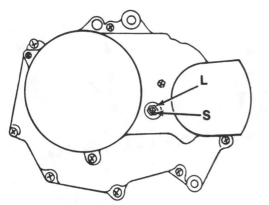

Fig. Y1-15—View identifying clutch adjuster screw (S) and locknut (L). Refer to text for adjustment procedure.

clockwise until slight resistance is felt. Turn screw 1/8 turn counterclockwise, hold position of adjuster screw (S) and tighten locknut (L) to secure adjustment.

FRONT BRAKE ASSEMBLY

BRAKE LEVER FREE PLAY. Recommended brake lever free travel measured at outer end of brake lever (L—Fig. Y1-19) should be 10-20 mm (0.4-0.8 in.). Brake lever free travel is adjusted by loosening locknuts (N) at equalizer bracket and rotating brake cable adjuster nuts (A) equally until recommended free travel is obtained. Equalizer bar must be parallel to bracket when lever free play is removed, if not loosen locknuts (N) on each brake cable and rotate cable adjuster nut (A) to reposition cable in bracket. Tighten locknuts (N) to retain adjustment on each cable, then recheck brake lever free travel and adjust brake cables in equal increments, if needed, to obtain recommended free travel.

OVERHAUL. Lining thickness may be determined externally by actuating brake and noting position of pointer (P—Fig. Y1-20) on each front brake actuating

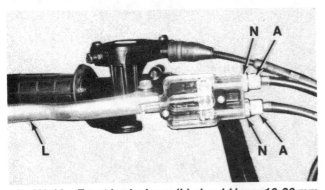

Fig. Y1-19—Front brake lever (L) should have 10-20 mm (0.4-0.8 in.) of free travel measured at outer end. Refer to text for adjustment procedures on cable adjuster nuts (A) and locknuts (N).

Fig. Y1-20—Pointer (P) should not rotate beyond mark (M) when front brake lever is applied or excessive brake lining wear is indicated and renewal of front brake shoes is required.

lever. There is sufficient brake lining if pointer does not reach brake lining limit mark (M) on brake backing plate.

WARNING: Inhaling asbestos brake dust is injurious to human health. Approved OSHA respiration equipment must be worn when working on or around brake components. DO NOT use compressed air to clean brake drums, shoes or nearby components as brake dust will be blown into air. Only vacuum equipment designed to pick up brake dust should be used.

Each front brake assembly is accessible after removing the respective brake drum. Renew the brake shoes if they are damaged or if the lining thickness is less than 2.0 mm (0.08 in.).

FRONT AXLE

The left and right front knuckle assemblies pivot on the end of each side of front axle tube. A grease fitting is located on the side of each knuckle. The manufacturer recommends injecting a lithium soap-based grease into fittings every six months.

Remove front wheel to service knuckle assembly. If excessive play between king pin and bushings is noted, then excessively worn components should be renewed. After servicing king pin assembly, tighten king pin nut to 30 N·m (22 ft.-lbs.) and install a new cotter pin.

On YFM100 models, install mounting bolts for front swing arm and shock absorbers so nut is to inside and tighten to 45 N·m (32 ft.-lbs.).

STEERING

TOE-IN SETTING. Place the steering handlebars in a straight ahead position. Use a suitable measuring tool

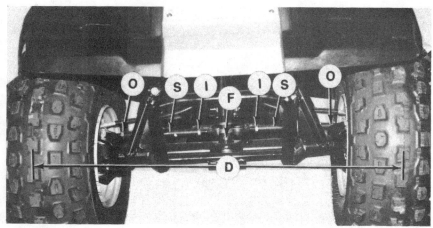

Fig. Y1-21—For correct toe-in setting, measured distance (D) should be shorter on the front than the measured distance on the rear. See text. Loosen inside (I) and outside (O) tie rod end locknuts and rotate tie rod shafts (S) in equal increments to adjust. Inject a lithium soap-based grease into lower steering shaft bushing through grease fitting (F) every six months.

and measure distance (D—Fig. Y1-21), at the spindle height, between the center of the tires on the front and rear sides. On YFM80 models, the measured distance (D) on the front side should be 0-3 mm (0-0.12 in.) shorter than the measured distance on the rear side. On YFM100 models, the difference should be 0-10 mm (0-0.4 in.). If not, loosen inside (I) and outside (O) locknuts on the left and right tie rod assemblies and rotate tie rod shafts (S) equally until measured distance is within recommended range.

After obtaining the correct setting, securely tighten the locknuts to retain tie rod settings.

INSPECTION. Rotate the handlebars from one extreme to the other and note if any binding or roughness is felt. Periodically inspect the steering components for looseness or any other damage. Renew any damaged component. Clean and grease components if excessive effort is noted. The manufacturer recommends injecting a lithium soap-based grease into lower steering shaft bushing through grease fitting (F—Fig. Y1-21) every six months.

OVERHAUL. To withdraw the steering shaft, loosen front carburetor intake clamp and disconnect ignition switch. Remove the handlebar assembly, front guard bar, front fender, tie rod ends from steering shaft, upper bushing holder and lower bushing holder cotter pin and nut, then withdraw steering shaft assembly.

Inspect components for excessive wear or any other damage and renew if needed. Grease upper and lower steering shaft bushings with a lithium soap-based grease prior to installing steering shaft. Tighten upper bushing holder cap screws to 23 N·m (17 ft.-lbs.) and bend tab on washer to retain cap screws. Tighten steering shaft lower nut to 30 N·m (22 ft.-lbs.) and install a new cotter pin. Tighten tie rod end nuts to 45 N·m (32 ft.-lbs.) and retain the new cotter pins. Complete reassembly in reverse order of disassembly.

REAR BRAKE ASSEMBLY

INSPECTION AND ADJUSTMENT. All models are equipped with a two-shoe internal expanding drum brake mounted on rear axle and actuated by either left handlebar lever or brake pedal on right side of vehicle.

Lining thickness may be determined externally by actuating brake and noting position of pointer (P—Fig. Y1-23) on actuating lever. There is sufficient brake lining if pointer does not reach or rotate beyond limit indicator (E) on backing plate.

Rear brake should be checked and adjusted after the first month of operation and then after every three months of operation. Brake lever (B—Fig. Y1-22) should have 10-20 mm (0.4-0.8 in.) of tree travel (F) on early models or 5-8 mm (0.2-0.4 in.) on later models. To adjust brake lever free travel, loosen locknut (N) and rotate adjuster nut (A) until recommended free travel is obtained. If adjuster nut (A) is near adjustment limit, loosen locknut (N) and rotate adjuster nut (A) completely inward. Rotate wing nut (W—Fig. Y1-23) at rear brake assembly until free travel is near recommended setting, then make final adjustment with adjuster nut (A—Fig.

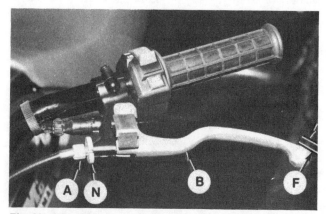

Fig. Y1-22—Rear brake lever (B) should have 10-20 mm (0.4-0.8 in.) of free travel (F) measured at outer end. Minor adjustments can be made by loosening locknut (N) and rotating adjuster nut (A).

Fig. Y1-23—Pointer (P) on actuating lever should not align or rotate beyond backing plate ear (E) when rear brake is applied. Rotate wing nut (R) to adjust brake pedal free travel and rotate wing nut (W) to adjust brake lever free travel.

Y1-22) and retain with locknut (N). Brake pedal should be adjusted to have 20-30 mm (0.8-1.2 in.) of free travel measured at pad end of brake pedal. Rotate wing nut (R—Fig. Y1-23) at rear brake assembly to adjust brake pedal free travel.

R&R AND OVERHAUL. To remove brake shoes and drum, support rear of vehicle and remove right rear axle cotter pin and nut. Detach right rear tire, wheel and hub assembly from axle.

WARNING: Inhaling asbestos brake dust is injurious to human health. Approved OSHA respiration equipment must be worn when working on or around brake components. DO NOT use compressed air to clean brake drums, shoes or nearby components as brake dust will be blown into air. Only vacuum equipment designed to pick up brake dust should be used.

Remove outer and inner axle shaft nuts. Remove brake drum cover (C—Fig. Y1-23). Slide brake drum off axle. Carefully remove brake shoes and springs from backing plate.

Brake shoes should be renewed if lining is worn to 2.0 mm (0.08 in.) or less. Brake drum should be renewed if inside diameter exceeds 130.5 mm (5.14 in.).

Reinstall by reversing removal procedure. On Models YFM80U and YFM100U, tighten axle shaft nuts using following procedure: Lightly tighten inner axle nut, then hold nut and tighten outer nut to 110 N·m (80 ft.-lbs.). Hold outer nut and rotate inner nut toward outer nut until a torque of 145 N·m (105 ft.-lbs.) is applied. On Models YFM100W, YFM100A and YFM100B, tighten axle shaft nuts using following procedure: Tighten inner axle nut to 110 N·m (80 ft.-lbs.). Hold inner nut and tighten outer axle nut to 130 N·m (96 ft.-lbs.). Place a mark across the two nuts. Tighten inner nut against outer nut until torque reading on inner nut is 160 N·m (118 ft.-lbs.). Distance between marks on nuts should be at least 3 mm (0.12 in.), if not retighten inner nut. Tighten axle shaft hub nut on all models to 85 N·m (61 ft.-lbs.) and install a new cotter pin. Adjust brake as outlined in INSPECTION AND ADJUSTMENT paragraphs.

FINAL DRIVE ASSEMBLY

Final drive service should be performed by a factory trained service technician as Yamaha special tools are required.

YAMAHA
YFA1

NOTE: Metric fasteners are used throughout vehicle.

CONDENSED SERVICE DATA

MODEL	YFA1
General	
Engine Make	Yamaha
Engine Type	Four-Stroke; Air-Cooled
Number of Cylinders	1
Bore	49.0 mm
	(1.93 in.)
Stroke	66.0 mm
	(2.60 in.)
Displacement	124 cc
	(7.56 cu. in.)
Compression Ratio	9.0:1
Engine Lubrication	Wet Sump; Oil Pump
Engine Oil	SAE 10W-40
Transmission Positions	Forward, Neutral & Reverse
Transmission Speeds	Variable
Transmission Lubrication	Sump
Transmission Oil	SAE 10W-40
Tire Size:	
Front	20 × 7-8
Rear	22 × 10-8
Tire Pressure:	
Front	20 kPa
	(2.9 psi)
Rear	25 kPa
	(3.6 psi)
Battery	12V-12AH
Vehicle Weight W/Full Fuel Tank	144 kg
	(317 lbs.)
Tune-Up	
Engine Idle Speed	1650-1750 rpm
Compression Pressure	850 kPa
	(123 psi)
Spark Plug:	
NGK	C7HSA
Electrode Gap	0.6-0.7 mm
	(0.024-0.028 in.)
Ignition:	
Type	Breakerless
Timing	7° BTDC @ 1700 rpm
	27° BTDC @ 5000 rpm
Carburetor:	
Make	Mikuni
Model	VM18SH
Jet Needle	4H36

Tune-Up (Cont.)

Carburetor: (Cont.)

Clip Position......................	3rd Groove From Top
Throttle Cut-Away	2.5
Pilot Jet	#12.5
Needle Jet	N-6
Main Jet..........................	#82.5
Float Height	21.8-22.8 mm
	(0.858-0.898 in.)
Idle Mixture Setting	2½ Turns
Throttle Lever Free Play	1-4 mm
	(0.04-0.16 in.)

Sizes-Clearances

Valve Clearance (cold):	
Intake...........................	0.08-0.12 mm
	(0.003-0.005 in.)
Exhaust	0.10-0.14 mm
	(0.004-0.006 in.)
Valve Face & Seat Angle:	
Intake & Exhaust	45°
Valve Seat Width	0.9-1.1 mm
	(0.035-0.043 in.)
Valve Margin (Min.):	
Intake...........................	0.4 mm
	(0.016 in.)
Exhaust	0.8 mm
	(0.031 in.)
Valve Stem Diameter:	
Intake...........................	4.975-4.990 mm
	(0.1960-0.1965 in.)
Exhaust	4.960-4.975 mm
	(0.1953-0.1960 in.)
Valve Guide Bore Diameter:	
Intake & Exhaust	5.000-5.012 mm
	(0.1969-0.1973 in.)
Valve Stem-to-Guide Clearance:	
Intake...........................	0.010-0.037 mm
	(0.0004-0.0015 in.)
Exhaust	0.025-0.052 mm
	(0.0010-0.0020 in.)
Valve Spring Free Length (Min):	
Intake & Exhaust	28.63 mm
	(1.127 in.)
Rocker Arm Bore	10.00-10.15 mm
	(0.394-0.400 in.)
Rocker Shaft Diameter	9.981-9.991 mm
	(0.3930-0.3933 in.)
Rocker Arm Bore-to-Shaft Clearance	0.009-0.034 mm
	(0.0004-0.0013 in.)
Camshaft Lobe Height:	
Intake & Exhaust	26.17-26.27 mm
	(1.030-1.034 in.)
Camshaft Journal Diameter:	
Intake & Exhaust	21.06-21.17 mm
	(0.829-0.833 in.)
Camshaft Runout (Max.)	0.03 mm
	(0.0012 in.)

Sizes-Clearances (Cont.)

Piston Diameter:
  Measured 6 mm (0.24 in.) From
  Skirt Bottom & 90° to Pin Bore . . . .   48.96-49.00 mm
                                             (1.928-1.929 in.)

Piston-to-Cylinder Clearance. . . . .   0.020-0.040 mm
                                         (0.0008-0.0016 in.)

Cylinder Bore. . . . .   49.030-49.045 mm
                                         (1.9303-1.9309 in.)

Piston Ring End Gap:
  Top & Second Rings . . . .   0.15-0.30 mm
                                           (0.006-0.012 in.)
  Oil Ring . . . .   0.30-0.90 mm
                                           (0.012-0.035 in.)

Piston Ring Side Clearance:
  Top. . . . .   0.03-0.07 mm
                                           (0.0012-0.0028 in.)
  Second. . . . .   0.02-0.06 mm
                                           (0.0008-0.0024 in.)

Connecting Rod Big End
  Side Clearance . . . .   0.05-0.45 mm
                                           (0.002-0.018 in.)

Connecting Rod Small
  End Side Shake. . . . .   0.8-1.0 mm
                                           (0.03-0.04 in.)

Crankshaft Runout at
  Main Bearing Journal. . . . .   0.03 mm
                                           (0.0012 in.)

Capacities

Fuel Tank . . . .   7.0 L
                                           (1.8 gal.)
Engine Sump . . . .   See Text
Transmission Sump . . . .   0.60 L
                                           (0.63 qt.)

Tightening Torques

Axle Nut:
  Front . . . .   70 N•m
                                           (51 ft.-lbs.)
  Rear. . . . .   120 N•m
                                           (85 ft.-lbs.)

Camshaft Sprocket . . . .   26 N•m
                                           (19 ft.-lbs.)

Crankcase . . . .   7 N•m
                                           (62 in.-lbs.)

Cylinder Base Screws . . . .   10 N•m
                                           (88 in.-lbs.)

Cylinder Head:
  6 mm . . . .   10 N•m
                                           (88 in.-lbs.)
  8 mm . . . .   22 N•m
                                           (16 ft.-lbs.)

Drive Clutch Nut.   55 N•m
                                           (40 ft.-lbs.)

Driven Clutch Pulley Nut . . . .   90 N•m
                                           (66 ft.-lbs.)

Driven Clutch Housing Nut . . . .   60 N•m
                                           (44 ft.-lbs.)

Tightening Torques (Cont.)

Engine Mounting Nuts . . . . 42 N·m
(31 ft.-lbs.)

Flywheel . . . . 70 N·m
(51 ft.-lbs.)

Rear Sprocket . . . . 62 N·m
(46 ft.-lbs.)

Spark Plug . . . . 13 N·m
(115 in.-lbs.)

Transmission Sprocket . . . . 75 N·m
(55 ft.-lbs.)

Wheel Nuts:
Front & Rear . . . . 55 N·m
(40 ft.-lbs.)

Standard Screws:
6 mm . . . . 6 N·m
(53 in.-lbs.)

8 mm . . . . 15 N·m
(133 in.-lbs.)

10 mm . . . . 30 N·m
(22 ft.-lbs.)

12 mm . . . . 55 N·m
(40 ft.-lbs.)

14 mm . . . . 85 N·m
(61 ft.-lbs.)

16 mm . . . . 130 N·m
(94 ft.-lbs.)

LUBRICATION

ENGINE. The engine is lubricated by a crankshaft-driven oil pump. Recommended oil is SAE 10W-30 with an API classification of SE and/or SF. The engine is not equipped with an oil filter.

Oil level should be maintained at upper mark on dipstick attached to fill plug (F—Fig. Y3-1). Do not screw plug in when checking oil level. Fill sump through opening for fill plug (F). Drain oil by removing drain plug on underside of crankcase.

The manufacturer recommends changing the oil after the first month of operation and every six months thereafter. Fill crankcase with 1.25 L (1.32 qt.) when changing oil. Crankcase capacity totally dry is 1.45 L (1.53 qt.).

TRANSMISSION. The transmission oil should be checked after the first month of operation. Change oil annually. Oil level should be maintained at hole for level screw (L—Fig. Y3-1). Add oil through hole for fill plug (P). Recommended oil is SAE 10W-30 with an API classification of SE and/or SF. Transmission oil capacity is 0.6 L (0.63 qt.).

DRIVE CHAIN. The drive chain should be lubricated with SAE 30-50 gear oil after first month of operation and after every 30 days of operation thereafter. The chain utilizes "O" rings to seal the chain rollers and pins. Incorrect lubrication may damage the "O" rings resulting in premature chain failure.

Fig. Y3-1—A dipstick is attached to fill plug (F) to check oil level in engine sump. The oil in the transmission should be level with hole for oil level screw (L). Add oil to transmission through opening for fill plug (P).

Remove and clean the drive chain when excessive dirt is evident. Remove chain as outlined in DRIVE CHAIN AND SPROCKETS section. The chain should be thoroughly washed in kerosene and wiped dry. The use of any cleaning solution other than kerosene may damage "O" rings. Lubricate chain with SAE 30-50 gear oil, then install and adjust chain as outlined in DRIVE CHAIN AND SPROCKETS section.

SUSPENSION AND STEERING. The grease fittings on suspension components should be injected with lithium base grease after initial month of operation and every three months thereafter. Grease fittings are located at lower steering shaft bearing, front suspension control arms, steering knuckles and swing arm.

The upper steering shaft bushing should be lubricated with lithium base grease every six months.

CABLES AND LEVERS. All cables and levers should be inspected and lubricated after first month of operation and every three months thereafter.

AIR CLEANER ELEMENT

All models are equipped with a foam-type air cleaner element located underneath the seat. The air cleaner element should be removed and cleaned every three months or more frequently if operating conditions are severe.

To remove air cleaner element, remove seat, detach cover and remove filter element. Thoroughly clean the foam element in a nonflammable solvent. Compress element between hands to remove solvent. Do not wring or twist element. Saturate element in clean SAE 10W-30 engine oil, then compress element to remove excess oil.

FUEL SYSTEM

CARBURETOR. The engine is equipped with a Mikuni VM18SH carburetor. Initial setting of idle mixture

screw (I—Fig. Y3-5) is 2½ turns out from a lightly seated position. Final adjustment must be performed with engine at normal operating temperature. Adjust idle speed screw (S) so engine idles at 1650-1750 rpm. Rotate idle mixture screw (I) so engine runs at highest idle speed, then readjust idle speed screw (S) so engine idles at specified rpm.

When servicing carburetor, refer to Fig. Y3-7 for an exploded view of carburetor and to carburetor specifications in CONDENSED SERVICE DATA section while

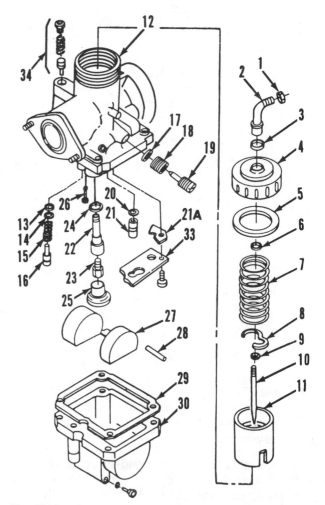

Fig. Y3-7—Exploded view of Mikuni VM18SH carburetor.

1. Nut
2. Cable guide
3. Washer
4. Cap
5. Washer
6. "E" ring
7. Spring
8. Retainer
9. Jet needle clip
10. Jet needle
11. Throttle slide
12. Body
13. "O" ring
14. Washer
15. Spring
16. Idle mixture screw
17. "O" ring
18. Spring
19. Idle speed screw
20. Washer
21. Inlet valve
21A. Retainer
22. Needle jet
23. Main jet
24. Washer
25. Cover
26. Pilot jet
27. Float
28. Pin
29. Gasket
30. Fuel bowl
33. Retainer
34. Starter valve assy.

Fig. Y3-5—Initial setting for idle mixture screw (I) is 2-1/2 turns out. Adjust idle speed screw (S) so engine idles at 1650-1750 rpm.

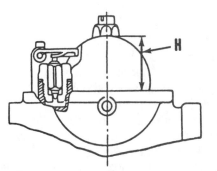

Fig. Y3-8—Float height (H) should be 21.8-22.8 mm (0.858-0.898 in.). Bend float arm tang to adjust float height.

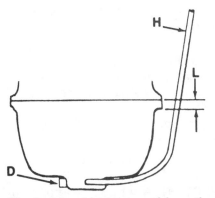

Fig. Y3-9—The fuel level is measured from the bottom edge of the carburetor body. Fuel level (L) should be 2.0-4.0 mm (0.08-0.16 in.) below carburetor body edge.

noting the following: Jet needle clip (9) should be installed in third groove from top of jet needle. Installing clip in a lower groove on jet needle will richen mid-range fuel mixture. Invert carburetor and measure float height as shown in Fig. Y3-8. Bend float arm tang to adjust float height. Make sure groove in side of throttle slide is aligned with pin in carburetor body when inserting slide in carburetor.

With the carburetor installed, the fuel level should be checked. Attach Yamaha fuel level gauge YM-01312 or a suitable clear hose (H—Fig. Y3-9) to fuel bowl nozzle. Hose should be long enough to extend above the bottom edge of carburetor body without kinking. Open fuel bowl drain screw (D). Run the engine at idle speed until fuel level in hose stabilizes, then stop engine. Measure distance from the bottom edge of carburetor body (fuel bowl contact surface) to fuel level in hose to determine fuel level (L). Fuel level check will not be accurate if hose is moved after fuel level is stabilized. Fuel level (L) should be 2.0-4.0 mm (0.08-0.16 in.) below carburetor body edge. To adjust fuel level, remove the fuel bowl and carefully bend float arm tang.

THROTTLE LEVER FREE PLAY. Free play (F—Fig. Y3-10) at the end of throttle lever should be 1-4 mm (0.04-0.16 in.). To adjust free play, slide back rubber

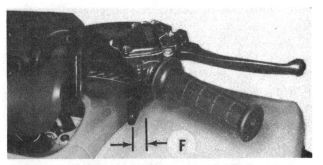

Fig. Y3-10—Free play (F) at the end of throttle lever should be 1-4 mm (0.04-0.16 in.). To adjust free play, slide back rubber boot, loosen locknut and rotate cable adjuster at top of carburetor.

boot, loosen locknut and rotate cable adjuster at top of carburetor. Retighten locknut.

IGNITION SYSTEM

The engine is equipped with a breakerless, capacitor discharge ignition system. The electronic ignition circuit consists of the flywheel, CDI module, source coil, pickup coil, ignition coil, spark plug, ignition switch and engine stop switch. To check ignition timing, remove right footboard and timing plug (P—Fig. Y3-12). Connect a power timing light to engine. Ignition timing (7° BTDC) at idle speed should occur when "H" mark on flywheel is aligned with pointer on case. Ignition timing is not adjustable. If ignition timing is not as specified, check condition of ignition components as described in the following test procedures and renew faulty or questionable components.

To check the pickup coil, disconnect connector between the pickup coil and the CDI module. Connect an ohmmeter lead to the grey lead from the pickup coil and the other ohmmeter lead to the red lead from the pickup coil. Ohmmeter reading should be 280-420 ohms.

To check the source coil, disconnect the connector between the source coil and the CDI module. Connect an ohmmeter between brown wire and green wire leads

Fig. Y3-12—Remove plug (P) to view ignition timing marks.

from source coil. Source coil resistance should be 310-400 ohms.

Ignition coil resistance reading should be 0.56-0.84 ohms for primary windings and 5.7-8.5k ohms for secondary windings.

If the ignition system malfunctions and all components test satisfactory, replace CDI module with a new or good unit and recheck ignition system.

ELECTRICAL SYSTEM

The vehicle is equipped with a charging system, battery and electric starter. The system is protected by a 5 amp fuse.

BATTERY. The battery is accessible after removing the seat. The negative terminal is grounded. The battery is a 12-volt unit with 12 amp-hour capacity.

CHARGING SYSTEM. The charging circuit consists of an alternator and a regulator/rectifier. The alternator rotor (flywheel) is attached to the right end of the crankshaft while the stator is mounted behind the rotor on the side of the right crankcase half. The regulator/rectifier module is mounted on the front of the vehicle frame.

The charging circuit should produce 14-15 VDC at 5000 rpm.

NOTE: Do not disconnect battery terminal wires while the engine is running as excessive alternator output will damage the regulator/rectifier.

To check the alternator stator coils, disconnect the connector with white, black and yellow leads from the alternator. Measure resistance between white wire and black wire. Resistance should be 0.56-0.84 ohm.

If previous tests prove satisfactory and fuse, wiring and connections are all good, replace regulator/rectifier with a good unit and recheck operation.

ELECTRIC STARTER. The starting circuit consists of the starter, starter relay, starter switch, cutoff relay, neutral switch and main switch. The cutoff relay and neutral switch prevent energizing starter relay unless neutral switch is in correct position.

The starter relay and cutoff relay are near the battery. The neutral switch is located on the left side of the engine. The electric starter motor is mounted on the front of the engine.

The starter motor can be removed after detaching the battery leads, starter motor leads and unscrewing the two screws securing the motor. Note the "O" ring on the front of the motor. Minimum brush length is 3.5 mm (0.14 in.). Minimum commutator diameter is 22 mm (0.866 in.). Armature coil resistance should be 0.016-0.024 ohm.

LIGHTING CIRCUIT. The lighting coil along with the alternator coils is located behind the flywheel to provide electrical power for the lights.

The lighting coil can be checked using an ohmmeter. Connect an ohmmeter to yellow wire and black wire leads to engine. Resistance should be 0.32-0.48 ohms.

To check the voltage regulator, disconnect the green wire and black wire leads to headlight. Connect positive lead of a voltmeter to green wire and negative voltmeter lead to black wire. Place headlight switch in low position. The voltmeter should indicate at least 12 volts with engine running at 3000 rpm and less than 14.8 volts at 8000 rpm. If specified voltage is not produced, renew voltage regulator with a new or good unit and recheck voltage.

The headlight is a 12V 25W/25W unit while the taillight is a 12V 3.8W unit.

WIRING. If wiring requires repair, always install wire that is the same gauge as original wire. Wires should be routed away from areas of extreme heat or sharp edges. Attach or hold wires in their original position using plastic tie straps to prevent short circuits.

DRIVE BELT

INSPECTION. A V-type drive belt transfers power through the torque convertor from the engine to the transmission. To inspect the drive belt, remove the seat, fuel tank cover and front fender deck. Remove the left foot board and bracket. Remove the air duct and left engine side cover. Wipe off any dirt or grease on the drive belt and inspect it for cracks, tears and other damage. Renew the belt if damaged or belt width is less than 18.1 mm (0.712 in.).

FASTENERS

After the first month of operation and every three months thereafter, the vehicle should receive an overall inspection. All screws, nuts and other fasteners should be checked and tightened to proper torque specification shown in CONDENSED SERVICE DATA section or in the appropriate maintenance section.

FRONT BRAKE SYSTEM

BRAKE LEVER FREE PLAY. Recommended brake lever free travel is 10-12 mm (0.39-0.47 in.) measured at gap between lever housing (H—Fig. Y3-14) and brake equalizer bar (B). Adjust lever free play by loosening locknut (N) and rotating brake cable adjuster (A) for each front brake. Gap between bar (B) and housing (H) should be the same for each cable.

OVERHAUL. Brake lining thickness may be checked externally by operating brake and noting position of

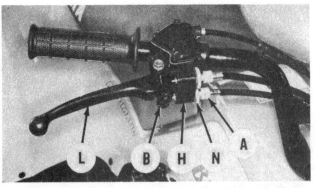

Fig. Y3-14—Brake lever free travel should be 10-12 mm (0.39-0.47 in.) measured at gap between lever housing (H) and equalizer bar (B). Adjust lever free play by loosening locknut (N) and rotating brake cable adjuster (A) for each front brake. Gap between equalizer bar (B) and housing (H) should be equal for each cable.

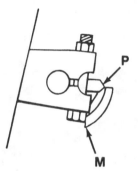

Fig. Y3-15—Brake linings are worn excessively if pointer (P) passes end of wear range scale (M) when brake is actuated.

pointer (P—Fig. Y7-15) on each front brake actuating lever. There is sufficient brake lining remaining if pointer does not align with or pass mark (M).

WARNING: Inhaling asbestos brake dust is injurious to human health. Approved OSHA respiration equipment must be worn when working on or around brake components. DO NOT use compressed air to clean brake drums, shoes or nearby components as brake dust will be blown into air. Only vacuum equipment designed to pick up brake dust should be used.

Each front brake assembly is accessible after removing the brake drum/hub. Renew the brake shoes if damaged or if lining is worn to less than 2.0 mm (0.08 in.). Renew the brake drum assembly if inside diameter exceeds 111.0 mm (4.37 in.). Tighten hub retaining nut to 70 N·m (51 ft.-lbs.). Tighten wheel retaining nuts to 55 N·m (40 ft.-lbs.).

FRONT AXLE

Both front steering knuckle assemblies pivot on king pins at the end of a control arm. The control arm pivots vertically and is attached to the vehicle frame by bolts. A shock absorber with a coil spring is attached to the vehicle frame and the control arm.

Remove front wheel for access to hub and spindle. Unscrew hub nut to remove wheel hub. The hub and brake drum are one piece. Renew bearings if rough or otherwise damaged. Be sure to install spacer between bearings when reassembling components. Tighten hub retaining nut to 70 N·m (51 ft.-lbs.). Tighten wheel retaining nuts to 55 N·m (40 ft.-lbs.).

Remove the front wheel to service the knuckle assembly. If excessive play between king pin and bushings is noted, then components should be renewed. Grease king pin prior to installation. Tighten castle nut securing king pin bolt to 30 N·m (22 ft.-lbs.) and install a new cotter pin. If control arm was removed, tighten control arm mounting bolts to 32 N·m (24 ft.-lbs.). Tighten retaining nut for tie rod end to 25 N·m (18 ft.-lbs.). Tighten shock absorber upper and lower mounting bolts to 45 N·m (33 ft.-lbs.).

STEERING

INSPECTION. Rotate the handlebar from one extreme to the other and note if any binding or roughness is felt. Periodically inspect the steering components for looseness or any other damage. Renew any damaged component. Clean and grease components if binding or excessive effort is noted.

TOE-IN SETTING. Place the handlebar in a straight ahead position. Use a suitable measuring tool and measure distance (B—Fig. Y3-17) at spindle height

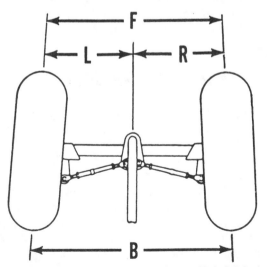

Fig. Y3-17—Toe-in should be 0-10 mm (0.0-0.4 in.). Refer to text for measurement and adjustment procedures.

between the center of the tires on the rear sides. Locate the same tire centerline points on front side of tires and measure front distance (F). The toe-in distance on the front side (F) should be shorter than the measured distance on the rear side (B). Specified toe-in is 0-10 mm (0.0-0.4 in.). Note that the distance from a projected vehicle centerline to left (L) and right (R) tire centerlines should also be equal.

To adjust, loosen inside and outside locknuts on the left and right tie rod assemblies and rotate tie rod shaft on each side equally until distance is within recommended range. After obtaining the correct setting, tighten locknuts to 30 N·m (22 ft.-lbs.).

OVERHAUL. To expose steering shaft, remove seat, fuel tank cover and front fender deck. Detach headlight unit. Disconnect any cables or wires that will prevent separation of handlebar from steering shaft and remove handlebar. Unscrew the two cap screws securing the steering shaft clamp halves. Clean the old grease from the steering shaft. Inspect the clamp halves and steering shaft for damage. Renew components if needed. Grease inside of steering shaft clamp halves with a lithium base grease and install. Tighten the retaining clamp cap screws to 23 N·m (17 ft.-lbs.).

To remove steering shaft, expose steering shaft as outlined in preceding paragraph. Remove the lower steering shaft retaining cotter pin and nut. Detach inner tie rod ends from steering shaft and withdraw the steering shaft. Note "O" rings adjacent to bushings and renew if damaged. Inspect the bushings and renew if needed. Apply a lithium base grease to bushings before installation of steering shaft. Tighten the lower steering shaft retaining nut to 30 N·m (22 ft.-lbs.). Tighten retaining nuts for tie rod ends to 25 N·m (18 ft.-lbs.).

When installing handlebar, install upper clamp so punch mark is toward front of handlebar. Tighten front screw on handlebar clamps first, then tighten the rear clamp screws. If properly tightened, there should be no gaps at the front of the clamps and even gaps at the rear of the clamps. Tighten clamp screws to 20 N·m (15 ft.-lbs.).

REAR BRAKE SYSTEM

INSPECTION AND ADJUSTMENT. The rear brake lever should have 5-8 mm (0.2-0.3 in.) free play measured at gap (G—Fig. Y3-19) between lever and housing. Adjust free play by rotating cable adjusters at lever or brake end of brake cable.

A rear brake lining indicator (I—Fig. Y3-20) is attached to brake cam. To externally check brake lining wear, apply rear brake and note position of indicator (I) with mark (M) on backing plate. Brake shoes should be renewed if indicator aligns or passes mark (M).

R&R AND OVERHAUL. To remove brake shoes and drum, support rear of vehicle and remove left rear axle

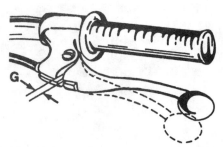

Fig. Y3-19—The rear brake lever should have 5-8 mm (0.2-0.3 in.) free play measured at gap (G) between lever and housing.

Fig. Y3-20—To check brake lining wear, apply rear brake and note position of indicator (I) with mark (M) on backing plate. Brake shoes should be renewed if indicator aligns or passes mark (M). To adjust drive chain tension, loosen upper (U) and lower (L) screws. Loosen locknuts and rotate chain tension adjuster screws (C) until specified chain tension is obtained.

cotter pin and nut. Detach left rear tire, wheel and hub assembly from axle.

WARNING: Inhaling asbestos brake dust is injurious to human health. Approved OSHA respiration equipment must be worn when working on or around brake components. DO NOT use compressed air to clean brake drum, shoes or nearby components as brake dust will be blown into air. Only vacuum equipment designed to pick up brake dust should be used.

Remove outer brake drum cover, then remove inner brake drum cover. Unscrew retaining nuts and remove brake drum. Carefully remove brake shoes and springs from backing plate.

Brake shoes should be renewed if lining is worn to 2.0 mm (0.08 in.) or less. Brake drum should be renewed if inside diameter exceeds 131 mm (5.16 in.).

Reinstall by reversing removal procedure. Tighten brake drum retaining nuts to 21 N·m (186 in.-lbs.).

Tighten axle shaft hub nut to 120 N·m (88 ft.-lbs.) and install a new cotter pin. Adjust brake as outlined in INSPECTION AND ADJUSTMENT paragraphs.

DRIVE CHAIN AND SPROCKETS

INSPECTION AND ADJUSTMENT. The final drive chain should be inspected and adjusted after the first month of operation and every six months thereafter. Improper maintenance and neglect can cause early failure of both drive chain and sprockets. With vehicle unloaded, measure drive chain travel at a point midway between sprockets. Drive chain free play should be approximately 30 mm (1 3/16 in.).

To adjust chain tension, loosen rear axle housing retaining screws (L and U—Fig. Y3-20), loosen adjusting screw locknut and rotate tension adjusting screw (C). Early models are equipped with a single adjusting screw while later models are equipped with adjusting screws on both ends of axle housing. Tighten upper axle housing retaining screws (U) to 85 N·m (63 ft.-lbs.) and lower axle housing retaining screws (L) to 60 N·m (44 ft.-lbs.) and recheck drive chain tension. Renew drive chain if recommended tension adjustment cannot be obtained. Refer to LUBRICATION for drive chain lubrication requirements.

R&R AND OVERHAUL. To remove the drive chain and both sprockets, remove left foot board and bracket. Use a location at rear of vehicle frame and lift rear wheels off the ground. Remove right rear wheel and hub. Detach shock absorber from lower mount. Loosen rear axle housing screws (L and U—Fig. Y3-20) and back off chain tension adjuster screws (C) to slacken chain. Remove nut securing swing arm pivot shaft. Support swing arm assembly and withdraw swing arm pivot shaft. Withdraw swing arm assembly far enough to provide clearance for drive chain removal. Remove front (engine) sprocket and drive chain. Remove front sprocket if needed. To remove rear sprocket, unscrew sprocket retaining nuts and remove sprocket.

Carefully examine sprockets for excessive wear. Worn sprockets will usually have a hooked tooth profile. A good test is to place a new chain on a used sprocket and check the fit. If sprockets require renewal due to wear, always renew drive chain. Sprockets should be renewed as a set. Renew drive chain if distance between 10 link pins exceeds 150.1 mm (5.91 in.) with chain straight and all slack removed.

Reassemble by reversing disassembly procedure. Tighten engine sprocket retaining nut to 75 N·m (55 ft.-lbs.). Tighten rear sprocket retaining nuts to 62 N·m (46 ft.-lbs.). Tighten swing arm pivot screw to 80 N·m (59 ft.-lbs.). Tighten axle hub nut to 120 N·m (88 ft.-lbs.). Refer to previous INSPECTION AND ADJUSTMENT paragraphs for recommended drive chain adjustment procedures.

FINAL DRIVE ASSEMBLY

R&R AND OVERHAUL. Support rear of vehicle and remove rear brake assembly and drive chain as previously outlined. Unscrew axle nuts next to sprocket hub and remove sprocket hub. Withdraw axle.

Renew seals, bearings and other damaged or excessively worn components as needed. Maximum axle runout with axle supported at bearing journals is 1.5 mm (0.060 in.). Reassembly is reverse order of disassembly. Lubricate splined areas with lithium base grease. When tightening axle nuts adjacent to sprocket hub, use the following procedure. Apply Loctite to nuts and tighten inner nut to 55 N·m (40 ft.-lbs.). Hold inner nut and tighten outer nut to 190 N·m (140 ft.-lbs.). Hold outer nut and tighten inner nut toward outer nut to 240 N·m (176 ft.-lbs.). Tighten axle hub nuts to 120 N·m (88 ft.-lbs.).

YAMAHA

YFM200DX, YFM225, YFM250, YFU1 AND YFU1T

NOTE: Metric fasteners are used throughout vehicle.

CONDENSED SERVICE DATA

MODELS	YFM200DX	YFM225	YFM250, YFU1, YFU1T
General			
Engine Make	Yamaha	Yamaha	Yamaha
Engine Type	Four-Stroke; Air-Cooled	Four-Stroke; Air-Cooled	Four-Stroke; Air-Cooled
Number of Cylinders	1	1	1
Bore	67 mm (2.64 in.)	70 mm (2.76 in.)	71 mm (2.80 in.)
Stroke	55.7 mm (2.19 in.)	58 mm (2.28 in.)	58 mm (2.28 in.)
Displacement	196 cc (12.0 cu. in.)	223.2 cc (13.6 cu. in.)	229.6 cc (14.0 cu. in.)
Compression Ratio	8.5:1	8.8:1	8.8:1
Engine Lubrication	Wet Sump; Oil Pump	Wet Sump; Oil Pump	Wet Sump; Oil Pump
Transmission Lubrication	Common With Engine	Common With Engine	Common With Engine
Engine/Transmission Oil	SAE 10W-40	SAE 10W-40	SAE 10W-40
Forward Speeds	5	5	5
Reverse Speeds	1	1	1
Tire Size:			
Front	22x8-10	22x8-10	22x8-10
Rear	22x10-8	25x13-9	22x12-9
Tire Pressure:			
Front	19.6 kPa (2.8 psi)	19.6 kPa (2.8 psi)	20 kPa* (2.9 psi)
Rear	16.7 kPa (2.4 psi)	16.7 kPa (2.4 psi)	20 kPa* (2.9 psi)
Battery	12V-14AH	12V-14AH	12V-14AH
Vehicle Weight W/Full Fuel Tank	184 kg (405 lbs.)	216 kg (475 lbs.)	216 kg** (475 lbs.)

*Recommended tire pressure for YFU1 and YFU1T models is 30 kPa (4.3 psi) for front tires and 40 kPa (5.8 psi) for rear tires.
**Vehicle weight for YFU1 and YFU1T models is 282 kg (620 lbs.).

Tune-Up			
Engine Idle Speed	1350-1450 rpm	1350-1450 rpm	1450-1550 rpm*
Compression Pressure	883 kPa (128 psi)	883 kPa (128 psi)	883 kPa (128 psi)
Spark Plug:			
NGK	D7EA	D7EA	D7EA
Nippon Denso	X22ES-U	X22ES-U	X22ES-U
Electrode Gap	0.6-0.7 mm (0.024-0.028 in.)	0.6-0.7 mm (0.024-0.028 in.)	0.6-0.7 mm (0.024-0.028 in.)
Ignition:			
Type	Breakerless	Breakerless	Breakerless

MODELS	YFM200DX	YFM225	YFM250, YFU1, YFU1T

Tune-Up (Cont.)

Ignition: (Cont.)

	YFM200DX	YFM225	YFM250, YFU1, YFU1T
Timing	10° BTDC @ 1000 rpm 30° BTDC @ 6000 rpm	10° BTDC @ 1000 rpm 30° BTDC @ 6000 rpm	10° BTDC @ 1000 rpm 30° BTDC @ 6000 rpm

Carburetor:

	YFM200DX	YFM225	YFM250, YFU1, YFU1T
Make	Mikuni	Mikuni	Mikuni
Model.	VM22SH	VM24SH	VM22SH*
Jet Needle	4DI1	5L10	5CP2*
Clip Position	3rd Groove From Top	4th Groove From Top	4th Groove From Top
Needle Jet	N-6	O-0	N-6**
Pilot Jet	#20	#20	#17.5*
Main Jet.	#117.5	#112.5	#130*
Float Height.	21.0-22.0 mm (0.83-0.87 in.)	20.5-22.5 mm (0.81-0.88 in.)	21.0-22.0 mm (0.83-0.87 in.)
Idle Mixture Setting	2 Turns	1¾ Turns	3¼ Turns*
Throttle Lever Free Play	3-5 mm (0.12-0.20 in.)	3-5 mm (0.12-0.20 in.)	3-5 mm (0.12-0.20 in.)

*On YFM250 models, these carburetor specifications are same as YFM225 models.
**On YFM250 models, the needle jet is a O-2.

Sizes-Clearances

Valve Clearance (cold):

	YFM200DX	YFM225	YFM250, YFU1, YFU1T
Intake.	0.05-0.09 mm (0.0020-0.0035 in.)	0.05-0.09 mm (0.0020-0.0035 in.)	0.05-0.09 mm (0.0020-0.0035 in.)
Exhaust	0.11-0.15 mm (0.0043-0.0060 in.)	0.11-0.15 mm (0.0043-0.0060 in.)	0.11-0.15 mm (0.0043-0.0060 in.)

Valve Face & Seat Angle:

	YFM200DX	YFM225	YFM250, YFU1, YFU1T
Intake & Exhaust	45°	45°	45°

Valve Seat Width:

	YFM200DX	YFM225	YFM250, YFU1, YFU1T
Intake & Exhaust	0.9-1.1 mm (0.035-0.043 in.)	0.9-1.1 mm (0.035-0.043 in.)	0.9-1.1 mm (0.035-0.043 in.)

Valve Margin:

	YFM200DX	YFM225	YFM250, YFU1, YFU1T
Intake.	0.8-1.2 mm (0.031-0.047 in.)	0.8-1.2 mm (0.031-0.047 in.)	0.8-1.2 mm (0.031-0.047 in.)
Exhaust	0.8-1.2 mm (0.031-0.047 in.)	0.8-1.2 mm (0.031-0.047 in.)	0.8-1.2 mm (0.031-0.047 in.)

Valve Stem Diameter:

	YFM200DX	YFM225	YFM250, YFU1, YFU1T
Intake.	5.975-5.990 mm (0.2352-0.2358 in.)	5.975-5.990 mm (0.2352-0.2358 in.)	5.975-5.990 mm (0.2352-0.2358 in.)
Exhaust	5.960-5.975 mm (0.2346-0.2352 in.)	5.960-5.975 mm (0.2346-0.2352 in.)	5.960-5.975 mm (0.2346-0.2352 in.)

Valve Guide Bore Diameter:

	YFM200DX	YFM225	YFM250, YFU1, YFU1T
Intake & Exhaust	6.000-6.012 mm (0.2362-0.2367 in.)	6.000-6.012 mm (0.2362-0.2367 in.)	6.000-6.012 mm (0.2362-0.2367 in.)
Maximum	6.03 mm (0.2374 in.)	6.03 mm (0.2374 in.)	6.03 mm (0.2374 in.)

Valve Stem-to-Guide Clearance:

	YFM200DX	YFM225	YFM250, YFU1, YFU1T
Intake.	0.010-0.037 mm (0.0004-0.0015 in.)	0.010-0.037 mm (0.0004-0.0015 in.)	0.010-0.037 mm (0.0004-0.0015 in.)
Maximum	0.1 mm (0.0039 in.)	0.1 mm (0.0039 in.)	0.1 mm (0.0039 in.)
Exhaust	0.025-0.052 mm (0.0010-0.0020 in.)	0.025-0.052 mm (0.0010-0.0020 in.)	0.025-0.052 mm (0.0010-0.0020 in.)

MODELS	YFM200DX	YFM225	YFM250, YFU1, YFU1T
Sizes-Clearances (Cont.)			
Valve Stem-to-Guide Clearance: (Cont.)			
Maximum....................	0.1 mm (0.0039 in.)	0.1 mm (0.0039 in.)	0.1 mm (0.0039 in.)
Valve Spring Free Length:			
Inner........................	35.5 mm (1.40 in.)	35.5 mm (1.40 in.)	35.5 mm (1.40 in.)
Outer.......................	37.2 mm (1.46 in.)	37.2 mm (1.46 in.)	37.2 mm (1.46 in.)
Rocker Arm Bore Diameter:			
Intake & Exhaust.................	12.000-12.018 mm (0.4724-0.4731 in.)	12.000-12.018 mm (0.4724-0.4731 in.)	12.000-12.018 mm (0.4724-0.4731 in.)
Rocker Shaft Diameter:			
Intake & Exhaust.................	11.981-11.991 mm (0.4717-0.4720 in.)	11.981-11.991 mm (0.4717-0.4720 in.)	11.981-11.991 mm (0.4717-0.4720 in.)
Camshaft Lobe Height:			
Intake & Exhaust.................	36.537-36.637 mm (1.4385-1.4424 in.)	36.537-36.637 mm (1.4385-1.4424 in.)	36.537-36.637 mm (1.4385-1.4424 in.)
Camshaft Runout (Max.).............	0.03 mm (0.0012 in.)	0.03 mm (0.0012 in.)	0.03 mm (0.0012 in.)
Cylinder Head Distortion (Max.).......	0.03 mm (0.0012 in.)	0.03 mm (0.0012 in.)	0.03 mm (0.0012 in.)
Cylinder Bore Diameter.............	66.97-67.02 mm (2.637-2.638 in.)	69.97-70.02 mm (2.755-2.757 in.)	70.97-71.02 mm (2.794-2.796 in.)
Cylinder Taper (Max.)...............	0.05 mm (0.002 in.)	0.05 mm (0.002 in.)	0.05 mm (0.002 in.)
Piston Diameter: Measured 4.0 mm* (0.16 in.) From Skirt Bottom & 90° to Pin Bore.......	66.935-66.985 mm (2.6352-2.6372 in.)	69.935-69.985 mm (2.7533-2.7553 in.)	70.92-70.97 mm (2.792-2.794 in.)
Piston-to-Cylinder Clearance........	0.025-0.045 mm (0.0010-0.0018 in.)	0.035-0.055 mm (0.0014-0.0022 in.)	0.040-0.060 mm (0.0016-0.0023 in.)
Piston Ring End Gap:			
Top & Second Rings..............	0.15-0.30 mm (0.006-0.012 in.)	0.15-0.30 mm (0.006-0.012 in.)	0.15-0.30 mm (0.006-0.012 in.)
Oil Ring......................	0.3-0.9 mm (0.012-0.035 in.)	0.3-0.9 mm (0.012-0.035 in.)	0.3-0.9 mm (0.012-0.035 in.)
Piston Ring Side Clearance:			
Top Ring.....................	0.03-0.07 mm (0.0012-0.0028 in.)	0.03-0.07 mm (0.0012-0.0028 in.)	0.03-0.07 mm (0.0012-0.0028 in.)
Second Ring...................	0.02-0.06 mm (0.0008-0.0024 in.)	0.02-0.06 mm (0.0008-0.0024 in.)	0.02-0.06 mm (0.0008-0.0024 in.)
Connecting Rod Big End Side Clearance (Max.).............	0.35-0.65 mm (0.014-0.026 in.)	0.35-0.65 mm (0.014-0.026 in.)	0.35-0.65 mm (0.014-0.026 in.)
Connecting Rod Small End Shake.....	0.08-1.0 mm (0.031-0.039 in.)	0.08-1.0 mm (0.031-0.039 in.)	0.08-1.0 mm (0.031-0.039 in.)
Crankshaft Runout (Max.)............	**	**	0.06 mm (0.0024 in.)
Clutch Friction Plate Thickness (Min.)..	2.8 mm (0.110 in.)	2.8 mm (0.110 in.)	2.8 mm (0.110 in.)
Clutch Steel Plate Warpage Limit......	0.2 mm (0.008 in.)	0.2 mm (0.008 in.)	0.2 mm (0.008 in.)

MODELS	YFM200DX	YFM225	YFM250, YFU1, YFU1T

Sizes-Clearances (Cont.)

Clutch Spring Free Length (Min.)	32.9 mm (1.30 in.)	32.9 mm (1.30 in.)	32.9 mm (1.30 in.)

*Measure piston diameter on YFM200DX models at a point 7.5 mm (0.30 in.) from bottom of piston skirt.
**On YFM200DX and YFM225 models, maximum allowable crankshaft runout with crankshaft supported at main bearings is 0.02 mm (0.0008 in.) at flywheel taper and 0.06 mm (0.0024 in.) at outer right end.

Capacities

Engine/TransmissionSump	See Text	See Text	See Text
Fuel Tank.	9.5 L (2.5 gal.)	12.0 L (3.2 gal.)	11 L* (2.9 gal.)

*Fuel tank capacity on YFU1 and YFU1T models is 13 L (3.4 gal.).

Tightening Torques

Axle Nut:			
Front	85 N·m (61 ft.-lbs.)	85 N·m (61 ft.-lbs.)	85 N·m* (61 ft.-lbs.)
Rear.	20 N·m (88 ft.-lbs.)	120 N·m (88 ft.-lbs.)	150 N·m (110 ft.-lbs.)

*Front axle nut tightening torque on YFU1 and YFU1T models is 70 N·m (51 ft.-lbs.).

Balancer Shaft Nut	50 N·m (37 ft.-lbs.)	50 N·m (37 ft.-lbs.)	75 N·m (55 ft.-lbs.)
Camshaft Sprocket	60 N·m (43 ft.-lbs.)	60 N·m (43 ft.-lbs.)	60 N·m (43 ft.-lbs.)
Clutch Nut:			
Centrifugal Clutch	78 N·m (57 ft.-lbs.)	78 N·m (57 ft.-lbs.)	78 N·m (57 ft.-lbs.)
Disc Clutch	50 N·m (37 ft.-lbs.)	50 N·m (37 ft.-lbs.)	50 N·m (37 ft.-lbs.)
Crankcase:			
6 mm	7 N·m (62 in.-lbs.)	7 N·m (62 in.-lbs.)	7 N·m (62 in.-lbs.)
8 mm	....	22 N·m (16 ft.-lbs.)	22 N·m (16 ft.-lbs.)
Cylinder Base Screws.	10 N·m (88 in.-lbs.)	10 N·m (88 in.-lbs.)	10 N·m (88 in.-lbs.)
Cylinder Head:			
Flange Screw	22 N·m (16 ft.-lbs.)	22 N·m (16 ft.-lbs.)	22 N·m (16 ft.-lbs.)
Hex Screw.	7 N·m (62 in.-lbs.)	7 N·m (62 in.-lbs.)	7 N·m (62 in.-lbs.)
Engine Mounting Nuts.	33 N·m (24 ft.-lbs.)	33 N·m (24 ft.-lbs.)	33 N·m (24 ft.-lbs.)
Flywheel	50 N·m (37 ft.-lbs.)	50 N·m (37 ft.-lbs.)	50 N·m (37 ft.-lbs.)
Spark Plug	17.5 N·m (155 in.-lbs.)	17.5 N·m (155 in.-lbs.)	17.5 N·m (155 in.-lbs.)
Wheel Nuts:			
Front & Rear	28 N·m (21 ft.-lbs.)	28 N·m (21 ft.-lbs.)	55 N·m (40 ft.-lbs.)
Standard Screws:			
6 mm	6 N·m (53 in.-lbs.)	6 N·m (53 in.-lbs.)	6 N·m (53 in.-lbs.)
8 mm	15 N·m (133 in.-lbs.)	15 N·m (133 in.-lbs.)	15 N·m (133 in.-lbs.)

MODELS	YFM200DX	YFM225	YFM250, YFU1, YFU1T
Tightening Torques (Cont.)			
Standard Screws: (Cont.)			
10 mm	30 N·m (22 ft.-lbs.)	30 N·m (22 ft.-lbs.)	30 N·m (22 ft.-lbs.)
12 mm	55 N·m (40 ft.-lbs.)	55 N·m (40 ft.-lbs.)	55 N·m (40 ft.-lbs.)
14 mm	85 N·m (61 ft.-lbs.)	85 N·m (61 ft.-lbs.)	85 N·m (61 ft.-lbs.)
16 mm	130 N·m (94 ft.-lbs.)	130 N·m (94 ft.-lbs.)	130 N·m (94 ft.-lbs.)

LUBRICATION

All Models

ENGINE AND TRANSMISSION. The engine and transmission are lubricated by a crankshaft-driven oil pump. On YFM250, YFU1 and YFU1T models, the sub-transmission is lubricated by engine oil provided by an external oil line routed to the sub-transmission case. The engine and transmission share a common sump. On YFM250, YFU1 and YFU1T models, oil for the sub-transmission is contained in a separate case. Recommended oil is SAE 10W-30 with an API classification of SE and/or SF.

Oil level should be maintained at upper mark on dipstick attached to fill plug (F—Fig. Y5-1). Do not screw plug in when checking oil level. Note that if there is sufficient oil in engine sump then sufficient oil should be present for sub-transmission. Fill sump through opening for fill plug (F). Drain oil by removing drain plug (D—Fig. Y5-2) on underside of crankcase. On YFM250, YFU1 and YFU1T models, drain oil in sub-transmission by removing drain plug on bottom of sub-transmission case.

The manufacturer recommends changing the oil and oil filter after the first month of operation and every six months thereafter. Remove oil filter cover (C—Fig. Y5-1) for access to oil filter. Clean the drain plug oil strainer in a suitable solvent. Renew the strainer if damaged or contaminated.

On YFM200DX models, fill crankcase with 1.5 L (1.6 qt.) of oil if oil and oil filter are changed. Crankcase capacity totally dry is 1.8 L (1.9 qt.).

On YFM225 models, fill crankcase with 1.5 L (1.6 qt.) of oil if oil and oil filter are changed. Crankcase capacity totally dry is 2.4 L (2.5 qt.).

On YFM250, YFU1 and YFU1T models, fill crankcase with 2.1 L (2.2 qt.) of oil if only oil is changed or 2.2 L (2.3 qt.) if oil and oil filter are changed. Crankcase capacity totally dry is 2.8 L (2.95 qt.).

To be sure the oil pump is pumping oil to the engine, slightly unscrew oil passage screw (W—Fig. Y5-3). Start

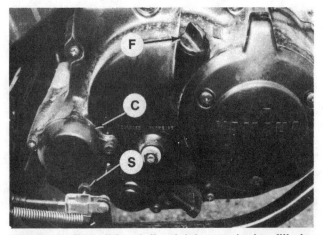

Fig. Y5-1—The oil level dipstick is attached to fill plug (F). The oil filter is located behind cover (C). Unscrewing lower cover screw (S) will allow oil to drain from filter compartment.

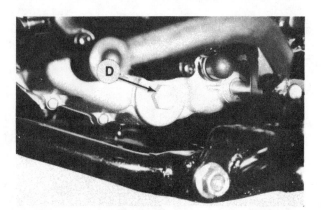

Fig. Y5-2—Remove plug (D) to drain oil from engine/transmission sump.

Fig. Y5-3—With engine running at idle speed, oil should seep around screw (W) when loosened.

and run engine at idle speed. Oil should just seep past screw after one minute. Retighten screw if oil seeps from hole. If no oil is present, stop engine and determine cause.

FINAL DRIVE HOUSING. To check oil level in final drive housing, remove fill plug (F—Fig. Y5-4). Oil should reach bottom edge of fill plug hole with vehicle on a level surface. Recommended oil is SAE 80 hypoid gear oil with API classification GL-4.

Oil in rear drive housing should be changed annually.

Unscrew drain plug to drain oil from housing. Oil capacity of final drive housing is 130 mL (4.4 oz.) on YFM200DX models, 230 mL (7.8 oz.) on YFM225 models and 380 mL (12.8 oz.) on YFU1 and YFU1T models. On YFM250 models, if oil is changed, refill with 210 mL (7.1 oz.) of oil. If final drive is completely dry (disassembled) on YFM250 models, refill with 250 mL (8.4 oz.) of oil.

SUSPENSION AND STEERING. The grease fittings on suspension components should be injected with lithium base grease after initial month of operation and

Fig. Y5-4—Pour oil into final drive housing through opening for oil fill plug (F). Oil level should be even with opening. Unscrew drain plug (D) to remove oil.

every six months thereafter. Grease fittings are located at lower steering shaft bearing, front suspension control arms and steering knuckles.

The upper steering shaft bushing should be lubricated with lithium base grease every six months.

CABLES AND LEVERS. All cables and levers should be inspected and lubricated after first month of operation and every three months thereafter.

AIR CLEANER ELEMENT

All Models

All models are equipped with a foam type air cleaner element. On YFM200DX models the air cleaner element is accessible after removing cover at rear of air cleaner housing. On all other models the air cleaner element is located underneath the seat. The air cleaner element should be removed and cleaned every three months or more frequently if operating conditions are severe.

To remove air cleaner element, remove seat on all models except YFM200DX models, detach cover and remove filter element. Thoroughly clean the foam element in a nonflammable solvent. Compress element between hands to remove solvent. Do not wring or twist element. Saturate element in clean SAE 10W-30 engine oil, then compress element to remove excess oil.

FUEL SYSTEM

All Models

CARBURETOR. The engine on YFM200DX, YFU1 and YFU1T models is equipped with a Mikuni VM22SH carburetor. The engine on YFM225 and YFM250 models is equipped with a Mikuni VM24SH carburetor.

Free play at the end of throttle lever should be 3-5 mm (0.12-0.20 in.). To adjust free play, slide back rubber boot, loosen locknut and rotate cable adjuster at throttle or at top of carburetor. Retighten locknut.

Initial setting of idle mixture screw (I—Fig. Y5-5) is 2 turns out from a lightly seated position on YFM200DX

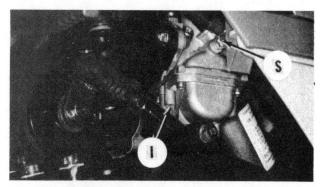

Fig. Y5-5—Adjust idle mixture screw (I) and idle speed screw (S) as outlined in text.

models, 1¾ turns out on YFM225 and YFM250 models, and 3¼ turns out on YFU1 and YFU1T models. Final adjustment must be performed with engine at normal operating temperature. Adjust idle speed screw (S) so engine idles at 1450-1550 rpm on YFU1 and YFU1T models and 1350-1450 on all other models. Rotate idle mixture screw (I) so engine runs at highest idle speed, then readjust idle speed screw (S) so engine idles at specified rpm.

When servicing carburetor, refer to Fig. Y5-6 for an exploded view of carburetor and to carburetor specifications in CONDENSED SERVICE DATA section while noting the following: Jet needle clip (9) should be installed in third groove from top of jet needle on YFM200DX models and in fourth groove from top of jet needle on all other models. Installing clip in a lower groove on jet needle will richen mid-range fuel mixture. Invert carburetor and measure float height as shown in Fig. Y5-7. Bend float arm tang to adjust float height. Make sure groove in side of throttle slide is aligned with pin in carburetor body when inserting slide in carburetor.

With the carburetor installed, the fuel level should be checked. Attach Yamaha fuel level gauge YM-01312 or a suitable clear hose (H—Fig. Y5-8) to fuel bowl nozzle. Hose should be long enough to extend above the bottom edge of carburetor body without kinking. Open fuel bowl drain screw (D). Run the engine at idle speed until fuel level in hose stabilizes, then stop engine. Measure distance from the bottom edge of carburetor body (fuel bowl contact surface) to fuel level in hose to determine fuel level (L). Fuel level check will not be accurate if hose is moved after fuel level is stabilized. Fuel level (L) should be 2.5-3.5 mm (0.10-0.14 in.) below carburetor body edge. To adjust fuel level, remove the fuel bowl and carefully bend float arm tang.

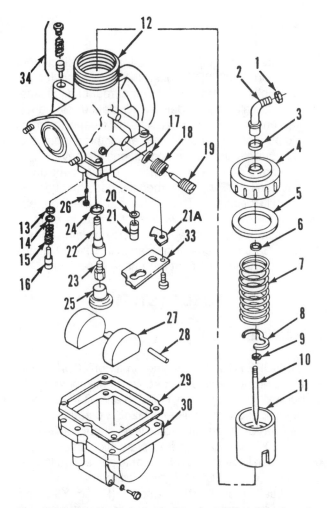

Fig. Y5-6—Exploded view of typical Mikuni carburetor used on all models.

1. Nut
2. Cable guide
3. Washer
4. Cap
5. Washer
6. "E" ring
7. Spring
8. Retainer
9. Jet needle clip
10. Jet needle
11. Throttle slide
12. Body
13. "O" ring
14. Washer
15. Spring
16. Idle mixture screw
17. "O" ring
18. Spring
19. Idle speed screw
20. Washer
21. Inlet valve
21A. Retainer
22. Needle jet
23. Main jet
24. Washer
25. Cover
26. Pilot jet
27. Float
28. Pin
29. Gasket
30. Fuel bowl
33. Retainer
34. Starter valve assy.

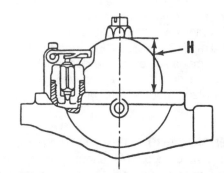

Fig. Y5-7—Refer to text for float height (H) adjustment.

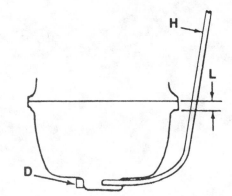

Fig. Y5-8—The fuel level is measured from the bottom edge of the carburetor body. Fuel level (L) should be 2.5-3.5 mm (0.10-0.14 in.) below carburetor body edge.

FUEL STRAINER. A strainer is mounted on the end of each pickup tube that extends into the fuel tank from the fuel valve. To inspect the strainers, the fuel in the fuel tank must be drained. Disconnect the fuel hose from the fuel valve. Unscrew fuel valve retaining screws and remove fuel valve. Clean and inspect the strainers. Reinstall the valve while noting that sealing washers are used on the retaining screws to prevent fuel leakage.

IGNITION SYSTEM

All Models

The engine is equipped with a breakerless, capacitor discharge ignition system. The electronic ignition circuit consists of the flywheel, CDI module, source coil, pickup coil, ignition coil, spark plug, ignition switch and engine stop switch. To check ignition timing, remove timing plug (P—Fig. Y5-9) and connect a power timing light to engine. Ignition timing (10° BTDC) at idle speed should occur when "F" mark on flywheel is aligned with notch (N) on case. Ignition timing is not adjustable. If ignition timing is not as specified, check condition of ignition components as described in the following test procedures and renew faulty or questionable components.

To check the pickup coil, disconnect connector between the pickup coil and the CDI module. Connect an ohmmeter lead to the white/green wire from the pickup coil and the other ohmmeter lead to the white/red wire from the pickup coil. Ohmmeter reading should be 180-220 ohms.

To check the source coil, disconnect the connector between the source coil and the CDI module. Connect

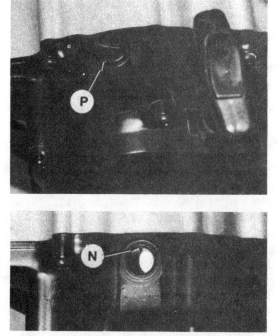

Fig. Y5-9—Remove plug (P) to view timing marks on flywheel and notch (N) in crankcase cover.

an ohmmeter between brown wire and black wire leads from source coil. Source coil resistance should be 343-352 ohms on YFM200DX models and 288-352 ohms on all other models.

Ignition coil resistance readings for YFM200DX, YFM225 and YFM250 models should be 0.72-0.98 ohms for primary windings and 5.0k-6.8k ohms for secondary windings. Ignition coil resistance readings for YFU1 and YFU1T models should be 0.85-1.15 ohms for primary windings and 5.0k-6.8k ohms for secondary windings.

If the ignition system malfunctions and all components test satisfactory, replace CDI module with a new or good unit and recheck ignition system.

ELECTRICAL SYSTEM

All Models

The vehicle is equipped with a charging system, battery and electric starter. The system is protected by a 10 amp fuse on YFM200DX models, a 30 amp fuse on YFM225 and YFM250 models, and a 20 amp fuse on YFU1 and YFU1T models.

BATTERY. The battery is accessible after removing the rear fender. The negative terminal is grounded. The battery is a 12-volt unit with 14 amp-hour capacity.

CHARGING SYSTEM. The charging circuit consists of an alternator and a regulator/rectifier. The alternator rotor is attached to the left end of the crankshaft while the stator is mounted on the inside of the left crankcase cover. The regulator/rectifier module is mounted on a panel near the battery on YFU1 and YFU1T models and on the rear of the vehicle frame on all other models.

The charging circuit should produce 14-15 VDC at 2000 rpm.

NOTE: Do not disconnect battery terminal wires while the engine is running as excessive alternator output will damage the regulator/rectifier.

To check the alternator stator coils on YFM200DX models, disconnect the connector with white, black and yellow leads from the alternator. Measure resistance between white wire and black wire. Resistance should be 0.36-0.50 ohm.

To check the alternator stator coils on YFM225, YFM250, YFU1 and YFU1T models, disconnect the connector with three white leads from the alternator. Measure resistance between any pair of white wires, then repeat test with another pair of wires. Resistance between any pair of white wires should be 0.4-0.5 ohms. Resistance between any white wire and vehicle ground must be infinity.

If previous tests prove satisfactory and fuse, wiring and connections are all good, replace regulator/rectifier with a good unit and recheck operation.

ELECTRIC STARTER. The starting circuit consists of the starter, starter relay, starter switch, cutoff relay, neutral switch, brake switch (not used on YFU1 and YFU1T models) and main switch. The cutoff relay, neutral switch and brake switch prevent energizing starter relay unless switches are in correct position.

On YFM200DX models, the starter relay and cutoff relay are attached to the rear of the frame under the rear fenders. On YFM225 models, the starter relay is located near the air cleaner box and the cutoff relay is attached to the rear of the frame. On YFM250 models, the starter relay is located next to the battery and the cutoff relay is attached to the rear of the frame. On YFU1 and YFU1T models, the starter relay and cutoff relay are mounted on a panel near the battery. On all models, the neutral switch is located on the left side of the engine and the brake switch is mounted on the handlebar. The electric starter motor is mounted on the front of the engine.

The starter motor can be removed after detaching the battery leads, starter motor leads, starter motor bracket and unscrewing the two screws securing the motor. Note the "O" ring on the front of the motor. Minimum brush length is 5.0 mm (0.20 in.) on YFM200DX models and 3.5 mm (0.14 in.) on all other models. Minimum commutator diameter is 22 mm (0.866 in.) on YFM200DX models and 21 mm (0.827 in.) on all other models. Armature coil resistance should be 0.023 ohm on YFM200DX models and 0.015-0.022 ohm on all other models.

WIRING. If wiring requires repair, always install wire that is the same gauge as original wire. Wires should be routed away from areas of extreme heat or sharp edges. Attach or hold wires in their original position using plastic tie straps to prevent short circuits.

FASTENERS

All Models

After the first month of operation and after every 30 days of operation thereafter, the vehicle should receive an overall inspection. All screws, nuts and other fasteners should be checked and tightened to proper torque specification shown in CONDENSED SERVICE DATA section or in the appropriate maintenance section.

VALVE SYSTEM

All Models

The valves are actuated via rocker arms by a single overhead camshaft. The camshaft is driven by a roller chain attached to the left end of the crankshaft. Valve clearance should be adjusted after the first month of operation and then after every six months of operation. Adjust valve clearance with engine cold.

To obtain access to valve adjustment covers proceed as follows. On YFM200DX models, remove seat, fuel tank cover and fuel tank. On YFM225 models, detach handlebar and remove fuel tank cover, seat, front carrier, front fender and fuel tank. On YFM250 models, remove front carrier, seat, handlebar, fuel tank cover, front fender and fuel tank. On YFU1 and YFU1T models, valve adjustment covers are accessible without removing adjacent parts.

To adjust valve clearance, remove timing plug (P—Fig. Y5-9) and valve adjustment covers at front and rear of cylinder head. The "T" mark on the flywheel indicates top dead center when aligned with notch (N) in plug hole. Rotate crankshaft and align top dead center mark with notch (N) with piston on compression stroke. To ensure piston is on compression stroke, rotate crankshaft past top dead center and observe intake (rear) rocker arm. If intake rocker arm movement is observed, continue to rotate crankshaft until marks are again aligned.

Clearance between rocker arm adjusting screw and valve stem should be 0.05-0.09 mm (0.0020-0.0035 in.) for the intake valve and 0.11-0.15 mm (0.0043-0.0060 in.) for the exhaust valve. Measure clearance with a suitable feeler gauge. Adjust clearance by loosening the adjusting screw locknut and turning the adjusting screw. Be sure to recheck clearance after tightening locknut. Install valve covers so "V" ridge on inside is towards top and points down when installed.

CAMSHAFT CHAIN

All Models

Camshaft chain adjustment is not required. The cam chain tensioner automatically adjusts chain tension.

CLUTCH

All Models

The engine is equipped with two automatically actuated clutches. A three-shoe centrifugal clutch is mounted on the right end of the crankshaft. The centrifugal clutch is disengaged at idle speed and engages when crankshaft speed increases. A multiple-disc clutch is attached to the transmission input shaft and is actuated by the gear shift mechanism. When the gear shift lever is operated, the multiple-disc clutch is disengaged to allow smooth transmission gear movement.

The clutch should be adjusted after the first month of operation and every six months thereafter. The clutch adjusting screw is located in right side cover. To adjust clutch, loosen locknut (N—Fig. Y5-10) then turn adjusting screw (S) counterclockwise until internal resistance is felt. Turn screw 1/8 turn clockwise. Secure adjusting screw with locknut (N).

The dual-clutch system should automatically disengage at engine idle speed. When selecting gears, clutch should engage and disengage freely without excess slippage. Difficult shifting, clutch grabbing or clutch slipping may indicate overhaul is necessary.

MANUAL STARTER

Model YFM200DXU

R&R AND OVERHAUL. Refer to Fig. Y5-11 for an exploded view of manual starter used on Model YFM200DXU. Starter can be removed from engine as a complete unit after removing the six cap screws that

Fig. Y5-10—Loosen locknut (N) and turn adjusting screw (S) as outlined in text to adjust clutch.

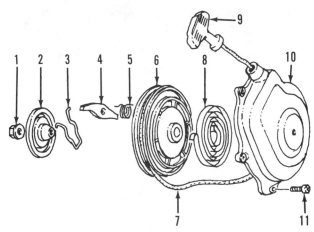

Fig. Y5-11—Exploded view of manual starter.

1. Nut
2. Drive housing
3. Clip
4. Pawl
5. Spring
6. Pulley
7. Rope
8. Rewind spring
9. Rope handle
10. Starter housing
11. Screw

retain the starter. If starter rope remains under tension, pull starter rope and hold rope pulley with notch adjacent to rope outlet. Pull a loop of rope back through outlet so rope engages notch in pulley and allow pulley to slowly unwind. Unscrew nut and disassemble unit. Be careful when removing rewind spring; a rapidly uncoiling starter spring can cause serious injury.

Rewind spring is wound into starter housing in a clockwise direction. Rope is wound on rope pulley in a clockwise direction as viewed with pulley in housing. Reassemble starter by reversing disassembly procedure. During reassembly, lightly grease pulley shaft and starter pawl. Insert long end of drive pawl spring in hole in pulley as shown in Fig. Y5-12. Install drive pawl and hook outer end of drive pawl spring under drive pawl and into notch on drive pawl. Turn drive pawl one turn counterclockwise and push drive pawl into recess in pulley. Apply a light coat of grease to spring clip (3—Fig. Y5-13) and install spring in groove of drive housing (2). Install drive housing and spring clip as shown in Fig. Y5-14.

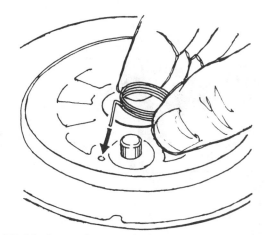

Fig. Y5-12—Insert long end of pawl spring in hole in pulley.

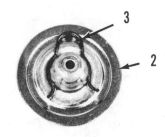

Fig. Y5-13—Apply grease to clip (3) and install in groove on drive housing (2).

To place tension on rewind spring after starter assembly, pass rope through rope outlet in housing and install rope handle. Pull a loop of rope back through starter housing outlet and into pulley notch in pulley. Turn pulley clockwise three or four complete revolutions to place tension on spring. Release rope from notch and allow rope to wind onto pulley. Do not place more tension on

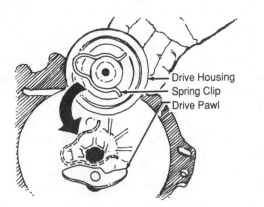

Fig. Y5-14—Install drive housing with clip on pulley as shown.

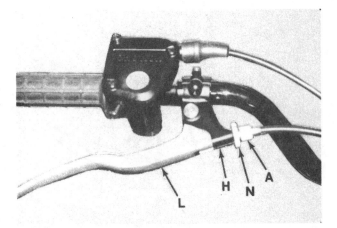

Fig. Y5-15—Brake lever free travel is measured at gap between lever housing (H) and brake lever (L). Adjust lever free play by loosening locknut (N) and rotating brake cable adjuster (A).

Fig. Y5-16—The front brake equalizer is attached to the front frame.

rewind spring than is necessary to draw rope handle up against housing. Check operation of starter before installation.

FRONT BRAKE SYSTEM

All Models

BRAKE LEVER FREE PLAY. Brake lever free travel is measured between lever housing (H—Fig. Y5-15) and brake lever (L). Recommended brake lever free travel is 3-5 mm (0.12-0.20 in.) for YFM250A and YFM250B models and 5-8 mm (0.20-0.31 in.) for all other models. Adjust lever free play by loosening locknut (N) and rotating brake cable adjuster (A). Operate brake lever while observing equalizer bar attached to front frame as shown in Fig. Y5-16. If equalizer bar does not remain level, adjust position of wing nut (W—Fig. Y5-17) at brake end of brake cable on appropriate brake. Readjust brake lever free play.

OVERHAUL. Brake lining thickness may be checked externally by operating brake and noting position of pointer (P—Fig. Y5-18) on each front brake actuating lever. There is sufficient brake lining remaining if pointer does not align with or pass mark (M).

Fig. Y5-17—Rotate wing nut (N) at end of each front brake cable to equalize brake action.

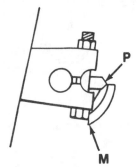

Fig. Y5-18—Brake linings are worn excessively if pointer (P) passes end of wear range scale (M) when brake is actuated.

WARNING: Inhaling asbestos brake dust is injurious to human health. Approved OSHA respiration equipment must be worn when working on or around brake components. DO NOT use compressed air to clean brake drums, shoes or nearby components as brake dust will be blown into air. Only vacuum equipment designed to pick up brake dust should be used.

Each front brake assembly is accessible after removing the brake drum/hub. Renew the brake shoes if damaged or if lining is worn to less than 2.0 mm (0.08 in.). Renew the brake drum assembly if inside diameter exceeds 111.0 mm (4.37 in.) on YFM200DX and YFM225 models, or if inside diameter exceeds 161 mm (6.34 in.) on YFM250, YFU1 and YFU1T models. Tighten hub retaining nut to 70 N·m (51 ft.-lbs.) on YFU1 and YFU1T models and 85 N·m (61 ft.-lbs.) on all other models. Tighten wheel retaining nuts to 28 N·m (21 ft.-lbs.) on YFM200DX and YFM225 models, and 55 N·m (40 ft.-lbs.) on YFM250, YFU1 and YFU1T models.

FRONT AXLE

All Models

Both front steering knuckle assemblies pivot on king pins at the end of a control arm. The control arm pivots vertically and is attached to the vehicle frame by bolts. A shock absorber with a coil spring is attached to the vehicle frame and the control arm.

Remove front wheel for access to hub and spindle. Unscrew hub nut to remove wheel hub. The hub and brake drum are one piece. Renew bearings if rough or otherwise damaged. Be sure to install spacer between bearings when reassembling components. On YFM250,

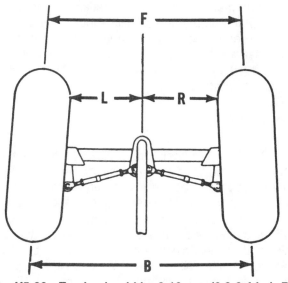

Fig. Y5-20—Toe-in should be 0-10 mm (0.0-0.4 in.). Refer to text for adjustment procedure.

YFU1 and YFU1T models, tapered end of spacer must be towards wheel side of hub. Tighten hub retaining nut to 70 N·m (51 ft.-lbs.) on YFU1 and YFU1T models and 85 N·m (61 ft.-lbs.) on all other models. Tighten wheel retaining nuts to 28 N·m (21 ft.-lbs.) on YFM200DX and YFM225 models, and 55 N·m (40 ft.-lbs.) on YFM250, YFU1 and YFU1T models.

Remove the front wheel to service the knuckle assembly. If excessive play between king pin and bushings is noted, then components should be renewed. Grease king pin prior to installation. Tighten castle nut securing king pin bolt to 35 N·m (26 ft.-lbs.) and install a new cotter pin. On all models except YFM200DX, install lower control arm mounting bolts so bolt heads are to outside. Tighten control arm mounting bolts to 68 N·m (50 ft.-lbs.) on YFM200DX models and 45 N·m (33 ft.-lbs.) on all other models. Tighten retaining nut for tie rod end to 25 N·m (18 ft.-lbs.) on YFU1 and YFU1T models and 40 N·m (29 ft.-lbs.) on all other models. Tighten shock absorber upper and lower mounting bolts to 45 N·m (33 ft.-lbs.).

STEERING

All Models

INSPECTION. Rotate the handlebar from one extreme to the other and note if any binding or roughness is felt. Periodically inspect the steering components for looseness or any other damage. Renew any damaged component. Clean and grease components if binding or excessive effort is noted.

TOE-IN SETTING. Place the handlebar in a straight ahead position. Use a suitable measuring tool and measure distance (B—Fig. Y5-20) at spindle height between the center of the tires on the rear sides. Locate the same tire centerline points on front side of tires and measure front distance (F). The distance on the front side (F) should be 0-10 mm (0.0-0.4 in.) shorter than the measured distance on the rear side (B). Note that the distance from a projected vehicle centerline to left (L) and right (R) tire centerlines should also be equal.

To adjust, loosen locknuts on the left and right tie rod assemblies and rotate tie rod shaft on each side equally until distance is within recommended range. After obtaining the correct setting, tighten locknuts to 30 N·m (22 ft.-lbs.).

OVERHAUL. To expose the steering shaft on YFM200DX models, remove handlebar, fuel tank, front carrier and front fender. To expose the steering shaft on all other models, remove handlebar, fuel tank cover, seat, front carrier and front fender. On YFM225 and YFM250 models remove dash panel. Unscrew the two cap screws securing the steering shaft clamp halves. Clean the old grease from the steering shaft. Inspect the clamp halves and steering shaft for damage. Renew components if needed. Grease inside of steering shaft clamp halves with a lithium base grease and install. Tighten the retaining clamp cap screws to 23 N·m (17 ft.-lbs.).

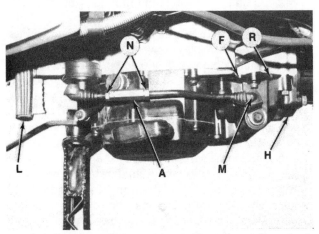

Fig. Y5-22—On YFM200DX models, rotate shift rod adjuster (A) so marks (F and R) on crankcase align with mark (M) on shift arm cover. Refer to text.

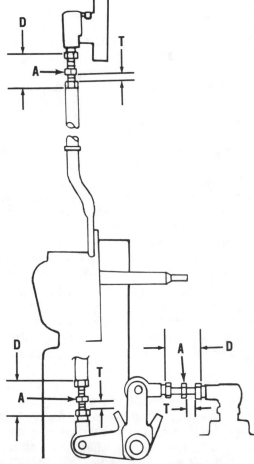

Fig. Y5-24—On YFM250W models, after loosening locknuts, rotate each shift rod adjuster (A) so distance (D) is 29.5-30.5 mm (1.16-1.20 in.) and distance (T) between face of adjuster and locknut is 7.0-10.0 mm (0.28-0.39 in.).

To remove steering shaft, remove steering shaft clamps as outlined in previous paragraph. Remove the lower steering shaft retaining cotter pin and nut. Detach inner tie rod ends from steering shaft and withdraw the steering shaft. On models so equipped, note "O" rings adjacent to bearing holder and renew if damaged. Inject lithium base grease in grease fitting after installation. Tighten the lower steering shaft retaining nut to 34 N·m (25 ft.-lbs.) on YFM200DX and YFM225 models, and 30 N·m (22 ft.-lbs.) on YFM250, YFU1 and YFU1T models. Tighten retaining nut for tie rod end to 25 N·m (18 ft.-lbs.) on YFU1 and YFU1T models and 40 N·m (29 ft.-lbs.) on all other models.

When installing handlebar, install upper clamp so punch mark is towards front of handlebar. Tighten front screw on handlebar clamps first, then tighten the rear clamp screws. If properly tightened, there should be no gaps at the front of the clamps and even gaps at the rear of the clamps. Tighten clamp screws to 20 N·m (15 ft.-lbs.).

FORWARD-REVERSE SHIFT LINKAGE

Model YFM200DX

All YFM200DX models are equipped with a reverse gear that is engaged by operating forward-reverse shift lever (L—Fig. Y5-22). The shift linkage operates a dog clutch inside gear housing (H). The dog clutch engages either the forward or reverse gear. Forward gear is selected when shift lever (L) is down, while reverse gear is engaged when the shift lever is up. The transmission must be in first gear when shifting to reverse as a pin in the shift linkage must index in a hole in the transmission shift drum.

To obtain proper gear engagement, adjust forward-reverse shift linkage as follows: Note mark (M) on shift arm cover and marks (F and R) on crankcase. Move shift lever (L) and note that mark (M) should point towards marks (F and R) on crankcase when forward and reverse gears are engaged. If marks do not align, loosen locknuts (N) and rotate shift rod adjuster (A) as required. Retighten locknuts (N).

Model YFM250W

All YFM250W models are equipped with a reverse gear and a high-low sub-transmission. The shift linkage operates dog clutches inside the sub-transmission to provide high, low and reverse gear operation.

To obtain proper gear engagement, the length of the shift links must be adjusted. Loosen locknuts at end of links and rotate adjusters (A—Fig. Y5-24) to obtain specified lengths. Distance (D) measured from opposite sides of locknuts should be 29.5-30.5 mm (1.16-1.20 in.). Distance (T) between faces of adjuster and locknut

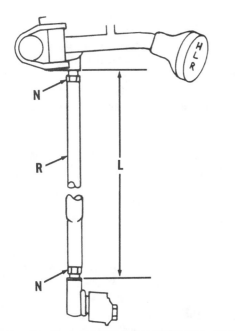

Fig. Y5-25—On Models YFM250A, YFM250B, YFU1 and YFU1T, loosen locknuts (N) on shift rod (R) and rotate rod so length (L) is 288.6-289.6 mm (11.36-11.40 in.).

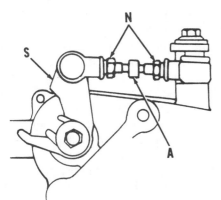

Fig. Y5-26—On Models YFM250A, YFM250B, YFU1 and YFU1T, loosen locknuts (N) on rear shift link and rotate adjuster (A) to synchronize shift control lever with shift arm (S). The shift control lever must fully engage each gear.

should be 7.0-10.0 mm (0.28-0.39 in.). Retighten locknuts after adjustment.

Models YFM250A, YFM250B, YFU1 And YFU1T

Models YFM250A, YFM250B, YFU1 and YFU1T are equipped with a reverse gear and a high-low sub-transmission, while YFU1T models are equipped with a reverse gear and low range transmission. On both models, the shift linkage operates dog clutches inside the sub-transmission to select the desired gear.

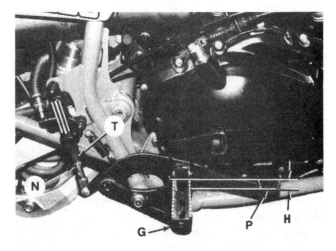

Fig. Y5-28—Brake pedal (P) height (H) on YFU1 and YFU1T models should be 5 mm (0.20 in.) below footpeg (G) in the released position when measured from the top of the footpeg to the top of the foot pad on the brake pedal. Loosen locknut (N) and rotate master cylinder actuator rod nut (T) to adjust pedal height.

To obtain proper gear engagement, the length of the shift rod must be adjusted. Loosen locknuts (N—Fig. Y5-25) and rotate shift rod (R) so length (L) is 288.6-289.6 mm (11.36-11.40 in.). Retighten locknuts (N). Loosen locknuts (N—Fig. Y5-26) on rear shift link and rotate adjuster (A) to synchronize shift control lever with shift arm (S). Be sure shift arm properly engages gear detents.

REAR BRAKE SYSTEM

Models YFU1 And YFU1T

The rear brakes consist of two-shoe hydraulically-actuated drum brakes mounted on both ends of the rear axle housing. The brakes are actuated by a brake pedal near the right footpeg.

Brake fluid must be rated DOT 3 or 4. Maintain brake fluid level above "LOW" mark on side of brake fluid reservoir. Do not overfill. To avert spillage, be sure reservoir is horizontal before removing cover.

BRAKE PEDAL HEIGHT ADJUSTMENT. Brake pedal (P—Fig. Y5-28) should be 5 mm (0.20 in.) below footpeg (G) in the released position when measured from the top of the footpeg to the top of the foot pad on the brake pedal as shown in Fig. Y5-28. To adjust, loosen locknut (N) and rotate master cylinder actuator rod nut (T) until recommended pedal height (H) is obtained, then tighten locknut (N) to retain adjustment. After adjustment, the end of the master cylinder push rod must be visible in the hole in the side of the clevis.

BRAKE PEDAL FREE PLAY. If brake pedal travel is excessive, adjust rear brakes as follows: Remove rear wheels and remove check plug on outside of brake drum. Rotate brake drum so hole is aligned with star wheel on brake shoe adjuster. Use a suitable tool and rotate star wheel until brake shoes lock against drum, then rotate star wheel in opposite direction four adjustment teeth. Adjust brake shoes on opposite wheel. Make sure no brake drag is noted after adjustment. If brake lever free play is still excessive, then bleed hydraulic system as outlined in BLEEDING section.

PARKING BRAKE ADJUSTMENT. A pull-type parking brake lever actuates the rear brakes via two cables. Adjust braking action for each brake by rotating wing nut at brake lever end of parking brake cables. If brakes are properly adjusted, the equalizer bar that pulls the cables should be parallel to bracket.

BLEEDING. Make sure brake fluid reservoir is full. Connect a bleed hose to bleed valve on back side of wheel cylinder. Route the bleed hose into a suitable

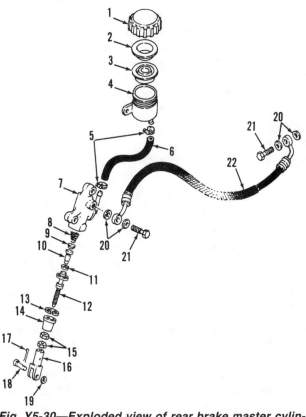

Fig. Y5-30—Exploded view of rear brake master cylinder.

1. Cap
2. Seal
4. Diaphragm
5. Clip
6. Hose
7. Body
8. Spring
9. Primary cup
10. Piston
11. Secondary cup
12. Push rod
13. Snap ring
14. Dust boot
15. Nuts
16. Clevis
17. Cotter pin
18. Pin
19. Washer
20. Sealing washers
21. Union bolt
22. Hose

container. Operate brake pedal until resistance is felt, then open bleed valve (rotate counterclockwise). Close bleed valve prior to releasing brake lever. Continue bleeding procedure until no air bubbles are noted in fluid discharged from bleed valve.

NOTE: Make sure reservoir remains full during bleeding procedure.

When bleeding procedure is completed, add brake fluid to reservoir as needed.

R&R AND OVERHAUL. To remove rear brake shoes and drum, support rear of vehicle and remove tire and wheel.

WARNING: Inhaling asbestos brake dust is injurious to human health. Approved OSHA respiration equipment must be worn when working on or around brake components. DO NOT use compressed air to clean brake drum, shoes or nearby components as brake dust will be blown into air. Only vacuum equipment designed to pick up brake dust should be used.

Unscrew axle nut and remove wheel hub from axle, then remove brake drum.

Renew the brake shoes if thickness is less than 1.0 mm (0.04 in.). Renew the brake drum if inside diameter exceeds 166 mm (6.54 in.). Disassemble and inspect wheel cylinder. Renew complete wheel cylinder if bore is scored, pitted or excessively worn. Superficial damage in wheel cylinder bore may be removed using a suitable cylinder hone. After honing, rinse bore with clean brake fluid. Shake out excess fluid but do not wipe dry. Using a shop towel or rag to dry cylinder will leave lint particles in bore. Renew boots and piston cups. During reassembly, lubricate components with clean brake fluid.

Reassemble by reversing disassembly procedure. Clean brake adjuster and lubricate with silicon grease before installing in housing. Screw adjuster completely in to allow installation of new brake shoes. Apply a light coat of silicone grease to three points on backing plate that will contact edge of brake shoe. Apply a light coat of grease to parking brake actuator. Do not allow grease on brake shoe linings. Tighten wheel hub retaining nut to 150 N·m (110 ft.-lbs.). Tighten wheel nuts to 55 N·m (40 ft.-lbs.). Adjust rear brake as previously outlined.

MASTER CYLINDER. To remove rear brake master cylinder (7—Fig. Y5-30), disconnect brake plunger from pedal. Detach brake lines from master cylinder and plug line to reservoir. Brake fluid will remove paint; be careful when removing master cylinder. Unscrew retaining screws and remove master cylinder. Remove dust boot (14) and snap ring (13). Disassemble piston assembly while noting location and direction of components. Renew complete master cylinder if bore is scored, pitted or excessively worn. Superficial damage in master cylinder bore may be removed using a suitable cylinder hone. After honing, rinse bore with clean brake fluid. Shake out excess fluid but do not wipe dry. Using a shop towel or rag to dry cylinder will leave lint particles in bore. Renew boots and piston cups. During reassembly, lubricate components with clean brake fluid. Reassembly is reverse of disassembly. Install spring (8) so small end contacts primary cup (9). Bleed brakes as previously outlined. Do not operate vehicle until brakes are tested and functioning properly.

All Other Models

ADJUSTMENT. To adjust rear brake pedal height, loosen locknut (N—Fig. Y5-32) and rotate adjuster screw (S). Brake pedal height should be 5 mm (0.2 in.) below top of footpeg. Step on brake pedal three times. Loosen cable adjuster at handlebar lever for rear brake cable and loosen both cable adjusters at rear brake. There must be sufficient free play in the brake cables so adjustment is not affected. Loosen brake arm locknut (N—Fig. Y5-33) and adjuster screw (S). Rotate handlebar brake cable adjuster (H) so pointer (R) is aligned with mark (M). Turn in adjuster screw (S) until tight then back it out ¼ turn. Tighten locknut (N) while holding adjuster screw. If the adjuster screw bottoms against the locknut, the brake pads are worn and should be renewed. Turn in pedal cable adjuster (P) until there is a 0-1 mm (0.00-0.04 in.) gap (G—Fig. Y5-35) between cable pin and front end of slot in brake arm. To adjust handlebar brake lever free play, except on Models YFM250A and YFM250B, turn cable adjuster at brake lever or at brake end of cable so there is a 5-8 mm (0.20-0.32 in.) gap (G—Fig. Y5-36) between lever and housing. On Models YFM250A and YFM250B, turn

Fig. Y5-32—To adjust rear brake pedal height on all models except YFU1 and YFU1T, loosen locknut (N) and rotate adjuster screw (S). Brake pedal height should be 5 mm (0.2 in.) below top of footpeg.

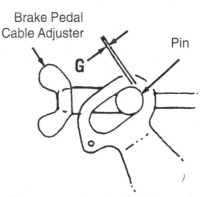

Fig. Y5-35—When properly adjusted, there should be a 0-1 mm (0.00-0.04 in.) gap (G) between actuating pin and end of slot in running brake actuating arm. On Models YFM250A and YFM250B, there should be a 4-5 mm (0.16-0.20 in.) gap (G) between cable pin and front end of slot in parking brake actuating arm. See text.

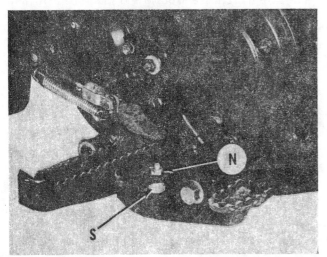

Fig. Y5-33—View of rear brake assembly.

H. Handlebar brake cable adjuster	P. Brake pedal cable adjuster
M. Alignment mark	R. Pointer
N. Locknut	S. Adjusting screw

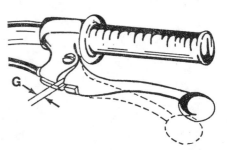

Fig. Y5-36—To adjust handlebar brake lever free play, turn cable adjuster at brake lever or at brake end of cable so there is a 5-8 mm (0.20-0.32 in.) gap (G) between lever and housing.

cable adjuster at brake lever or at brake end of cable so there is a 4-5 mm (0.16-0.20 in.) gap (G—Fig. Y5-35) between cable pin and front end of slot in parking brake actuating arm.

Block up rear end of vehicle so wheels can turn freely and check for brake drag while rotating wheels. If brake drags, repeat brake adjustment procedure.

OVERHAUL. All models are equipped with a cable-actuated rear disc brake. The brake assembly is located on the right side of the final drive housing. The brake cover must be removed to inspect the brake assembly. The brake actuating arm assembly must be removed before the brake cover can be removed. The right wheel and hub must be removed to remove the brake disc. Renew brake pads if thickness is less than 1.5 mm (0.060 in.) on YFM200DX models and 2.0 mm (0.08 in.) on YFM225 and YFM250 models. Renew brake disc if thickness is less than 3.0 mm (0.12 in.). Maximum allowable disc runout is 0.5 mm (0.020 in.).

Reverse removal procedure to install brake components. Apply lithium base grease to brake cam. Tighten caliper retaining nuts to 50 N·m (37 ft.-lbs.). Tighten actuator plate retaining nuts to 9 N·m (80 in.-lbs.). Tighten wheel hub nut to 120 N·m (88 ft.-lbs.) on YFM200DX and YFM225 models and 150 N·m (110 ft.-lbs.) on YFM250 models. Tighten wheel retaining nuts to 28 N·m (21 ft.-lbs.) on YFM200DX and YFM225 models and 55 N·m (40 ft.-lbs.) on YFM250 models.

DIFFERENTIAL LOCK CABLE

Models YFU1 And YFU1T

All YFU1 and YFU1T models are equipped with a differential in the final drive. A cable-actuated locking device permits locking the differential so power is transferred to both rear wheels and a single wheel cannot slip.

Cable free play measured at connection between spring at rear of cable and cable end should be 5-10 mm (0.2-0.4 in.). To adjust cable free play, loosen locknut and turn cable adjuster at cable bracket located at front of final drive housing.

FINAL DRIVE

All Models

Service on the final drive should be performed by a Yamaha service technician equipped with the special tools required for overhaul.

YAMAHA
YFS200

NOTE: Metric fasteners are used throughout vehicle.

CONDENSED SERVICE DATA

MODEL	YFS200
General	
Engine Make	Yamaha
Engine Type	Two-Stroke; Air-Cooled
Number of Cylinders	1
Bore	66.0 mm (2.60 in.)
Stroke	57.0 mm (2.24 in.)
Displacement	195 cc (11.9 cu. in.)
Compression Ratio	6.6:1
Engine Lubrication	Oil Injection
Engine Oil	Air-Cooled, Two-Stroke Engine Oil
Transmission Oil	SAE 10W-30
Forward Speeds	6
Tire Size:	
Front	21 × 7-10
Rear	21 × 10-8
Tire Pressure:	
Front	30 kPa (4.3 psi)
Rear	25 kPa (3.6 psi)
Vehicle Weight W/Full Fuel Tank	150 kg (331 lbs.)
Tune-Up	
Engine Idle Speed	1450-1550 rpm
Spark Plug:	
NGK	B8ES
Nippon Denso	W24ES
Electrode Gap	0.7-0.8 mm (0.028-0.031 in.)
Ignition:	
Type	Breakerless
Timing	16° BTDC
Carburetor:	
Make	Mikuni
Model	VM26SS
Jet Needle	5J22
Clip Position	2nd Groove From Top
Needle Jet	P-6
Pilot Jet	#32.5
Main Jet	#230

Tune-Up (Cont.)
Carburetor: (Cont.)

Float Height	20.0-21.5 mm
	(0.79-0.85 in.)
Idle Mixture Setting	1½ Turns Out
Throttle Lever Free Play	4-6 mm
	(0.16-0.24 in.)

Sizes-Clearances

Cylinder Head Distortion (Max.)	0.03 mm
	(0.0012 in.)
Cylinder Bore Diameter	66.00-66.02 mm
	(2.598-2.599 in.)
Wear Limit	66.1 mm
	(2.602 in.)
Cylinder Bore Taper (Max.)	0.08 mm
	(0.003 in.)
Cylinder Bore Out-of-Round (Max.)	0.05 mm
	(0.002 in.)
Piston-to-Cylinder Wall Clearance	0.035-0.040 mm
	(0.0014-0.0016 in.)
Piston Diameter Measured 10 mm (0.4 in.) From Skirt Bottom	65.965-66.000 mm
	(2.5970-2.5984 in.)
Piston Ring End Gap	0.20-0.35 mm
	(0.008-0.014 in.)
Piston Ring Side Clearance	0.03-0.05 mm
	(0.0012-0.0020 in.)
Connecting Rod Big End Side Clearance	0.4-0.7 mm
	(0.016-0.028 in.)
Connecting Rod Small End Side Shake	0.8-1.0 mm
	(0.031-0.040 in.)
Connecting Rod Big End Radial Clearance	0.021-0.035 mm
	(0.0008-0.0014 in.)
Crankshaft Runout (Max.)	0.03 mm
	(0.0012 in.)
Clutch Friction Plate Thickness (Min.)	2.8 mm
	(0.110 in.)
Clutch Steel Plate Warpage Limit	0.05 mm
	(0.002 in.)

Capacities

Fuel Tank	9.0 L
	(2.4 gal.)
Transmission Sump: Drained	0.65 L
	(0.69 qt.)
Dry	0.7 L
	(0.74 qt.)
Engine Oil Tank	1.3 L
	(1.37 qt.)

Tightening Torques
Axle Nut:

Front	70 N•m
	(51 ft.-lbs.)

Tightening Torques (Cont.)

Axle Nut: (Cont.)

Rear	120 N·m (88 ft.-lbs.)
Clutch Nut	80 N·m (59 ft.-lbs.)
Crankcase	8 N·m (71 in.-lbs.)
Cylinder	25 N·m (18 ft.-lbs.)
Cylinder Head	27 N·m (20 ft.-lbs.)
Engine Sprocket	10 N·m (88 in.-lbs.)
Flywheel	73 N·m (54 ft.-lbs.)
Primary Drive Gear	80 N·m (59 ft.-lbs.)
Rear Sprocket	24 N·m (18 ft.-lbs.)
Spark Plug	25 N·m (18 ft.-lbs.)
Wheel Retaining Nut	45 N·m (33 ft.-lbs.)
Standard Screws:	
6 mm	6.0 N·m (53 in.-lbs.)
8 mm	15 N·m (133 in.-lbs.)
10 mm	30 N·m (22 ft.-lbs.)
12 mm	55 N·m (40 ft.-lbs.)
14 mm	85 N·m (63 ft.-lbs.)
16 mm	130 N·m (96 ft.-lbs.)

LUBRICATION

ENGINE. The engine is lubricated by oil injected into the fuel:air mixture at the carburetor. An oil pump mounted on the right side of the engine pumps oil from the oil tank to the carburetor. Oil is metered by the pump in direct relation to engine speed and throttle setting.

Recommended oil is Yamalube or a good quality oil designed for air-cooled, two-stroke engines. Oil tank capacity is 1.3 L (1.37 qt.).

Refer to OIL PUMP section if pump control cable adjustment or bleeding of the oil system is required. Note that bleeding the oil system is required if the oil tank runs dry, if lines are disconnected or if the vehicle lies on its side.

TRANSMISSION. Recommended transmission oil is SAE 10W-30 oil with API classification SF. The manufacturer recommends changing the transmission oil after first month of operation and then every six months thereafter.

Transmission oil level is checked at sight glass (G—Fig. Y7-1). With vehicle level, oil level should be between two marks on sight glass. Pour oil into transmission through opening for fill plug (F). Drain oil by unscrewing drain plug on underside of engine. Dry capacity of transmission sump is 0.7 L (0.74 qt.). Refilling transmission will only require 0.65 L (0.69 qt.) of oil

Fig. Y7-1—Transmission oil level should be between marks on sight glass (G). Pour oil through opening of fill plug (F).

because some oil will be trapped inside case. After refilling transmission, check oil level.

DRIVE CHAIN. The drive chain should be lubricated with SAE 30-50 gear oil after the first week of operation and after every 30 days of operation thereafter. The chain utilizes "O" rings to seal the chain rollers and pins. Incorrect lubrication may damage the "O" rings resulting in premature chain failure.

Remove and clean the drive chain when excessive dirt is evident. Remove chain as outlined in DRIVE CHAIN AND SPROCKETS section. The chain should be thoroughly washed in kerosene and wiped dry. The use of any cleaning solution other than kerosene may damage "O" rings. Lubricate chain with SAE 30-50 gear oil, then install and adjust chain as outlined in DRIVE CHAIN AND SPROCKETS section.

SUSPENSION AND STEERING. The grease fittings on suspension components should be injected with lithium base grease after first month of operation and every three months thereafter. Grease fittings are located at inner ends of control arms and lower end of steering shaft.

The swing arm bushings and upper steering shaft bushing should be lubricated with lithium base grease after first month of operation and every three months thereafter.

CABLES AND LEVERS. All cables and levers should be inspected and lubricated after the first month of operation and after every three months of operation thereafter.

AIR CLEANER ELEMENT

All models are equipped with a foam type air cleaner element located underneath the seat. The air cleaner

element should be removed and cleaned every three months or more frequently if operating conditions are severe.

To remove air cleaner element, remove seat and unscrew cover. Unscrew element retaining screw and remove element. Thoroughly clean the foam element in a nonflammable solvent. Compress element between hands to remove solvent. Do not wring or twist element. Saturate element in clean SAE 10W-30 engine oil, then compress element to remove excess oil. Apply grease to seating surface of element and reinstall element.

FUEL SYSTEM

CARBURETOR. The engine is equipped with a Mikuni VM26SS carburetor. Initial setting of idle mixture screw (I—Fig. Y7-3) is $1\frac{1}{2}$ turns out from a lightly seated position. Final adjustment must be performed with engine at normal operating temperature. Remove seat for access to idle speed screw (S—Fig. Y7-4) which is located in carburetor switch housing mounted on top of carburetor. Adjust idle speed screw (S) so engine idles at 1450-1550 rpm. Rotate idle mixture screw (I—Fig. Y7-3) so engine runs at highest idle speed, then readjust idle speed screw (S—Fig. Y7-4) so engine idles at specified rpm.

When servicing carburetor, refer to Fig. Y7-5 for an exploded view of carburetor and to carburetor specifications in CONDENSED SERVICE DATA section while noting the following: When removing carburetor, loosen retainer (18) and unscrew cap (5) to separate throttle slide and switch assembly from carburetor. Remove needle jet (14) by carefully forcing towards top of carburetor. Jet needle clip (11) should be installed in second groove from top of jet needle. Installing clip in a lower groove on jet needle will richen mid-range fuel mixture. Groove in side of needle jet (14) must index with pin in carburetor. When measuring float height, tilt carburetor

Fig. Y7-3—Adjust idle mixture screw (I) as outlined in text.

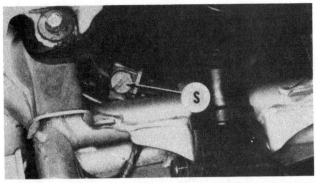

Fig. Y7-4—The seat must be removed for access to idle speed screw (S).

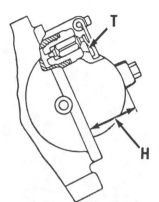

Fig. Y7-6—Tilt carburetor when measuring float height so tang (T) just touches inlet valve and valve spring is not compressed. Float height (H) should be 20.0-21.5 mm (0.79-0.85 in.). Bend tang (T) to adjust float height.

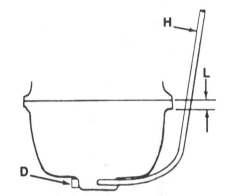

Fig. Y7-7—The fuel level is measured from the bottom edge of the carburetor body. Fuel level (L) should be 0.5-1.5 mm (0.020-0.060 in.) above carburetor body edge.

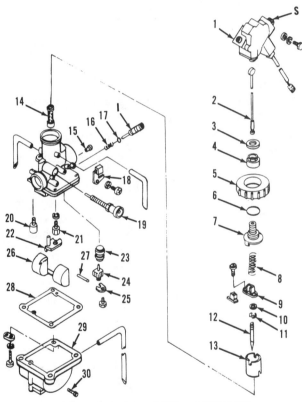

Fig. Y7-5—Exploded view of Mikuni VM26SS.

I. Idle mixture screw	15. Air jet
S. Idle speed screw	16. Spring
1. Throttle switch assy.	17. "O" ring
2. Throttle cable	18. Retainer
3. Washer	19. Starter plunger
4. Nut	20. Pilot jet
5. Cap	21. Main jet
6. "O" ring	22. Baffle
7. Coupler	23. Fuel inlet seat
8. Spring	24. Fuel inlet valve
9. Connector	25. Retainer
10. Washer	26. Float
11. Clip	27. Float pin
12. Jet needle	28. Gasket
13. Throttle slide	29. Fuel bowl
14. Needle jet	30. Drain screw

as shown in Fig. Y7-6 so float arm tang (T) just contacts fuel inlet valve and spring in valve is not compressed. Bend float arm tang to adjust float height. Make sure groove in side of throttle slide is aligned with pin in carburetor body when inserting slide in carburetor.

With the carburetor installed, the fuel level should be checked. Attach Yamaha fuel level gauge YM-01312 or a suitable clear hose (H—Fig. Y7-7) to fuel bowl nozzle. Hose should be long enough to extend above the bottom edge of carburetor body without kinking. Open fuel bowl drain screw (D). Run the engine at idle speed until fuel level in hose stabilizes, then stop engine. Measure distance from the bottom edge of carburetor body (fuel bowl contact surface) to fuel level in hose to determine fuel level (L). Fuel level check will not be accurate if hose is moved after fuel level is stabilized. Fuel level (L) should be 0.5-1.5 mm (0.020-0.060 in.) above carburetor body edge. To adjust fuel level, remove the fuel bowl and carefully bend float arm tang (T—Fig. Y7-6).

THROTTLE LEVER FREE PLAY. Free play at the end of throttle lever (T—Fig. Y7-8) should be 4-6 mm

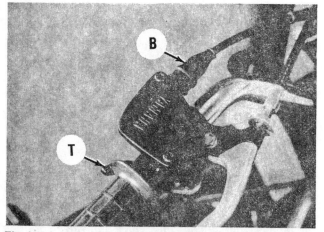

Fig. Y7-8—Throttle lever (T) free play should be 4-6 mm (0.16-0.24 in.). Slide back boot (B) for access to adjuster.

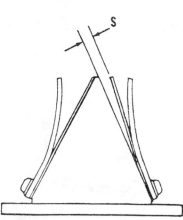

Fig. Y7-9—Reed valve petals may stand open a maximum of 0.5 mm (0.020 in.).

(0.16-0.24 in.). To adjust free play, slide back rubber boot (B), loosen knurled nut and rotate cable adjuster. Retighten knurled nut.

REED VALVE. A "V" type reed valve assembly is located between the intake manifold and engine. The reed valve assembly is accessible after removing the carburetor and intake manifold.

Reed petal seats must be smooth and flat. Renew reed petals if bent, broken or otherwise damaged. Do not attempt to straighten reed petals.

Reed valve petals may stand open (S—Fig. Y7-9) a maximum of 0.5 mm (0.020 in.). The reed petals and stops can be renewed individually. Notches on corners of reed petals and stops must be aligned. Apply Loctite to reed stop retaining screws. Tighten intake manifold screws to 8 N.m (71 in.-lbs.).

FUEL STRAINER. A strainer is mounted on the end of each pickup tube that extends into the fuel tank from the fuel valve. To inspect the strainers, the fuel in the fuel tank must be drained. Disconnect the fuel hose from

the fuel valve. Unscrew fuel valve retaining screws and remove fuel valve. Clean and inspect the strainers. Reinstall the valve while noting that sealing washers are used on the retaining screws to prevent fuel leakage.

IGNITION AND ELECTRICAL

IGNITION SYSTEM. Model is equipped with a pointless, capacitor discharge ignition system. A charge coil located behind the flywheel provides electrical power for the ignition system. The pickup coil is also located behind the flywheel. The CDI module is attached to the front of the frame while the ignition coil is attached to the middle of the frame. The ignition circuit includes a control unit attached to the front of the frame and switches located in the throttle housing and attached to the top of the carburetor.

Ignition timing is not adjustable. Ignition timing should be correct if components operate properly.

Some ignition components can be checked using an ohmmeter. To check the pickup coil, disconnect white/red wire and black wire leads to engine. Pickup coil resistance should be 72-108 ohms.

To check the charge coil, disconnect the black/red wire and black wire leads to engine. Charge coil resistance should be 192-288 ohms.

Ignition coil resistance readings should be 1.44-1.76 ohms for primary windings and 5.28k-7.92k ohms for secondary windings.

To check for a problem in the control unit circuit, disconnect three-wire connector to control unit. If engine starts with control unit disconnected, then circuit is faulty. Check operation of throttle switch and carburetor switches, which are on-off type switches. If switches operate properly, then replace control unit with a new or good unit.

If the ignition system malfunctions and all components test satisfactory, replace CDI module with a new or good unit and recheck ignition system.

ELECTRICAL SYSTEM. A lighting coil is located behind the flywheel to provide electrical power for the lights.

The lighting coil can be checked using an ohmmeter. Connect an ohmmeter to yellow/red wire and black wire leads to engine. Resistance should be 0.16-0.24 ohms.

To check the voltage regulator, disconnect the yellow wire and black wire leads to headlight. Connect positive lead of a voltmeter to yellow wire and negative voltmeter lead to black wire. Place headlight switch in high position. The voltmeter should indicate 13.5-14.1 volts with engine running at 5000 rpm. If specified voltage is not produced, renew voltage regulator with a new or good unit and recheck voltage.

The headlight is a 12V 45W/45W unit while the taillight is a 12V 3.8W unit.

Fig. Y7-10—Unscrew bleed screw (B) and allow oil to run out until oil is free of air bubbles.

OIL PUMP

The engine is equipped with an oil pump that meters oil to the carburetor where it is injected into the air:fuel mixture thereby lubricating the engine. The oil pump is located behind a cover on the right front portion of the engine.

BLEEDING. The oil system must be bled if the oil tank runs dry, the vehicle lies on its side, oil lines are disconnected or the oil pump is removed. To bleed air from the oil and the oil line leading to the pump, unscrew bleed screw (B—Fig. Y7-10) and allow oil to run out until oil is free of air bubbles. Install bleed screw. Disconnect oil line from carburetor and fill line with recommended engine oil, then reattach line to carburetor.

REMOVE AND REINSTALL. To remove oil pump, remove right front engine cover. Detach oil hoses from pump and plug hoses. Unscrew and remove oil pump. When reinstalling pump, tighten retaining screws to 5 N•m (44 in.-lbs.). Bleed oil pump and lines as outlined in previous section.

FASTENERS

After the first month of operation and every three months thereafter, the vehicle should receive an overall inspection. All screws, nuts and other fasteners should be checked and tightened to proper torque specification shown in CONDENSED SERVICE DATA section or in the appropriate maintenance section.

CLUTCH

The engine is equipped with a multiple-disc clutch that is located behind the right crankcase cover.

Clutch lever free play (F—Fig. Y7-11) should be 5-8 mm (0.20-0.31 in.). To adjust clutch lever free play, push back dust boot, loosen locknut and rotate adjuster (A). Retighten locknut.

To adjust clutch, loosen clutch cable and on early models, detach parking brake cable from handlebar

Fig. Y7-11—Clutch lever free play (F) should be 5-8 mm (0.20-0.31 in.). Loosen locknut and rotate adjuster (A) to adjust free play. Parking brake cable used on early models is not shown.

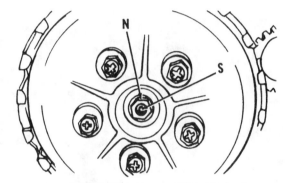

Fig. Y7-12—Adjust clutch as outlined in text.

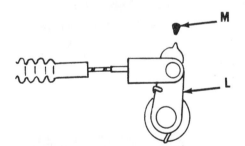

Fig. Y7-13—Pointer on lever (L) is aligned with mark (M) by turning clutch adjusting screw (S—Fig. Y7-12). See text.

lever. Detach right footpeg assembly for access to crankcase cover. Remove oil pump as previously outlined. Remove kick starter lever from shaft. Detach right crankcase cover from engine. Loosen locknut (N—Fig. Y7-12) then push operating lever (L—Fig. Y7-13) forward until it stops. Rotate screw (S—Fig. Y7-12) so point on lever end aligns with mark (M) on crankcase, then hold screw and retighten locknut (N). Reassemble components. It may be necessary to rotate oil pump drive shaft so gears mesh when installing crankcase side cover. Tighten side cover screws to 10 N·m (88 in.-lbs.). Be sure kick starter is properly installed and will not contact engine during operation. Tighten kick starter retaining nut to 65 N·m (48 ft.-lbs.). Bleed and install oil pump as previously outlined. Adjust clutch lever free play as previously outlined. On early models with parking brake on clutch lever, adjust parking brake as outlined in REAR BRAKE section.

FRONT BRAKE SYSTEM

BRAKE LEVER FREE PLAY. Recommended brake lever free travel is 5-8 mm (0.20-0.31 in.) measured between lever housing (H—Fig. Y7-15) and brake lever (L). Adjust lever free play by loosening locknut (N) and rotating brake cable adjuster (A). Remove cover on front fender and operate brake lever while observing equalizer bar shown in Fig. Y7-16. If equalizer bar does not remain level, adjust position of wing nut at brake end of

Fig. Y7-15—Front brake lever free travel is measured at gap between lever (L) and housing (H). Free travel should be 5-8 mm (0.20-0.31 in.). Adjust free travel by loosening locknut (N) and turning adjuster (A). Parking brake cable (P) is located on clutch lever on early models.

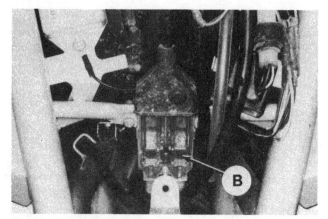

Fig. Y7-16—Equalizer bar (B) must remain level when actuating front brakes.

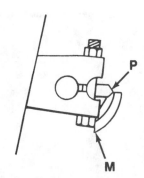

Fig. Y7-17—Brake linings are worn excessively if pointer (P) passes end of wear range scale (M) when brake is actuated.

brake cable on appropriate brake. Readjust brake lever free play.

OVERHAUL. Brake lining thickness may be checked externally by operating brake and noting position of pointer (P—Fig. Y7-17) on each front brake actuating lever. There is sufficient brake lining remaining if pointer does not align with or pass mark (M).

WARNING: Inhaling asbestos brake dust is injurious to human health. Approved OSHA respiration equipment must be worn when working on or around brake components. DO NOT use compressed air to clean brake drums, shoes or nearby components as brake dust will be blown into air. Only vacuum equipment designed to pick up brake dust should be used.

Each front brake assembly is accessible after removing the brake drum/hub. Renew the brake shoes if damaged or if lining is worn to less than 2.0 mm (0.08 in.). Renew the brake drum assembly if inside diameter exceeds 111.0 mm (4.37 in.). Tighten hub retaining nut to 70 N·m (51 ft.-lbs.). Tighten wheel retaining nuts to 45 N·m (33 ft.-lbs.).

FRONT AXLE

Both front steering knuckle assemblies pivot on ball joint assemblies at the end of each upper and lower control arm. The control arms are bolted at the ends to the vehicle frame and a shock absorber is used to limit and cushion the up and down movement of the control arms. The shock absorbers are adjustable to alter shock absorber spring setting for different terrain and load conditions.

Remove front wheel for access to hub and spindle. Unscrew hub nut to remove wheel hub. The hub and brake drum are one piece. Renew bearings if rough or otherwise damaged. Be sure to install spacer between bearings when reassembling components. Tapered end of spacer must be towards wheel side of hub. Tighten hub retaining nut to 70 N·m (51 ft.-lbs.). Tighten wheel retaining nuts to 45 N·m (33 ft.-lbs.).

Remove the front wheel to service the ball joint assemblies. Note that removing the brake components will allow greater access to ball joint assemblies. If any ball joint or control arm is excessively worn or any other damage is noted, then ball joint and control arm must be renewed as a unit assembly. Lower control arm and upper control arm retaining nuts should be tightened to 30 N·m (22 ft.-lbs.). Tighten ball joint to steering knuckle clamp bolts to 48 N·m (35 ft.-lbs.). Shock absorber retaining nuts should be tightened to 45 N·m (33 ft.-lbs).

STEERING

TOE-IN SETTING. Place the handlebar in a straight ahead position. Use a suitable measuring tool and measure distance (B—Fig. Y7-18) at spindle height between the center of the tires on the rear sides. Locate the same tire centerline points on front side of tires and measure front distance (F). The distance on the front side (F) should be 0-10 mm (0.0-0.4 in.) shorter than the measured distance on the rear side (B). Note that the distance from a projected vehicle centerline to left (L) and right (R) tire centerlines should also be equal.

To adjust, loosen inside and outside locknuts on the left and right tie rod assemblies and rotate tie rod shaft on each side equally until distance is within recommended range. After obtaining the correct setting, tighten locknuts to 30 N·m (22 ft.-lbs.).

INSPECTION. Rotate the steering handlebar from one extreme to the other and note if any binding or roughness is felt. Periodically inspect the steering components for looseness or any other damage. Renew any damaged component. Clean and grease components if binding or excessive effort is noted.

OVERHAUL. To expose the steering shaft, remove the front fender cover. Unscrew the two cap screws securing the clamp halves. Clean the old grease from the steering shaft. Inspect the clamp halves and steering shaft for damage. Renew components if needed. Grease inside of steering shaft clamp halves with a lithium base grease and install. Tighten the retaining clamp cap screws to 23 N·m (17 ft.-lbs.).

To remove steering shaft, remove the front fender cover and detach the handlebar assembly from the steering shaft flange. Detach headlight bracket from steering shaft flange. Detach inner tie rod ends from steering shaft. Remove the lower steering shaft retaining cotter pin and nut and withdraw the steering shaft. Inspect the lower bushings and "O" rings and renew if needed. Apply a lithium base grease to lower bushings before installation. Tighten the lower steering shaft retaining nut to 30 N·m (22 ft.-lbs.). Tighten the retaining nut for either tie rod end to 25 N·m (18 ft.-lbs.).

When installing handlebar, tighten front screw on handlebar clamps first, then tighten the rear clamp screws. If properly tightened, there should be no gaps at the front of the clamps and even gaps at the rear of the clamps. Tighten clamp screws to 20 N·m (15 ft.-lbs.).

REAR BRAKE SYSTEM

ADJUSTMENT. The rear brake and parking brake are adjusted simultaneously. On early models, the parking brake cable is routed to the clutch lever on the handlebar, while on later models, the parking brake cable is routed to the front brake lever assembly. Apply rear brake pedal several times. Slide back boot from parking brake cable at lever, loosen locknut and turn cable adjuster in. Slide back boot on brake end of rear brake cable. Loosen locknut (N—Fig. Y7-19) and turn cable adjuster (A) out so free play at parking brake lever is zero. Additional adjustment is possible at parking brake lever. Hold adjusters and tighten locknuts. Reinstall

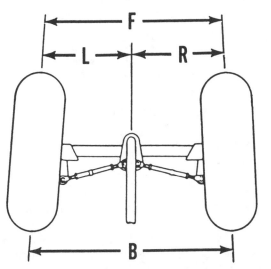

Fig. Y7-18—Toe-in should be 0-10 mm (0.0-0.4 in.). Refer to text for measurement and adjustment procedures.

Fig. Y7-19—Loosen locknut (N) and rotate adjuster (A) to adjust parking brake cable free play as outlined in text.

boots. Be sure brake does not drag by rotating rear wheels with rear of vehicle supported.

OVERHAUL. To remove rear brake caliper, support rear of vehicle and remove right rear wheel.

WARNING: Inhaling asbestos brake dust is injurious to human health. Approved OSHA respiration equipment must be worn when working on or around brake caliper and pads. DO NOT use compressed air to clean brake caliper, pads or nearby components as brake dust will be blown into air. Only vacuum equipment designed to pick up brake dust should be used.

Turn brake cable adjusters clockwise at parking brake lever and brake so tension on brake cable is removed. Unscrew the actuator from the caliper and detach the brake cable. Unscrew the caliper mounting screws and remove the caliper. Renew brake pads if pad thickness is less than 1.0 mm (0.04 in.).

Inspect brake disc and renew if excessively worn or damaged. The wheel hub must be removed before removing disc hub. Note that boots covering disc hub are retained by wire clips. Tighten brake disc retaining screws to 28 N·m (21 ft.-lbs.). Apply lithium base grease to splines of disc hub and wheel hub.

DRIVE CHAIN AND SPROCKETS

INSPECTION AND ADJUSTMENT. The final drive chain should be inspected and adjusted after the first month of operation and every six months thereafter. Improper maintenance and neglect can cause early failure of both drive chain and sprockets. To measure drive chain free play, support rear of frame near swing

Fig. Y7-20—Loosen drive housing retaining nuts (N), loosen locknuts on chain tension adjusting screws (C) and turn screws to adjust chain tension.

arm pivot so rear wheels are off ground. Measure drive chain travel at a point midway between rub block at swing arm and rear sprocket. Drive chain free play should be 30-40 mm ($1\frac{3}{16}$-$1\frac{9}{16}$ in.).

To adjust chain tension, loosen rear axle housing retaining nuts (N—Fig. Y7-20), loosen adjusting screw locknuts and rotate tension adjusting screws (C). Note axle alignment marks on swing arm and maintain axle alignment by aligning same marks on each side of axle housing. Tighten axle housing retaining nuts to 50 N·m (36 ft.-lbs.) and recheck drive chain tension. Renew drive chain if recommended tension adjustment cannot be obtained. Refer to LUBRICATION for drive chain lubrication requirements.

R&R AND OVERHAUL. The drive chain is sealed by "O" rings and fitted with a master link. To remove the drive chain and both sprockets, support rear of vehicle and remove left wheel. Remove chain guard under rear sprocket. Loosen rear axle housing nuts (N—Fig. Y7-20) and back off chain tension adjuster screws (C) to slacken chain. Remove left engine side cover. Remove drive chain master link while taking care not to damage or lose "O" rings. Remove drive chain. To remove rear sprocket, unscrew sprocket retaining nuts and remove sprocket. To remove engine sprocket, unscrew retaining screws and remove sprocket.

Carefully examine sprockets for excessive wear. Worn sprockets will usually have a hooked tooth profile. A good test is to place a new chain on a used sprocket and check the fit. If sprockets require renewal due to wear, always renew drive chain. Sprockets should be renewed as a set. Renew drive chain if distance between 10 link pins exceeds 150.1 mm (5.91 in.) with chain straight and all slack removed.

Reassemble by reversing disassembly procedure. Tighten engine sprocket retaining screws to 10 N·m (88 in.-lbs.). Tighten rear sprocket retaining nuts to 24 N·m (18 ft.-lbs.). When assembling chain, be sure "O" rings are properly installed on master link. Install master link clip as shown in Fig. Y7-21. Tighten wheel retaining nuts to 45 N·m (33 ft.-lbs.). Refer to previous INSPECTION AND ADJUSTMENT paragraphs for recommended drive chain adjustment procedure.

FINAL DRIVE ASSEMBLY

R&R AND OVERHAUL. Support rear of vehicle. Apply parking brake and loosen axle nuts adjacent to sprocket hub. Release the parking brake and remove brake caliper as previously outlined. Remove drive chain as previously outlined. Remove left wheel hub. Remove axle nuts (A—Fig. Y7-20) and sprocket hub. Withdraw axle from right side (brake side) of housing. If required, remove brake disc from axle while noting wire clips that retain boots around disc hub.

Renew seals, bearings and other damaged or excessively worn components as needed. Maximum axle

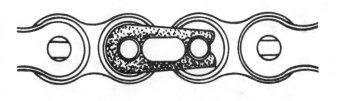

← CHAIN TRAVEL

Fig. Y7-21—Install drive chain master link clip with closed end towards direction of chain travel.

runout with axle supported just outside inner splined areas is 1.5 mm (0.060 in.). Reassembly is reverse order of disassembly. Lubricate splined areas with lithium base grease. When tightening axle nuts adjacent to sprocket hub, use the following procedure. Tighten inner nut to 55 N•m (40 ft.-lbs.). Hold inner nut and tighten outer nut to 190 N•m (140 ft.-lbs.). Hold outer nut and tighten inner nut towards outer nut to 240 N•m (176 ft.-lbs.). Tighten axle hub retaining nuts to 120 N•m (88 ft.-lbs.).

YAMAHA
YFB250

NOTE: Metric fasteners are used throughout vehicle.

CONDENSED SERVICE DATA

MODEL	YFB250
General	
Engine Make	Yamaha
Engine Type	Four-Stroke; Air-Cooled
Number of Cylinders	1
Bore	71 mm
	(2.80 in.)
Stroke.	58 mm
	(2.28 in.)
Displacement	229.6 cc
	(14.0 cu. in.)
Compression Ratio	8.7:1
Engine Lubrication	Wet Sump; Oil Pump
Transmission Lubrication	Common With Engine
Engine/Transmission Oil	SAE 10W-40
Forward Speeds.	5
Reverse Speeds	1
Tire Size:	
Front	22 × 7-10
Rear.	22 × 10-10
Tire Pressure:	
Front	20 kPa
	(2.9 psi)
Rear.	25 kPa
	(3.6 psi)
Battery	12V-12AH
Vehicle Weight W/Full Fuel Tank	188 kg
	(414 lbs.)
Tune-Up	
Engine Idle Speed	1350-1450 rpm
Compression Pressure	900 kPa
	(130 psi)
Spark Plug:	
NGK.	D7EA
Nippon Denso	X22ES-U
Electrode Gap	0.6-0.7 mm
	(0.024-0.028 in.)
Ignition:	
Type.	Breakerless
Timing	10° BTDC @ 1000 rpm
	30° BTDC @ 6000 rpm
Carburetor:	
Make	Mikuni
Model.	VM24SH
Jet Needle	5L10

Tune-Up (Cont.)

Carburetor: (Cont.)

Clip Position......................	4th Groove From Top
Needle Jet	O-4
Pilot Jet	#20
Main Jet	#85
Float Height	21.0-22.0 mm
	(0.83-0.87 in.)
Idle Mixture Setting	1¼ Turns
Throttle Lever Free Play	3-5 mm
	(0.12-0.20 in.)

Sizes-Clearances

Valve Clearance (cold):	
Intake............................	0.05-0.09 mm
	(0.0020-0.0035 in.)
Exhaust	0.11-0.15 mm
	(0.0043-0.0060 in.)
Valve Face & Seat Angle:	
Intake & Exhaust	45°
Valve Seat Width:	
Intake & Exhaust	0.9-1.1 mm
	(0.035-0.043 in.)
Valve Margin:	
Intake............................	0.8-1.2 mm
	(0.031-0.047 in.)
Exhaust	0.8-1.2 mm
	(0.031-0.047 in.)
Valve Stem Diameter:	
Intake............................	5.975-5.990 mm
	(0.2352-0.2358 in.)
Exhaust	5.960-5.975 mm
	(0.2346-0.2352 in.)
Valve Guide Bore Diameter:	
Intake & Exhaust	6.000-6.012 mm
	(0.2362-0.2367 in.)
Maximum......................	6.03 mm
	(0.2374 in.)
Valve Stem-to-Guide Clearance:	
Intake............................	0.010-0.037 mm
	(0.0004-0.0015 in.)
Maximum......................	0.1 mm
	(0.0039 in.)
Exhaust	0.025-0.052 mm
	(0.0010-0.0020 in.)
Maximum......................	0.1 mm
	(0.0039 in.)
Valve Spring Free Length:	
Inner............................	35.5 mm
	(1.40 in.)
Outer	37.2 mm
	(1.46 in.)
Rocker Arm Bore Diameter:	
Intake & Exhaust	12.000-12.018 mm
	(0.4724-0.4731 in.)

Sizes-Clearances (Cont.)

Rocker Shaft Diameter:
Intake & Exhaust .... 11.985-11.991 mm
(0.4718-0.4720 in.)

Camshaft Lobe Height:
Intake........................... 36.587 mm
(1.4404 in.)

    Minimum .... 36.487 mm
(1.4365 in.)

  Exhaust .... 36.632 mm
(1.4422 in.)

    Minimum .... 36.532 mm
(1.4383 in.)

Camshaft Runout (Max.) .... 0.03 mm
(0.0012 in.)

Cylinder Head Distortion (Max.)......... 0.03 mm
(0.0012 in.)

Cylinder Bore Diameter .... 70.97-71.02 mm
(2.794-2.796 in.)

Cylinder Taper (Max.)................ 0.05 mm
(0.002 in.)

Piston Diameter:
Measured 4.0 mm (0.16 in.) From
Skirt Bottom & 90° to Pin Bore .... 70.92-70.97 mm
(2.792-2.794 in.)

Piston-to-Cylinder Clearance........... 0.040-0.060 mm
(0.0016-0.0023 in.)

Piston Ring End Gap:
Top & Second Rings .... 0.15-0.30 mm
(0.006-0.012 in.)

  Oil Ring .... 0.3-0.9 mm
(0.012-0.035 in.)

Piston Ring Side Clearance:
Top Ring........................ 0.03-0.07 mm
(0.0012-0.0028 in.)

  Second Ring .... 0.02-0.06 mm
(0.0008-0.0024 in.)

Connecting Rod Big End
Side Clearance (Max.)............... 0.35-0.65 mm
(0.014-0.026 in.)

Connecting Rod Small
End Shake...................... 0.08-1.0 mm
(0.031-0.039 in.)

Crankshaft Runout (Max.):
Clutch End...................... 0.06 mm
(0.0024 in.)

  Flywheel End.................... 0.03 mm
(0.0012 in.)

Clutch Friction Plate
Thickness (Min.) .... 2.8 mm
(0.110 in.)

Clutch Steel Plate Warpage Limit .... 0.2 mm
(0.008 in.)

Clutch Spring Free Length (Min.)........ 32.9 mm
(1.30 in.)

Capacities

Engine/Transmission Sump............ See Text
Fuel Tank .... 9.7 L
(2.6 gal.)

Tightening Torques

Axle Nut:

Front	70 N·m (51 ft.-lbs.)
Rear	150 N·m (110 ft.-lbs.)
Balancer Shaft Nut	75 N·m (55 ft.-lbs.)
Camshaft Sprocket	60 N·m (43 ft.-lbs.)

Clutch Nut:

Centrifugal Clutch	78 N·m (57 ft.-lbs.)
Disc Clutch	50 N·m (37 ft.-lbs.)
Crankcase	7 N·m (62 in.-lbs.)
Cylinder Base Screws	10 N·m (88 in.-lbs.)

Cylinder Head:

Flange Screw	22 N·m (16 ft.-lbs.)
Hex Screw	7 N·m (62 in.-lbs.)
Engine Mounting Nuts	33 N·m (24 ft.-lbs.)
Flywheel	50 N·m (37 ft.-lbs.)
Spark Plug	17.5 N·m (155 in.-lbs.)

Wheel Nuts:

Front	45 N·m (33 ft.-lbs.)
Rear	55 N·m (40 ft.-lbs.)

Standard Screws:

6 mm	6 N·m (53 in.-lbs.)
8 mm	15 N·m (133 in.-lbs.)
10 mm	30 N·m (22 ft.-lbs.)
12 mm	55 N·m (40 ft.-lbs.)
14 mm	85 N·m (61 ft.-lbs.)
16 mm	130 N·m (94 ft.-lbs.)

LUBRICATION

ENGINE AND TRANSMISSION. The engine and transmission are lubricated by a crankshaft-driven oil pump. The engine and transmission share a common sump. Recommended oil is SAE 10W-30 with an API classification of SE and/or SF.

Oil level should be maintained at upper mark on dipstick attached to fill plug (F—Fig. Y9-1). Do not screw plug in when checking oil level. Fill sump through opening for fill plug (F). Drain oil by removing drain plug (D—Fig. Y9-2) on underside of crankcase.

The manufacturer recommends changing the oil and oil filter after the first month of operation and every six months thereafter. Remove oil filter cover (C—Fig. Y9-2) for access to oil filter. Clean the drain plug oil strainer in a suitable solvent. Renew the strainer if damaged or contaminated.

Fill crankcase with 1.5 L (1.6 qt.) of oil if only oil is changed or 1.6 L (1.7 qt.) if oil and oil filter are changed. Crankcase capacity totally dry is 1.8 L (1.9 qt.).

To be sure the oil pump is pumping oil to the engine, slightly unscrew oil passage screw (W—Fig. Y9-3). Start and run engine at idle speed. Oil should just seep past screw after one minute. Retighten screw if oil seeps from hole. If no oil is present, stop engine and determine cause.

FINAL DRIVE HOUSING. To check oil level in final drive housing, remove fill plug (F—Fig. Y9-4). Oil should reach bottom edge of fill plug hole with vehicle on a level surface. Recommended oil is SAE 80 hypoid gear oil with API classification GL-4.

Oil in rear drive housing should be changed annually.

Unscrew drain plug (D) to drain oil from housing. If oil is changed, refill with 120 mL (4.1 oz.) of oil. If final drive is completely dry (disassembled), refill with 130 mL (4.4 oz.) of oil.

SUSPENSION AND STEERING. The grease fittings on suspension components should be injected with

Fig. Y9-3—With engine running at idle speed, oil should seep around screw (W) when loosened.

Fig. Y9-1—The oil level dipstick is attached to fill plug (F). The oil filter is located behind cover (C). Unscrewing lower cover screw (S) will allow oil to drain from filter compartment.

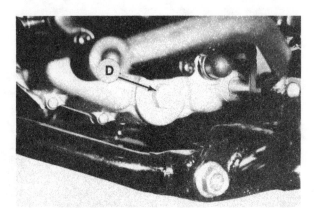

Fig. Y9-2—Remove plug (D) to drain oil from engine/transmission sump.

Fig. Y9-4—Pour oil into final drive housing through opening for oil fill plug (F). Oil level should be even with opening. Unscrew drain plug (D) to remove oil.

lithium base grease after initial month of operation and every six months thereafter.

The upper steering shaft bushing should be lubricated with lithium base grease every six months.

CABLES AND LEVERS. All cables and levers should be inspected and lubricated after first month of operation and every three months thereafter.

AIR CLEANER ELEMENT

Model is equipped with a foam-type air cleaner element. The air cleaner element is located underneath the seat. The air cleaner element should be removed and cleaned every three months or more frequently if operating conditions are severe.

To remove air cleaner element, remove seat, detach cover and remove filter element. Thoroughly clean the foam element in a nonflammable solvent. Compress element between hands to remove solvent. Do not wring or twist element. Saturate element in clean SAE 10W-30 engine oil, then compress element to remove excess oil.

FUEL SYSTEM

CARBURETOR. The engine is equipped with a Mikuni VM24SH carburetor.

Free play at the end of throttle lever should be 3-5 mm (0.12-0.20 in.). To adjust free play, slide back rubber boot, loosen locknut and rotate cable adjuster at throttle or at top of carburetor. Retighten locknut.

Initial setting of idle mixture screw (I—Fig. Y9-5) is 1¼ turns out from a lightly seated position. Final adjustment must be performed with engine at normal operating temperature. Adjust idle speed screw (S) so engine idles at 1350-1450 rpm. Rotate idle mixture screw (I) so engine runs at highest idle speed, then readjust idle speed screw (S) so engine idles at specified rpm.

When servicing carburetor, refer to Fig. Y9-6 for an exploded view of carburetor and to carburetor specifications in CONDENSED SERVICE DATA section while noting the following: Jet needle clip (9) should be in-

stalled in fourth groove from top of jet needle. Installing clip in a lower groove on jet needle will richen mid-range fuel mixture. Invert carburetor and measure float height as shown in Fig. Y9-7. Bend float arm tang to adjust float height. Make sure groove in side of throttle slide is aligned with pin in carburetor body when inserting slide in carburetor.

With the carburetor installed, the fuel level should be checked. Attach Yamaha fuel level gauge YM-01312 or a suitable clear hose (H—Fig. Y9-8) to fuel bowl nozzle.

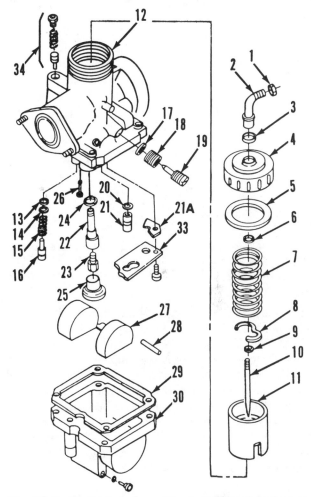

Fig. Y9-6—Exploded view of typical Mikuni carburetor used on all models.

1.	Nut	18.	Spring
2.	Cable guide	19.	Idle speed screw
3.	Washer	20.	Washer
4.	Cap	21.	Inlet valve
5.	Washer	21A.	Retainer
6.	"E" ring	22.	Needle jet
7.	Spring	23.	Main jet
8.	Retainer	24.	Washer
9.	Jet needle clip	25.	Cover
10.	Jet needle	26.	Pilot jet
11.	Throttle slide	27.	Float
12.	Body	28.	Pin
13.	"O" ring	29.	Gasket
14.	Washer	30.	Fuel bowl
15.	Spring	33.	Retainer
16.	Idle mixture screw	34.	Starter valve assy.
17.	"O" ring		

Fig. Y9-5—Adjust idle mixture screw (I) and idle speed screw (S) as outlined in text.

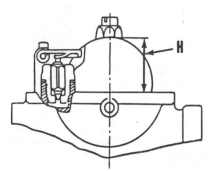

Fig. Y9-7—Float height (H) should be 21.0-22.0 mm (0.83-0.87 in.).

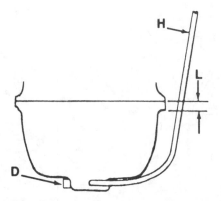

Fig. Y9-8—The fuel level is measured from the bottom edge of the carburetor body. Fuel level (L) should be 2.0-4.0 mm (0.08-0.16 in.) below carburetor body edge.

Hose should be long enough to extend above the bottom edge of carburetor body without kinking. Open fuel bowl drain screw (D). Run the engine at idle speed until fuel level in hose stabilizes, then stop engine. Measure distance from the bottom edge of carburetor body (fuel bowl contact surface) to fuel level in hose to determine fuel level (L). Fuel level check will not be accurate if hose is moved after fuel level is stabilized. Fuel level (L) should be 2.0-4.0 mm (0.08-0.16 in.) below carburetor body edge. To adjust fuel level, remove the fuel bowl and carefully bend float arm tang.

FUEL STRAINER. A strainer is mounted on the end of each pickup tube that extends into the fuel tank from the fuel valve. To inspect the strainers, the fuel in the fuel tank must be drained. Disconnect the fuel hose from the fuel valve. Unscrew fuel valve retaining screws and remove fuel valve. Clean and inspect the strainers. Reinstall the valve while noting that sealing washers are used on the retaining screws to prevent fuel leakage.

IGNITION SYSTEM

The engine is equipped with a breakerless, capacitor discharge ignition system. The electronic ignition circuit consists of the flywheel, CDI module, source coil, pickup coil, ignition coil, spark plug, ignition switch and engine

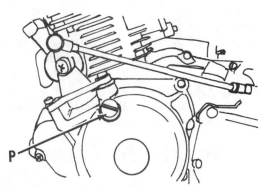

Fig. Y9-9—Remove plug (P) to view timing marks on flywheel.

stop switch. To check ignition timing, remove timing plug (P—Fig. Y9-9) and connect a power timing light to engine. Ignition timing (10° BTDC) at idle speed should occur when pointer on crankcase is aligned with double marks on flywheel. Ignition timing is not adjustable. If not as specified, check condition of ignition components as described in the following test procedures and renew faulty or questionable components.

To check the pickup coil, disconnect connector between the pickup coil and the CDI module. Connect an ohmmeter lead to the white/green wire from the pickup coil and the other ohmmeter lead to the white/red wire from the pickup coil. Ohmmeter reading should be 189-231 ohms.

To check the source coil, disconnect the connector between the source coil and the CDI module. Connect an ohmmeter between brown wire and black wire leads from source coil. Source coil resistance should be 428-523 ohms.

Ignition coil resistance readings should be 0.36-0.48 ohms for primary windings and 5.4k-7.4k ohms for secondary windings.

If the ignition system malfunctions and all components test satisfactory, replace CDI module with a new or good unit and recheck ignition system.

ELECTRICAL SYSTEM

The vehicle is equipped with a charging system, battery and electric starter. The system is protected by a 10 amp fuse on YFM200DX models, a 30 amp fuse on YFM225 and YFM250 models, and a 20 amp fuse on YFU1 and YFU1T models.

BATTERY. The battery is accessible after removing the rear fender. The negative terminal is grounded. The battery is a 12-volt unit with 12 amp-hour capacity.

CHARGING SYSTEM. The charging circuit consists of an alternator and a regulator/rectifier. The alternator rotor is attached to the left end of the crankshaft while the stator is mounted on the inside of the left crankcase cover. The regulator/rectifier module is mounted on a panel near the air cleaner box.

The charging circuit should produce 14-15 VDC at 2000 rpm.

NOTE: Do not disconnect battery terminal wires while the engine is running as excessive alternator output will damage the regulator/rectifier.

To check the alternator stator coils, disconnect the connector with white wire from the alternator. Measure resistance between white wire and ground. Resistance should be 0.72-0.88 ohm.

If previous tests prove satisfactory and fuse, wiring and connections are all good, replace regulator/rectifier with a good unit and recheck operation.

ELECTRIC STARTER. The starting circuit consists of the starter, starter relay, starter switch, cutoff relay, neutral switch, brake switch and main switch. The cutoff relay, neutral switch and brake switch prevent energizing starter relay unless switches are in correct position.

The starter relay and cutoff relay are attached to a panel near the air cleaner box. The neutral switch is located on the left side of the engine and the brake switch is mounted on the handlebar. The electric starter motor is mounted on the front of the engine.

The starter motor can be removed after detaching the battery leads, starter motor leads, starter motor bracket and unscrewing the two screws securing the motor. Note the "O" ring on the front of the motor. Minimum brush length is 5.0 mm (0.20 in.). Minimum commutator diameter is 22 mm (0.866 in.). Armature coil resistance should be 0.023 ohm.

WIRING. If wiring requires repair, always install wire that is the same gauge as original wire. Wires should be routed away from areas of extreme heat or sharp edges. Attach or hold wires in their original position using plastic tie straps to prevent short circuits.

FASTENERS

After the first month of operation and after every 30 days of operation thereafter, the vehicle should receive an overall inspection. All screws, nuts and other fasteners should be checked and tightened to proper torque specification shown in CONDENSED SERVICE DATA section or in the appropriate maintenance section.

VALVE SYSTEM

The valves are actuated via rocker arms by a single overhead camshaft. The camshaft is driven by a roller chain attached to the left end of the crankshaft. Valve clearance should be adjusted after the first month of operation and then after every six months of operation. Adjust valve clearance with engine cold.

To obtain access to valve adjustment covers remove seat, fuel tank cover and fuel tank.

To adjust valve clearance, remove timing plug (P—Fig. Y9-9) and valve adjustment covers at front and rear of cylinder head. The single mark on the flywheel indicates top dead center when aligned with pointer in plug hole (double marks are for ignition timing). Rotate crankshaft and align top dead center mark with pointer with piston on compression stroke. To ensure piston is on compression stroke, rotate crankshaft past top dead center and observe intake (rear) rocker arm. If intake rocker arm movement is observed, continue to rotate crankshaft until marks are again aligned.

Clearance between rocker arm adjusting screw and valve stem should be 0.05-0.09 mm (0.0020-0.0035 in.) for the intake valve and 0.11-0.15 mm (0.0043-0.0060 in.) for the exhaust valve. Measure clearance with a suitable feeler gauge. Adjust clearance by loosening the adjusting screw locknut and turning the adjusting screw. Be sure to recheck clearance after tightening locknut. Install valve covers so "V" ridge on inside is toward the top and points down when installed.

CAMSHAFT CHAIN

Camshaft chain adjustment is not required. The cam chain tensioner automatically adjusts chain tension.

CLUTCH

The engine is equipped with two automatically actuated clutches. A three-shoe centrifugal clutch is mounted on the right end of the crankshaft. The centrifugal clutch is disengaged at idle speed and engages when crankshaft speed increases. A multiple-disc clutch is attached to the transmission input shaft and is actuated by the gear shift mechanism. When the gear shift lever is operated, the multiple-disc clutch is disengaged to allow smooth transmission gear movement.

The clutch should be adjusted after the first month of operation and every six months thereafter. The clutch adjusting screw is located in right side cover. To adjust clutch, loosen locknut (N—Fig. Y9-10) then turn adjusting screw (S) counterclockwise until internal resistance is felt. Turn screw 1/8 turn clockwise. Secure adjusting screw with locknut (N).

The dual-clutch system should automatically disengage at engine idle speed. When selecting gears, clutch should engage and disengage freely without excess slippage. Difficult shifting, clutch grabbing or clutch slipping may indicate overhaul is necessary.

Fig. Y9-10—Loosen locknut (N) and turn adjusting screw (S) as outlined in text to adjust clutch.

FRONT BRAKE SYSTEM

BRAKE LEVER FREE PLAY. Recommended brake lever free travel is 5-8 mm (0.20-0.31 in.) measured between lever housing (H—Fig. Y9-12) and brake lever (L). Adjust lever free play by loosening locknut (N) and rotating brake cable adjuster (A). Operate brake lever while observing equalizer bar attached to front frame as shown in Fig. Y9-13. If equalizer bar does not remain level, adjust position of wing nut at brake end of brake cable on appropriate brake. Readjust brake lever free play.

OVERHAUL. Brake lining thickness may be checked externally by operating brake and noting position of pointer (P—Fig. Y9-15) on each front brake actuating lever. There is sufficient brake lining remaining if pointer does not align with or pass mark (M).

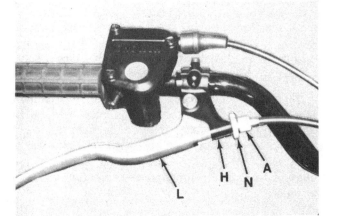

Fig. Y9-12—Front brake lever free travel should be 5-8 mm (0.20-0.31 in.) measured at gap between lever housing (H) and brake lever (L). Adjust lever free play by loosening locknut (N) and rotating brake cable adjuster (A).

Fig. Y9-13—The front brake equalizer is attached to the front frame.

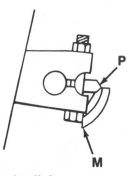

Fig. Y9-15—Brake linings are worn excessively if pointer (P) passes end of wear range scale (M) when brake is actuated.

WARNING: Inhaling asbestos brake dust is injurious to human health. Approved OSHA respiration equipment must be worn when working on or around brake components. DO NOT use compressed air to clean brake drums, shoes or nearby components as brake dust will be blown into air. Only vacuum equipment designed to pick up brake dust should be used.

Each front brake assembly is accessible after removing the brake drum/hub. Renew the brake shoes if damaged or if lining is worn to less than 2.0 mm (0.08 in.). Renew the brake drum assembly if inside diameter exceeds 111.0 mm (4.37 in.). Tighten hub retaining nut to 70 N·m (51 ft.-lbs.). Tighten wheel retaining nuts to 45 N·m (33 ft.-lbs.).

FRONT AXLE

Both front steering knuckle assemblies pivot on a ball joint at the end of a lower control arm. The lower control arm pivots vertically and is attached to the vehicle frame by bolts. A strut that incorporates a shock absorber with a coil spring is attached to the vehicle frame and the steering knuckle.

Remove front wheel for access to hub and spindle. Unscrew hub nut to remove wheel hub. The hub and brake drum are one piece. Renew bearings if rough or otherwise damaged. Be sure to install spacer between bearings when reassembling components. Tapered end of spacer must be toward wheel side of hub. Tighten hub retaining nut to 70 N•m (51 ft.-lbs.). Tighten wheel retaining nuts to 45 N•m (33 ft.-lbs.).

Remove the front wheel to service the knuckle assembly. If excessive play in ball joint is noted, then ball joint should be renewed. Ball joint and lower control arm are available only as a unit. If control arm was removed, install mounting bolts so bolt heads are to outside and tighten to 45 N•m (33 ft.-lbs.). Tighten nut securing upper end of strut to 55 N•m (40 ft.-lbs.). Install bolts that secure strut to steering knuckle so bolt head is to front of vehicle and tighten to 70 N•m (51 ft.-lbs.). Tighten ball joint nut to 25 N•m (18 ft.-lbs.). Tighten retaining nut for tie rod end to 25 N•m (18 ft.-lbs.).

STEERING

INSPECTION. Rotate the handlebar from one extreme to the other and note if any binding or roughness is felt. Periodically inspect the steering components for looseness or any other damage. Renew any damaged component. Clean and grease components if binding or excessive effort is noted.

TOE-IN SETTING. Place the handlebar in a straight ahead position. Use a suitable measuring tool and measure distance (B—Fig. Y9-17) at spindle height between the center of the tires on the rear sides. Locate the same tire centerline points on front side of tires and measure front distance (F). The distance on the front side (F) should be 0-10 mm (0.0-0.4 in.) shorter than the measured distance on the rear side (B). Note that the distance from a projected vehicle centerline to left (L) and right (R) tire centerlines should also be equal.

To adjust, loosen locknuts on the left and right tie rod assemblies and rotate tie rod shaft on each side equally until distance is within recommended range. After obtaining the correct setting, tighten locknuts to 30 N•m (22 ft.-lbs.).

OVERHAUL. To expose the steering shaft, remove front bumper, front fender and handlebar. Unscrew the two cap screws securing the steering shaft clamp halves. Clean the old grease from the steering shaft. Inspect the clamp halves and steering shaft for damage. Renew components if needed. Grease inside of steering shaft clamp halves with a lithium base grease and install. Tighten the retaining clamp cap screws to 23 N•m (17 ft.-lbs.).

To remove steering shaft, remove steering shaft clamps as outlined in previous paragraph. Remove the lower steering shaft retaining cotter pin and nut. Detach inner tie rod ends from steering shaft and withdraw the steering shaft. Note "O" rings adjacent to bearing holder and renew if damaged. Inject lithium base grease in grease fitting after installation. Tighten the lower steering shaft retaining nut to 30 N•m (22 ft.-lbs.). Tighten retaining nut for tie rod end to 25 N•m (18 ft.-lbs.).

When installing handlebar, install upper clamp so punch mark is toward front of handlebar. Tighten front screw on handlebar clamps first, then tighten the rear clamp screws. If properly tightened, there should be no gaps at the front of the clamps and even gaps at the rear of the clamps. Tighten clamp screws to 20 N•m (15 ft.-lbs.).

FORWARD-REVERSE
SHIFT LINKAGE

All models are equipped with a reverse gear that is engaged by operating forward-reverse shift lever (L—Fig. Y9-19). The shift linkage operates a dog clutch inside gear housing (H). The dog clutch engages either the forward or reverse gear. Forward gear is selected when shift lever (L) is down, while reverse gear is engaged when the shift lever is up. The transmission must be in first gear when shifting to reverse as a pin in the shift linkage must index in a hole in the transmission shift drum.

To obtain proper gear engagement adjust forward-reverse shift linkage as follows: Note mark (M) on shift arm cover and marks (F and R) on crankcase. Move shift lever (L) and note that mark (M) should point toward marks (F and R) on crankcase when forward and reverse gears are engaged. If marks do not align, loosen locknuts (N) and rotate shift rod adjuster (A) as required. Retighten locknuts (N).

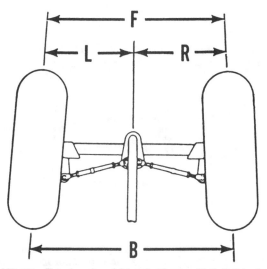

Fig. Y9-17—Toe-in should be 0-10 mm (0.0-0.4 in.). Refer to text for adjustment procedure.

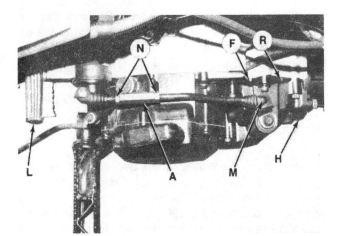

Fig. Y9-19—Rotate shift rod adjuster (A) so marks (F and R) on crankcase align with mark (M) on shift arm cover. Refer to text.

REAR BRAKE SYSTEM

INSPECTION AND ADJUSTMENT. The vehicle is equipped with a two-shoe internally expanding drum brake mounted on the rear axle housing. The brake may be operated by either a handlebar lever or a brake pedal.

To adjust brake, step on brake pedal three times. Loosen cable adjuster at handlebar lever and loosen both cable adjusters at rear brake. There must be sufficient free play in the brake cables so adjustment is not affected. Turn in pedal cable adjuster (R—Fig. Y9-21) so brake pedal free travel is 20-30 mm (0.79-1.18 in.). To adjust handlebar brake lever free play, turn cable adjuster (W) at brake end of cable so there is a 0-1 mm (0.00-0.04 in.) gap (G—Fig. Y9-22) between cable pin

Fig. Y9-21—Refer to text for rear brake pedal and lever adjustment. Brake shoes are worn excessively if pointer (P) passes mark on backing plate when brake is applied.

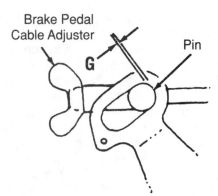

Fig. Y9-22—When properly adjusted, there should be a gap (G) of 0-1 mm (0.00-0.04 in.) between actuating pin and end of slot in actuating arm. See text.

and front end of slot in brake arm. Turn cable adjuster at handlebar lever so gap (G—Fig. Y9-23) between lever and housing is 5-8 mm (0.2-0.3 in.).

A rear brake lining indicator (P—Fig. Y9-21) is attached to the brake cam. To externally check brake lining wear, apply rear brake and note position of pointer (P) with mark on backing plate. Brake shoes should be renewed if indicator aligns or passes mark.

R&R AND OVERHAUL. To remove brake shoes and drum, support rear of vehicle and remove right rear wheel.

WARNING: Inhaling asbestos brake dust is injurious to human health. Approved OSHA respiration equipment must be worn when working on or around brake components. DO NOT use compressed air to clean brake drum, shoes or nearby components as brake dust will be blown into air. Only vacuum equipment designed to pick up brake dust should be used.

Unscrew axle nut and remove brake drum. Carefully remove brake shoes and springs from backing plate.

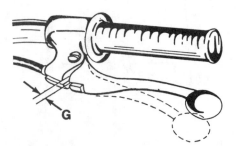

Fig. Y9-23—To adjust rear brake lever free play, turn cable adjuster at brake lever or at brake end of cable so there is a 5-8 mm (0.20-0.32 in.) gap (G) between lever and housing.

Brake shoes should be renewed if lining is worn to 2.0 mm (0.08 in.) or less. Brake drum should be renewed if inside diameter exceeds 161 mm (6.34 in.).

Reassemble by reversing disassembly procedure and noting the following: Tighten backing plate retaining screws to 28 N.m (20 ft.-lbs.). Apply a light coat of grease to brake shoe cam and anchor pin. Do not allow grease on brake shoe linings. Be sure to install spacer between brake drum and axle. Tighten axle nut to 150 N.m (110 ft.-lbs.). Tighten wheel retaining nuts to 55 N.m (40 ft.-lbs.). Adjust rear brake as previously outlined.

FINAL DRIVE

Service on the final drive should be performed by a Yamaha service technician equipped with the special tools required for overhaul.

YAMAHA
YFM350ER AND YFM350FW

NOTE: Metric fasteners are used throughout vehicle.

CONDENSED SERVICE DATA

MODELS	YFM350ER & YFM350FW
General	
Engine Make	Yamaha
Engine Type	Four-Stroke; Air-Cooled
Number of Cylinders	1
Bore	83.0 mm
	(3.27 in.)
Stroke	64.5 mm
	(2.54 in.)
Displacement	348 cc
	(21.2 cu. in.)
Compression Ratio	8.6:1
Engine Lubrication	Wet Sump; Oil Pump
Transmission Lubrication	Common With Engine
Engine/Transmission Oil	SAE 10W-40
Forward Speeds	5
Reverse Speeds	1
Tire Size:	
Front:	
YFM350ER	22 × 8-10
YFM350FW	25 × 8-12
Rear:	
YFM350ER	25 × 12-9
YFM350FW	25 × 10-12
Tire Pressure:	
Front:	
YFM350ER	30 kPa
	(4.3 psi)
YFM350FW	20 kPa
	(2.9 psi)
Rear	20 kPa
	(2.9 psi)
Battery	12V-14AH
Vehicle Weight	
W/Full Fuel Tank:	
YFM350ER	237 kg
	(521 lbs.)
YFM350FW	264 kg
	(581 lbs.)
Tune-Up	
Engine Idle Speed	1450-1550 rpm
Compression Pressure	834 kPa
	(121 psi)
Spark Plug:	
NGK	D8EA
Nippon Denso	X24ES-U

Tune-Up (Cont.)

Spark Plug: (Cont.)

Electrode Gap	0.6-0.7 mm (0.024-0.028 in.)

Ignition Type	Breakerless
Timing	10° BTDC @ 1000 rpm 33° BTDC @ 5000 rpm

Carburetor:

Make	Mikuni
Model	BTM32SH
Jet Needle	5H26
Clip Position	3rd Groove From Top
Needle Jet	N-8
Pilot Jet	#45
Main Jet	#117.5*
Float Height	11.4-13.4 mm (0.45-0.53 in.)
Idle Mixture Setting	2¼ Turns*
Throttle Lever Free Play	3-5 mm (0.12-0.20 in.)

*Main jet size on Model YFM350FW is #122.5; idle mixture screw setting is 2¾ turns.

Sizes-Clearances

Valve Clearance (cold):

Intake	0.06-0.10 mm (0.0023-0.0039 in.)
Exhaust	0.16-0.20 mm (0.0063-0.0078 in.)

Valve Face & Seat Angle:

Intake & Exhaust	45°

Valve Seat Width:

Intake & Exhaust	1.0-1.2 mm (0.039-0.047 in.)

Valve Margin:

Intake	1.0-1.4 mm (0.039-0.055 in.)
Exhaust	0.8-1.2 mm (0.031-0.047 in.)

Valve Stem Diameter:

Intake	6.975-6.990 mm (0.2746-0.2752 in.)
Exhaust	6.955-6.970 mm (0.2738-0.2744 in.)

Valve Guide Bore Diameter:

Intake & Exhaust	7.000-7.012 mm (0.2756-0.2761 in.)
Maximum	7.03 mm (0.277 in.)

Valve Stem-to-Guide Clearance:

Intake	0.010-0.037 mm (0.0004-0.0015 in.)
Maximim	0.1 mm (0.0039 in.)
Exhaust	0.030-0.057 mm (0.0012-0.0022 in.)
Maximum	0.1 mm (0.0039 in.)

Sizes-Clearances (Cont.)

Valve Spring Free Length:
   Inner............................ 39.9 mm
                                             (1.57 in.)
   Outer........................... 43.27 mm
                                             (1.70 in.)

Rocker Arm Bore Diameter:
   Intake & Exhaust.................. 12.000-12.018 mm
      (0.4724-0.4731 in.)

Rocker Shaft Diameter:
   Intake & Exhaust.................. 11.981-11.991 mm
      (0.4717-0.4720 in.)

Camshaft Lobe Height:
   Intake & Exhaust.................. 40.29-40.39 mm
      (1.586-1.590 in.)

Camshaft Runout (Max.)............. 0.03 mm
      (0.0012 in.)

Cylinder Head Distortion (Max.)........ 0.03 mm
      (0.0012 in.)

Cylinder Bore Diameter.............. 82.97-83.02 mm
      (3.267-3.269 in.)

Cylinder Taper (Max.)............... 0.05 mm
      (0.002 in.)

Piston Diameter:
 Measured 5.5 mm (0.22 in.) From
   Skirt Bottom & 90° to Pin Bore........ 82.92-82.97 mm
      (3.2646-3.2665 in.)

Piston-to-Cylinder Clearance........... 0.040-0.060 mm
      (0.0016-0.0024 in.)

Piston Ring End Gap:
   Top & Second Rings............... 0.20-0.40 mm
      (0.008-0.016 in.)
   Oil Ring...................... 0.3-0.9 mm
      (0.012-0.035 in.)

Piston Ring Side Clearance:
   Top Ring...................... 0.04-0.08 mm
      (0.0016-0.0032 in.)
   Second Ring.................... 0.03-0.07 mm
      (0.0012-0.0028 in.)

Connecting Rod Big End Side
   Clearance (Max.).................. 0.35-0.85 mm
      (0.014-0.033 in.)

Connecting Rod Small End
   Shake........................ 0.08-1.0 mm
      (0.031-0.039 in.)

Crankshaft Runout (Max.)............. 0.06 mm
      (0.0024 in.

Capacities

Engine/Transmission Sump............ See Text
Fuel Tank:
   YFM350ER..................... 11 L
      (2.9 gal.)
   YFM350FW..................... 10 L
      (2.6 gal.)

Tightening Torques

Axle Nut:
  Front:
    YFM350ER . . . .   115 N·m
                                            (84 ft.-lbs.)
    YFM350FW . . . .   130 N·m
                                             (96 ft.-lbs.)

  Rear:
    YFM350ER . . . .   115 N·m
                                             (84 ft.-lbs.)
    YFM350FW . . . .   150 N·m
                                           (110 ft.-lbs.)

Balancer Shaft Nut. . . . .   60 N·m
                                           (43 ft.-lbs.)
Camshaft Sprocket . . . .   60 N·m
                                           (43 ft.-lbs.)
Chain Tensioner End Cap Screw. . . . . . .   25 N·m
                                           (18 ft.-lbs.)
Clutch Nut (both clutches) . . . .   79 N·m
                                           (58 ft.-lbs.)
Crankcase . . . .   10 N·m
                                           (88 in.-lbs.)
Cylinder Base Screws . . . .   10 N·m
                                           (88 in.-lbs.)

Cylinder Head:
  Flange Screw.   40 N·m
                                           (29 ft.-lbs.)
  Hex Screw . . . .   20 N·m
                                           (14 ft.-lbs.)
Engine Mounting Nuts . . . .   40 N·m
                                           (29 ft.-lbs.)
Spark Plug . . . .   18 N·m
                                           (159 in.-lbs.)

Wheel Nuts:
  Front & Rear . . . .   55 N·m
                                           (40 ft.-lbs.)

Standard Screws:
  6 mm . . . .   6 N·m
                                           (53 in.-lbs.)
  8 mm . . . .   15 N·m
                                           (133 in.-lbs.)
  10 mm . . . .   30 N·m
                                           (22 ft.-lbs.)
  12 mm . . . .   55 N·m
                                           (40 ft.-lbs.)
  14 mm . . . .   85 N·m
                                           (61 ft.-lbs.)
  16 mm . . . .   130 N·m
                                           (94 ft.-lbs.)

LUBRICATION

All Models

ENGINE AND TRANSMISSION. The engine and transmission are lubricated by a crankshaft-driven oil pump. The engine, transmission and output gears share a common sump. Recommended oil is SAE 10W-30 with an API classification of SE and/or SF.

Oil level should be maintained at upper mark on dipstick attached to fill plug (F—Fig. Y13-1). Do not screw plug in when checking oil level. Fill sump through opening for fill plug (F). Drain oil by removing drain plug on underside of crankcase.

Fig. Y13-1—The oil level dipstick is attached to fill plug (F).

Fig. Y13-2—The oil filter is located behind cover (C).

Fig. Y13-3—With engine running at idle speed, oil should seep around screw (W) when loosened.

The manufacturer recommends changing the oil and oil filter after the first month of operation and every six months thereafter. Fill crankcase with 2.7 L (2.85 qt.) of oil if oil and oil filter are changed. Crankcase capacity totally dry is 3.4 L (3.6 qt.).

Remove oil filter cover (C—Fig. Y13-2) for access to oil filter. Be sure "O" rings are not damaged and properly positioned during assembly. Clean the drain plug oil strainer in a suitable solvent. Renew the strainer if damaged or contaminated.

To be sure the oil pump is pumping oil to the engine, slightly unscrew oil passage screw (W—Fig. Y13-3). Start and run engine at idle speed. Oil should just seep past screw after one minute. Retighten screw if oil seeps from hole. If no oil is present, stop engine and determine cause.

FRONT DRIVE HOUSING. Model YFM350FW. To check oil level in front drive housing, remove fill plug (F—Fig. Y13-5). Oil should reach bottom edge of fill plug hole with vehicle on a level surface. Recommended oil is SAE 80 hypoid gear oil with API classification GL-4.

Oil in front drive housing should be changed annually.

The front drive housing is equipped with two drain plugs. Both plugs must to removed to completely drain oil from housing. Oil capacity of front drive housing is 500 mL (16.8 oz.).

REAR DRIVE HOUSING. To check oil level in rear drive housing, remove fill plug (F—Fig. Y13-5). Oil should reach bottom edge of fill plug hole with vehicle on a level surface. Recommended oil is SAE 80 hypoid gear oil with API classification GL-4.

Oil in rear drive housing should be changed annually.

Unscrew drain plug to drain oil from housing. Oil capacity of rear drive housing is 250 mL (8.4 oz.).

SUSPENSION AND STEERING. The grease fittings on suspension components should be injected with lithium base grease after initial month of operation and every three months thereafter.

Fig. Y13-5—Pour oil into front and rear drive housings through opening for oil fill plug (F). Oil level should be even with opening.

CABLES AND LEVERS. All cables and levers should be inspected and lubricated after first month of operation and every three months thereafter.

AIR CLEANER ELEMENT

All Models

All models are equipped with a foam-type air cleaner element located underneath the seat. The air cleaner element should be removed and cleaned every three months or more frequently if operating conditions are severe.

To remove air cleaner element, remove seat, detach cover and remove filter element. Thoroughly clean the foam element in a nonflammable solvent. Compress element between hands to remove solvent. Do not wring or twist element. Saturate element in clean SAE 10W-30 engine oil, then compress element to remove excess oil. Apply grease to seating surface of element and reinstall element.

FUEL SYSTEM

All Models

CARBURETOR. The carburetor is connected to the throttle lever by a cable. Throttle lever free play (F—Fig. Y13-7) should be 3-5 mm (0.12-0.20 in.) measured at end of lever. To adjust throttle lever free play, slide dust boot (B) down cable, loosen locknut (N) and rotate cable adjuster (A). Tighten locknut and slide dust boot back over adjuster.

The engine is equipped with a Mikuni BTM32SH. Refer to CONDENSED SERVICE DATA for carburetor specifications. Initial setting of idle mixture screw (M—Fig. Y13-9) is 2 turns out from a lightly seated position. Final adjustment must be performed with engine at normal operation temperature. Adjust idle speed screw (S) so engine idles at 1350-1450 rpm. After adjusting

carburetor, adjust throttle free play as outlined in previous paragraph.

To check float height, remove carburetor and fuel bowl. Invert carburetor and measure float height as shown in Fig. Y13-10. Float height (H) should be 11.4-13.4 mm (0.45-0.53 in.). Adjust float height by carefully bending float tang (T).

With the carburetor installed, the fuel level should be checked. Attach Yamaha fuel level gauge YM-01312 or a suitable clear hose (H—Fig. Y13-11) to fuel bowl nozzle. Hose should be long enough to extend above the bottom edge of carburetor body without kinking. Open fuel bowl drain screw (D). Run the engine at idle speed until fuel level in hose stabilizes, then stop engine. Measure distance from the bottom edge of carburetor body (fuel bowl contact surface) to fuel level in hose to determine fuel level (L). Fuel level check will not be accurate if hose is moved after fuel level is stabilized. Fuel level (L) should be 1-2 mm (0.039-0.079 in.) above

Fig. Y13-9—Adjust idle mixture screw (M) and idle speed screw (S) as outlined in text. Unscrew drain screw (D) to remove fuel in fuel bowl.

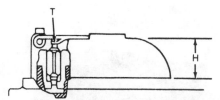

Fig. Y13-10—Float height (H) should be 11.4-13.4 mm (0.45-0.53 in.) mm. Bend tang (T) to adjust float height.

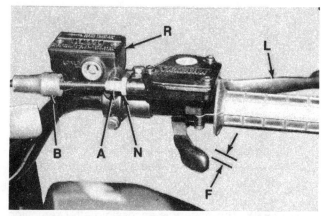

Fig. Y13-7—Throttle lever free play (F) should be 3-5 mm (0.12-0.20 in.). To adjust, slide dust boot (B) down cable, loosen locknut (N) and rotate adjuster (A).

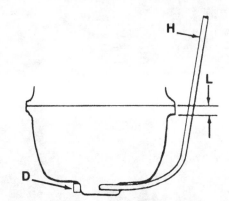

Fig. Y13-11—The fuel level is measured from the bottom edge of the carburetor body. Fuel level (L) should be 1-2 mm (0.039-0.079 in.) above carburetor body edge.

carburetor body edge. To adjust fuel level, remove the fuel bowl and carefully bend float arm tang (T—Fig. Y13-10).

FUEL STRAINER. A strainer is mounted on the end of each pickup tube that extends into the fuel tank from the fuel valve. To inspect the strainers, the fuel in the fuel tank must be drained. Disconnect the fuel hose from the fuel valve. Unscrew fuel valve retaining screws and remove fuel valve. Clean and inspect the strainers. Reinstall the valve while noting that sealing washers are used on the retaining screws to prevent fuel leakage.

IGNITION SYSTEM

All Models

The engine is equipped with a breakerless, capacitor discharge ignition system. The electronic ignition circuit consists of the flywheel, CDI module, source coil, pickup coil, ignition coil, spark plug, ignition switch and engine stop switch. To check ignition timing, remove timing plug (P—Fig. Y13-13) and connect a power timing light to engine. Ignition timing (10° BTDC) at idle speed should occur when "F" mark on flywheel is aligned with notch (N) on case. Ignition timing is not adjustable. If not as specified, check condition of ignition components as described in the following test procedures and renew faulty or questionable components.

To check pickup coil on Models YFM350ERT, YFM350ERU, YFM350FWT and YFM350FWU, disconnect connector between the pickup coil and the CDI

Fig. Y13-13—Remove plug (P) to view timing marks on flywheel and notch (C) in crankcase cover.

module. Connect an ohmmeter lead to the grey lead from the pickup coil and the other ohmmeter lead to the blue lead from the pickup coil. Ohmmeter reading should be 180-220 ohms. Connect one ohmmeter lead to the yellow lead from the pickup coil and the other ohmmeter lead to the green lead from the pickup coil. Ohmmeter reading should be 180-220 ohms.

To check pickup coil on Models YFM350ERW and YFM350FWW, disconnect connector between pickup coil and CDI module. Connect an ohmmeter lead to the yellow lead from the pickup coil and the other ohmmeter lead to the blue lead from the pickup coil. Ohmmeter reading should be 170-210 ohms. Connect one ohmmeter lead to the yellow lead from the pickup coil and the other ohmmeter lead to the green lead from the pickup coil. Ohmmeter reading should be 170-210 ohms.

To check pickup coil on Models YFM350ERA, YFM350ERB, YFM350FWA and YFM350FWB, disconnect connector between the pickup coil and the CDI module. Connect an ohmmeter to the blue wire and yellow wire leads from the pickup coil. Ohmmeter reading should be 171-209 ohms.

To check the source coil, disconnect the connector between the source coil and the CDI module. On Models YFM350ERT, YFM350ERU, YFM350ERW, YFM350FWT, YFM350FWU and YFM350FWW, connect an ohmmeter between brown wire and red wire leads from source coil. On Models YFM350ERA, YFM350ERB, YFM350FWA, YFM350FWB, YFM350XB and YFM350XD, connect an ohmmeter between white/green wire and red wire leads to source coil. Source coil resistance should be 270-330 ohms on all models.

Ignition coil resistance readings for Models YFM350ERT, YFM350ERU YFM350ERW, YFM350FWT, YFM350FWU and YFM350FWW should be 0.72-0.98 ohms for primary windings and 5.0-6.8k ohms for secondary windings. Ignition coil resistance readings for Models YFM350ERA, YFM350ERB, YFM350FWA and YFM350FWB should be 0.36-0.48 ohms for primary windings and 5.4-7.4k ohms for secondary windings.

If the ignition system malfunctions and all components test satisfactory, replace CDI module with a new or good unit and recheck ignition system.

ELECTRICAL SYSTEM

All Models

The vehicle is equipped with a charging system, battery and electric starter. The system is protected by a 30 amp fuse.

BATTERY. The battery is accessible after removing the seat. The negative terminal is grounded. The battery is a 12-volt unit with 14 amp-hour capacity.

CHARGING SYSTEM. The charging circuit consists of an alternator and a regulator/rectifier. The alternator rotor is attached to the left end of the crankshaft while the stator is mounted on the inside of the left crankcase cover. The regulator/rectifier module is mounted on the rear of the vehicle frame.

The charging circuit should produce 14-15 VDC at 5000 rpm.

NOTE: Do not disconnect battery terminal wires while the engine is running as excessive alternator output will damage the regulator/rectifier.

To check the alternator stator coils, disconnect the connector with three white leads from the alternator. Measure resistance between any pair of white wires, then repeat test with another pair of wires. Resistance between any pair of white wires should be 0.32-0.39 ohms on Models YFM350ERT, YFM350ERU and YFM350ERW, and 0.70-0.86 ohms on all other models. Resistance between any white wire and vehicle ground must be infinity.

If previous tests prove satisfactory and fuse, wiring and connections are all good, replace regulator/rectifier with a good unit and recheck operation.

ELECTRIC STARTER. The starting circuit consists of the starter, starter relay, starter switch, cutoff relay, neutral switch, reverse switch, clutch switch and main switch. The cutoff relay, neutral switch and reverse switch prevent energizing starter relay unless switches are in correct position.

The starter relay and cutoff relay are near the battery. The neutral switch is located on the left side of the engine. The clutch switch is located in the clutch lever housing. The electric starter motor is mounted on the front of the engine.

The starter motor can be removed after detaching the battery leads, starter motor leads and unscrewing the two screws securing the motor. Note the "O" ring on the front of the motor. Minimum brush length is 8.5 mm (0.33 in.). Minimum commutator diameter is 27 mm (1.06 in.). Armature coil resistance should be 0.011-0.013 ohm.

WIRING. If wiring requires repair, always install wire that is the same gauge as original wire. Wires should be routed away from areas of extreme heat or sharp edges. Attach or hold wires in their original position using plastic tie straps to prevent short circuits.

FASTENERS

All Models

After the first month of operation and after every 30 days of operation thereafter, the vehicle should receive an overall inspection. All screws, nuts and other fasteners should be checked and tightened to proper torque specification shown in CONDENSED SERVICE DATA section or in the appropriate maintenance section.

VALVE SYSTEM

All Models

The valves are actuated via rocker arms by a single overhead camshaft. The camshaft is driven by a roller chain attached to the left end of the crankshaft. Valve clearance should be adjusted after the first month of operation and then after every six months of operation. Adjust valve clearance with engine cold.

To adjust valve clearance, remove seat, front fender assembly and fuel tank. Remove timing plug (P—Fig. Y13-13) and valve adjustment covers at front and rear of cylinder head. The "T" mark on the flywheel indicates top dead center when aligned with notch (N) in plug hole. Rotate crankshaft and align top dead center mark with notch (N) with piston on compression stroke. To ensure piston is on compression stroke, rotate crankshaft past top dead center and observe intake (rear) rocker arm. If intake rocker arm movement is observed, continue to rotate crankshaft until marks are again aligned.

Clearance between rocker arm adjusting screw and valve stem should be 0.06-0.10 mm (0.0023-0.0039 in.) for the intake valve and 0.16-0.20 mm (0.0063-0.0078 in.) for the exhaust valve. Measure clearance with a suitable feeler gauge. Adjust clearance by loosening the adjusting screw locknut and turning the adjusting screw. Be sure to recheck clearance after tightening locknut. Install valve covers so "V" ridge on inside is toward top and points down when installed.

CAMSHAFT CHAIN

All Models

Camshaft chain adjustment is not required. The cam chain tensioner automatically adjusts chain tension.

CLUTCH

All Models

The engine is equipped with two automatically actuated clutches. A four-shoe centrifugal clutch is mounted on the right end of the crankshaft. The centrifugal clutch is disengaged at idle speed and engages when crankshaft speed increases. A multiple-disc clutch is attached to the transmission mainshaft and is actuated by the gear shift mechanism. When the gear shift lever is operated, the multiple-disc clutch is disengaged to allow smooth transmission gear movement.

The clutch should be adjusted after first month of operation and every six months thereafter. The clutch

Fig. Y13-15—Loosen locknut (L) and turn adjusting screw (S) as outlined in text to adjust clutch.

Fig. Y13-17—Rotate nuts (N) so hole in clevis (C—Fig. Y13-16) is aligned with hole in shift arm (A) and install clevis pin (P).

adjusting screw is located in right side cover. To adjust clutch, loosen locknut (L—Fig. Y13-15) then turn adjusting screw (S) counterclockwise until internal resistance is felt. Turn screw 1/8 turn clockwise. Secure adjusting screw with locknut (L).

The dual-clutch system should automatically disengage at engine idle speed. When selecting gears, clutch should engage and disengage freely without excess slippage. Difficult shifting, clutch grabbing or clutch slipping may indicate overhaul is necessary.

FORWARD-REVERSE SHIFT CABLE

All Models

All models are equipped with a sub-transmission that contains high and low gears as well as reverse gear. The shift linkage must be adjusted so the gears are properly engaged when gears are selected using the shift lever.

CAUTION: The engine must be at idle speed when shifting sub-transmission, otherwise, clutch may be engaged and damage to gears may result.

Fig. Y13-16—Refer to text for adjustment of forward-reverse shift cable.

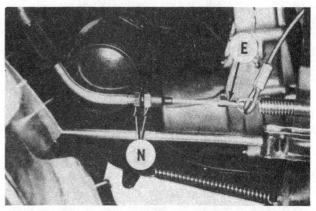

Fig. Y13-18—Refer to text for adjustment of reverse lockout cable.

To adjust shift cable, place shift lever in LOW position. Remove clevis pin (P—Fig. Y13-16) and make sure shift arm (A) is in LOW position. Confirm that shift lever is in LOW position, then rotate nuts (N—Fig. Y13-17) so hole in clevis (C—Fig. Y13-16) is aligned with hole in shift arm (A) and install clevis pin (P). Tighten nuts and check adjustment.

It should not be possible to move shift lever to RE-VERSE position unless the rear brake pedal is depressed. To adjust reverse lockout cable, move shift lever to LOW position. Rotate nuts (N—Fig. Y13-18) so slack is removed from cable and tension is just applied to spring. With brake pedal depressed, cable end (E) travel should be at least 5 mm (0.2 in.).

MANUAL STARTER

All Models So Equipped

R&R AND OVERHAUL. Refer to Fig. Y13-20 for an exploded view of manual starter used on early models. Starter can be removed from engine as a complete unit after removing the four cap screws that retain the starter. If starter rope remains under tension, pull starter rope

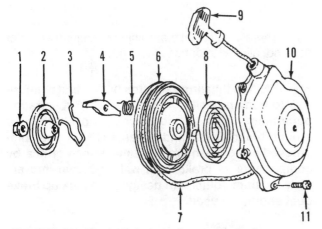

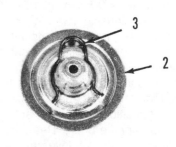

Fig. Y13-20—*Exploded view of manual starter.*

1. Nut	7. Rope
2. Drive housing	8. Rewind spring
3. Clip	9. Rope handle
4. Pawl	10. Starter housing
5. Spring	11. Screw
6. Pulley	

Fig. Y13-22—*Apply grease to clip (3) and install in groove on drive housing (2).*

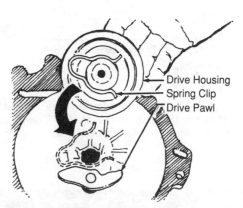

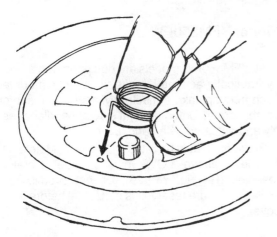

Fig. Y13-21—*Insert long end of pawl spring in hole in pulley.*

Fig. Y13-23—*Install drive housing with clip on pulley as shown.*

Y13-22) and install spring in groove of drive housing (2). Install drive housing and spring clip as shown in Fig. Y13-23.

To place tension on rewind spring after starter is assembled, pass rope through rope outlet in housing and install rope handle. Pull a loop of rope back through starter housing outlet and into pulley notch in pulley. Turn pulley clockwise three or four complete revolutions, putting tension on spring. Release rope from notch and allow rope to wind onto pulley. Do not place more tension on rewind spring than is necessary to draw rope handle up against housing. Check starter operation before installation.

and hold rope pulley with notch adjacent to rope outlet. Pull a loop of rope back through outlet so rope engages notch in pulley and allow pulley to slowly unwind. Unscrew nut and disassemble unit. Be careful when removing rewind spring; a rapidly uncoiling starter spring can cause serious injury.

Rewind spring is wound into starter housing in a clockwise direction. Rope is wound on rope pulley in a clockwise direction as viewed with pulley in housing. Reassemble starter by reversing disassembly procedure. During reassembly, lightly grease pulley shaft and starter pawl. Insert long end of drive pawl spring in hole in pulley as shown in Fig. Y13-21. Install drive pawl and hook outer end of drive pawl spring under drive pawl and into notch on drive pawl. Turn drive pawl one turn counterclockwise and push drive pawl into recess in pulley. Apply a light coat of grease to spring clip (3—Fig.

FRONT BRAKE SYSTEM

Model YFM350ER

All YFM350ER models are equipped with cable-actuated drum-type brakes at each front wheel. The front brakes are operated by a lever attached to the right handlebar.

The handlebar lever operates front and rear wheel brakes. If either brake is adjusted, then the other brake should be adjusted to ensure maximum braking effectiveness.

YAMAHA YFM350ER AND YFM350FW

BRAKE LEVER FREE PLAY. Recommended brake lever free travel is 3-5 mm (0.12-0.20 in.) measured between lever housing (H—Fig. Y13-25) and brake lever (L). Loosen both locknuts (N) and both cable adjusters (A). Rotate front brake cable adjuster (A) to adjust brake lever free play. Operate brake lever while observing equalizer bar attached to front of frame and shown in Fig. Y13-26. If equalizer bar does not remain level, adjust position of wing nut at brake end of brake cable on appropriate brake. Readjust brake lever free play. Adjust rear brake lever as outlined in REAR BRAKE section.

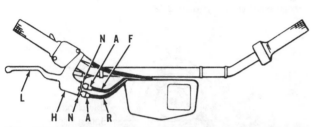

Fig. Y13-25—The right handlebar lever operates the brakes through the front brake cable (F) and rear brake cable (R). Refer to text for adjustment.

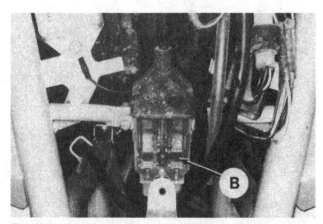

Fig. Y13-26—The front brake equalizer (B) is attached to the front frame. (The equalizer used on YFM350ER models is similar to the one shown.)

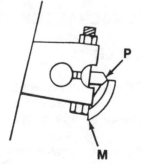

Fig. Y13-27—Brake linings are worn excessively if pointer (P) passes end of wear range scale (M) when brake is actuated.

OVERHAUL. Brake lining thickness may be checked externally by operating brake and noting position of pointer (P—Fig. Y13-27) on each front brake actuating lever. There is sufficient brake lining remaining if pointer does not align with or pass mark (M).

WARNING: Inhaling asbestos brake dust is injurious to human health. Approved OSHA respiration equipment must be worn when working on or around brake drums and shoes. DO NOT use compressed air to clean brake drums, shoes or nearby components as brake dust will be blown into air. Only vacuum equipment designed to pick up brake dust should be used.

Each front brake assembly is accessible after removing the brake drum/hub. Renew the brake shoes if damaged or if lining is worn to less than 2.0 mm (0.08 in.). Renew the brake drum if inside diameter exceeds 161.0 mm (6.34 in.). Tighten hub retaining nut to 115 N•m (84 ft.-lbs.). Tighten wheel retaining nuts to 55 N•m (40 ft.-lbs.).

Model YFM350FW

All YFM350FW models are equipped with a two-shoe hydraulically-actuated brake assembly mounted on each front spindle. A master cylinder and reservoir assembly are mounted on right side of handlebar assembly and actuated by a hand lever.

Brake fluid must be rated DOT 3 or 4. Maintain brake fluid level above "LOW" mark on side of brake fluid reservoir (R—Fig. Y13-29). Do not overfill. To avert spillage, be sure reservoir is horizontal before removing cover.

BRAKE LEVER FREE PLAY. Front brake lever free play before screw in lever contacts master cylinder piston should be 3-5 mm (0.12-0.20 in.) measured at outer end of brake lever (L—Fig. Y13-29). To adjust,

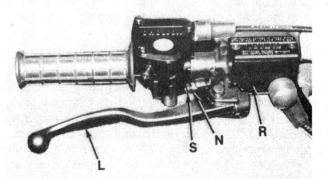

Fig. Y13-29—Loosen locknut (N) and rotate screw (S) to adjust front brake lever (L) free play.

loosen locknut (N) and rotate screw (S) until recommended free play is obtained. Retighten locknut (N).

Brake lever free play before brakes are applied should be 25-30 mm (1.0-1.2 in.). Adjust by removing rubber plug on outside of brake drum and rotate brake drum so hole is aligned with star wheel on brake shoe adjuster. Use a suitable tool and rotate star wheel until brake shoe locks against drum, then rotate star wheel in opposite direction three adjustment teeth. Repeat adjustment on remaining brake shoe, then adjust both brake shoes on opposite wheel. Make sure no brake drag is noted after adjustment. If brake lever free play is still excessive, then bleed hydraulic system as outlined in BLEEDING section.

BLEEDING. Make sure reservoir (R—Fig. Y13-29) is full. Connect a bleed hose to bleed valve on back side of wheel cylinder. Route the bleed hose into a suitable container. Operate brake lever until resistance is felt, then open bleed valve (rotate counterclockwise). Close bleed valve prior to releasing brake lever. Continue bleeding procedure until no air bubbles are noted in fluid discharged from bleed valve.

NOTE: Make sure reservoir (R) remains full during bleeding procedure.

When bleeding procedure is completed, add brake fluid to reservoir until fluid level is at upper level line in reservoir. Make sure fluid level is kept above lower level line adjacent to reservoir sight glass.

R&R AND OVERHAUL. Determining brake shoe thickness is possible by removing "CHECK" plug on outside of brake drum. Brake shoes should be renewed if lining thickness is 1 mm (0.04 in.) or less.

WARNING: Inhaling asbestos brake dust is injurious to human health. Approved OSHA respiration equipment must be worn when working on or around brake drum and shoes. DO NOT use compressed air to clean brake drum, shoes or nearby components as brake dust will be blown into air. Only vacuum equipment designed to pick up brake dust should be used.

Support front of vehicle so wheel is off ground and remove wheel. Unscrew axle nut and remove brake drum/hub. While noting location of components, disassemble brake assembly. Detach brake line from wheel cylinder and plug line to reduce fluid loss.

Renew the brake drum if inside diameter exceeds 161.0 mm (6.34 in.). Disassemble and inspect wheel cylinder. Renew complete wheel cylinder if bore is scored, pitted or excessively worn. Superficial damage in wheel cylinder bore may be removed using a suitable cylinder hone. After honing, rinse bore with clean brake fluid. Shake out excess fluid but do not wipe dry. Using a shop towel or rag to dry cylinder will leave lint particles in bore. Renew boots and piston cups. During reassembly, lubricate components with clean brake fluid.

Apply a suitable sealer to wheel cylinder contact area on backing plate and install wheel cylinder. Attach brake line. Clean brake adjuster and lubricate with silicon grease before installing in housing. Screw adjusters completely in to allow installation of new brake shoes. Apply a light coat of silicone grease to three points on backing plate that will contact edge of brake shoe. Install brake shoes and springs and secure brake shoes with pins and clips. Tighten axle nut to 130 N.m (96 ft.-lbs.). Tighten wheel nuts to 55 N.m (40 ft.-lbs.).

Adjust and bleed brakes as previously outlined.

MASTER CYLINDER. To remove front brake master cylinder (9—Fig. Y13-31), detach brake line from master cylinder. Brake fluid will remove paint; be careful when removing master cylinder. Unscrew two retaining screws and remove master cylinder. Remove brake lever, reservoir cover (7) and diaphragm (8). Remove dust boot (1) and snap ring (2). Disassemble piston assembly while noting location and direction of components. Renew complete master cylinder if bore is scored, pitted or excessively worn. Superficial damage in master cylinder bore may be removed using a suitable cylinder hone. After honing, rinse bore with clean brake fluid. Shake out excess fluid but do not wipe dry. Using a shop towel or rag to dry cylinder will leave lint particles in bore. Renew boots and piston cups. During reassembly, lubricate components with clean brake fluid. Reassembly is reverse of disassembly. Install spring (6) so small end contacts primary cup (5). Bleed brakes as previously outlined. Do not operate vehicle until brakes are tested and functioning properly.

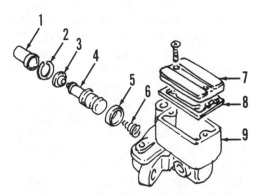

Fig. Y13-31—Exploded view of front brake master cylinder.

1. Dust boot
2. Snap ring
3. Secondary cup
4. Piston
5. Primary cup
6. Spring
7. Cover
8. Diaphragm
9. Body

FRONT AXLE

Model YFM350ER

Both front steering knuckle assemblies pivot on king pins at the end of a control arm. The control arm pivots vertically and is attached to the vehicle frame by bolts. A shock absorber with a coil spring is attached to the vehicle frame and the control arm.

Remove front wheel for access to hub and spindle. Unscrew hub nut to remove wheel hub. The hub and brake drum are one piece. Renew bearings if rough or otherwise damaged. Be sure to install spacer between bearings when reassembling components. Tighten hub retaining nut to 115 N•m (84 ft.-lbs.). Tighten wheel retaining nuts to 55 N•m (40 ft.-lbs.).

Remove the front wheel to service the knuckle assembly. If excessive play between king pin and bushings is noted, then components should be renewed. Grease king pin prior to installation. Tighten castle nut securing king pin bolt to 35 N•m (26 ft.-lbs.) and install a new cotter pin. If control arm was removed, tighten control arm mounting bolts to 45 N•m (33 ft.-lbs.). Tighten retaining nut for tie rod end to 40 N•m (29 ft.-lbs.). Tighten shock absorber upper and lower mounting bolts to 45 N•m (33 ft.-lbs.).

Model YFM350FW

Both front steering knuckles pivot on ball joints at the end of the upper control arm and in the lower arm of the steering knuckle. The control arm ends are bolted to the vehicle frame. A shock absorber on each side limits and cushions vertical movement of the control arms. A spring on the shock absorber supports the vehicle. The axle shaft is supported by ball bearings in the steering knuckle.

To remove axle hub, remove wheel and brake drum. Unscrew axle hub retaining nut and pull hub off of axle shaft. The axle shaft is supported by bearings in the steering knuckle. The axle shaft must be removed for access to bearings. Refer to FRONT AXLE SHAFTS section for axle shaft removal. When reinstalling axle hub, tighten retaining nut to 130 N•m (96 ft.-lbs.). Tighten wheel retaining nuts to 55 N•m (40 ft.-lbs.).

The control arms can be removed without separating axle shaft and steering knuckle. The ball joint and control arm are renewable only as a unit assembly. Inspect, and if necessary, renew bearings in steering knuckle. Pack bearing with grease before installation. Inspect, and if necessary, renew bearing seals. Be sure to install spacer between bearings. Tighten control arm bolts to 43 N•m (32 ft.-lbs.). Tighten upper ball joint nut to 25 N•m (18 ft.-lbs.). Tighten lower ball joint clamp bolt to 35 N•m (26 ft.-lbs.). Tighten tie rod end nut to 25 N•m (18 ft.-lbs.). Tighten axle nut to 130 N•m (96 ft.-lbs.). Tighten wheel retaining nuts to 55 N•m (40 ft.-lbs.).

STEERING

All Models

INSPECTION. Rotate the handlebar from one extreme to the other and note if any binding or roughness is felt. Periodically inspect the steering components for looseness or any other damage. Renew any damaged component. Clean and grease components if binding or excessive effort is noted.

TOE-IN SETTING. Place the handlebar in a straight ahead position. Use a suitable measuring tool and measure distance (B—Fig. Y13-33) at spindle height between the center of the tires on the rear sides. Locate the same tire centerline points on front side of tires and measure front distance (F). The toe-in distance on the front side (F) should be shorter than the measured distance on the rear side (B). Specified toe-in is 0-10 mm (0.00-0.39 in.) on YFM350ER models and 5-15 mm (0.20-0.60 in.) on YFM350FW models. Note that the distance from a projected vehicle centerline to left (L) and right (R) tire centerlines should also be equal.

To adjust, loosen inside and outside locknuts on the left and right tie rod assemblies and rotate tie rod shaft on each side equally until distance is within recommended range. After obtaining the correct setting, tighten locknuts to 30 N•m (22 ft.-lbs.).

OVERHAUL. To expose steering shaft, remove seat and fuel tank cover. Unscrew and remove forward-reverse shift handle. Remove headlights and carrier rack, if so equipped. Remove front fender deck. Disconnect any cables or wires that will prevent separation of handlebar from steering shaft and remove handlebar. Remove dash panel on YFM350ER models and tripme-

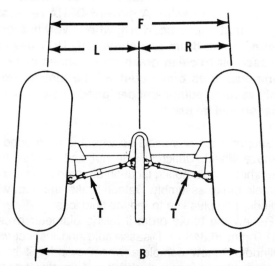

Fig. Y13-33—Toe-in should be 0-10 mm (0.00-0.39 in.) on YFM350ER models and 5-15 mm (0.20-0.60 in.) on YFM350FW models. Refer to text for adjustment procedure.

ter on YFM350FW models. Unscrew the two cap screws securing the steering shaft clamp halves. Clean the old grease from the steering shaft. Inspect the clamp halves and steering shaft for damage. Renew components if needed. Grease inside of steering shaft clamp halves with a lithium base grease and install. Tighten the retaining clamp cap screws to 23 N·m (17 ft.-lbs.).

To remove steering shaft, expose steering shaft as outlined in preceding paragraph. Remove the lower steering shaft retaining cotter pin and nut. Detach inner tie rod ends from steering shaft and withdraw the steering shaft. On YFM350ER models, note "O" rings adjacent to bushings and renew if damaged. On YFM350FW models, remove seal and unscrew bearing retaining nut to remove lower bearing. Inspect the bushings or lower bearing and seals and renew if needed. Apply a lithium base grease to bushings or bearing before installation. On YFM350FW models, tighten bearing retaining nut to 40 N·m (29 ft.-lbs.). On all models, tighten the lower steering shaft retaining nut to 30 N·m (22 ft.-lbs.). Tighten retaining nuts for tie rod ends to 40 N·m (29 ft.-lbs.) on YFM350ER models and 25 N·m (18 ft.-lbs.) on YFM350FW models.

When installing handlebar, install upper clamp so punch mark is toward front of handlebar. Tighten front screw on handlebar clamps first, then tighten the rear clamp screws. If properly tightened, there should be no gaps at the front of the clamps and even gaps at the rear of the clamps. Tighten clamp screws to 20 N·m (15 ft.-lbs.).

FRONT AXLE SHAFTS

Model YFM350FW

Model YFM350FW is equipped with a front-wheel-drive system that uses an axle shaft between the front drive housing and steering knuckle. Each axle shaft is equipped with a ball joint at each end.

To remove axle shaft, first remove front brake drum as previously outlined. Using a suitable ball joint removal tool, separate lower ball joint from steering knuckle. Move steering knuckle and brake assembly away while withdrawing axle shaft from steering knuckle. Use a suitable puller to disengage inner axle shaft end from gear inside the drive housing.

Move shaft in normal range of motion and check for excessive wear and damage. Note that ball joint is not serviceable and must be renewed as a unit assembly. Boots and retaining rings should be available. Boot bands should be renewed if removed. Boots should be renewed if cracked, torn or otherwise damaged. Note that inner ball joint must be disassembled to install a new outer boot. To inspect ball joints, detach boot bands and slide back boots. Clean joint assembly and inspect for damage and excessive wear. Pack inner ball joint and boots with molybdenum disulfide grease.

Before installing shaft be sure the circlip is fitted in the circumferential groove around the end of the inner drive shaft. Install the axle in the drive housing while positioning the inner shaft so the circlip fits into the groove of the gear inside the drive housing. Insert the axle in the knuckle and attach the knuckle to the lower control arm ball joint. Tighten lower ball joint clamp bolt to 35 N·m (26 ft.-lbs.). Tighten axle nut to 130 N·m (96 ft.-lbs.). Tighten wheel retaining nuts to 55 N·m (40 ft.-lbs.).

FRONT DRIVE

Model YFM350FW

Service on the front drive should be performed by a Yamaha service technician equipped with the special tools required for overhaul.

REAR BRAKE

All Models

ADJUSTMENT. To adjust rear brake pedal height, loosen locknut (N—Fig. Y13-35) and rotate adjuster screw. Brake pedal height should be 5 mm (0.2 in.) below top of footpeg. Step on brake pedal three times. Loosen cable adjuster at handlebar lever (Fig. Y13-25) for rear brake cable (R) and loosen both cable adjusters at rear brake. There must be sufficient free play in the brake cables so adjustment is not affected. Loosen brake arm locknut (N—Fig. Y13-36) and adjuster screw (S). Rotate handlebar brake cable adjuster (H) so pointer (R) is aligned with mark (M). Turn in adjuster screw (S) until tight, then back out ¼ turn. Tighten locknut (N) while holding adjuster screw. If the adjuster screw bottoms against the locknut, the brake pads are worn and should be renewed. Turn in pedal cable adjuster (P) until there is a 0-1 mm (0.00-0.04 in.) gap (G—Fig. Y13-37) between cable pin and front end of slot in brake arm. To adjust handlebar brake lever free play, turn cable adjuster at brake lever or at brake end of cable

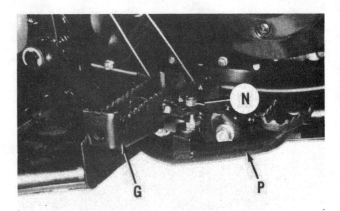

Fig. Y13-35—Brake pedal (P) should be 5 mm (0.2 in.) below footpeg (G) in the released position.

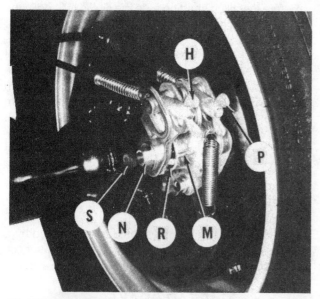

Fig. Y13-36—View of rear brake assembly.

H. Handlebar brake cable adjuster	P. Brake pedal cable adjuster
M. Alignment mark	R. Pointer
N. Locknut	S. Adjusting screw

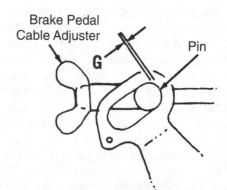

Fig. Y13-37—When properly adjusted, there should be a gap (G) between actuating pin and end of slot in actuating arm. See text.

so there is a 4-5 mm (0.16-0.20 in.) gap (G—Fig. Y13-37) between cable pin and front end of slot in brake arm.

Block up rear end of vehicle so wheels can turn freely and check for brake drag while rotating wheels. If brake drags, repeat brake adjustment procedure.

OVERHAUL. All models are equipped with a cable-actuated rear disc brake. The brake assembly is located on the right side of the final drive housing. The brake cover must be removed to inspect the brake assembly. The brake actuating arm assembly must be removed before the brake cover can be removed. The right wheel and hub must be removed to remove the brake disc. Renew brake pads if thickness is less than 2.0 mm (0.08 in.). Renew brake disc if thickness is less than 3.0 mm (0.12 in.). Maximum allowable disc runout is 0.5 mm (0.020 in.).

Reverse removal procedure to install brake components. Apply lithium base grease to brake cam. Tighten caliper retaining nuts to 50 N·m (37 ft.-lbs.). Tighten actuator plate retaining nuts to 9 N·m (80 in.-lbs.). Tighten wheel hub nut to 115 N·m (84 ft.-lbs.) on YFM350ER models and 150 N·m (110 ft.-lbs.) on YFM350FW models. Tighten wheel retaining nuts to 55 N·m (40 ft.-lbs.).

REAR DRIVE

Model YFM350FW

Service on the rear drive should be performed by a Yamaha service technician equipped with the special tools required for overhaul.

YAMAHA
YFM350X

NOTE: Metric fasteners are used throughout vehicle.

CONDENSED SERVICE DATA

MODEL	YFM350X
General	
Engine Make	Yamaha
Engine Type	Four-Stroke; Air-Cooled
Number of Cylinders	1
Bore	83.0 mm
	(3.27 in.)
Stroke	64.5 mm
	(2.54 in.)
Displacement	348 cc
	(21.2 cu. in.)
Compression Ratio	9.2:1
Engine Lubrication	Wet Sump; Oil Pump
Transmission Lubrication	Common With Engine
Engine/Transmission Oil	SAE 10W-40
Forward Speeds	6
Reverse Speeds	1
Tire Size:	
Front	21 × 7-10*
Rear	22 × 10-9*
Tire Pressure:	
Front	30 kPa
	(4.3 psi)
Rear	25 kPa
	(3.6 psi)
Battery	12V-12AH
Vehicle Weight W/Full Fuel Tank	188 kg
	(414 lbs.)

*On Model YFM350XT, front tire size is 21 × 8-10 and rear tire size is 22 × 11-9.

Tune-Up	
Engine Idle Speed	1450-1550 rpm
Compression Pressure	834 kPa
	(121 psi)
Spark Plug:	
NGK	D8EA
Nippon Denso	X24ES-U
Electrode Gap	0.6-0.7 mm
	(0.024-0.028 in.)
Ignition:	
Type	Breakerless
Timing	10° BTDC @ 1000 rpm
	33° BTDC @ 5000 rpm
Carburetor:	
Make	Mikuni
Model	BTM36SH

Tune-Up (Cont.)
Carburetor: (Cont.)

Jet Needle	5J18
Clip Position	3rd Groove From Top
Needle Jet	0-6
Pilot Jet	#42.5
Main Jet	#145
Float Height	11.4-13.4 mm
	(0.45-0.53 in.)
Idle Mixture Setting	1¼ Turns
Throttle Lever Free Play	3-5 mm
	(0.12-0.20 in.)

Sizes-Clearances

Valve Clearance (cold):	
Intake	0.06-0.10 mm
	(0.0023-0.0039 in.)
Exhaust	0.16-0.20 mm
	(0.0063-0.0078 in.)
Valve Face & Seat Angle:	
Intake & Exhaust	45°
Valve Seat Width:	
Intake & Exhaust	1.2-1.4 mm
	(0.047-0.055 in.)
Valve Margin:	
Intake	1.0-1.4 mm
	(0.039-0.055 in.)
Exhaust	0.8-1.2 mm
	(0.031-0.047 in.)
Valve Stem Diameter:	
Intake	6.975-6.990 mm
	(0.2746-0.2752 in.)
Exhaust	6.955-6.970 mm
	(0.2738-0.2744 in.)
Valve Guide Bore Diameter:	
Intake & Exhaust	7.000-7.012 mm
	(0.2756-0.2761 in.)
Maximum	7.03 mm
	(0.277 in.)
Valve Stem-to-Guide Clearance:	
Intake	0.010-0.037 mm
	(0.0004-0.0015 in.)
Maximum	0.1 mm
	(0.0039 in.)
Exhaust	0.030-0.057 mm
	(0.0012-0.0022 in.)
Maximum	0.1 mm
	(0.0039 in.)
Valve Spring Free Length:	
Inner	39.9 mm
	(1.57 in.)
Outer	43.27 mm
	(1.70 in.)
Rocker Arm Bore Diameter:	
Intake & Exhaust	12.000-12.018 mm
	(0.4724-0.4731 in.)

Sizes-Clearances (Cont.)

Rocker Shaft Diameter:
Intake & Exhaust . . . .
11.981-11.991 mm
(0.4717-0.4720 in.)

Camshaft Lobe Height:
Intake & Exhaust . . . .
40.62-40.72 mm
(1.599-1.603 in.)

Camshaft Runout (Max.) . . . .
0.03 mm
(0.0012 in.)

Cylinder Head Distortion (Max.) . . . .
0.03 mm
(0.0012 in.)

Cylinder Bore Diameter . . . .
82.97-83.02 mm
(3.267-3.269 in.)

Cylinder Taper (Max.) . . . .
0.05 mm
(0.002 in.)

Piston Diameter:
Measured 5.5 mm (0.22 in.) From
Skirt Bottom & 90° to Pin Bore . . . .
82.94-82.95 mm
(3.2653-3.2657 in.)

Piston-to-Cylinder Clearance . . . .
0.040-0.060 mm
(0.0016-0.0024 in.)

Piston Ring End Gap:
Top & Second Rings . . . .
0.20-0.40 mm
(0.008-0.016 in.)

Oil Ring . . . .
0.3-0.9 mm
(0.012-0.035 in.)

Piston Ring Side Clearance:
Top Ring . . . .
0.04-0.08 mm
(0.0016-0.0032 in.)

Second Ring . . . .
0.03-0.07 mm
(0.0012-0.0028 in.)

Connecting Rod Big End
Side Clearance (Max.) . . . .
0.35-0.85 mm
(0.014-0.033 in.)

Connecting Rod Small End Shake . . . . . .
0.08-1.0 mm
(0.031-0.039 in.)

Crankshaft Runout (Max.) . . . .
0.06 mm
(0.0024 in.)

Clutch Friction Plate Thickness (Min.) . . . .
2.8 mm
(0.110 in.)

Clutch Steel Plate Warpage Limit . . . .
0.2 mm
(0.008 in.)

Clutch Spring Free Length (Min.) . . . .
46.5 mm
(1.83 in.)

Capacities

Engine/Transmission Sump . . . .
See Text

Fuel Tank . . . .
9.5 L
(2.5 gal.)

Tightening Torques

Axle Nut:
Front . . . .
85 N•m
(61 ft.-lbs.)

Rear . . . .
120 N•m
(85 ft.-lbs.)

Tightening Torques (Cont.)

Balancer Shaft Nut	60 N·m (43 ft.-lbs.)
Camshaft Sprocket	60 N·m (43 ft.-lbs.)
Chain Tensioner End Cap Screw	38 N·m (27 ft.-lbs.)
Clutch Nut	80 N·m (58 ft.-lbs.)
Crankcase	10 N·m (88 in.-lbs.)
Cylinder Base Screws	10 N·m (88 in.-lbs.)
Cylinder Head:	
Flange Screw	40 N·m (29 ft.-lbs.)
Hex Screw	20 N·m (14 ft.-lbs.)
Engine Mounting Nuts	33 N·m (24 ft.-lbs.)
Spark Plug	17.5 N·m (155 in.-lbs.)
Wheel Nuts:	
Front & Rear	45 N·m (32 ft.-lbs.)
Standard Screws:	
6 mm	6 N·m (53 in.-lbs.)
8 mm	15 N·m (133 in.-lbs.)
10 mm	30 N·m (22 ft.-lbs.)
12 mm	55 N·m (40 ft.-lbs.)
14 mm	85 N·m (61 ft.-lbs.)
16 mm	130 N·m (94 ft.-lbs.)

LUBRICATION

All Models

ENGINE AND TRANSMISSION. The engine and transmission are lubricated by a crankshaft-driven oil pump. The engine and transmission share a common sump. Recommended oil is SAE 10W-30 with an API classification of SE and/or SF.

Oil level should be maintained at upper mark on dipstick attached to fill plug (F—Fig. Y15-1). Do not screw plug in when checking oil level. Fill sump through opening for fill plug (F). Drain oil by removing drain plug on underside of crankcase.

The manufacturer recommends changing the oil and oil filter after the first month of operation and every six months thereafter. Fill crankcase with 2.5 L (2.64 qt.) of oil if oil and oil filter are changed. Crankcase capacity totally dry is 3.2 L (3.4 qt.).

Remove oil filter cover (C—Fig. Y15-2) for access to oil filter. Clean drain plug oil strainer in a suitable solvent. Renew the strainer if damaged or contaminated.

To be sure the oil pump is pumping oil to the engine, slightly unscrew oil passage screw (W—Fig. Y15-3). Start and run engine at idle speed. Oil should just seep past screw after one minute. Retighten screw if oil seeps from hole. If no oil is present, stop engine and determine cause.

DRIVE CHAIN. The drive chain should be lubricated with SAE 30-50 gear oil after first month of operation and after every 30 days of operation thereafter. The chain uses "O" rings to seal the chain rollers and pins. Incorrect lubrication may damage the "O" rings resulting in premature chain failure.

Remove and clean the drive chain when excessive dirt is evident. Remove chain as outlined in DRIVE CHAIN AND SPROCKETS section. The chain should be thoroughly washed in kerosene and wiped dry. The use of any cleaning solution other than kerosene may damage "O" rings. Lubricate chain with SAE 30-50 gear oil, then install and adjust chain as outlined in DRIVE CHAIN AND SPROCKETS section.

Fig. Y15-1—The oil level dipstick is attached to fill plug (F).

Fig. Y15-2—The oil filter is located behind cover (C).

Fig. Y15-3—With engine running at idle speed, oil should seep around screw (W) when loosened.

SUSPENSION AND STEERING. The grease fittings on suspension components should be injected with lithium base grease after initial month of operation and every three months thereafter. Grease fittings are located at lower steering shaft bearing, rear shock absorber links and inner ends of control arms.

The swing arm bearings and upper steering shaft bushing should be lubricated with lithium base grease every six months.

CABLES AND LEVERS. All cables and levers should be inspected and lubricated after first month of operation and every three months thereafter.

AIR CLEANER ELEMENT

All Models

All models are equipped with a foam-type air cleaner element located beneath the seat. Air cleaner element should be removed and cleaned every three months or more frequently if operating conditions are severe.

To remove air cleaner element, remove seat, detach cover and remove filter element. Thoroughly clean foam element in a nonflammable solvent. Compress element between hands to remove solvent. Do not wring or twist. Saturate element in clean SAE 10W-30 engine oil, then compress element to remove excess oil. Apply grease to seating surface of element and reinstall element.

FUEL SYSTEM

All Models

CARBURETOR. The carburetor is connected to the throttle lever by a cable. Throttle lever free play (F—Fig. Y15-5) should be 3-5 mm (0.12-0.20 in.) measured at end of lever. To adjust throttle lever free play, slide dust boot (B) down cable, loosen locknut (N) and rotate cable

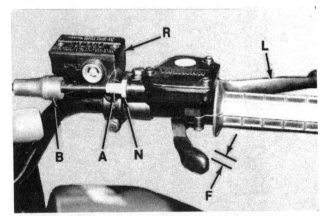

Fig. Y15-5—Throttle lever free play (F) should be 3-5 mm (0.12-0.20 in.). To adjust, slide dust boot (B) down cable, loosen locknut (N) and rotate adjuster (A).

adjuster (A). Tighten locknut and slide dust boot back over adjuster.

The engine is equipped with a Mikuni BTM36SH. Refer to CONDENSED SERVICE DATA for carburetor specifications. Initial setting of idle mixture screw (M—Fig. Y15-6) is 1¼ turns out from a lightly seated position. Final adjustment must be performed with engine at normal operation temperature. Adjust idle speed screw (S) so engine idles at 1450-1550 rpm. After adjusting carburetor, adjust throttle free play as outlined in previous paragraph.

To check float height, remove carburetor and fuel bowl. Invert carburetor and measure float height as shown in Fig. Y15-7. Float height (H) should be 11.4-13.4 mm (0.45-0.53 in.). Adjust float height by carefully bending float tang (T).

With the carburetor installed, the fuel level should be checked. Attach Yamaha fuel level gauge YM-01312 or a suitable clear hose (H—Fig. Y15-8) to fuel bowl nozzle. Hose should be long enough to extend above the bottom edge of carburetor body without kinking. Open fuel bowl drain screw (D). Run engine at idle speed until fuel level in hose stabilizes, then stop engine. Measure distance from bottom edge of carburetor body (fuel bowl contact surface) to fuel level in hose to determine fuel level (L). Fuel level check will not be accurate if hose is moved after fuel level is stabilized. Fuel level (L) should be 3-4 mm (0.012-0.016 in.) above carburetor body edge. To adjust fuel level, remove fuel bowl and carefully bend float arm tang (T—Fig. Y15-7).

FUEL STRAINER. A strainer is mounted on the end of each pickup tube that extends into the fuel tank from the fuel valve. To inspect the strainers, the fuel in the fuel tank must be drained. Disconnect the fuel hose from the fuel valve. Unscrew fuel valve retaining screws and remove fuel valve. Clean and inspect the strainers. Reinstall the valve while noting that sealing washers are used on the retaining screws to prevent fuel leakage.

IGNITION SYSTEM

All Models

The engine is equipped with a breakerless, capacitor discharge ignition system. The electronic ignition circuit consists of the flywheel, CDI module, source coil, pickup coil, ignition coil, spark plug, ignition switch and engine stop switch. To check ignition timing, remove timing plug (P—Fig. Y15-9) and connect a power timing light to

Fig. Y15-6—Adjust idle mixture screw (M) and idle speed screw (S) as outlined in text. Unscrew drain screw (D) to remove fuel in fuel bowl.

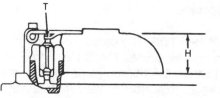

Fig. Y15-7—Float height (H) should be 11.4-13.4 mm (0.45-0.53 in.) mm. Bend tang (T) to adjust float height.

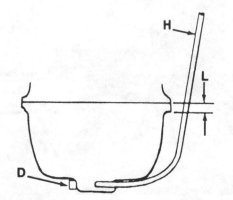

Fig. Y15-8—The fuel level is measured from the bottom edge of the carburetor body. Fuel level (L) should be 3-4 mm (0.012-0.016 in.) above carburetor body edge.

Fig. Y15-9—Remove plug (P) to view timing marks on flywheel and notch (N) in crankcase cover.

engine. Ignition timing (10° BTDC) at idle speed should occur when "F" mark on flywheel is aligned with notch (N) on case. Ignition timing is not adjustable. If not as specified, check condition of ignition components as described in the following test procedures and renew faulty or questionable components.

To check the pickup coil on Model YFM350XT, disconnect connector between the pickup coil and the CDI module. Connect an ohmmeter lead to the grey lead from the pickup coil and the other ohmmeter lead to the blue lead from the pickup coil. Ohmmeter reading should be 180-220 ohms. Connect one ohmmeter lead to the yellow lead from the pickup coil and the other ohmmeter lead to the green lead from the pickup coil. Ohmmeter reading should be 180-220 ohms.

To check pickup coil on Models YFM350XU and YFM350XW, disconnect connector between pickup coil and CDI module. Connect an ohmmeter lead to the yellow lead from the pickup coil and the other ohmmeter lead to the blue lead from the pickup coil. Ohmmeter reading should be 170-210 ohms. Connect one ohmmeter lead to the yellow lead from the pickup coil and the other ohmmeter lead to the green lead from the pickup coil. Ohmmeter reading should be 170-210 ohms.

To check pickup coil on Models YFM350XA, YFM350XB and YFM350XD, disconnect connector between pickup coil and CDI module. Connect an ohmmeter to the blue wire and yellow wire leads from the pickup coil. Ohmmeter reading should be 171-209 ohms.

To check the source coil, disconnect the connector between the source coil and the CDI module. On Models YFM350XT and YFM350XU, connect an ohmmeter between brown wire and red wire leads from source coil. On Models YFM350XW, YFM350XA, YFM350XB and YFM350XD, connect an ohmmeter between white/green wire and red wire leads to source coil. Source coil resistance should be 270-330 ohms on all models.

Ignition coil resistance readings for Models YFM350XT, YFM350XU and YFM350XW should be 0.72-0.98 ohms for primary windings and 5.0-6.8k ohms for secondary windings. Ignition coil resistance readings for Models YFM350XA and YFM350XB should be 0.36-0.48 ohms for primary windings and 5.4-7.4k ohms for secondary windings.

If the ignition system malfunctions and all components test satisfactory, replace CDI module with a new or good unit and recheck ignition system.

ELECTRICAL SYSTEM

All Models

The vehicle is equipped with a charging system, battery and electric starter. The system is protected by a 15 amp fuse.

BATTERY. The battery is accessible after removing the seat. The negative terminal is grounded. The battery is a 12-volt unit with 12 amp-hour capacity.

CHARGING SYSTEM. The charging circuit consists of an alternator and a regulator/rectifier. The alternator rotor is attached to the left end of the crankshaft while the stator is mounted on the inside of the left crankcase cover. The regulator/rectifier module is mounted on the rear of the vehicle frame.

The charging circuit should produce 14-15 VDC at 5000 rpm.

NOTE: Do not disconnect battery terminal wires while the engine is running as excessive alternator output will damage the regulator/rectifier.

To check the alternator stator coils, disconnect the connector with three white leads from the alternator. Measure resistance between any pair of white wires, then repeat test with another pair of wires. Resistance between any pair of white wires should be 0.70-0.86 ohms. Resistance between any white wire and vehicle ground must be infinity.

If previous tests prove satisfactory and fuse, wiring and connections are all good, replace regulator/rectifier with a good unit and recheck operation.

ELECTRIC STARTER. The starting circuit consists of the starter, starter relay, starter switch, cutoff relay, neutral switch, reverse switch, clutch switch and main switch. The cutoff relay, neutral switch, reverse switch and clutch switch prevent energizing starter relay unless switches are in correct position.

The starter relay and cutoff relay are near the battery. The neutral switch is located on the left side of the engine. The clutch switch is located in the clutch lever housing. The electric starter motor is mounted on the front of the engine.

The starter motor can be removed after detaching the battery leads, starter motor leads and unscrewing the two screws securing the motor. Note the "O" ring on the front of the motor. Minimum brush length is 8.5 mm (0.33 in.). Minimum commutator diameter is 27 mm (1.06 in.). Armature coil resistance should be 0.011-0.013 ohm.

WIRING. If wiring requires repair, always install wire that is the same gauge as original wire. Wires should be routed away from areas of extreme heat or sharp edges. Attach or hold wires in their original position using plastic tie straps to prevent short circuits.

FASTENERS

All Models

After the first month of operation and after every 30 days of operation thereafter, the vehicle should receive an overall inspection. All screws, nuts and other fasteners should be checked and tightened to proper torque specification shown in CONDENSED SERVICE DATA section or in the appropriate maintenance section.

VALVE SYSTEM

All Models

The valves are actuated via rocker arms by a single overhead camshaft. The camshaft is driven by a roller chain attached to the left end of the crankshaft. Valve clearance should be adjusted after the first month of operation and then after every six months of operation. Adjust valve clearance with engine cold.

To adjust valve clearance, remove seat, front fender assembly and fuel tank. Remove timing plug (P—Fig. Y15-9) and valve adjustment covers at front and rear of cylinder head. The "T" mark on the flywheel indicates top dead center when aligned with notch (N) in plug hole. Rotate crankshaft and align top dead center mark with notch (N) with piston on compression stroke. To ensure piston is on compression stroke, rotate crankshaft past top dead center and observe intake (rear) rocker arm. If intake rocker arm movement is observed, continue to rotate crankshaft until marks are again aligned.

Clearance between rocker arm adjusting screw and valve stem should be 0.06-0.10 mm (0.0023-0.0039 in.) for the intake valve and 0.16-0.20 mm (0.0063-0.0078 in.) for the exhaust valve. Measure clearance with a suitable feeler gauge. Adjust clearance by loosening the adjusting screw locknut and turning the adjusting screw. Be sure to recheck clearance after tightening locknut. Install valve covers so "V" ridge on inside is toward top and points down when installed.

CAMSHAFT CHAIN

All Models

Camshaft chain adjustment is not required. The cam chain tensioner automatically adjusts chain tension.

CLUTCH

All Models

The engine is equipped with a multiple-disc clutch that is located behind the right crankcase cover.

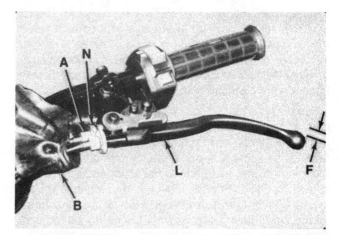

Fig. Y15-10—Clutch lever free play (F) should be 5-10 mm (0.2-0.4 in.). To adjust, push back dust boot (B), loosen locknut (N) and rotate adjuster (A).

Clutch lever free play (F—Fig. Y15-10) should be 5-10 mm (0.2-0.4 in.). To adjust clutch lever free play, push back dust boot (B), loosen locknut (N) and rotate adjuster (A). Retighten locknut. If adjustment limit is reached at handlebar lever, additional adjustment is available using adjuster at engine end of clutch cable.

Properly operated, the clutch should disengage and engage freely. Difficult shifting, clutch grabbing or slipping may indicate clutch repair is required.

MANUAL STARTER

All Models So Equipped

R&R AND OVERHAUL. Refer to Fig. Y15-11 for an exploded view of manual starter used on early models. Starter can be removed from engine as a complete unit

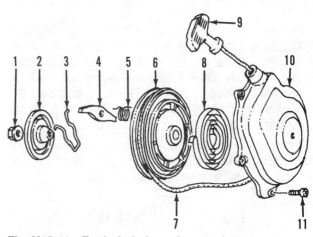

Fig. Y15-11—Exploded view of manual starter.

1. Nut
2. Drive housing
3. Clip
4. Pawl
5. Spring
6. Pulley
7. Rope
8. Rewind spring
9. Rope handle
10. Starter housing
11. Screw

after removing the four cap screws that retain the starter. If starter rope remains under tension, pull starter rope and hold rope pulley with notch adjacent to rope outlet. Pull a loop of rope back through outlet so rope engages notch in pulley and allow pulley to slowly unwind. Unscrew nut and disassemble unit. Be careful when removing rewind spring; a rapidly uncoiling starter spring can cause serious injury.

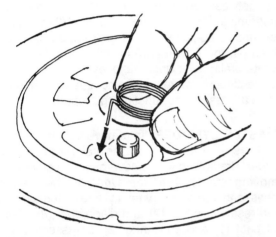

Fig. Y15-12—Insert long end of pawl spring in hole in pulley.

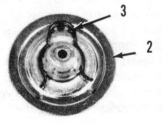

Fig. Y15-13—Apply grease to clip (3) and install in groove on drive housing (2).

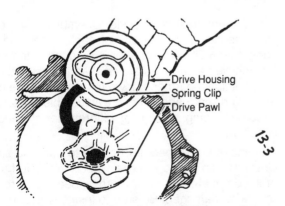

Fig. Y15-14—Install drive housing with clip on pulley as shown.

Rewind spring is wound into starter housing in a clockwise direction. Rope is wound on rope pulley in a clockwise direction as viewed with pulley in housing. Reassemble starter by reversing disassembly procedure. During reassembly, lightly grease pulley shaft and starter pawl. Insert long end of drive pawl spring in hole in pulley as shown in Fig. Y15-12. Install drive pawl and hook outer end of drive pawl spring under drive pawl and into notch on drive pawl. Turn drive pawl one turn counterclockwise and push drive pawl into recess in pulley. Apply a light coat of grease to spring clip (3—Fig. Y15-13) and install spring in groove of drive housing (2). Install drive housing and spring clip as shown in Fig. Y15-14.

To place tension on rewind spring after starter is assembled, pass rope through rope outlet in housing and install rope handle. Pull a loop of rope back through starter housing outlet and into pulley notch in pulley. Turn pulley clockwise three or four complete revolutions to place tension on spring. Release rope from notch and allow rope to wind onto pulley. Do not place more tension on rewind spring than is necessary to draw rope handle up against housing. Check operation of starter before installation.

FRONT BRAKE ASSEMBLY

All Models

A disc brake assembly is used on both front wheels. Front brake adjustment for disc pad wear is not required due to the compensating action of the piston in the caliper.

Brake fluid must be rated DOT 3 or 4. Maintain brake fluid level above "LOW" mark on side of brake fluid reservoir (R—Fig. Y15-15). Do not overfill. To avoid spillage, be sure reservoir is horizontal before removing cover.

BRAKE LEVER FREE PLAY. Front brake lever free play should be 4-8 mm (0.16-0.31 in.) measured at outer end of brake lever (L—Fig. Y15-15). To adjust, loosen

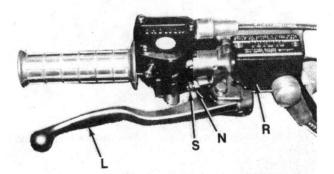

Fig. Y15-15—Loosen locknut (N) and rotate screw (S) to adjust front brake lever (L) free play.

locknut (N) and rotate screw (S) until recommended free play is obtained. Retighten locknut (N).

BLEEDING. Make sure reservoir (R—Fig. Y15-15) is full. Connect a bleed hose to bleed valve on both front brake caliper assemblies. Route the bleed hoses into suitable containers. Operate the brake lever until hard resistance is felt, then open one bleed valve. Close bleed valve prior to releasing brake lever. Continue bleeding procedure on both wheels until no air bubbles are noted in discharged fluid from bleed valve.

NOTE: Make sure reservoir remains full during bleeding procedure.

When bleeding procedure is completed, add brake fluid to reservoir until fluid level is at upper level line in reservoir.

OVERHAUL. The brake pads on later models are equipped with a wear indicator on the pad to indicate when the service limit has been reached and pad should be renewed. Brake pads should be renewed if pad thickness is 1.0 mm (0.039 in.) or less.

WARNING: Inhaling asbestos brake dust is injurious to human health. Approved OSHA respiration equipment must be worn when working on or around brake calipers and pads. DO NOT use compressed air to clean brake calipers, pads or nearby components as brake dust will be blown into air. Only vacuum equipment designed to pick up brake dust should be used.

On early models, the caliper housing is two-piece, while the caliper housing on later models is single-piece. On early models, the brake pads can be renewed without removing the caliper by unscrewing the caliper

housing screw and swinging the caliper half away for access to the brake pads. Retighten caliper housing screw to 23 N·m (17 ft.-lbs.).

Brake components are accessible after removing wheel, caliper mounting screws and withdrawing caliper. Brake disc should be renewed if thickness is less than 3 mm (0.118 in.) or runout exceeds 0.15 mm (0.006 in.). Tighten brake disc mounting bolts to 28 N·m (21 ft.-lbs.). Push piston by hand back into caliper to allow clearance for new brake pads. On later models, install shim between brake pad and piston. Tighten brake caliper mounting screws on to 28 N·m (21 ft.-lbs.). On later models equipped with a brake pad retaining pin, tighten pin to 18 N·m (160 in.-lbs.). After reassembly, operate brake lever until brake lever will not pump up after continuous operation. Do not operate vehicle until brakes are tested and functioning properly.

MASTER CYLINDER. To remove front brake master cylinder (9—Fig. Y15-17), detach brake line from master cylinder. Brake fluid will remove paint; be careful when removing master cylinder. Unscrew two retaining screws and remove master cylinder. Remove brake lever, reservoir cover (7) and diaphragm (8). Remove dust boot (1) and snap ring (2). Disassemble piston assembly while noting location and direction of components. Renew complete master cylinder if bore is scored, pitted or excessively worn. Superficial damage in master cylinder bore may be removed using a suitable cylinder hone. After honing, rinse bore with clean brake fluid. Shake out excess fluid but do not wipe dry. Using a shop towel or rag to dry cylinder will leave lint particles in bore. Renew boots and piston cups. During reassembly, lubricate components with clean brake fluid. Reassembly is reverse of disassembly. Install spring (6) so small end contacts primary cup (5). Bleed brakes as previously outlined. Do not operate vehicle until brakes are tested and functioning properly.

FRONT AXLE

All Models

Both front steering knuckle assemblies pivot on ball joint assemblies at the end of each upper and lower control arm. The control arms are bolted at the ends to the vehicle frame and a shock absorber is used to limit and cushion the up and down movement of the control arms. The shock absorbers are adjustable to alter shock absorber spring setting for different terrain and load conditions.

Remove front wheel for access to hub and spindle. Unscrew hub nut to remove wheel hub. The hub and brake drum are one piece. Renew bearings if rough or otherwise damaged. Be sure to install spacer between bearings when reassembling components. Tapered end of spacer must be toward wheel side of hub. Tighten hub

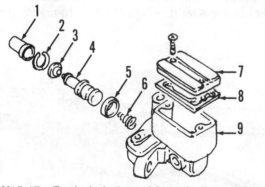

Fig. Y15-17—Exploded view of front brake master cylinder.

1. Dust boot
2. Snap ring
3. Secondary cup
4. Piston
5. Primary cup
6. Spring
7. Cover
8. Diaphragm
9. Body

retaining nut to 85 N·m (62 ft.-lbs.). Tighten wheel retaining nuts to 45 N·m (33 ft.-lbs.).

Remove the front wheel to service the ball joint assemblies. Note that removing the brake components will allow greater access to ball joint assemblies. Ball joints are threaded into control arms and should be tightened to 85 N·m (61 ft.-lbs.). Tighten control arm retaining nuts to 45 N·m (33 ft. lbs.). Tighten ball joint retaining nuts to 25 N·m (18 ft.-lbs.). Shock absorber retaining nuts should be tightened to 45 N·m (33 ft.-lbs).

STEERING

All Models

INSPECTION. Rotate the handlebar from one extreme to the other and note if any binding or roughness is felt. Periodically inspect the steering components for looseness or any other damage. Renew any damaged component. Clean and grease components if binding or excessive effort is noted.

TOE-IN SETTING. Place the handlebar in a straight ahead position. Use a suitable measuring tool and measure distance (B—Fig. Y15-18) at spindle height between the center of the tires on the rear sides. Locate the same tire centerline points on front side of tires and measure front distance (F). The distance on the front side (F) should be 17-27 mm (0.67-1.06 in.) shorter than the measured distance on the rear side (B). Note that the distance from a projected vehicle centerline to left (L) and right (R) tire centerlines should also be equal.

To adjust, loosen inside (I—Fig. Y15-19) and outside locknuts (O) on the left and right tie rod assemblies and rotate tie rod shaft (S) on each side equally until distance is within recommended range. After obtaining the correct setting, tighten locknuts to 30 N·m (22 ft.-lbs.).

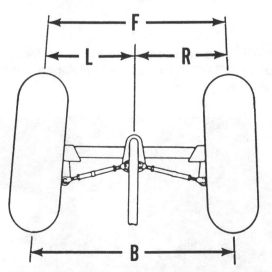

Fig. Y15-18—Toe-in should be 17-27 mm (0.67-1.06 in.). Refer to text for measurement and adjustment procedures.

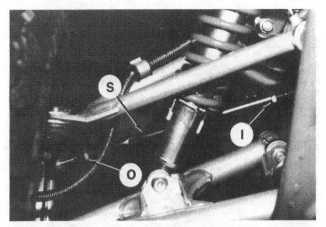

Fig. Y15-19—Loosen inside (I) and outside locknuts (O) on the left and right tie rod assemblies and rotate tie rod shaft (S) on each side to adjust toe-in.

OVERHAUL. To expose the steering shaft, remove front fender cover and handlebar. Unscrew the two cap screws securing the steering shaft clamp halves. Clean the old grease from the steering shaft. Inspect the clamp halves and steering shaft for damage. Renew components if needed. Grease inside of steering shaft clamp halves with a lithium base grease and install. Tighten the retaining clamp cap screws to 23 N·m (17 ft.-lbs.).

To remove steering shaft, remove steering shaft clamps as outlined in previous paragraph. Remove the lower steering shaft retaining cotter pin and nut. Detach inner tie rod ends from steering shaft and withdraw the steering shaft. On early models, note "O" rings adjacent to bearing holder and renew if damaged. On later models, remove seal and unscrew bearing retaining nut to remove lower bearing. Inspect the lower bearing and seals and renew if needed. Apply a lithium base grease to bearing before installation. On later models, tighten bearing retaining nut to 40 N·m (29 ft.-lbs.). On all models, tighten the lower steering shaft retaining nut to 30 N·m (22 ft.-lbs.). Tighten retaining nuts for tie rod ends to 25 N·m (18 ft.-lbs.). Tighten handlebar clamp screws to 20 N·m (15 ft.-lbs.).

REAR BRAKE ASSEMBLY

All Models

A single disc brake assembly is used for both rear wheels. The running brake is operated hydraulically by a foot pedal on the lower right side. The parking brake is mechanically operated by a cable and handlebar components in conjunction with the clutch lever. Rear brake adjustment for disc pad wear is not required due to the compensating action of the piston in the caliper.

Brake fluid must be rated DOT 3 or 4. Maintain brake fluid level above "LOW" mark on side of brake fluid reservoir (R—Fig. Y15-23). Do not overfill. To avoid

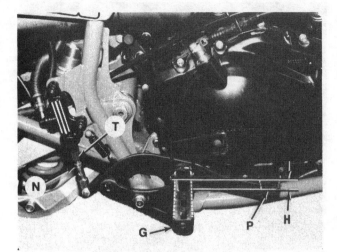

Fig. Y15-20—Brake pedal (P) should be 10 mm (3/8 in.) below footpeg (G) in the released position. Loosen locknut (N) and rotate master cylinder actuator rod nut (T) to adjust pedal height.

Fig. Y15-22—Loosen locknut (L) and turn adjuster screw (S) as outlined in text to adjust parking brake. Attach a hose to bleed screw (B) to bleed rear brake system.

spillage, be sure reservoir is horizontal before removing cover.

BRAKE PEDAL HEIGHT ADJUSTMENT. Brake pedal (P—Fig. Y15-20) should be 10 mm (3/8 in.) below footpeg (G) in the released position when measured from the top of the footpeg to the top of the foot pad on the brake pedal as shown in Fig. Y15-20. To adjust, loosen locknut (N) and rotate master cylinder actuator rod nut (T) until recommended pedal height (H) is obtained, then tighten locknut (N) to retain adjustment. After adjustment, the end of the master cylinder push rod must be visible in the hole in the side of the clevis.

PARKING BRAKE ADJUSTMENT. Make sure parking brake/clutch lever is in the released position. Slide dust boot (B—Fig. Y15-21) down cable. Loosen locknut (N) and rotate cable adjuster (A) completely inward. Loosen locknut (L—Fig. Y15-22) and adjuster screw

(S). Turn in adjuster screw (S) until tight, then back out ¼ turn. Tighten locknut (L) while holding adjuster screw. If the adjuster screw bottoms against the locknut, then the brake pads are worn and should be renewed. Block up rear end of vehicle so wheels can turn freely and check for brake drag while rotating wheels. If brake drag is present, repeat preceding brake adjustment.

BLEEDING. Make sure rear brake master cylinder reservoir is full. Connect a bleed hose to bleed valve (B—Fig. Y15-22) on brake caliper assembly. Route the bleed hose into a suitable container. Operate foot pedal until firm resistance is felt, then open bleed valve (B). Close bleed valve prior to releasing foot pedal. Continue bleeding procedure until no air bubbles are noted in discharged fluid from bleed valve.

NOTE: Make sure rear brake master cylinder reservoir (R—Fig. Y15-23) remains full during bleeding procedure.

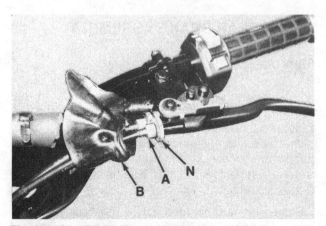

Fig. Y15-21—Slide dust boot (B) down cable to expose parking brake cable locknut (N) and adjuster (A).

Fig. Y15-23—Maintain level of brake fluid in rear brake fluid reservoir above "LOW" mark on reservoir.

When bleeding procedure is completed, add brake fluid to rear brake master cylinder reservoir as needed.

OVERHAUL. The brake pads are equipped with a wear indicator on the pad to indicate when the service limit has been reached and pad should be renewed. Brake pads should be renewed if pad thickness is 1.0 mm (0.039 in.) or less.

WARNING: Inhaling asbestos brake dust is injurious to human health. Approved OSHA respiration equipment must be worn when working on or around brake calipers and pads. DO NOT use compressed air to clean brake calipers, pads or nearby components as brake dust will be blown into air. Only vacuum equipment designed to pick up brake dust should be used.

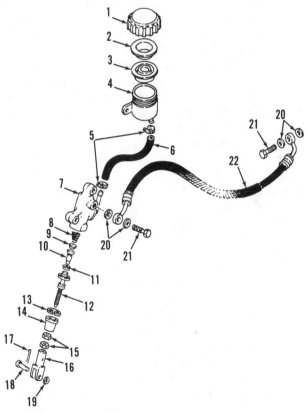

Fig. Y15-24—Exploded view of rear brake master cylinder.

1. Cap	13. Snap ring
2. Seal	14. Dust boot
4. Diaphragm	15. Nuts
5. Clip	16. Clevis
6. Hose	17. Cotter pin
7. Body	18. Pin
8. Spring	19. Washer
9. Primary cup	20. Sealing washers
10. Piston	21. Union bolt
11. Secondary cup	22. Hose
12. Push rod	

Brake components are accessible after removing caliper mounting screws and withdrawing caliper. Brake disc should be renewed if thickness is 3.0 mm (0.118 in.) or less or disc runout is 0.15 mm (0.006 in.) or more. Push piston by hand back into caliper to allow clearance for new brake pads. Tighten brake pad retaining pins to 12 N·m (160 in.-lbs.). Tighten brake caliper mounting screw to 23 N·m (17 ft.-lbs.). After reassembly, operate brake pedal until pedal will not pump up after continuous operation. Do not operate vehicle until brakes are tested and functioning properly.

MASTER CYLINDER. To remove rear brake master cylinder (7—Fig. Y15-24), disconnect brake plunger from pedal. Detach brake lines from master cylinder and plug line to reservoir. Brake fluid will remove paint; be careful when removing master cylinder. Unscrew retaining screws and remove master cylinder. Remove dust boot (14) and snap ring (13). Disassemble piston assembly while noting location and direction of components. Renew complete master cylinder if bore is scored, pitted or excessively worn. Superficial damage in master cylinder bore may be removed using a suitable cylinder hone. After honing, rinse bore with clean brake fluid. Shake out excess fluid but do not wipe dry. Using a shop towel or rag to dry cylinder will leave lint particles in bore. Renew boots and piston cups. During reassembly, lubricate components with clean brake fluid. Reassembly is reverse of disassembly. Install spring (8) so small end contacts primary cup (9). Bleed brakes as previously outlined. Do not operate vehicle until brakes are tested and functioning properly.

DRIVE CHAIN AND SPROCKETS

All Models

INSPECTION AND ADJUSTMENT. The final drive chain should be inspected and adjusted after initial break-in and after every month of operation thereafter. Improper maintenance and neglect can cause early failure of both drive chain and sprockets. To measure drive chain free play, support rear of frame near swing arm pivot so rear wheels are off ground. Measure drive chain travel at a point midway between rub block at swing arm and rear sprocket. Drive chain free play should be 30-40 mm (1.18-1.57 in.).

To adjust chain tension, loosen upper rear axle housing retaining screws (U—Fig. Y15-25) and lower screws (L). Loosen adjusting screw locknuts (N) and rotate tension adjusting screws (S) equally. Note axle alignment marks adjacent to adjusting screws and maintain axle alignment by aligning same marks on each side of axle housing. Tighten upper axle housing retaining screws (U) to 100 N·m (72 ft.-lbs.) and lower screws (L) to 50 N·m (36 ft.-lbs.). Recheck drive chain tension. Renew drive chain if recommended tension adjustment

Fig. Y15-25—To adjust drive chain tension, loosen upper (U) and lower (L) screws. Loosen locknuts (N) and rotate screws (S) until specified chain tension is obtained.

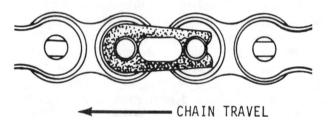

← CHAIN TRAVEL

Fig. Y15-26—Install drive chain master link clip with closed end towards direction of chain travel.

cannot be obtained. Refer to LUBRICATION for drive chain lubrication requirements.

R&R AND OVERHAUL. The drive chain is sealed by "O" rings and fitted with a master link. To remove the drive chain and both sprockets, remove engine sprocket cover and loosen engine sprocket retaining nut. Support rear of vehicle and remove left wheel. Remove chain guard under rear sprocket. Loosen chain tension as outlined in previous section. Remove drive chain master link while taking care not to damage or lose "O" rings. Remove drive chain. To remove rear sprocket, unscrew sprocket retaining nuts and remove sprocket. Remove engine sprocket.

Carefully examine sprockets for excessive wear. Worn sprockets will usually have a hooked tooth profile. A good test is to place a new chain on a used sprocket and check the fit. If sprockets require renewal due to wear, always renew drive chain. Sprockets should be renewed as a set.

Reassemble by reversing disassembly procedure. Tighten engine sprocket retaining nut to 75 N·m (54 ft.-lbs.). Tighten rear sprocket retaining nuts and secure by bending tabs of lockplate against nuts. When assembling chain, be sure "O" rings are properly installed on master link. Install master link clip as shown in Fig. Y15-26. Tighten wheel retaining nuts to 45 N·m (33 ft.-lbs.). Refer to previous INSPECTION AND ADJUSTMENT paragraphs for recommended drive chain adjustment procedures.

FINAL DRIVE ASSEMBLY

All Models

R&R AND OVERHAUL. Support rear of vehicle. Remove rear brake caliper. Remove drive chain as previously outlined. Remove both rear wheels and hubs. Remove upper rear axle housing retaining screws (U—Fig. Y15-25) and lower retaining screws (L). Unscrew rear axle retaining nuts (H), then lightly tap left end of axle with a soft-faced mallet to drive axle shaft out of axle housing. DO NOT strike threaded end of axle.

Inspect axle housing seals and bearings and renew if required. Maximum axle runout with axle supported just outside inner splined area for brake hub and just outside threads for inner axle nuts (H) is 1.5 mm (0.060 in.). Reassembly is reverse order of disassembly. Lubricate splined areas with lithium base grease.

When tightening inner axle nuts (H) on Models YFM350XT and YFM350XU use the following procedure: Apply Loctite to threads of inner axle nuts. Tighten inner nut to 55 N·m (40 ft.-lbs.). Hold inner nut and tighten outer nut to 190 N·m (140 ft.-lbs.). Hold outer nut and tighten inner nut toward outer nut to 240 N·m (176 ft.-lbs.).

When tightening inner axle nuts (H) on Models YFM350XW, YFM350XA, YFM350XB and YFM350XD, use the following procedure: Apply Loctite to threads of inner axle nuts. Tighten inner nut to 55 N·m (40 ft.-lbs.). Hold inner nut and tighten outer nut to 190 N·m (140 ft.-lbs.). Place a mark across the two nuts. Tighten inner nut against outer nut until torque reading on inner nut is 240 N·m (176 ft.-lbs.). Distance between marks on nuts should be at least 3 mm (0.12 in.). If not, retighten inner nut.

Tighten axle shaft hub nut on all models to 120 N·m (88 ft.-lbs.) torque.

YAMAHA
YFZ350

NOTE: Metric fasteners are used throughout vehicle.

CONDENSED SERVICE DATA

MODEL	YFZ350
General	
Engine Make	Yamaha
Engine Type	Two-Stroke; Liquid-Cooled
Number of Cylinders	2
Bore	64.0 mm
	(2.51 in.)
Stroke	54.0 mm
	(2.12 in.)
Displacement	347 cc
	(21.2 cu. in.)
Compression Ratio	6.5:1
Engine Lubrication	Fuel:Oil Premix
Engine Fuel:Oil Ratio	24:1
Engine Oil	Good Quality 2-Stroke Oil
Transmission Oil	SAE 10W-30
Forward Speeds	6
Tire Size:	
Front	21 × 7-10
Rear	22 × 10-9*
Tire Pressure:	
Front	30 kPa
	(4.3 psi)
Rear	25 kPa
	(3.6 psi)
Vehicle Weight W/Full Fuel Tank	182 kg
	(400 lbs.)

*Later models are equipped with 20 × 11-10 rear tires.

Tune-Up	
Engine Idle Speed	1450-1550 rpm
Spark Plug:	
NGK	B8ES
Nippon Denso	W24ES
Electrode Gap	0.7-0.8 mm
	(0.028-0.031 in.)
Ignition:	
Type	Breakerless
Timing	17° BTDC
Carburetor:	
Make	Mikuni
Model	VM26SS
Jet Needle	5N7
Clip Position	3rd Groove From Top
Needle Jet	O-8
Pilot Jet	#25

Tune-Up (Cont.)
Carburetor: (Cont.)

Main Jet	#210
Float Height	20.0-22.0 mm
	(0.79-0.87 in.)
Idle Mixture Setting	2 Turns Out
Throttle Lever Free Play	4-6 mm
	(0.16-0.24 in.)

Sizes-Clearances

Cylinder Head Distortion (Max.).	0.03 mm
	(0.0012 in.)
Cylinder Bore Diameter	64.00-64.02 mm
	(2.5197-2.5205 in.)
Wear Limit	64.1 mm
	(2.524 in.)
Cylinder Bore Taper (Max.)	0.05 mm
	(0.002 in.)
Cylinder Bore Out-of-Round (Max.)	0.01 mm
	(0.0004 in.)
Piston-to-Cylinder Wall Clearance	0.060-0.065 mm
	(0.0024-0.0026 in.)
Piston Diameter Measured 10 mm	
(0.4 in.) From Skirt Bottom	63.94-64.00 mm
	(2.5173-2.5197 in.)
Piston Ring End Gap	0.30-0.45 mm
	(0.012-0.018 in.)
Piston Ring Side Clearance	0.02-0.06 mm
	(0.0008-0.0024 in.)
Connecting Rod Big End	
Side Clearance	0.25-0.75 mm
	(0.010-0.030 in.)
Connecting Rod Small	
End Side Shake	0.36-0.98 mm
	(0.014-0.038 in.)
Connecting Rod Big End	
Radial Clearance	0.021-0.035 mm
	(0.0008-0.0014 in.)
Crankshaft Runout (Max.)	0.05 mm
	(0.0020 in.)
Clutch Friction Plate Thickness (Min.)	2.7 mm
	(0.106 in.)
Clutch Steel Plate Warpage Limit	0.05 mm
	(0.002 in.)

Capacities

Cooling System	2.5 L
	(2.6 qt.)
Fuel Tank	12.0 L
	(3.2 gal.)
Transmission Sump:	
Drained	1.5 L
	(1.6 qt.)
Dry	1.7 L
	(1.8 qt.)

Tightening Torques
Axle Nut:

Front	85 N•m
	(62 ft.-lbs.)

Tightening Torques (Cont.)

Axle Nut: (Cont.)

Rear	120 N·m (88 ft.-lbs.)
Clutch Nut	90 N·m (66 ft.-lbs.)

Crankcase:

6 mm	10 N·m (88 in.-lbs.)
8 mm	25 N·m (18 ft.-lbs.)
Cylinder	28 N·m (21 ft.-lbs.)
Cylinder Head	28 N·m (21 ft.-lbs.)
Engine Sprocket	80 N·m (59 ft.-lbs.)
Flywheel	80 N·m (59 ft.-lbs.)
Primary Drive Gear	65 N·m (48 ft.-lbs.)
Rear Sprocket	60 N·m (44 ft.-lbs.)
Spark Plug	20 N·m (15 ft.-lbs.)
Wheel Retaining Nut	45 N·m (33 ft.-lbs.)

Standard Screws:

6 mm	6.0 N·m (53 in.-lbs.)
8 mm	15 N·m (133 in.-lbs.)
10 mm	30 N·m (22 ft.-lbs.)
12 mm	55 N·m (40 ft.-lbs.)
14 mm	85 N·m (63 ft.-lbs.)
16 mm	130 N·m (96 ft.-lbs.)

LUBRICATION

ENGINE. The engine is lubricated by oil mixed with the fuel. Recommended oil is a good quality two-stroke oil designed for use in motorcycles. Specified fuel:oil ratio is 20:1.

TRANSMISSION. Recommended oil is SAE 10W-30 engine oil. Oil level should be maintained at upper mark on dipstick attached to fill plug. Do not screw plug in when checking oil level. Fill transmission through open-ing for fill plug (F). Drain oil by removing drain plug on underside of crankcase. If oil is changed, fill sump with 1.5 L (1.6 qt.) of oil. Transmission oil quantity required after disassembly is 1.7 L (1.8 qt.).

Manufacturer recommends changing transmission oil after initial break-in and annually thereafter.

DRIVE CHAIN. The drive chain should be lubricated with SAE 30-50 gear oil after initial break-in and after every 30 days of operation thereafter. The chain utilizes "O" rings to seal the chain rollers and pins. Incorrect lubrication may damage the "O" rings resulting in premature chain failure.

Remove and clean the drive chain when excessive dirt is evident. Remove chain as outlined in DRIVE CHAIN AND SPROCKETS section. The chain should be thoroughly washed in kerosene and wiped dry. The use of any cleaning solution other than kerosene may damage "O" rings. Lubricate chain with SAE 30-50 gear oil, then install and adjust chain as outlined in DRIVE CHAIN AND SPROCKETS section.

SUSPENSION AND STEERING. The grease fittings on suspension components should be injected with lithium base grease after initial break-in and every three months thereafter. Grease fittings are located at inner ends of control arms and rear shock absorber links.

The swing arm bushings and upper steering shaft bushing should be lubricated with lithium base grease after initial break-in and every three months thereafter.

CABLES AND LEVERS. All cables and levers should be inspected and lubricated after initial break-in and after every three months of operation thereafter.

AIR CLEANER ELEMENT

Model is equipped with a foam-type air cleaner element located underneath the seat. The air cleaner element should be removed and cleaned every three months or more frequently if operating conditions are severe.

To remove air cleaner element, remove seat, detach cover and remove filter element. Thoroughly clean the foam element in a nonflammable solvent. Compress element between hands to remove solvent. Do not wring or twist element. Saturate element in clean SAE 10W-30 engine oil, then compress element to remove excess oil. Apply grease to seating surface of element and reinstall element.

FUEL SYSTEM

CARBURETOR. The engine is equipped with two Mikuni VM26SS carburetors. The carburetors should be adjusted in the following order: synchronization, idle adjustment and throttle free play. Performing only part of the sequence or reversing its order may result in poor performance.

Adjustment. The carburetors must be synchronized so throttle slide positions on the carburetors are the same. Remove screw in side of carburetor to view throttle slide. Operate throttle several times, then push throttle so circular mark on throttle slide can be viewed through screw hole. Position throttle so mark is at top of hole on either carburetor. Remove seat and turn adjuster in throttle cable to adjust position of throttle slide on opposite carburetor so marks are in identical posi-

tion. Operate throttle several times and recheck position of marks.

Initial setting of idle mixture screw (I—Fig. Y17-1) is 2 turns out from a lightly seated position. Rotating idle mixture screw clockwise will richen idle mixture. Final adjustment must be performed with engine at normal operating temperature. Remove seat for access to idle speed screws (S) which are located in carburetor switch housings mounted on top of both carburetors. Adjust idle speed screws (S) so engine idles at 1450-1550 rpm. Idle speed screws must be in same position. Adjust each idle mixture screw (I) so engine runs at highest idle speed. Position of idle mixture screws on both carburetors should be in same position. Readjust idle speed screws (S) so engine idles at specified rpm.

Overhaul. When overhauling carburetor, refer to Fig. Y17-1 for an exploded view of carburetor and to carbu-

Fig. Y17-1—Exploded view of Mikuni VM26SS.

I.	Idle mixture screw	15.	Air jet
S.	Idle speed screw	16.	Spring
1.	Throttle switch assy.	17.	"O" ring
2.	Throttle cable	18.	Retainer
3.	Washer	19.	Starter plunger
4.	Nut	20.	Pilot jet
5.	Cap	21.	Main jet
6.	"O" ring	22.	Baffle
7.	Coupler	23.	Fuel inlet seat
8.	Spring	24.	Fuel inlet valve
9.	Connector	25.	Retainer
10.	Washer	26.	Float
11.	Clip	27.	Float pin
12.	Jet needle	28.	Gasket
13.	Throttle slide	29.	Fuel bowl
14.	Needle jet	30.	Drain screw

retor specifications in CONDENSED SERVICE DATA section while noting the following: When removing carburetor, loosen retainer (18) and unscrew cap (5) to separate throttle slide and switch assembly from carburetor. Remove needle jet (14) by carefully forcing towards top of carburetor. Jet needle clip (11) should be installed in second groove from top of jet needle. Installing clip in a lower groove on jet needle will richen mid-range fuel mixture. Groove in side of needle jet (14) must index with pin in carburetor. When measuring float height, tilt carburetor as shown in Fig. Y17-5 so float arm tang (T) just contacts fuel inlet valve and spring in valve is not compressed. Bend float arm tang to adjust float height. Make sure groove in side of throttle slide is aligned with pin in carburetor body when inserting slide in carburetor.

With the carburetor installed, the fuel level should be checked. Attach Yamaha fuel level gauge YM-01312 or a suitable clear hose (H—Fig. Y17-9) to fuel bowl nozzle. Hose should be long enough to extend above the bottom edge of carburetor body without kinking. Open fuel bowl drain screw (D). Run the engine at idle speed until fuel level in hose stabilizes, then stop engine. Measure distance from the bottom edge of carburetor body (fuel bowl contact surface) to fuel level in hose to determine fuel level (L). Fuel level check will not be accurate if hose is moved after fuel level is stabilized. Fuel level (L) should be 0.5-1.5 mm (0.020-0.060 in.) above carburetor body edge. To adjust fuel level, remove the fuel bowl and carefully bend float arm tang (T—Fig. Y17-5).

THROTTLE LEVER FREE PLAY. Free play (F—Fig. Y17-12) at the end of the throttle lever should be 4-6 mm (0.16-0.24 in.). To adjust free play, slide back rubber boot (B), loosen knurled nut (N) and rotate cable adjuster (A). Retighten knurled nut.

REED VALVE. A "V" type reed valve assembly is located between the intake manifold and engine. The reed valve assembly is accessible after removing the carburetor and intake manifold.

Reed petal seats must be smooth and flat. Renew reed petals if bent, broken or otherwise damaged. Do not attempt to straighten reed petals.

Reed valve petals may stand open (S—Fig. Y17-17) a maximum of 0.5 mm (0.020 in.). The reed petals and stops can be renewed individually. Notches on corners of reed petals and stops must be aligned. Apply Loctite to reed stop retaining screws. Tighten intake manifold screws to 10 N·m (88 in.-lbs.).

FUEL STRAINER. A strainer is mounted on the end of each pickup tube that extends into the fuel tank from the fuel valve. To inspect the strainers, the fuel in the fuel tank must be drained. Disconnect the fuel hose from the fuel valve. Unscrew fuel valve retaining screws and remove fuel valve. Clean and inspect the strainers. Reinstall the valve while noting that sealing washers are used on the retaining screws to prevent fuel leakage.

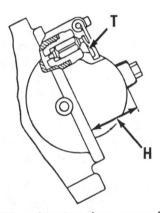

Fig. Y17-5—Tilt carburetor when measuring float height so tang (T) just touches inlet valve and valve spring is not compressed. Float height (H) should be 20.0-21.5 mm (0.79-0.85 in.). Bend tang (T) to adjust float height.

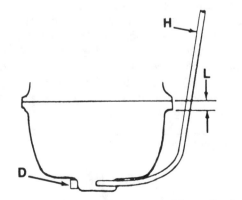

Fig. Y17-9—The fuel level is measured from the bottom edge of the carburetor body. Fuel level (L) should be 0.5-1.5 mm (0.020-0.060 in.) above carburetor body edge.

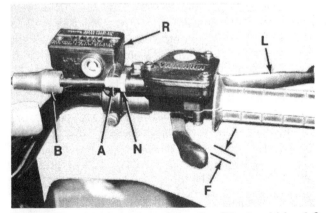

Fig. Y17-12—Throttle lever free play (F) should be 4-6 mm (0.16-0.24 in.). To adjust, slide dust boot (B) down cable, loosen locknut (N) and rotate adjuster (A).

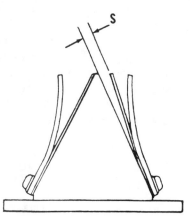

Fig. Y17-17—Reed valve petals may stand open a maximum of 0.5 mm (0.020 in.).

COOLING SYSTEM

INSPECTION. The engine is liquid-cooled by a pressurized cooling system that consists of a radiator, water pump and hoses. System components should be inspected periodically. Replace hoses if cracked, split or otherwise damaged. Inspect radiator for signs of leakage and remove any obstructions.

CHANGING COOLANT. Coolant should be changed every two years. The manufacturer recommends a mixture of 50 percent distilled water and 50 percent antifreeze. Cooling system capacity is 2.5 L (2.6 qt.).

NOTE: Distilled water must be used to prevent corrosion and clogging in the radiator. Only antifreeze designed for aluminum engines and radiators may be used. A mixture of antifreeze and distilled water must be present at all times. Use of only distilled water will cause corrosion and subsequent damage.

To drain coolant, remove radiator cap and unscrew drain plug at bottom of each cylinder. Catch coolant in a suitable container and dispose of according to prevailing ordinances. Disconnect lower hose from reserve tank then drain and collect coolant. Tip vehicle side-to-side to drain trapped coolant. Reconnect hose to reserve tank and reinstall drain plugs.

To refill cooling system, pour coolant into radiator until full. Tip vehicle side-to-side to release trapped air bubbles. Refill radiator. Start and run engine at fast idle, then stop engine. Refill radiator, if necessary, and fill reserve tank to full mark. Install radiator cap and run engine until warm, then stop engine, check for leaks and allow engine to cool. Refill radiator, if necessary, and fill reserve tank to full mark.

RADIATOR CAP. The radiator cap should have a relief opening pressure of 93-123 kPa (13.5-18 psi).

IGNITION AND ELECTRICAL

IGNITION SYSTEM. Model is equipped with a pointless, capacitor discharge ignition system. A charge coil located behind the flywheel provides electrical power for the ignition system. The pickup coil is also located behind the flywheel. The CDI module is attached to the front of the frame while the ignition coil is attached to the middle of the frame. The ignition circuit includes a control unit attached to the front of the frame and switches located in the throttle housing and attached to the top of the carburetor.

Ignition timing is not adjustable. Ignition timing should be correct if components operate properly.

Some ignition components can be checked using an ohmmeter. To check the pickup coil, disconnect white/red wire and white/green wire leads to engine. Pickup coil resistance should be 94-140 ohms.

To check the charge coil, disconnect the green wire and red wire leads to engine. Charge coil resistance should be 13.7-20.5 ohms.

Ignition coil resistance readings should be 0.28-0.38 ohms for primary windings and 4.7k-7.1k ohms for secondary windings.

To check for a problem in the control unit circuit, disconnect three-wire connector to control unit. If engine starts with control unit disconnected, then circuit is faulty. Check operation of throttle switch and carburetor switches, which are on-off type switches. If switches operate properly, then replace control unit with a new or good unit.

If the ignition system malfunctions and all components test satisfactory, replace CDI module with a new or good unit and recheck ignition system.

ELECTRICAL SYSTEM. A lighting coil is located behind the flywheel to provide electrical power for the lights. The lighting coil can be checked using an ohmmeter. Connect an ohmmeter to yellow wire and black wire leads to engine. Resistance should be 0.28-0.38 ohms.

To check the voltage regulator, disconnect the yellow wire and black wire leads to headlight. Connect positive lead of a voltmeter to yellow wire and negative voltmeter lead to black wire. Place headlight switch in high position. The voltmeter should indicated 11.5 volts with engine running at 5000 rpm and 16.3 volts with engine running at 8000 rpm. If voltage exceeds 16.3 volts, renew voltage regulator with a new or good unit and recheck voltage.

Each headlight is a 12V 30W/30W unit while the taillight is a 12V 3.8W unit.

FASTENERS

After initial break-in and every three months thereafter, the vehicle should receive an overall inspection. All screws, nuts and other fasteners should be checked and

tightened to proper torque specification shown in CON-
DENSED SERVICE DATA section or in the appropriate
maintenance section.

CLUTCH

The engine is equipped with a multiple-disc clutch that
is located behind the right crankcase cover.

Clutch lever free play (F—Fig. Y17-21) should be
10-15 mm (0.4-0.6 in.). To adjust clutch lever free play,
push back dust boot (B), loosen locknut (N) and rotate
adjuster (A). Retighten locknut.

To adjust clutch, loosen clutch cable at handlebar
lever. Detach right footpeg assembly and dismount
master cylinder for rear brake from frame. Drain transmission oil and coolant. Detach radiator hose from water
pump (water pump is in right crankcase side cover).
Disconnect breather hose to right crankcase side cover.
Remove kick starter lever from shaft. Detach right crankcase side cover from engine. Loosen locknut (N—Fig.
Y17-23) then push operating lever (L—Fig. Y17-25)
forward until it stops. Rotate screw (S—Fig. Y17-23) so
point on lever end (L—Fig. Y17-25) aligns with mark (M)
on crankcase, then hold screw and retighten locknut.
Reassemble components. Tighten side cover screws to

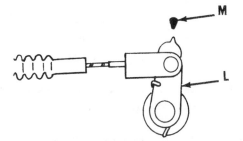

*Fig. Y17-25—Pointer on lever (L) is aligned with mark
(M) by turning clutch adjusting screw (S—Fig. Y17-23).
See text.*

7 N·m (62 in.-lbs.). Be sure kick starter is properly
installed and will not contact engine during operation.
Tighten kick starter retaining nut to 25 N·m (18 ft.-lbs.).
Fill transmission and cooling system as previously outlined. Adjust clutch lever free play as previously outlined.

FRONT BRAKE ASSEMBLY

A disc brake assembly is used on both front wheels.
Front brake adjustment for disc pad wear is not required
due to the compensating action of the piston in the
caliper.

Brake fluid must be rated DOT 3 or 4. Maintain brake
fluid level above "LOW" mark on side of brake fluid
reservoir. Do not overfill. To avert spillage, be sure
reservoir is horizontal before removing cover.

BRAKE LEVER FREE PLAY. Front brake lever free
play should be 4-8 mm (0.16-0.31 in.) measured at outer
end of brake lever (L—Fig. Y17-27). To adjust, loosen
locknut (N) and rotate screw (S) until recommended free
play is obtained. Retighten locknut (N).

BLEEDING. Make sure reservoir (R—Fig. Y17-27) is
full. Connect a bleed hose to bleed valve on both front
brake caliper assemblies. Route the bleed hoses into
suitable containers. Operate the brake lever until hard

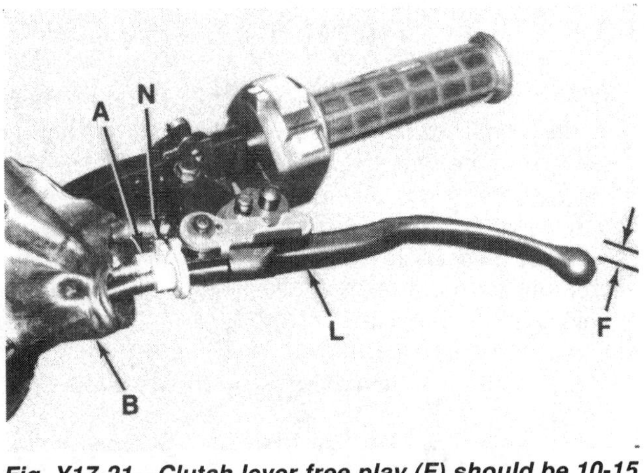

*Fig. Y17-21—Clutch lever free play (F) should be 10-15
mm (0.4-0.6 in.). To adjust, push back dust boot (B),
loosen locknut (N) and rotate adjuster (A).*

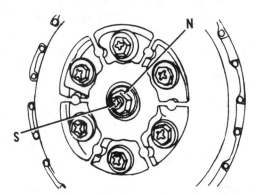

Fig. Y17-23—Adjust clutch as outlined in text.

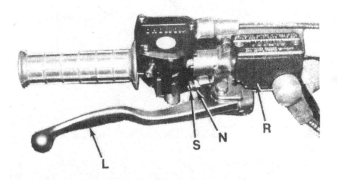

*Fig. Y17-27—Loosen locknut (N) and rotate screw (S) to
adjust front brake lever (L) free play.*

resistance is felt, then open one bleed valve. Close bleed valve prior to releasing brake lever. Continue bleeding procedure on both wheels until no air bubbles are noted in discharged fluid from bleed valve.

NOTE: Make sure reservoir remains full during bleeding procedure.

When bleeding procedure is completed, add brake fluid to reservoir until fluid level is at upper level line in reservoir.

OVERHAUL. The brake pads are equipped with a wear indicator on the pad to indicate when the service limit has been reached and pad should be renewed. Brake pads should be renewed if pad thickness is 1.0 mm (0.039 in.) or less.

WARNING: Inhaling asbestos brake dust is injurious to human health. Approved OSHA respiration equipment must be worn when working on or around brake calipers and pads. DO NOT use compressed air to clean brake calipers, pads or nearby components as brake dust will be blown into air. Only vacuum equipment designed to pick up brake dust should be used.

Brake components are accessible after removing wheel, caliper mounting screws and withdrawing caliper. Brake disc should be renewed if thickness is less than 3 mm (0.118 in.) or runout exceeds 0.5 mm (0.020 in.). Tighten brake disc mounting bolts to 28 N·m (21 ft.-lbs.). Push piston by hand back into caliper to allow clearance for new brake pads. Tighten brake caliper mounting screws on Models YFZ350U and YFZ350W to 23 N·m (17 ft.-lbs.). Tighten brake caliper mounting screws on Models YFZ350A, YFZ350B and YFZ350D to 28 N·m (21 ft.-lbs.). On later models equipped with a

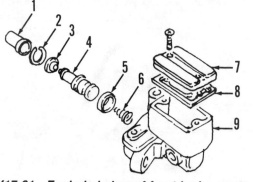

Fig. Y17-31—Exploded view of front brake master cylinder.

1. Dust boot
2. Snap ring
3. Secondary cup
4. Piston
5. Primary cup
6. Spring
7. Cover
8. Diaphragm
9. Body

brake pad retaining pin, tighten pin to 18 N·m (160 in.-lbs.). After reassembly, operate brake lever until brake lever will not pump up after continuous operation. Do not operate vehicle until brakes are tested and functioning properly.

MASTER CYLINDER. To remove front brake master cylinder (9—Fig. Y17-31), detach brake line from master cylinder. Brake fluid will remove paint; be careful when removing master cylinder. Unscrew two retaining screws and remove master cylinder. Remove brake lever, reservoir cover (7) and diaphragm (8). Remove dust boot (1) and snap ring (2). Disassemble piston assembly while noting location and direction of components. Renew complete master cylinder if bore is scored, pitted or excessively worn. Superficial damage in master cylinder bore may be removed using a suitable cylinder hone. After honing, rinse bore with clean brake fluid. Shake out excess fluid but do not wipe dry. Using a shop towel or rag to dry cylinder will leave lint particles in bore. Renew boots and piston cups. During reassembly, lubricate components with clean brake fluid. Reassembly is reverse of disassembly. Install spring (6) so small end contacts primary cup (5). Bleed brakes as previously outlined. Do not operate vehicle until brakes are tested and functioning properly.

FRONT AXLE

Remove front wheel for access to hub and spindle. Unscrew hub nut to remove wheel hub. The hub and brake drum are one piece. Renew bearings if rough or otherwise damaged. Be sure to install spacer between bearings when reassembling components. Tapered end of spacer must be towards wheel side of hub. Tighten hub retaining nut to 85 N·m (62 ft.-lbs.). Tighten wheel retaining nuts to 45 N·m (33 ft.-lbs.).

STEERING

TOE-IN SETTING. Place the handlebar in a straight ahead position. Use a suitable measuring tool and measure distance (B—Fig. Y17-33) at spindle height between the center of the tires on the rear sides. Locate the same tire centerline points on front side of tires and measure front distance (F). The distance on the front side (F) should be 0-10 mm (0.0-0.4 in.) shorter than the measured distance on the rear side (B). Note that the distance from a projected vehicle centerline to left (L) and right (R) tire centerlines should also be equal.

To adjust, loosen inside and outside locknuts on the left and right tie rod assemblies and rotate tie rod shaft on each side equally until distance is within recommended range. After obtaining the correct setting, tighten locknuts to 30 N·m (22 ft.-lbs.).

INSPECTION. Rotate the handlebar from one extreme to the other and note if any binding or roughness

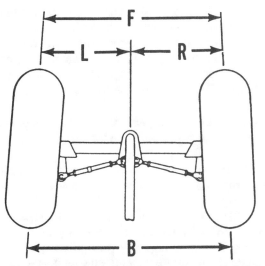

Fig. Y17-33—Toe-in should be 0-10 mm (0.0-0.4 in.). Refer to text for measurement and adjustment procedures.

is felt. Periodically inspect the steering components for looseness or any other damage. Renew any damaged component. Clean and grease components if binding or excessive effort is noted.

OVERHAUL. To expose the steering shaft, remove radiator cover, fuel tank cover, front fender and handlebar. Drain cooling system and remove radiator. Unscrew the two cap screws securing the steering shaft clamp halves. Clean the old grease from the steering shaft. Inspect the clamp halves and steering shaft for damage. Renew components if needed. Grease inside of steering shaft clamp halves with a lithium base grease and install. Tighten the retaining clamp cap screws to 23 N·m (17 ft.-lbs.).

To remove steering shaft, remove steering shaft clamps as outlined in previous paragraph. Remove the lower steering shaft retaining cotter pin and nut. Detach inner tie rod ends from steering shaft and withdraw the steering shaft. Remove seal and unscrew bearing retaining nut to remove lower bearing. Inspect the lower bearing and seals and renew if needed. Apply a lithium base grease to bearing before installation. Tighten bearing retaining nut to 40 N·m (29 ft.-lbs.). Tighten the lower steering shaft retaining nut to 30 N·m (22 ft.-lbs.). Tighten retaining nuts for tie rod ends to 25 N·m (18 ft.-lbs.). Tighten handlebar clamp screws to 20 N·m (15 ft.-lbs.).

FRONT SUSPENSION

Both front steering knuckle assemblies pivot on ball joint assemblies at the end of each upper and lower control arm. The control arms are bolted at the ends to the vehicle frame and a shock absorber is used to limit and cushion the up and down movement of the control arms. The shock absorbers are adjustable to alter shock

absorber spring setting for different terrain and load conditions.

Remove the front wheel to service the ball joint assemblies. Note that removing the brake components will allow greater access to ball joint assemblies. If any ball joint or control arm is excessively worn or any other damage is noted, then ball joint and control arm must be renewed as a unit assembly. Tighten lower control arm retaining nuts to 32 N·m (24 ft. lbs.). On early models with a strut type upper control arm (YFZ350U and YFZ350W), tighten retaining bolt to 32 N·m (24 ft.-lbs.). On models with a wishbone type upper control arm (YFZ350A, YFZ350B and YFZ350D), tighten retaining bolt to 38 N·m (28 ft.-lbs.). Tighten ball joint retaining nuts to 25 N·m (18 ft.-lbs.). Shock absorber retaining nuts should be tightened to 45 N·m (33 ft.-lbs.).

REAR BRAKE ASSEMBLY

A single disc brake assembly is used for both rear wheels. The running brake is operated hydraulically by a foot pedal on the lower right side. The parking brake is mechanically operated by a cable and handlebar components in conjunction with the clutch lever. Rear brake adjustment for disc pad wear is not required due to the compensating action of the piston in the caliper.

Brake fluid must be rated DOT 3 or 4. Maintain brake fluid level above "LOW" mark on side of brake fluid reservoir. Do not overfill. To avert spillage, be sure reservoir is horizontal before removing cover.

BRAKE PEDAL HEIGHT ADJUSTMENT. Brake pedal (P—Fig. Y17-35) should be 10 mm (3/8 in.) below footpeg (G) in the released position when measured from the top of the footpeg to the top of the foot pad on the brake pedal as shown in Fig. Y17-35. To adjust, loosen locknut (N) and rotate master cylinder actuator

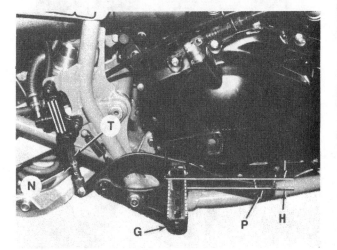

Fig. Y17-35—Brake pedal (P) should be 10 mm (3/8 in.) below footpeg (G) in the released position. Loosen locknut (N) and rotate master cylinder actuator rod nut (T) to adjust pedal height.

rod nut (T) until recommended pedal height is obtained, then tighten locknut (N) to retain adjustment. After adjustment, the end of the master cylinder push rod must be visible in the hole in the side of the clevis.

PARKING BRAKE ADJUSTMENT. Make sure parking brake/clutch lever is in the released position. Slide dust boot (B—Fig. Y17-37) down cable. Loosen locknut (N) and rotate cable adjuster (A) completely inward. Loosen locknut (L—Fig. Y17-39) and adjuster screw (S). Turn in adjuster screw (S) until tight, then back out 1/8 turn. Tighten locknut (L) while holding adjuster screw. If the adjuster screw bottoms against the locknut, then the brake pads are worn and should be renewed. Block up rear end of vehicle so wheels can turn freely and check for brake drag while rotating wheels. If brake drag is present, repeat preceding brake adjustment.

BLEEDING. Make sure rear brake master cylinder reservoir is full. Connect a bleed hose to bleed valve

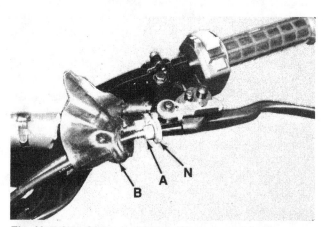

Fig. Y17-37—Slide dust boot (B) down cable to expose parking brake cable locknut (N) and adjuster (A).

Fig. Y17-39—Loosen locknut (L) and turn adjuster screw (S) as outlined in text to adjust parking brake. Attach a hose to bleed screw (B) to bleed rear brake system.

(B—Fig. Y17-39) on brake caliper assembly. Route the bleed hose into a suitable container. Operate foot pedal until firm resistance is felt, then open bleed valve (B). Close bleed valve prior to releasing foot pedal. Continue bleeding procedure until no air bubbles are noted in discharged fluid from bleed valve.

NOTE: Make sure rear brake fluid reservoir remains full during bleeding procedure.

When bleeding procedure is completed, add brake fluid to rear brake master cylinder reservoir as needed.

OVERHAUL. The brake pads are equipped with a wear indicator on the pad to indicate when the service limit has been reached and pad should be renewed. Brake pads should be renewed if pad thickness is 1.0 mm (0.039 in.) or less.

WARNING: Inhaling asbestos brake dust is injurious to human health. Approved OSHA respiration equipment must be worn when working on or around brake calipers and pads. DO NOT use compressed air to clean brake calipers, pads or nearby components as brake dust will be blown into air. Only vacuum equipment designed to pick up brake dust should be used.

Brake components are accessible after removing caliper mounting screws and withdrawing caliper. Brake disc should be renewed if thickness is 3.0 mm (0.118 in.) or less or disc runout is 0.15 mm (0.006 in.) or more. Push piston by hand back into caliper to allow clearance for new brake pads. Tighten brake pad retaining pins to 18 N·m (160 in.-lbs.). Tighten brake caliper mounting screw to 23 N·m (17 ft.-lbs.). After reassembly, operate brake pedal until pedal will not pump up after continuous operation. Do not operate vehicle until brakes are tested and functioning properly.

MASTER CYLINDER. To remove rear brake master cylinder (7—Fig. Y17-41), disconnect brake plunger from pedal. Detach brake lines from master cylinder and plug line to reservoir. Brake fluid will remove paint; be careful when removing master cylinder. Unscrew retaining screws and remove master cylinder. Remove dust boot (14) and snap ring (13). Disassemble piston assembly while noting location and direction of components. Renew complete master cylinder if bore is scored, pitted or excessively worn. Superficial damage in master cylinder bore may be removed using a suitable cylinder hone. After honing, rinse bore with clean brake fluid. Shake out excess fluid but do not wipe dry. Using a shop towel or rag to dry cylinder will leave lint particles in bore. Renew boots and piston cups. During reassembly, lubricate components with clean brake fluid. Reassembly is reverse of disassembly. Install spring (8) so small end contacts primary cup (9). Bleed brakes as

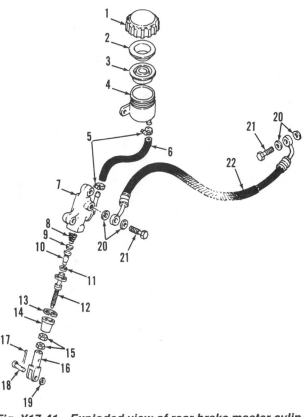

Fig. Y17-41—*Exploded view of rear brake master cylinder.*

1. Cap	13. Snap ring
2. Seal	14. Dust boot
4. Diaphragm	15. Nuts
5. Clip	16. Clevis
6. Hose	17. Cotter pin
7. Body	18. Pin
8. Spring	19. Washer
9. Primary cup	20. Sealing washers
10. Piston	21. Union bolt
11. Secondary cup	22. Hose
12. Push rod	

previously outlined. Do not operate vehicle until brakes are tested and functioning properly.

DRIVE CHAIN AND SPROCKETS.

INSPECTION AND ADJUSTMENT. The final drive chain should be inspected and adjusted after initial break-in and after every month of operation thereafter. Improper maintenance and neglect can cause early failure of both drive chain and sprockets. To measure drive chain free play, support rear of frame near swing arm pivot so rear wheels are off ground. Measure drive chain travel at a point midway between rub block at swing arm and rear sprocket. Drive chain free play should be 15-20 mm (0.59-0.79 in.).

To adjust chain tension, loosen upper rear axle housing retaining screws (U—Fig. Y17-43) and lower screws (L). Loosen adjusting screw locknuts (N) and rotate tension adjusting screws (S) equally. Note axle align-

Fig. Y17-43—*To adjust drive chain tension, loosen upper (U) and lower (L) screws. Loosen locknuts (N) and rotate screws (S) until specified chain tension is obtained.*

ment marks adjacent to adjusting screws and maintain axle alignment by aligning same marks on each side of axle housing. Tighten upper axle housing retaining screws (U) to 120 N·m (88 ft.-lbs.) and lower screws (L) to 60 N·m (44 ft.-lbs.). Recheck drive chain tension. Renew drive chain if recommended tension adjustment cannot be obtained. Refer to LUBRICATION for drive chain lubrication requirements.

R&R AND OVERHAUL. The drive chain is sealed by "O" rings and fitted with a master link. To remove the drive chain and both sprockets, remove left engine side cover and loosen engine sprocket retaining nut. Support rear of vehicle and remove left wheel. Remove chain guard under rear sprocket. Loosen chain tension as outlined in previous section. Remove drive chain master link while taking care not to damage or lose "O" rings. Remove drive chain. To remove rear sprocket, unscrew sprocket retaining nuts and remove sprocket. Remove engine sprocket.

Carefully examine sprockets for excessive wear. Worn sprockets will usually have a hooked tooth profile. A good test is to place a new chain on a used sprocket and check the fit. If sprockets require renewal due to wear, always renew drive chain. Sprockets should be renewed as a set.

Reassemble by reversing disassembly procedure. Tighten engine sprocket retaining nut to 80 N·m (59 ft.-lbs.). Tighten rear sprocket retaining nuts to 60 N·m (44 ft.-lbs.). When assembling chain, be sure "O" rings are properly installed on master link. Install master link clip as shown in Fig. Y17-45. Tighten wheel retaining nuts to 45 N·m (33 ft.-lbs.). Refer to previous INSPECTION AND ADJUSTMENT paragraphs for recommended drive chain adjustment procedures.

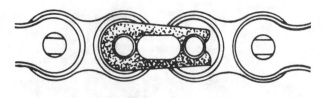

← CHAIN TRAVEL

Fig. Y17-45—Install drive chain master link clip with closed end towards direction of chain travel.

FINAL DRIVE ASSEMBLY

R&R AND OVERHAUL. Support rear of vehicle. Remove rear brake caliper. Remove drive chain as previously outlined. Remove both rear wheels and hubs. Remove upper rear axle housing retaining screws (U—Fig. Y17-43) and lower retaining screws (L). Unscrew rear axle retaining nuts (H), then lightly tap left end of axle with a soft-faced mallet to drive axle shaft out of axle housing. DO NOT strike threaded end of axle.

Inspect axle housing seals and bearings and renew if required. Maximum axle runout with axle supported just outside inner splined area for brake hub and just outside threads for inner axle nuts (H) is 1.5 mm (0.060 in.). Reassembly is reverse order of disassembly. Lubricate splined areas with lithium base grease.

When tightening inner axle nuts (H) on Models YFZ350T, YFZ350U and YFZ350W, use the following procedure: Apply Loctite to threads of inner axle nuts. Tighten inner nut to 130 N•m (96 ft.-lbs.). Hold inner nut and tighten outer nut to 190 N•m (140 ft.-lbs.). Hold outer nut and tighten inner nut towards outer nut to 240 N•m (176 ft.-lbs.).

When tightening inner axle nuts (H) on Models YFZ350A, YFZ350B and YFZ350D, use the following procedure: Apply Loctite to threads of inner axle nuts. Tighten inner nut to 55 N•m (40 ft.-lbs.). Hold inner nut and tighten outer nut to 190 N•m (140 ft.-lbs.). Place a mark across the two nuts. Tighten inner nut against outer nut until torque reading on inner nut is 240 N•m (176 ft.-lbs.). Distance between marks on nuts should be at least 3 mm (0.12 in.), if not retighten inner nut.

Tighten axle shaft hub nut on all models to 120 N•m (88 ft.-lbs.).

METRIC CONVERSION

Square centimeters	x	.155	= Square inches
Square centimeters	=	6.4515	x Square inches
Square meters	x	10.7641	= Square feet
Square meters	=	.0929	x Square feet
Cubic centimeters	x	.061025	= Cubic inches
Cubic centimeters	=	16.387	x Cubic inches
Cubic meters	x	35.3156	= Cubic feet
Cubic meters	=	.0283	x Cubic feet
Cubic meters	x	1.308	= Cubic yards
Cubic meters	=	.765	x Cubic yards
Liters	x	61.023	= Cubic inches
Liters	=	.0164	x Cubic inches
Liters	x	.2642	= U.S. gallons
Liters	=	3.7854	x U.S. gallons
Grams	x	15.4324	= Grains
Grams	=	.0648	x Grains
Grams	x	.03527	= Ounces avoirdupois
Grams	=	28.3495	x Ounces avoirdupois
Kilograms	x	2.2046	= Pounds
Kilograms	=	.4536	x Pounds
Kilograms per square centimeter	x	14.2231	= Pounds per square inch

Kilograms per square centimeter	=	.0703	x Pounds per square inch
Kilograms per cubic meter	x	.06243	= Pounds per cubic foot
Kilograms per cubic meter	=	16.0189	x Pounds per cubic foot
Metric tons (1000 kilograms)	x	1.1023	= Tons (2000 pounds)
Metric tons (1000 kilograms)	=	.9072	x Tons (2000 pounds)
Kilowatts	=	.746	x Horsepower
Kilowatts	x	1.3405	= Horsepower
Millimeters	x	.03937	= Inches
Millimeters	=	25.4	x Inches
Meters	x	3.2809	= Feet
Meters	=	.3048	x Feet
Kilometers	x	.62138	= Miles
Kilometers	=	1.6093	x Miles

METRIC CONVERSION

MM.	INCHES			MM.	INCHES			MM.	INCHES			MM.	INCHES			MM.	INCHES			MM.	INCHES		
1	0.0394	1/32	+	51	2.0079	2.0	+	101	3.9764	3 31/32	+	151	5.9449	5 15/16	+	201	7.9134	7 29/32	+	251	9.8819	9 7/8	+
2	0.0787	3/32	−	52	2.0472	2 1/16	−	102	4.0157	4 1/32	−	152	5.9842	5 31/32	+	202	7.9527	7 15/16	+	252	9.9212	9 29/32	+
3	0.1181	1/8	−	53	2.0866	2 3/32	−	103	4.0551	4 1/16	−	153	6.0236	6 1/32	−	203	7.9921	8.0	−	253	9.9606	9 31/32	−
4	0.1575	5/32	+	54	2.1260	2 1/8	+	104	4.0945	4 3/32	+	154	6.0630	6 1/16	+	204	8.0315	8 1/32	+	254	10.0000	10.0	
5	0.1969	3/16	+	55	2.1654	2 5/32	+	105	4.1339	4 1/8	+	155	6.1024	6 3/32	+	205	8.0709	8 1/16	+	255	10.0393	10 1/32	+
6	0.2362	1/4	−	56	2.2047	2 7/32	−	106	4.1732	4 3/16	−	156	6.1417	6 5/32	−	206	8.1102	8 1/8	−	256	10.0787	10 3/32	−
7	0.2756	9/32	−	57	2.2441	2 1/4	−	107	4.2126	4 7/32	−	157	6.1811	6 3/16	−	207	8.1496	8 5/32	−	257	10.1181	10 1/8	−
8	0.3150	5/16	+	58	2.2835	2 9/32	+	108	4.2520	4 1/4	+	158	6.2205	6 7/32	+	208	8.1890	8 3/16	+	258	10.1575	10 5/32	+
9	0.3543	11/32	+	59	2.3228	2 5/16	+	109	4.2913	4 9/32	+	159	6.2598	6 1/4	+	209	8.2283	8 7/32	+	259	10.1968	10 3/16	+
10	0.3937	13/32	−	60	2.3622	2 3/8	−	110	4.3307	4 11/32	−	160	6.2992	6 5/16	−	210	8.2677	8 9/32	−	260	10.2362	10 1/4	−
11	0.4331	7/16	−	61	2.4016	2 13/32	−	111	4.3701	4 3/8	−	161	6.3386	6 11/32	−	211	8.3071	8 5/16	−	261	10.2756	10 9/32	−
12	0.4724	15/32	+	62	2.4409	2 7/16	−	112	4.4094	4 13/32	+	162	6.3779	6 3/8	+	212	8.3464	8 11/32	+	262	10.3149	10 5/16	+
13	0.5118	1/2	+	63	2.4803	2 15/32	+	113	4.4488	4 7/16	+	163	6.4173	6 13/32	+	213	8.3858	8 3/8	+	263	10.3543	10 11/32	+
14	0.5512	9/16	−	64	2.5197	2 17/32	−	114	4.4882	4 1/2	−	164	6.4567	6 15/32	−	214	8.4252	8 7/16	−	264	10.3937	10 13/32	−
15	0.5906	19/32	−	65	2.5591	2 9/16	−	115	4.5276	4 17/32	−	165	6.4961	6 1/2	−	215	8.4646	8 15/32	−	265	10.4330	10 7/16	−
16	0.6299	5/8	+	66	2.5984	2 19/32	+	116	4.5669	4 9/16	+	166	6.5354	6 17/32	+	216	8.5039	8 1/2	+	266	10.4724	10 15/32	+
17	0.6693	21/32	+	67	2.6378	2 5/8	+	117	4.6063	4 19/32	+	167	6.5748	6 9/16	+	217	8.5433	8 17/32	+	267	10.5118	10 1/2	+
18	0.7087	23/32	−	68	2.6772	2 11/16	−	118	4.6457	4 21/32	−	168	6.6142	6 5/8	−	218	8.5827	8 19/32	−	268	10.5512	10 9/16	−
19	0.7480	3/4	−	69	2.7165	2 23/32	−	119	4.6850	4 11/16	−	169	6.6535	6 21/32	−	219	8.6220	8 5/8	−	269	10.5905	10 19/32	−
20	0.7874	25/32	+	70	2.7559	2 3/4	+	120	4.7244	4 23/32	+	170	6.6929	6 11/16	+	220	8.6614	8 21/32	+	270	10.6299	10 5/8	+
21	0.8268	13/16	+	71	2.7953	2 25/32	+	121	4.7638	4 3/4	+	171	6.7323	6 23/32	+	221	8.7008	8 11/16	+	271	10.6693	10 21/32	+
22	0.8661	7/8	−	72	2.8346	2 27/32	−	122	4.8031	4 13/16	−	172	6.7716	6 25/32	−	222	8.7401	8 3/4	−	272	10.7086	10 23/32	−
23	0.9055	29/32	−	73	2.8740	2 7/8	−	123	4.8425	4 27/32	−	173	6.8110	6 13/16	−	223	8.7795	8 25/32	−	273	10.7480	10 3/4	−
24	0.9449	15/16	+	74	2.9134	2 29/32	+	124	4.8819	4 7/8	+	174	6.8504	6 27/32	+	224	8.8189	8 13/16	+	274	10.7874	10 25/32	+
25	0.9843	31/32	+	75	2.9528	2 15/16	+	125	4.9213	4 29/32	+	175	6.8898	6 7/8	+	225	8.8583	8 27/32	+	275	10.8268	10 13/16	+
26	1.0236	1 1/32	−	76	2.9921	3.0	−	126	4.9606	4 31/32	−	176	6.9291	6 15/16	−	226	8.8976	8 29/32	−	276	10.8661	10 7/8	−
27	1.0630	1 1/16	+	77	3.0315	3 1/32	+	127	5.0000	5.0		177	6.9685	6 31/32	−	227	8.9370	8 15/16	−	277	10.9055	10 29/32	−
28	1.1024	1 3/32	+	78	3.0709	3 1/16	+	128	5.0394	5 1/32	+	178	7.0079	7.0	+	228	8.9764	8 31/32	+	278	10.9449	10 15/16	+
29	1.1417	1 5/32	−	79	3.1102	3 1/8	−	129	5.0787	5 3/32	−	179	7.0472	7 1/16	−	229	9.0157	9 1/32	−	279	10.9842	10 31/32	−
30	1.1811	1 3/16	−	80	3.1496	3 5/32	−	130	5.1181	5 1/8	−	180	7.0866	7 3/32	−	230	9.0551	9 1/16	−	280	11.0236	11 1/32	−
31	1.2205	1 7/32	+	81	3.1890	3 3/16	+	131	5.1575	5 5/32	+	181	7.1260	7 1/8	+	231	9.0945	9 3/32	+	281	11.0630	11 1/16	+
32	1.2598	1 1/4	−	82	3.2283	3 7/32	+	132	5.1968	5 3/16	−	182	7.1653	7 5/32	+	232	9.1338	9 1/8	+	282	11.1023	11 3/32	+
33	1.2992	1 5/16	−	83	3.2677	3 9/32	−	133	5.2362	5 1/4	−	183	7.2047	7 7/32	−	233	9.1732	9 3/16	−	283	11.1417	11 5/32	−
34	1.3386	1 11/32	+	84	3.3071	3 5/16	−	134	5.2756	5 9/32	−	184	7.2441	7 1/4	−	234	9.2126	9 7/32	−	284	11.1811	11 3/16	−
35	1.3780	1 3/8	−	85	3.3465	3 11/32	+	135	5.3150	5 5/16	+	185	7.2835	7 9/32	+	235	9.2520	9 1/4	+	285	11.2204	11 7/32	+
36	1.4173	1 13/32	+	86	3.3858	3 3/8	+	136	5.3543	5 11/32	+	186	7.3228	7 5/16	+	236	9.2913	9 9/32	+	286	11.2598	11 1/4	+
37	1.4567	1 15/32	−	87	3.4252	3 7/16	−	137	5.3937	5 13/32	−	187	7.3622	7 3/8	−	237	9.3307	9 11/32	−	287	11.2992	11 5/16	−
38	1.4961	1 1/2	−	88	3.4646	3 15/32	−	138	5.4331	5 7/16	−	188	7.4016	7 13/32	−	238	9.3701	9 3/8	−	288	11.3386	11 11/32	−
39	1.5354	1 17/32	+	89	3.5039	3 1/2	+	139	5.4724	5 15/32	+	189	7.4409	7 7/16	+	239	9.4094	9 13/32	+	289	11.3779	11 3/8	+
40	1.5748	1 9/16	+	90	3.5433	3 17/32	+	140	5.5118	5 1/2	+	190	7.4803	7 15/32	+	240	9.4488	9 7/16	+	290	11.4173	11 13/32	+
41	1.6142	1 5/8	−	91	3.5827	3 19/32	−	141	5.5512	5 9/16	−	191	7.5197	7 17/32	−	241	9.4882	9 1/2	−	291	11.4567	11 15/32	−
42	1.6535	1 21/32	−	92	3.6220	3 5/8	−	142	5.5905	5 19/32	−	192	7.5590	7 9/16	−	242	9.5275	9 17/32	−	292	11.4960	11 1/2	−
43	1.6929	1 11/16	+	93	3.6614	3 21/32	+	143	5.6299	5 5/8	+	193	7.5984	7 19/32	+	243	9.5669	9 9/16	+	293	11.5354	11 17/32	+
44	1.7323	1 23/32	+	94	3.7008	3 11/16	+	144	5.6693	5 21/32	+	194	7.6378	7 5/8	+	244	9.6063	9 19/32	+	294	11.5748	11 9/16	+
45	1.7717	1 25/32	−	95	3.7402	3 3/4	−	145	5.7087	5 23/32	−	195	7.6772	7 11/16	−	245	9.6457	9 21/32	−	295	11.6142	11 5/8	−
46	1.8110	1 13/16	−	96	3.7795	3 25/32	−	146	5.7480	5 3/4	−	196	7.7165	7 23/32	−	246	9.6850	9 11/16	−	296	11.6535	11 21/32	−
47	1.8504	1 27/32	+	97	3.8189	3 13/16	+	147	5.7874	5 25/32	+	197	7.7559	7 3/4	+	247	9.7244	9 23/32	+	297	11.6929	11 11/16	+
48	1.8898	1 7/8	−	98	3.8583	3 27/32	+	148	5.8268	5 13/16	+	198	7.7953	7 25/32	+	248	9.7638	9 3/4	+	298	11.7323	11 23/32	+
49	1.9291	1 15/16	−	99	3.8976	3 29/32	−	149	5.8661	5 7/8	−	199	7.8346	7 27/32	−	249	9.8031	9 13/16	−	299	11.7716	11 25/32	−
50	1.9685	1 31/32	−	100	3.9370	3 15/16	−	150	5.9055	5 29/32	−	200	7.8740	7 7/8	−	250	9.8425	9 27/32	−	300	11.8110	11 13/16	−

NOTE: The + or − sign indicates that the decimal equivalent is larger or smaller than the fractional equivalent.